Principles of Pharmaceutical Marketing

Third Edition

Principles
of Pharmaceutical
Marketing

MICKEY C. SMITH, Ph.D.

Professor, Department of Health Care Administration, University of Mississippi School of Pharmacy, University, Mississippi

Routledge
Taylor & Francis Group
New York   London

First published by

LEA & FEBIGER
600 Washington Square
Philadelphia, PA 19106
U.S.A.

This edition published 2013 by Routledge

711 Third Avenue, New York, NY 10017

2 Park Square, Milton Park, Abingdon, Oxon OX14 4RN

Routledge is an imprint of the Taylor & Francis Group, an informa business

Library of Congress Cataloging in Publication Data
Smith, Mickey C.
    Principles of pharmaceutical marketing
    Bibliography: p.
    Includes index.
    1. Drug trade—United States.   I. Title.
HD9666.5.S56 1983   615'.1'0688   82-6624
ISBN 0-8121-0858-2   AACR2

Dedicated to the memory of Dr. Charles W. Hartman
thinker, teacher, and friend

Preface

In his remarkable book *White Collar*, C. Wright Mills has likened authors of textbooks to *wholesalers*, "who while they do not produce ideas do distribute them ... to other academic men (retailers), who in turn sell them directly to student consumers."* Certainly this observation is a doubly appropriate means of introducing the present volume. Wholesalers occupy an important place in marketing, and the nature of pharmaceutical marketing is such that explanation, more than theory, is presently needed.

This text is designed for (1) undergraduate students in pharmacy whose background in marketing is limited, (2) those actually involved in pharmaceutical marketing, and (3) anyone desiring an introduction to the intricacies involved in the marketing of pharmaceutical products.

The absence of a *textbook* related specifically to the general field of pharmaceutical marketing has necessitated the use of a nonpharmacy-oriented textbook, the use of outside reading materials, or a combination of the two. None of these methods is completely satisfying, either to the instructor or to the student.

If a nonpharmacy-oriented textbook is used, the student is presented with ideas whose applications do not necessarily hold true for the pharmaceutical industry. It is then necessary for the instructor to supply examples relating basic marketing principles to the distribution of pharmaceutical products. The use of outside readings, although providing examples of pharmaceutical marketing practices, does not provide students with the underlying principles of marketing. The task of presenting these principles is

*New York: Oxford University Press, 1951, p. 132.

then left to the instructor. The implementation of either approach demands that the lecturer bridge the gap that exists between reading and didactic materials. If the two methods are combined it is likely that the student will be overwhelmed with reading material, much of which is duplication. This textbook represents an attempt to bring more efficiency into this process.

It will be immediately obvious to those acquainted with previous editions of *Principles of Pharmaceutical Marketing* that this third edition has a new look. Although the earlier books did benefit from additions by expert contributors, the present edition was consciously planned to offer the perspectives both of those who teach and of those who practice pharmaceutical marketing. This reflects the need for and the effort to provide the most relevant "real world" approach to this complex and fascinating field.

Although the *principles* of pharmaceutical marketing have not and will not change, their implementation changes with astonishing and sometimes annoying regularity. New marketing institutions, new prescribers, and new classes of drugs have appeared, each requiring adaptation by marketers. Indeed, two new chapters, one on generic drugs and one on institutional and government marketing, reflect such changes. The increasingly international character of the pharmaceutical industry is recognized in a new chapter devoted to that topic.

Many of the changes have resulted from suggestions from readers, for which I am grateful. Particularly important to me for a number of years has been the counsel of my friend and colleague, Dr. Max Ferm, who also contributed to the text. Dr. T. Donald Rucker spent a great deal of time in providing valuable criticism, which is much appreciated. My graduate students at Ole Miss have contributed immeasurably to my continuing education in pharmaceutical marketing.

The contributors and their affiliations are noted elsewhere in this book, but their participation is gratefully acknowledged here. The authors lend to this work their considerable expertise and writing skills, and have done so in timely fashion. They have all accepted suggestions, editing (admittedly only minor), and coaxing about deadlines, with good grace. I am pleased and honored to have had the opportunity to work with them. One word is due to those who contributed chapters to this text. I have had every opportunity to alter their work without granting them reciprocal privileges. Therefore, responsibility for errors or omission remains mine alone.

Individual acknowledgment of those who assisted in other ways in preparing this text risks important omissions. I must, however, mention Mary Ervin, Beverly Brown, Frieda McDonald, and Myrna Heimer, all of whom assisted in preparation of the manuscript. In addition to myself, I believe that the industry as a whole owes a debt to *Medical Marketing and Media* for their long-term commitment to providing a vehicle for marketing communications. Finally, my thanks to Certified Medical Representatives Institute for their continued interest in the text.

MICKEY C. SMITH

Contributors

With chapters and/or material contributed by:

ROGER K. BECKER
Manager of Hospital Sales
Pharmaceutical Division
Abbott Laboratories

STEPHEN C. CHAPPELL
Group Vice-President and
Assistant to the Chairman
IMS America, Ltd.

DOUGLAS L. COCKS, PH.D.
Manager of Corporate Affairs
Research
Eli Lilly and Company

ROBERT J. DESALVO, PH.D.
Assistant Dean and Associate Professor
of Pharmacy Administration
College of Pharmacy
University of Cincinnati

RICHARD E. FAUST, PH.D.
Director of Research Planning
and Development
Hoffman-LaRoche, Inc.

JACK T. FAY, JR. PH.D.
Vice-President, Retail Services
Foremost-McKesson

MAX A. FERM, O.D.
Consultant
Generix Drug

JEAN PAUL GAGNON, PH.D.
Professor of Pharmacy
School of Pharmacy
University of North Carolina

DEWEY D. GARNER, PH.D.
Professor of Health-Care
Administration
School of Pharmacy
University of Mississippi

BARRIE G. JAMES, PH.D.
Vice-President of Business
Development
Biogen
Geneva, Switzerland

TED KLEIN
President
Ted Klein & Company and
Medical Marketing Distaff, Inc.

ARTHUR KOORHAN
Divisional Vice-President,
Pharmacy Operations
Cunningham Drug Stores, Inc.

DAVID W. KRUGER

Manager of Trade and Customer Relations
Pharmaceutical Division
Abbott Laboratories

RUSSELL F. LEHN

Manager of Pricing
Pharmaceutical Division
Abbott Laboratories

ALFRED A. MANNINO, R.PH.

Vice-President, Corporate Affairs
Marion Laboratories, Inc.

ALAN W. MERCILL, J.D.

Vice-President, Technical Affairs
The Proprietary Association

DEV. S. PATHAK, D.B.A.

Professor and Chairman
Division of Administrative and
    Social Sciences in Pharmacy
College of Pharmacy
The Ohio State University

MICHAEL A. PIETRANGELO, J.D.

*Senior Vice-President,
    Administration*
Schering-Plough, Inc.

GARY C. WILKERSON, J.D.

Senior Counsel
Schering-Plough, Inc.

PHILLIP C. ZARLENGO

*Manager of Governmental Health
    Programs*
Pharmaceutical Division
Abbott Laboratories

Contents

PART ONE: *The Pharmaceutical Market*

  1. Introduction to Pharmaceutical Marketing 5

  2. Identification of the Market 25

  3. Market Behavior 48

  4. Physician Prescribing Habits 68

  5. Patient Motivation 88

  6. Market Analysis 115

PART TWO: *The Pharmaceutical Product*

  7. Drug Development and the Marketing-Research Interface 141

  8. Diversification and Specialization 172

  9. Marketing Generic Drugs 190

  10. Nonprescription Drugs 206

PART THREE: *Distribution Channels*

  11. The Manufacturer 231

  12. The Wholesaler 248

  13. The Retailer 272

  14. Hospitals and Government Agencies 301

Part Four: *Competitive Practices*

15. Economic and Competitive Aspects of the
    Pharmaceutical Industry   343

16. Advertising   369

17. Detailing and Other Forms of Promotion   400

18. Retail Competition—The Community Level   418

19. International Marketing   448

Part Five: *Controls*

20. Internal Controls   459

21. External Controls   485

Suggested Readings   514

Index   517

Principles of Pharmaceutical Marketing

## PART I

The Pharmaceutical Market

## CHAPTER 1

Introduction to Pharmaceutical Marketing

DEV S. PATHAK

The twentieth century will be remembered for many technological achievements, including a greater understanding of the atom's structure, the information explosion that has resulted from advances in computer technology, and the information obtained from space explorations. When measured in terms of its impact on people's lives, though, the twentieth century "might just as well be called the 'drug age'."[1]

Although drugs and drugs alone cannot be considered to be the sole reason for the progress in medicine achieved in the twentieth century, a glance back to as recently as 40 years ago indicates that "At that time, there were no antibiotics, no corticoids, few sulfa drugs, few vitamins, no tranquilizers, no antihypertensives, no antihistamines, no oral contraceptive drugs, no effective oral diabetic drugs, no prophylactic drugs for gout, no potent active oral diuretics, no drugs to lower the level of blood lipids and cholesterol in the plasma, and no vaccines against polio, measles or mumps."[2] Many great strides, however, have been made in the last 40 years. Not only have many of the debilitating diseases now been controlled or eradicated, but many experts agree that by the end of this century pharmaceuticals may be of even greater importance in our lives because of anticipated major breakthroughs in the fields of neurobiology, immunology, molecular biology, cellular differentiation, cell membrane studies, and genetics.[3, 4] No wonder Chain, the Nobel prize-winning biochemist, has labeled drugs as "one of the greatest blessings—perhaps *the* greatest blessing—of our time."[5]

Although everyone, whether friend or foe of the pharmaceutical industry, recognizes the contribution of the industry to the health and welfare of the public, it is important to realize that all the developments in the pharmaceutical field and the availability of pharmaceuticals to the general public have not merely occurred by chance. Although most of the praise is accorded to those in the pharmaceutical industry concerned with research and development, few appreciate the contributions made by the pharmaceutical marketing system (and by many working within this system) in making these drugs available at the right time, at the right place, in the right quantity, at a reasonable price, and with the right information. This lack of appreciation for the pharmaceutical marketing function or system stems from many misconceptions and barriers to marketing in the pharmaceutical industry, and from the lack of understanding of the meaning of the term "pharmaceutical marketing."

Misconceptions About and Barriers to Marketing in the Pharmaceutical Industry

After having read this book you will be able to evaluate and criticize pharmaceutical marketing practices, so some of the most common misconceptions about and barriers to marketing in the pharmaceutical industry will be discussed in this section.

Marketing for Drug Products, Not for Pharmaceutical Services

The term "marketing" is commonly associated with the marketing of goods—i.e., physical products only. Thus, a common myth in regard to marketing is that only physical products can be marketed, and not services. This is why many professionals, including clinical pharmacists, believe that only pharmaceutical manufacturers and distributors such as wholesalers and "druggists" should deal with marketing of pharmaceuticals, and that professionals involved in providing clinical services should avoid marketing. Marketing approaches are now being adopted by various service professions, such as insurance, banking, and hospitals. Marketing activities are essential for all exchanges undertaken for the purposes of want satisfaction. Although many of these exchanges involve physical products, such as goods, marketing can be used for all products—goods, services, and ideas—that have want-satisfying capabilities.[6]

Commercialism and Lack of Professionalism

Many health-care professionals have a strong disdain for commercialism because they believe that their primary motivation for adopting the profession was not "money" but "service." Regardless of their motivation, all professionals, including clinical pharmacists, recognize the inevitable fact that some equitable charge must be established for the services provided. The charge establishment—pricing—is an integral part of the marketing of any product.

This disdain for marketing is further enhanced by some professional organizations, as has been done by the American Pharmaceutical Association (APhA), through prohibitions on soliciting professional practice by means of advertising by their members. The pros and cons of such prohibitions on professionals could be argued at length, and the courts have now recognized that such prohibitions are unconstitutional.[7]

"Drug Pushing"

Many critics of pharmaceutical marketing have argued that marketing efforts, especially the advertising and promotional practices of the pharmaceutical industry, encourage pill-taking or pill-prescribing behavior in all problem situations. Such irrational behavior on the part of patients and physicians is blamed on the "drug-pushing" efforts of the pharmaceutical companies, who create an artificial demand for products. Instead of outlining the details of these allegations, the following reflection by Dr. Halberstam on the issue may be worth remembering:

> The reliable studies which have been done on both OTC and prescription drugs used in the United States have shown that Americans tend to be conservative in the use of drugs, and that there is strong Puritan ethic which operates to make Americans endure suffering when they would otherwise seek pharmaceutical relief. . . . The accusation that we are an overmedicated society or a nation of "junkies" is just a little slogan that people who know a little bit about pharmaceutical usage have picked up. . . . Rather than being junkies, we are a nation of puritans, who somehow feel that it is proper to suffer.[8]

Unproductive Use of Resources

Because pharmaceutical marketing expenditures do not result in any visible change in the form of the product, it has been argued that all these expenditures should be considered as an unproductive use of resources. What is not recognized in this argument is that these marketing activities create the intangible utilities of time, place, and possession. Although the intangible utilities do not visibly change the drug product, they add significantly to the value of the product from the purchaser's viewpoint.

Some critics have not only ignored the intangible values created by pharmaceutical marketing expenditures, but have argued that these expenditures are designed to give suppliers control over the demand curve. Because "such outlays are not likely to enhance the intrinsic value of the prescription and hence, improve the patient's welfare,"[9] they should be viewed as "redundant." This analysis does not take into consideration the fact that value in use is only one of the demand factors that affects the price determination. Furthermore, the patient's welfare, from his own and the physician's perspective, is a function of the perceived value as well as of the intrinsic value of the prescription. Because the perceived value can be viewed as a simple ratio of perceived quality and perceived price, the "value" of a drug (and thus the patient's welfare) can be improved by pharmaceutical marketing expenditures that lead to an increase in the perceived quality of the prescription.*

Inefficiency and Ineffectiveness

The term "efficiency" refers to the achievement of objectives through minimum resource expenditures, and the term "effectiveness" refers to the maximization of stated objectives. Table 1-1 illustrates the relationship of efficiency and effectiveness criteria to a few pharmacy-related activities. If patient welfare is the ultimate objective, it can be argued that the existence of too many marginal pharmacies and too many "me-too" drugs provide evidence of the inefficiency of our pharmaceutical marketing system. Similarly, the existence of too many drugs for the treatment of a single disease and the absence of drugs for the treatment of many of the known diseases can be regarded as the ineffectiveness of pharmaceutical marketing. Although this criticism, of the existence of the inefficiency and ineffectiveness of pharmaceutical marketing, is not completely unfounded, it should be recognized that this is the price to be paid for selecting freedom of enterprise under a market economy over the alternative of paternalism

---

*The quality of a drug may be viewed as an additive effect of many variables. Thus, "quality = efficiency + safety + clinical evidence + experience + information communicated to doctors and other professionals + reputation of manufactures based on performance of prior products." For this definition, see Weston, J. F.: Pricing in the Pharmaceutical Industry, in *Issues in Pharmaceutical Economics*, edited by R. I. Chien, Lexington, MA: Lexington Books, 1979, p. 76.

TABLE 1-1. *Efficiency vs. Effectiveness*

| | EFFECTIVENESS* | |
	HIGH	LOW
HIGH (EFFICIENCY†)	Training 5 clinical pharmacists a year for ambulatory care setting to work with physicians in a group medical practice, with the American Medical Association obtaining employment for them upon graduation.	Training pharmacists to provide only drug distribution services.
LOW	Requiring 30 minutes of pharmacist consultation with *all* patients for *any* symptom.	Spending $10 million on a campaign to pass a legislation requiring every chain drugstore to have a Pharm. D. on duty in Ohio, and not finding anybody to sponsor the bill.

*Effectiveness is the optimum attainment of the stated objective.
†Efficiency is the minimization of resource expenditure necessary to achieve objective.

under a centrally directed economy. The alternative, however, does not guarantee optimal efficiency and effectiveness for the pharmaceutical marketing system either.

Market, Marketing, and Pharmaceutical Marketing

Because pharmaceutical marketing is only a branch of the field of marketing, it is essential to define the term "marketing". Furthermore, because all theoreticians and businessmen would agree that marketing definitely has something to do with "dealing in a market," this section begins by discussing four different connotations of the term "market": place connotation, size connotation, economic connotation, and business opportunity connotation.*

A common use of the term "market" is in terms of a place. For example, the Columbus, Ohio, market for over-the counter drugs (OTCs) refers to a specific geographic area in which the exchange of drugs takes place between buyers and sellers. Although geographic market area determination for a firm is logically appeal-

*Discussion of the terms "market" and "marketing" is based upon the work by McInnis, W.: A Conceptual Introduction to Marketing, in *Theory in Marketing*, 2nd Ed., edited by R. Cox, W. Alderson, and S. J. Shapiro, Homewood, IL: Richard D. Irwin, 1964, pp. 54–65.

ing and necessary for many small businesses, modern communication technology obviates the fundamental requirement of place connotation of market, that exchange between buyers and sellers takes place in a specific geographic area.

The size connotation of market is normally explained in terms of number of people or dollars, or quantity volume of a product. This definition of market is commonly used by researchers who are interested in investigating the pharmaceutical market place. Although some have used the four-digit Standard Industrial Classification (SIC) of the Bureau of the Census, "Pharmaceutical Preparations," as a basis for their analysis,[10] others have used the classification of therapeutic drugs as markets, resulting in 10,[11] 19,[12] or 69[13] markets, depending upon the researcher's definition. There is no general agreement as to how to define a market using this approach, because it provides no explanation of the underlying processes leading to the formation of any market.

The economic connotation of market avoids viewing the market from either size or place perspective, and treats the concept of market as a process "actuated by the interplay of actions of the various individuals cooperating under the division of labor."[14] The market mechanism—the process of objective exchange valuation—is the basis of any economic theory. The problem with the economic connotation of market, however, is that it fails to recognize that valuation is only one of the many dimensions, and not the only dimension, of the market. The inevitable result of the emphasis on the valuation dimension of the market is that most economic analyses eventually translate all market forces into costs and prices, even when these forces may not be synonymous with either. Such an approach adds precision to economic analysis, but only at the expense of marketing analyses.

The business opportunity connotation of market considers market to be a multidimensional concept; it views valuation as only one of the dimensions necessary to understand the concept of market. From a marketer's viewpoint, market is the gap that separates the parties interested in an exchange.[15] The major gaps or separations that can indicate an existence of a market are spatial, time, perceptual, ownership, and value separations. McCarthy has added two more discrepancies to this list, discrepancy of quantity and of assortment.[16] Each of these separations constitutes an obstacle as well as an opportunity for a marketer—the larger the separation, the larger the market. A brief explanation of each of these separations and an example of one opportunity as it relates to each of these separations in pharmaceutical marketing is provided in Table 1-2. The astute reader has probably already recognized that this concept of market incorporates the other three connotations of market discussed previously.

TABLE 1-2. *Opportunities in Pharmaceutical Market Due to Market Separations*

MARKET SEPARATION	DESCRIPTION	EXAMPLES OF PHARMACEUTICAL CARE
Spatial	Physical separation of providers and recipients	Rural pharmacy
Time	Pharmaceutical care not available when needed, or available when not needed	Home health care
Perceptual	Recipient not familiar with provider services or availability of pharmaceutical care; providers not aware of who needs the care they provide	Clinical services by clinical pharmacists; drug abuse counseling
Ownership	Lack of resources for the title exchange when purchasing pharmaceutical goods and services	Third-party programs; pharmacy cooperatives; drug product selection
Value	Differences in value assigned to a pharmaceutical good or service by providers and recipients	Many clinical services; patient profiles
Quantity discrepancy	Differences in preference for producing large quantities of a good or service by producer/provider due to specialization of labor vs. what is needed by individual purchaser/recipient	"Orphan" drugs
Assortment discrepancy	Individual producer/provider specializing in producing/providing a few goods/services; purchaser/recipient needing a variety of goods/services	Drug discount houses; group practice sites for pharmacists and physicians, and for clinical pharmacists

Market and Marketing

Although the existence of a gap between parties interested in an exchange (i.e., the existence of a market) is necessary, it is not by itself sufficient to result in an exchange. A market is a potential and is not a reality until it is actualized. The process involved in converting the potential market into a real market is called "marketing." Marketing, thus, is "a process by which markets are actualized."[15] Because markets may be viewed as gaps that separate the parties interested in an exchange, marketing as a discipline is a study of how various gaps or separations between parties interested in an exchange are anticipated and removed. Consequently, the process of market actualization (Fig. 1-1) requires that various activities (called marketing activities) remove the gaps between parties interested in an exchange. Some of these points require careful examination.

The essence of marketing is exchange. "The existence of a market is the foundation for an exchange and not a substitute for it."[15] Every exchange requires that (1) there are two or more parties who (2) are interested in satisfying their unfulfilled desires, (3) have something of value to offer to each other, and (4) are capable of communication and delivery.[16]

The process of market actualization may be initiated by either party interested in an exchange. In the normal economic sense, the party with goods is called a "producer" and the party with money is called a "consumer." This is why markets, as defined from the producer's view, are viewed as people with money (purchasing power) and felt or quiescent need.[17]

If the party interested in providing goods or services is labeled as a producer or seller, and the party interested in receiving and consuming goods or services is labeled as a buyer or seller, we find that four major exchange flows (Fig. 1-1) occur in the process of market actualization: product flow, information flow, payment flow, and use right flow.[18] Although the direction of product flow and use right flow is normally from producer to consumer, the direction of payment flow is toward the producer, and information flows both ways. Various activities, such as advertising, pricing, transportation, and marketing research, which are undertaken to identify the gaps between parties interested in an exchange and to facilitate the exchange flows to complete the exchange are called marketing activities. Marketers are those individuals and institutions involved in anticipating and removing separations between parties interested in an exchange. Marketing activities may be undertaken by any party involved in the process of market actualization; one does not have to be a manufacturer to be involved in marketing.

Although most definitions of exchange and marketing revolve around dyadic or restricted exchanges (two-party reciprocal relationships), exchange relationships in modern society are becoming more complicated because of specialization due to division of labor, the use of money as a medium of exchange, and the increasing number of participants.[19] Complex exchanges (a system of mutual relationships between at least three parties) and inter-

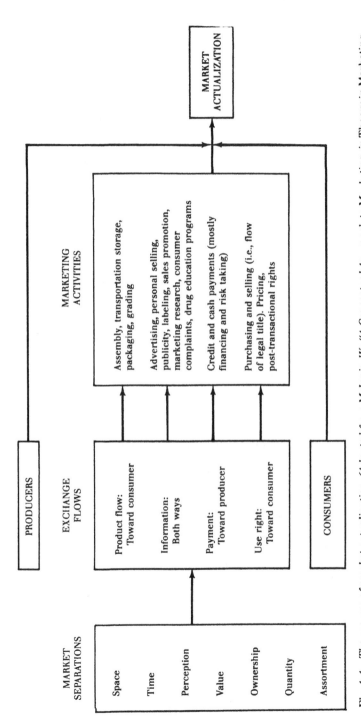

Fig. 1-1. *The process of market actualization. (Adapted from McInnis, W.: "A Conceptual Approach to Marketing, in Theory in Marketing, edited by R. Cox, W. Alderson, and S. J. Shapiro. Homewood, IL: Richard D. Irwin, 1964, p. 51; McCarthy, E. J.: Basic Marketing, 7th Ed., Homewood, IL: Richard D. Irwin, 1981, p. 20.)*

13

active exchanges (combination of complex and univocal reciprocity* arrangements) are more commonplace in today's society, especially in the pharmaceutical marketplace.[19] Figure 1-2 illustrates various types of exchanges in the pharmaceutical market. It is important to realize that while separations (gaps) between parties interested in exchanges are getting larger, the need for exchange makes them dependent on each other.

In marketing, as in any field of investigation, it is important to recognize the distinction between the positive theory and the normative theory of marketing.[20, 21] The positive theory approach to marketing explains "what is" the process of market actualization. This approach leads to the understanding, analysis, and development of verifiable hypotheses of the process of market actualization; it is by no means a mere description of the process. The normative theory approach, on the other hand, leads to an explanation of "what should be," according to some objective. Managerial and public policy scholars in marketing are usually concerned with approaches for controlling and improving the market actualization process so as to achieve their goals *best*.[21] Although marketing as an investigative field is a positive science, marketing management is a normative science that attempts to use the understanding of market actualization to achieve some goals best, such as to maximize sales, market share, or profit. Those who do not fulfill the goals of normative theory are simply practicing the *art* of marketing. It should be noted here that the normative approach to marketing is not independent of the positive approach. Positive theory is also dependent on normative theory. All positive theories are also continually revised and updated according to real world experiences. The answer to a normative question such as "What is the best price of a new antibiotic?" requires understanding of many positive marketing theory questions, such as "What is the market for this antibiotic?" "What are the determinants that lead to a prescription for such a product?" and "What is the relationship of communication of information regarding the product to physicians and sales of this type of product?"

Marketing and Pharmaceutical Marketing

Pharmaceutical marketing, as a subspecialty of marketing, can be defined as *a process by which market for pharmaceutical care is actualized.* It encompasses all the activities carried out by various

*Univocal reciprocity occurs "if the reciprocations involve at least three actors and if the actors do not benefit each other directly but only indirectly." See Ekeh, P. P.: *Social Exchange Theory: The Two Traditions*, Cambridge, MA: Harvard University Press, 1974, pp. 50–52.

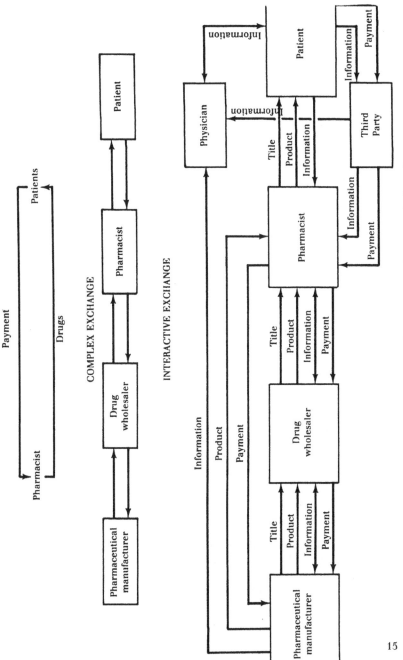

SIMPLE EXCHANGE

Payment

Pharmacist   Patients

Drugs

COMPLEX EXCHANGE

Pharmaceutical manufacturer — Drug wholesaler — Pharmacist — Patient

INTERACTIVE EXCHANGE

Fig. 1-2. *Examples of types of exchanges in the pharmaceutical market.*

15

individuals or organizations to actualize markets for pharmaceutical care. Let us examine this definition closely.

The emphasis in pharmaceutical marketing is on pharmaceutical care, and not just on drugs. Any article, service, or idea needed to anticipate and to remove gaps in pharmaceutical care should be included in the discussion of pharmaceutical marketing. The marketing of many clinical pharmaceutical services and programs is as much a part of pharmaceutical marketing as is the marketing of drug products. In other words, pharmaceutical marketing is not synonymous with, but is significantly broader than, the marketing of pharmaceuticals.

The emphasis in this definition is on pharmaceutical care, indicating that the justification for the existence of pharmaceutical marketing is the patient, and not the manufacturer or the pharmacist.

Any party interested in the exchange for pharmaceutical care may undertake pharmaceutical marketing activities. Hospital pharmacies, community pharmacies, third-party insurance companies, consulting pharmacies, and many other organizations and individuals, in addition to pharmaceutical manufacturers and drug wholesalers, are involved in pharmaceutical marketing.

Pharmaceutical marketing, as a field of investigation, is amoral or goal-free. The definition does not indicate any other goal than the process involved in completing the exchange for pharmaceutical care. Value judgments regarding efficiency or effectiveness of the pharmaceutical marketing system or any of its activities are not an inherent part of the study of the field.

The actualization of markets for pharmaceutical care indicates that all activities involved in anticipating, enlarging, facilitating, and completing or removing gaps in pharmaceutical care are within the scope of the field of pharmaceutical marketing. In other words, pharmaceutical marketing is not a static passive process but a dynamic active process.

Approaches to the Study of Pharmaceutical Marketing

Pharmaceutical marketing, like any other field of investigation, can be studied from various perspectives, with each perspective providing a different approach. Following is a discussion of the five traditional approaches normally used in the study of any type of marketing.

Managerial Approach

This is the most widely adopted approach for the study of marketing.[16, 22, 23] It essentially consists of assisting a marketing manager in selecting the best combination of marketing activities for achieving organizational goals. The major steps involved in any *good* marketing management are (1) formulation of objectives, (2) identification of a target market by market opportunity assessment, resource, and environment analysis, and by selection of specific segmentation or product differentiation strategy, (3) development of an optimal marketing mix, a combination of four controllable marketing variables—product, price, place, and promotion—commonly known as the four Ps,[16] to achieve marketing goals through the target market, and (4) implementation and evaluation of marketing strategy. In effect, management of marketing functions can be described as providing the *right* product, at the *right* price, at the *right* place, with the *right* information, to the *right* market to achieve the organizational objectives. The Task Force on Prescription Drugs endorsed this approach when it described rational prescribing as "Prescribing the right drug for the right patient, at the right time, in the right amounts, and with due consideration of relative costs."[24]

In the formulation of objectives the management, using this approach, may be guided by many orientations, such as production, finance, sales, or customer orientation. The customer orientation, according to the marketing concept, is considered the cornerstone of modern marketing management.[6, 16, 22] Although its advocates have usually discussed the application of this approach only from a manufacturer's perspective, there is nothing inherent in the approach indicating that it cannot be adopted by parties other than pharmaceutical manufacturers, such as community pharmacies. In effect, this approach can be successfully adopted by hospital pharmacies interested in developing reimbursable clinical pharmacy programs.[25]

The major limitation of this approach is that it views marketing as a tool for achieving organizational objectives (a normative view), and not as a field of investigation (a positive theory view). Furthermore, emphasis on achievement of organizational goals through the appropriate identification of target market(s) in the pharmaceutical marketplace may lead to the development of many "me-too" drugs, and may create a class of many needed "orphan" drugs. In other words, achievement of organizational goals at the microlevel in the pharmaceutical marketplace may not always be the most beneficial for society.

Functional Approach

The functional approach concentrates on the study of various marketing activities and functions in completing the major exchange flows leading to market actualization. Table 1-3 shows the relationship of various functions and exchange flows. Although marketing scholars do not agree on how many functions are essential to the field of marketing, marketing functions are traditionally broken down into four categories: (1) transaction functions, including buying and selling; (2) logistics functions, including transportation and storage; (3) facilitating functions, including grading, risk-taking, financing, and market information; and (4) quasimarketing functions, including product development and pricing.[26] Because all these functions must be performed by one or more institutions during the marketing of any commodity, this approach is an integral part of the field of pharmaceutical marketing. There is no definitive statement available, however, that describes which specific functions are essential tasks and which ones are not in the pharmaceutical marketplace.

Institutional Approach

The institutional approach examines the emergence and inter-relationships of various marketing institutions, such as retailers, wholesalers, agents, and producers. In its purest form it may explain the evolution of marketing structure at the firm level as well as at the market level. Emphasis in such an approach is on exchange flows that take place "between entire channels rather than between individual entities along the channel."[27] Doody and Revzan have discussed this approach in its most complex form, and have shown that it can be used to examine various structures and behavioral patterns of various institutions in a marketplace.[28] The only research that has come closest to applying this approach to pharmaceutical marketing was done by Smith and colleagues, who analyzed distribution channels and their relationship to the pharmaceutical industry.[29] Because the emphasis in this approach is on group behavior, it has a tendency to "overlook the individual forces that, collectively, make up institutional behavior; nor does it explain the relationship between the two."[15]

Industrial Organization (Economic, Commodity) Approach

This approach is popular among economists interested in analyzing the relationship between market structure, conduct, and performance of "organizations" involved in the marketplace.[30]

TABLE 1-3. *Functional Approach and its Relationship to Exchange Flows*

FUNCTIONAL CATEGORY	SPECIFIC MARKETING FUNCTIONS	EXCHANGE FLOW RELATIONSHIP
Transactional functions	Buying	Use right flow
	Selling	Use right flow
Logistics functions	Transportation	Product flow
	Sorting	Product flow
Facilitating functions	Grading	Product flow
	Financing	Payment flow
	Risk-taking	Payment flow
	Market information	Information flow
Quasimarketing functions	Product development	Product flow
	Pricing	Use right flow
Other functions	Assembling	Product flow
	Packaging	Product flow

The fundamental assumption behind the analysis used in this approach is that market relationships are actualized by valuation process only; hence, pricing of a commodity is given significant attention (the commodity approach). As shown in Figure 1-3, the causation implied by this analysis is that market structure affects market conduct, which in turn affects market performance. The higher the concentration, a few firms controlling a large portion of the market, the lesser the competition, leading to poor efficiency and effectiveness of marketing functions.

Many economic studies of the pharmaceutical industry have adopted this approach. Those cited by Jadlow concluded that the pharmaceutical market is highly concentrated,[30] and were critical of the behavior and performance of the pharmaceutical industry. However, the recent studies emphasizing Schumpeterian-type competition have challenged the implications of earlier studies that used static competition measures.[31] The dynamic analysis of the pharmaceutical industry indicates that the market structure and performance of the industry are not atypical. The industry is, in effect, innovation-prone, and has improved consumer welfare and competition by providing therapeutic advances, a dynamic form of price competition, and promotional activities that facilitate rather than erect barriers to entry.

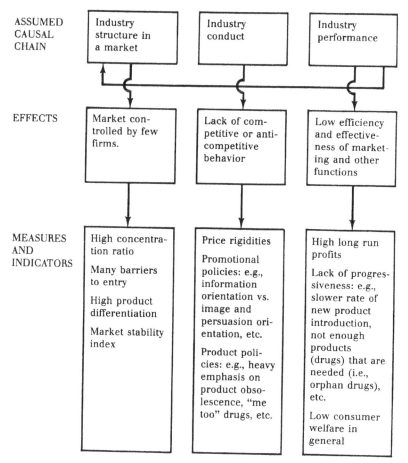

Fig. 1-3. *Industrial organization approach.*

Systems Analysis Approach

Recently a few marketing scholars have attempted to apply systems analysis to marketing. A system can be defined as "a set of objects together with a relationship between their attributes."[32] From a management perspective, "a system is a set of regularly interacting or independent groups coordinated in such a way as to form a unified whole and organized so as to accomplish a set of goals."[33]

It is important to realize that a system is usually a part of larger

Fig. 1-4. *Levels of marketing systems.*

systems. For example, as can be seen from Figure 1-4, management of pharmaceutical marketing may be part of a pharmaceutical organization system, which in turn is part of a health-care marketing system, and so on. If pharmaceutical marketing is viewed as part of the health-care marketing system, it can be depicted as a simplified network of relationships between various institutions and their attributes, leading to actualization of markets for pharmaceutical care through exchange flows and marketing functions within the bounds established by external systems (Fig. 1-5). In order to study a marketing system, it should be recognized that the description of a system should specify the environmental constraints, resources, components (including structure, functions, and goals), performance measures, and management and control of the system.[33]

As can be seen from this outline of the systems analysis approach, it is inclusive of all other approaches used to study pharmaceutical marketing. Additionally, the systems analysis approach allows both positive and normative studies of pharmaceutical marketing at the microlevel (pharmaceutical organization) as well as at the macrolevel (pharmaceutical marketing system) to be used.

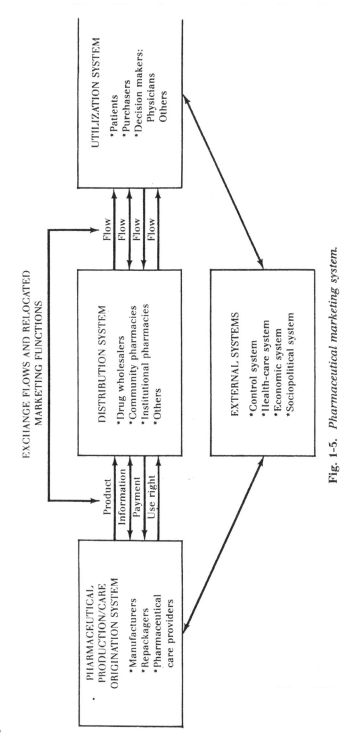

Fig. 1-5. *Pharmaceutical marketing system.*

References

1. Fuchs, V.: *Who Shall Live? Health, Economics and Social Choice,* New York: Basic Books, 1974, p. 106.
2. Siskind, D. A.: Contributions of the Pharmaceutical Industry to Improved Health, in *The Pharmaceutical Industry,* edited by C. M. Lindsay, New York: John Wiley & Sons, 1978.
3. Thomas, L.: Biomedical Science and Human Health, quoted in Bezold, C.: *The Future of Pharmaceuticals,* New York: John Wiley & Sons, 1981, pp. 4–6.
4. Denkewalter, R. G., and Tishler M.: Drug Research—Whence and Whither, in *Progress in Drug Research,* edited by E. Jucker, Basel: Birkhauser, 1966.
5. Chain, E. B.: Academic and Industrial Contribution to Drug Research, *Nature, 200* (No. 4905):441, 1963.
6. Enis, B. M.: *Marketing Principles,* 3rd Ed., Santa Monica: Goodyear Publishing, 1980, pp. 8–15.
7. Virginia State Board of Pharmacy v. Virginia Citizens Consumer Council, [1976] 200 United States 321, 337.
8. Halberstam, Michael J., quoted in Cope J. D.: The Charges Against OTC Medicine Advertising—Are They Deserved? *Journal of the American Pharmaceutical Association, 16*:502 1976.
9. Rucker, T. D.: Public Policy Considerations in the Pricing of Prescription Drugs, *California Pharmacist, 22* (No. 3):8, 1978.
10. Grabowski, H. G., and Vernon, J. M.: Structural Effects of Regulation on Innovation in the Ethical Drug Industry, in *Essays on Industrial Organization in Honor of Joe S. Bain,* edited by R. T. Masson and P. D. Qualls, Cambridge, MA: Ballinger, 1976.
11. Cocks, D. L., and Vihts, J. R.: Pricing Behavior of the Ethical Pharmaceutical Industry, *Journal of Business, 47*:349, 1974.
12. Vernon, J. M.: Concentration, Promotion, and Market Share Stability in the Pharmaceutical Industry, *Journal of Industrial Economics, 19*:246, 1971.
13. Hornbrook, M. C.: Market Domination and Promotional Intensity in the Wholesale-Retail Sector of the U.S. Pharmaceutical Industry, Washington, DC, National Center for Health Services Research, Technical Paper Series, No. 5, 1976.
14. Von Mises, L.: *Human Action,* New Haven: Yale University Press, 1949, p. 258.
15. McInnis, W.: A Conceptual Introduction to Marketing, in *Theory in Marketing,* 2nd Ed., edited by R. Cox, W. Alderson, and S. J. Shapiro, Homewood, IL: Richard D. Irwin, 1964.
16. McCarthy, E. J.: *Basic Marketing: A Managerial Approach,* 7th Ed., Homewood, IL: Richard D. Irwin, 1981, p. 20.
17. Gist, R. R.: *Marketing and Society,* 2nd Ed., Hinsdale, IL: The Dryden Press, 1974, p. 7.
18. Enis, B. M.: *Marketing Principles,* Pacific Palisades, CA: Goodyear Publishing, 1974, p. 90.
19. Bagozzi, R. P.: Marketing as Exchange, *Journal of Marketing, 39*:32, 1979.
20. Keynes, J. M.: *The Scope and Method of Political Economy,* London: McMillan Publications, 1891, pp. 34–35.

21. Narver, J. C., and Savitt, R.: *The Marketing Economy: An Analytical Approach*, New York: Holt, Rinehart and Winston, 1971, pp. 9–10.
22. Kotler, P.: *Marketing Management: Analysis, Planning and Control*, Englewood Cliffs, NJ: Prentice-Hall, 1972.
23. Cravens, D. W., Hills, G. E., and Woodruff, R. B.: *Marketing Decision Making: Concepts and Strategy*, Homewood IL: Richard D. Irwin, 1980.
24. Task Force On Prescription Drugs: *The Drug Makers and The Drug Distributors.* Washington, DC: U.S. Government Printing Office, 1968, p. vii.
25. Pathak, D. S., and Nold, E. G.: Developing Reimbursable Clinical Pharmacy Programs: A Goal-Oriented Approach, *American Journal of Hospital Pharmacy, 36*:1548, 1979.
26. Beckman, T. N., Davidson, W. R., and Talarzyk, W. W.: *Marketing*, 9th Ed., New York: The Ronald Press, 1973, pp. 19–21.
27. Cox, Reavis: Quantity Limits and the Theory of Economic Opportunity, in *Theory in Marketing*, edited by W. Alderson and R. Cox, Homewood, IL: Richard D. Irwin, 1950.
28. Doody, E. A., and Revzan, D. A.: *Marketing: An Institutional Approach*, 2nd Ed., New York: McGraw-Hill, 1953.
29. Smith, M. C., Roberts, K. B., and MacLayton, D.: The Pharmaceutical Industry: Distribution Channels and Relationship—
    a. Part I, *Medical Marketing and Media, 11*:32, 1976;
    b. Part II, *Medical Marketing and Media, 11*:26, 1976;
    c. Part III, *Medical Marketing and Media, 11*:30, 1976.
30. For a review of these studies, see Jadlow, J. M.: A Summary and Critique of Economic Studies of the Ethical Drug Industry: 1962–68, in *Issues in Pharmaceutical Economics*, edited by R. I. Chien, Lexington, MA: Lexington Books, 1979, pp. 13–27.
31. For a review of these studies, see Grabowski, H. G., and Vernon, J. M.: "New Studies on Market Definition, Concentration, Theory of Supply, Entry and Promotion, in *Issues in Pharmaceutical Economics*, edited by R. I. Chien, Lexington, MA: Lexington Books, 1979, pp. 29–52.
32. Lewis, R. J., and Erickson, L. G.: Marketing Functions and Marketing Systems: A Synthesis, *Journal of Marketing. 33*:13, 1970.
33. Carman, J. M. and Uhl, K. P.: *Marketing: Principles and Methods*, 7th Ed., Homewood, IL: Richard D. Irwin, 1973, pp. 16–17.

## CHAPTER 2

Identification of the Market

MICKEY C. SMITH

Even the most colloquial use of the term marketing implies the existence, somewhere, of a "market." But what constitutes a market? If this question were asked of 100 marketing executives in the pharmaceutical industry, almost certainly 100 different answers would be given. Even the American Marketing Association has, through the years, provided as many as four definitions for the term:

1. The aggregate of forces or conditions within which buyers and sellers make decisions that result in the transfer of goods and services.

2. The aggregate demand of the potential buyers of a commodity or service.

3. The place or area in which buyers and sellers function.

4. (As a verb) To perform business activities that direct the flow of goods and services from producer to consumer or user.[1, 2]

Probably the most useful of these definitions is the second, which emphasizes the importance of demand for the product. This in no way negates the correctness of the other definitions, which are proper in suitable context. The particular advantage of the second definition lies in its ability, upon clarification, to serve simultaneously as a definition and as an introduction to market segmentation.

Aggregate demand refers to the composite of the individual demands of all the potential buyers of a product. Each market is made up of a number of different market segments, each composed of a group of buyers or buying units (in the special case of the pharmaceutical industry, prescribers, or prescribing units), who share qualities that make that segment distinct and give it significance to marketing. Another way of stating this is that a market is not only an aggregate demand for a product but consists of the sum of the demands of different market segments.

Even a single characteristic common to a group of people is sufficient to classify this group as a "market." For example, the use of cosmetics is great enough to group a population of women into the "cosmetic market." Past use of cosmetics is not a sufficient qualification for marketing purposes. The marketer is also interested in those who may buy cosmetics in the future. For this portion of the market it would perhaps be better to use the term "prospect," rather than market. Differentiation within the market, however, does not end here. Continuing with the cosmetic example we might speak of the "luxury cosmetic market" when referring to a specific segment of those who use (or may use) cosmetics. The "door-to-door" market is a further type of qualification that may be desirable, which may be broken down to "the Avon market," the "Vivian Woodard market," and others.

The importance of subclassifications within the "market" is easily exemplified within the ethical pharmaceutical industry. It seems safe to state that no one within the entire population is immune from being classified in some portion of the prescription drug market, particularly if we are to include "prospects." Thus, if we are to speak only of the ethical drug market in its most general terms, we must include the entire population.

The pharmaceutical market is unique in the importance of the influence of a nonpurchaser on the purchasing habits of the ultimate consumer. Because of the "veto power" of physicians in regard to the acceptance of a prescription drug, it becomes necessary to classify physicians as thoroughly as the patients. A further peculiarity of the pharmaceutical market is the importance of the disease entity. With a few exceptions, such as the oral contraceptives, incidence of disease is an important classificatory device for identifying and quantifying a "market" for a prescription drug product.

Because of the almost limitless possibilities in identifying the various pharmaceutical "markets" it is, perhaps, the best course for us to limit our discussion to the prescription pharmaceutical market as a whole in the United States.

The Consumer

In a population that is changing and growing as rapidly as ours, the use of statistics in a text such as this seem almost pointless, because data become immediately obsolete. Statistics can be used as examples, however, to point out relationships, even though the numbers themselves may be outdated.

Study of the size and character of the market obviously involves more than mere nose counting (although this may be of paramount importance to the antihistamine manufacturer). The demographic data that may be necessary for any evaluation of the consumer market for prescription drugs must include, among other factors, the sex, age, and income of the population. For other types of products a great many other considerations, such as occupation, religion, educational status, and mobility must also be considered. These must in fact be studied by prescription drug manufacturers as well, but at a step removed from the market—in the physician's office.

From the manufacturer's viewpoint, sex is an important demographic characteristic. It has been shown that women comprise somewhat more than their expected half of the population, and this trend is expected to continue. Perhaps even more important, as far as the manufacturer is concerned, is the finding that women account for significantly more than their share of the health care market, prescription drugs included. The obvious special interest in the sexual makeup of the population by the manufacturers of such drug products as estrogens, vaginal creams, and oral contraceptives would seem to require little elaboration.

Data on age are of interest in a general way to all of industry. The relative proportion of the population in each age category is important not only for purposes of forecasting demand for an individual class of prescription products (e.g., antispasmodics for infant colic), but also to help direct research efforts. Particularly important trends for the pharmaceutical industry are found in the 0- to 19-year and 60- to 79-year categories. Not only do these groups offer specialized product development opportunities, but they are the two categories most frequently considered in the development of government health care programs. Both of these considerations must enter into the long-range planning of pharmaceutical manufacturers. A further consideration is the fact that these two segments of the population demand proportionately more health care than do other segments of the population.

Because level of income determines the total available monies for expenditure on drug products, this statistic becomes extremely

Principles of Pharmaceutical Marketing

important. A further consideration is the importance of income levels in determining the type and level of health-care purchases. For example, the greater the affluence of a given family unit, the more likely for its members to seek medical attention (with the potential of resultant prescriptions) for increasingly minor ailments. Those in the lower income brackets lean more heavily toward self-medication for such things as colds and aches and pains.

Table 2-1 considers both age and income variables, as well as racial factors, by showing per capita numbers of physician visits.

TABLE 2-1. *Physician Visits per Person per Year, According to Age, Color, and Economic status: United States, 1964, 1973, and 1978*

AGE AND YEAR	TOTAL		WHITE		ALL OTHER	
	POOR	NON-POOR*	POOR	NON-POOR	POOR	NON-POOR
All ages[†]			Number of visits			
1964	3.9	4.8	4.2	4.9	3.3	3.9
1973	5.3	5.0	5.4	5.1	5.3	4.6
1978	5.6	4.7	5.7	4.7	5.6	4.5
Under 17 years						
1964	2.3	4.0	2.6	4.1	1.9	2.4
1973	3.8	4.3	4.2	4.4	3.2	2.9
1978	4.0	4.2	4.3	4.3	3.5	3.3
17–44 years						
1964	4.1	4.7	4.5	4.8	3.3	4.2
1973	5.7	5.0	5.8	5.0	5.6	4.8
1978	5.8	4.4	5.7	4.4	6.1	4.8
45–64 years						
1964	5.1	5.1	5.2	5.1	4.9	4.6
1973	6.3	5.4	6.1	5.4	7.1	5.3
1978	7.5	5.0	7.6	5.0	7.3	4.8
65 years and over						
1964	6.0	7.3	6.2	7.3	4.9	6.5
1973	6.5	6.9	6.4	6.8	7.0	8.6
1978	6.2	6.8	6.2	6.8	6.8	7.0

*Definition of poor and nonpoor are based on family income for each year as follows:

YEAR	POOR	NONPOOR
1964	less than $3,000	$3,000 or more
1973	less than $6,000	$6,000 or more
1978	less than $7,000	$7,000 or more

[†]Age adjusted by the direct method to the 1970 civilian noninstitutionalized population, using four age intervals.

Source: Division of Health Interview Statistics, National Center for Health Statistics: Data from the National Health Interview Survey, 1980.

The greater number of visits by those in upper age groups is obvious, as is the greater number of visits by whites. It should be noted, however, that the passage of time has brought increased utilization of physicians' services by the poor, almost certainly the result of the Medicaid program.

The National Center for Health Statistics conducted interviews during 1977 to investigate the relationships between age, income, place of residence, and other factors and expenditures for prescribed and nonprescribed medication. (Unfortunately, no more recent study of this scope has been published.) Table 2-2 summarizes some of their findings.

Certain facts become obvious when these figures are examined. Females spend more for medication than do males for prescribed medications. Whites spend more for medication than do nonwhites. This is at least partly explained by the difference in family incomes. As family income rises, expenditures for medicine decline. It should be pointed out that the dollar amounts involved here are not nearly as important as the relationships that are described. Changes in drug prices, inflation, and other factors can be expected to change the dollar figures. The relationships, however, seem to remain essentially the same, at least in the near term.

Further detail on the reasons for prescription use can be found in Table 2-3, which shows the number of prescriptions by medical condition. Table 2-4 describes physician visits by source of care.

The Physician

Gosselin has called prescription drugs "directed consumer goods."[3] Another way of stating this is that prescription medication sales result from derived demand—that is, the sale of a prescription drug is not based on any choice of the consumer but rather on that of the physician. For this reason, the physician also constitutes a "market" for prescription drugs. Many of the same factors that affect consumer purchase patterns also affect the prescribing habits of the physician. Other recognized factors also influence the physician's decision to prescribe a given medication.

Perhaps no other group in the United States or the world has been so thoroughly classified, categorized, and identified as has the American physician. An example of just how thoroughly this has been done is shown in Table 2-5, in which 400,000 physicians are classified by age, primary specialty, and type of practice. Although there is no point in presenting them here, data are available from the same source that show all the figures presented in Table 2-5, and that provide a further breakdown by geographic area. *(Text continues on p. 38.)*

TABLE 2-2. *Annual Expenditures and Sources of Payment for Prescribed Medicines: Mean Expense per Person with Expense and Percentage Paid by Source of Payment (NMCES household data: United States, 1977)*

POPULATION CHARACTERISTICS	TOTAL POPULATION WITH EXPENSE FOR PRESCRIBED MEDICINES (IN THOUSANDS)	MEAN EXPENSE PER PERSON WITH EXPENSE $	SOURCE OF PAYMENT			
			FAMILY	PRIVATE HEALTH INSURANCE	MEDICAID	OTHER*
			Percentage distribution			
Total[†§‖]	120,424	46	73.0	13.6	7.7	5.6
Age in years						
Less than 6	11,736	20	73.6	10.2	9.9	6.2
6 to 18	21,905	20	74.7	12.2	7.6	5.5
19 to 24	11,424	27	71.4	11.8	9.6	7.2
25 to 54	45,062	44	70.6	15.8	6.0	7.5
55 to 64	13,720	79	71.5	16.2	7.0	5.3
65 or older	16,577	93	77.0	10.3	9.5	3.2
Sex						
Male	50,952	41	71.8	15.5	4.8	8.0
Female	69,472	50	73.8	12.5	9.4	4.3
Ethnic/racial background						
White	90,162	46	74.4	14.9	5.5	5.2
Black	9,895	44	60.7	6.7	25.3	7.3
Hispanic	4,718	35	58.1	6.9	26.5	8.5
Family income						
Less than $12,000	42,807	57	71.9	8.4	14.5	5.2
$12,000 to $19,999	31,880	42	74.8	16.8	3.2	5.2
$20,000 or more	45,395	39	73.2	18.5	1.6	6.6

Education of family head					
Less than 9 years	23,501	65	70.9	9.0	15.5	4.6
9 to 11 years	18,851	49	71.8	12.7	10.0	5.5
12 years	38,564	42	73.7	15.6	4.5	6.1
13 to 15 years	16,065	38	73.9	16.9	2.2	6.9
16 or more years	18,777	39	76.3	17.7	0.4*	5.5
Employment status					
Employed	48,929	39	75.3	16.5	2.0	6.3
Unemployed	3,244	35	70.1	13.5	9.1	7.3
Not in labor force	43,101	71	71.7	12.2	10.9	5.1
Place of residence					
SMSA	83,157	45	71.4	14.7	8.0	5.8
Other	37,266	49	76.4	11.3	6.9	5.4
U.S. Census region					
Northeast	26,315	42	74.6	13.5	8.3	3.7
North Central	32,717	44	72.7	17.0	6.0	4.2
South	39,692	51	75.5	10.5	8.1	5.9
West	21,701	47	67.1	15.0	8.4	9.3

*Includes CHAMPUS, CHAMPVA, the Indian Health Service, the Veterans Administration, the military, other federal, state, city or county payers, philanthropic institutions, and unknown sources of payment.

†Includes all other ethnic/racial groups not shown separately.

‡Includes persons with negative income.

§Includes persons with unknown education.

‖Includes all those not in the labor force but less than 16 years of age.

*Relative standard error is equal to or greater than 30%.

Source: National Center for Health Services Research.

TABLE 2-3. *Percentage Distribution of Drug Mentions by Therapeutic Category, according to Sex and Age of the Patient: United States, 1980*

THERAPEUTIC CATEGORY*	ALL PATIENTS	SEX OF PATIENT		AGE OF PATIENT				
		FEMALE	MALE	UNDER 15 YEARS	15–24 YEARS	25–44 YEARS	45–64 YEARS	65 YEARS AND OVER
All categories	679,593	413,570	266,023	115,643	75,213	148,126	175,572	165,038
				Number in thousands				
Total	100.00	100.00	100.00	100.00	100.00	100.00	100.00	100.00
				Percent distribution				
Antihistamine drugs	6.47	5.94	7.28	14.60	7.75	7.16	3.90	2.29
Anti-infective agents	15.44	14.36	17.11	29.49	26.10	17.17	8.73	6.30
Antibiotics	13.26	11.99	15.22	27.03	23.68	14.41	7.01	4.46
Antineoplastic agents	0.79	0.99	0.47	*0.07	*0.18	*0.45	1.48	1.14
Autonomic drugs	3.71	3.70	3.73	2.78	3.09	4.91	4.14	3.12
Blood formation and coagulation	1.22	1.38	0.97	*0.46	1.42	1.19	1.18	1.75
Cardiovascular drugs	9.49	8.55	10.94	*0.34	*0.53	2.90	13.66	21.44
Cardiac drugs	3.87	3.23	4.87	*0.15	*0.36	1.09	5.28	9.08
Hypotensive agents	3.35	3.42	3.19	*0.11	*0.12	1.32	5.46	6.59
Vasodilating agents	2.16	1.79	2.72	*0.06	*0.05	*0.38	2.78	5.52
Central nervous system drugs	16.29	17.06	15.09	5.84	11.55	21.75	20.72	16.16
Analgesics and antipyretics	8.51	8.35	8.74	4.47	6.42	9.89	10.33	9.10
Psychotherapeutic agents	2.41	2.62	2.10	*0.29	1.44	3.39	3.58	2.22
Sedatives and hypnotics	3.68	4.05	3.12	0.70	2.25	4.76	4.98	4.09
Electrolytic, caloric, and water balance	7.65	8.05	7.02	*0.56	1.59	4.62	11.67	13.81
Diuretics	6.30	6.70	5.69	*0.21	*0.93	3.85	9.63	11.69

DRUG MENTIONS

32

Expectorants and cough preparations	2.78	2.53	3.17	6.49	3.30	2.69	1.80	1.07
Eye, ear, nose, and throat preparations	3.84	3.58	4.24	4.01	3.10	3.46	3.28	4.98
Gastrointestinal drugs	3.55	3.47	3.67	2.13	2.41	3.42	4.14	4.56
Hormones and synthetic substances	8.22	9.98	5.48	1.93	9.76	9.37	10.44	8.52
Adrenals	2.69	2.67	2.74	1.45	2.42	3.03	3.48	2.56
Serums, toxoids, and vaccines	3.49	2.94	4.34	14.50	2.52	0.81	0.99	1.28
Skin and mucous membrane preparations	8.12	7.86	8.53	8.43	15.77	10.75	5.72	4.61
Spasmolytic agents	1.70	1.40	2.15	1.77	*0.53	1.03	1.84	2.64
Vitamins	3.57	4.67	1.86	0.75	6.57	4.87	2.95	3.66
Other therapeutic categories	2.22	2.04	0.97	4.82	2.37	1.82	1.52	1.42
Unknown	1.47	1.49	1.45	1.03	1.47	1.64	1.84	1.25

*Based on the pharmacologic therapeutic classification of the American Society of Hospital Pharmacists. Selected categories reproduced with the Society's permission.

Source: National Center for Health Statistics.

TABLE 2-4. *Physician Visits, According to Source or Place of Care and Selected Patient Characteristics: United States, 1973 and 1978*

(Data are based on household interviews of a sample of the civilian noninstitutionalized population)

CHARACTERISTIC	ALL SOURCES OR PLACES*		DOCTOR'S OFFICE OR CLINIC OR GROUP PRACTICE		HOSPITAL OUTPATIENT DEPARTMENT†		TELEPHONE	
	1973	1978	1973	1978	1973	1978	1973	1978
			Visits per 1000 population					
Total†, §, ‖	4991.0	4717.0	3440.7	3158.3	533.6	642.7	640.8	569.8
Age								
Under 17 years	4184.6	4108.3	2595.1	2579.5	494.9	554.6	778.5	689.8
17–44 years	5045.9	4528.3	3486.7	2995.4	553.4	652.8	581.6	495.1
45–64 years	5454.5	5286.2	4019.3	3688.3	553.2	751.8	538.9	498.5
65 years and over	6542.3	6294.2	4911.0	4618.6	547.7	669.3	615.9	599.4
Sex‡								
Male	4363.8	4100.0	2964.2	2655.8	501.5	650.5	500.2	451.2
Female	5552.5	5280.9	3870.8	3617.7	562.2	637.7	767.1	675.0
Race‡								
White	5053.4	4723.6	3535.7	3230.2	458.2	566.0	699.0	622.3
Black	4723.6	4859.4	2833.5	2788.7	1145.0	1188.8	252.8	245.8
Family income†, #								
Less than $7,000	5435.2	5587.2	3343.9	3264.7	883.5	1060.0	528.0	549.1
$7,000–$9,999	4752.1	4891.4	3374.2	3213.2	562.2	836.1	464.6	515.1
$10,000–$14,999	4848.7	4673.0	3455.3	3061.4	486.9	657.4	627.5	620.7
$15,000–$24,999	5092.4	4671.1	3466.7	3249.7	508.5	522.0	751.3	654.1
$25,000 or more	5142.2	4591.1	3588.3	3330.8	457.9	435.3	721.8	561.9

34

Geographic region‡							
Northeast	4904.6	4874.3	3206.8	3001.3	626.1	753.7	633.6	694.0
North Central	5022.3	4593.6	3514.6	3163.2	470.3	564.5	727.4	613.0
South	4829.0	4470.0	3326.2	3067.8	529.4	589.2	581.3	436.5
West	5351.1	5164.7	3858.3	3525.5	514.9	721.5	620.0	594.3
Location of residence‡							
Within SMSA	5230.3	4905.3	3501.1	3207.9	605.3	715.6	712.7	613.3
Outside SMSA	4468.0	4321.7	3308.3	3060.1	374.9	486.2	483.2	480.4

*Includes all other sources or places of care not shown separately.
†Includes hospital outpatient clinic or emergency room.
‡Age adjusted by the direct method to the 1970 civilian noninstitutionalized population, using four age intervals.
§Includes all other races not shown separately.
‖Includes unknown family income.
#Family income categories for 1978. Corresponding income categories in 1973, adjusting for inflation, were: less than $5,000; $5,000–$6,999; $7,000–$9,999; $10,000–$14,999; and $15,000 or more.

Source: Division of Health Interview Statistics, National Center for Health Statistics: Data from the National Health Interview Survey, 1980.

TABLE 2-5. *Primary Specialty of Federal and Nonfederal Physicians, Selected Years 1970–1979*

SPECIALTY	1970	1975	1978	1979	CHANGE (%) 1970–1979	1978–1979
Total Physicians*	310,845	340,280	375,811	393,729	26.6	4.8
Aerospace medicine	1,188	684	584	577	−51.4	−1.2
Allergy	1,719	1,716	1,537	1,509	−12.2	−1.8
Anethesiology	10,860	12,861	14,246	15,367	41.5	7.9
Cardiovascular diseases	6,476	6,933	8,506	8,767	35.4	3.1
Child psychiatry	2,090	2,581	2,926	3,163	51.3	8.1
Colon and rectal surg.	667	661	679	721	8.1	6.2
Dermatology	4,003	4,661	5,105	5,483	37.0	7.4
Diagnostic radiology	1,968	3,544	5,431	6,532	231.9	20.3
Forensic pathology	200	190	234	234	17.0	—
Emergency medicine	N/A	2,340	5,007	5,538	N/A	19.6
Family practice	†	11,461	21,611	24,924	‡	15.3
Gastroenterology	2,010	2,381	3,314	3,495	73.8	5.5
General practice	57,948	45,096	34,586	33,206	‡	−4.0
General preventive med.	804	789	756	769	−4.4	1.7
General surgery	29,761	31,562	32,059	33,217	11.6	3.6
Internal medicine	41,872	54,331	62,641	68,591	59.0	6.3
Neurological surgery	2,578	2,926	3,098	3,268	26.8	5.5
Neurology	3,074	4,131	4,923	5,381	75.0	9.3

Obstetrics/gynecology	18,876	21,751	23,963	25,215	33.6	5.2
Occupational medicine	2,713	2,355	2,351	2,356	-13.1	0.2
Opthalmology	9,927	11,129	11,933	12,619	27.1	5.7
Orthopedic surgery	9,620	11,379	12,657	13,506	40.4	6.7
Otorhinolaryngology	5,409	5,745	6,117	6,410	18.5	4.8
Pathology	10,283	11,720	12,620	13,302	29.3	5.4
Pediatrics	17,941	21,746	24,545	26,696	48.8	8.8
Pediatric allergy	391	446	437	454	16.1	3.9
Pediatric cardiology	487	558	588	632	29.8	7.5
Phys. medicine/rehab.	1,479	1,664	1,900	2,084	40.9	9.7
Plastic surgery	1,600	2,236	2,624	2,883	80.1	9.9
Psychiatry	21,146	23,922	25,596	26,860	27.0	4.9
Public health	3,029	2,665	2,340	2,312	-23.7	-1.2
Pulmonary diseases	2,315	2,335	3,070	3,225	39.3	5.0
Radiology	10,524	11,527	11,579	11,712	11.3	1.1
Therapeutic radiology	868	1,169	1,397	1,516	74.6	8.5
Thoracic surgery	1,809	1,979	2,042	2,215	22.4	8.5
Urological surgery	5,795	6,667	7,242	7,561	30.5	4.4
Other specialties	6,929	4,957	5,129	5,185	-25.2	1.0
Unspecified	12,486	7,542	10,438	6,244	-50.0	-40.2

These figures do not include: inactive, not classified and address unknown; 23,183 (1970); 53,462 (1975); 61,675 (1978); 60,835 (1979).
†In 1970 family practice was combined with general practice.
‡Due to the combination of family practice and general practice in 1970, data are not comparable.
N/A indicates not applicable.

Sources: *AMA Physician Masterfile*, 1979; Division of Survey and Data Resources, American Medical Association, 1980. Center for Health Services Research and Development: *Physician Distribution and Medical Licensure in the U.S., 1978*, American Medical Association, 1979. Also prior editions.

These data are obtained from such sources as the American Medical Association, and are constantly being updated. By using computers, changes resulting from deaths, relocations, and changes in practice can be noted and reflected in tabular form within days. Some ways in which these data are used will be presented here.

Physician Specialty

The number of physicians in a given specialty is important, if for no other reason than budgeting of advertising expenditures. It can be determined without too much difficulty who among the physician specialists are most likely to use a certain prescription drug in their practice. Identification of physicians by specialty can be helpful to advertisers in determining the size of the physician audience and in finding the relative use of a product by specialists as opposed to general practitioners.

Age

Pharmaceutical advertisers frequently omit physicians over 65 years of age from their direct mail advertising. This is based on the assumption that this group of physicians is less active in practice than their younger counterparts. Age, however, cannot always predict the activity or importance of the physician. Patients, particularly the elderly, tend to continue going to the older physician, with whom they have built up an accord over the years. Nevertheless, age is a factor in promotional decisions.

The Academic Market

The teacher is of interest to manufacturers who are attempting to have their products accepted as a standard item. Insofar as he influences the future prescribing habits of his students, the medical school instructor is important for marketing activity far beyond that justified by his sometimes limited practice.

In addition to demographic factors, methods have been devised for identifying other segments of the physician market. Fisher-Stevens has developed a profile of physicians based on their tendency to try new drugs. An example of such a profile is shown in Table 2-6.

Other profiles are available from this and other firms, so we have a "high prescribers" market. Another publication is sent to residents, interns, and "decision makers" in the hospital. The "decision makers" market includes chiefs of service, directors of intern and residency training, directors of medical education, pro-

TABLE 2-6. *Fisher-Stevens Physicians' Practice Profile—Innovator/Traditionalist Counts*

SPECIALTY	INNOVATOR	EARLY ADOPTER	EARLY MAJORITY	LATE MAJORITY	TRADI- TIONALIST	TOTAL
General Practice	323	2,879	3,135	5,593	1,737	13,667
General practice subspecialty*	163	584	616	1,077	468	2,908
Family Practice	182	1,772	2,280	3,062	638	7,934
Internal Medicine	404	2,276	2,512	4,365	1,187	10,744
Internal medicine subspecialty†	506	578	446	743	282	2,555
Osteopathy	274	1,651	1,878	2,477	804	7,084
Psychiatry‡	408	1,087	1,214	2,086	1,101	5,896
Cardiology	516	541	447	690	251	2,245
General Surgery	239	1,482	1,610	2,761	1,179	7,271
Orthopedic Surgery	91	662	856	1,296	442	3,347
Pediatrics	230	1,244	1,348	3,250	1,561	7,633
Urology	103	532	417	606	174	1,832
Obstetrics/Gynecology§	480	2,063	2,197	3,462	1,376	9,578
All Other Spec.||	47	85	93	153	76	454
Unspecified	68	395	358	574	311	1,706
Grand Total	3,834	17,831	19,407	32,195	11,587	84,854

*Emergency medicine, general preventive medicine, occupational medicine, public health, physical medicine, pulmonary diseases.
†Diabetes, endocrinology, gastroenterology, geriatrics, hematology, infectious diseases, neoplastic diseases, nutrition, rheumatology.
‡Child neurology, child psychiatry, neurology, psychiatry.
§Gynecology, obstetrics and gynecology, obstetrics.
||Other recognized AMA specialties that are not in one of the above groups or who are not a GP, FP, IM, DO, PD, CD, GS, ORS, U, US.

Source: Fisher-Stevens, Inc., 1981.

The PPP Data Base is an unpublished data compilation registered under the Copyright Laws of the United States.

fessors in the university-affiliated teaching hospital, and medical consultants to the Armed Forces. Another source has identified such groups as "known steroid users," "known tetracycline users," etc. The possibilities for identifying and segmenting physicians in the United States seem to be endless. It seems certain that efforts to find new ways of identifying submarkets among physicians will continue.

Other Doctors and Health-Care Personnel

The physician is not the only "doctor" who is influential in the ultimate destination of prescription pharmaceuticals. Others who must be considered include osteopaths, dentists, podiatrists, veterinarians, nurses, physician assistants, and chiropractors.

Osteopathic Physicians

The osteopath is becoming increasingly important as a prescriber. His status has improved over the years and, in many states, he is legally considered equal to the physician as far as his ability to prescribe, practice surgery, and practice as a member of the hospital staff. In many states the osteopath takes the same board examination for licensure as does the physician.

There are fewer osteopaths than physicians, but the importance of this group in the pharmaceutical market cannot be ignored. Indeed, some statistics would indicate that, on a per-capita basis, the osteopath is a greater source of prescriptions than the physician. It is estimated that there will be approximately 30,000 osteopaths in practice by 1990 in the United States. It has been projected that the more than 10,000 osteopathic physicians account for more than 50 million new prescriptions annually, or roughly 104 prescriptions per week per physician. These physicians, according to one study, are similar in total patient and prescription volume to their allopathic counterparts.[4]

Dentists

There are presently more than 130,000 practicing dentists in the United States, with nearly one third of them having staff affiliation in hospitals. In the limited sphere of their use of drugs dentists can be an important source of prescriptions.

Dentists are estimated to account for nearly 40 million prescriptions annually.[5] Among the types of medications administered, prescribed, and dispersed by dentists are narcotic analgesics, nonnarcotic analgesics, antibiotics, nasal decongestants, sedatives, tranquilizers, maintenance vitamins, fluoride tablets, fluoride gels, fluoride solutions, fluoride/vitamin combinations, and topical steroids.

Podiatrists

Podiatrists or chiropodists treat a variety of conditions, including ingrowing toenails, tumors, bone growths or deformities, abcess drainage, and cysts. The method of treatment by podiatrists sometimes includes drugs, although in some states their use of drugs and anesthetics is limited. Degrees awarded to this group include Doctor of Surgical Chiropody (DSC), Doctor of Podiatry (PodD or PD), and Doctor of Podiatric Medicine (DPM).

There are approximately 8000 podiatrists in the United States, the majority in solo practice. They are concentrated in the Northeast and on the West Coast. Podiatrists are estimated to use as many as 15 drugs per day, with 3 or more of those uses being in the form of prescriptions. A study in one state showed that more than half of podiatric prescriptions were in the following therapeutic categories: oral antibiotics, topical antifungals, non-narcotic analgesics, topical antibiotics, and escharotics.[6]

Veterinarians

Although the area of market opportunity in the field of veterinary medicine is considerably different from that for humans, many of the same drugs are employed, sometimes in the same packages and dosage forms. The field has grown rapidly in recent years, particularly in the small animal field as the nation's pet population has grown in numbers and received increasingly more medical attention.

There are more than 25,000 Doctors of Veterinary Medicine in the United States, and they are permitted to prescribe medications for animal use only.

Nurses

There are more than one million nurses in this country and, while it is difficult to quantify their influence on both prescription and nonprescription drug use, it is certainly substantial. There is a special class of nurse practitioners who have prescribing privileges in several states, and their practices are just beginning to be studied.

One study by the *American Journal of Nursing* indicated that nearly 90% of hospital nurses make suggestions about drugs or-

TABLE 2-7. *Expenditures for Health Services and Supplies under Public Programs by Program, Type of Expenditure, and Source of Funds (in millions of dollars) 1979*

| | TOTAL | HEALTH SERVICES AND SUPPLIES | | | | | | | | | | |
| | | PERSONAL HEALTH CARE | | | | | | | | | ADMINISTRATION | GOVERNMENT PUBLIC HEALTH ACTIVITIES |
PROGRAM AREA		TOTAL	HOSPITAL CARE	PHYSICIANS' SERVICES	DENTISTS' SERVICES	OTHER PROFESSIONAL SERVICES	DRUGS AND MEDICAL SUNDRIES	EYE-GLASSES AND APPLIANCES	NURSING HOME CARE	OTHER HEALTH SERVICE		
All public programs Total federal expenditures	85,237	75,884	47,692	10,624	559	1,200	1,420	409	10,102	3,897	3,306	6,047
Total federal expenditures	56,439	53,311	34,886	7,999	298	848	705	332	5,461	2,783	1,787	1,341
Total state and local expenditures	28,798	22,575	12,806	2,625	241	352	716	77	4,642	1,114	1,519	4,706
Major program areas:												
Medicare[*]	30,538	29,328	21,651	6,407	—	552	—	249	373	97	1,010	—
Medicaid[†]	22,796	21,683	8,009	2,217	448	459	1,226	—	8,796	528	1,113	—
Federal expenditures	12,464	11,770	4,347	1,203	243	249	665	—	4,775	287	694	—
State and local expenditures	10,332	9,915	3,662	1,015	205	210	560	—	4,021	241	419	—
Other public assistance payments for medical care	1,530	1,530	565	157	32	52	86	—	621	57	—	—
Federal expenditures	—	—	—	—	—	—	—	—	—	—	—	—
State and local expenditures	1,530	1,530	565	157	32	52	86	—	621	57	—	—

Veterans' medical care	5,355	5,305	4,444	61	36	—	15	48	315	391	50	—
Department of Defense medical care[‡]	4,025	4,000	2,837	107	2	103	11	—	—	1,043	25	—
Workers' compensation medical care[*]	4,442	3,542	1,696	1,411	—	6	66	66	—	—	1,100	—
Federal employees	108	108	71	27	—	—	2	2	—	—	—	—
State and local programs	4,333	5,233	1,625	1,384	—	96	64	64	—	—	1,100	—
Other public hospitals (net)[§]	6,828	6,828	6,828	—	—	—	—	—	—	—	—	—
Other public expenditures for personal health care[||]	3,879	3,869	1,662	265	22	55	18	46	—	1,801	10	—
Federal	2,810	2,800	1,536	195	17	40	14	35	—	965	10	—
State and local	1,069	1,069	125	70	5	14	5	15	—	856	—	—
Government public health activities	6,047	—	—	—	—	—	—	—	—	—	—	6,047
Federal	1,341	—	—	—	—	—	—	—	—	—	—	1,341
State and local	4,706	—	—	—	—	—	—	—	—	—	—	4,706

[*]Represents total expenditures from trust funds for benefits and administrative costs. Trust fund income includes premium payments paid by or on behalf of beneficiaries.

[†]Includes funds paid into Medicare trust funds by states under "buy-in" agreements to cover premiums for public assistance recipients and for persons who are medically indigent.

[‡]Includes care for retirees and military dependents. Payments for services other than hospital care and other health services represent only those made under contract medical programs.

[§]Expenditures for state and local government hospitals not offset by other revenues.

[||]Includes program spending for maternal and child health; Vocational Rehabilitation medical payments; temporary disability insurance medical payments; PHS and other federal hospitals; Indian health services; alcoholism, drug abuse, and mental health; and school health.

Source: *Health Care Financing Review, 2:21,* 1980.

dered as they are required. In addition nurses reported that they recommend initiating therapy in such drug classes as psychotropics, analgesics, laxatives, and antiemetics.

Physician Assistants

Physician assistants (PAs) is another group of nonphysicians who influence drug use. They have the right to prescribe in the majority of states, usually with some form of physician supervision. In a study conducted by the journal, *Physician Assistant,* it was found that half of those responding issued 20 or more prescriptions per day.[8] Among the most frequently prescribed drug categories were analgesics, antibiotics, antihistamines, antihypertensives, and cough and cold remedies.

Chiropractors

Although chiropractors do not represent a market force for prescription medications, the more than 14,000 members of this group do wield some influence among their patients. In many states they are limited to hand manipulation, and in a few states they are not granted licenses at all. In other states, however, they have branched into other methods of treatment, such as electrotherapy and diet.

The Government as a Market

Various government agencies serve as both direct and indirect markets for drugs. A thorough discussion of the direct marketing of drugs to government agencies is provided in Chapter 14. The indirect segment is largest because of the Medicaid vendor programs. Altogether, federal and state expenditures for drugs are now approaching 1.5 billion dollars (Table 2-7).

Incidence of Disease

In attempting to identify characteristics common to consumers for purposes of focusing the marketing effort, one characteristic is immediately obvious to the prescription drug manufacturer. Unfortunately for the patient he is just that—a patient. One type of characteristic that is perhaps the most useful for identifying consumer markets is the incidence of disease.

The value of disease incidence as part of market intelligence is probably obvious. Nevertheless, the relationship of the statistics of disease to marketing decision making, and more particularly to market-related research decisions, may be less apparent.

Both mortality (total deaths and death rate in proportion to the population) and morbidity (prevalence of disease in proportion to the population) are determinants in deciding the importance of this characteristic as a market factor. An examination of vital statistics reveals some major causes of death today and changes in the death rates from some diseases that are directly attributable to the development and use of new pharmaceuticals. Table 2-8 shows the death rate for selected diseases over a 28-year period, 1950 to 1977. Some changes are dramatic, and some are disappointing. For some conditions, the death rate is actually increasing.

TABLE 2-8. *Age-Adjusted Death Rates* for Selected Causes of Death: United States Selected Years 1950–1977*
(Data are based on the national vital registration system)

CAUSE OF DEATH	YEAR							
	1950	1955	1960	1965	1970	1975	1976	1977
	Deaths per 100,000 resident population							
All causes	841.5	764.5	760.9	739.0	714.3	658.3	627.5	612.3
Diseases of the heart	307.6	287.5	286.2	273.9	253.6	220.5	216.7	210.4
Cerebrovascular disease	88.8	83.0	79.7	72.7	66.3	54.5	51.4	48.2
Malignant neoplasms	125.4	125.8	125.8	127.0	129.9	130.9	132.3	133.0
Respiratory system	12.8	16.0	19.2	23.0	28.4	32.5	33.5	34.3
Digestive system	47.7	43.5	41.1	38.3	35.2	33.6	33.6	33.4
Breast†	22.2	22.7	22.3	22.8	23.1	22.8	23.1	23.5
Influenza and pneumonia	26.2	21.0	28.0	23.5	22.1	16.6	17.4	14.2
Bronchitis, emphysema, and asthma	—	—	—	—	11.6	8.6	7.9	7.2
Tuberculosis	21.7	8.4	5.4	3.6	2.2	1.2	1.1	1.0
Cirrhosis of liver	8.5	9.4	10.5	12.1	14.7	13.8	13.6	13.1
Diabetes mellitus	14.3	13.0	13.6	13.4	14.1	11.6	11.1	10.4
All accidents	57.5	54.4	49.9	53.3	53.7	44.8	43.2	43.8
Motor vehicle accidents	23.3	24.6	22.5	26.5	27.4	21.3	21.5	22.4
Suicide	11.0	9.9	10.6	11.4	11.8	12.6	12.3	12.9
Homicide	5.4	4.8	5.2	6.2	9.1	10.5	9.5	9.6

*Age-adjusted rates are computed by the direct method to the total population of the United States as enumerated in 1940, using 11 age groups.
†Female only.

Sources: National Center for Health Statistics: *Vital Statistics Rates in the United States, 1940–1960,* by R. D. Grove and A. M. Hetzel, Department of Health, Education and Welfare Pub. No. (PHS) 1677, Public Health Service, Washington, DC: U.S. Government Printing Office, 1968. Unpublished data from the Division of Vital Statistics.

What is the significance of these data for the pharmaceutical marketer? At the most basic level they indicate direction for future product research. Combined with other data, such as sales of competitive products, effectiveness of a new product, and success of new products in the past, they can provide the basis for forecasting success of new entries into the marketplace.

The "Intermediate Consumer" Market

Most of the discussion involving the marketing of prescription drug products usually revolves around the ultimate consumer, the patient, and the decision maker, the physician. Often neglected are the various agencies that McCarthy has called the "intermediate consumers."[9] Most of this group is made up of what we normally consider "middlemen," but other agencies are also involved.

The point to be made, which is often overlooked, is that each segment of the industry represents a "market" for one or more of the other elements. Thus, in addition to the retailer, the hospital, the industrial infirmary, and government agencies, all represent markets for the wholesaler. Also note that even the retailer is not necessarily limited in marketing activities to the ultimate consumer. A great deal of buying and selling occurs long before the consumer obtains a prescription from the community pharmacy. When it is remembered that within each of these markets there exists considerable variation, the real complexity of the pharmaceutical market becomes evident. Identifying, describing, and serving these markets is the function of marketing. This job is further complicated by the fact that the purchasing behavior of the decision makers in these markets is considerably different from that of the ultimate consumer.

Probably no one has done a better job of indicating the primary importance of the market to the whole philosophy of running a business than Theodore Levitt. In his short but remarkably incisive book, *Innovation in Marketing,* he has brought the whole situation into perspective.

> The view that an industry is a customer-satisfying process, not a goods-producing process, is vital for all businessmen to understand. An industry begins with the customer and his needs, not with a patent, a raw material, or a selling skill. Given the customer's needs, the industry develops backwards, first concerning itself with the physical delivery of customer satisfactions. Then it moves back further to creating the things by which these satisfactions are in part achieved. How these materials are created is a matter of indifference to the customer, hence the particular form of manufacturing, processing, or what-

have-you cannot be considered as a vital aspect of the industry. Finally, the industry moves back still further to finding the raw materials necessary for making its products.

The irony of some industries oriented toward technical research and development is that the scientists who occupy the high executive positions are totally unscientific when it comes to defining their companies' over-all needs and purposes. They violate the first two rules of the scientific method—being aware of defining their companies' problems, and then developing testable hypotheses about solving them. They are scientific only about convenient things, such as laboratory and product experiments. The reason that the customer (and the satisfaction of his deepest needs) is not considered as being "the problem" is not because there is any certain belief that no such problem exists, but because an organizational lifetime has conditioned management to look in the opposite direction. Marketing is a stepchild.[10]

Pharmaceutical marketing seems to be moving away from the mistakes of the past as described by Professor Levitt. There is convincing evidence that, in fact, a great preoccupation with the market as a first step in product development rather than the last is now the rule rather than the exception.

References

1. Committee on Definitions: *Marketing Definitions,* Chicago: American Marketing Association, 1960, p. 15.
2. Report of the Definitions Committee of the American Marketing Association, *The Journal of Marketing, 13*(No. 2):202, 1948.
3. Gosselin, R. A.: Pharmaceutical Marketing Research, paper presented at the University of Texas College of Pharmacy, February 20, 1962.
4. Reisman, R.: The Practice of Osteopathic Physicians, *Medical Marketing and Media, 12*:126, 1977.
5. Smiler, B.: Drugs in Dentistry, *Medical Marketing and Media, 10*:13, 1975.
6. Freeman, R. A., Temple, T. R., and Ringstrom, R.: The Podiatrist as a Drug Prescriber, *Medical Marketing and Media, 13*:3, 1978.
7. O'Conner, A. B.: The Nurses' Role in Pharmaceutical Therapy, *Medical Marketing and Media, 15*:37, 1980.
8. Rubin, L. A.: Physician Assistants and Their Prescribing Practices, *Medical Marketing and Media, 12*:50, 1977.
9. McCarthy, E.: *Basic Marketing, A Managerial Approach,* Homewood, IL: Richard D. Irwin, 1960.
10. Levitt, T.: *Innovation in Marketing,* New York: McGraw-Hill, 1962, pp. 66–70.

## CHAPTER 3

Market Behavior

MICKEY C. SMITH

In Chapter 2 several definitions of the term "market" were presented. One of these was more or less synonymous with the term "marketplace"—that is, the environment within which the functions of buying and selling are conducted. The very fact that two parties are willing to buy and to sell is a reflection of their differing evaluations of what they are exchanging (the goods of the seller and the funds of the buyer).

Obviously each party in the exchange must want that which the other offers more than that which he has at the moment. One does not give 20 dollars for a shirt unless that shirt is more valuable to him than his 20 dollars. The comparative willingness of the seller to sell his goods is known as *supply*. Similarly, the willingness of the buyer to buy is known as *demand*.

Supply and demand are affected by many economic, social, and environmental factors. The characteristics of the goods themselves, the nature of the sales outlet, the socioeconomic status of the buyer, and the availability of other goods and alternate sources of supply are a few of the factors that may affect supply.

The prescription drug industry is affected by the basic characteristics of supply and demand, as are other industries. However, drugs are somewhat peculiar in that the demand may be affected to a considerable degree by the influence of third and even fourth parties to the traditional buyer-seller relationship.

Changes and the Nature of Supply and Demand

Both supply and demand may be influenced by various internal and external factors. Furthermore, it should be noted that the demand and supply curves for major sectors of industry or for the consumer population are actually a composite of what may often be many thousands of individual supply curves of single products. Figure 3-1 shows a supply curve.

For the sake of precision it should be pointed out that when the term "change in demand" is used it should refer to a change in the quantity demanded at all prices. When a change occurs at only one or two points on the demand curve, we are seeing a change in the "quantity demanded" and not in "demand." Most marketing activities result in a change in quantity demanded rather than demand per se. There are cases in which marketing activity has resulted in actual changes in demand. If *demand* can be stimulated through promotion alone, it is said to be "expansible."[1] This expansibility should not be confused with demand elasticity. Expansibility of demand is determined by the magnitude of increase in sales of a product or brand, resulting from promotion, without any change in price. This characteristic has also been referred to as "promotional elasticity."[2]

The most frequently discussed relationship in the supply-demand interface is that between price and quantity. There is an obvious although not always effective tendency for the quantity of a commodity demanded to vary inversely with the price. This relationship however, will vary. Some reasons for variation include (1) changes in consumer tastes, (2) changes in total income and its distribution in the population, (3) changes in the prices of other commodities, particularly those which may be substituted easily for the one under consideration, and (4) (especially in the field of prescription drugs) changes in the character and source of payment for the commodity.

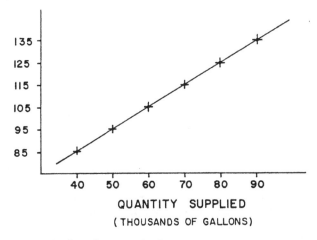

Fig. 3-1. *Supply curve for beer.*

Price has traditionally been the least efficient means of competition for industry. As a consequence most marketers prefer to concentrate on the potential for variations in demand previously mentioned in preference to engaging in price competition. Nevertheless, price and quantity continue to be associated in most demand analyses.

Elasticity of Demand

Elasticity of demand is a term frequently used to indicate the effect of price changes on the quantity demanded of a given commodity. The proportionality of the change is the means used to measure elasticity. As many as five classifications are used to describe various degrees of elasticity:

1. Perfectly elastic demand.

2. Elastic demand.

3. Unit elasticity of demand.

4. Inelastic demand.

5. Perfectly inelastic demand.[3]

Figure 3-2 shows the demand curves indicating these variations: A–A' represents perfect elasticity, B–B' elasticity, C–C' unit elasticity, D–D' inelasticity, and E–E' perfect inelasticity. The most frequently encountered states are the elastic and inelastic, in which price changes result in, respectively, greater than and less than proportionate changes in the quantity demanded. Unit elasticity represents exactly proportionate changes in quantity demanded corresponding with changes in price. Perfect elasticity is the situation in which any price change would result in an infinite change in the quantity demanded, while perfect inelasticity reflects the situation in which changes in price have no effect on quantity demanded.

It is possible to find situations in the prescription drug industry in which each type of elasticity exists. The most frequent case, at least under present drug marketing conditions, would be that of inelasticity. Changes in price of prescription drugs do not normally result in proportionate inverse changes in the quantity demanded. During the course of a rapid increase in the price of quinidine some years ago, for example, there was little change in the number of units sold. The principal reason for inelasticity of demand is the nature of the product itself. Prescription drugs are necessary to health and, within reasonable limits, will be purchased in spite of price increases. Furthermore, there is little reason for purchasing more of a drug than is needed regardless of how much the price decreases.

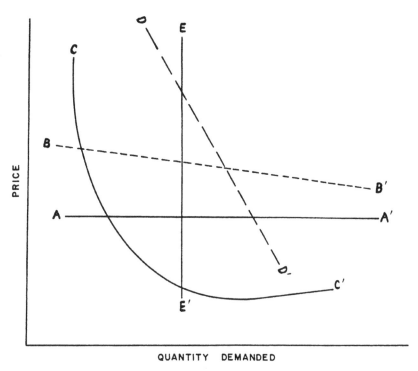

Fig. 3-2. *Types of elasticity of demand.*

In addition to the nature of the product at least two other factors contribute to price inelasticity. The physician's role as the decision maker in the choice of prescription drugs tends to make price a secondary consideration. Moreover, the efforts of the pharmaceutical industry toward product differentiation, either through promotion or actual product changes, reduce the importance of price as a consideration in drug choice and consequently reduce the elasticity of demand.

Probably the least likely type of elasticity to be found within the drug market would be perfect elasticity. It is improbable that any situation would exist in which any price change, either up or down, would affect the quantity demanded so dramatically. Perfect inelasticity is possible within the industry, however, particularly when the demand schedule for a single product is considered. Given a product, the only one of its kind effective in life-threatening situations, it is highly unlikely that routine changes in price would have any effect on the quantity sold.

The case of elasticity of demand is encountered infrequently in the pharmaceutical industry, except in cases of products that are satisfactory substitutes for each other, and whose substitutability is well known to those who make the drug choice. Again, promotional and product development efforts are often aimed at minimizing this substitutability.

One characteristic of the future market for prescription drugs that should be mentioned here is the probable influence of third-party payment on the nature of demand. It is possible to project considerable differences in the behavior of demand for product classes compared with individual products sold on a brand-name basis. It might be expected that the product class (e.g., antibiotics) would continue to exhibit a relatively inelastic demand schedule. The individual products (Msyteclin-F, Squibb; tetracycline HCl, McKesson) might have elastic demand schedules, however, depending upon the effectiveness of efforts to induce physicians to prescribe drugs by generic name.

Interestingly enough, federal and state programs to supply prescription drugs to certain groups of patients would have almost completely opposite effects on the elasticity of demand for prescription drugs as a total class and on the demand for individual, easily substitutable drugs. When it is known that a third party will foot the bill, cost considerations ("Should I see the doctor, or try to get something at the drugstore?") become less important. Consequently the total demand for drugs by the groups affected will probably increase with less elasticity. In efforts to offset the effects of this increase, third-party payers can be expected, and indeed have begun, to build in price elasticity by product in an effort to bring these prices down.

Other Demand Characteristics

SEASONAL DEMAND

Although, as has been pointed out, total demand is less likely to change than is quantity demanded, the latter may be affected significantly by seasonal variations.* The importance of seasonal variations to planning of production and marketing should be emphasized. Both of these functions depend upon accurate forecasting of seasonal change in quantity demanded for individual products. From the production point of view this is important for scheduling and purchasing. In marketing, sales quotas and plans, advertising campaigns, and budgets are all factors that are significantly affected by seasonal patterns.

It will come as no surprise to learn that some pharmaceuticals, such as cold remedies, are sold in larger quantities during

---

*I am indebted to James A. Visconti for much of the material presented here on seasonal demand.

the winter months. The seasonality of demand of other products is less obvious. Figure 3-3 shows the seasonality of four types of prescription drug products—diuretics, cardiovascular drugs, dermatologic preparations, and anti-allergic drugs. It can readily be seen from these trends that extreme temperatures may be expected to affect the heart patient and his consequent use of medication. The high rates of use for dermatologic preparations and anti-allergic drugs during the summer months can presumably be explained by the increased exposure to allergy-aggravating substances during this period of outdoor living.

DERIVED DEMAND

The term "derived demand" is usually applied to the industrial goods market. Commodities used for industrial rather than household purposes are said to exhibit derived demand—that is, they depend for their very existence upon products sold to consumers.[4]

In the pharmaceutical industry an individual heart medication could be followed backward to the production plant. In order to produce the particular tablet in quantity, the manufacturer may have had to purchase punching machines, coating machines, excipients, and other materials. The demand for these materials is "derived" from the demand for the drug itself. Considerable study has been made of this phenomenon, with one development being the construction of input-output tables to quantify the interdependence of different industries and the extent of their reliance on derived demand.

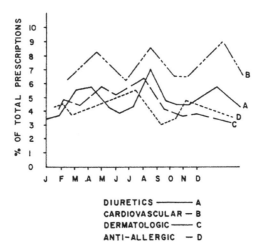

DIURETICS ——— A
CARDIOVASCULAR — B
DERMATOLOGIC —— C
ANTI-ALLERGIC — D

Fig. 3-3. *Seasonal prescription trends.*

It may be stretching a point to mention that a great deal of the demand for our present commodities is "derived" from the ability of prescription pharmaceuticals to help the customer stay alive and in comparatively good health.

DIRECTED DEMAND

Gosselin was the first to classify prescription drugs as "directed consumer goods."[5] The description is particularly apt. Almost any product can be said to benefit from directed demand, at least insofar as it is possible to direct this demand through advertising. It is doubtful, however, whether or not any other good or service except for public utilities is less a matter of consumer choice than of prescription pharmaceuticals.

The principal director, of course, is the prescribing physician. In most cases this physician still finds it feasible to make a choice on his own. For a number of reasons the trend, if one exists, is for less discretion of choice by the physician. Drug committees, government agencies, and even individual pharmacies are helping in this "direction" demand.

There have been few attempts by or for the consumer to give *him* the choice of prescription drug. *The Handbook of Prescription Drugs* probably goes farther in this direction than has any such effort in the past.[6] In this book the author compares prices of generic-named drugs as offered by different manufacturers, and encourages the patient to request generic prescriptions.

In any case, from the marketing viewpoint, the directed demand for prescription drugs would seem to offer little reason for consumer advertising by prescription drug manufacturers at present, although some of them are running institutional advertisements in lay journals. It has been suggested that more active promotion to the public may occur in the future.

PRIMARY AND SELECTIVE DEMAND

The difference between primary and selective demand is particularly important to the marketing function. Primary demand is the demand for the type of product as distinguished from the demand for specific brands. In the drug field we might speak of the demand for antibiotics, for diuretics, or for oral contraceptives. We might differentiate various segments of this type of demand even more (e.g., the demand for *sequential* oral contraceptives, the demand for *mercurial* diuretics, the demand for *broad-spectrum* antibiotics). Yet each of these is a part of primary demand. As we shall see, every major new concept in product types and many major product type changes require the stimulation of primary demand. The change, innovation, or even the *concept* must first be validated within the mind of the decision maker before any effort is made to sell the benefits of one brand over another. It is clear that the first marketer of a new product line, if successful, must do much of the primary demand stimulation for competitors who will follow. Indeed, the number of such competitors may be a direct reflection of the innovator's success in primary demand stimulation.

We are all much more familiar with selective demand. Instead of promoting features and benefits of the product type or class, the manufacturer emphasizes the advantages of his own brands in comparison with competitors' brands. All primary demand stimulation, however, does not necessarily stop.

Not only do the messages differ but so does the nature of the promotional activities aimed, respectively, at primary and selective demand stimulation. The former tends toward a much higher informational content. In the pharmaceutical industry it is almost instructional in character. It is important, particularly when a product is new, to be certain that the physician is thoroughly versed in the proper dosage and administration. Potential trouble areas must be adequately explained to him. The physician who tries a new type of treatment for the first time and is disappointed in the results is not likely to try it again soon. The introduction of the oral contraceptives was certainly a good example of thorough explanations of the mechanism of action being given to both the physician and to the patient. Additional primary demand stimulation was required when the sequential versions were introduced.

Stimulation of selective demand attempts to capitalize on product or company differentiation. Promotion with this aim may depend less on "hard" information, although there is considerable side-by-side comparison of products in this type of promotion. Innovations in dosage form (e.g., Spansules, micronized particles) can be exploited. Promotion of the corporate image is favored as a means of blanketing a group of products with selective demand stimuli.

Market Behavior

A frequently heard axiom in pharmacy goes something like "Ninety percent of today's prescriptions could not have been filled 15 years ago." Whether or not the figures are exactly accurate, this expression sums up succinctly the dynamic nature of the prescription drug market. It is true that the available prescription product assortment is in a constant state of flux. Indeed, it has been estimated that the average life of a prescription drug after marketing is approximately 5 years.

The mortality rate of new drug products can be seen in Table 3-1. In this table we have shown the products marketed in the years 1957 to 1958, about 25 years before the present edition of this text appeared. Those products still actively marketed, as well as those appearing in a recent list of the 100 most prescribed drugs (see Table 3-2), are indicated.

It is obvious from the data in Table 3-1 that the years 1957 and 1958 were unusually productive in terms of the number of new chemical entities marketed. Many of these products have now disappeared from the market; few can be said to be continuing successes. These products were mainly new chemical formulations and did not include many combination products and product duplications that would have even a lesser chance of success.

The effective life of pharmaceutical products can be further demonstrated by examination of the histories of those drugs that have been most successful. Each year IMS America publishes a list of the most prescribed drugs, as determined by its market research. The top 100 for 1980 are presented in Table 3-2, accounting for more than half of all prescriptions in this country.

Product Life Cycle

The pharmaceutical market is not the only one characterized by periodic replacement of top-selling products by new entries. The industry is committed, however, to the pursuit of growth primarily through the research and development of new products. As we will see in Chapter 7, a "new" product may be either a new chemical entity or a modification of an existing product.

Because of their own active research and development programs and, more importantly, because of similar programs of competing companies, most firms find that their new products experience some variation of a basic life cycle, depicted in Figure 3-4. Variations on this cycle occur primarily in the length of the five phases and in the magnitude of the sales volume. There seems to be little doubt that the concept of product life cycle can be applied to pharmaceuticals as well.

The mandate of this cycle for research development is clear. New drugs are necessary for survival. No firm can afford the luxury of resting on its laurels following the successful development and introduction of a new product. History has proven that competing firms will quickly make such rest an uneasy one.

Table 3-3 shows market shares of the top five drugs in each of three therapeutic categories for the years 1968, 1973, and 1978. In the systemic anti-arthritic market we can see the decline of the two products (B, D) and the roller-coaster performance of another

TABLE 3-1. *Fate of New Drugs Marketed in 1957–1958*

DRUGS	MARKETER	NO LONGER ACTIVELY MARKETED	STILL MARKETED	TOP 200 DRUGS 1980
Megimide	Abbott	X		
Leritine	Merck, Sharpe, & Dohme	X		
Darvon	Lilly		X	X
Zactane	Wyeth	X		
Viadril	Pfizer	X		
Fluothane	Ayerst	X		
Delvex	Lilly	X		
Sintrom	Geigy	X		
Liquamar	Organon		X	
Celontin	Parke-Davis		X	
Peganone	Abbott		X	
Dimetane	Robins		X	X
Actidil	Burroughs Wellcome		X	
Polaramine	Schering		X	X
Spontin	Abbott	X		
TAO	Roerig	X		
Ilosone	Lilly		X	X
Kantrex	Bristol		X	
Vancocin	Lilly		X	
Benzapas	Smith-Dorsey	X		
Fungizone	Squibb		X	
Kynex	Lederle	X		
Madribon	Roche	X		
Dartal	Searle	X		
Pacatal	Warner-Chilcott	X		
Suavitil	Merck, Sharpe, & Dohme	X		
Trilafon	Schering		X	
Ultran	Lilly	X		
Vesprin	Squibb		X	
Quiactin	Merrell	X		
Stelazine	Smith, Kline, & French		X	X
Suvren	Ayerst	X		
Trancopal	Winthrop	X		
Vistaril	Pfizer		X	X
Leukeran	Burroughs Wellcome	X		
Harmonyl	Abbott		X	
Protalba	Pitman-Moore	X		
Singoserp	Ciba	X		
Cylospasmol	Ives		X	
Clarin	Leeming	X		
Saff	Abbott	X		
Cothera	Ayerst		X	
Tessalon	Ciba		X	
Bradisol	Ciba	X		
Enzactin	Ayerst		X	
Capsebon	Pitman-Moore	X		

TABLE 3-1. (*Continued*)

DRUGS	MARKETER	NO LONGER ACTIVELY MARKETED	STILL MARKETED	TOP 200 DRUGS 1980
Orinase	Upjohn		X	X
Diabinese	Pfizer		X	X
Cardrase	Upjohn		X	
Diuril	Merck, Sharpe, & Dohme		X	X
Dornavac	Merck, Sharpe, & Dohme	X		
Neutrapen	Riker	X		
Daranide	Merck, Sharpe, & Dohme	X		
Darbid	Smith, Kline, & French		X	
Elorine	Lilly	X		
Tricoloid	Burroughs Wellcome	X		
Tral	Abbott	X		
Atratan	Irwin Neisler	X		
Murel	Ayerst	X		
Furoxone	Eaton		X	
Ilopan	Warren-Teed		X	
Dulcolax	Geigy		X	
Polykol	Upjohn	X		
Imferon	Lakeside		X	
Halotestin	Upjohn		X	
Medrol	Upjohn		X	X
Hydeltrasol	Merck, Sharpe, & Dohme		X	
Aristocort	Lederle		X	
Kenalog	Squibb		X	X
Decadron	Merck, Sharpe, & Dohme		X	
Estradurin	Ayerst		X	
Norlutin	Parke-Davis		X	
Enovid	Searle		X	
Robaxin	Robins		X	X
Paraflex	McNeil		X	
Sinaxar	Armour	X		
Disipal	Riker		X	
Deaner	Riker		X	

Sources: de Haen, P.: *Review of Drugs, 1941–1961,* Washington, DC: Pharmaceutical Manufacturers Association, 1962, and IMS America, Inc., 1980.

(C). Two products (A, E) in the top five in 1978 were not even marketed in 1968.

The oral contraceptive market obviously felt the effects of new product development. None of the 1978 products were on the market 10 years before, and 3 of the 5 were already showing erosion of market shares in the 1973 to 1978 period.

The nonbarbiturate sedative market illustrates the effect of a dominating product innovation. Product A, not available in 1973 had, by 1978, garnered nearly three fourths of the market.

TABLE 3-2. *The Top 100 Most Prescribed Drugs in 1980*

RANK	PRODUCT NAME	MANUFACTURER
1	Valium	Roche
2	Inderal	Ayerst
3	Tylenol with codeine	McNeil
4	Dyazide	Smith, Kline, & French
5	Lasix oral	Hoechts-Roussel
6	Ampicillin	Unspecified
7	Lanoxin	Burroughs Wellcome
8	Tetracycline systemic	Unspecified
9	Motrin	Upjohn
10	Dimetapp	Robins
11	Penicillin VK	Unspecified
12	Dalmane	Roche
13	Aldomet	Merck, Sharpe, & Dohme
14	Actifed	Burroughs Wellcome
15	Tagamet	Smith, Kline, & French
16	Keflex	Dista
17	Darvocet-N 100	Lilly
18	Erythromycin systemic	Unspecified
19	Amoxicillin	Unspecified
20	HydroDiuril	Merck, Sharpe, & Dohme
21	Empirin with codeine	Burroughs Wellcome
22	E.E.S.	Abbott
23	V-Cillin K	Lilly
24	Indocin	Merck, Sharpe, & Dohme
25	Premarin oral	Ayerst
26	Slow-K	Ciba
27	Clinoril	Merck, Sharpe, & Dohme
28	Donnatal	Robins
29	Hydrochlorothiazide	Unspecified
30	Hygroton	USV
31	Prednisone oral	Unspecified
32	Isordil	Ives
33	Benadryl capsules/tablets	Parke-Davis
34	Synthroid	Flint
35	Dilantin sodium	Parke-Davis
36	Librium	Roche
37	Elavil	Merck, Sharpe, & Dohme
38	Fiorinal	Sandoz
39	Diabinese	Pfizer
40	Phenobarbital	Unspecified
41	Tranxene	Abbott
42	Aldoril	Merck, Sharpe, & Dohme
43	Mycolog	Squibb
44	Antivert	Roerig
45	Drixoral	Schering
46	Lomotil	Searle
47	Ortho-Novum 1/50-21	Ortho
48	Amoxil	Beecham

TABLE 3-2. (*Continued*)

RANK	PRODUCT NAME	MANUFACTURER
49	Vibramycin	Pfizer
50	E-mycin	Upjohn
51	Ovral	Wyeth
52	Naprosyn	Syntex
53	Librax	Roche
54	Aldactazide	Searle
55	Lopressor	Geigy
56	Percodan	Endo
57	Mellaril	Sandoz
58	Thyroid	Unspecified
59	Zyploprim	Burroughs Wellcome
60	Monistat-7	Ortho
61	Digoxin	Unspecified
62	Butazolidin Alka	Geigy
63	Ativan	Wyeth
64	Timoptic	Merck, Sharpe, & Dohme
65	Lo/Ovral	Wyeth
66	Atarax	Roerig
67	Ornade	Smith, Kline, & French
68	Darvon compound-65	Lilly
69	Persantine	Boehringer
70	Phenergan expectorant with codeine	Wyeth
71	Triavil	Merck, Sharpe, & Dohme
72	Naidecon	Bristol
73	Ser-Ap-Es	Ciba
74	Pen-Vee-K	Wyeth
75	Diuril Oral	Merck, Sharpe, & Dohme
76	Bactrim DS	Roche
77	Valisone	Schering
78	Parafon Forte	McNeil
79	Sinequan	Roerig
80	Macrodantin	Norwich-Eaton
81	Cortisporin Otic	Burroughs Wellcome
82	Meprobamate	Unspecified
83	Minipress	Pfizer
84	Ilosone	Dista
85	Apresoline	Ciba
86	Synalgos-DC	Ives
87	Nalfon	Dista
88	Septra DS	Burroughs Wellcome
89	Nitrobid	Marion
90	Nitroglycerin	Unspecified
91	Phenaphen with codeine	Robins
92	Coumadin oral	Endo
93	Achromycin-V	Lederle
94	Tuss-Ornade	Smith, Kline, & French
95	Talwin tablets	Winthrop
96	Phenergan VC expectorant with codeine	Wyeth

TABLE 3-2. (*Continued*)

RANK	PRODUCT NAME	MANUFACTURER
97	Orinase	Upjohn
98	Tenuate	Merrell Dow
99	Serax	Wyeth
100	Pavabid	Marion

Source: IMS America, Inc., 1981.

TABLE 3-3. *Market Shares of Top Drugs in Selected Categories*

DRUG CLASS	DRUG	1978 RANK (%)	1973 RANK (%)	1968 RANK (%)
Anti-arthritic	A	1 (33.5)	*	*
Systemic	B	2 (27.5)	1 (36.5)	1 (38.5)
	C	3 (17.8)	2 (22.6)	2 (16.4)
	D	4 (5.2)	4 (7.9)	4 (8.4)
	E	5 (3.7)	*	*
Top 5 total %†		87.7	82.7	81.5
Oral contraceptives	A	1 (16.3)	1 (22.6)	*
Estrogen/progestin	B	2 (13.5)	3 (9.9)	*
	C	3 (8.8)	*	*
	D	4 (7.5)	2 (12.4)	*
	E	5 (7.1)	4 (9.5)	*
Top 5 total %†		53.2	61.8	50.1
Nonbarbiturate	A	1 (74.5)	*	*
Sedatives	B	2 (7.9)	2 (11.7)	1 (20.2)
	C	3 (7.7)	1 (17.7)	1 (36.9)
	D	4 (4.6)	4 (9.1)	3 (15.7)
	E	5 (3.4)	3 (10.0)	6 (2.8)
Top 5 total %†		98.1	55.5	89.0

*Product *not* marketed in year indicated.
†Includes products *not* shown in 1978 top five.

Source: IMS America, Inc., 1979.

The product life cycle also has significant effects on the marketing activities of the firm. Each stage of the life cycle of a particular type of product is characterized by differing market conditions and marketing activities. Conversely, the marketing activities of the firm affect the life cycle. In a modest study of firms characterized as successful and unsuccessful in terms of market

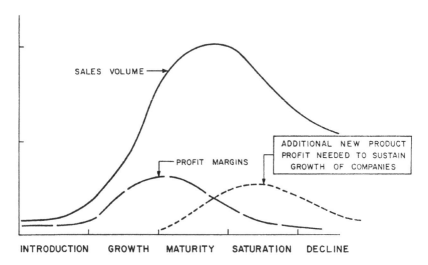

Fig. 3-4. *The basic life cycle of new products. (Adapted from Jones, R. W.: Management of New Products,* The Journal of Industrial Engineering, *9: 647, 1958; reprinted in Lazer W., and Kelly, E. J.* Managerial Marketing: Perspectives and Viewpoints, *Homewood, IL: Richard D. Irwin, 1962, p. 224.)*

failure rates of new products introduced between 1958 and 1964 certain differences were found:

> Analysis of the data indicated that companies which are successful in introducing new products use sources of ideas for new products marketed which are not significantly different from those of the unsuccessful new product introducers.
>
> Although a larger proportion of successful companies employed fixed procedures for evaluating new products than unsuccessful introducers the difference was not large enough to be significant. Likewise a higher proportion of successful new product introducers utilized formal scheduling tools but the differential was not significant to be statistically significant.
>
> The one characteristic in which successful companies differed significantly from nonsuccessful companies in terms of new product introduction was in the employment of concept testing. A significantly larger proportion of companies which were successful in introducing new products used concept testing of the new product than did firms which were unsuccessful in introducing new products.
>
> The proportion of successful firms using one department or individual for new product coordination was larger than the proportion among the companies which were unsuccessful. Likewise a larger percentage of successful firms were marketing concept-oriented products than unsuccessful firms.[8]

Introduction Stage

In the introduction stage the new class of product is presented to the physician for the first time. Usually this will be a product that does something old in a new way (e.g., long-acting tablets), or does something that was not possible before (measles vaccine). Sales generally increase slowly in this stage. Physician habits must be broken, at least to the extent of trying the new product. Unless the medical profession has been awaiting this type of development for a long time (such as in the case of the oral contraceptives) this can be a slow process. As we shall see in Chapter 4, the market for the product during this phase will be comprised of a small percentage of the medical population that is normally the first to try new drugs, and who are quite influential with their colleagues. If the product is as effective and safe as this core group wishes, word can be expected to filter down to the rest of the medical community.

The ease of introduction of a new product class can be expected to be affected by the relative success of any previous efforts in this product class. The beta blockers serve as an example.

In the introductory stage direct competition may not be a problem although, if the product merely does a job in a new or better way, there may be difficulty in convincing the physician of the value of a change. Production cost, marketing costs, and prices are traditionally high during the introduction stage. Unless the product can be produced efficiently using existing equipment and in the face of unpredictable sales, the economics of mass production will be hard to realize. Marketing costs will reflect the special nature of promotion to stimulate *primary* demand. The promotional level usually maintained in later stages would probably not be sufficient to introduce the new concept properly. If the new product represents a sufficiently radical departure from traditional therapy, it may conceivably be necessary to familiarize the general public, as well as the physician, with the new concept. The distribution portion of marketing costs will also be higher than normal, with the special problems of initial stocking of pharmacies and hospitals.

Although pricing will be discussed in Chapter 15, it is worthwhile to point out here that the usual pricing pattern finds the new product at its highest price upon its introduction. This reflects both the lack of direct competition and the uncertain sales future. Even at this highest price, in the face of high production and marketing costs and with the buildup of past research and development costs, management may plan on operating at a loss on the product during the introductory stage.

Growth Stage

During the growth stage there is widespread approval of the product concept. If the product successfully survives the introduction stage, which many do not, it can be expected that many more physicians will "get on the bandwagon." During this stage the number of competitors will begin to increase. Either modifications of the original product or completely different products for the same purpose will appear. By this time production methods will have been established, with a frequent lowering of costs. Prices will tend to go down for two main reasons:

1. Increased sales will make some economies of scale possible.

2. The increase in the number of competing firms leads to both a theoretical and an actual tendency toward lower prices.

The growth stage sees promotional activities devoted to the stimulation primarily of selective demand. The advertiser no longer finds it expedient to promote the benefits and qualities of the product class, but rather to promote the advantages of his own brand in comparison with those of his competitors.

Maturity Stage

During the maturity stage competition reaches its peak. By this point all of the firms that have any hope of receiving a share of the market will be pursuing it. By virtue of the numbers involved some of these companies will be marginal from either a financial or technological standpoint. The total sales of the product class, which have been rising through the early stages, continue to increase, but at a decreasing rate. During this stage the struggle for sales to the large volume buyers (hospitals and government agencies) becomes heated. The net effect is price competition for this business. As shall be seen in later chapters, promotion tends to change in emphasis, as does media, with less reliance on the detail man and more on journal advertising and direct mail.

Saturation Stage

Saturation marks the point at which the drug product has been tried and used for all remotely feasible indications (either with or without the blessing of the Food and Drug Administration or of the manufacturer), and has found its place in the therapeutic resources of the physician. New sales from this point on are strictly a function of population and incidence of disease. In addition, the past success of the product class may now be mitigated by products of a new type or changes in medical thinking. It is possible for the medical community to realize after a sufficient period of time that a product is simply not doing all of the things they thought it would.

During this phase all the product variations may be expected to appear. It is now seemingly desirable to have tablets, capsules, and liquid. A dermatologic form may be prepared, or a long-acting form, or a combination. The promotion may now attempt to add some vitality through efforts to segment the market by using special messages to separate physician specialties.

In the saturation stage the number of competitors of any importance stabilizes. Indeed, because of the effectiveness of earlier selective demand stimulation, it would probably be difficult for any new firm to penetrate the market at all.

Decline

There can be a number of reasons for the decline of a product class, most of them related to the effectiveness of the product as compared to other means of therapy. If the decline is caused by a new product development, the decline may be rapid, with only those who are slow to change in *any* direction continuing to prescribe the product.

Promotion during this stage may again be aimed at stimulation of primary demand. The effort may be half-hearted, and may be aimed at only a core of physician-users. Some firms may now drop from the competition, leaving a potential marketing opportunity for those remaining. The profits may be slim, however, with many of the economies gone.

Length of Product Life Cycle

It is necessary to point out that the life cycle for a class of pharmaceutical products is neither predictable nor uniform. Some product types come and go so quickly as to achieve almost "fad" status. Others seem to remain in vogue for decades. Neither is there any real uniformity in the respective length of the stages. As has been noted, decline may be rapid or quite slow. The use of pills, for example, has now all but disappeared.

Molecular Manipulation

One of the criticisms of the drug industry in previous years past was in regard to its use of "molecular manipulation" to produce new drugs. The criticism takes the form of viewing the marketing of sometimes slightly different chemical forms of a basic molecule as being responsible for a glut of drugs, often with little therapeutic advantage over existing drug products. Neglecting for the moment this issue of free enterprise and competition, the potential benefits of such chemical variation and experimentation require attention.

Schneller has described in cogent fashion the social benefits of 40 years of molecular modification of the sulfa drugs.[9] Beginning with the first sulfonamide capable of combating an infection (Prontosil, in 1952), Schneller has traced the following progression:

- Sulfanilamide

- Sulfapyridine

- Sulfathiazole

- Sulfasalazine

- Sulfasoxazole

- Sulfamethizole

Other drug categories directly discovered as a result of sulfa drug research were carbonic anhydrase inhibitors and antidiabetic compounds. Clearly, molecular manipulation has its positive aspects.

Halberstam, in another article on molecular manipulation, has pointed out that "While most molecular modification does not result in clinically dramatic improvement, most clinically significant improvement results from molecular modification."[10] It seems reasonable to state also that the market behavior described in this chapter is, itself, frequently a consequence of the same practice. But Halberstam also noted that:

> Despite the apparently large amounts spent on drug advertising, it is rare for a product to achieve widespread sales unless it does, in fact, show clinical superiority to existing competitors. The dry skeletons of many highly promoted products which failed to survive lie along the path to clinical popularity.[10]

Planned Obsolescence

Planned obsolescence of products has been a matter of some apparent concern to social critics. The term usually refers to a purposeful outmoding of new products at periodic intervals, either through the introduction of new models or by deliberate underengineering during the product's manufacture. Planned obsolescence in this sense does not exist in the pharmaceutical industry. There is a plan, however, on the part of most major drug manufacturers to make most of the drug products now existing obsolete, including their own. There is nothing sinister about this plan. The only way this can be accomplished, and a direct result of the plan, is the development of safer, more effective drug products to replace those now on the pharmaceutical market. This effort to improve the quality of pharmaceuticals, admittedly a direct result of the profit motive, has the side-effect of providing better drugs.

References

1. Cundiff, E. W., and Still, R. R.: *Basic Marketing,* Englewood Cliffs, NJ: Prentice-Hall, 1964, p. 492.
2. Dean, J.: *Managerial Economics,* Englewood Cliffs, NJ: Prentice-Hall, 1951, pp. 161–163.
3. Guthrie, J. A.: *Economics,* Homewood, IL: Richard D. Irwin, 1957, p. 252.
4. Fisk, G.: *Marketing Systems, An Introductory Analysis,* New York: Harper & Row, 1967, p. 171.
5. Gosselin, R. A.: Pharmaceutical Marketing Research, Speech presented at the University of Texas, February 20, 1962.
6. Burack, R.: *The Handbook of Prescription Drugs,* New York: Pantheon Books, 1967.
7. Vetz, R. A.: A. H. Robins Conducts Two Ad Campaigns to Reach Its Three Publics, *Public Relations Journal, 18:*23, 1961.
8. Norwood, F. J., and Smith, M. C.: New Product Marketing Practices by Pharmaceutical Firms, *Medical Marketing and Media, 5:*28, 1970.
9. Schneller, G. H.: Forty Years of Molecular Modification, *Drug Development and Industrial Pharmacy, 3:*131, 1977.
10. Halberstam, M. J.: Too Many Drugs? *Forum on Medicine, 2:*284, 1979.

## CHAPTER 4

Physician Prescribing Habits

JEAN PAUL GAGNON

You have probably realized from discussions in the previous three chapters that the prescription drug market is unique because consumers have little input into the ethical drug selection process. Approximately 300,000 physicians in various specialties located throughout the United States decide which chemical entity should be taken for a diagnosed illness. This chapter focuses on the decision-making process that these physicians go through when prescribing drugs. It presents a background on decision making and on models of physician prescribing behavior, a review of studies and surveys on factors affecting physician prescribing, and concludes with an explanation of observed behavior and suggestions for improvement.

Decision Making

Daniel Albert has suggested that:

> Decision theory is a group of related constructs that seek to describe or prescribe how individuals or groups of people choose a course of action when faced with several alternatives and a variable amount of knowledge about the determinance of the outcomes of those alternatives.[1]

Albert went on to state that decision theory is either descriptive (how people do behave) or prescriptive (how people should behave), and that decisions can be classified by the amount of knowledge possessed by the decision maker—for instance, decisions of certainty, in which each alternative course of action has a single well-specified outcome, uncertainty, in which each alternative course of action has a well-defined set of possible outcomes, each with a particular probability of occurrence, or ignorance, in which each action results in a range of possible outcomes but the probability of occurrence of each outcome is unknown. Using this classification of decision making, medical decisions, especially those concerning prescribing, are probably made under conditions of risk—uncertainty.

Others who have studied decision making have classified the behavior of decision makers into two types, rational and emotional. A rational buyer evaluates all alternatives completely, matches his needs with the respective abilities of the products available to fulfill these needs and, theoretically at least, makes his purchase with clear goals in mind. The emotional buyer, on the other hand, may be swayed by product attributes (or the advertising) having nothing to do with the actual need-satisfying properties of the product.

Some qualifications need to be made at this point. For one thing, there is the tendency to equate rational buying with intelligent buying. This assumes too great an ability on the part of the buyer to identify the important product qualities necessary for his complete satisfaction intelligently. In essence, then, the buyer may be rational but inept. It should also be pointed out that rational and emotional motives may occasionally be combined. A physician, for example, may use the most rational therapeutic approach when choosing the proper chemical entity for treating a given condition, and then may use completely emotional criteria for the choice of the brand of that drug to employ. The basic motivations behind a physician's choice of drug therapy must be considered to be rational. He would be expected to select the product that would do the most good with the least possible side-effects, and perhaps the lowest cost. In most cases of drug selection, however, physicians try to make a rational decision under conditions of uncertainty. It is this process that is examined in this chapter.

Physician Prescribing Models

A few researchers have proposed prescriptive models of prescribing behavior, while others have conducted descriptive studies of physician prescribing behavior. There are many interacting variables that influence a physician's ultimate selection of a drug. Thus,

> Whether it takes place in the office of a general practitioner or that of a psychiatrist, it is never a simple operation involving only symptom and a treatment intended to eradicate the symptom. It always includes a multiplicity of components.[2]

Included among the variables in the prescribing process are the clinical and behavioral characteristics of the patient, the patient's needs and expectations regarding treatment in the use of medication, the attitudes, expectations, and training of the treating physician, and the organizational and contextual constraints placed upon the doctor-patient relationship by features of the treatment and of the institution. Because physician prescribing is a system, it can be best understood by employing the methods of systems research.

Five researchers have examined the decision-making process behind physician prescribing and have proposed explanations for it. Knapp and Oeltjen, in an experimental study of risk-benefit assessment by general practitioners and internists regarding drug selection, posited that the probability of a practitioner prescribing a drug for a particular case was a function of (1) physician expectancy that a beneficial effect on a patient's condition would occur if the drug were prescribed, (2) the amount of beneficial effect to be gained, (3) the expectancy of drug side-effects, and (4) the magnitude of these side-effects.[3] Utilizing this analytic framework, the authors found "disease seriousness" and medical specialty to be highly related to perceived risks in the decision to medicate a patient in four hypothetical cases of hypertension.

Hemminki has reported that the major influences on prescribing are research and the pressures from drug firms, and proposed the simplified model in Figure 4-1 to describe the decision-making process for prescribing drugs. She observed that:

> Research and drug firms are closely dependent on each other, and may affect physicians through education, scientific journals, and advertising according to the doctor's personal characteristics, his work and his therapeutic opportunities and that patient demands and expectations are controversial and might be largely created by doctors themselves.[4]

Lilja, in a Swedish study, has examined the product decision-making priorities of 118 general practitioners employed by the government.[5] Using the method of regression analysis, he found that "high curing effect" was uniformly the most important consideration in the selection of a drug to treat hypothetical cases of adult diabetes and pneumonia. "Low side-effects" were found to be second in importance in selecting an antidiabetic medication, while "low cost" was found to be more important in selecting an antibiotic. Based on this study, Lilja proposed that physicians select drugs through a habitual or nonhabitual choice. Most of the drug choices a physician makes are habitual, and it was suggested that, in explaining how a physician may adopt a new drug, it is important to consider the habitual process outlined in Figure 4-2.

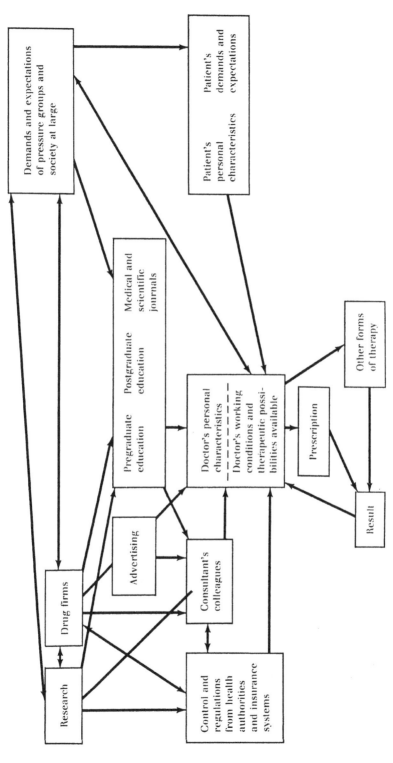

Fig. 4-1. *A simplified model of the factors that affect drug prescription. Note: Diagnosis considered constant. (Hemminki, C.: The Role of Prescriptions in Therapy,* Medical Care, 13:151, 1975.)

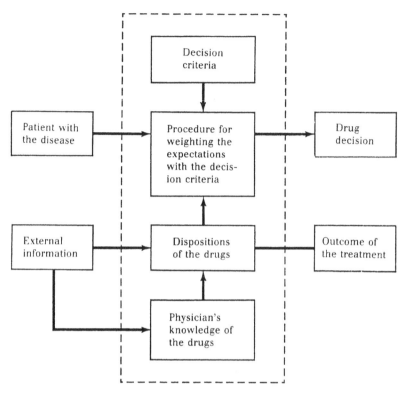

Fig. 4-2. *The physician's nonhabitual choice process. (Lilja, J.: How Physicians Choose Their Drugs,* Social Science and Medicine, 10:363, 1976.)

The components within the dotted line in Figure 4-2 are in the physician's mind.

Miller, drawing upon an extensive review, has also constructed a model for depicting the system for adoption of a new drug by a physician.[6] He conceded that aspects of his model cannot be verified with research studies. The model in Figure 4-3 has three major subdivisions: (1) antecedents—factors present in the situation prior to the introduction of innovation; (2) process; and (3) results. Antecedents fall into two major categories, the individual's identity and his perceptions of the situation (cultural and social influences, patients, and organizations). (Figure 4-3 appears on page 82.) Miller hypothesized that:

> The drug adoption process is the process through which an individual physician passes from his first hearing of a new drug to his adoption of it. The process can be viewed as consisting of five stages: awareness, interest, evaluation, trial, and adoption. In the awareness stage the

physician reads or hears about a new drug but he has incomplete information about it. He may become interested in the drug and actively seek information in the interest stage. In the evaluation stage the physician mentally applies the new drug to his situation and decides whether or not to try it. In the trial stage the new drug is prescribed on a trial basis to determine its value. In the adoption stage the physician begins using the new drug regularly for all new, and perhaps older, patients.

The evidence for the existence of stages in the drug adoption process is derived from studies on the differential use of various sources of information. Although the evidence is not unequivocal, it appears that commercial and formal sources are most influential in the early adoption stages and the more professional and informal sources are used in what corresponds to the later stages of the adoption process.[6]

Miller believed that the model is sufficiently comprehensive to accommodate not only different drugs but other kinds of innovations.

Benson has stated that there are two major defects in the models described above that limit their usefulness.[7] First, most of them are based on studies that did not measure actual physician prescribing behavior but that used physician responses to simulate clinical situations. Inferring that such "proxy" behavior measures approximate actual clinical behaviors is highly problematic and thus limits study findings derived from the use of such a methodology. A second major problem with physician decision making, according to Benson, is that none of the studies attempted to examine simultaneously the influence of all interactive variables on the treatment decision-making process. Examining the influence of one or two variables separately severely restricts the interpretations that can be formulated.

At this point it is appropriate to examine the studies that were used to construct the decision diagrams in Figures 4-1 to 4-3.

Review of Studies of Physician Prescribing Behavior

It is obvious that a prescriber's drug selection decision process, like any consumer purchasing decision, involves the input of many variables. Unlike a consumer, however, the physician's decision to prescribe involves the input of unique parameters and carries with it a high degree of responsibility. Specifically, what motivates physicians to select a specific drug? Since the late 1940s there have been approximately 100 studies done that examined the influence of specific variables or groups of variables on physician prescribing behavior. In addition to these studies, 3 reviews have been written that collated the results obtained.

The first review of physician prescriber studies, published in 1974 by Worthen, examined the effect of six variables that influence physician prescribing: (1) patients, (2) pharmacists, (3) journals, (4) advertising, (5) drug representatives, and (6) peer groups.[8] Patients were found to have only a slight influence on physician prescribing. The pharmacist was found to have a real influence in some communities but the incidence was low and did not seem to be increasing at an appreciable rate. Journal articles were found to be important as a source of information for the prescriber because they offer the advantages of providing commercial messages and of educating the physician to the latest advances in the art of medicine through scholarly and professional articles. Printed advertising may function more to inform than to convince, but it ranked high in importance in notifying physicians of a new drug product. Drug representatives were found to be of high importance in informing physicians of the availability of the product and other drug data, such as dosage forms and schedules. Peers were found to be a legitimizing channel who influenced prescribing habits by bestowing some kind of approval on the physician's use of a product.

Coleman, Menzel, and Katz, in a classic study of peer influence on physician prescribing, determined the social structure of a community of physicians in four midwestern towns by using social economic techniques. By means of personal interviews they were able to determine which physicians in selecting communities were most often contacted by their colleagues for social purposes, consultation of a formal nature, and ordinary discussion in the course of a normal work day. Having identified the physicians in this fashion, the investigators were able to diagram these relationships.[9]

Miller, in the second review of physician prescribing habits performed in 1974, found discussions with peers to be important in drug adoptions in both large and small cities.[10] He also reported the following: (1) physicians use more professional sources, particularly colleagues, when called upon to treat difficult conditions in which the effects of drug therapy are less clearly defined; (2) they tend to treat wealthier patients with newer and more expensive drugs; (3) colleagues sharing an office with a physician will use a colleague as a source of information for drugs not presently used by the physician; (4) the attendance at hospital staff meetings seems to influence the adoption of new drugs positively; and (5) formularies probably have a significant effect on prescribing.

Miller further noted that the drug attributes affecting adoption of a new drug are social reward, consistency of therapeutic response, communicability, pharmaceutical attractiveness, and relative advantage. Negative factors influencing physician prescribing are risk and a high continuing cost of therapy. Factors affecting the prescribing of established drugs include initial cost, continuing cost, social reward, time savings, consistency of therapeutic response, clarity of results, pharmaceutical attractiveness, length of drug name, and name and reputation of manufacturer.

Miller noted further that specialists and younger, scientifically oriented physicians who share offices, who have large practices, and who in general tend to have questioning and critical attitudes towards prescribing and medical practice, use new drugs early in the course of treatment and may be better prescribers. In addition, attendance at specialty meetings, receipt of many medical journals, and integration into social networks appear to be correlated with early adoption of a new drug. Miller hypothesized that there are five phases through which physicians pass before they adopt a drug: awareness, interest, evaluation, trial, and adoption. He concluded his review by stating that drug company representatives appear to be unrivaled as a source of influence for creating an initial *awareness* of a drug. Sources important for responding to *interest* are detail men, journal articles, journal advertising, colleagues, and the *Physicians' Desk Reference*. In the *evaluation* phase physicians use the *Physicians' Desk Reference,* journal advertisements, house organs, direct mail, and samples to obtain data on dosage, frequency of administration, etc.

The last literature review of physician prescribing studies was published in 1975 by Hemminki, who reported the following: (1) education appears to influence the quality of prescribing positively; (2) the contribution of advertising to prescribing is debatable in that a positive attitude towards advertising can be expected to influence prescribing; (3) colleagues do have a positive effect on prescribing, but the influence of a colleague is always secondary to other factors, such as advertising and education; (4) control and regulatory measures may have a positive effect on prescribing; (5) patient and society demands on physicians for drugs may be exaggerated in the case of ethical drugs; and (6) no generalizations can be made from studies examining the influence of physician characteristics on prescribing behavior.[11]

In addition to these reviews, other articles were subsequently published between 1975 and 1980 that examined specific elements associated with physician prescribing. Lowery and colleagues, in a survey of 220 physicians, found that many physicians had limited knowledge of the cost of antimicrobial agents.[12] Linn and Davis reported that physicians who preferred professional sources as their source of new drug information were significantly more likely to express conservative attitudes as to when drugs should be used than were physicians who preferred commercial sources, and were less likely to feel that medical advice from sources other than a physician was acceptable.[13] Mapes and Litt used four criteria of appropriateness, economics, effectiveness, and safety to evaluate proper prescribing in Britain.[14] They reported that effectiveness and safety considerations are not entirely independent and that, as workload increases there is a tendency to use outmoded prescriptions. Examining sources of information on new drugs in a health maintenance organization, Christensen and Wertheimer found that physicians primarily use literature sources for general information and colleagues for information on new drugs, but found that the use of colleagues was not consistent among time periods or practice settings.[15]

In a follow-up study, Hartzema and Christensen examined variables that influence the prescribing volume of 80 family practitioners in a large HMO.[15a] Patient panel size and age composition explained most of the observed variance. In addition, these researchers found that female patients tend to select female physicians, and that older physicians tend to have older patients. Thus, a physician's age may be a proxy for older panels of patients with chronic conditions.

Applied Management Sciences, in an intensive study for the Food and Drug Administration (FDA), distributed a relatively lengthy 5-page questionnaire to 15,000 physicians in the United States who represented 22 medical specialties.[16] Over 10,000, or 73%, of the eligible sample responded. The significant findings from this study were the following: (1) estimated readership among physicians for national journals is highest for specialty journals (the *Journal of the American Medical Association* has the highest overall readership); (2) the most widely used and most often consulted source of drug information is the *Physicians' Desk Reference;* (3) package inserts are the most used source of information among drug company materials, (4) peer colleagues followed by consultants are the most often used sources among personal contacts, (5) textbooks are used less frequently for drug information, and (6) sources of drug information strong in believability, currency, and provision of the best clinical guidance are national journal articles, meetings, and courses.

The most recent studies of physician prescribing behavior were done by Melville and Shearer. Melville hypothesized that low job satisfaction among general practitioners may be associated with poor quality prescribing.[17] After surveying 124 general practitioners in England and Wales, he found that the prescribing of drugs that are prone to cause adverse reactions or that are deemed inappropriate by medical consensus was associated with low job satisfaction. Physicians with low satisfaction were also more likely to permit ancillary staff to write prescriptions for potentially hazardous drugs. Shearer examined the use of drug information sources for various types of drug information with a mail questionnaire.[18] One half of the sample practiced at a tertiary level university hospital and one half practiced in community hospitals. This researcher reported the following:

1. Physicians in the university hospital sought more drug information that did their community counterparts.

2. There is a significant difference in the mean reliability scores of information sources between university- and community-affiliated hospitals (Table 4-1).

3. Physicians do discriminate in their uses of drug information sources for different types of information (Table 4-2).

4. Physicians do not appear to vary significantly their uses of drug information sources by disease category or by length of time that a drug has been on the market.

5. There were significant differences in the use of clinical, hospital, and community pharmacists for various types of drug information.

TABLE 4-1. *Mean Score for Reliability of Information Source**

INFORMATION SOURCE	UNIVERSITY HOSPITAL[†]		COMMUNITY HOSPITAL[‡]	
	MEAN	RANK	MEAN	RANK
Physician specialist	4.509	1	4.494	1
Textbooks	4.377	2	4.465	2
Clinical pharmacologist[§]	4.346	3	4.060	5
Journal articles	4.208	4	4.290	4
Clinical pharmacist[§]	4.113	5	3.675	9
Hospital pharmacist	3.943	6	4.000	7
Peer physician	3.916	7	4.011	6
Physicians' desk reference[§]	3.752	8	4.323	3
Drug information center[§]	3.721	9	3.938	8
Community pharmacist[§]	2.971	10	3.549	10
Direct mail[§]	2.434	11	3.402	11
Journal advertising[§]	2.425	12	3.326	12
Detail man[§]	2.173	13	3.043	13

*Rank order not statistically different.
[†]Sample size = 107.
[‡]Sample size = 96.
[§]Statistically different means 5 = very reliable; 4 = reliable; 3 = no opinion; 2 = unreliable; 1 = very unreliable.

Source: Shearer, S. W.: Evaluation of the Hospital Pharmacist as a physician's Drug Information Source, M.S. Thesis, School of Pharmacy, University of North Carolina, 1977, p. 12.

TABLE 4-2. *Primary Sources of Drug Information Used by Community (C) and University (U) Hospital Physicians**

	COMMUNITY PHARMACIST		HOSPITAL PHARMACIST		PHYSICIANS' DESK REFERENCE		PHYSICIAN SPECIALIST		PHARMACEUTICAL/ MEDICAL TEXTBOOKS		MEDICAL JOURNAL ARTICLES	
	U (%)	C (%)	U (%)	C (%)	U (%)	C (%)	U (%)	C (%)	U (%)	C (%)	U (%)	C (%)
Absorption						62.5						
Compatibilities						55.2						
Ingredients					80.4	86.5						
Toxicities					71.0	82.3						
Dosage					73.8	84.4						
Evaluation											67.3	50.0
Availability		45.8	54.2									
Choice							55.1					45.8
Administration method					53.3	64.6						

*University hospital sample size = 107; community hospital sample size = 96.
†Percentages do not total 100% due to multiple answers.

Source: Shearer, S. W.: Evaluation of the Hospital Pharmacist as a Physician's Drug Information Source, M.S. Thesis, School of Pharmacy, University of North Carolina, 1977, p. 79.

Table 4-2 provides some insight into how physicians do behave. It would appear that convenience—availability and type of information desired—has a pronounced effect on the use of drug information sources. Both groups of physicians tend to use third-party sources, such as clinical pharmacologists, peer physicians, clinical hospital and community pharmacists, textbooks and medical journals, for absorption, dosage, evaluation, choice, compatibility, and availability information. Toxicity, ingredients, dosage, and availability information are also obtained from commercial sources. However, community-based physicians, because of the lack of third-party sources, rely heavily on the *Physicians' Desk Reference* for drug information.

In addition to studies examining the effects of internal and external variables on physician prescribing behavior, researchers have investigated the behavior of other health personnel as well as specific drug categories, especially psychotropics.

Prescribing Patterns of Other Professionals

Other professionals, such as optometrists, physicians' assistants, dentists, osteopaths, allopathic physicians, podiatrists, veterinarians, and nurse practitioners, write prescriptions in all or many states. However, few studies or surveys have been performed to evaluate the sources of information used by these professionals for prescription drugs. One survey by the Bureau of Economic Research examined sources of drug information for 4243 dentists.[19] The results of this survey revealed that published or editorial matter ranked first among dentists surveyed, and detail men and advertisements in dental publications ranked second. The former received a higher percentage of first-place rankings and the latter received more third-place rankings. Recently, the National Center for Health Services Research funded a grant to examine the prescribing patterns of 400 nurse practitioners in four states. The results of this study will be compared to physician prescribing patterns.

Psychotropic Drugs

A drug category that has received extensive study and review with regard to physician prescribing behavior is psychotropics. Overall and co-workers, in 1972, studied the prescribing behavior of 60 psychiatric residents in the adult outpatient clinic of a Southwestern university hospital. These researchers reported patient symptom profiles that were systematically different for patients treated with different classes of psychotropic medication.[20] Another study performed by Sheppard and colleagues examined the drug treatment preferences of 312 New York and 107 California psychiatrists by mail questionnaire.[21] The questionnaires included a simulated case history of a 34-year-old paranoid schizophrenic. An important result of this study was that, as the condition of their patient's deteriorated, the 419 psychiatrists began to use more and more drugs, suggesting that as treatment procedures fail, treatment becomes unconventional or experimental.

Zowadski and co-workers studied the use of psychotropic drugs among the aged in the California Medicaid program.[22] These researchers reported high usage of psychotropic drugs in the study sample, but found that use was related not to age but to institutional residence.

Prien and colleagues, in a review of surveys on psychotherapeutic drug prescription practices, reached the following conclusions: (1) these surveys uniformly fail to provide adequate information for evaluating the appropriateness of prescription practices with psychiatric patients; and (2) recommendations for remedial action based on the survey findings are, at best, premature because they are preoccupied with what treatment is being prescribed to the virtual neglect of why the treatment is being prescribed.[23] It was suggested that data be obtained about longitudinal treatment patterns and reasons for treatment decisions.

Benson hypothesized the psychiatric decision-making process as a three-stage sequence: (1) whether or not to prescribe any type of psychiatric drug for the patient; (2) whether or not to prescribe a neuroleptic or some other form of medication, and (3) what dose to prescribe.[7] He obtained information on the prescribing behavior of 55 psychiatrists and data on 1003 of their patients, and divided the various factors posited to influence the decision-making process into several related sets of variables: physician characteristics, sociodemographic education and training, attitudinal characteristics, patient characteristics, sociodemographic clinical and behavioral characteristics, and treatment setting and contextual characteristics. A series of preliminary questions were then asked at each level of the decision-making process. What variables are important? Does the influence of particular variables differ significantly across the decision-making process? What sets of variables (patient characteristics, physician characteristics, or setting characteristics) appear to be most important and does their relative importance vary at different points in the process Benson summed up his research by stating that:

> Different factors appear to be working at varying phases of the drug treatment process with physician and contextual influences exerting their strongest (although moderate) influence, compared to patient

characteristics, at the initial phase of the process where the decision to use psychotropic medication or not is made. As the process narrows, patient characteristics, particularly clinical and behavioral characteristics, tend to dominate the decision-making process.

Because of the high degree of subjectivity employed in the diagnosis and treatment of psychic disorders, this area of drug prescribing continues to be open to discussion.

Explanation of Observed Behavior

It is apparent from the results of these studies on physician prescribing behavior that physicians use various drug information sources in the different stages of the drug selection decision-making process. What motivates a physician to decide on a particular drug? What is the decision-making scheme used by physicians?

The decision diagram outlined by Miller (Fig. 4-3) may partially explain the process used by physicians to select a drug. First, a physician becomes aware of a particular drug through drug company advertisements or journal articles. Interest is piqued because of encounters with clinical situations that may warrant use of the drug or by an increased frequency of reports on the drug. At some point the physician decides to consider using the drug and begins an evaluation process. At this stage the physician looks for third-party endorsement of the drug and seeks information on the costs versus benefits associated with the drug's use. If all the information received is positive, the drug may be tried on a few patients. If the outcomes of these trials are acceptable, the physician may switch and may begin to prescribe the drug regularly. In essence, this is probably the scenario followed by most physicians.

We have seen that different drug information sources, for certain types of information, are used at different stages in the drug selection process.[18] The problems with this process relate to the frequency of exposure and the convenience and availability of the various sources. Physicians place a high value on convenience and availability of information. Thus, the first sources used are those located in their offices. Drug companies, who recognized this fact years ago, orient their advertising and promotional campaigns around the physician's office. The main objective of drug companies is to have free product information available to the physician within the office. This is accomplished by direct mail pamphlets, journal articles, and a well-trained force of representatives. The advantages of the drug industry's information program are that it is free and convenient. Unfortunately, however, it may be biased.

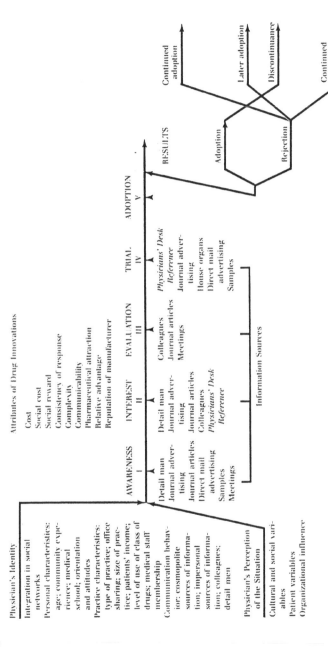

Fig. 4-3. *Model for the adoption of a drug innovation by an individual physician within a social system. (Miller, R. R.: Prescribing Habits of Physicians, Drug Intelligence and Clinical Pharmacy, 8:88, 1974.)*

The major complaint that government regulators and consumerists have with the existing drug information system for physicians is that an imbalance exists between physician exposure to third-party and proprietary information sources. To understand how to solve this problem information about how it evolved must be available. Initially, as seen in Figure 4-4, prescribers obtained most drug information from research-based companies.[24] Because of the undesirability of this system, however, checks and balances were instituted and prescribers sought out independent sources of drug information; the system in Figure 4-5 then evolved. Today, governmental regulators believe that the system can be further improved by increasing the availability of thirdparty drug informational sources through a governmental agency, such as a national center for drug science.[25] Thus they see a structure similar to that shown in Figure 4-6 as the ultimate solution for promoting good prescribing practices.

In reality, a system such as the one in Figure 4-6 creates many new problems that could be as detrimental as those that presently exist. For example, without any contact with drug manufacturers, physicians would not have up to date specifications, such as the composition, dosage, and availability of drugs. What, then, is the answer? Is there room for a pluralistic approach to providing drug information to physicians?

The prescribing studies that have been conducted indicate that each source of information available to a physician is active in the drug selection process. Proprietary information from drug companies contains an accurate description of a drug's characteristics—ingredients, dosages, frequency of administration, sideeffects, contraindications, and use. Third-party sources—journals, specialists, and clinical pharmacists—provide comparison information on drugs within a drug category. The well-trained practitioner knows how to use both sources in his decision making. It is

Fig. 4-4. *Prescribing information: typical flow patterns of the 1950s. (Office of Health Economics:* Sources of Information for Prescribing Doctors in Britain, *London: Office of Health Economics, 1977, p. 42.)*

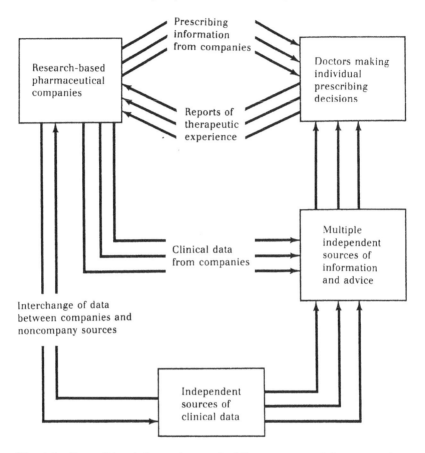

Fig. 4-5. *Prescribing information: typical flow patterns of the 1970s. (Office of Health Economics:* Sources of Information for Prescribing Doctors in Britain, *London: Office of Health Economics, 1977, p. 43.)*

imperative for medical schools to familiarize students with the various drug information sources available so that they can be used properly. It is also important for the government and third-party insurers to seek ways to compensate practitioners for providing third-party drug information.

Over the last 10 years various third-party information sources have evolved, including hospital drug information centers and clinical pharmacists. The problem that exists today centers around the convenience and availability of these services to physicians. Today, as in the past, the drug industry provides drug information more conveniently than does any other source. In order to

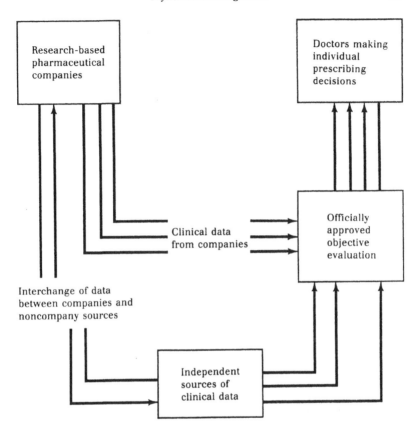

Fig. 4-6. *Prescribing information: flow patterns based on governmental concept. (Office of Health Economics:* Sources of Information for Prescribing Doctors in Britain, *London: Office of Health Economics, 1977, p. 43.)*

improve the availability of third-party drug information sources, the government as well as the pharmaceutical and medical professions should concentrate on making this type of information conveniently available to practitioners.

Sound decision making involves the same processes, whether or not it is for drugs, food, or other convenience items. The decision maker should collect information on the product specifications from the manufacturer, and should obtain information on the effectiveness and usefulness of the product from knowledgeable third-party sources. The role of government in this process should not be to stifle one source in favor of another, but to ensure that what is provided is accurate.

It is up to the professions of pharmacy and medicine to educate practitioners about the various information sources and to stress when they should be used. It is also imperative for the professions to consolidate and concentrate their efforts on increasing the availability and convenience of third-party drug information sources. Prescribing can be improved with accurate drug information; it remains to be seen whether or not the system can be.

References

1. Albert, D. A.: Decision Theory in Medicine, *Milbank Memorial Fund Quarterly, 56* (No. 3):362, 1978.
2. Brodsky, C. M.: The Pharmacotherapy System, *Psychosomatics, 11*:24, 1969.
3. Knapp, D. E., and Oeltjen, P. D.: Benefits to Risks Ratio in Physician Drug Selection, *American Journal of Public Health, 62* (No. 10):1346, 1972.
4. Hemminki, C.: The Role of Prescriptions in Therapy, *Medical Care, 13* (No. 2):150, 1975.
5. Lilja, J.: How Physicians Choose Their Drugs, *Social Science and Medicine, 10*:363, 1976.
6. Miller, R. R.: Prescribing Habits of Physicians—A Review of Studies and Prescribing of Drugs, Parts 7 and 8, *Drug Intelligence and Clinical Pharmacy, 8*:81, 1974.
7. Benson, P.: An Analysis of the Psychiatric Drug Prescription Decision Process, Ph.D. Thesis, Department of Sociology, University of North Carolina, 1980, p. 6.
8. Worthen, D. B.: Prescribing Influences: An Overview, *British Journal of Medical Education, 7*:109, 1974.
9. Coleman, J. S., Menzel, H., and Katz, E.: Social Processes in Physicians' Adoption of a New Drug, *Journal of Chronic Diseases, 9*:1, 1959.
10. Miller, R. R.: Prescribing Habits of Physicians—A Review of Studies and Prescribing of Drugs, Parts 1–6, *Drug Intelligence and Clinical Pharmacy, 7*:492, 557, 1973.
11. Hemminki, C.: Review of Literature on the Factors Affecting Drug Prescribing, *Social Science and Medicine, 9*:111, 1975.
12. Lowery, D. R., Lowy, L., and Warner, R. S.: A Survey of Physicians' Awareness of Drug Costs, *Journal of Medical Education, 47*:349, 1972.
13. Linn, L. S., and Davis, M. S.: Physicians' Orientation Toward the Legitimacy of Drug Use and Their Preferred Source of New Drug Information, *Social Sciences and Medicine, 6*:199, 1972.
14. Mapes R., and Litt, B.: Aspects of British General Practitioners' Prescribing, *Medical Care, 15* (No. 5):371, 1977.
15. Christensen, D. G., and Wertheimer, A. L.: Sources of Information and Influence on New Drug Prescribing Among Physicians, *Social Science and Medicine, 13A*:313, 1979.
15a. Hartzema, B., and Christensen, D.: Physician Prescribing Rate Determinants, *Medical Care,* in press.
16. Applied Management Sciences: Survey of Drug Information Need and Problems Associated with Communications, Directed to Practicing Physicians, Part I, Washington, DC: Physician Information Survey Journal and Drug Administration, 1974.

17. Melville, A.: Job Satisfaction in General Practice: Implications for Prescribing, *Social Science and Medicine, 14A*:495, 1980.
18. Shearer, S. W.: Evaluation of the Hospital Pharmacist as a Physician's Drug Information Source, M.S. Thesis, School of Pharmacy, University of North Carolina, 1977.
19. Bureau of Economic Research Statistics: Survey of Drug Usage in Dental Practice 1969. I. Introduction, *Journal of the American Dental Association, 81*:1179, 1970.
20. Overall, J. E., Henry, B. W., Markett, J. R., and Emken, R. L.: Decisions About Drug Therapy. I. Prescriptions for Adult Psychiatric Outpatients, *Archives of General Psychiatry, 26* (No. 2):140, 1968.
21. Sheppard, C., Moan, E., Beyel, V., et al.: Comparative Survey of Psychiatrist Treatment Preferences: California and New York, *Comprehensive Psychiatry, 15*:213, 1974.
22. Zowadski, R. T., Glazer, G. B., and Lurie, E.: Psychotropic Drug Use Among Institutionalized and Noninstitutionalized Medicaid Aged in California, *Journal of Gerontology, 33* (No. 6):825, 1978.
23. Prien, R. F., Bolter, M. B., and Coffey, E. M.: Hospital Surveys of Prescribing Practices with Psychotherapeutic Drugs, *Archives of General Psychiatry, 35*:1271, 1978.
24. Office of Health Economics: Sources of Information for Prescribing Doctors in Britain, Luton, England: Office of Health Economics, 1977.
25. Anonymous, Medical News: Physician Prescribing Practices Criticized; Solutions in Question, *Journal of the American Medical Association, 241*:2353, 1979.

## CHAPTER 5

Patient Motivation

MICKEY C. SMITH

In the emphasis on the prescriber in the pharmaceutical industry it is easy to lose track of the importance of the patient. To do so is a serious mistake. Despite the importance of the physician as a director in the choice of prescription medications, consumer choice still demands thorough consideration. Usually a person has a choice in what he does about his health. Should I have a checkup? Will this pain go away or should I see a doctor about it? Would a chiropractor do me any good? What about that new medicine I heard about on TV? The consumer chooses his physician, his pharmacist and, ultimately, although his influence may be indirect, determines the components of total health care. In the area of self-medication, of course, the consumer's choice becomes much more important. In the face of these facts, study of the consumer's motivations seems logical. If further justification is needed for study of consumer motivations, it might be well to point out that *consumer* motivations may help to determine:

1. The self-medication-prescription mixture for that individual.

2. The ultimate future of drug distribution.

3. Social and legal pressures on present and future marketing systems.

Consumer Motivation

Psychologic studies indicate that human activity, including human behavior, is directed toward satisfaction of certain basic needs. Some, although not total, agreement exists among clinical psychologists concerning the nature of these needs. Maslow has enumerated these needs in order of their importance to most people. According to this psychologist, an individual normally tries to satisfy the most basic needs first and, satisfying these, he is then free to devote his attention to the next on the list:

1. *The Physiologic Needs.* This group includes hunger, thirst, sleep, and so forth. These are the most basic needs, and until they are satisfied other needs are of no importance.

2. *The Safety Needs.* In modern society these needs are more often reflected in the needs for economic and social security rather than in needs for physical safety.

3. *The Belongingness and Love Needs.* The need for affectionate relations with individuals and a place in society is so important that its lack is a common cause of maladjustment.

4. *The Esteem Needs.* People need both self-esteem, a high evaluation of self, and the esteem of others in our society. Fulfillment of these needs provides a feeling of self-confidence and usefulness to the world; failure to fulfill these needs produces feelings of inferiority and helplessness.

5. *The Need for Self-Actualization.* This is the desire to achieve to the maximum of one's capabilities and, although it may be present in everyone, its fulfillment depends upon the prior fulfillment of the more basic needs.

6. *The Desire to Know and Understand.* These needs refer to the process of searching for meaning in the things around us.

7. *The Aesthetic Needs.* These needs may not appear to be present among many individuals because of their failure to satisfy more basic needs, but among some individuals the need for beauty is an important one.[1]

At first glance it would seem that pharmaceuticals solve only the physiologic needs. New developments in prescription drugs, however, give promise of meeting more and more of these needs. Certainly many other products *currently* offered in pharmacies are designed to meet these specific needs.

Consumer Decision Making in Health Matters

There are a number of models of consumer behavior available. We have chosen to use as a framework for this chapter the model developed by Andrew Twaddle,[2] shown in Figure 5-1. It is simple but comprehensive, and is based on the concept that sickness is a decision-making career. Twaddle's premise is that illness is an altered state of well-being about which an individual makes a series of decisions, which appear on page 90:

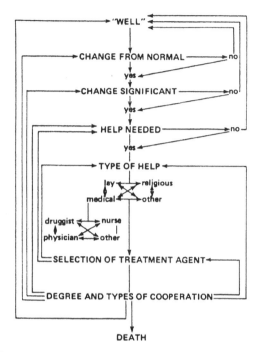

Fig. 5-1. *Decision steps in sickness career. (Twaddle, A. C., and Hessler, R. M.:* A Sociology of Health, *St. Louis: C. V. Mosby, 1977, p. 124.)*

1. That some change from normal health has occurred.

2. That the change is significant.

3. That help is needed.

4. That a particular type of help is preferable.

5. That a particular treatment agent or setting is appropriate.

6. That certain types and degrees of cooperation with the treatment agent are appropriate.

Has a Change from Normal Occurred?

Trying to define "normal" for society is difficult, but is not really necessary for the present discussion. *Normal*, for our purposes, and for those of the patient, is whatever the patient perceives it to be. For that reason, of course, the characteristics of normality vary from individual to individual.

In any case, *changes* from normal can take several forms. The most typical one is what we usually call "symptoms." For most people *pain* is not normal, nor is dizziness, nor is constipation. Thus, these symptoms represent a change from normality. Another kind of change is altered capacity—for instance, the inability to cut the grass without becoming winded. This kind of change may, of course, be attributed to something other than illness, such as aging. (Indeed some such changes *should* be so attributed, but stereotyping can result in misdiagnosis.)

It should be obvious that some people enter the health care system without experiencing any change from normality. Many hypertensive patients, for example, are diagnosed even though they are asymptomatic. Such patients begin their sickness careers as a result of routine checkups or screening programs.

Drug manufacturers and public health proponents also are concerned with "helping" people decide that a change has occurred. "Cancer's Seven Danger Signals" are described in terms of deviations from normality, while some commercials for nonprescription drugs describe, or at least imply, physical changes that should (or should not) occur in a normal individual.

The role of tolerance threshold should be obvious. Some people stoically "grin and bear" levels of pain that would send others immediately for help. Some variations are cultural—men are supposed to be "macho"—but ethnic variations in response to pain have also been demonstrated.

Symptoms are likely to be defined as serious in a direct relationship to their unfamiliarity to the patient or to the degree to which they seem threatening. Mechanic has also found that symptoms that persist or recur tend to be viewed as serious.[4]

Assumptions about cause include a component of ambiguity. The seriousness attached to back pain, for example, may differ depending on whether the patient believes it is due to muscle pain or to a kidney disorder. The same is true for assumptions about prognosis. Symptom seriousness appears to be related directly to the length of time it is expected to last, to the degree of incapacity expected to be associated with it, and to the degree to which death is thought to be a likely outcome.

Interpersonal influence often takes the form of what has been referred to as the "lay referral system"—that is, the network of friends and relatives who are consulted when a symptom is experienced. It should be apparent that the influence of these significant others is in turn a function of the degree to which *they* are influenced by their personal perceptions of the factors under discussion.

It is well known that many symptoms are experienced routinely by the population, yet many never do anything to relieve these symptoms. Some studies have shown that social stress from other life crises may be a trigger to action. A person who has lived with intermittent bouts of stomach pain may, stimulated by a divorce action, suddenly decide to seek medical care.

Treatability apparently affects perception of seriousness in that conditions perceived as untreatable are likely to take on the identity of handicaps rather than of sickness. Physical manifestations (such as visibility to the patient and to others) are likely to result in attaching greater seriousness to symptoms. The same is true for the way the patient handles his symptoms. Grimaces and groans by the patient, whether voluntary or involuntary, are likely to lead to a greater level of severity being attached to the condition by those around him.

It should be clear from the foregoing that health decisions are complex, subjective, often emotional, and subject to influence by others.

Significance of the Change

Among the factors that appear to enter into the patient's decisions concerning symptoms are the following:

1. Extent of interference with normal activities or characteristics.

2. The clarity of the symptoms.

3. The tolerance threshold of the symptomatic person.

4. The familiarity and seriousness of the symptoms.

5. Assumptions about cause.

6. Assumptions about prognosis.

7. Interpersonal influence.

8. Other life crises of the symptomatic person.

9. Assumptions about treatability.

10. Physical manifestations.

11. Impression management.[3, 4]

This list is not necessarily exhaustive, and the evidence supporting the impact of each factor is sometimes equivocal. Nevertheless, there is some evidence in each case that these factors play some (usually unquantified) role in the complex decision-making process of the patient as he pursues his sickness career.

It has also been found that the more a condition inconveniences an individual (or sometimes those with whom he relates), the more likely it is to be viewed as significant. The same is apparently true for symptom clarity—the more obvious the meaning of the symptom, to the patient or to those around him, the more significance will be attached to it.

Need for Help

We have shown that there are a number of often related factors involved in the decision that a symptom is significant. Even having made that decision, however, it is by no means universally true that the patient will decide to seek aid as opposed to self-treatment or even capitulation to the illness. Examples of the behavior variations involved can be seen in the results of the following studies.[5]

The methods used a sampling procedure that employed geographic stratification by supervisor district. Random sampling within each district, using the grid technique, was then used for household selection. The 603 households interviewed represented approximately 5.3% of the households in the 3 counties.

Interviews were conducted with the head of the household or with another responsible adult living in the house. The respondents answered questions for themselves as well as for the others living in the household.

The household interviews were extensive. Questions pertained to demographic characteristics, utilization of and attitudes toward primary care, hospital, emergency medical, dental, and pharmacy services, availability of health insurance and other third-party resources, current health status and behavior (including a 53-item symptoms checklist), attitudes and expectations toward a nurse practitioner serving in the community, and general satisfaction with current medical services.

Table 5-1 presents comparative data on the proportion of those covered by the surveys who experienced each symptom as well as on the proportion of those who sought the care of a physician in response to the symptom. The data are organized in decreasing order of total number of individuals reporting the symptom in the combined study population.

Table 5-2 displays a ranking of the symptoms by both frequency of reporting and by the proportion of individuals with those symptoms who saw a physician. Upon comparing the data in the two studies, using the Spearman rank order correlation coefficient (ρ), a significant correlation was found regarding both symptom frequency ($\rho = 0.8227$; $P < 0.001$) and proportion of persons who saw a physician for the symptom ($\rho = 0.7612$; $P < 0.001$). These results show consistency in both the frequency of appearance of symptoms and the response to those symptoms by the patients in the two studies.

In another study Bush and Osterweis used a quantitative technique called Path Analysis to determine some of the factors in-

(Text continues on p. 100.)

TABLE 5-1. *Frequency of Symptoms and Proportion Seeking Medical Care*

SYMPTOM DESCRIPTION	STUDY 1 (N = 3645)		STUDY 2 (N = 1845)		TOTAL (N = 5488)	
	A NO. REPORTING (% OF N)	B NO. VISITING MD (% OF A)	C NO. REPORTING (% OF N)	D NO. VISITING MD (% OF C)	E NO. REPORTING (% OF N)	F NO. VISITING MD (% OF E)
1. Repeated attacks of sinus trouble (etc.)	467 (12.8)	276 (59.0)	247 (13.4)	101 (40.9)	714 (13.5)	377 (52.8)
2. High blood pressure	376 (10.3)	312 (83.0)	225 (12.2)	208 (92.4)	601 (11.0)	520 (86.5)
3. Arthritis or rheumatism	371 (10.2)	204 (55.0)	222 (12.2)	130 (57.5)	593 (10.8)	334 (56.3)
4. Hay fever or allergy	288 (7.9)	66 (22.9)	106 (5.7)	38 (35.8)	394 (7.2)	104 (26.4)
5. Chronic (repeated) nervous trouble	186 (5.1)	144 (77.4)	88 (4.8)	66 (75.0)	274 (5.0)	210 (76.6)
6. Trouble seeing, even with glasses	154 (4.2)	68 (44.1)	90 (4.9)	40 (44.4)	244 (4.4)	108 (44.3)
7. Ear infections or problems	189 (5.2)	136 (71.9)	52 (2.8)	38 (73.1)	241 (4.4)	174 (72.2)
8. Overweight	159 (4.4)	60 (37.8)	81 (4.4)	33 (40.7)	240 (4.4)	93 (38.8)
9. Swelling of the ankles	136 (3.7)	70 (51.5)	63 (3.4)	46 (73.0)	199 (3.6)	116 (58.3)
10. Bad shortness of breath	108 (3.0)	68 (63.0)	87 (4.7)	56 (64.4)	195 (3.6)	124 (63.6)
11. Insomnia (trouble sleeping often)	143 (3.9)	51 (35.7)	45 (2.4)	23 (51.1)	188 (3.4)	74 (39.4)
12. Serious backaches	95 (2.6)	59 (62.1)	77 (4.2)	40 (51.9)	172 (3.1)	99 (57.6)
13. Serious headaches almost every day	86 (2.4)	54 (62.8)	80 (4.3)	49 (61.3)	166 (3.0)	103 (62.0)
14. Severe pain in or around heart or chest	79 (2.2)	53 (67.1)	84 (4.6)	65 (77.4)	163 (3.0)	118 (72.4)
15. Serious gas pain in stomach	116 (3.2)	51 (44.0)	42 (2.3)	23 (54.8)	158 (2.9)	74 (46.8)
16. Stomach ulcers	72 (2.0)	59 (81.9)	81 (4.4)	64 (79.0)	153 (2.8)	123 (80.4)
17. Painful or swollen joints	101 (2.8)	51 (50.5)	48 (2.6)	34 (70.8)	149 (2.7)	85 (57.0)
18. Diabetes (sugar)	92 (2.5)	81 (88.0)	50 (2.7)	48 (96.0)	142 (2.6)	129 (90.8)

19. Trouble with varicose veins (stinging or dark spots on legs)	84 (2.3)	44 (52.4)	41 (2.2)	23 (56.1)	125 (2.3)	67 (53.6)
20. Urinated (gone to bathroom more than twice a night every night)	77 (2.1)	33 (42.9)	48 (2.6)	26 (54.2)	125 (2.3)	59 (47.2)
21. Hardening of arteries	60 (1.6)	50 (84.4)	55 (3.0)	39 (70.9)	115 (2.1)	89 (77.4)
22. Kidney stones or chronic (repeated) kidney trouble (dribbling)	70 (1.9)	56 (80.0)	43 (2.3)	38 (88.4)	113 (2.1)	94 (83.2)
23. Anemia (low blood)	45 (1.2)	35 (77.8)	55 (3.0)	46 (83.6)	100 (1.8)	81 (81.0)
24. Asthma	81 (2.2)	59 (72.8)	18 (1.0)	12 (66.7)	99 (1.8)	71 (71.7)
25. Frequent diarrhea (loose bowels)	74 (1.3)	26 (35.1)	21 (1.1)	11 (52.4)	95 (1.7)	37 (38.9)
26. Chronic bronchitis or frequent coughing	52 (1.4)	42 (80.8)	32 (1.7)	21 (65.6)	84 (1.5)	65 (75.0)
27. "Female" troubles	48 (1.3)	42 (87.5)	36 (1.9)	22 (61.1)	84 (1.5)	64 (76.2)
28. Fainting or blackout spells	49 (1.3)	31 (63.3)	28 (1.5)	24 (85.7)	77 (1.4)	55 (71.4)
29. Tumor, cyst, or growth	48 (1.3)	41 (85.4)	23 (1.2)	21 (91.3)	71 (1.3)	62 (87.3)
30. Nausea and vomiting	43 (1.2)	30 (69.8)	24 (1.3)	10 (41.7)	67 (1.2)	40 (59.7)
31. Prostate trouble (trouble making water)	48 (1.3)	26 (58.1)	18 (1.0)	15 (83.3)	66 (1.2)	41 (62.1)
32. Chronic (repeated) gall bladder or liver trouble	37 (1.0)	26 (70.3)	22 (1.2)	17 (77.3)	59 (1.1)	43 (72.9)
33. Hernia or rupture (large navel in children)	33 (0.9)	22 (66.7)	26 (1.4)	14 (53.8)	59 (1.1)	36 (61.0)
34. Thyroid trouble or goiter (swollen place on neck)	40 (1.1)	31 (77.5)	18 (1.0)	15 (83.3)	58 (1.1)	46 (79.3)
35. Pain or burning, when going to the bathroom	40 (1.1)	24 (60.0)	17 (0.9)	14 (82.4)	57 (1.0)	38 (66.7)

TABLE 5-1. *(Continued)*

SYMPTOM DESCRIPTION	STUDY 1 (N = 3643)		STUDY 2 (N = 1845)		TOTAL. (N = 5488)	
	A. NO. REPORTING (% OF N)	B. NO. VISITING MD (% OF A)	C. NO. REPORTING (% OF N)	D. NO. VISITING MD (% OF C)	E. NO. REPORTING (% OF N)	F. NO. VISITING MD (% OF E)
36. Underweight	30 (0.8)	16 (53.3)	24 (1.3)	12 (50.0)	54 (1.0)	28 (51.9)
37. Pregnancy	22 (0.6)	20 (90.9)	31 (1.7)	29 (93.5)	53 (1.0)	49 (92.5)
38. Paralysis of any kind (been paralyzed, weakness, numbness on one side)	23 (0.6)	16 (69.5)	27 (1.5)	22 (81.5)	50 (0.9)	38 (76.0)
39. Any broken bones	31 (0.8)	29 (93.3)	14 (0.8)	13 (92.9)	45 (0.8)	42 (93.3)
40. Bad reaction to prescription drug	31 (0.8)	25 (80.6)	11 (0.6)	10 (90.9)	42 (0.7)	35 (83.3)
41. Cancer	17 (0.5)	15 (88.3)	18 (1.0)	18 (100.0)	35 (0.6)	33 (94.3)
42. Epilepsy (fits or seizures)	15 (0.4)	11 (75.3)	9 (0.5)	8 (88.9)	24 (0.4)	19 (79.2)
43. Stroke	10 (0.3)	10 (100.0)	9 (0.5)	9 (100.0)	19 (0.3)	19 (100.0)
TOTAL	4299	2623 (61.0)	2440	1501 (61.5)	6739	4124 (61.2)

Source: Smith, M. C., Sharpe, T. R., and Banahan, B. F.: Patient Response to Symptoms, *Journal of Clinical and Hospital Pharmacy*, 6:267, 1981.

TABLE 5-2. *Rank of Symptoms by Frequency and Proportion Seeing Physician*

SYMPTOM	RANK BY SYMPTOM FREQUENCY			RANK BY PROPORTION SEEING PHYSICIAN		
	STUDY 1	STUDY 2	TOTAL	STUDY 1	STUDY 2	COMBINED
1. Repeated attacks of sinus trouble (etc.)	1	1	1	30	41	35
2. High blood pressure	2	2	2	9	6	7
3. Arthritis or rheumatism	3	3	3	33	30	33
4. Hay fever or allergy	4	4	4	43	43	43
5. Chronic (repeated) nervous trouble	6	6	5	16	20	16
6. Trouble seeing, even with glasses	8	5	6	37	39	39
7. Ear infections or problems	5	16	7	19	21	21
8. Overweight	7	9(T)*	8	40	42	42
9. Swelling of the ankles	10	13	9	35	22	30
10. Bad shortness of breath	12	7	10	26	27	25
11. Insomnia (trouble sleeping often)	9	20	11	41	37	40
12. Serious backaches	14	12	12	28	36	31
13. Serious headaches almost every day	16	11	13	27	28	27
14. Severe pain in or around heart or chest	19	8	14	23	18	20
15. Serious gas pain in stomach	11	22	15	38	32	38

TABLE 5-2. *(Continued)*

SYMPTOM	RANK BY SYMPTOM FREQUENCY			RANK BY PROPORTION SEEING PHYSICIAN		
	STUDY 1	STUDY 2	TOTAL	STUDY 1	STUDY 2	COMBINED
16. Stomach ulcers	22	9(T)	16	10	17	11
17. Painful or swollen joints	13	18(T)	17	36	24	32
18. Diabetes (sugar)	15	17	18	5	3	5
19. Trouble with varicose veins (stinging or dark spots on legs)	17	23	19(T)	34	31	34
20. Urinated (gone to bathroom more than twice a night every night)	20	18(T)	19(T)	39	33	37
21. Hardening of arteries	24	14(T)	21	8	23	15
22. Kidney stones or chronic (repeated) kidney trouble (dribbling)	23	21	22	13	10	9
23. Anemia (low blood)	30	14(T)	23	15	12	10
24. Asthma	18	35(T)	24	18	25	22
25. Frequent diarrhea (loose bowels)	21	34	25	42	35	41
26. Chronic bronchitis or frequent coughing	25	25	26(T)	11	26	12
27. "Female" troubles	27(T)	24	26(T)	6	29	17
28. Fainting or blackout spells	26	27	28	25	11	23
29. Tumor, cyst, or growth	27(T)	32	29	7	7	6
30. Nausea and vomiting	31	30(T)	30	21	40	29

31. Prostate trouble (trouble making water)	27(T)	35(T)	31	31	13(T)	26
32. Chronic (repeated) gall bladder or liver trouble	34	33	32(T)	20	19	19
33. Hernia or rupture (large navel in children)	35	29	32(T)	24	34	28
34. Thyroid trouble or goiter (swollen place on neck)	32(T)	35(T)	34	15	13(T)	13
35. Pain or burning, when going to the bathroom	32(T)	39	35	29	15	24
36. Underweight	38	30(T)	36	33	38	36
37. Pregnancy	40	26	37	3	4	4
38. Paralysis of any kind (been paralyzed, weakness, numbness on one side)	39	28	38	22	16	18
39. Any broken bones	36(T)	40	39	2	5	3
40. Bad reaction to prescription drug	36(T)	41	40	12	8	8
41. Cancer	41	35(T)	41	4	1(T)	2
42. Epilepsy (fits or seizures)	42	42(T)	42	17	9	14
43. Stroke	43	42(T)	43	1	1(T)	1

*T = tie in rank.

Source: Smith, M. C., Sharpe, T. R., and Banahan, B. F.: Patient Response to Symptoms, *Journal of Hospital and Clinical Pharmacy*, 6:267, 1981.

volved in the use of prescribed and nonprescribed medicines.[6] A simplified version of the "path diagram" that they produced is shown in Figure 5-2; the arrows in the diagram indicate the direction of influence. (The degree of influence has been omitted in the interest of simplicity.)

The main findings of this study of more than 2300 people in Baltimore were as follows:

- Perceived morbidity is the principal predictor of medicine use, especially prescribed medicine with physician intervention.

- Anxiety has an effect on the use of prescribed medicine.

- The more convenient and available medical care is perceived to be, the more likely persons are to use nonprescribed medicines.

- Age, sex and race *are* factors in both types of medicine use, with males, nonwhites, and the young using fewer drugs.

- Neither Medicare, Medicaid, nor economic class had significant effects on drug use.

Type of Help Needed

Once the decision to seek help has been made the patient is still faced with a decision as to type. Although the physician is our society's model for primary care, he is by no means the only alternative. There are, for example, dentists, podiatrists, optometrists, chiropractors, clinical psychologists, and many other nonphysician health care providers. Choice of type will be a function of social, cultural, economic, educational, emotional, geographic, and legal factors.

Svarstad has offered a process explanation of one such decision, the decision to self-medicate.[7] From her review of the literature she suggested the following:

- As high as 20% of people use nonprescription drugs in response to an illness episode.

- Females make greater use of all types of drugs than do males.

- Little is known (or at least published) about the nature of individuals' decisions to use particular drug products or to follow a particular drug regimen.

Svarstad suggested the need for more research to be done on the decision process regarding drug use.

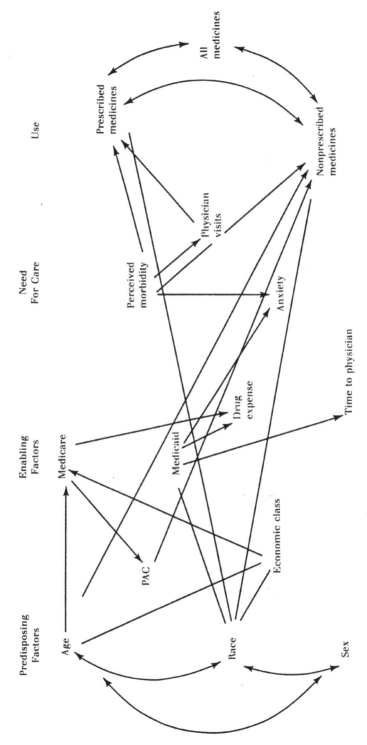

Fig. 5-2. *Path diagram of factors related to medicine use. (Bush, P. J., and Osterweis, M.: Pathways to Medicine Use, Journal of Health and Social Behavior, 19: 179, 1978.)*

Appropriateness of a Particular Treatment or Type of Setting

For our purposes this type of decision will be examined in the form of pharmacy patronage motives. Consumers are motivated toward purchase in a particular outlet, as well as toward the purchase of a particular item. The same subconscious and overt motives may be factors in patronage of a particular pharmacy or in the purchase of a product.

Gagnon has reviewed studies on the reasons patients utilize a particular pharmacy.[8] He found common factors in several studies, leading to the following list of significant patronage motives:

Convenient location:
  Close to home;
  Close to work;
  Close to physician;
  Close to shopping.
Like the personnel.
Price better than other
  pharmacies.

Parking.
Less waiting time.
Professional and convenient
  services.
Quality and merchandise
  assortment.

If we assume that the pharmacist is successful in motivating his clients to patronize his pharmacy, we can assume further that he would have some interest in the motivating factors behind their purchase. The motivation behind their prescription purchases is obvious. They have no choice other than the choice of having it filled or not, and which pharmacist to fill it. Inherent in this situation is the potential for considerable customer dissatisfaction that the pharmacist would do well to recognize.

It can be shown that patients strongly dislike the bother, delay, and experience of purchasing prescriptions. People actually do not buy prescription *drugs*. They do not really taste them, never analyze them, seldom appreciate them, or really test them. What they buy is the *right* to continue to be healthy. The pharmacy is like a tax collector to whom people are compelled to pay a periodic toll as a price for their health. This makes the pharmacy a basically unpopular institution. It can *never* be made popular or pleasant—only less unpopular, less unpleasant. Nobody likes a tax collector, not even a handsome Adonis or a seductive Venus.

The above principles are reflected in customer complaints. The customer did not want the prescription, had no choice of the product, and could not judge the quality of his prescription. Further, he was bombarded constantly with editorials and cartoons in the mass media inferring or directly stating that prescription prices are too high.

The prescription is different from most other purchases. Generally speaking, a product should be more than a means of achieving objective utility. Even the other necessities of life offer more than this. Food can be purchased in everchanging packages and variations. Clothing and shelter may be stylish and can be changed to suit the whims of the consumer. None of this is true of prescription drugs. Practically the only way to build in any *subjective* utility is through the services that the pharmacy offers. The object of a company's efforts ought to be to offer a cluster of such value satisfactions that people will want to deal with it rather than its competitors. This involves (1) making a careful calculation regarding what it is that the customer really values, (2) supplying services that meet these needs, and (3) communicating to the consumer the fact that you are so doing.

In 1973 the American Pharmaceutical Association (APhA) published the results of a major study aimed at determining the level of consumer's awareness of the nature and value of comprehensive community pharmacy services. In the course of that study a number of interesting discoveries were made that have marketing implications.

In this study, slightly different reasons were found to be involved in the choice of a pharmacy. Weighted scores for reasons were as follows:

Professional service	2302
Lower prices	2192
Personal attention	1980
A pharmacist who knows your physician	1653
A ready source of drug information	1632
A large variety of merchandise	1437
Advertised drug prices	1259

Because this was one of the most comprehensive studies of patients' attitudes toward pharmacies, we believe that a verbatim reproduction of other major findings is justified here:

Patients expect—and indeed *want*—professional attention and services, since the central issue is the patient's health, a matter of deep concern.

Patients are the focus of a "push/pull" effect. On the one hand they have been *pushed* away by increasingly negative feelings toward their community pharmacist. At the same time, they are *pulled* to the mass merchandiser and discount houses by the allure of perceived lower prices for prescription medication. However, the psychological satisfaction which the patient sees as missing in his relationships with the community pharmacist is even more lacking in dealing with the mass merchandiser. Direct personal contact between the community pharmacist and his patient—on a *professional* level—is indicated. For example, prescription medication should be delivered to the patient by the pharmacist himself so as to create a feeling of personal interest and to answer any questions.

The public is unaware of what services the modern community pharmacist performs. And equally important, it is unaware of the value of these services. Further, today's patient reacts positively to a program of comprehensive pharmaceutical services when he is informed of its features. It should be borne in mind that consumers generally will base purchase decisions on more than a price *if* they receive equivalent perceived value or satisfaction in return. Retention of the present prescription price structure depends on restoration of the pharmacist's professionalism.

The pharmacist has lost his professional standing primarily because the patient cannot visualize him as a tradesman and a professional simultaneously. Even the type of establishment in which pharmacies are usually located detracts from the pharmacist's professionalism, since physicians and lawyers and dentists perform their services in offices. Also, the use of the terms "drug store" and "druggist" are detrimental and not as conducive to building an image of professionalism as are "pharmacy" and "pharmacist."

Patients feel the pharmacist should share in the physician's responsibility for the appropriateness of the prescription medication and they rely on the pharmacist for the proper directions for medication use. This is considered an essential service.

The ideal practicing pharmacist is one who closely resembles patient's concepts of the "old-fashioned" family pharmacist—one who will provide the kinds of personal services covered by the term "comprehensive pharmaceutical services." Further, today's pharmacist, particularly among older patients (who, after all, require more prescription medication), has a "carry-forward" credit in terms of a favorable impression created by "the older corner drug store." The community pharmacist should build on this foundation.

The positive image of the "old-fashioned" pharmacy is not as widespread among younger patients. Also, since the professional image of pharmacy has lost many of its positive elements, reinforcement of these positive perceptions will make acceptance by young people more likely and progressively easier to achieve.

The inter-relationships among patient, pharmacist, manufacturer and physician indicate a close alliance between the pharmacist and the physician, not always to the pharmacist's advantage. A principal complaint is that physicians get "kickback money" for promoting a particular pharmacy and might actually have a financial interest in that pharmacy.

Since most patients realize it is the physician who prescribes the drug product and the manufacturer who sets the cost to the pharmacist, both the physician and the manufacturer are to a large degree held responsible for high prices.

Advertising of prescription drug prices is not looked upon favorably, since this imparts a "sale" dimension to a product which, by its association with the patient's health, is a most serious matter. However, *posting* of prices and of fees would be welcome by many patients, since it would alleviate mistrust and allay misconceptions about the cost of prescription medication. Also required is the establishment and communication of the availability and value of a program of comprehensive pharmaceutical services, including maintenance of patient medication records.

In general, patients do not shop for comparative prescription prices. However, due to recent publicity, personal experience in some cases and word-of-mouth, the community pharmacist is *perceived* by many patients as charging more for comparable prescription medication than the mass merchandiser. Further, because they are dealing with an item that concerns their health, patients tend to rationalize the higher cost. It is up to the pharmacist to provide the comprehensive pharmaceutical services which will help the patient absolve any feelings of guilt he might have. Since the patient must trust the pharmacist in health matters, he wants to be able to apply that trust in terms of what he pays for prescription medication.

One of our major recommendations is that the program of comprehensive pharmaceutical services be identified by an APhA seal. This seal would serve the patient as a ready identification for those pharmacies providing comprehensive pharmaceutical services with all the advantages such a program provides the participating community pharmacist, including a boost in his professionalism as perceived by the patient.

Many patients want to be participants in matters affecting their health. The community pharmacist should be able to identify these people and to consult with them, helping them in whatever way he can in order to build a better relationship with the patient.

The community pharmacy itself is psychologically warmer and more inviting to the patient. When compared to "discount drug counters," both the "pharmacy" and the "drug store" were seen as offering more pleasant surroundings, although the "pharmacy" was rated higher in this regard than the "drug store." Further the "discount drug counter" was considered more circus-like, hence noisier, less relaxing, and less inviting.[9]

Patient Compliance

Patient compliance is crucial to successful therapy. It is also important to call attention to certain economic factors—notably, the various cost dimensions related to drugs—that may affect the compliance performance of the patient either positively or negatively.

FACTORS AFFECTING COMPLIANCE

A patient cannot comply unless he takes the important first step of having the prescription filled. Little is known about the phenomenon of unfilled prescriptions, perhaps because of the methodologic difficulties associated with trying to study the dimensions of this problem.

In the early 1960s it was alleged that 20 to 50% of all prescribed medications were never dispensed, partly because of high drug prices. However, formal study of four Wisconsin communities revealed that only slightly more than 3% of prescription orders remained unfilled,[10] and that failure on the part of the patient to have them filled was not related to price or patient income.[11] Most other studies found similarly low rates, although one recent New England investigation did report that approximately 6% of the prescriptions written were apparently never filled.[12] Nevertheless, the problem has not been extensively studied in a controlled situation.

Patient Income. Recent reviews of studies of compliance have shown little relationship between compliance and patient income,[13] although cost of therapy is occasionally a factor.[14] What is still lacking are definitive studies isolating the interrelationship between income, drug costs, and compliance. Perhaps even more intriguing, and also not studied, is the role of third-party payments, particularly Medicaid, in the compliance situation.

It seems logical to expect that the relatively (and "relatively" is a pregnant term here) high cost for drugs would deter compliance in one or more of the following ways:

· Failure to have prescriptions filled.

· Failure to obtain needed refills.

· Failure to take the medication as frequently as instructed.

· Premature discontinuance of medication to "save some" for a future episode of illness.

On the other hand, it might be concluded that the patient who pays a high price for a drug might, all other factors being equal, treat the drug and its use with respect, and therefore be more compliant. (A corollary to this line of thought is that patients whose drugs are paid for by third parties would tend, again everything else being equal, to be less compliant.)

Compliance Behavior Model. After reviewing much of the literature on compliance, Becker and Maiman postulated a model for predicting and explaining compliance behavior.[14] An adaptation of their model, with the role of cost highlighted, is shown in Figure 5-3. Although it is important to recognize that cost is just one of many factors determining compliance, it is also important to recognize that this is one over which the physician can exercise some control. Furthermore, there has been a tendency to view the concept of "cost" in terms that are too simplistic.

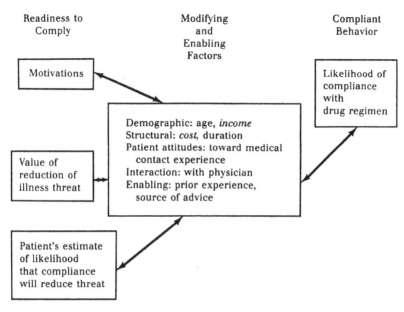

Fig. 5-3. *Factors in compliant behavior. (Adapted from Becker, M. H., and Maiman, L. A.: Socio-Behavioral Determinants of Compliance with Health and Medical Care Recommendations,* Medical Care, *13: 10, 1975.)*

Many considerations are involved in determining what drug costs really mean to the patient. They include the following: (1) cost of the prescription; (2) cost of drug per day; (3) cost for partially versus entirely filling the prescription; (4) cost of total treatment; (5) proportion of total treatment cost; (6) its position in cost sequence; (7) perceived cost; (8) expected cost; (9) past cost experiences; (10) importance of the cost, based on ability to pay; (11) opportunity cost—what is given up to purchase the drug; (12) inconvenience or convenience of dosage form used in improving compliance; (13) psychic or symbolic cost; (14) cost of alternatives, including noncompliance; (15) cost of competing products, their generic equivalence or nonequivalence, and their therapeutic effectiveness. Each of these items warrants the physician's consideration inasmuch as each alone, or in combination with others, may affect whether or not the patient ever receives the drug or takes it properly. It should be noted that some of the factors that may inhibit the patient from getting the prescription filled initially may actually promote compliance once that step is taken.

Cost Factors. As described previously, there are numerous ways to look at cost as a factor in compliance. The first factor is the most usual, simply the initial expense of the prescription. The average prescription today costs something over six dollars, roughly the price of five commercial hamburgers.

Once the initial cost is considered, however, there may be a wide variation in what it costs the patient to use the drug each day. Although it is unlikely that the patient has considered this in terms of the few cents that are usually spent daily for needed medication, he may have looked into how much "half" of the prescription will cost. Such partial prescription filling is often tried by low-income patients who either cannot pay the full cost or who are unsure whether or not the medicine will "work." The patient should be made aware that he will actually be penalizing himself by filling only part of the prescription if the pharmacist uses the professional fee rather than a markup system.

Another factor relates to the duration of treatment. The physician should be aware that in writing a prescription, authorizing five refills, and expecting the patient to get them all, he is writing an order of $25 to $30 of medication. The patient's experience and perceptions also have something to do with the role of cost in compliance. A $5 prescription charge means different things to different people. Income, the nature of the illness, the physician's indications of what charges to expect, and the level of prescription charges paid by the patient in the past all affect his reaction to the charge for each new prescription.

Noneconomic costs include the time the patient spends to get a prescription filled. There may be psychologic costs in admitting that one is ill enough to need a prescription and, indeed, the prescription itself may symbolize that weakness. On the other hand, some patients may feel that receiving and taking medicine is necessary to gain attention or to prove that they are really sick.

Patient Response. What is the price of alternatives to drug therapy, including noncompliance? Drug charges may not seem excessive if the alternative is an extra 2 or 3 days away from work. How the patient responds to the cost factors described is almost certainly affected in some way by (1) the proportion of the total treatment cost that goes for medications and (2) at which point the drug costs actually appear in the "cost-of-illness" sequence. For example, the average patient is unlikely to notice a $50 drug charge on a $1200 hospital bill, but even a $3 prescription fee may become the "last straw" if it follows charges for physician services and x-ray and laboratory studies.

ENCOURAGING COMPLIANCE

Physicians should be aware that seemingly minor differences in similar drugs may have major implications for compliance. The ease of administration, comparatively rapid onset of effect, or appearance of the drug product may make the difference in whether or not the patient follows the physician's intended drug regimen.

In some cases the physician's choice has a dual effect on encouraging compliance. For example, certain psychotropic drugs can be prescribed in larger doses twice a day, rather than in smaller doses three or four times a day, with a cost saving to the patient.[15] Both the lower cost and the less frequent dose would favor compliance.

Fortunately, there are a number of other cost-related steps that the physician may take to encourage compliance. One of the most important is to learn something about drug prices. One study involving more than 200 California physicians showed they had only a limited knowledge of the costs of certain antimicrobial agents, and usually their estimates were too low. Furthermore, these physicians listed the *patient* as their most important source of information on drug prices.[16] Given the normal sequence of drug prescribing and dispensing, it can only be assumed in such a situation that information is obtained as the patient returns to the physician complaining about the price of the last prescription.

A final issue in this type of decision is what, in fact, the patient really expects from the physician in terms of drug therapy. The data on this are not consistent. Stimson,[16] in a British study, found that patients were not as prescription-oriented when visiting the physician as many seem to believe.[17] Rappoport, also in England, found that 56% of a sample of patients expected to receive a prescription.[17] Perhaps more interesting was the finding that 24% intended to buy an over-the-counter (OTC) product from a pharmacy after leaving the physician's office. Perhaps most interesting, 50% of those who expected a prescription but did not obtain one intended to purchase a product for self-medication. To further confuse this issue, Wartman and colleagues have reported finding that patients who did not receive prescriptions reported more satisfaction with the communicative aspects of their visits to physicians than did patients who received prescriptions.[19]

A Special Note About the Prescription

It is possible that the prescription has become so commonplace that we may have lost sight of some of its many functions, yet the prescription is the clear focal point of a great deal of pharmacy-medicine interaction and conflict. Certainly it is central to the practice of pharmacy. In this section we will review some of the obvious or manifest functions that prescriptions serve. We will then examine some of the less obvious or latent functions that may be filled by prescriptions and, finally, suggest some implications.

According to Merton, the manifest functions of an institution are "Those objective consequences contributing to the adjustment or adaptation of the system which are intended and recognized by participants in the system" and latent functions are those consequences "which are neither intended nor recognized."[20]

It might also be wise to offer a few definitions, because "prescription" may be defined in a number of ways:

1. According to *The Art of Compounding,* the prescription "is an order written by a physician, dentist, veterinarian, or other licensed practitioner directing the pharmacist to compound and dispense medication for a patient, and usually accompanied by directions for its administration or use."[21] This definition probably serves as well as any other to describe the traditional usage of the term.

2. Prescription may also refer to the finished product—that which is dispensed pursuant to the order just described. Thus, the patient enters the pharmacy with one prescription in hand and leaves with another.

3. As a verb form, "prescription" may also refer to the act of issuing the order by the licensed practitioner.

4. By dictionary definition, "prescription" may refer to the directions for administration. Thus: "Take one tablet three times daily" is a prescription.

This discussion will refer mainly to the first two definitions, although some use may be made of the others.

Manifest Functions

In Table 5-3 are listed the manifest functions of the prescription as we perceive them. These are the functions with which most are familiar. The prescription serves as the method by which the physician communicates to both the patient and to the pharmacist his wishes concerning drug therapy. It is the legal authorization for dispensing "legend" drugs and, when filed, particularly in a medication profile, serves as a therapeutic record.

The prescription (referring to the drug itself) is a therapeutic tool that, when properly dispensed and used, allows the physician some control over patient therapy even after he leaves the office or hospital. Prescriptions also serve as a convenient means of drug sampling and as a method of trying new drugs.

TABLE 5-3. *Manifest Functions of the Prescription*

---

    1. Means of communication
    2. Legal document
    3. Record source
    4. Method of therapy
    5. Means of medical control of therapy*
    6. Sample mechanism*
    7. Means of clinical trial*

---

*These functions have latent components as well.

Latent Functions

In one of the most important papers in recent times on the sociology of drug use, Pellegrino has presented an eloquent examination of the symbolic importance of the prescription.[22] He examined "three interacting levels of symbolism": the actual ingestion of the drug, the enhancement by the fact of illness, and the investiture of symbolism by the act of prescribing by the physician. From our reading of Pellegrino's work we were able to identify 14 different uses of the prescription, the act of prescribing, or the drug itself (Table 5-4).

Also included in Table 5-4 are a number of other functions of the prescription that we have identified as "latent." Some of these have appeared in the literature and others are simply the result of personal observation or theorizing. A few of these will be discussed in turn.

Evidence of prescription legitimization of sick role status is slight. In a small study, Jackson, Smith, and Liao found that the existence of a prescription resulted in a greater likelihood of mentally ill patients being accorded the two "rights" of the sick role—freedom from blame and exemption from normal duties.[23]

> The crucial points to be noted about the sick role are: its passive orientation which may provide latent rewards to certain types of individuals, particularly those from cultural backgrounds emphasizing passive value orientations; and its potential for helping people cope with failure to perform social roles adequately.[24]

Gallagher has observed that "many individuals use a variety of drugs as a supportive resource in the pursuit and attainment of socially-approved goals" and has described this phenomenon as "routine drug use as an adaptive resource in goal attainment."[25]

As Shuval has noted, professional legitimization is necessary to prevent large scale avoidance of social responsibility by feigning illness. "It is not enough for the individual to claim to be sick; before entering the sick role it is necessary to obtain 'official'

TABLE 5-4. *Latent Functions of the Prescription*

1. Visible sign of the physician's power to heal (drug)
2. Symbol of the power of modern technology (drug)
3. Sign that the patient is "really" ill (drug)
4. Legitimizes the long-term illness without cure
5. Concrete expression that physician has fulfilled his contract
6. Reasonable excuse for human contact with physician
7. Satisfactorily terminates the visit
8. Fits the concept of modern man that he can control his own destiny
9. Expression of physician's control
10. Indication of physician's concern
11. Medium of communication between physician and patient
12. Forestalls lengthy discussions
13. Source of satisfaction to the physician
14. Identifies the clinical situation as legitimately medical
15. Legitimizes sick role status
16. Symbol of patient control
17. Means of patient goal attainment
18. Excuse for failure
19. Symbol of patient stability
20. Evidence of physician as an activist
21. Evidence of pharmacist activity
22. Research source of utilization and treatment
23. Political tool
24. Medium of exchange
25. Sampling medium
26. Method of clinical trial
27. Method of differentiating legal drug status

recognition that one is indeed 'ill'."[26] Shuval also noted that in Israel a document attesting to a legitimized illness is required for a number of special situations. The humanely oriented doctor is under pressure to accede to requests for the document (known as *petek*), "particularly when they come from hard-pressed welfare recipients, housewives and others."[26]

Berle has stated that "illness may be an aspect of lack of success and may therefore become a justification for failure. Failure is almost inevitable when there is a discrepancy between an individual's aspirations and the limited opportunities opened to him. To prove illness, so that one may be cared for, is then a vital necessity.[27]

Balint and his associates in England studied the special case of "repeat" prescriptions and tested a model consisting of three stages. In the first stage the patient, feeling a need for someone or something reliable, engages in a polemic with his doctor, "offering" various symptoms in search of a stable relationship. A truce (Stage II) is reached when the physician prescribes and continues to supply a satisfactory drug. This is followed by an uneasy peace (Stage III), an uneasiness caused by the physician's knowledge that it is often bought at the price of irrational prescribing.

In these cases the prescription becomes a symbol of the stability sought by the patient. This symbol is characterized by "the ambivalent over-evaluation of the drug that has become the representative of the 'something' he so badly needs, and therefore must be good, reliable, unchanging, and, above all, available."[24]

The same study provided evidence of the value of the prescription as a symbol of patient control of the doctor. Sometimes the control was more tangible, with the patient selecting the drug type and the physician admitting that he cheerfully acceded to the patient's wishes.[24]

The prescription has been called a "too easy measure of what the pharmacist does."[28] Prescriptions have been used to study treatment patterns and to predict and analyze market structures. Prescriptions and their payment have therefore been the subject of political battles, and are used as a medium of exchange. As noted previously, they are involved in drug sampling and in individual clinical trials by the physician.

Finally, the prescription serves to identify the legal status of drugs.[29]

It should now be apparent that the prescription serves a remarkable range of functions, many of them little recognized.

References

1. Maslow, A. H.: *Motivation and Personality,* New York: Harper and Brothers, 1954, p. 80.
2. Twaddle, A. C.: *Sickness Behavior and the Sick Role,* Boston: G. K. Hall and Company, 1979, p. 134.
3. Twaddle A. C., and Hessler, R. M.: *A Sociology of Health,* St. Louis: C. V. Mosby, 1977, p. 108.
4. Mechanic, D.: *Medical Sociology,* New York: The Free Press, p. 201.
5. Smith, M. C., Sharpe, T. R., and Banahan, B. F.: Patient Response to Symptoms, *Journal of Clinical and Hospital Pharmacy,* 6:116, 1981.
6. Bush, P. J., and Osterweis, M.: Pathways to Medicine Use, *Journal of Health and Social Behavior, 19:*179, 1978.
7. Svarstad, B. L.: Self-Medication: A Sociopsychological Perspective, Paper presented at the Ohio Pharmaceutical Seminar, Columbus, 1978.
8. Gagnon, J. P.: Pharmacy Patronage Motives: Review and Results of Recent Investigations, Paper presented to the Academy of Pharmaceutical Sciences, New Orleans, 1976.
9. American Pharmaceutical Association: *Communicating the Value of Comprehensive Pharmaceutical Services to the Consumer,* Washington, DC: American Pharmaceutical Association, 1973, pp. 41–42.
10. Hammel, R. W., et al.: Unfilled Prescriptions in Your Community? *Journal of the American Pharmaceutical Association, NSI:*155, 1961.
11. Hammel, R. W., and Williams, P. O.: Do Patients Receive Prescribed Medication? *Journal of the American Pharmaceutical Association, NSI:* 332, 1964.

12. Taubman, A. H., et al.: Non-compliance in Initial Prescription Filling, *The Apothecary, 87*:14, 1975.
13. Mikeal, R. I., and Sharpe, T.: *Patient Compliance,* in Pharmacy Practice, edited by A. I. Wertheimer and M. C. Smith. Baltimore, University Park Press, 1974, pp. 170–194.
14. Becker, M. H., and Maiman, I. A.: Socio-Behavioral Determinants of Compliance with Health and Medical Care Recommendations, *Medical Care, 13*:10, 1975.
15. Marder, J. E., and Dimascio, A.: Improving Scheduling and Reducing Costs of Psychotropic Drugs for Out-Patients, *Hospital Community Psychiatry 24*:556, 1973.
16. Lowry, D. R., et al.: A Survey of Physicians' Awareness of Drug Costs, *Journal of Medical Education 47*:349, 1972.
17. Stimson, G. V.: Doctor-Patient Interaction and Some Problems for Prescribing, *Journal of the Royal College of General Practitioners, 29*:468, 1979.
18. Rappoport, J.: Patients' Expectations and Intentions to Self-Medicate, *Journal of the Royal College of General Practitioners, 26*:88, 1976.
19. Wartman, P. R., et al.: Do Prescriptions Adversely Affect Doctor-Patient Interactions? *American Journal of Public Health, 71*:1358, 1981.
20. Merton, R. K.: *Social Theory and Social Structure,* New York: The Free Press, 1949.
21. Jenkins, G. L., et al.: *Scoville's The Art of Compounding,* New York: McGraw-Hill, 1957, p. 3.
22. Pellegrino, E. D.: Prescribing and Drug Ingestion: Symbols and Substances, *Drug Intelligence and Clinical Pharmacy, 10*:624, 1976.
23. Jackson, J. D., Smith, M. C., and Liao, W. C.: Validation of Sick Role Rights for Mental Illness, *Psychological Reports, 43*:426, 1978.
24. Balint, M., et al.: *Treatment or Diagnosis,* Philadelphia: J. B. Lippincott, 1970, pp. 41, 47, 90.
25. Gallagher, E. B.: Lines of Reconstruction and Extension in Parsonian Sociology of Illness, *Social Science and Medicine, 10*:207, 1976.
26. Shuval, J. T.: *Social Functions of Medical Practice,* San Francisco: Jossey-Bass, 1970, p. 11.
27. Berle, B. B.: *Eighty Puerto Rican Families in New York City,* New York: Columbia University Press, 1958, p. 256.
28. Smith, M. C.: General Practice Pharmacy in the United Kingdom and the USA: Some Comparisons and Contrasts, *The Pharmaceutical Journal, 208*:9, 1973.
29. Marinker, M.: The Doctor's Role in Prescribing, *Journal of the Royal College of General Practitioners, 23*:22, 1973.

## CHAPTER 6

Market Analysis

STEPHEN C. CHAPPELL

Measurement of Markets

As noted in Chapter 2, "market" is a frequently used term that may mean a number of things. The average dictionary, in fact, will list some 20 different meanings or applications of the term. Even within the framework of a single industry, there are multiple applications, some very broad, others finite. One hears reference to the pharmaceutical market, the prescription market, the hospital market, the antibiotic market, and the tetracycline market. A geographic or regional connotation may be applied, such as the Atlanta or Philadelphia market. We may speak of the general practitioner market or the urologist market, or the unit dose market, or the injectable market, and so on.

Whatever the term "market" implies in a given situation, its size, growth patterns, and characteristics are of vital import in the conduct of business. Management requires knowledge of the markets in which they participate or contemplate. Thus, there is a need for "market research" to define and characterize markets as a forerunner to the broader term of "marketing research."

Most markets tend to be of such magnitude that measurement can be accomplished only by statistical inference from observations of merely a sample of all the events occurring within them. The design and execution of proper statistical samples require a great deal of knowledge, thought, and planning. Well-meaning but partially informed people make classic mistakes in attempting to draw samples of the pharmaceutical market. Samples are often well designed and, in statistical theory, are faultless. If, however, these designs cannot be executed in the field, as is often the case, the effort is worthless. It is quite easy to make the mistake of drawing an excellent sample of the wrong universe, and often the results from a good sample of a proper universe are invalidated because the wrong variables were measured in relation to the problem at hand.

These points apply to both periodic and continuing audits and surveys and to special purpose, nonrepetitive research projects. There is greater danger in the second area, for there is often a tendency to accept results at face value in the absence of historical data with which to make comparisons.

Descriptive statistics and census data are available from many excellent sources and serve to describe, in numerical terms, many of the population characteristics of given fields of interest. Among these sources are the United States Census data, the *Statistical Abstract of the United States,* the United States Tariff Commission Reports, and several excellent references prepared and issued by private firms. Any full service library can assist the analyst in locating these services. It behooves the researcher to check sources carefully to determine their applicability to the particular problem. Some data, which have the appearance of being "census" data, may in fact have been based upon sample findings. It is important to know the details of how the data were obtained in order to evaluate their acceptability and validity for a given analysis.

The measurement of product movement at the final point of sale in the long distribution line is a fundamental function of marketing research. Measurement may be the number of times an item is sold, the number of units of an item that have been sold, or the dollar value of the total sales from one time period to another. The aggregate figures for all similar products measure individual product fields, and the combination of all fields yields the measurement of a market. From these data can be computed:

1. The size of a market expressed in numbers of transactions or individual sales, total units, or dollars.

2. Growth or decline trends of total markets, individual field, individual products, and product forms.

3. Regional or geographic variations in markets.

4. Time series analysis—secular trend, cyclical variation, seasonal pattern, and episodic movement.

5. Singular, partial, or multiple correlation with other series or factors.

Measurement data are historical data. An audit conducted today is history at the very moment it is conducted. Historical data, however, are the basis for extrapolation or projection into the future. Analysis of past performance is the foundation for planning future action.

Pharmaceutical Market and Marketing Research

It has often been stated that, with regard to the marketplace in which it operates, the pharmaceutical industry is perhaps the most "data rich" of all industries. As a result it is one of, if not the most, sophisticated users of market and marketing research information. To a large degree, this wealth of data regarding the pharmaceutical marketplace is a function of the many inherently unique aspects of the pharmaceutical marketing process.

In order to explain this statement, let us review some of the basic characteristics of pharmaceutical marketing. In a broad sense, pharmaceutical companies produce and market two types of products. One type is the prescription or legend product that may be obtained by consumers only upon the presentation of authorization by a licensed prescriber. The other type is the over-the-counter product that may be purchased without a prescription.

There has been an expansion of the over-the-counter pharmaceutical market in recent years, but the most fundamental business of pharmaceutical companies still remains the production and marketing of prescription pharmaceuticals. In the marketing segment of this activity, the industry is unique in that it does *not* market its products to the ultimate consumer, the patient, but instead to an intermediary, the physician (or other prescriber, such as a dentist). Although it is the patient who ultimately purchases and consumes a prescription drug, it is the physician who makes the decision as to which, if any, drug or product the patient is to have, how much he is to have, in what form he is to take it, and for how long. The primary target, then, of the marketing effort for these products is the population of licensed prescribers in the country, rather than the consumers of the products. Another target of the marketing effort for prescription pharmaceuticals is the population of licensed pharmacists in the country, this group having assumed more importance recently because of their increased role as decision makers with regard to the specific brand of drug to be dispensed to the patient. Here too, however, the focus is on an intermediary rather than on the ultimate consumer.

The selling of prescription pharmaceuticals to the public also involves some atypical characteristics. Professional licensure is required for an establishment to stock and sell prescription products. Further, the seller (or dispenser) of these products must himself be licensed to do so. The selling of prescription pharmaceuticals to the public is thus restricted to the comparatively small numbers of pharmacists and pharmacies in the country rather than to the substantially larger number of retailers and retail outlets that would normally be the case for a consumer product.

Uniqueness also characterizes prescription products in the sense that, as mentioned previously, purchase of these products by consumers requires the presentation of authorization by a licensed prescriber in the form of a written prescription. A record of every transaction involving the sale or dispensing of a prescription drug to the consumer is therefore created and maintained, with these records being specific to the patient, physician, pharmacy, and product.

In effect, product choice decisions and product movement in the multibillion dollar prescription drug industry are accounted for or represented by what basically amounts to a relative handful of the population. The number of licensed prescribers of medication in the United States is probably about 500,000, and the number of registered pharmacists is roughly 140,000. There are approximately 55,000 retail pharmacies in the country and slightly more than 7,000 hospitals. Contrast these numbers, for example, to the potential hundred million decision makers who might be involved in a consumer product, and to the many hundreds of thousands of outlets that might sell a consumer product with few, if any, records maintained regarding these decisions or sales.

These examples, along with other unique aspects of prescription product marketing, are of considerable importance in the gathering of data regarding the marketplace. In one sense, there is virtually no difficulty in finding physicians, pharmacists, pharmacies, or hospitals. Primarily because of professional licensure requirements, all are on continually maintained lists of one type or another. Additionally, the number of members in each of these groups is known to within a very small degree of error. The person who wants to know the number of physicians in the country does not have to initiate a study to find out this information. Consider this as compared to the problems that would be encountered by the researcher who wanted to know the number of coffee drinkers in the United States and wanted to conduct research among them—no list of coffee drinkers exists.

There is relatively little required of the researcher in the pharmaceutical marketplace in terms of characterizing potential research subjects. Information is available, for example, on the physician's type of practice, specialty, year graduated from medical school, medical school attended, and location of practice. Information is also available on retail pharmacies in terms of their type, size, and location. Hospitals are identified by type, bed size, affiliation with learning institutions, presence of a formulary, and whether or not certain types of equipment are available. This precharacterizing of research subjects is generally not available to the researcher in the consumer marketplace.

Another element that facilitates the conduct of market research in the pharmaceutical marketplace is the fair amount of homogeneity that is found within and among the various groups of participants in the marketplace. Physicians and pharmacists, for example, have received the same basic education as other physicians or pharmacists. As with most purchasers of consumer products, no wide variations from physician to physician are found in terms of socioeconomic considerations. Most participants in the health care area are professionals and tend to communicate on an inter- and intragroup basis better than the average consumer does with other consumers. Similarity in thinking and activity among the members of a particular group generally tends to facilitate researching of the group.

The conduct of market research in the prescription product area is also made somewhat easier than doing the same in the consumer sector because most of the decisions made by principals in the market are based on knowledge rather than on emotion or whim.

Finally, in many segments of pharmaceutical market research, the researcher does not have to create or search extensively for records of fact regarding decision or activity. As pointed out earlier, for instance, records are required to exist for every transaction regarding the sale of a prescription product to a consumer.

In summary, many of the unique characteristics of prescription product marketing have the effect in one fashion or another of eliminating or minimizing many of the requirements and effort associated with market research in the general sense. This is certainly a major reason for the enormous amount of data available regarding the prescription product marketplace.

You, of course, should not carry away the impression that market research in the pharmaceutical industry is an effortless undertaking. Although there are many areas of advantage relative to other industries, many of the peculiar aspects found in pharmaceutical marketing create complications with which the researcher has to deal. As one illustration, the construction of a sample of retail pharmacies has to take into consideration the fact that pharmacies vary a great deal in the composition of their sales volume. Some may fill only a few prescriptions yet have an extremely high volume of business overall. Others may do a negligible business in items other than prescriptions. Some fill the prescriptions of only a small number of physicians while others have files containing prescriptions from several hundred physicians. The customary probability or random statistical sample of the drugstores in the country may not necessarily constitute a representative sample of the prescription market in the country.

Market and Marketing Research Services

A large number of market and marketing research services have been developed for the pharmaceutical industry by independent research companies, sometimes referred to as service agencies or suppliers. Many of these services have been in continuous operation since the 1950s; others were initiated over the years in response to changes in the marketplace and to concomitant changes in the information needs of the industry. A relatively new service offered to the pharmaceutical marketer, for example, is one that depicts the frequency and characteristics of substitution in retail pharmacies. This information is important in today's market, but was obviously of no relevance prior to the repeal of antisubstitution legislation. Advances in technology have also been responsible for the development of new services by facilitating the collection and processing of information that was either not available previously or was too difficult to collect and process. As an illustration, the recent advent of pharmacy service systems has provided as a by-product millions of records of prescription dispensing information stored on computers, easily accessible for very detailed analyses.

The services provided by independent research companies are generally classified into two major categories—*syndicated* or *custom*. A syndicated service is defined here as one in which all subscribers receive identical information. These services are generally supported by a large number of subscribers. The custom service, on the other hand, is supported by only one client to whose specific needs the service or project is tailored. Only the contracting client receives the information in a custom project. Another categorization of these services is based on their periodicity or continuity. They may be periodic, continuing (and periodic), or ad hoc in nature.

Periodic and Continuing Audits and Surveys

There are seven general types of continuing audits or surveys of the pharmaceutical marketplace:

1. Retail pharmacy purchase audit.

2. Hospital purchase audit.

3. Warehouse withdrawal audit.

4. Retail pharmacy prescription audit.

5. Physician panels.

6. Promotional media audit.

7. Retail sales audit.

Broadly defined, these services are nationwide in scope, each covering one aspect of the pharmaceutical marketplace on a regular, periodic basis—monthly, quarterly, etc. With some exceptions, which will be noted, these audits present national (continental United States) estimates of activity—dollars, prescriptions, detail calls. These estimates represent projections of data collected from a sample constructed to be representative of the population, or *universe*—physician, hospitals, pharmacies—being studied. Again, in general, data are presented at the product level. Product level data are then summarized to therapeutic category or to manufacturer level, and these ultimately to a total marketplace figure. In addition to absolute volume estimates, market share and trend information are customarily provided.

RETAIL PHARMACY PURCHASE AUDIT

This is designed to provide a measurement of pharmaceutical product purchases by retail pharmacies. A purchase audit is, in effect, an "inflow" audit, measuring the flow of product (either directly from a manufacturer or from a wholesaler) *into* retail pharmacies. This is in contrast to an "outflow" audit such as the prescription audit, which monitors the flow of a product out of the pharmacy into the hands of the consumer. In theory, at any one point in time, the difference between an inflow audit and an outflow audit is represented by inventory on the shelf.

The methodology employed to collect purchase information is essentially one of invoice auditing. Individual pharmacies on the panel are audited monthly for all records of purchase. The scope of the retail pharmacy purchase audit is not limited to prescription, or to legend, pharmaceuticals, but includes proprietary and ethical over-the-counter medications as well. The latter group of products is becoming increasingly important in the marketplace. In 1980, close to one third of total retail pharmacy purchase dollars was represented by over-the-counter pharmaceuticals. The increasing orientation of the public toward self-medication, combined with growth in the "de-$R_x$ing" movement, suggests that this segment will grow even more in the future. Table 6-1 shows examples of retail and hospital audits.

HOSPITAL PURCHASE AUDIT

In general methodology, style, and form, this is a replica of the retail pharmacy purchase audit. The obvious difference is that this audit focuses on hospital purchases of pharmaceutical products. The hospital sector has increased substantially over the past decade as a market for pharmaceutical products. The growth in pur-

TABLE 6-1. *Hospital and Drugstore Purchase Audit*

184 ——— 184

11000 ANTICOAGULANTS

	12 MONTHS 1975 DRUG $000S	HOSP. $000S	COMBINED $000S	SHARE	12 MONTHS 1976 DRUG $000S	SHARE	HOSPITAL $000S	SHARE	COMBINED $000S	SHARE	COMBINED % CHGE 76/75 VOL.	SHARE
11000 ANTICOAGULANTS	9,700	25,983	35,683	100%	10,311	100%	28,375	100%	38,686	100%	+8.4	
11200 ANTICOAGULANTS INJECT	769	25,349	26,117	73.2	797	7.7	27,564	97.1	28,361	73.3	+8.6	+0.2
11100 ANTICOAGULANTS ORAL	8,931	635	9,565	26.8	9,514	92.3	812	2.9	10,325	26.7	+7.9	-0.4

• • • • • • • • • • • • • • • • •

	12 MONTHS 1975 DRUG $000S	HOSP. $000S	COMBINED $000S	SHARE	12 MONTHS 1976 DRUG $000S	SHARE	HOSPITAL $000S	SHARE	COMBINED $000S	SHARE	COMBINED % CHGE 76/75 VOL.	SHARE
11200 ANTICOAGULANTS INJECT	769	25,369	26,117	100%	797	100%	27,564	100%	28,361	100%	+8.6	
WYETH HEPARIN SODIUM TUBEX	25	2,726	2,752	10.5	30	3.8	6,173	22.4	6,203	21.9	+125.5	+101.6
0278-01 TUBEX 5MU 1CC 10	3	1,350	1,353	5.2	3	0.3	2,572	9.3	2,574	9.1	+90.3	+75.2
0277-01 TUBEX 10MU 1CC 10	15	748	763	2.9	12	1.5	874	3.2	885	3.1	+16.1	+6.9
0275-01 TUBEX 1MU 1CC 10		123	123	0.5	1	0.1	514	1.9	515	1.8	+320.0	+287.4
0276-01 TUBEX 20MU 1CC 10	1	77	79	0.3	14	1.8	149	0.5	163	0.6	+107.3	+91.3
W/NS 1CC 50				0.0		0.0	923	3.3	923	3.3		
25MU 1CC 10		282	282	1.1		0.0	528	1.9	528	1.9	+87.4	+72.6
5MU 1CC 1	6	76	82	0.3		0.0	272	1.0	272	1.0	+232.0	+206.4
10MU 1CC 1		3	3	0.0	1	0.1	231	0.8	232	0.8	+999.9	+999.9
15MU 1CC 10		67	67	0.3		0.0	62	0.2	62	0.2	-7.9	-15.2
1MU 1CC 1				0.0		0.0	49	0.2	49	0.2		
UPJOHN HEPARIN SODIUM	56	7,045	7,100	27.2	76	9.5	5,913	21.5	5,989	21.1	-15.7	-22.3
VIAL	42	6,946	6,988	26.8	71	8.9	5,894	21.4	5,965	21.0	-14.6	-21.4
1MU/CC 10CC	18	4,217	4,234	16.2	10	1.3	3,050	11.1	3,060	10.8	-27.7	-33.6
50 LNG		3,478	3,478	13.3		0.0	1,277	4.6	1,277	4.5	-63.3	-66.2
5 LNG		16	16	0.1		0.0	785	2.8	785	2.8	+999.9	+999.9
1 LNG	3	146	150	0.6	7	0.8	609	2.2	615	2.2	+310.6	+278.5
50 INT		414	414	1.6	1	0.1	286	1.0	286	1.0	-30.9	-36.3
25 INT		83	83	0.3	1	0.1	44	0.2	45	0.2	-45.5	-50.0
5 INT	12		13	0.0		0.0	36	0.1	36	0.1	+184.4	+166.0
1 INT	2	71	72	0.3	2	0.2	10	0.0	12	0.0	-83.3	-84.8
25 INT	8		8	0.0		0.0	4	0.0	4	0.0	-56.0	
10MU/CC 6CC	13	2,515	2,528	9.7	38	4.7	1,607	5.8	1,644	5.8	-35.0	-50.1
50 LNG		1,395	1,395	5.3		0.0	490	1.8	490	1.7	-64.9	-67.7
5 LNG		49	49	0.2		0.0	477	1.7	477	1.7	+869.5	+794.1
1 LNG	12	156	167	0.6	23	2.9	246	0.9	269	1.0	+61.0	+48.4
50 INT		187	187	0.7		0.0	181	0.7	181	0.6	-3.1	-10.8
25 INT		700	700	2.7		0.0	171	0.6	171	0.6	-75.6	-77.5
5 INT		4	4	0.0		0.0	40	0.1	40	0.1	+805.3	+768.8
1 INT	1		1	0.0	14	1.8	2	0.0	17	0.1	+999.9	+999.9
10MU/CC 1CC	11	51	62	0.2	8	1.0	723	2.6	731	2.6	+999.9	+591.9
1 LNG	2		2	0.0	4	0.4	419	1.5	422	1.5	+999.9	+999.9
5 LNG		3	3	0.0	3	0.4	197	0.7	200	0.7	+999.9	+999.9
50 LNG		14	14	0.1		0.0	49	0.2	49	0.2	+261.2	+232.7
1 INT	1	7	7	0.0		0.0	22	0.1	23	0.1	+178.7	+154.8
50 INT	8	20	28	0.1		0.0	18	0.1	18	0.1	-35.8	-41.1
25 INT		7	7	0.0		0.0	9	0.0	9	0.0	+32.3	
1 LNG				0.0		0.0	7	0.0	7	0.0		
5 INT				0.0		0.0	3	0.0	3	0.0		
5MU/CC 10CC		103	103	0.4	2	0.3	261	0.9	268	0.9	+160.2	+135.5
50 LNG		22	22	0.1		0.0	185	0.7	185	0.7	+741.1	+677.4
5 LNG				0.0		0.0	70	0.3	70	0.2		
1 LNG				0.0	7	0.9		0.0	7	0.0		
5 INT				0.0		0.0	3	0.0	3	0.0		
1 LNT				0.0		0.0	1	0.0	1	0.0		
25 INT				0.0		0.0	1	0.0	1	0.0	+101.0	
5MU/CC 1CC				0.0		0.0	177	0.6	177	0.6		
5 LNG 7/73				0.0		0.0	72	0.3	72	0.3		
5INT 1/73				0.0		0.0	105	0.4	105	0.4		
1MU/CC 30CC		53	53	0.2	6	0.7	45	0.2	51	0.2	-6.3	-11.8
5 LNG		7	7	0.0		0.0	25	0.1	25	0.1	+234.9	+207.1
1 INT				0.0		0.0	18	0.1	18	0.1		
5 INT				0.0	5	0.7	1	0.0	6	0.0		
50 INT		13	13	0.1		0.0	2	0.0	2	0.0	-86.3	-88.0
20MU/CC 1CC		5	5	0.0	2	0.3	31	0.1	33	0.1	+580.1	+538.9

Source: IMS America, Inc.

chases of pharmaceuticals by hospitals has on a relative basis far exceeded that of the retail pharmacy segment. There are a number of reasons for this, but of probably prime importance to the pharmaceutical marketer is the fact that in many communities around the country the hospital has become more of a factor in routine patient care. The increase in the number of patient visits to hospital outpatient facilities has been remarkable in the past 10 years, as has been the growth in the filling of prescriptions by hospital pharmacies for these outpatients.

Given the focus of this text, descriptions of the above two audit types have been within the context of pharmaceutical products. Other related product areas are covered within the framework of retail pharmacy and hospital purchase auditing. From the former, purchase data are collected and compiled for toiletry and beauty aid products, and for veterinary pharmaceuticals. The latter yields data on purchases of hospital supplies (needles, sutures, drapes, x-ray film) and diagnostic reagents.

WAREHOUSE WITHDRAWAL AUDIT

This is a service that measures the withdrawal of pharmaceutical products from the pharmaceutical wholesaler and from major drug chain warehouses. Although this audit monitors withdrawal or outflow from warehouses, you will note that this is basically the same as measuring inflow to the pharmacy or hospital. Because it is, this service is actually similar to the purchase audits described above, and you may question the need for both types of services. Major differences, however, do exist. The purchase audits reflect all purchases by a pharmacy or hospital whether or not they were purchased directly from a manufacturer or from a wholesaler. Given the focus of the warehouse withdrawal audit on the warehouse segment only, purchases directly from the manufacturer are not represented in the auditing process.

On the other hand, although the purchase audits are based on *samples* of hospitals and pharmacies, the warehouse withdrawal study is, for all intents and purposes, a *census* of warehouse withdrawal activity for pharmaceutical products. The amount of data available from such a census is enormous as compared to that developed with the purchase audit. This mass of data provides the capability to isolate and analyze small segments of the marketplace, such as zip code or specific sales territories. This capability is quite valuable in dealing with questions of individual territory potential and performance, needs for territorial realignment, or differential selling techniques.

RETAIL PHARMACY PRESCRIPTION AUDITS

This is designed to measure the outflow of prescription drugs from the pharmacy into the hands of the consumer. In many ways, it may be logically argued that prescription audit data are the most sensitive indicators of prescription product performance in the marketplace. The prescription is not an expression of opinion, attitude, or speculation on the part of the prescriber but is a matter of record. As prescribers collectively change their minds about individual drugs or areas of therapy these changes are, in essence, automatically recorded in the prescription files of pharmacies. Prescriptions, further, are indicators of what is presently occurring in terms of demand. Purchase data, for example, may record a pharmacy's purchase of antibiotics in the month of August in anticipation of the antibiotic "season." That purchase record, however, does not signify current physician demand for antibiotics.

Prescription data are also viewed by most pharmaceutical marketers as the best indicators of the results of marketing or promotional efforts to create new business. If one looks at purchase data for an antihypertensive product it is impossible to sort out that portion of dollars representative of new business as opposed to that portion reflective of patients who are already using the product. New prescription volume for the same product, however, is a reasonably good indicator of the trend in generating new patient business for the product.

There are presently two primary methods of collecting data for continuing syndicated prescription audits. One method relies on a sample of retail pharmacies, with pharmacists in each of these pharmacies recording information regarding prescriptions filled by the pharmacy (Table 6-2). The other method takes advantage of pharmacy service system-generated prescription records, and extracts required information from records stored on computers. Each method has inherent advantages and disadvantages. Pharmacy service system data is voluminous, and easily and quickly collected and processed. These data, however, represent information only on what is dispensed by the pharmacy. The method that relies on pharmacist reporting of information produces a smaller volume of data and takes more time to collect and process, but yields information on what was prescribed by the physician as well as on what was dispensed by the pharmacist. The ideal prescription audit will combine the advantages offered by both methods.

TABLE 6-2. *Prescription Audit*

NATIONAL PRESCRIPTION AUDIT

THERAPEUTIC CATEGORY REPORT
Add (000) to all figures

DECEMBER 1976   11100 ANTICOAG, ORAL   PAGE 49

PRODUCT MFR Dose-Form Strength	MOVING THREE MONTH AVERAGES					% CAT 76	% CO 76	% CHG 76-75		YEAR-TO-DATE				CURRENT MONTHS					
	RX SIZE	RX PRICE $	DACON	# DAYS THERAPY	COST per DAY $					1974	1975	1976		JUL	AUG	SEP	OCT	NOV	DEC
								1	N RX	1167	1213	1220	RX	108	102	119	103	97	91
								-2	P RX	2920	2908	2861	RX	256	204	218	234	250	240
								-1	T RX	4087	4121	4081	RX	364	306	337	337	347	331
								9	T $	10235	10778	11729	$	1059	918	1073	948	963	1041
ATHROMBIN-K PURDUE-F																			
TABLET 5MG						•	•	-80	N RX	1	5	1	RX	1	0	0	0	0	0
						•	•	-80	P RX	2	10	2	RX	2	0	0	0	0	0
						•	•	-80	T RX	3	15	3	RX	3	0	0	0	0	0
						•	•	-83	T $	9	36	6	$	6	0	0	0	0	0
COUMADIN ORAL ENDO																			
TABLET 2MG 60.0	5.01	1.6	37.5	0.13		5	1	2	N RX	45	63	64	RX	7	4	6	4	9	1
						7	5	10	R RX	204	174	191	RX	21	12	16	11	22	3
TABLET 2.50MG 50.4	4.24	1.1	45.8	0.09		12	1	9	N RX	139	138	150	RX	9	15	16	16	13	12
						10	7	-1	R RX	293	295	293	RX	19	28	25	30	25	23
TABLET 5MG 62.4	5.35	1.2	52.0	0.10		65	7	3	N RX	737	770	793	RX	68	70	75	63	57	60
						61	44	4	R RX	1666	1672	1747	RX	150	125	113	139	145	160
TABLET 7.50MG 39.3	4.83	1.0	39.3	0.12		4	•	13	N RX	50	48	54	RX	6	1	4	7	5	5
						6	6	5	R RX	159	153	160	RX	16	3	11	19	14	14
TABLET 10MG 41.1	5.38	1.0	41.1	0.13		4	•	-18	N PX	58	55	45	RX	5	2	7	5	1	4
						3	2	-39	R RX	105	132	81	RX	9	3	12	9	2	7
						91	10	3	N RX	1031	1076	1108	RX	95	92	108	95	85	82
						87	63	2	R RX	2433	2432	2478	RX	215	171	178	206	208	207
						88	24	2	T RX	3464	3508	3586	RX	310	263	286	303	293	289
						90	25	11	T $	9084	9546	10550	$	964	816	951	836	846	973
DICUMAROL UNSPEC																			
CAP 25MG 100.0	4.15					•	•	50	N RX	4	4	6	RX	1	0	0	0	1	0
						•	•	46	R RX	13	13	19	RX	3	0	0	0	3	0
CAP 50MG 6.0	1.50	1.0	6.0	0.25		1	•	100	N RX	4	4	8	RX	0	0	0	0	1	0
						1	•	125	R RX	12	12	27	RX	0	0	0	0	3	0
TABLET 25MG 74.7	3.53	1.3	57.5	0.06		1	•	-25	N RX	10	8	6	RX	1	0	1	0	1	1
						1	•	-31	R RX	32	26	18	RX	3	0	3	0	3	3
TABLET 50MG 22.0	2.99	1.5	14.7	0.20		1	•	-35	N RX	13	20	13	RX	2	2	2	1	1	1
						2	•	-35	R RX	44	66	43	RX	7	7	7	3	3	3
TABLET 100MG						•	•	-50	N RX	1	2	1	RX	1	0	0	0	0	0
						•	•	-50	R RX	3	6	3	RX	3	0	0	0	0	0
						3	•	-11	N RX	32	38	34	RX	5	2	3	1	4	2
						4	•	-11	R RX	104	123	110	RX	16	7	10	3	12	6
						4	•	-11	T RX	136	161	144	RX	21	9	13	3	16	8
						1	•	-22	T $	97	170	132	$	16	4	8	4	16	8
DIPAXIN UPJOHN																			
TABLET 5MG 100.0	8.15					•	•	-50	N RX	7	6	3	RX	1	0	0	0	0	1
						•	•	-50	P RX	14	12	6	RX	2	0	0	0	0	2
						•	•	-50	T RX	21	18	9	RX	3	0	0	0	0	3
						•	•	-39	T $	42	54	33	$	6	0	0	0	0	12
HEDULIN MERRLNATNL																			
TABLET 50MG 100.0	6.50					•	•	0	N RX	6	3	3	RX	1	0	0	0	1	0
						•	•	0	P RX	24	12	12	RX	4	0	0	0	4	0
						•	•	0	T PX	30	15	15	RX	5	0	0	0	5	0
						1	•	8	T $	85	60	65	$	30	0	0	0	15	0
LIQUAMAR ORGANON																			
TABLET 3MG 50.0	4.23	0.5	0.0	0.00		•	2	67	N PX	2	3	5	RX	0	1	0	0	1	0
						1	7	67	P RX	10	15	25	RX	0	5	0	0	5	0
						1	3	67	T RX	12	18	30	RX	0	6	0	0	6	0
						1	3	100	T $	24	42	84	$	0	24	0	0	12	0
PANWARFIN OP'A ABBOTT																			
TABLET 2 MG						•	•	100	N PX	0	1	2	RX	1	0	0	0	0	0
						•	•	100	R RX	0	1	2	RX	4	0	0	0	0	0
TABLET 2.50MG 16.0	3.08	0.5	32.0	0.10		1	•	20	N RX	12	5	6	RX	0	1	2	0	0	1
						1	•	21	P RX	44	19	23	RX	0	4	7	0	0	4
TABLET 5MG 51.8	4.30	1.0	51.8	0.08		2	•	-38	N RX	35	40	25	RX	2	2	4	2	3	3
						4	1	-37	P RX	189	182	115	RX	9	9	18	9	14	14
TABLET 7.5MG 40.0	4.30	0.5	80.0	0.05		•	•	-33	N RX	4	3	2	RX	0	0	0	1	0	1
						•	•	-33	R RX	15	12	8	RX	0	0	0	4	0	4
						3	•	-33	N RX	52	55	37	RX	3	13	6	3	3	5
						6	1	-33	R RX	252	240	162	RX	13	25	13	13	14	22
						5	1	-33	T PX	304	295	199	RX	16	16	31	16	17	27
						5	•	-20	T $	629	683	547	$	16	44	89	53	55	32
SINTROM GEIGY																			
TABLET 4MG 37.2	7.35	0.9	46.5	0.16		1	•	67	N PX	6	4	10	RX	0	0	1	2	1	1
						1	•	67	P PX	12	19	30	RX	0	0	3	6	3	3
						1	•	97	T PX	18	24	40	RX	0	0	4	8	4	4
						1	•	122	T $	68	72	150	$	0	0	16	40	4	16
WARFARIN SODIUM UNSPEC																			
TABLET 2.5MG 80.0	5.85	1.0	80.0	0.07		•	•	50	N RX	4	2	3	RX	0	0	1	0	1	0
						•	•	50	R RX	8	4	6	RX	0	0	2	0	2	0
TABLET 5MG 62.5	4.77	1.2	52.1	0.09		1	•	180	N RX	17	5	14	RX	2	4	0	2	1	0
						1	•	180	R RX	34	13	28	RX	4	8	0	4	2	0
						2	•	90	N PX	22	10	19	RX	2	4	1	2	2	0
						1	•	125	R RX	44	16	36	RX	4	8	2	4	4	0
						1	•	112	T RX	56	25	55	RX	6	12	3	6	6	0
						1	•	162	T $	144	58	152	$	21	30	9	15	15	0

• Less than 0.5%   ■ Not computable   + More than 999%
EFFECTIVE 1973 Rx DOLLARS ARE AT PHARMACY COST LEVELS

Source: IMS America, Inc.

PHYSICIAN PANELS

These represent research services of a somewhat different type. One physician panel is a study of medical practice in the United States. Although most of the services discussed thus far are oriented toward the depiction of product movement in one way or another, this physician panel goes somewhat further in that it portrays *usage* of pharmaceutical products along a number of variables.

A sample of physicians is utilized. Each physician in the sample is asked to provide specific information regarding each patient seen during an assigned reporting period. Information requested includes diagnosis, patient characteristics, location of visit, drugs, if any, used to treat the condition, and action desired from these drugs. Beyond simple estimates of volume and trend of drug usage, data resulting from this study are used to determine such considerations as which conditions a drug is used for, by what specialty of physician, in what frequency, and for what patient type (Tables 6-3 to 6-5).

Another type of physician panel is designed to collect the daily new prescription output of individual physicians. Followed over time, data from this panel can demonstrate changes in prescribing habits by physician or groups of physicians based on specialty, age, location of practice, and prescribing volume. These data are often used to track new products, in which physicians are identified as to certain characteristics and monitored as to if and when they began to prescribe a new product, in what volume, for how long and how, if at all, previous prescribing patterns were altered.

Still other physician panels are maintained that are narrower in scope in terms of drug use or diagnosis areas, but that are more detailed in the information provided within these more limited parameters.

PROMOTIONAL MEDIA AUDIT

Three segments of promotional activity in the pharmaceutical marketplace are monitored by continuing audits—detailing, journal advertising (Chap. 16), and direct mail advertising. Projections of detailing effort as perceived by physicians in office-based practice, and the receipt of direct mail advertisements by this group of physicians, are made from information provided by samples of physicians who report on these respective promotional approaches (Table 6-6). An audit that depicts the detailing of pharmacists is also available. The amount of dollars spent by pharmaceutical companies for the placement of advertising in professional journals is monitored for the industry, with the dollar estimate based on a census of all publications that carry ethical pharmaceutical product advertising.

(*Text continues on p. 131.*)

TABLE 6-3. *Office Visit Audit—Drug Class*

	12 Mos.	Qtr.						
Est. U. S. Appear. (,000)	11107	3040		ANTICOAGULANTS			JAN 76 – DEC 76	
Sample Data:							Class 11000	Page 233
Drug Appearances	2304	613						
Drug Uses	2439	649						

Age

Age	TOTAL 12 Mos. No. %	Male 12 Mos. No. %	Female 12 Mos. No. %	Unspec. 12 Mos. No.
2 & Under	1 -	- -	1 -	-
3-9	1 -	- -	1 -	-
10-19	66 1	23 -	43 1	-
20-39	1146 11	364 7	756 15	26
40-59	3693 34	2142 38	1500 29	52
60-64	1260 12	690 12	540 10	30
65 +	4737 43	2362 43	2282 44	73
TOTAL	10936 100	5600 100	5153 100	183
Unspec.	171	48	42	81

Form

Form	12 Mos. No. %	Qtr. %
Tab/Cap	7292 67	66
Liquid	- -	-
Oph	- -	-
Otic	- -	-
Nasal	- -	-
Inj.	3449 32	34
Top.	- -	-
Supp.	- -	-
A. O.	86 1	-
TOTAL	10826 100	100
Unspec.	282	

Concomitancy

Concomitancy	12 Mos. No. %
Use Alone	5727 52
W/ DIGITALIS PREP	1180 11
W/ VASODL,COR,NITRITE	865 8
W/ MIN,TRNQ,BENZODIAZ	585 5
W/ ANTICOAG,,INJECT	457 4
W/ ANTICOAG,,ORAL	449 4
W/ DIUR,OTHER NON-INJ	343 3
W/ ANTI-ARRHYTHMIA	286 3

Specialty

Specialty	12 Mos. No. %	Qtr. %	Drugs/ Phy./Yr.
GP/FP/PT	3036 27	26	67
Int. Med.	5006 45	44	198
Card.	1397 13	14	309
Gastro	90 1	-	68
Gen. Surg.	703 6	7	40
Ortho. Surg.	184 2	2	24
A.O. Surg	155 1	2	25
Ob/Gyn.	14 -	-	1
Ped.	19 -	1	2
ENT.	6 -	-	1
Ophth.	10 -	-	1
Derm.	- -	-	-
Allerg.	29 -	1	17
Urology	11 -	-	2
Psych.	- -	-	-
Neur.	62 1	-	37
Osteo.	38 r 3	2	43
TOTAL	11107 100	100	62

Location

Location	12 Mos. No. %	Qtr. %
Office	3432 33	33
Home	23 -	-
Hosp	6267 60	60
Teleph.	715 7	6
Nurse Hm.	50 -	1
Other	13 -	-
TOTAL	10522 100	100
Unspec.	585	

Region

Region	12 Mos. No. %	Qtr. %
East	2655 24	26
Midwest	3076 28	21
South	3390 31	35
West	1976 18	19
TOTAL	11107 100	100

Visit

Visit	12 Mos. No. %	Qtr. %
First	765 7	6
Subseq.	9773 93	92
TOTAL	10637 100	100
Unspec.	570	

Issuance

Issuance	12 Mos. No. %	Qtr. %
Hosp. Ord.	6479 67	69
Admin.	119 1	2
Disp.	58 1	1
Rx	2910 30	28
Sample	- -	-
Samp w Rx	- -	-
Rec'm'nd	34 -	-
TOTAL	9596 100	100
Unspec.	1512	

Therapy

Therapy	12 Mos. No. %	Qtr. %
New	1046 10	11
Continued	8985 90	89
TOTAL	10032 100	100
Unspec.	1076	

Diagnosis

Diagnosis	12 Mos. No. %	Qtr. %
07 CIRCULATORY DISORDERS	7673 65	63
4650 PULM EMBOLISM INFARCTION	1805 16	17
4640 PHLEB THROMB OTH SITES	1613 14	16
4205 CARD MYOCARD VENTRICLE	1032 9	10
4630 PHLEB THROMB LOW EXTREM	710 6	4
4201 CORONARY ARTERY HEART D	389 3	3
4200 ARTERIOSCLEROTIC HEART D	267 2	4
4331 DISORDERS HEART RHYTHM	162 1	1
4160 MISC RHEUMATIC HEART DIS	151 1	1
4207 CARD MYO VENTRIC W COMPL	149 1	1
4203 CORON ARTERY W SEL COMPL	141 1	1
4341 CONGESTIVE HEART FAILURE	105 1	1
4205 ARTERIO CORON ARTERY	99 1	1
4209 ARTERIO CARD MYO VENTRIC	97 1	-
4431 HYPERT ARTERIO HEART OTH	80 1	1
4200 ARTERIOSCLER WO GANGRENE	78 1	-
4540 ARTERIAL EMBOL THROMBOS	75 1	-
4208 HYPERT CARD MYO VENTRIC	75 1	-
4202 ANGINA PECTORIS	64 1	-
4221 CARDIO ARTERIOSCLEROSIS	63 1	-
4222 OTH MYOCARD DEGENERAT	58 -	-
4672 CIRC DIS OTHER UNSPEC	56 -	-
4204 HYPERTEN CORONARY ARTERY	83 -	-
4602 VARICOSE ULCER UNSPEC	52 -	1
4440 HYPERT ESSENTIAL BENIGN	46 -	-
4560 OTH VENOUS EMBOL THROMB	46 -	-
4100 DISEASES OF MITRAL VALVE	39 -	-
4430 HYPERT HEART DIS OTHER	32 -	-
4211 NON RHEUM AORTIC ENDOCAR	25 -	-
4214 OTH NON RHEUM VALVE DIS	21 -	1
4344 UNSPEC HEART DISEASE	19 -	-
4140 OTH RHEUM ENDOCARDITIS	14 -	-
4470 HYPERTENSION NO MENT HT	13 -	-
4210 NON RHEUM MITRAL ENDOCAR	12 -	-
4560 OTHER DIS OF ARTERIES	12 -	-
18 SPEC COND W O SICKNESS	2410 20	23
Y100 SURGICAL AFTERCARE	1334 11	14
Y105 MEDICAL AFTERCARE	1076 9	9
06 DIS OF CNS SENSE ORGS	1067 9	8
3310 CEREBRAL HEMORRHAGE	389 3	3
3341 CERE ARTERIO CONGESTION	311 3	2
3320 CEREBRAL EMBOLISM THROMB	261 2	2
3347 STROKE NOS	66 -	-
3680 UNSPEC DISEASE OF EYE	44 -	-
3340 UNSPECIFIED CNS LESION	16 -	-
16 SYMPTOMS AND SENILITY	239 2	3
7950 OTH ILL DEF CONDITIONS	183 1	1
7825 SYNCOPE OR COLLAPSE	80 1	1
7837 PAIN IN CHEST	23 -	-
08 DIS OF RESP SYSTEM	123 1	1
5272 OTH DIS LUNG PLEUR CAV	34 -	-
4930 PNEUMONIA OTHER UNSPEC	16 -	-
5220 PULM CONGEST HYPOSTASIS	16 -	-
17 ACCIDENTS AND POISONING	73 1	1
8000 FRACTURES	37 -	-
9800 OTH ACCIDENTS POISONINGS	15 -	-
11 DELIV CUMPL OF PREGNANCY	32 -	-
6620 PUERP PHLEBIT THROMBOS	32 -	-
09 DIGESTIVE DISORDERS	30 -	-
04 G U DISORDERS	27 -	-
6034 RENAL INSUFF KID URETER	27 -	-
04 BLOOD & BLOOD FORM ORG	24 -	-
2940 POLYCYTHEMIA	13 -	-
02 NEOPLASMS	16 -	-
15 CERT DIS EARLY INFANCY	14 -	-
7730 ILL DEF INF DIS NO IMM	14 -	-
13 DIS BONES ORGS OF MOVEMT	12 -	-
12 DIS SKIN CELLULAR TISSUE	9 -	-
36 DIABETES MELLITUS	8 -	-
14 CONGENITAL MALFORMATIONS	7 -	-
05 MENTAL DISORDERS	5 -	-
TOTAL	11757 100	100

Desired Action

Desired Action	12 Mos No. %	Qtr. %
ANTICOAGULANT	7080 87	85
PROPHYLAXIS	769 9	11
DISSOLVE CLOT	108 1	1
SYMPTOMATIC	86 1	1
ANTICONVULSANT	20 -	-
ANTICOAGULANT & PROPHYLAXIS	10 -	-
ANTICOAGULANT & SYMPTOMATIC	9 -	-
LIPOTROPIC	8 -	-
DISSOLVE CLOT & ANTIINFLAMMATORY	6 -	-
PAIN RELIEF & PROPHYLAXIS	6 -	-
REDU CHOLESTEROL	5 -	-
ANTICOAGULANT & DISSOLVE CLOT	5 -	-
RED LIPID LEVEL	4 -	-
ANTICOAGULANT & MYOCARD STIMUL	4 -	-
ANTIEMETIC	4 -	-
ANTICOAGULANT & SEDATIVE UNSPEC	4 -	-
ANTIHEMORRHAGIC	4 -	-
ANTIINFLAMMATORY	4 -	-
ANTINAUSEANT	4 -	-
INC MYOCARD CONT	4 -	-
PERIPH VASODILAT	4 -	-
CEREBR VASODILAT	4 -	-
INC CIRCULATION	4 -	-
CHELATING AGENT	3 -	-
MYOCARD STIMUL	3 -	-
ANTICOAGULANT & PERIPH VASODILAT	3 -	-
TOTAL	8138 100	100
NO REASON GIVEN	2969	

TABLE 6-4. *Office Visit Audit—Individual Drug*

	12 Mos.	Qtr.				
Est. U. S. Appear. (,000)	291	97	PANWARFIN ORAL	77034	ABBOT	JAN 76 – DEC 76
Sample Data					Class 11100	Page 238
Drug Appearances	66	23				
Drug Uses	66	23				

Age	TOTAL 12 Mos.		Male 12 Mos.		Female 12 Mos.		Unspec. 12 Mos.
	No.	%	No.	%	No.	%	No.
2 & Under	–	–	–	–	–	–	–
3-9	–	–	–	–	–	–	–
10-19	–	–	–	–	–	–	–
20-39	13	5	3	2	10	8	–
40-59	70	25	29	20	37	30	3
60-64	50	18	40	27	10	8	–
65 +	148	52	74	50	69	56	6
TOTAL	281	100	147	100	126	100	8
Unspec	10				10		

Form	12 Mos.		Qtr.
	No.	%	%
Tab/Cap	291	100	100
Liquid	–	–	–
Oph	–	–	–
Otic	–	–	–
Nasal	–	–	–
Inj.	–	–	–
Top.	–	–	–
Supp.	–	–	–
A O	–	–	–
TOTAL	291	100	100
Unspec.	–		

Concomitancy	12 Mos.	
	No.	%
Use Alone	144	50
W/ DIGITALIS PREP	53	18
W/ MIN.TRNQ,BENZODIAZ	30	10
W/ VASODL,COR,NITHITE	20	7
W/ DIUR,OTHER NON-INJ	20	7
W/ DIUR,K-SPARING	14	5
W/ ANTICOAG,,INJECT	10	3
W/ ANTIARTHRTCS,SYST,	10	3

Specialty	12 Mos.		Qtr.	Drugs/
	No.	%	%	Phy./Yr.
GP/FP/PT	124	42	28	3
Int Med.	45	16	–	2
Card.	111	38	63	24
Gastro	–	–	–	–
Gen. Surg.	–	–	–	–
Ortho Surg.	–	–	–	–
A O. Surg.	–	–	–	–
Ob/Gyn.	–	–	–	–
Ped.	–	–	–	–
ENT	–	–	–	–
Ophth.	–	–	–	–
Derm	–	–	–	–
Allerg.	–	–	–	–
Urology	–	–	–	–
Psych.	–	–	–	–
Neur	–	–	–	–
Osteo.	13	5	9	1
TOTAL	291	100	100	2

Diagnosis		12 Mos.		Qtr.
		No.	%	%
07	CIRCULATORY DISORDERS	241	83	90
4440	PHLEB THROMB OTH SITES	68	23	28
4280	CARD MYOCARD VENTRICLE	84	19	23
4630	PHLEB THROMB LOW EXTREM	28	10	9
4201	CORONARY ARTERY HEART D	26	9	10
4200	ARTERIOSCLEROTIC HEART D	13	4	7
4680	PULM EMBOLISM INFARCTION	11	4	–
4222	OTH MYOCARD DEGENERAT	9	3	8
4341	CONGESTIVE HEART FAILURE	9	3	4
4208	ANGINA PECTORIS	6	2	–
4207	CARD MYO VENTRIC W COMPL	6	2	6
4208	ARTERIO CORON ARTERY	5	2	–
4440	HYPERT ESSENTIAL BENIGN	4	1	–
4203	CORON ARTERY W SEL COMPL	3	1	–
18	SPEC COND W O SICKNESS	40	14	7
Y109	MEDICAL AFTERCARE	32	11	7
Y100	SURGICAL AFTERCARE	8	3	–
06	DIS OF CNS SENSE ORGS	7	2	3
3310	CEREBRAL HEMORRHAGE	7	2	3
09	DIGESTIVE DISORDERS	3	1	–
5350	DISEASES TEETH OTHER	3	1	–
	TOTAL	291	100	100

Desired Action	12 Mos.		Qtr.
	No.	%	%
ANTICOAGULANT	182	75	100
PROPHYLAXIS	43	18	–
DISSOLVE CLOT	15	6	–
SYMPTOMATIC	3	1	–
TOTAL	243	100	100
NO REASON GIVEN	48		

Location	12 Mos.		Qtr.
	No.	%	%
Office	117	44	31
Home	–	–	–
Hosp.	131	50	63
Teleph.	14	5	6
Nurse Hm.	3	1	–
Other	–	–	–
TOTAL	265	100	100
Unspec.	26		

Region	12 Mos.		Qtr.
	No.	%	%
East	14	5	9
Midwest	143	49	28
South	120	41	63
West	14	5	–
TOTAL	291	100	100

Visit	12 Mos.		Qtr.
	No.	%	%
First	23	9	6
Subseq.	249	91	94
TOTAL	274	100	100
Unspec.	19		

Issuance	12 Mos.		Qtr.
	No.	%	%
Hosp. Ord.	135	58	67
Admin.	–	–	–
Disp.	3	1	–
Rx	96	41	33
Sample	–	–	–
Samp w Rx	–	–	–
Rec'm'nd	–	–	–
TOTAL	233	100	100
Unspec.	58		

Therapy	12 Mos.		Qtr.
	No.	%	%
New	–	–	–
Continued	269	100	100
TOTAL	269	100	100
Unspec.	22		

Source: IMS America, Inc.

TABLE 6-5. *Office Visit Audit—Diagnosis*

	12 Mos.	Qtr.
Est. U. S. Visits (,000)	129437	29088
Patient Visits w/Drugs	107278	24220
Patient Visits w/o Drugs	22159	4868
Sample Data - Total Visits	23767	5231

CIRCULATORY DISORDERS

JAN 77 - DEC 77 Class 07 Page 281

Age

Age	TOTAL 12 Mos. No.	%	Male 12 Mos. No.	%	Female 12 Mos. No.	%	Unspec. 12 Mos. No.
2 & Under	161	–	78	–	75	–	8
3-9	506	–	288	–	210	–	9
10-19	968	1	476	1	451	1	41
20-39	7680	6	3471	6	4060	6	149
40-59	34464	27	16444	30	17341	25	679
60-64	15142	12	6826	13	8022	11	294
65 +	68181	54	26504	49	40296	57	1381
TOTAL	127102	100	54086	100	70454	100	2562
Unspec.	2335		472		565		1298

Specialty

Specialty	12 Mos. No.	%	Qtr. No.	%	Visits/ Phy./Yr.
GP/FP/PT	49982	39	40		1120
Int. Med.	47988	37	36		1830
Card.	12258	9	10		2598
Gastro	1003	1	1		671
Gen. Surg.	5410	4	3		310
Ortho. Surg.	280	–	–		35
A.O. Surg.	1672	1	1		231
Ob/Gyn.	809	1	1		53
Ped.	563	–	–		44
ENT	445	–	1		107
Ophth.	259	–	–		30
Derm.	180	–	–		53
Allerg.	28	–	–		16
Urology	1027	1	–		191
Psych.	132	–	–		11
Neur	199	–	–		111
Osteo.	7202	6	6		799
TOTAL	129437	100	100		704

Location

Location	12 Mos. No.	%	Qtr. %
Office	72078	60	61
Home	1485	1	1
Hosp.	38330	32	31
Teleph.	5871	5	5
Nurse Hm.	2201	2	2
Other	378	–	–
TOTAL	120345	100	100
Unspec.	9092		

Region

Region	12 Mos. No.	%	Qtr. %
East	35910	28	27
Midwest	31576	24	25
South	41629	32	33
West	20322	16	15
TOTAL	129437	100	100

Visit

Visit	12 Mos. No.	%	Qtr. %
First	12333	10	10
Refer.	3956	32**	
Subseq.	108682	90	90
TOTAL	121015	100	100
Unspec.	8422		

** % of First Visits

Surgery

Surgery	12 Mos. No.	%	Qtr. %
Yes	1124	1	1
No	128313	99	99
TOTAL	129437	100	100
Unspec.	–		

Desired Action

Desired Action	12 Mos. No.	%	Qtr. %
LOWER BLOOD PRES	20437	16	17
ANTIHYPERTENSIVE	16151	13	13
DIURETIC	13022	10	10
DIGITALIS EFFECT	8380	7	9
CURB CARD ARRYTH	7012	6	6
REL ANGINAL PAIN	5920	5	6
ANTICOAGULANT	4405	4	3
CORONARY VASODIL	3646	3	2
MAINTAIN BL PRES	3449	3	3
CONTROL HEART RT	2998	2	3
CORRECT K IMBAL	2957	2	2
INC MYOCARD CONT	2612	2	2
VASODILATOR	2574	2	2
CARDIOTONIC	2312	2	2
MYOCARD STIMUL	2191	2	1
PROPHYLAXIS	2060	2	1
SYMPTOMATIC	1951	2	1
PAIN RELIEF	1735	1	1
DIURETIC & ANTIHYPERTENSIVE	1448	1	1
REDUCE SWELLING	1235	1	1
ANTIINFLAMMATORY	1074	1	1
SEDATIVE UNSPEC	1052	1	1
SEDATIVE NIGHT & PROMOTE SLEEP	695	1	–
REDUCE ANXIETY	689	1	–
INC CIRCULATION	666	1	1
REDU FLUID RETEN	638	1	1
TRANQUILIZER	638	1	1
SEDATIVE NIGHT	614	–	1
ANALGESIC	572	–	1
ANTIBIOTIC	566	–	–
COMBAT INFECTION	543	–	–
DIURETIC & LOWER BLOOD PRES	511	–	1
RELIEVE DYSPNEA	456	–	1
RELAXANT	329	–	1
CARDIAC COMPEN	291	–	–
SEDATIVE DAY	287	–	–
REDU NERVOUSNESS	273	–	–
REDUCE TENSION	259	–	–
FECAL SOFTENER	259	–	–
PERIPH VASODILAT	256	–	–
BRONCHODILATOR	237	–	–
VIT MIN SUPPL	234	–	–
RELIEVE HEADACHE	220	–	–
CEREBR VASODILAT	217	–	–
ANTIBACTERIAL	215	–	–
CURB CARD ARRYTH & DIGITALIS EFFECT	172	–	–
CALMING EFFECT	165	–	–
DISSOLVE CLOT	154	–	–
GENERAL TONIC	142	–	–
ANTIDEPRESSANT	141	–	–
CONTROL VERTIGO	139	–	–
LAXATIVE	138	–	–
URICOSURIC ACT	125	–	–
ANTICONVULSANT	122	–	–
RAISE BLOOD PRES	122	–	–
CONTROL HEART RT & CURB CARD ARRYTH	120	–	–
PROMOTE SLEEP	117	–	–
PRE OP PREP	114	–	–
CONTROL EDEMA	112	–	–
CONTROL DIZZINES	104	–	–
SHRINK HEMORROID	102	–	–
ANTINAUSEANT	102	–	–
ALL OTHERS	4951	4	4
TOTAL	125425	100	100
NO REASON GIVEN	56977		

Drugs

Drugs	12 Mos. No	%	Qtr. %
31500 DIGITALIS PREP	28922	22*	23*
74014 LANOXIN	16100	12	12
74040 DIGOXIN	10965	8	9
74012 DIGITOXIN	913	1	1
74002 CRYSTODIGIN	357	–	–
41210 DIUR.THIAZ & REL	21409	17*	17*
79017 HYDRODIURIL	6977	5	4
79061 HYGROTON	4349	3	3
79006 DIURIL ORAL	2831	2	2
79027 HYDROCHLOROTHIAZIDE	2489	2	3
79026 ESIDRIX	1550	1	1
79070 ENDURON	1182	1	1
79073 METAHYDRIN	369	–	–
79079 RENESE	313	–	–
41230 DIUR.OTHER NON-INJ	15891	12*	13*
79097 LASIX ORAL	15037	12	12
79124 ZAROXOLYN	640	–	–
31211 VASOOL.COR.NITRITE	15320	10*	10*
72068 ISORDIL	5643	4	4
72014 NITROGLYCERINE	3978	3	3
72118 NITROBID	1403	1	1
72139 SORBITRATE	1154	1	1
72021 PERITRATE	965	1	1
72252 NITROSTAT	800	1	1
72026 NITROL OINTMENT	349	–	–
72001 CARDILATE	327	–	–
31140 ANTIHYPRTNS, OTHRS	12536	5*	6*
71769 ALDOMET	8211	6	6
71701 APRESOLINE	1711	1	1
71794 CATAPRES	1062	1	1
71806 MINIPRESS	796	1	1
71762 ISMELIN	722	1	–
41220 DIUR.K-SPARING	12145	9*	10*
79095 DYAZIDE	7497	6	7
79087 ALDACTAZIDE	2957	2	2
79084 ALDACTONE	1239	1	1
79091 DYRENIUM	413	–	–
31400 BETA-BLOCKING	10559	8*	9*
76055 INDERAL	9889	8	8
71671 PROPRANOLOL	665	1	1
31110 RAUWOLF W/DIURETCS	9570	7*	8*
71518 SER AP ES	3274	3	3
71513 HYDROPRES	1886	1	2
71538 REGROTON	916	1	1
71522 SALUTENSIN	791	1	1
71506 DIUPRES	673	1	–
71529 ENDURONYL	625	–	–
71542 RAUZIDE	339	–	1
71530 ENDURONYL FORTE	337	–	–
31130 ANTIHYPRTNS/DIURET	5004	4*	4*
71772 ALDORIL	3072	2	2
71807 APRESAZIDE	550	–	1
71776 ESIMIL	408	–	–
71796 COMBIPRES	388	–	–
71778 ALDOCLOR	328	–	–
31300 ANTI-ARRHYTHMIA	4716	4*	4*
76007 QUINIDINE	2385	2	2
76006 PRONESTYL	1479	1	1
76039 QUINAGLUTE	485	–	–
64121 MIN.TRNQ.BENZODIAZ	4375	3*	3*
07061 VALIUM	3243	3	2
07041 LIBRIUM	576	–	–
07102 TRANXENE	312	–	–
60110 POTAS.SUP,CHLORIDE	4328	3*	4*
87217 SLOW-K	1627	1	1
87066 POT CHLORIDE ORAL	1459	1	1
K-LOR	310	–	–
11100 ANTICOAG.,ORAL	4063	3*	2*
77000 COUMADIN ORAL	3653	3	2
31120 RAUWOLF W/O DIURET	2710	2*	2*
70024 RESERPINE	1333	1	1
70023 RAUWOLFIA SERP	599	–	1
70021 SERPASIL	375	–	–
11200 ANTICOAG.,INJECT	2616	2*	2*
77006 HEPARIN SOD	2588	2	2
41100 DIUR.INJECT.	1435	1*	1*
79097 LASIX INJECT	1240	1	1
31220 PERIPHERAL VASOOL	1226	1*	1*
73037 VASODILAN	352	–	–
73011 CYCLOSPASMOL	322	–	–
31230 PAPAVERINE VASOOL	1182	1*	1*
72093 PAVABID	845	1	1
ALL OTHERS	23993	18*	17*
TOTAL	182403	1.4	1.4

* THERAPEUTIC CLASS PERCENTAGES ELIMINATE DOUBLE COUNTING, I.E., THE PATIENT RECEIVING MAALOX AND GELUSIL IS ONLY PERCENTAGED ONCE

Source: IMS America, Inc.

TABLE 6-6. *Detail Audit*

THERAPEUTIC CLASS DETAIL REPORT   # DETAILS AND # TOTAL MINUTES (000)   DEC 1978   PAGE E 016

		1976	1977	JAN	FEB	MAR	APR	MAY	JUN	JUL	AUG	SEP	OCT	NOV	DEC	CURRENT 12 MOS	YEAR TO DATE
10100-PTY ANTIARTHRT TOP																	
BANALG ONEAL J F	# DETAILS	14	14	1	1	5	3	2	2	2	2	2	2	2	2	25	25
	# MINUTES	18	28	3	0	8	2	2	4	2	2	3	5	3	4	42	42
DERMOLIN MALLARE	# DETAILS					0								0		1	1
	# MINUTES					1			0							1	1
IODEX LAMBDA PH	# DETAILS								0							0	0
	# MINUTES																
IODEX METHYL SAL LAMBDA PH	# DETAILS								0							0	0
	# MINUTES																
TOT 10100-PTY ANTIARTHR T TOP	# DETAILS	14	14	2	1	5	3	2	3	2	2	2	2	2	2	26	26
	# MINUTES	18	28	3	0	8	2	2	4	2	2	3	5	3	4	42	42
11000-ANTICOAGULANTS																	
COUMADIN ENDO	# DETAILS	4	18	1	0	2	1	0	1	1	2	2	0	0		10	10
	# MINUTES	12	46	11	0	3	1	0	1	1	2	3	0	0		23	23
HEPARIN ORGANON	# DETAILS					2	1							0		1	1
	# MINUTES					3	1							1		3	3
HEPARIN UPJOHN	# DETAILS	4	3	0	0				0		2					1	1
	# MINUTES	16	5	0					2		3					3	3
HEPARIN SOD WYETH	# DETAILS	2	1									2				1	1
	# MINUTES	7	1													6	6
LIPO HEPIN RIKER LABS	# DETAILS	0		1												0	0
	# MINUTES	1														1	1
PAN-HEPRIN ABBOTT LAB	# DETAILS	1			1				0				0	1		0	0
	# MINUTES	5							0				0	2		1	1
SINTROM GEIGY	# DETAILS								2		2			0		0	0
	# MINUTES								6		3			0		0	0
TOT 11000-ANTICOAGULANTS	# DETAILS	13	26	2	1	2	1	1	5	8	4	2	5	3	1	14	14
	# MINUTES	46	71	12	2	8	1	0	15	27	5	2	13	6	4	37	37
12000-ANTICONVUL SANTS																	
CLONOPIN ROCHE	# DETAILS	5	0			1	12	10	2							0	0
	# MINUTES	14	0			0	61	40	6							0	0
DEPAKENE ABBOTT LAB	# DETAILS															58	58
	# MINUTES															196	196

RETAIL SALES AUDIT

This has historically been used primarily for nonprescription pharmaceuticals. One type of retail sales audit may be described as "opening inventory plus delivered purchases minus ending inventory." Mainly because of time and cost considerations, this type of audit is conducted for selected products of interest to the subscriber as opposed to the "all products, all categories" approach of most of the audit services already described.

These descriptions are of the general types of continuing audits and surveys offered to the pharmaceutical marketer. Although each has one major objective, you will readily understand that each of these provides data or information ancillary to the main objective but still of considerable use. Because the purchase audits, for example, collect unit and dollar information at the package size level, the opportunity exists for performing pricing analysis. The main use of prescription audits is to provide prescription counts by product, but information may also be collected on daily dosage, patient price, and number of units of drug prescribed. An analysis of dosage is, therefore, capable of being done.

It should also be pointed out that a great deal of work is done using segments of a particular study. Prescription data, for example, are studied to obtain both prescribing and dispensing information.

Finally, in recent years, much progress has been made in combining the information available in the individual audits into one general data base that offers the potential for an almost unlimited number of cross tabulations and interrelating exercises.

Noncontinuing Audits and Surveys

Independent research companies also perform and provide audits and surveys of a noncontinuing nature. Some of these may be of a scope similar to that of the continuing projects, while others tend to have a much narrower focus. These are primarily done to provide information on market segments that are either not particularly dynamic, or are of major interest, and that therefore do not require month-to-month or quarter-to-quarter monitoring. Others are performed to address a given problem or issue that may arise, while still others are carried out to make initial observations of an area. In the past 5 years, for example, one-time studies have been prepared on hospital outpatient clinics in terms of patient visits and drug use, on the mail order portion of the prescription market, and on the provision of audio-visual materials in promotion. In many cases, of course, these one-time studies have produced information suggesting that the area of study is of sufficient import to warrant ongoing monitoring.

Other Services and Information Sources

There are many other market and marketing research services offered to the industry. Indeed, an entire book could be devoted to a listing and discussion of all these services. Some are done by auditing or surveying while others involve individual in depth personal interviewing or the use of the "focus group" technique. Focus groups basically represent bringing together a small number of subjects to interact with one another regarding a specific question. The following represents only a sample of such services: advertising copy testing, readership studies, promotional effectiveness analyses, attitudinal studies, concept testing, awareness and use studies, test market analysis, high prescriber identification, acquisition and licensing studies, forecasting and strategic planning studies.

In addition to market and marketing research offerings, there are various other sources of information regarding pharmaceuticals, the pharmaceutical marketplace, and the population in general available to the pharmaceutical marketer or market researcher. These usually provide background information or intelligence, or are reference works. The *Pink Sheet* and the *Green Sheet* are examples of publications that provide news or intelligence regarding the industry. Publications such as the *Merck Manual, Merck Index, AMA Drug Evaluations, Facts and Comparisons,* and *Remington's Practice of Pharmacy* are excellent for obtaining background information on diseases and drugs. The *Journal of the American Hospital Association* and its *Annual Guide* issue provide a wealth of demographic information on the hospital universe in the United States. Finally, many government agencies publish a variety of reports and studies of potential interest, such as United States Census Data, the *Statistical Abstract of the United States* and, of more specific interest to the pharmaceutical market researcher, studies such as those of specific diseases and health care financing.

Company Market and Marketing Research Activities

Because of the abundance of market and marketing research services offered to the pharmaceutical industry, you may be left with the impression that these offerings satisfy all the needs of companies, and that the function of the market research department within the company is simply to analyze the data provided in these services. This is not the case; many research studies are initiated, carried out, and analyzed by in house personnel. In some cases this is due to requirements of confidentiality. In others, company personnel may have more knowledge of a particular subject area. Third, there may be a need for correlation of the market research study with other areas of the company such as research and development or sales, and this is often more easily accomplished by in house staff. Finally, a company may view the use of its own staff as being less costly than contracting out a project. Analyses of internal company data such as factory sales, promotional spending, and detailing call reports, also generally fall within the market research department's area of responsibility. A third major segment of activity is the analysis of data provided by independent research companies who work with these outside suppliers on particular projects.

Marketing Data

Analysis and Interpretation

The successful analysis and interpretation of marketing data or, for that matter, any data, is contingent upon a number of factors. These factors are relevant whether the analyst is working with data reflecting a group of five physicians, or with data on the millions of transactions that are represented in the warehouse withdrawal audit.

Perhaps most of the significant factors in successful use of marketing data can be summarized by one word—*understanding*. The first element of understanding relates to understanding the question to be answered, or the problem to be solved. You might be surprised to learn how much effort is wasted in providing answers to the wrong question, or solutions to the wrong problem. Before beginning any research or analytic effort, the astute analyst hones in on the specific question to be answered. The analyst, for example, should not be satisfied with a request to "find out how physicians use product X." As a first step, what is meant by the term "use?" Does it mean used by diagnosis, by strength or dosage, for how long, singly or in combination with other products? The analyst should also determine whether the requestor means physicians in general or specialists, their use of the product overall or within a specific diagnosis, in the office or hospital, now or over a period of time. It is simply common sense that the more detailed and specific the request, the more accurate will be the response to the request.

Understanding is also required of the information or data with which the analyst works. A primary requirement is a comprehension of the methodology employed to collect data or to compile information. If, for example, the data are collected from a sample of a population, the analyst must understand the makeup of that sample. What specific activities or characteristics of the population is the sample designed to reflect? How are potential participants in the sample selected? What is the response to the recruiting effort? Do the answers to the latter two questions suggest a bias in the results of the study? What device or method is used to collect the data? If a document, what pieces of information are requested on the document? What instructions are given to the participant for recording information?

Although these questions may appear to be more technical than practical, they are of utmost importance to the data analyst. An analyst familiar with the data collection methodology of a study, audit, or survey will better understand the objectives of the study, what questions it can answer and, equally important, what questions it *cannot* answer. The analyst responding to the request discussed above, as an example, will have to determine if data are available to answer the question and, if not, how to obtain the data.

As another element, if the data being analyzed are projected from a sample to represent a total population or activity, the user of these data should be familiar with the projection technique utilized, and the reliability of the resultant estimates. Meaningless data are frequently given the status of meaningful data by the analyst who is unaware of its limitations.

Furthermore, there should be a familiarity with the units of measurement or terminology used in an audit or study. Frequently, analysis of physician practice data involves the number of *patients* with a given disorder. The physician panel does not measure patients; it measures *patient visits*. The analyst who labels dollars found in the pharmacy purchase audit as manufacturer sales dollars for a product is incorrect. This audit measures purchases of a product by retail pharmacies. The difference might sound unimportant but, according to whether or not the product is purchased directly from a manufacturer or through a wholesaler, it could amount to 15%.

A complete understanding of each of the pieces of data used by the analyst is important not only within the context of successful use of an individual set of data, but also because of the differences that occur in conjunctive use of different sets of data. Often retail pharmacy prescription data will indicate activities or trends dissimilar to those in the retail pharmacy purchase audits. If it is recalled that one of these audits measures outflow and the other measures inflow, many of these apparent differences can be easily understood and explained.

Beyond the necessity of understanding data, there is an equally important factor involved in working with data—the need to understand that all data are not to be taken at face value. The successful analyst is a questioning analyst. Although no one purposely causes errors to be made, errors do occur or, if not errors, then anomalies occur. The competent analyst does not accept these simply because they appear in black and white, but instead questions them and attempts to find out why they have occurred. In sum, defining and understanding the question or problem, understanding the data to be worked with, and possessing the ability to question are three major requirements for successful analysis and interpretation of marketing data.

There are other elements that contribute to proper as opposed to mediocre or complete as opposed to incomplete analytic efforts. Data should not be viewed in an isolated sense, but as part of different pieces or sources of data. The determination that new prescriptions for a product have increased is, by itself, an interesting point. Taking into account the fact that the number of new prescriptions has increased without any additional promotion of the product is more interesting. Further analysis that shows that new prescriptions have increased without any additional promotion of the product but with a doubling of promotion for a competitive product is even more interesting and of more importance.

The analyst will also try to explain as fully as possible the reasons for an occurrence. If sales of a product have risen 15% the analyst should try to determine if this is the result of real growth (growth in units) or simply the result of a price increase. If the growth is real, is it because there was seasonal stocking of the product or can it be determined that new prescriptions for the same time period showed the same kind of increase, indicating that physician demand was increasing? In general, the analyst understands the point that the answer to one question usually leads to other questions to be answered.

Applications and Uses

The services and data that have been discussed throughout this chapter have been labeled as market research, marketing research, or marketing services and data. Although these data are designed to measure or portray the marketplace in one way or another, and are perhaps of special importance to the marketer, their utility and application extend well beyond the sector of the marketing department. There are probably few areas in any pharmaceutical company that do not, at one time or another, have use for these services and data.

As an example, a major strategic question that companies have to deal with is research and development planning. What disease or product areas appear to warrant long-term research and development investment? Which seem to suggest the plausibility of short-term involvement? Marketing data can aid in this planning process in such areas as identifying market size and potential, whether or not there is available therapy, where therapy is available but not used, and what is to be the next logical step in therapy. Short-term focus is illustrated by analyzing the data to help identify areas that may be available for subdivision. The analgesic market, for example, is a broad one. Some companies have been successful in orienting their development efforts toward a segment of that market, such as migraine headache analgesia. Similarly, there has been success in the segmenting of the respiratory condition area by offering products specifically for sinusitis. Data analysis may help identify product sectors in which more convenient dosing of a drug would be beneficial to the patient and to marketing.

These data may be useful with regard to the serendipitous research and development discovery. Should the company that finds itself with a compound that appears effective in the treatment of a particular disorder pursue the study of the compound? Available data can help in this decision by delineating such parameters as the prevalence of this disorder, the potential market size, or drugs presently employed. It should be pointed out here that for neither directed nor serendipitous research results is market size or potential necessarily the key determinant in deciding whether to continue studying a product. Many companies have marketed drugs for treating miniscule patient populations.

There are other segments of the broadly defined development process that benefit from the use of marketing data. Diverse conditions such as osteoarthritis and hypertension are often found in the same patients. If an antiarthritic compound has a blood pressure-elevating property, this compound would not be used to treat arthritic patients who are also hypertensive. Data from physician panels on medical practice can quantify how frequently these conditions exist together, and thus suggest the minimization of usage potential that would be caused by this property of the compound. Questions on the need for specific dosage forms required for a product may be answered by reviewing marketing data. Diagnosis data, for instance, would indicate that otitis media is mainly a disorder of pediatric patients. If an anti-infective with efficacy in otitis media cannot be formulated in liquid form, it would be used infrequently.

Data are useful in planning clinical trials. If a product demonstrates activity in more than one condition, data showing the relative importance of the various conditions might be used to determine for which condition clinical testing should be performed. Seasonality, regionality, and specialty data are also of interest in planning clinical trials. Companies may determine the combination of region, season, and specialty that are most likely to produce large numbers of patients with a specific condition.

Assuming that a product is to be marketed, or is on the market, the manufacturing area of a company needs direction in regard to how much of the product is required. Marketing data can be used to assist in these determinations. The need for samples, for instance, in terms of such factors as overall quantity or package size, is often decided by analysis of competitive sampling as shown by audits of promotional activity.

Corporate development departments rely on marketing data in many cases to analyze potential company or product acquisitions and licensing opportunities. Financial and legal personnel also have occasion to view market data as an aid in their activities.

The most frequent use of market data occurs, of course, in the marketing area of the company. One major use is for premarketing planning. Much of this use is involved with analysis of the market that the drug is to enter. A marketer needs to know various pieces of information to ensure successful marketing of a product. What physician specialties are important in a given therapy or diagnosis category? Is the hospital an important sector? What patient characteristics are apparent? What is the present state of the market in terms of competition? How do competitors promote their products? Are there presently unsatisfied portions of the market? Attitudinal research is generally carried out to determine how physicians perceive a proposed product or the advantages and disadvantages of currently available products. Advertising personnel study data to depict in print media a patient type that the physician finds relevant to the condition for which a drug is to be used.

Once a product is on the market, the main use of marketing data is to monitor the performance of a product across all the various aspects of the marketplace. Product sales, prescriptions, overall physician usage or by specialty or high prescribers, diagnosis, and location, for example, are all analyzed continuously to monitor progress of a product by itself as well as in relation to the market in which it competes. Invariably, this monitoring process reveals information that suggests the need for additional information or action, and the market or marketing research process takes another turn.

Future Considerations

As Gosselin has so aptly stated, the task of market and marketing research is to keep those who need to be kept informed supplied with all the facts possible to amass. The extraordinarily dynamic nature of the pharmaceutical industry, coupled with the ever increasing ability to collect facts, suggest the need for and ability of the market research function to contribute even more significantly in the future. Although the pharmaceutical industry is, in fact, a "data-rich" industry, and much is presently known, much more needs to be known.

PART II

The Pharmaceutical Product

Drug Development and the Marketing-Research Interface

RICHARD E. FAUST

Environment for Research and Product Development

Although the pharmaceutical industry is an old one, the modern research-oriented firm did not really become established until after World War II. The introduction of antibiotic therapy in the 1940s was followed by the development of important cardiovascular drugs, diuretics, steroids, and other drugs that affected the central nervous system, including antidepressants and tranquilizers. The peak of new product introductions occurred around 1960. Following the passage of the New Drug Amendments in 1962, there was precipitous decline in the flow of new drug products of all types. Some have put forth the theory that this decline was due to the lack of fundamental new biologic and biomedical knowledge from which new drug leads are generated. Most observers feel, however, that in general both the complexity of modern drug development and the impact of regulatory testing requirements account for the decline in research productivity.

The success of a pharmaceutical firm is the result of more than just the efficiency of its research and development (R & D) laboratories, however, because the input of research is essentially information that is used by manufacturing and marketing to make and to sell products. For the pharmaceutical firm to be successful, these three key functions must operate in an integrated and pro-

ductive manner. Therefore, all regulations, such as Good Manufacturing Practices and those enforced by such groups as the Occupational Safety and Health Administration (OSHA), the
Environmental Protection Agency (EPA), and the Toxic Substances Control Act (TOSCA) that influence production will also
have an impact on the research process. All regulatory and pricing
policies that make it difficult for marketing to compete successfully will also affect the research process indirectly. Consequently,
the technoscientific success of the pharmaceutical company is
dependent upon the integration of key functions and the profi-
ciency of research "to create," manufacturing "to make," and
marketing "to sell" new and improved products (Fig. 7-1).

Most observers agree that the pharmaceutical industry is in the
midst of change that will have a profound effect upon its organization and product line. The industry has moved through the "fabu-
lous 50s," with the advent of major new therapeutic breakthroughs, into the "sobering 60s," with the passage of the New
Drug Amendments of 1962 and the subsequent decline in the flow
of new products, to the "stabilizing 70s," and is at the start of the
"exciting 80s," with many new product possibilities emerging as a
result of research in such areas as molecular biology, brain chemistry, and immunology. The success of each firm in exploiting
these and related scientific accomplishments depends in part
upon the nature and efficiency of the working relationships between its research and marketing functions, and upon their joint
efforts in responding to a changing and often challenging environment.

The United States health-care market is changing rapidly. The
traditional delivery of health care is being challenged, as is the
procurement, dispensing, and utilization of pharmaceutical products. Today, more than ever before, individuals other than the
physician (e.g., formulary members, medical administrators, and
group practice administrators) have greater influence on the
pharmaceutical selection process. Purchasing is becoming more
centralized in an effort to realize economies in procurement practices. The emergence of third-party financiers of pharmaceutical
products has created new decision makers with different needs,
who have influence over product availability and purchase price.
Although the relative efficacy of pharmaceutical products must
certainly affect the decision-making process, economy and efficiency are also viewed as important factors. These factors may
influence research project selection and development goals, and
are vital points of discussion between a firm's research and marketing operations.

The business environment, which today is dominated by regulation and legislation designed to benefit various segments of society, influences marketing efforts and has an impact on the mar-

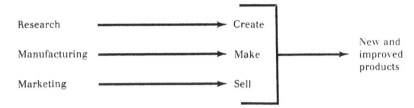

Fig. 7-1. *Corporate technoscientific success.*

keting-research interface. Environmental factors that affect the success of marketing groups in research-oriented firms include more generic prescribing, increased substitution, and governmental efforts to reduce the cost of health care through such cost-containment measures as maximum allowable cost (MAC). Other trends that place pressure on drug prices include formulary restrictions, central procurement operations, and volume purchase plans. If a firm cannot compete successfully in the marketplace as a result of all these factors, funds will not be available to support large R & D investments, especially for more exploratory and innovative programs designed to discover major new therapeutic agents.

Corporate Planning Perspectives

"Corporate development" is a relatively new term that refers to a planned utilization of a corporation's creative resources to capitalize fully on existing business strengths, to adjust itself to the changing world, and to create growth opportunities. More attention is being given to the development of the total corporation through managed creativity applied to every business function. In addition to new and improved products and processes, corporations may seek growth and efficiency through new distribution channels and customers, new financial and administrative practices, and new marketing strategies. Close interaction with and collaboration between R & D and marketing is therefore needed to support various corporate development plans and objectives.

In a survey of ten of the world's larger research-oriented pharmaceutical firms, the increasing influence of corporate management and marketing on R & D decision making and directions was noted.[1] This greater involvement of corporate planners, financial personnel, and marketing management has come about in part because of the escalating costs and greater risks presently associated with drug discovery and development. Taking into account the "time value" of money and research failures during development, the cost of developing a new single chemical entity (NCE) was $54 million in 1978.[2] One study concluded that three fourths of the NCEs introduced from 1967 to 1976 failed to generate cash flows large enough to recover the cost of capital or original R & D investment.[3] Therefore, during the past two decades, many pharmaceutical firms have diversified into other business areas (e.g., foods, cosmetics, and agrochemicals) in order to maintain sales and profit streams and to minimize risk. Others have accelerated licensing activities aimed at acquiring new products and product leads from other groups in order to augment internal R & D productivity. In 1980 nearly 300 products were the subject of licensing or joint development agreements worldwide.[4] Close collaboration between research and marketing personnel is essential in all these diversification and acquisition activities if the effort is to complement internal research most efficiently and provide for future corporate growth.

Unquestionably, investing in long-range R & D requires an act of faith by top management. In spite of all the elaborate models available for identifying market opportunities, establishing research priorities, and forecasting return on investment (ROI), research investment still requires the judgment of top level managers. Increasingly, there is no effective measurement system that can prove that the investment will be paid back. There is little doubt, however, that the success of a major new drug product can have a profound impact on a firm's sales and profit profile, and it is this possibility that often encourages continued investments in R & D in many firms. The introduction of Tagamet, the new drug for the treatment of ulcer disease contributed significantly to a near doubling in sales and profit for the SmithKline Corporation for the 9 months ending September 30, 1978, as compared to the same period a year earlier.[5] Merck went through a dry spell with no single significant new drug being introduced from 1965 to 1975.[6] The firm continued to invest heavily in research that is now developing important new products that will probably provide an excellent revenue stream in the 1980s.

The growing trend for corporate planning and operations groups to examine the research function is reflected in excerpts from two job notices in a leading newspaper. "We have two openings in our Corporate Planning Analysis Services Group . . . ." One position, described as a "senior planning consultant," indicated that the candidate "must have doctorate in Operations Research or Business Administration" and "should have working knowledge in applying statistical and mathematical techniques to research, distribution, marketing and manufacturing activities." The other described " . . . an exceptional opening for a professional who combines a doctorate in Operations Research with (preferably) a lower degree in Chemistry, Chemical Engineering, or a closely related field." The position was described as one in which the candidate " . . . will plan and carry out internal consulting assignments that apply O.R. to a variety of problems, including R & D projects and their evaluation . . . ."

Marketing and Research Perspectives

There are obvious conceptual differences between R & D and marketing groups, the most apparent of which is the constant conflict between the long- and short-term demands for the firm's resources. Marketing wants "bottom line" performance and output today, while the goals of research are often focused on the future. Moreover, in many firms, at least in the past, R & D has traditionally been treated with unusual deference by management. Left to pursue its own ways the research function sometimes acquires its own mystique, which serves as a protective cloak over its inner workings and prevents managment from providing adequate direction and monitoring. Research philosophy frequently adheres to the traditional spirit of the freedom of scientific inquiry and independence. The conceptual differences between R & D and marketing sometimes contribute to an antagonistic and mutually suspicious relationship in which they may compete in fixing the blame on each other for the lack of new products or new product success. Increasingly, new organizational approaches and communication channels are being developed within companies to create improved rapport between marketing and research operations. The penalties for lack of coordination can be severe in terms of costly, unproductive, or scattered research and commercialization efforts.

The Project Management Institute (PMI) has established a forum in which project management personnel in the pharmaceutical industry interact and develop information of mutual interest. Table 7-1, developed by this group, compares the perceptions of "research" versus "development" (and also marketing) personnel to items of management concern.[7]

Research and Business Planning

Research Plan

The nature of the "research planning" function varies considerably within pharmaceutical firms but, in general, it focuses on the allocation of research resources involving project selection

TABLE 7-1. *Contrasting Perspectives of "Research" and "Development" Personnel*

ITEM	RESEARCH PEOPLE	DEVELOPMENT PEOPLE
Definition of goals	Prefer fewer statements	Prefer well-defined statements
Relationships with others	Usually more independent	Usually more "team aware"
Reaction to organization structure	Prefer less	Work well in structured environment
Management orientation	Usually less	Usually more
Comfort with estimating timing	Usually difficult	Usually less difficult
Possessiveness	Usually less willing to share with those outside specialty	Usually less possessive than research type
Work perspective	Usually happy with "problem" orientation	Probably prefer "product" orientation

Source: Adapted from Staples, R.: Project Management in the Pharmaceutical Industry . . . A Statement of Issues and Observations, *Project Management Quarterly,* 10:24, 1979.

and monitoring. It may also encompass such activities as those associated with generating R & D budgets and forecasting output, personnel administration, and organizational development. Firms vary in their approaches to planning with regard to complexity and sophistication. At one end of the spectrum, a generally liberal philosophy characterizes a serendipitous and somewhat less structured approach to such tasks as project selection and monitoring and to setting priorities. At the other end, a more quantitative and systematized approach is used to aid decision making and to help analyze alternatives. The tone is usually set by the senior research executive of the firm, although he is often influenced by his peers in other functional areas, especially marketing.

In some firms research management feels that unfettered scientific endeavors patterned after those of the academic world will be most productive in the long term. In many firms, however, there is a growing tendency to develop a more controlled and detailed research approach using quantitative and computerized planning techniques. Such approaches must be installed carefully, because, in one sense there can be no true "research planning." Genuine planning presupposes that the operations, available resources, and timetables have been worked out in advance and are known at each research level. By its nature, though, research is a field of activity in which the unknown and unexpected can never be excluded. Therefore, it will always be impossible to assemble all existing information at the outset and to establish an absolutely hard and fast schedule. Research activities must be carefully guided to avoid the danger of submerging the creative and innovative spirit in bureaucratic "administrivia" and "planning overkill."

Research functional or operational plans are often designed to convey the status of research activities and commitments, to present a profile of the use of research resources, and to generate a picture of outputs both in the near and long term. Most research plans seek to create a balance between programs yielding near-term results (1 to 5 years) and those providing rewards further out in time (5 to 10 years). In addition, the major research-oriented firms invest in more exploratory or basic programs that may be termed "new horizon research," in which the payback may not occur for at least 15 to 20 years. The contents of a typical strategic or functional research plan may be outlined as follows:

I. Introduction: A statement of the orientation of the plan, its relationship to previous and related plans, and current information being developed in research.

II. Objectives: A statement of research objectives and their relationship to corporate and business objectives.

III. Research Environment: An overview of research and how it is affected by competitive R & D trends, political-legislative pressures, various major scientific and technological factors, and socioeconomic forces. Strategies to respond to these dynamic environmental elements are presented.

IV. Research Resource Analysis: An analysis of research personnel, expenses, and facilities, including recent growth patterns, current allocations, and present needs.

V. Drug Development Project Analysis
   A. Drug development projects (year 1 to 5)
   B. Drug development projects (year 5 to 10): The compounds projected in the pharmaceutical business plan are analyzed using a "one-pager" format that encompasses such information as the project objective, sales projections, patent status, development timetable, and competitive products.

VI. Exploratory Research Activities
   A. Overview of exploratory effort: Perspectives on magnitude of the effort, emerging trends and changing patterns, and commentary on research activities that have an impact on broad areas, such as aging.

B. Important research areas and activities: A review of current important and emerging research efforts and integrated programs aimed at generating significant new products and product leads beyond those of the current project planning period.

VII. Support for Marketed Products: A summary of research efforts aimed at developing new dosage forms and indications, as well as special clinical and other studies that support current products.

VIII. Research Operational Improvement Strategies and Goals: An elaboration of research actions, plans, and strategies aimed at improving operations and the probability of success over the planning board; an assessment of broad trends, patterns, and considerations to aid in evaluating research output and contributions to corporate success.

IX. Research Requirements and Resource Projections: A profile of personnel, funding, and facility needs during the next 5 years, including perspectives on alternative output patterns influenced by the magnitude of budget and personnel increases.

X. Planning Highlights and Summary: An overview and summary of planning goals, operating strategies, and achievements projected for the near, mid, and long term.

Business Plan

A strategic business plan is designed to convey the thrust of the business operation. The areas covered usually include an analysis of environmental forces and other factors that influence the success of the enterprise and indirectly impact on R & D. The contents of a typical pharmaceutical strategic business plan may be outlined as follows:

I. Description and Purpose of the Business: A statement of the basic business growth strategy and goals of the marketing area that presents a picture of the business and its general plans for the planning period, usually 5 to 10 years.

II. Environmental Analysis: An overview of the environmental forces affecting the business, such as increased substitution, more generic prescribing, efforts to reduce health care costs, inflation, patent expirations, concern for "orphan" drugs, increased competition, and various governmental regulations.

III. Critical Issues: Many plans contain a description of important issues that will affect the success of the business over the planning period. These issues and concerns will vary with the firm, but they might include such topics as

A. The impact of various special regulations, such as Drug

Efficacy Study Implementation (DESI) and Controlled Substances Act (CSA) on the product line.

B. The patent status of marketed products

C. Special bulk manufacturing capacity needed for various new products.

D. Changing marketing strategies caused by certain trends, such as the increasing number of physicians and shifts in health-care delivery systems.

IV. Strategies and Programs: Once critical operational areas have been identified, strategic plans usually describe how the business intends to meet these challenges and to ensure growth and profits. Because one critical issue usually centers on the flow of new products from research over the planning period, various strategies are often mentioned that are designed to improve research productivity and to enhance the functional interface between research and marketing groups. Under a plan to "improve research productivity," one might find such action strategies as the following:

A. Improve criteria for product candidate selection for development and evaluate compliance to criteria throughout development.

B. Improve the priority-setting process and communication of priorities for research and product development programs.

C. Inventory current research programs and commitments to improve allocation of resources.

D. Establish mechanisms for research program review to ensure consistency with business objectives and goals.
These various action strategies in a business plan are similar to those found in a typical research planning document. They illustrate dramatically the need for close collaboration between R & D planners and those marketing personnel responsible for generating the business plan.

V. Resource Requirements: This section of the planning document presents a detailed analysis of the projected output over the planning period, including sales from existing and new products and dosage forms. The resources needed (e.g., facilities, capital, and personnel) for this are also projected over the planning period. Often probabilities are used to forecast output and, in some cases, an "optimistic," "pessimistic," and "most likely" forecast is presented that is also closely connected to research productivity.

The Research Process

As drug industry R & D expenditures increased to about $2 billion in 1981, the pressure on research and marketing groups to recoup these enormous investments also increased. Most large firms need a major product success periodically to cover the cost of project failures and increasing research budgets. A typical large pharmaceutical firm may synthesize 2000 to 3000 compounds yearly and, after primary screening of many of these, will take about 300 through advanced pharmacologic testing. Of these, about 50 "leads" may emerge, but only 6 or 7 of the most promising are selected for extended toxicologic studies and are filed as investigational new drugs (INDs). From these few only 1 to 2 new drug applications (NDAs) evolve and are approved for marketing. Unless one approved NDA is a major success every 10 to 15 years, generating several hundred million dollars in annual sales, research costs can become prohibitive for those firms that invest heavily in R & D.

Pharmaceutical R & D involves various possible approaches to the discovery of new drugs: (1) the random screening of large numbers of chemical compounds thought to have potential therapeutic properties; (2) the selective molecular modification of existing compounds in order to reduce side-effects or improve efficacy; and (3) basic research in such areas as cellular biology and biomolecular structures that elucidate disease processes and provide clues to help the chemist in designing molecules having therapeutic properties. Related to this are new approaches to genetic research, which have the potential of producing significant advances in medical research and drug development. Recombinant DNA research is now used in industry to produce various proteins and macromolecules, such as insulin, somatostatin, and interferon. Recombinant DNA technology can also work to cure underlying defects through gene replacement therapy. This approach to disease, described as altering the underlying physiologic causes of illness, may be important for developing agents to treat many disease states.

The usual approach to drug discovery thus involves interactions between chemists, biologists, and pharmacologists, in which compounds are synthesized and screened in animals for various properties having potential value in human disease. Another approach that has been successfully employed in the past may be described as "clinical serendipity," or the accidental or unexpected discovery of various clinical effects when drugs are tested in man. Many examples may be noted. Chlorpromazine, tested as an antimotion sickness preparation, was found to be an ataraxic. Meprobamate, designed as a muscle relaxant, proved to be a tranquilizer, and procaine, used widely as a local anesthetic, was later found useful as an anti-arrhythmic. More recently propranolol, used since 1967 as an anti-arrhythmic, as an anti-anginal in 1973, and as an antihypertensive agent in 1976, was found to be effective as an antimigraine agent in 1979.[8] It is now also being used to prevent second heart attacks. Such usefulness, discovered through unexpected clinical observations, has been the method by which an impressive variety of new drugs and drug uses have been discovered in the past. The fact that certain therapeutic applications may be revealed after a product is introduced provides another rationale for close collaboration between research and marketing and sales personnel who monitor the use of products by the medical profession.

Exploratory Research

The decision to explore research areas from which new leads may emerge is essentially made by research management, although it is influenced by broad marketing considerations. Some factors that influence these research decisions within a firm include the following:

- Use of the existing bank of skills and resources within the firm.
- "Breakthrough" or emerging research areas.*
- "Visceral" knowledge and experience of research managers and scientists.
- The persistence of the project "champion."*
- Need for "critical mass" of expertise internally.
- New animal pharmacologic screens developed to provide novel leads.
- Competitive research activity and strengths.*
- External consultants—their role in providing expert opinion, guidance, and ideas.
- Influence of university research, a source of ideas and cooperative ventures.
- Medical need and market potential.*
- Serendipity and its unexpected role in the discovery process.
- Some development projects that may generate new basic knowledge/leads.
- Project and research synergies—one research area influencing another.

*Marketing information, inputs, and support may be especially important in addressing these factors.

Drug Development

After a product has been produced by chemical synthesis or isolation, compounds of interest are screened by pharmacologists using a sophisticated range of techniques, from subcellular particles to intact animals. Compounds with potential therapeutic applications are submitted for various toxicologic examinations, including determinations of lethal doses in several species of animals and pathologic studies for detection of organ toxicity. Potentially useful compounds are next considered for clinical pharmacology. This is a critical step in the life of a new chemical entity, because only a few compounds among the hundreds synthesized will be investigated in humans. Deciding which of several possible analogues of a series of compounds should be developed can be extremely difficult. In addition to judgments regarding potential therapeutic efficacy and safety, a number of marketing-oriented factors must be considered, including possible advantages over competitive products and the cost of production. Compounds chosen for human study undergo extensive toxicologic evaluation (e.g., tests for carcinogenicity, teratogenicity, and mutagenicity) and pharmacokinetic studies to assess how the drug is metabolized and excreted in animals.

The clinical pharmacologist is responsible for giving the drug to a human being for the first time (Phase I). These are essentially safety tests performed on well volunteers. Before this is done the Food and Drug Administration (FDA) must review and evaluate all preclinical studies done with animals and must approve an IND application filed by the firm. After completion of these Phase I studies, the drug is administered for the first time to patients who have the disease (Phase II). Relatively small numbers of patients are monitored closely by specialized studies tailored to the type of disease treated. Compounds then move into full scale clinical tests, in which hundreds or thousands of patients are investigated (Phase III). These studies take place under conditions approximating the environment in which the drug will be used. Placebo controls are used and great care is taken to detect adverse reactions, including interactions of the new drug with other medications.

Following the completion of Phase III studies, the firm prepares and files an NDA with the FDA. Such an NDA may be composed of as many as 200 2-inch thick volumes containing many thousands of pages. If approved, the drug is made available to the medical profession. The entire process is a tortuous and uncertain one, and the attrition rate for new chemical entities is high.

Tables 7-2 through 7-8 summarize the events, timing, and costs associated with the development of a typical oral systemic drug for long-term administration.[9] The expenditures for various activities

(*Text continues on p. 156.*)

TABLE 7-2. *New Drug Development of an Oral Systemic Drug for Long-term Administration: I. Research*

DISCIPLINE	STAGE OF DEVELOPMENT	COST $(000)
Chemistry	Synthesis of many compounds	500
Biology, animal pharmacology	Screening of many compounds	400
Toxicology	—	—
Pharmacy	—	—
Clinical medicine	—	—
Marketing regulatory project management	Market survey project initiation	100
Total	Year 0 to 2	$1000

Source: Adapted from Katz. M.: The Birth Pangs of a New Drug, *Drug and Cosmetic Industry, 128*:40, 1980. Copyright by Harcourt Brace Jovanovich, Inc. Reprinted by permission of the publisher.

TABLE 7-3. *New Drug Development of an Oral Systemic Drug for Long-Term Administration: II. Pre-Industrial*

DISCIPLINE	STAGE OF DEVELOPMENT	COST $(000)
Chemistry	Process development, lead compound, analytic methodology, synthesis-radiotracers	500
Biology, animal pharmacology	Extended screening, lead compound, pharmacology, ADME-short-term	400
Toxicology	Acute, subacute, mutagenicity	400
Pharmacy	Pre-formulation dosage design, analytical methodology	500
Clinical medicine	Data for IND	200
Marketing regulatory project management	IND compilation, project planning	200
Total	Year 2 to 4	$2000

Source: Adapted from Katz, M.: The Birth Pangs of a New Drug. *Drug and Cosmetic Industry, 128*:40, 1980. Copyright by Harcourt Brace Jovanovich, Inc. Reprinted by permission of the publisher.

TABLE 7-4. *New Drug Development of an Oral Systemic Drug for Long-Term Administration: III. Phase I*

DISCIPLINE	STAGE OF DEVELOPMENT	COST $(000)
Chemistry	Synthesis, pilot plant scale-up, process development	400
Biology, animal pharmacology	ADME-long-term, many species	300
Toxicology	Subacute, teratology	1000
Pharmacy	Dosage design, analytic methodology, clinical manufacturing	700
Clinical medicine	Safety tolerance, bioavailability	1300
Marketing regulatory project management	Planning control status reports	300
Total	Year 4 to 6	$4000

Source: Adapted from Katz, M.: The Birth Pangs of a New Drug. *Drug and Cosmetic Industry,* *128*:40, 1980. Copyright by Harcourt Brace Jovanovich, Inc. Reprinted by permission of the publisher.

TABLE 7-5. *New Drug Development of an Oral Systemic Drug for Long-Term Administration: IV. Phase II*

DISCIPLINE	STAGE OF DEVELOPMENT	COST $(000)
Chemistry	Production for Phase III, scale-up continued, specifications, development	300
Biology, animal pharmacology	ADME continues, mechanism of action studied	200
Toxicology	Reproductive toxicology, carcinogenicity	1600
Pharmacy	Clinical manufacturing scale-up, processing, stability studies	800
Clinical medicine	Dose-range studies, controlled efficacy	5700
Marketing regulatory project management	Market research status reports	400
Total	Year 6 to 8	$9000

Source: Adapted from Katz, M.: The Birth Pangs of a New Drug. *Drug and Cosmetic Industry,* *128*:40, 1980. Copyright by Harcourt Brace Jovanovich, Inc. Reprinted by permission of the

TABLE 7-6. *New Drug Development of an Oral Systemic Drug for Long-Term Administration: V. Phase III*

DISCIPLINE	STAGE OF DEVELOPMENT	COST $(000)
Chemistry	Processing, scale-up, quality control methods	200
Biology, animal pharmacology	Special studies, drug interactions	100
Toxicology	Long-term carcinogenicity	1000
Pharmacy	Manufacturing scale up, quality control methods, line extensions	600
Clinical medicine	Clinical efficacy, long-term safety	3700
Marketing regulatory project management	Planning, NDA compilation	400
Total	Year 8 to 10	$6000

Source: Adapted from Katz, M.: The Birth Pangs of a New Drug. *Drug and Cosmetic Industry*, *128*:40, 1980. Copyright by Harcourt Brace Jovanovich, Inc. Reprinted by permission of the publisher.

TABLE 7-7. *New Drug Development of an Oral Systemic Drug for Long-Term Administration: VI. NDA Wait*

DISCIPLINE	STAGE OF DEVELOPMENT	COST $(000)
Chemistry	Processing scale-up	300
Biology, animal pharmacology	Special studies, responses to FDA queries	100
Toxicology	—	—
Pharmacy	Processing scale-up, packaging scale-up	400
Clinical medicine	Long-term follow-up, Claims/indications, extensions, Start Phase IV studies	1100
Marketing regulatory project management	Prepare launch, labeling negotiation	100
Total	Year 10 to 12	$2000

Source: Adapted from Katz, M.: The Birth Pangs of a New Drug. *Drug and Cosmetic Industry*, *128*:40, 1980. Copyright by Harcourt Brace Jovanovich, Inc. Reprinted by permission of the publisher.

TABLE 7-8. *New Drug Development of an Oral Systemic Drug for Long-Term Administration: I.–VI. Research to NDA*

DISCIPLINE	STAGE OF DEVELOPMENT	COST $(000)
Chemistry		2000
Biology, animal pharmacology		1500
Toxicology		4000
Pharmacy		3000
Clinical medicine		12000
Marketing regulatory project management		1500
Total	Year 0 to 12	$24000

Source: Adapted from Katz, M.: The Birth Pangs of a New Drug. *Drug and Cosmetic Industry,* *128*:40, 1980. Copyright by Harcourt Brace Jovanovich, Inc. Reprinted by permission of the publisher.

are "direct." They do not include the costs of discovery (exploratory research), the costs associated with other compounds that do not survive the development process (estimated to be seven failures per success), or the "time value" of money. Note that the tables present various marketing and project management activities as a compound moves through the development stages.

Marketing Inputs to Research

It is obvious that the impact of marketing on the R & D process varies with the stage of the process. As we move from the exloratory end of the R & D spectrum to the point at which leads are identified and a decision is made to pursue an IND and an NDA, the goals of projects become better defined and the role of marketing increases. At any point either inadequate marketing inputs or attempts to exert excessive control over the research process can create major problems. Difficulties may also arise when research programs are too unstructured and are not in tune with marketing strategies and the near-term concern for increased revenues and profits. Once projects are formalized, marketing needs to monitor progress and to provide important insights concerning (1) the nature of the clinical studies to be undertaken and the desired claim structure for the product, (2) dosage forms to be developed, and their characteristics, and (3) the timing of the NDA submission.

Marketing should also exert considerable influence on research activities in support of existing products, including broad-
ened claims, new dosage forms, and overall defensive efforts. Because of the decline in the evolution of new chemical entities over
the past two decades, there has been more emphasis on "defensive" projects, those aimed at prolonging the life cycle of currently
marketed products. Even in the large research-based firms, as
much as 20 to 25% of the R & D budget may be directed to such
defensive activities.[10]

In some firms a formal statement of marketing interests and
opportunities in various therapeutic categories is developed by
marketing specialists, and is presented to research scientists as a
guide to research decision making in the selection of R & D programs and projects. The marketing overview usually includes
such information as market definition and potential, patient prevalence, current sales data and projections, leading marketed products, prescribing patterns, and competitive trends. In some cases
marketing experts may provide specific suggestions to research
such as those on Table 7-9, noting potential sales for products that
might be developed.[11]

Project Selection

Project selection decisions are often influenced by a number of
important considerations in addition to the size of the research
budget. In a study of the research planning methodologies and
approaches of six leading pharmaceutical firms, project selection
was found to be influenced by various scientific, marketing, and
organizational factors.[12] All of the factors in Table 7-10 are not of
concern in every decision influencing project selection and priorities, but the compilation represents a checklist of areas often considered before decisions are finalized.

From this table it may be noted that many research, manufacturing, and marketing concerns must be considered that influence
project selection decisions. Consider, for example, the following
factors for a firm wishing to develop a market position in antibiotics, essentially a new area for the firm that has a couple of exciting
research leads.

1. Do we have specific objectives in the antibiotic field with
   regard to market position by a targeted date? Can we obtain commitment of resources (e.g., people, funds, facilities) to obtain these objectives? Should our emphasis be
   near term (2 to 3 years) or long term (5 to 10 years)?

TABLE 7-9. *Market Potential of Possible New Products*

PRODUCT DESCRIPTION	FIFTH YEAR SALES POTENTIAL ($)
Single-entity hypotensive agent, with new mode of action, effective for mild to severe hypertension without significant side-effects (e.g., prostaglandin, ionophore).	150 million
Centrally acting hypotensive agent with a significant reduction in the incidence of sedation and sexual dysfunction occurring with current products.	75 to 100 million
A cardiospecific beta blocker with once- or twice-a-day dosage marketed within the near future.	70 to 80 million
A uricosuric potassium-sparing diuretic with hypotensive activity free of ticrynafen-like hepatic toxicity.	50 to 75 million
An agent with hypotensive activity that is effective in treating patients with severe hypertension but with a much lower incidence of side-effects than agents currently available	20 to 25 million
A new class of hypotensive agents with minor improvements in side-effect profile of existing products.	10 to 20 million

Source: Adapted from Statement of Marketing Interests and Opportunities, Project Management Department, Hoffman-La Roche, 1981.

2. What are the risks and uncertainties associated with the effort? What are the financial implications of these uncertainties?

3. What is the nature of the competition in terms of marketed products and current development efforts? What are their strengths, weaknesses, and abilities?

4. What other known antibiotics are actively being developed? What are their potential market advantages and disadvantages?

5. What are the competitive advantages of the products we are considering to develop? What is the expected market life cycle? Are there possible follow-up products?

(*Text continues on p. 160.*)

TABLE 7-10. *Factors Influencing Project Selection*

SCIENTIFIC FACTORS	MARKETING CONSIDERATIONS	ORGANIZATIONAL AND OTHER ELEMENTS
Interrelationship with other research activities—synergistic advantages or competition with other programs.	Projected sales and profits from effort.	Relationship to activities at other research centers or units within the company.
Probability of achieving project objectives.	Relationship to need as reflected by current state of consumer satisfaction.	Timing of project with respect to other activities in marketing, research, etc.
Time required to achieve project objective.	Status and efficacy of current competitive products or means of meeting consumer need.	Manufacturing capabilities and needs.
Impact on balance of short- and long-term programs within research.	Compatibility with current marketing capabilities and strengths.	Prestige and image value to the company.
Estimated cost of the project in the coming year and to completion.	Influence of new competitive products under development.	Effect on organizational ésprit de corps and attitudes.
Utilization of existing research talent and resources.		Impact of governmental and public opinion and other environmental pressures.
Value as a means of generating experience and gaining a technical expertise in a field—a foundation for future research activities.		Alternative uses of scientific personnel and facilities if project dropped after a few years.
Need for critical mass of expertise and activity to ensure progress.		Moral compulsion to develop drugs meeting medical need but having little or no profit potential.
Elasticity of resource input and probable output relationships.		
Patentability or exclusivity of discoveries from project.		
Competitive research effort in the area—in academic and government research centers.		

6. What are the pricing structure and profit trend with antibiotics?

7. Who are the customers (e.g., physicians, third-party payers, government) and what "value" is each looking for? How will value differences affect our market positioning and opportunities?

8. Can we market antibiotics more successfully with a dedicated sales group or through our existing field force? Are special promotional efforts needed?

9. How will products be produced? If agents are manufactured by us, where? How much investment is needed? Do we have adequate in-house technical expertise to manufacture? What are the new material requirements? Do we need specialized facilities?

10. What is the patent position for each of our potential market entities? Are areas of litigation of concern?

11. What is the R & D cost to support our strategy? Do we have the internal technical and scientific expertise to support the needed research effort? How will a move to antibiotic research impact on other research projects and programs?

12. If we accomplish our objectives, what is the likely response of our competitors? How will we respond to them and what will be the impact on our market share and profitability?

The interrelationship of scientific, social, and economic factors is of great significance in drug development. Certainly, the drug must possess some degree of clinical merit and, the less effective the product, the more vulnerable it is to replacement by a more effective agent. Sociologic factors are also important. For example, changing behavioral codes make contraceptive drugs much more saleable today than would have been possible several decades ago. Dietary patterns are another illustration of a sociologic change of potential significance to the drug industry; obesity is currently a major health problem. Many factors that will influence future industrial development involve intangibles in the areas of sociologic and consumer action, and it is difficult to identify and quantify these trends in terms that would help to guide specific managerial courses of action. One problem is that market research is almost completely based on retrospective data and extrapolations. It has great difficulty in coping with areas in which a market does not already exist. Increasingly, therefore, we are seeing the evolution of various techniques to forecast technologic, sociologic, and economic trends that will have an impact on the pharmaceutical industry. Various projections and scenarios about the future can be developed to aid in developing research and marketing strategies.

Project Management

Project management usually involves a form of organizational design in which the traditional hierarchy is supplemented by or integrated with subunits, usually called task forces or project teams. It has emerged as a formally recognized approach to organizational design only in the last 25 years. The distinctiveness of subunits lies in the fact that (1) they are designed to deal with specific problems or to achieve relatively explicit goals or objectives, (2) they cut across traditional departmental and disciplinary lines by using the expertise of personnel, and (3) they may be temporary so that when their goals or objectives are attained or abandoned personnel are reassigned or released. Figure 7-2 illustrates how project teams or task forces are designed to carry out product development missions by coordinating activities across

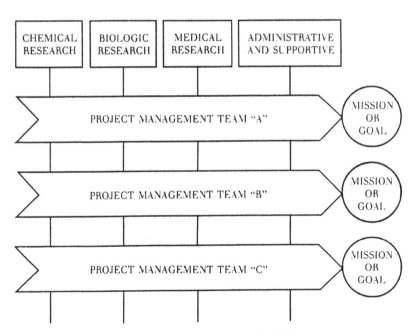

Fig. 7-2. *Project management interdisciplinary teams.*

several functional areas. The mission or goal of project management team A, for example, may be to guide the development of all cardiovascular compounds as they move through research and toward approved NDAs.

The Project Mangement Institute has reported the results of a survey of pharmaceutical R & D planning and project management operations in 22 firms.[13] R & D project planning teams were functional in 21 of the firms, and were active from the identification of a promising lead to NDA filing. The number of personnel involved in the direction of project planning operations ranged from 1 to 17 with 20% of the companies reporting 10 or more. Most of the project and planning managers had academic degrees in science (e.g., biology, chemistry), with 1 in 5 possessing an MBA degree. Various titles were used to describe the personnel working in this area, such as project coordinator, leader, consultant, analyst, or manager, network technician, planning analyst, and manager of R & D resource planning. In 18 of the 21 firms participating in the survey, the project planning function reported to the president or a vice president within the R & D organization.

Upjohn is one of the few pharmaceutical firms that has changed markedly from a traditional discipline-oriented organizational structure to one that is product-oriented.[14] In their reorganization they abolished their chemistry, pharmacology, and medical units and created several new product research units, each consisting of several persons from these and related functions. The more than 24 functional activities required to develop a new drug are organized under 7 product research units of about 30 to 70 people in the following areas of medicine: central nervous system (CNS) diseases, fertility, infectious diseases, cardiovascular diseases, diabetes, atherosclerosis, hypersensitivity diseases, and cancer. This project team concept is outlined in Table 7-11.

The product research manager has the responsibility of managing the product locating and development programs in his area of responsibility. He has line authority only over the A element. Therefore, he needs to solicit support and contributions from experts in the B and C categories. Contributors to new product development located administratively within research are in the A and B categories, while those in other functional units are listed under C. The characteristics and advantages of the Upjohn drug development system have been summarized as follows:[14]

1. The teams and the organization are quite stable in composition. Each man knows his boss and colleagues and hopefully learns to rely on their predictable behavior.

2. The responsibility for the development of a compound is centered in one man, the product research manager. In a discipline-oriented organization, responsibility is diffused, it

TABLE 7-11. *Project Team and Support Research and Staff Units Directed by the Product Research Manager*

CATEGORY A	CATEGORY B	CATEGORY C
Organic chemistry	Toxicology	Patent law
Biochemistry	Physical and analytical	Chemical production
Pharmacology	chemistry	Pharmaceutical production
Medicine	Pharmacy	Pharmaceutical marketing
	Pilot plant	Control
	Animal rearing	Purchasing
	Prison clinic	
	Hospital clinic	
	Field monitors	
	Computer center	
	Biostatistics	
	Clinical research laboratory	
	FDA liaison	
	Library and technical	
	information	
	Research services	
	Administrative services	

is passed from one man to another, or it resides high in the organization. Drug development activities are similar to the activity of a football team moving the ball under the direction of a quarterback. In a discipline-oriented organization, the drug development process resembles the activity of a relay team passing the baton from one solo performer to another.

3. In the organization attempts are made to foster a good understanding of objectives by careful program and project planning and by wide communication of the plans.

4. Prerogatives based on organizational position or academic background are avoided whenever possible.

5. Communications are kept open, and conscious attempts are made to keep members of the total organization well informed on technical and administrative activities and decisions.

The selection and organization of personnel at the marketing-research interface is critical in developing a successful drug development program. The project manager, whether functioning in the research or marketing organization or in a separate group, should possess an array of specific skills and personality traits. First, he must appreciate the complexity of science and technology, which usually requires direct exposure through education or work experience in the laboratory and the scientific process. Incidentally, a pharmaceutical education provides an excellent background for project management because it encompasses a broad array of subject material and courses in various scientific areas closely associated with drug development. The project manager must also have a goal- or mission-oriented perspective, characterized by a sense of urgency. In addition he must possess a keen sensitivity to the "people" element and motivational factors so essential in obtaining the cooperation needed to ensure the rapid evolution of drug development programs.

Various computerized PERT/CPM project planning systems are in use in the drug industry. The ideal computerized approach should (1) be simple and flexible, (2) generate documents that are of minimal size, easy to read and comprehend, and cover all essential information, (3) offer positive benefits for the users, (4) be cost-effective in performance, and (5) be easy to install and update. One such computerized project monitoring approach provides the following information, which is presented in five reports.[15]

    I. Status Report: This report is a communication medium between users and project planning. It includes:
        A. Activities in process.
        B. Activities completed.
        C. Activities due to start.
        D. Activities due to finish.
        E. Indication of early start and early finish.
        F. Duration of each activity.
        G. Status and comment.
    II. Critical Path Report: This identifies:
        A. All activities from start to finish, department, duration, early start, early finish, and final target date.
        B. The department that is responsible for the activities.
        C. Total duration of the critical activities.
        D. Successor activities.
    III. Multiproject Departmental Report
        A. All the multiproject activities are sorted by an early start date.
        B. Slack or float date is indicated for rescheduling.
        C. Critical activities are indicated for special attention.
        D. The early start date and finish date of these activities are identified.
    IV. Management Exception Report: This notes the:
        A. Critical path and noncritical activities that are delayed or are finished early.
        B. Problem areas that require attention from management.
    V. New Product Planning Chart: This is a total graphic illustration of a project from start to finish, in which:

A. All the critical paths are indicated.
B. The length of the band indicates duration, early start, and early finish date.
C. All interrelated activities are shown.
D. All the departmental activities are grouped into pertinent horizontal columns.
E. Major events and milestone activities are shown as flags.
F. Weekly, monthly, and annual scales are shown at the top of chart.

Some firms use simple "one-pager" forms to provide a brief status report of projects under development. Such a form presenting data on the status of an analgesic in Phase II clinical studies is illustrated in Figure 7-3.

Product Manager

In addition to the interactions between marketing and research that occur during the drug development stage in the category of project management, most firms have product directors or managers in marketing who are concerned with developing market plans for existing products and who have, in addition, a vital interest in new products moving toward NDA approval. Because these products, when approved, are assigned to the product planning function, personnel in this area seek to become involved during the latter stages of the drug development cycle. The job description for a product director at Hoffman-La Roche may be described as follows:[11]

The basic function of a product director is to plan for and manage the development of assigned, existing, and new pharmaceutical products as individual businesses by assessing marketing needs and opportunities, developing marketing strategies and responsibility, and directing the application of marketing resources in an optimal manner consistent with the goals of the firm. In this capacity he directs the product- or project-related activities of each member of the marketing teams, composed of the following personnel:

- Advertising manager

- Product sales manager

- Sales planning manager

- Professional services physician

- Professional services writer

- Professional services manager

THE MARKET: Analgesic   PROJECT NUMBER:
U.S. SALES $MILLIONS: GENERIC NAME:
                                         TRADE NAME:

MARKET LEADERS: 1.   2.   3.

THERAPEUTIC ADVANTAGE: As effective as market leader but safer, less risk
of CNS depression than others, possible less sedative effect.

DESIRED PRODUCT CLAIMS:		SUPPORT DATA TO DATE		
	Not Proved	Posi- ble	Proba- ble	Assured
Analgesic Oral				
50 mg qid effective		X		
100 mg qid effective		X		
200 mg qid effective		X		
100 mg bid effective	X			
200 mg bid effective	X			
Less CNS depression		X		
Less sedative effect		X		

AVAILABLE DOSE FORMS:

CLINICAL WORKUP TO DATE:

CURRENT PROGRAM OBJECTIVE:

CURRENT ACTIVITY: START . . . Progress to NDA . . . COMPLETE
Pharmaceutical formulation   XXXXXXXXXXXXXXXXXX
Pharmaceutical stability   XXXXXXXXXXXXXXXXXX
Analytical methods   XXXXXXXXXXXXXXXXXX
Chemical manufacturing   XXXXXXXXXX
Chronic toxicity
Phase I tolerance   XXXXXXXXXXXXXXXXXXXXXXXXXXXXXXXX
Phase II clinical efficacy   XXXXXXXXXX
Phase III efficacy in broad use
Phase III safety in broad use

ESTIMATED NDA SUBMISSION DATE:

COMMENT:
(Items of special interest concerning toxicity, clinical supplies, dosage form
development or others relating to various current activities.)

COSTS: To 1981:   INFORMATION DATE:
       1981 operating budget:
       Estimated to NDA:

Fig. 7-3. *New drug product development status summary.*

- Medical affairs physician
- Proofreader
- Marketing research analyst
- Copywriter
- Career development associate
- Other specific team members (as appropriate)

The principal functional responsibilities of the product director are the following:

- Develop annual, intermediate, and long-range marketing and business strategies and plans for the business.
- Manage and recommend to the marketing board strategies and plans relative to pricing, distribution, labeling, trademarking, and packaging associated with assigned products.
- Establish and achieve all quantifiable product/project/personnel objectives
- Develop unit and dollar sales projections to ensure appropriate planning to meet the anticipated needs of the marketplace and achievement of profit plans.
- Recommend and develop appropriate new dosage forms strategy and plans for assigned products to maximize opportunities.
- Conduct team meetings, foster communications among team members and departments, and issue appropriate and timely minutes.
- Work with sales management to achieve national and regional sales strategies and plans.
- Direct selected projects that will impact across product lines and influence future business policies of the firm.
- Ensure, through leadership and direction, that the planning, developing, implementation, and monitoring of marketing programs conform with and fully support the product plan.
- Initiate and maintain appropriate linkage between the product and project teams and other functional resources, such as distribution, drug regulatory affairs, finance, law, materials management, product development, packaging develop-

ment, production, manufacturing, facilities planning, research, public relations, public policy, business development, and strategic planning.

- Communicate and actively participate with research and project management to ensure that product research and development plans are implemented that fulfill agreed-to strategies for assigned products and therapeutic areas.

- Coordinate to achieve mutually satisfactory resolution of any actual or potential conflicts indentified between assigned product marketing strategies or programs and existing local, state, or federal laws and regulations.

- Monitor social, political, economic, regulatory, and legal trends affecting the pharmaceutical industry and assigned markets, and react with recommendations.

- Consult with and engage outside support, consultants, and agencies to ensure the continuous generation of new, innovative, and creative ideas for product and project objectives.

- Establish budgets, budget mix, and monitor expenditures by specific media and target audiences for products or projects.

- Anticipate and apprise management of changes in the marketplace and initiate modifications to the marketing plan based on evolving market dynamics.

- Exercise final team approval on promotional copy and field communications related to assigned products.

- Assume responsibility in concert with appropriate department heads to assist team members in the informal training process relative to team interactions and activities.

- Participate and interact with broad chartered committees, such as FDA production committee, product coordinating committee, project teams, and product management review committee.

- Coordinate the response to FDA relative to assigned marketed products with drug regulatory affairs and others.

- Input into project management to maximize potential marketing opportunities prior to issuance of the transfer document.

- Review and comment on selling emphasis programs.

- Recommend appropriate allocation of sales efforts for the pharmaceutical line to the sales department and marketing board for the current planning period.

- Launch new products.

Research Productivity

One of the most critical concerns of those working at the marketing-research interface is the assessment of R & D productivity. Certainly, in the long term, the ultimate criterion of success is the contribution that a research effort makes to the profit profile of the firm through new and improved products. There are valuable yardsticks available to help measure how well a research organization is doing toward achieving that goal. A careful analysis of research momentum and patterns can be helpful in answering the question: "Compared to the past, what are we doing better and what trends exist today within the research operation that support both short- and long-range goals, reflect research dynamism, and are indicative of progress? For example, quantitative data on publications, patents, and new compounds synthesized or screened when studied over time may show trends or milestones that together are indicative of past accomplishment and are of value in predicting future output. To rely on only one or two measures, however, may be misleading. Even the widespread practice used by many economists of evaluating a firm's R & D productivity solely in terms of the number of new single chemical entities introduced ignores such important factors as the market potential of the compounds, the magnitude of support directed to existing products, and the amount of exploratory research effort invested in programs that will generate major new breakthroughs in the future. When assessing the productivity of a research group and its contributions to marketing goals, a number of factors should be listed and evaluated. Some areas that should be assessed as indicators of R & D output and productivity may be outlined as follows:

I. New Product Sales and Profits.
II. New Product Potential:
   A. Number of NDAs submitted or approved.
   B. Number of INDs submitted or approved.
   C. New compounds synthesized.
   D. New compounds screened in animal tests.
   E. New screening methods.
   F. Patents filed or issued.
III. Support of Existing Products:
   A. New or improved indications.
   B. New or improved dosage forms.
   C. Studies to challenge adverse publicity.
   D. Effort to protect patent position.
IV. Support of Corporate Functions:
   A. New or improved syntheses and processes.
   B. Scientific data and advice.
   C. Information for public policy issues, etc.

V. Contributions to the Scientific Community:
   A. Number and type of publications.
   B. Support for academic research.
VI. Other Indicators of Progress:
   A. Positive organizational changes.
   B. Improved facilities.
   C. New research directions.
   D. Improved communications, motivation, management training, etc.

We have shown that one of the most critical areas of interaction and communication in the drug development process is the one between research and marketing. Special attention must be given to building bridges of understanding between these two vital groups because, as we examine the following seven key R & D functions, we can easily envision the valuable role of marketing insights and information in most of them:[16]

1. Solving problems.

2. Generating ideas.

3. Entrepreneuring ideas—that is, moving the idea past the initial evaluation stage and acquiring resources so that it can be developed into a commercial product or process.

4. Managing the project, acquiring additional support, and managing the resources necessary to realize the entrepreneur's dream.

5. Gatekeeping or acquiring and transmitting to others within the organization the necessary technical and other information.

6. Sponsoring or nurturing useful people and ideas.

7. Controlling the quality of the technical work. Individuals working in this area must know the science as well as the marketing and manufacturing environment in order to spot pitfalls and suggest ways of avoiding them.

Over the past few years, there has been a growing recognition of the need to provide more incentives for research and innovation in the United States. Some favorable patterns are emerging that will facilitate the drug approval process and that will support new drug discovery. For example, efforts have been made to restore up to 7 years of patent protection to compensate for the time taken to meet certain mandated governmental testing requirements and for regulatory review. Tax incentives have recently been passed that will provide credits for various research investments. Moreover, a number of programs are underway to develop means of accelerating the drug approval process so that new drugs will be available to the medical profession faster than the current development cycle, which takes as long as 10 to 12 years. Some changes being implemented may call for even greater collaboration between research and marketing groups. For example, any post-marketing surveillance system will necessitate close communication and information feedback mechanisms between research and experience in the marketplace. It appears that these and other trends continue to reaffirm the fact that the interactions between the marketing and research functions of the modern pharmaceutical firm are critical to its success.

References

1. Meyer, F. H., and Mika, T. R.: R & D Management in the Pharmaceutical Firm, *Drug and Cosmetic Industry, 128*:46, 1981.
2. Hansen, R. W.: The Pharmaceutical Development Process: Estimate of Current Development Costs and Times and the Effects of Regulatory Changes, in *Issues in Pharmaceutical Economics,* edited by R. I. Chen and D. C. Heath, 1979, p 151.
3. Virts, J., and Weston, J. F.: Returns to Research and Development in the U.S. Pharmaceutical Industry, *Managerial and Decision Economics, 1*:103, 1980.
4. *IMS Pharmaceutical Newsletter, 8* (No. 18):4, 1981.
5. *Shareholders' Financial News,* SmithKline Corporation, October 18, 1978.
6. Gibson, P.: Being Good Isn't Enough Anymore, *Forbes, 124*:40, 1979.
7. Staples, R., Project Management in the Pharmaceutical Industry . . . A Statement of Issues and Observations, *Project Management Quarterly, 10*:24, 1979.
8. *PMA Newsletter, 23* (No. 43):5, 1981.
9. Katz, M.: The Birth Pangs of a New Drug, *Drug and Cosmetic Industry, 128*: 40, 1980.
10. Faust, R. E.: The 1962 Drug Amendments: Challenge to the Research Process, *American Pharmacy, 19*:11, 1979.
11. Statement of Marketing Interests and Opportunities, Project Management Department, Hoffman-La Roche, 1981.
12. Faust, R. E.: Project Selection in the Pharmaceutical Industry, *Research Management, 14*:14, 1971.
13. Trautwein, C. A.: Results of a Survey of Pharmaceutical R & D Planning Departments, Presented at the Project Management Institute Meeting, Cherry Hill, NJ, September 29, 1981.
14. Weisblat, D. I., and Stucki, J. C.: Goal-Oriented Organization at Upjohn, *Research Management, 17*:34, 1974.
15. Yun, J. M.: Use of a Project Management System on New Drug Development, *Drug Information Journal, 10*:111, 1976.
16. Technology Management Group, Pugh-Roberts Associates, Cambridge, MA. Reported in *Inside R & D, 7*, No. 28, July 12, 1978.

## CHAPTER 8

Diversification and Specialization

ROBERT J. DeSALVO

The development of any industry is characterized by the growth of the individual firms within the industry. This growth is related to the firm's long-term objectives, and includes the product planning process. In keeping with the company objectives, management will have to decide the direction the firm must take according to the company's resources and current and near-term economic, legal, political, and social environments. Some or all of these so-called uncontrollable variables affect the diversification and specialization policies of the firm. Just as timing is critical for the release and promotion of a new product, timing in the broader sense of a company's expansion policy is critical to the long-term success of the firm. Economic or legal constraints, for example, may warrant a firm putting its resources in a product line or service that is totally unrelated to its principal business activity. Later in this chapter we will examine a brief chronologic history of expansion within the pharmaceutical industry that manifests trends into areas of diversification and specialization.

Growth and Expansion

Growth can result from one of two forms of expansions, internal expansion or external expansion. Firms within many industries such as the automotive, steel, drug, or cosmetic industry have reached their present size by utilizing these forms, either singly or in combination. In reality few dominant firms within the drug industry have not been involved with external expansion in some way or another. It should be noted also that expansion is not limited to firms producing and marketing a tangible product, but also to service-oriented firms and firms at different levels in the channel of distribution. Expansion to diversify or to specialize can be viewed as part of a total marketing strategy and may incorporate plans of product development, such as product differentiation or market segmentation. The internal form of expansion is the realization of the company's growth through the utilization of the already existing facilities and personnel of the firm. For example, a drug manufacturer may find that an additional market exists for an "extra strength" version of an existing product, or that a market exists for a product with which the firm has had no experience. The point here is that the firm can use its existing facilities and personnel to effect this expansion.

External Expansion

Types

External expansion is achieved by buying some or all of the assets of another firm. It is usually attained by the use of what is called the "business combination" and, in some cases, may be preceded by a joint venture or agreement. The assets obtained may range from some facility, personnel, or stock to the complete purchase of the firm, which may include subsidiaries. Obviously each proposed business combination is influenced by a great many legal, tax, and accounting considerations, and these factors determine the type and form of combination that takes place. Although management is concerned with these factors, the completion of the combination has important marketing ramifications in regard to fulfilling the expansion goals of the firm.

Table 8-1 exhibits the types of business combinations and Table 8-2 displays the categories of business combination forms. Some examples can illustrate the nature of business combinations. In 1970, Parke-Davis and Company was merged into Warner Lambert Company, with the latter becoming the parent or surviving company. In this case the merged company did not lose its name or identity, but did lose its former business entity status because it is currently a division of the parent company. Use of the consolidation is extremely limited in the drug industry. In a few cases two or more subsidiaries of a firm have been consolidated to form a division or unit.

The most frequently used method of external expansion is the acquisition. Over 95% of all business combinations in the drug industry utilize the acquisition type of business combination. This provides the most flexibility for achieving the mutual satisfaction of the firms involved, and in turn affects the tax considerations of

TABLE 8-1. *Types of Business Combinations*

STATUTORY MERGER	STATUTORY CONSOLIDATION	ACQUISITION	JOINT VENTURES
A reorganization of one or more corporations into an already existing entity through approval of the voting stockholders of the companies involved. The combining corporation loses its former entity status and the surviving corporation becomes responsible for all of the merging corporation's past and future actions.	A reorganization of two or more corporations into one previously nonexistent entity through a voting stockholders' approval of the corporations involved. All participating firms lose their former legal entity status, and a new corporation is created that becomes responsible for the past actions of the combining corporations.	An exchange of voting stock or assets, or a purchase of stock or assets for cash or other securities, in which there may or may not be a gain or loss recognized for tax purposes. "Asset" is meant to include inventories, distribution rights, patents, trademarks, brand names, goodwill, or other tangible or intangible items considered an asset under standard accounting procedures.	An association or agreement between firms to carry out a single or multiple business activity with no intent that the association be permanent or continuous. All firms involved remain autonomous business entities.

174

TABLE 8-2. *Forms of Business Combinations*

HORIZONTAL COMBINATION	VERTICAL COMBINATION		CONGLOMERATE COMBINATION		MIXED COMBINATION
A business combination between two companies selling identical, similar, or substitutable goods and services at the same stages of production or distribution to the same types of customers.	A business combination that combines two or more companies' operations at different levels in the channel of distribution, from extraction or production of raw materials to the marketing of the final products. Within this form of combination, there are two subgroups.		A business combination in which there is no relationship between the combining companies in regard to the stages of production or service furnished. Within this form there are two subgroups.		A business combination that includes characteristics of at least two of the other forms of combinations, even though one form may be more dominant.
	FORWARD VERTICAL COMBINATION	BACKWARD VERTICAL COMBINATION	CIRCULAR COMBINATION		
	A business combination between two or more companies engaged in different stages of production and distribution of the final product. The combining company's stage of production is subsequent to that of the parent company.	A business combination between two or more companies engaged in different stages of production and distribution of the final product. The parent company's stage of production is subsequent to that of the combining company.	A business combination by which the joining companies' products or services are unrelated but may be distributed through the same outlets.		

Source: Federal Trade Commission Report on the Merger Movement, 1978, p. 23.

the acquisition. The acquired may range from the entire firm, in which case it would appear to be similar to the merger, to the acquisition of certain assets. An example is the Dow Chemical Company's acquisition of the pharmaceutical business of Richardson-Merrell, Inc.

Although not a business combination in the true sense because there is no change of ownership, the joint venture has been utilized for a long time by many firms as a means of expansion. In some cases it serves as the precursor to an actual business combination. Usually the joint venture is an agreement between two or more firms to undertake some marketing function—for example, distribute products in a foreign country or to work together to develop some type of new delivery system. A large number of joint ventures have been undertaken with foreign firms, illustrating the interest of the drug industry in expanding markets on an international scale.

Forms

The combinations that drug industry firms have been involved in are usually horizontal or conglomerate in form. Although both of these forms characterize the business combinations that are taking place, the number of conglomerates has been increasing at a faster rate. Expansion of retail drug operations in local and interstate activities by acquisition is a good example of the horizontal form. Firms such as Revco, Walgreens, and Grays have expanded their operations in this manner. Business combinations between firms within the industry result in various degrees of product integration. The amount of integration depends upon the product similarity, identification of product with its manufacturer, size of the companies involved, outlets available, amount of distribution desired and the parent company's extent of control. An example of integration in the drug industry is the Pfizer purchase of J. B. Roerig Company. Both firms manufacture prescription-legend and nonprescription-legend drugs. In both cases the same outlets are available, but the J. B. Roerig Company has been operated as a fully owned subsidiary maintaining its own sales force.

The most representative business combination of the vertical form was the Merck & Company merger of Sharp & Dohme. Merck was primarily engaged in developing, manufacturing, and distributing chemicals, while Sharp & Dohme was primarily a pharmaceutical and biologic product manufacturer that processed chemicals into finished products and marketed them to members of the medical profession. Another example of vertical integration is that of drug wholesalers acquiring manufacturers of drugs as well as medical supplies and equipment.

There is a definite trend for some firms in the drug industry to follow a program of conglomerate diversification. In these cases the business activities of the acquired or merged firm are unrelated to that of the parent firm. Factors other than a proposed company's product line are given greater consideration, and the parent company's acquisition program specifications include factors such as size, growth prospects, earnings per share, industry position, and management. The type of firm is not limited by its product line. In general, the trend of conglomerate combinations by the firms of the drug industry has been complementary or related to the broader area of the health and beauty aid industry. This is not to say that some firms place greater emphasis on potential rather than on product line.

What Do We Mean by Diversification and Specialization?

Diversification, as the name implies, indicates that a firm has a variety of major or minor business activities that may be related or may be in completely separate industries. A few examples may help to clarify this. Table 8-3 presents a representative listing of three firms whose business activities place them, by definition, into the category of diversified firms. All the firms are involved in pharmaceuticals as well as in the broader area of health care. The distinguishing factor is the business activity that accounts for the largest percentage of sales. At one extreme of diversification is the holding company, which actually manufactures and sells nothing but owns and manages a group of firms similar to that of a stock portfolio. Among the best-known holding companies is American Home Products. It should be noted that the typical diversified pharmaceutical manufacturer has extensive foreign divisions and subsidiaries in addition to domestic holdings.

By specialization in the strict and narrow sense we are describing a firm with a single major business activity that accounts for the bulk of its sales. For example, most business activities of retail pharmacy operations are reported as sales of individual units. Expansion of firms at this level is usually horizontal in nature, involving the opening or the purchase of another unit(s). At the manufacturer's level the great majority of sales comes from a single type of product, such as pharmaceuticals. In an even more narrow sense some firms specialize in products for certain therapeutic categories, ailments, or anatomic structures.

Most benefits of specialization are self-evident. A firm becomes known for its expertise in the area; this results in the product line reaching the status of a specialty good with a relatively inelastic

TABLE 8-3. *Business Activities of Diversified Firms with Pharmaceutical Interests*

FIRM	BUSINESS DESCRIPTION	REPRESENTATIVE DIVISIONS AND SUBSIDIARIES
American Home Products	Company and subsidiaries are engaged in manufacture, distribution, and sale of diversified line of products in four major lines of business: prescription drugs; packaged drugs; houseware and household products; food products.	Adams Plastic Co. Inc. American Permanent Wave Co. Ayerst Laboratories Boyle-Midway, Inc. E. J. Brach & Sons Ekco Products Fort Dodge Labs Co. Ives Laboratories, Inc. Corometrics Medical Systems, Inc. Slaymaker Lock Co. Inc. Whitehall Laboratories, Inc. Wyeth Laboratories, Inc.
Bristol-Myers	Through its divisions and subsidiaries is a major producer and distributor of pharmaceuticals and medical products, toiletries and beauty aids, nonprescription health products, and household products.	Bristol Labs Bristol-Myers Products Clairol, Inc. Drackett Co. Mead Johnson & Co. Pelton & Crane Co. Unitek Corp. Westwood Pharmaceuticals, Inc. Zimmer Products
Johnson & Johnson	Engaged in the manufacture and sale of a broad range of products in the health care and other fields. Divided into four industry segments: consumer; professional; pharmaceutical; industrial.	Chicopee Mills, Inc. Devro, Inc. Ethicon, Inc. Extracorporeal Medical Specialties, Inc. Hancock Laboratories, Inc. Johnson & Johnson Baby Products Co. McNeil Laboratories Ortho Pharmaceutical Corp. Permacil Personal Products Co. Surgikos, Inc. Technicare Corp.

Source: Moody's Industrials, Standard & Poors, Directory of Corporate Affiliations, 1981, p. 342.

demand. Firms such as Alcon, Allergan, and Armour are examples of firms that have specialized in an area. Each of these firms was acquired by a larger diversified organization. Thus, in effect, we have a type of specialization occurring within the broader confines of the expansion policies of a diversified parent firm.

A negative aspect of specialization is that a firm may be labeled as a "one-product company," and may have significant dependence on a single product or therapeutic category. If there is no parent company to absorb setbacks, the growth potential and attraction to potential investors will be constrained.

Chronologic Review

Although important business combinations occurred in the drug industry prior to the 1900s, most manufacturers and suppliers of drug products had not developed any incorporated organizational structure. Many firms were small in number and in size, and were family-owned and managed by the founder and his sons and relatives. This is in contrast to other industries such as oil and railroads, which in the early 1900s were obtaining capital funds from investors. The drug industry at this time was financing its own expansion from earnings.

Between 1900 and 1917 two events affecting the drug industry occurred. First, the community pharmacist increased dependence upon the manufacturer. Second, the use of medicinal chemicals increased and began to replace the crude botanical drugs formerly used by practitioners to prepare tinctures, elixirs, and fluid extracts. Entry of the United States into World War I created an additional demand for drug products, and freed the industry from dependence upon foreign sources for drugs and chemicals.

During and after World War I, a two-way vertical integration existed between the drug and chemical manufacturers. Chemical manufacturers undertook a forward vertical integration to produce finished drug products. In contrast to this forward integration, the drug manufacturers began a backward integration to fill their own requirements for basic chemicals.

In contrast with the first two decades of the twentieth century, the 1920s exhibited a large increase in the number of acquisitions and mergers that occurred on a national level. The drug industry had developed its corporate structure sufficiently to figure predominantly in this merger era. The principle objective involved in the business combinations undertaken was that of diversification. Scientific activities resulting in new products expanded existing product lines. In addition, the opening of new merchandise outlets, characterized by the retail chain store expansion during this period and the increase in opportunity for profits due to a moderate prosperity of the industry, created a search for diversification that would afford an increase and protection of income.

Sharp & Dohme, Incorporated expanded into biologic manufacturing and increased its existing product line by utilizing the acquisition. Dermatological Research Laboratories, a developer of arsphenamines, was acquired in 1922 and was followed in 1928 by the acquisition of John T. Milliken and Company, a manufacturer of pharmaceutical preparations. In 1930, Swan-Myers Company, a biologic manufacturer, was purchased. In 1928 McKesson & Robbins, Incorporated undertook a large geographic expansion program. The purpose was to combine, under one ownership, a group of well-established and widely geographically distributed wholesale drug operations. By 1929 McKesson & Robbins had acquired 28 wholesale firms.*

In the 1940s drug industry firms could be categorized into one of four groups. The first consisted of a core of pharmaceutical manufacturers termed the "old line" companies, which provided the majority of sales of prescription-legend drugs. Abbott Laboratories, Eli Lilly and Company, and Parke-Davis and Company are examples. Closely allied to these firms was the second category, chemical manufacturers who supplied the bulk of drugs to the pharmaceutical manufacturer, such as Merck & Company. The third group consisted of nonprescription-legend drug manufacturers whose majority of sales were obtained from highly advertised drug products. Among these firms were Vick Chemical Company and Miles Laboratories. There were a few firms that had significant interest in both prescription-legend and nonprescription-legend drugs, such as American Home Products Corporation and Sterling Drug Incorporated. The fourth group of companies comprised more than 1000 small drug companies whose business was limited to specialty or regional markets.

By the time World War II ended, leadership in drug research, development, and manufacturing had passed from Europe to the United States. Also, there had been notable developments and improvements in the areas of anti-infective drugs, psychotherapeutic agents, diuretics, hormones, and biologic products. And, along with this leadership, firms were maturing from those that were family-owned and operated to the professionally managed type of corporations that were active in multiple areas of the drug industry as well as in other industries. The industry's growth was also being fostered by expanding population, rising income, increasing acceptance of drug therapy, automation, improved marketing techniques, and health insurance.

The dominant pharmaceutical manufacturers reflect their economic oligopolistic market structure in their representation among the largest industrial corporations in the United States, as shown in Table 8-4. Although the rankings in this table are based on total sales from all business activities of the firm, it appears that in general the firms responsible for most pharmaceutical sales are concentrated among the top 300 firms. Expansion via the business combination is partially responsible for the overall increase. Over

---

*An extensive historical review is presented in Williams Haynes: *American Chemical Industry,* New York: D. Van Nostrand and Company, 1954.

TABLE 8-4. *Ranking of Representative Pharmaceutical Manufacturers Among the Largest United States Industrial Corporations Based on Sales*

FIRM	YEAR													
	1955	1960	1965	1970	1971	1972	1973	1974	1975	1976	1977	1978	1979	1980
Abbott Laboratories	328	325	286	238	252	251	254	249	215	209	200	197	197	185
Eli Lilly & Company	249	256	216	199	172	172	173	176	167	171	169	156	163	154
Merck & Company	217	219	208	162	151	147	151	152	139	132	147	146	147	142
Pfizer, Incorporated	207	177	125	137	133	130	132	130	125	118	126	121	125	126
Parke-Davis & Company	272	234	296	Merged into Warner Lambert & Company										
Schering-Plough Corporation	NI,	462	475	266	265	259	259	266	247	254	254	250	220	209
G.D. Searle & Company	NI,	NI,	NI,	445	438	422	308	288	268	273	274	288	288	289
SmithKline Corporation	329	290	280	300	301	303	322	326	297	296	291	242	229	203
Squibb Corporation	A division of Olin Mathieson			167	150	154	189	201	183	188	187	190	188	196
Upjohn Company	NI,	275	282	263	264	258	249	242	223	220	217	211	212	206

Source: From Fortune 500 Annual Directories, © Time, Inc. All rights reserved.

TABLE 8-5. *Changes in Business Activity Descriptions for Three Firms in the Pharmaceutical Industry for 1960, 1970, and 1980*

YEAR	SMITHKLINE CORPORATION*	SCHERING-PLOUGH CORPORATION†	G. D. SEARLE & COMPANY
1960	Manufactures ethical pharmaceuticals, medical specialties, and various veterinary medicines.	Manufactures pharmaceutical, veterinary, and proprietary products.	Company manufactures ethical pharmaceuticals.
1970	Develops, manufactures, and sells prescription pharmaceuticals. Subsidiaries develop, manufacture, and sell antibiotics, sun care products, dairy and nondairy specialty food products, veterinary pharmaceuticals and biologicals, feed additives, cardiac monitoring and resuscitation equipment, medical diagnostic instruments, and equipment and ultrasonic instruments used in cleaning, nondestructive testing, and plastic welding. Also engaged in medical laboratory services field.	An international pharmaceutical company that markets a diversified product line including corticoids, cold products, antihistamines, psychopharmaceuticals, fungicides, cosmetics and toiletries, laxatives, animal health products, and medical laboratory diagnostic aids.	Company operates through four divisions; domestic pharmaceuticals, Searle International, Nuclear Chicago, and Corporate Development. Searle manufactures ethical pharmaceuticals, sells bulk steroids intermediates, and manufactures equipment for biomedical and chemical laboratories. Nuclear Chicago manufactures equipment to detect and measure radioactive materials, processes radioactive materials, conducts research on a contractual basis, and manufactures chromatography instruments.

1980

Company is engaged primarily in the research, development, manufacture, and marketing of prescription medicines, proprietary pharmaceuticals, and animal health products. Company also researches, manufactures, and markets ultrasonic and electronic instruments, and provides wide range of medical laboratory services through clinical laboratories.

Company is engaged in the development, manufacture, and marketing of ethical pharmaceuticals and proprietary medicines, cosmetics, toiletries, household products, animal health care products, and through subsidiaries is engaged in broadcasting operations. Company also conducts research in areas related to physical diagnosis, mental disorders, and immunology. Also engaged in the manufacture and distribution of foot and leg care products, shoes and footwear, and pressure-sensitive adhesive tape products for industrial and home application.

Company and its subsidiaries are principally engaged in pharmaceuticals, consumer products, medical products, specialty gases, blood gas monitoring equipment, medical forms, and retail optical products.

*Name changed in 1973 from Smith, Kline and French Laboratories to SmithKline Corporation.
†Name changed in 1971 from Schering Corporation to Schering-Plough Corporation.

Source: Moody Industrials

the years it has become more difficult to locate a major firm in the traditional drug industry channel of distribution that has not been involved in external expansion via the business combination.

The "merger fever" of the drug industry has been increasing, and in some cases it has become difficult to classify a firm as a representative of a single business activity because of its variety of holdings. Using the examples in Table 8-5, the trend for expansion for diversification during the 1960s and 1970s becomes readily apparent. It also appears that by 1980 there was some indication for firms to follow a divestiture program in order to concentrate or to specialize in selected areas. In a divestiture program, the parent firm sells off units, divisions, product lines, etc., in order to re-deploy assets—for example, from former diverse holdings to areas of specialization in keeping with company objectives.

Pharmaceutical manufacturers have experienced a trend for domestic expansion internally, and externally for overseas markets. Firms are now assuming a worldwide marketing strategy. Although much expansion has occurred in Europe, all continents have been invaded by the expansion policy of drug manufacturers. Business combinations in world markets are usually horizontal or vertical in form. Horizontal combinations provide an outlet for distributing domestic products abroad as well as manufacturing facilities for their products; these manufacturing facilities provide new bases for export purposes. Vertical combinations provide a source of supply for existing foreign operations and also serve as a source of supply for subsequent expansion.

Two areas in which drug manufacturers have shown special interest are animal health products and plastics. These later combinations have been partly vertical to secure a source of supply of enclosures for finished products of the parent firms. In other cases the expansions were for diversification outside of the drug industry.

Another type of integration occurred in the 1960s. During this period the prescription-legend manufacturer expanded, usually by a subsidiary or division, to handle and promote nonprescription-legend drugs. Firms such as SmithKline and Sandoz have followed this format. The structure of the industry started to change as the "old line" pharmaceutical manufacturer diversified. Attitudes toward promotion were changing, and it became "ethical" for the prescription-legend drug manufacturer to have subsidiaries in the fields of cosmetics and proprietary drugs that were promoted through mass media. In other cases the old line pharmaceutical manufacturer began mass media promotion under its own corporate title.

A major area of diversification for drug industry firms was the entry into the field of cosmetics. Starting in 1962, business combinations between dominant firms of the drug and cosmetic industries were transacted in which the drug firms became the surviving company. There is a mutual interest for combinations between drug and cosmetic firms, with one reason being that the existing outlets for distribution may be utilized. These combinations were therefore circular conglomerate in form. Through these combinations the drug and cosmetic industries established a closer relationship. The combined organization possesses access to the chemical and technical knowledge needed to achieve integration of the company's resources and skills; thus, the new relationship results in the production of "medicated cosmetics."

Table 8-6 exhibits the interest of drug manufacturers in diversifying into the area of cosmetics. The cosmetic industry has many characteristics of the drug industry, which may be the reason for the attraction. There also now exists a number of diversified firms with interests in both areas. With possibly one exception, dominant firms in the cosmetic industry have not become the parent or surviving firm of combinations with drug firms. The Revlon Company has diversified into a number of areas, including drugs. USV Laboratories, Armour Pharmaceuticals, Barnes Hind Pharmaceuticals, and Norcliff-Thayer are all units of Revlon's expansion program. Chemical manufacturers have continued their expansion into the area of finished drug products. Olin Mathieson merged E. R. Squibb & Sons, Dow Chemical acquired Pitman-Moore, and Rohm & Haas acquired Warren Teed.

TABLE 8-6. *Drug and Cosmetic Business Combinations*

PARENT FIRM	ACQUIRED OR MERGED
American Cyanamid Company	John H. Breck, Inc. Shulton, Inc. Geoffrey Beene, Inc.
Eli Lilly & Company	Elizabeth Arden
Pfizer, Inc.	Barbasol Company Coty, Inc. Pacquin, Inc.
Richardson-Merrell Inc.	Adams Group (Oil of Olay)
A. H. Robins Company	Societe Parfums Caron
Schering-Plough	Carl Hoeppner K. G. (West Germany) Sardeau, Inc.
SmithKline Corporation	Sea & Ski, Inc.
Squibb Corporation	Lanvin-Charles of the Ritz
Syntex Corporation	Fermodyl House of Westmore

The drug wholesaler was exposed to an institutional change in which an increase in retail outlets that was not serviced by these wholesalers appeared. These retail outlets, utilizing other sources and assuming marketing functions, forced wholesalers to re-evaluate their position in the marketing channel. As a result of this re-evaluation the drug wholesaler adopted a backward integration policy that consisted of combinations with manufacturers of drug and medical supplies. The results of these combinations permitted the drug wholesalers to provide their drug accounts with products formerly purchased from other sources. The availability of these products at competitive prices helped to establish a closer working relationship between retail and wholesale drug operations. In essence, these integrations permitted the drug wholesalers to absorb the previously existing marketing functions of the manufacturers in the distribution channel. The legal environment of substitution laws and government programs will greatly affect the future marketing strategy of the drug wholesaler.

The food chain store operation, in the retail segment of the distribution channel, demonstrated an interest in combining with retail drugstore chain operations. The acquirers established themselves as merchandisers of nonfood products that were formerly associated with the retail drugstore. The major attraction of the food and drug combinations was the prescription-dispensing aspect of the drug operation. The Kroger Company and the Jewel Company have been active in this type of diversification. It has provided the food chain operation with experienced management to incorporate prescription-dispensing facilities into existing or future outlets. With the advent of shopping centers and the one-stop shopping concept, the coalescing of the supermarket and drugstores into a one-stop shopping unit has provided economies in rent, utilities, purchasing, and personnel. At the same time, drugstores have continued to serve shopping districts as separate units in which a combination food-drugstore was not indicated.

Throughout the 1960s and 1970s the retail drug component of the marketing channel continued to manifest horizontal expansion, with some exploration into other retailing areas. The acceptance of optical units in department stores has spread to retail drug units. A number of retail pharmacies have added optical centers, and the tie-in of cosmetics and fashion goods may develop this into a major form of expansion for the retail drug component of the drug industry.

In the 1970s drug manufacturing firms showed a pronounced expansion into other areas of the health-care industry. Medical and surgical devices and instruments, optical interests (at various levels in the distribution channel), ultrasonic equipment, clinical laboratories, prosthetics, and dental equipment and supplies were among the areas of diversification sought by the dominant pharmaceutical manufacturers. These combinations manifest a type of integration in that the acquisitions are "related" in the wider business activities of the health-care industry. Although they may officially be considered as conglomerate in nature, they have a possibly synergistic effect of product integration when the entire product line is viewed from a health-care industry viewpoint.

Foreign expansion was accelerated during the 1970s as firms continued to seek a broader base for the protection of income (Chap. 19). The reversal of foreign expansion is noteworthy, namely that of investment of foreign dollars into the United States market. The decline of the United States dollar, along with the stability of the political environment, presented an excellent investment potential for foreign firms. Investment from abroad is threefold in nature. First, foreign firms' investments via the business combination have acquired a conglomerate of former United States-based manufacturing firms. This increased investment, however, was not limited to manufacturers; retailers, including discount chain operations, were also acquired. Second, foreign investment is manifested in the building of new plants in the United States. The third phase is the partial purchase of stock in United States companies, especially in the area of technology. Drugs have by no means been exempt from the expansion policy of foreign firms into the domestic marketplace (Table 8-7).

The number of business combinations in which drug industry firms have been involved over the years has varied with the economic environment of the nation. There is some evidence that the legal environment correlates somewhat with the expansion and diversification objectives of a firm. In 1962 pharmaceutical manufacturers were the subject of a series of governmental investigations and legislation, primarily concerned with the financial status and products of the prescription-legend drug manufacturers. In 1962, legislation was passed that resulted in more stringent control of the manufacturing, labeling, and marketing of prescription-legend drugs.

During these investigations and the subsequent passage of legislation, there was a decrease in the number of new prescription-legend drug products that reached the market. This decrease was paralleled by an increase in merger activity in the drug industry. Included in these combinations was an overall increase in the number of pharmaceutical manufacturers participating, as well as an increase in the number of combinations with foreign firms who had prescription-legend drug-manufacturing facilities. As patent protection expires, increased pressure for cost savings, additional government constraints, increased research, and development cost for new product entities confront the pharmaceutical manufacturer, the objectives of firms will be attained by expansion in the form of diversification.

TABLE 8-7. *Business Combinations by Foreign Firms into the Domestic Drug Market*

ACQUIRER	ACQUIRED OR MERGED
Bayer AG (West Germany)	Cutter Laboratories Helena Chemical Company Miles Laboratories
Beecham Group Ltd. (England)	S. E. Massengill Merck's Calgon Rohm & Haas Company (Animal Health Operations)
Boots Co. Ltd. (England)	Rucker Pharmacal
Fison Ltd. (England)	UVS Pharmaceutical Corporation (Acquired certain assets) Cooper Laboratories (Acquired certain assets)
Glaxo Holding Ltd. (England)	Meyer Laboratories, Inc.
Imperial Chemical Industries (England)	Atlas Chemical—Stuart Pharmaceuticals
Kali-Chemie AG (West Germany)	Purepac (majority interest)
Nestle SA (Switzerland)	Alcon Laboratories

Why Expand?

Regardless of the outward appearance of any financial gain or physical asset obtained, the most important reason for transacting a business combination of any type or form is that of buying time. By utilizing the business combination, companies add well-established profit-making products to their existing product lines faster than could be done by their own research and development. The combination can therefore achieve the research and development goals of a firm by acting as a substitute, with the same net results. The combination can also increase the market share for a firm and, at the same time, eliminate future problems of competition. Time is also a factor because, in addition to the products acquired, a segment of customers are acquired with brand loyalties at various levels in the channel of distribution. The brand loyalty of consumer acceptance is related to the element of time and therefore is an important consideration.

The parent firm may also find it easier to introduce and to market new products as part of an established line. Many businesses acquired by firms have product manufacturing processes and technologies that are protected by patents and trademarks. These assets represent a type of time protection and formula for achieving a market position and share.

In addition to the physical assets obtained, time is also important in those instances in which trained and experienced personnel and management are obtained. They are not only beneficial for the operation of the new combined firm, but also serve as a potential source of future executive talent.

Other reasons for external expansion are to obtain the control of a processing stage in a forward vertical combination and to procure a source of supply of raw materials in a backward vertical combination—that is, to establish a type of economies of scale. Financial reasons include tax considerations, personal objectives of the owners, and protection of income.

All external expansion programs are not successful. There are a number of pitfalls that can beset a firm following this form of expansion. Morale of the employees of the acquired or merged firm may be affected, key personnel may leave because of the combination, and there may be power struggles among executives. These are only a few of a wide range of problems that may accompany what looks promising in theory. Regardless of the type of firm or its position in the channel of distribution, the results of an external expansion program are expected to achieve, in whole or in part, the company's objectives for increasing or protecting its income.

## CHAPTER 9

Marketing Generic Drugs

MAX A. FERM*

A "drug" may be defined as a substance endowed with some action on living matter. This substance may have an established or nonproprietary or generic name, a chemical name, and one or more brand names. The American Medical Association (AMA) and the United States Pharmacopeia (USP) have established a combined nomenclature committee to meet with industry to provide a single and suitable established or nonproprietary or generic name for each drug in general use. The term "United States Adopted Name" or "USAN" is used to designate the established name.[1] Although the finite definition of "generic" means a class of substances having the same biologic properties, "generic" has customarily been used as a synonym for established or nonproprietary names.

Proprietaries are products that have a name of distinctive mark provided by the proprietor, who is usually the manufacturer. If the name or mark is registered as a registered trademark, then the product is trademarked or is a trademarked proprietary. The term "brand name" identifies the product of a seller, may be the trademark designation, and distinguishes the product from its competitors. When an established name is preceded or followed by the name of the manufacturer or distributor, however, the name is considered to be a brand name—e.g., Bayer Aspirin Tablets.

Health professionals now use the word "proprietary" for brand or trademark names and "nonproprietary" for generic or established names. The nonproprietary or generic name, rather than either the proprietary or chemical name, is used because scientific nomenclature is unwieldy, scientific names are meaningless

*The material on pages 190 to 198 was written by Dr. Edward Stempel and appeared as Drug-Product-Selection and Generic Products, *Drug Store News Continuing Education Program*, 3:1, 1981. It is adapted here by permission of the author and publisher.

to those who do not have expertise in a specific field, and the use of generic names also reduces the risk of having a proprietary name become distinctive of a particular product.

History of the Generic Market

The practice of assigning brand names is not new, as evidenced by the first recorded brand name, Epsom Salts, for magnesium sulfate in 1698 in England.[1] In the seventeenth and eighteenth centuries, brand-name medicines were generally called patent medicines, which were usually mixtures of several substances whose chemical composition was either unknown to the manufacturer or was a closely guarded secret.

The United States patent law was enacted in 1790 and has remained unchanged, even though efforts were made by Senator Kefauver to change the law in the early 1960s. The life of a patent is 17 years from the date of issue; trademarks, however, which are protected by the Lanham Trademark Act, are unlimited as to their life span.[1]

During the early years of the patent law, the market was flooded with medicines of questionable value under protected patent names or proprietary names used as trademarks. Many of these medicines were more poisonous than therapeutic. Therefore, such rampant quackery led to a decline in their use, and drugs of botanic origin gained importance.[1]

Generic Era: 1850–1920

During the late nineteenth and early twentieth centuries, pharmaceuticals were prescribed mostly by their generic names, those that were most commonly used were "galenicals," and product differentiation was achieved by manufacturers on the basis of advertising the quality of products and by ethical distribution practices. The USP VII (of 1908) did not permit the inclusion of monographs for substances that could only be produced by a patented process or protected by proprietary rights. Stated in another fashion, the USP of that time was opposed to proprietary products. However, this was revised in 1926, and was stated as policy in the USP X.[1]

Brand Era: 1921–1960

The so-called miracle drugs, such as the sulfonamides, the penicillins, and chloramphenicol, were discovered and then sheltered under the protective roof of patents to provide profit potential. The first broad-spectrum antibiotic to be marketed was Aureo-mycin (American Cyanamid-Lederle Laboratories), launched in 1948 as a brand-name product. It had no chemical name because none was assigned, and it could only be prescribed by its brand name. Only the manufacturer to whom the discoverer assigned the patent could legally produce the drug in this country unless others were licensed by the manufacturer who owned the patent. Thus, brand names became useful as a marketing tool.

In the decade 1950 to 1960, the development and marketing of drugs by brand names reached unprecedented proportions. Some of these drugs were diuretics, hormones, antihypertensives, non-narcotic analgesics, antibiotics, and tranquilizers. Because the investment of millions of dollars in research for new and better drugs was a risky prospect, manufacturers charged high prices to recover their invested capital and to counteract the obsolescence of their existing products.[1]

Increased Acceptance of Generics: 1961 to Present

In December, 1959, Senator Kefauver's much publicized hear-ings on monopoly in the drug industry began. Subsequently, Sena-tor Nelson's hearings suggested that generic drugs cost less than their brand-name counterparts. In 1966, the Task Force on Pre-scription Drugs recommended generic prescribing of drugs, and projected a wholesale cost savings of $41 million if 63 products were prescribed exclusively by generic names.[1] According to Dr. P. McKercher, Associate Professor of Pharmacy at Wayne State University in Detroit, Michigan residents saved approximately $6 million because of the state's drug product selection law. Savings accruing to other states vary according to the unique terms writ-ten into their drug product selection laws.

Generic Laws

During the years of the Brand Era, physicians became accus-tomed to prescribing trademarked products by brand name be-cause of the massive and successful promotional marketing pro-grams of pharmaceutical manufacturers. Manufacturers became concerned that prescriptions for their trademarked products might be filled with a substitute product, which is now popularly termed as the generic equivalent. In the 1950s the drug industry enjoyed much prestige, and there were some attempts at counter-feiting products. Through the impetus of national organizations, notably the American Pharmaceutical Association (APhA), phar-maceutical manufacturers went on record as supporting the en-actment of antisubstitution laws. By 1970 the APhA reversed its stand of favoring the repeal of antisubstitution laws because the justification for these laws was no longer valid, and pharmaceutical education was training pharmacists as the best health practitioners for selecting the brand of drug from among multisource products. Furthermore, the continued expiration of the many drug patents was coupled with the entry of large brand-name-oriented manufacturers into the "branded generics" line—nonproprietary or generic products manufactured and distributed by these large brand-name-oriented manufacturers. All these factors helped repeal antisubstitution laws and grant pharmacists responsibility for drug product selection.[2]

Manufacturer's Name on Label

It is a popular misconception that brand-name drugs are produced by large, well-known firms while generics are made by small companies. Both types of firms can market either or both brands and generics, and can supply the other with bulk materials and final dosage forms. As an example of the complexities of drug marketing, ampicillin is a widely used antibiotic available under 224 product labels and produced by only 24 formulators, whereas 219 conjugated estrogen products are produced by 45 manufacturers.[3]

Many manufacturer-distributors who strongly promote the brand-name concept are reluctant to have the name of the actual manufacturer on the drug product label because such manufacturer-distributors sell to repackagers and other distributors for sale under the name of the latter, and a sizable proportion of their drugs are actually manufactured in outside facilities by other companies. As indicated by Fink, the reputation of the manufacturer is one of the criteria that the pharmacist can utilize in his efforts to participate in drug product selection.[4] It is therefore surprising that drug laws have not required that the name of the manufacturer appear on the label. This requirement will change in time. For example, a section of the California Administrative Code requires that the name and place of business of the manufacturer appear in the labeling of any product manufactured after June 1, 1974. Furthermore, the Federal Register of October 3, 1978 (*43*:45614–45619) proposed requirements for designating the manufacturer's name on a drug's label or a drug product's label.

Drug Product Selection

Since 1972 many states have repealed existing antisubstitution laws by providing drug product selection legislation. These state laws often contain the elements listed on page 194.

- A formulary or drug list.
- A requirement of a two-line R_x form—substitution permissible or dispense as written.
- A requirement to advise the physician of substitution.
- The requirement of keeping records.
- A section exempting physicians from liability.
- A requirement of prior patient consent.
- A requirement of passing on a portion of the savings to the patient.

As of January, 1982, 49 states and the District of Columbia had enacted some form of drug product selection legislation.

In early 1979 the publication of a Model Drug Product Selection Law developed by the Federal Trade Commission (FTC), attempted to improve the piecemeal revisions of states' substitution laws. Some requirements of the model law are that (1) physicians write "medically necessary" on prescriptions of brand-name products when drug product selection is not permissible, (2) pharmacists are permitted to pass on a portion of the cost savings to the consumer (or to obtain an additional fee for dispensing drug product equivalents and counseling the patient), and (3) the patient must be informed that the pharmacist has selected a lower cost, equivalent drug product, and the patient has the right to refuse the selected product.

Lawler has indicated that the FTC devoted 2 years and close to $2 million to design a model substitution law, and he believes it to be a viable alternative to New York's existing law.[5] Some states have already adopted the Model Drug Product Selection Law.

Advent of Branded Generics

A pharmaceutical company registers numerous drug products with trademarked names to differentiate its products from similar competitive products. This extends some economic benefit beyond the patent life of a product. In addition, many pharmaceutical companies promote products with nonproprietary names as well as those with names of the manufacturers marketing them. Because they are multisource products, such products are known as branded generics.

Large pharmaceutical manufacturers have been reluctant to abandon or change their traditional marketing pattern, which was based on promotional efforts to encourage physicians to write for products on a brand-name basis. Nevertheless, manufacturers have prepared themselves for drug product selection by establishing an additional market of branded generics. It seems inevitable that the American competitive system of pricing of equivalent products will contribute to financial savings beneficial to patients as well as to third-party providers. Such savings result when pharmacists are able to take advantage of (1) cost savings obtainable through purchases of equivalent, multisource drug products and (2) inventory savings obtainable by stocking one or two rather than several products.[6]

Factors Influencing Pharmacist's Selection

Fink has reviewed pharmacists' view of generics, and has indicated the factors desired of manufacturers and used by pharmacists in drug product selection (Table 9-1).[4] Pharmacists seek a total package of services when evaluating sources of supply in addition to specific product information data such as dissolving properties and bioavailability. Fink prudently stated, "What good does it do for a pharmacist to select a particular brand of product to use when he has the option of drug product selection if he can only order it directly from the manufacturer or distributor and then wait for uncertain delivery?"[4]

A study in November 1979 indicated the criteria for pharmacists' selection of manufacturers in purchasing generic drugs on a scale of 1 to 10, with 10 being the most important.[7] These factors, in order of rating and decreasing importance to pharmacists, are as follows: (1) liability program (8.3); (2) bioavailability-information data (7.7); (3) availability of a full line of generics (7.6);

TABLE 9-1. *Factors Desired of Manufacturers by Pharmacists*

Bioavailability information	Organoleptic characteristics
Cost	Sales policies
Distribution policies	Professional involvement
Dosage data	Product quality
Indications of safety and effectiveness	Manufacturer's reputation
Manufacturing procedures	Return goods policies
Nature of the drug	Shipping and billing procedures

(4) well-known company (7.5); (5) availability from wholesalers (7.0); (6) price (6.2); (7) face-to-face contact with service representatives (5.3); and (8) minimum order requirements (4.8).

In summary, pharmacists desire efficacious products as well as suppliers' services.

Growth of Generic Prescribing and Substitution

Dibble indicated in 1979 that there are five factors operating to increase the share of the generic prescription drug market: (1) fewer new products; (2) expiration of patents; (3) generic prescribing; (4) maximum allowable cost (MAC) on government-paid prescriptions; and (5) drug-product selection.[8] Furthermore, 47% of new prescriptions are for single source products, leaving 53% for multiple source products. Of these 53% prescriptions, 43% specify brand names and are eligible for substitution under drug product selection laws, but only about 6% of the (43%) brand-name prescriptions for multiple source drugs are substituted.

Two audits funded by the Department of Health, Education and Welfare indicated that substitution was practiced in 1.5 to 2% of new prescriptions in Michigan and Florida in late 1977.[8] Although this seems low, it must be emphasized that this is about 2% (or 18 million prescriptions) of all new prescriptions. Furthermore, substitution increased 25% nationally in 1978, equivalent to about 4.5 million more prescriptions.[8] Indeed, it is estimated that the number of substituted new prescriptions reached 35 million in 1981.

Variations in laws among states result in different percentages of prescriptions substituted. In Michigan, under "permissive" drug product selection, one report that measured physicians' prescribing habits, but not pharmacists' dispensing practices, indicated that Michigan pharmacists substituted about 1.5% of prescriptions after having a drug product selection law for 1 year.[9] In New York, where substitution is mandatory if the physician checks the "substitution permissible" line, it was reported that prescriptions authorizing substitution declined from 25 to 22.5% during the first 10 months of the law.[10] Seven states account for two thirds of all product substitutions: California, Pennsylvania, New York, New Jersey, Michigan, Florida, and Ohio.[11]

The National Prescription Audit (NPA) of 1979 indicated that, of the total number of new prescriptions, the number of new generically written prescriptions has increased each year from a 6.4% share in 1966 to a 14.1% share in 1979.[12] The share of new and refill prescriptions written generically increased from 1977 to

1979, from about 8.7% of total prescriptions in 1977 to 12.1% in 1979, representing 165 million new and refill generically written prescriptions in 1979.

The NPA audit also indicated that about 80% of prescriptions with the source specified did not prohibit substitution, yet about 17% of the prescriptions that did have source specified were dispensed legally with a substitute product. This corroborates other reports that indicate pharmacists substitute in about 20% of total prescriptions that permit substitution—that is, substitution is permitted for 1 out of 10 prescriptions. Furthermore, the ratio of actual to potential substitution would be more prevalent in a state with a mandatory substitution law than in one in which the law is more permissive, or the pharmacist actually practices drug product selection.[13]

A 1979 report indicated that in 10 states that require mandatory substitution unless physicians indicate otherwise, 46% of pharmacists surveyed indicated that 30% of all prescriptions were designated "dispense as written" (curtailing substitution), whereas 20% of those surveyed indicated that about 70% of all their prescriptions bore the dispense as written (DAW) instructions.[7]

Basis for Equivalency

It is well known that bioavailability data are needed to evaluate drug products comparatively. Bioavailability is the rate and extent of a drug's release from a dosage form and its availability for absorption in the patient's blood.

Formulation factors affect the rate and extent of absorption from a dosage form. There are tests available that can provide a measure of drug release, such as disintegration tests, and there the more reliable dissolution tests for orally administered products. Drug concentrations in blood serum are used to measure absorption of a product at certain times after administration of a specific drug of the same strength from the same dosage forms that is administered by the same route in a cross-over type of study. Each subject, of a specific sex, weight, and ethnic origin, receives each product once to compensate for any unusual absorption pattern in a particular subject. These drug concentrations are then plotted as a standard point-to-point concentration against time, commonly referred to as a curve—although it may not resemble a true curve. The resultant curve indicates the time of onset, the intensity of action, and the duration of effectiveness. The area under the curve is referred to as the bioavailability profile. A series of curves of the same drug in a particular dosage form from different manufacturers is known as the bioequivalency profile.

These profiles are the basis for product interchangeability lists. These lists indicate those multiple source drug products (a drug supplied by different manufacturers) with dosage forms that have the least likelihood of exhibiting significant bioavailability differences; that is, their bioavailability profiles or curves are similar.

The Food and Drug Administration (FDA) Approved Drug Product List, published in 1979, included over 5000 prescription drug products approved by the FDA for marketing in the United States.[14] Of these, 3300 were multisource or available from more than one manufacturer, and 2400 of those were evaluated as being therapeutically equivalent. Of the 200 most frequently prescribed products in the United States, 83 were multisource, and 58 (about 70%) of these were therapeutically equivalent.[15] This FDA drug list of 5000 products was evaluated, and it was found that there were 261 multiple source products, with 134 (are about 52%) of these being eligible for substitution.[15]

Generic Market: 1982

Resolution of the Lannett Issue

In the early 1970s, the FDA issued regulations and procedures establishing an approval system for marketing the generic equivalent of drugs with new drug applications (NDAs) issued prior to 1962 and rated "effective" by the Drug Efficacy Study/Implementation (DESI) Committee. Depending upon the characteristics of the generic drug evaluated, bioequivalency requirements included an evaluation of the manufacturing facility, manufacturing procedure, dissolution studies, and clinical bioavailability. This established the mechanism for issuing an abbreviated new drug application (ANDA), and established the foundation for drugs produced by small, emerging generic companies.

By the late 1970s, most of the important products approved prior to 1962 whose patents had expired were available as multisource products. At the same time patents had expired for many high volume products marketed after 1962. This presented an opportunity and a major problem to generic suppliers. They proceeded to develop these products on the basis that such products already rated safe and effective would require no more development expenses than those previously incurred for approval of pre-1962 drugs. The indications were clear, but the problem was that federal regulations did not yet include post-1962 drugs in the ANDA process and the only mechanism left required a full protocol for NDAs, including expensive and time-consuming clinical trials.

A number of generic manufacturers, led by the Lannett Company, took the position that the intent of the existing regulations covering the issuance of ANDAs was sufficient justification for marketing products evaluated as safe and effective. In line with this premise they followed the established protocols and submitted applications. In the absence of an established procedure, the FDA could not offer an evaluation for approval.

Many of these products were subsequently marketed without FDA approval, and became known as "Lannett products." Within a short period of time the FDA, operating within its mandate and prompted by brand-name companies attempting to protect their franchises, exercised their right to seize unapproved drugs. This led to court cases that remained unresolved for a number of years. Early in 1981, at approximately the same time that the FDA promulgated a new policy (later known as the "paper NDA") for a shortened approval process, the courts ruled in favor of the FDA and so ended the Lannett issue.

The influence of brand-name companies in attempting to prevent the proliferation of shortened or abbreviated NDAs became apparent early in 1981 when the Upjohn Company took a strong opposing position against the issuance of FDA approval for the Boots Company submission of ibuprofen. Ibuprofen, known in this country as Motrin, is an original Boots compound licensed to Upjohn at a time when Boots (a British company) did not have any marketing capability in the United States.

Boots later purchased Rucker Laboratories, a Shreveport-based regional pharmaceutical company. Boots had already developed a wealth of product data on ibuprofen through their efforts in marketing the product in other parts of the world. However, Upjohn produced its own United States data for approval in this country. When Boots filed its application here, Upjohn formally objected on the basis that a full NDA was required and, as such, Boots would have to cross-reference its confidential data, which Upjohn was unwilling to provide. Ultimately Boots did get approval, but this incident clearly shows how important the issue of multiple source is to the brand-name companies.

Size, Shape, and Color Objection

Once realizing that the availability of a shortened NDA was inevitable, the brand-name companies embarked upon a new approach to inhibit the progress of generics. The issue became "product dress" or "look-alike". Clearly, imitation without notification to the user or buyer does infringe upon the rights of the original product and the company offering the product. Under usual circumstances, the test for infringement for packaged goods is to examine the outer package and label and, if the probability exists that the purchaser would mistake a copy for the original, then the manufacturer or owner of the original product would be justified in demanding removal of the copy product and receiving an award for damages. In the case of prescription drugs, however, there are in fact two buyers—the pharmacist who dispenses the product from the original package and the consumer who purchases the drug when it has been repackaged. Therefore, the manufacturer or supplier of the original drug contends that not only should the original package be distinctly different, but also the dosage form (tablet, capsule, liquid) should be distinctly different.

Generic manufacturers have argued that the possibility for mistaking the source of the drug is remote. Pharmacists know the source of the drug by its supplier and by the distinctive label on the bottle. Patients, by law, must be advised that a generic has been substituted, and in many instances the tablet is imprinted with the manufacturer's or distributor's logo and National Drug Code (NDC) number.

In spite of this, several brand-name manufacturers have been successful in having the courts (particularly in New Jersey, stronghold for brand-name manufacturers) issue restraining orders to generic companies to cease manufacturing look-alikes. Generic manufacturers have countered by arguing that look-alikes are important to the dispenser for recognizing the drug quickly. In the summer of 1982, the United States Supreme Court decided in favor of the generic manufacturers and ruled that the marketing of look-alikes does *not* constitute an infringement of the Lanham Act.

Generic Marketers

By any standards the generic pharmaceutical industry may be categorized as a cottage industry. Although it has received support in the form of promotion by the federal government, state governments, and various consumer advocate groups, it has not materially affected the growth and viability of brand-name manufacturers to the extent that no brand-name manufacturer has succumbed to the invasion of generics. The reasons may be the following:

1. Brand loyalty, particularly among physicians, is more important than cost savings.
2. Generic profit margins are not in sufficient excess to be worth promoting to the physicians.

3. No brand-name manufacturer represents a strong majority of the market.

4. There is an underlying concern that generics lack the quality of the brands.

Generic companies may be categorized as manufacturers, distributors, or manufacturers/distributors. A typical manufacturer of generic drugs produces between 20 and 40 different products, principally for generic distributors. The company will have a limited marketing organization directed toward the sale of its products to large purchasers such as distributors, the federal government, chain drug stores, and hospitals. Some also engage in selling to foreign government markets, particularly in less developed countries in which a generic industry has yet to develop. Because of limited physical capability, a highly competitive market, and broad product lines these manufacturers cannot afford to maintain large inventories. They must therefore be capable of switching their physical resources quickly to meet market demands. Generally, products are produced with the manufacturer's label, but it is not uncommon to find the distributor's label affixed for those who are capable of buying in larger quantities. In essence, they are private-labeling to a segment of their market, and it is not unusual to find a product manufactured by one company bearing a number of different labels. These are easy for the pharmacist to detect as a result of state laws requiring the manufacturer's name on the label. Prior to the institution of such laws, it could only be determined that the distributor was not the manufacturer by noting on the label the words "distributed by" or "manufactured for."

Distributors range in size from comparatively small operations, producing $200,000 to $1 million gross volume and serving a city or county, to companies with sales in excess of $40 million serving the country from one large regional center or from several distribution warehouses strategically located in various parts of the country. The larger companies can also be distinguished by the package, which usually includes the label of the distributor.

It is difficult if not impossible to count the number of generic distributors because many are small and unidentifiable. Moreover, the mortality rate of small- to medium-sized companies is high, a point worthy of further discussion.

Because price is the dominant factor for generic companies, the gross margins are small. A typical distributor margin may range from 20 to 30% (brands may range from 60 to 90%). All operating expenses must be deducted from this, including overhead, selling, distribution and, perhaps most important, inventory. Generic distributors are, in effect, specialty wholesalers who are expected to offer a full range of products in all dosage strengths and economical package sizes. As such they probably handle an inventory of 1000 or more different packages. The cost of maintaining a large inventory is extremely high in relation to the gross profit, and often requires supplemental financing. In the late 1970s, when interest rates reached into the double digits, this problem became evident by the number of failures due to undercapitalization. They were forced into a classic "Catch-22" situation whereby optimizing inventory turnover by lowering inventory led to frequent out of stock or back order situations. This, in turn, forced the retailers to switch their sources of supply. The companies lost business and eventually failed. The theory of greater turnover is practical and may be realized if the manufacturer's supply can be controlled. As previously noted, this would be impossible, because most manufacturers produced products on demand without attempting to build inventories of their own.

Another problem encountered is the time difference between prompt payment to manufacturers and accounts receivable. Retail pharmacies are attuned to payment for goods in a multisource marketplace that may range from 45 to 60 days or even more. They, too, have the problem of a large inventory but can obtain credit from "hungry" distributors whereby they may delay payment to one or more distributors while buying from an alternate source. In the meantime, with fewer manufacturers distributing the same products, the distributor is forced into prompt payment or else loses a principal source of supply. A receivable over 120 days plus financing at 20% or more could destroy the distributor's net profit. Inflation increases the demand for lower cost products, increases the competition, lowers the selling price, and increases the cost of doing business—another "Catch-22". But companies do survive and, in some cases, thrive. The answer appears to be a combination of rapid growth, adequate capitalization, tight control of expenses, and a degree of business, particularly financial, sophistication not commonly found in a "me-too" industry comprised of small companies.

The advantage of controlling manufacturing while engaging in broad market distribution appears obvious. Thus this combination offers the greatest potential for market penetration and success. Interestingly, when manufacturers venture into broad retail distribution, they do so on a limited basis with modest or no gain. However, when distributors acquire manufacturing, the combination appears to meet with greater success. It can be hypothesized that marketing acumen is more important than technological capability, and that a large customer base is more easily maximized by a dependable source of products than is a source of products attempting to find new outlets. On this basis, it makes sense that major brand-name manufacturers who enter the generic marketplace rely upon their own distribution resource and buy most of their generics from manufacturers rather than utilizing their own manufacturing facility.

Generic Promotion

Independents

Irrespective of the specific market segment, generic promotion has one major theme—*price.* For the most part, it is assumed that all products are created equal under the laws of the FDA. Therefore there is considerable shopping for price, which leads to multiple suppliers and relatively little loyalty on the part of the buyer. This further promotes intense competition and the necessity to reach the customer frequently.

Frequent contacts with the customer to get what is desired into the "Want Book" is the guiding light of full line wholesalers who first employed outside field representatives and later switched to the convenience of the telephone. It appears obvious that the wholesalers can control the generic market. Their initial interest was low, however, owing to their need for better margins. They viewed the generic drugs as a trade-off (since they already carried the brands) for lower margins. More recently, as generics have developed a mainstay business, wholesalers have re-entered the market on the basis that it is better to have some profit than none at all.

Generic suppliers, particularly small companies, similarly approach the market with personal selling. The larger, more established companies found that on a local basis personal selling was affordable, but increasing their field staff to widen their coverage became risky. The more conservative and cost-efficient approach of mail order was substituted until such time when an area generated sufficient business to warrant the commission salesperson. More aggressive suppliers found that with the advent of WATS lines (wide area telephone service) they could reach distant customers quickly and be cost-efficient. This then became the standard operation for marketing to the independent retailer.

Mail has remained a valuable tool for reaching those who would not readily listen to a "price pitch," such as dispensing physicians, dentists, veterinarians, and other licensed professionals. As prices stablized, customers began to seek other services. The larger companies who were successful in reaching the marketplace then supplemented the telephone and mail with commission salespeople who, like wholesalers, could provide personalized in-store service to check inventories, handle returns, and generally keep the independent aware of the generic market.

Chains

Multistore units with central buying were not receptive to either mail or telephone as a promotional medium. By virtue of their mode of operation, they were responsive to personal selling, which remains the promotional medium of choice. The traditional supplier, however, found little success in chains because the chain preferred to purchase from a manufacturer who could offer the lowest prices and maintain a consistency of supply. Chains quickly recognized the opportunity in generics and subsequently used these cost-saving products as a promotional tool to win customers for their stores. They also recognized that, although there was an additional cost involved in a double inventory, it was more than offset by their increased customer base and the increased return on investment provided by generics.

Promotional Themes

First price, then prompt delivery with personalized service, then what? Obviously, competition fosters differences. Another promotional ingredient that became essential as a result of the Lannett issue was reliability. The market was receptive to the high-volume Lannett products. However, when the FDA began to take action against these products, it proved embarrassing and uncomfortable for a pharmacy to have the product one day and the next day be out of it. This was particularly true for chains whose buyers were hard-pressed to maintain consistency of products and prices. As a result, the supplier who could assure the buyer that all generics were approved found favor in the chains and developed a reliability profile that became more meaningful when the Lannett issue was resolved in early 1981.

Reliability is coupled with another promotional theme—liability insurance. Retailers have become more aware of the proliferation of malpractice suits affecting physicians. Brand-name companies highlighted this issue, although there was little probability that pharmacists would be similarly effective when they were given the power of drug product selection. The dispensing of questionable Lannett products, and the fears of loss entailed in malpractice, however, made it mandatory for generic suppliers to back their products with substantial indemnification via liability insurance. Amounts being promoted ranged from anywhere between $5 and $25 million.

Almost every supplier has now met the requirements of price, delivery, reliability, and liability protection. It was necessary in order to survive. *New* differences are now being created; one in particular is the return goods policy. Generic suppliers traditionally provide free delivery and no-charge pickup on returns. However, because there appears to be a predominance of price orientation, the retailer can return a product in inventory purchased at a higher price for a comparable one currently being featured at a lower price, and do this at no cost. For this reason most return goods policies do not allow for return after 60 days from date of purchase. A new promotional position offering a more liberalized extended term for the return of merchandise is now appearing.

Finally, there appears to be a "prove it" attitude developing from some segments of pharmacy. The first major liability case against a pharmacist appeared in the national press during the summer of 1981. It was alleged that a patient died as a result of receiving an unapproved critical generic drug. This case has fostered a prompt response from generic suppliers that not only do all drugs meet federal and state requirements for marketing but also that, when required, the results of bioavailability studies are readily available to demonstrate comparability. In essence the challenge has become a promotional theme.

References

1. Gumbhir, A. K., and Rodowskas, C. A., Jr.: The Development of the Contemporary Generic-Brand Drug Controversy, Presented at American Institute of the History of Pharmacy, San Francisco, March 31, 1971, pp. 2–6.
2. Anonymous: DPS Now Extends to 46 States and D.C., *American Pharmaceutical Association Weekly, 18*:138, 1979.
3. Hecht, A.: Generic Drugs: How Good Are They? *FDA Consumer, 12*:18, 1978.
4. Fink, J. L., III: Marketing in a Generic Environment: A Pharmacist's Viewpoint, *Medicine Marketing and Media, 12*:42, 1979.
5. Lawler, B.: PSSNY Asks Regents Support for New Generic Law, *New York State Pharmacists, 54* (No. 10):8, 1979.
6. Colaizzi, J. L.: Drug Product Selection, in Perspectives of Medicine in Society, edited by A. I. Wertheimer and P. J. Bush, Hamilton, IL: Drug Intelligence Publications, 1977, p. 117.
7. 45% of MD Scripts Carry DAW Instructions, *Drug Store News, 1*:43, 1979.
8. Dibble, F. N.: Marketing in a Generic Environment, *Medical Marketing and Media, 14*:12, 1979.
9. Michigan Substitution Law Has Had Virtually No Effect on R$_x$ Buying Patterns, *Green Sheet, 25* (Nos. 51, 52):2, 1976.
10. NY Generic Substitution Declined From 25% to 22.5% in First 10 Months, *Green Sheet 22* (No. 12):2, 1979.
11. Syndicated Studies by Market Measures.
12. Top Twenty Generic Products, *Drug Store News, 2*:22, 1980.
13. Anonymous: R.Ph.'s Pass Up Most Opportunities to Substitute, A.D. Survey Discloses, *American Druggist, 178*:7, 1978.
14. FDA Drug List: Key to Generic Substitution, *FDA Consumer, 13*:15, 1979.
15. Only 134 (14%) of the 971 Drugs on FDA's Therapeutically Equivalent Drug List, *Green Sheet, 28* (No. 16):4, 1979.

## CHAPTER 10

Nonprescription Drugs

ALAN W. MERCILL

Background: An Industry's Roots

More often than not, authors of reports on nonprescription medicines begin their discussions by examining the so-called "patent medicine era," which reached its zenith (or nadir, depending on one's point of view) exactly 100 years ago, in the 1880s. Unfortunately, a common mistake of many of these writers is their assumption that the promotional techniques of the medicine purveyors were unique or somehow atypical. Instead, the use of flowery, outrageous prose to hawk medicinal products was generally reflective of the nation's general level of culture and taste as it then existed. Extravagant claims, including references to secret formulas, were commonplace in connection with selling packaged goods of many types, such as foods, beverages, cosmetics, household gadgets, and articles of clothing. The principle of *caveat emptor* (let the buyer beware) also extended to such fields as publishing, real estate promotion, land development, and the practices of "regular" medicine and pharmacy.

With respect to medicine and pharmacy, professional standards were abominably low in the late 1800s, and were frequently nonexistent west of the Mississippi River. It was the day of squabbling systems of medical philosophy. This was often confusing to the patient, who had to choose between such theories as "pepper and steam," "homeopathic," "eclectic," "botanic," "bleeding," and the use of calomel. No wonder the public often turned to home remedies for minor ailments, rather than consulting a doctor or pharmacist. Quackery abounded in all the health professions in the 1800s and, contrary to some prevailing opinion, was not confined to those who foisted "Wahoo Bitters" and similar products on an unsuspecting public.[1]

It would be a mistake today to assume that nonprescription medicines that carry the same names as they did in the last century also contain the same ingredients or have the same labeling. The fact that a few trade names are still in current use also should not be viewed as a commentary upon the social responsibility or moral stature of those who currently own trademarks that may have a colorful past. The present formulations have undergone many transformations and bear little or no relationship to the esoteric products that preceded them.

In fact, the term "patent medicine" is a misnomer, although it is deeply rooted in history. Early kings of England for centuries granted "patents of royal favor" to the bootmakers, tailors, and mediciners who served the Royal Family. The early American colonists, most of whom were loyal Englishmen, prized the medicines that bore the token of royal favor—the "patents." The term is now an American anachronism and has yielded to other terms, such as "nonprescription" or "over-the-counter" medicines (OTC).

What are Nonprescription Medicines?

Nonprescription medicines are those that are lawfully sold over the counter for the public to use in self-medication without professional supervision on the basis of labeling that provides adequate directions for proper use. Self-medication is considered in this chapter to indicate what is taken as a response to minor illness and injury. However, the term is also used to describe preventive health strategy—for example, the consumption of vitamins, the use of fluoridated toothpastes and rinses to prevent dental caries, and the use of sun screens to protect against reactions to intense sunlight.

The federal Food, Drug, and Cosmetic Act of 1938, the principal law regulating medicinal ingredients, separates drugs into two classes and sets up important distinctions and requirements for each. One class consists of nonprescription medicines, which are those drugs that are safe and are labeled for use without supervision of a physician or other professional. In the absence of professional advice, it is the consumer who selects a product, based on the nature of his symptoms. He relies on his general knowledge, including his personal experience with it and other products, and especially on the information supplied to him in labeling. Nonprescription medicines may be purchased in various retail outlets, including pharmacies, grocery and variety stores, and other types of convenience stores.

By contrast, prescription drugs are those that, because of their "potentiality for harmful effect," the "method of their use," or the "collateral measures" required, are *not safe for self-medication* and, accordingly, must be dispensed *only* under supervision of a prescribing physician or dentist. These products must bear the prescription legend and are restricted to sale in pharmacies only.

In sum, under federal law, habit-forming and potentially harmful drugs are limited to prescription sale, whereas drug products for use in self-medication are generally available and are labeled so that they may be used by the general public. The underlying rationale is that if a drug is safe for lay use on the basis of its labeling alone, it must be available over the counter.

Some nonprescription drugs are promoted to the general public and are often called proprietary medicines. Others are promoted only to those in health professions and are frequently called "ethical OTCs." The reasons for the differences in distribution are based solely upon manufacturers' marketing strategies. According to federal law, all nonprescription drugs are regulated in the same way. The concept of limiting OTCs only to pharmacy distribution by law or regulation—for example, the so-called "third class of drugs"—is not recognized in the federal Food, Drug, and Cosmetic Act.

Opponents of the third class believe that restriction of OTC drug products to pharmacies would be anticompetitive without any public benefit. Recent official statements from two government agencies share this view:

1. In 1974 the Department of Justice stated in a letter to the FDA that: "Preventing supermarkets and general merchandising stores from selling [nonprescription medicines] products would substantially lessen competition, and severely inconvenience the consumer by limiting access to these drugs. A most likely result of this market limitation would be an increase in the price the consumer must pay."[2]

2. FDA Commissioner Alexander M. Schmidt's reply to the Justice Department included the following sentence: "Restricting the sale of some or all [nonprescription] drugs only to pharmacies would decrease the number of outlets where the consumer could purchase [nonprescription] products, limit the competition, and raise some [nonprescription] drug prices, with no attendant public benefit."[3]

Food and Drug Administration's OTC Review

Background

On January 4, 1972 the Food and Drug Administration (FDA) embarked on a major program to ensure the safety, effectiveness, and adequate labeling of all nonprescription drugs and drug products on the domestic market. At the time FDA had no idea of the extent of the problem because the agency has little tangible information concerning the number of ingredients and products to be evaluated. In announcing the review, then FDA Commissioner Charles C. Edwards predicted that it would cover about 200 active ingredients contained in between 100,000 and 500,000 marketed products. As a result of manufacturers' submissions of data and information, as well as product reports filed pursuant to the Drug Listing Act, the FDA has now concluded that approximately 1100 active ingredients are contained in about 350,000 marketed OTC products.

It is fair and accurate to say that no other program in the FDA's 75-year history has been more demanding in its scientific, organizational, and legal requirements. One industry spokesman has called the OTC review a "giant bureaucratic sponge"—soaking up industry's energies, funds, and talents.[4] The same could also be said of agency time.

The review was the third and final major step undertaken by the FDA to implement the 1962 Kefauver-Harris amendments to the federal Food, Drug, and Cosmetic Act. The first step was a requirement that all new prescription drugs and over-the-counter drugs that were not generally recognized as safe (GRAS) and effective (GRAE) as defined in Section 505 of the Act must be shown to be effective for the purposes claimed for them on the label before appearing on the market.

The second step, which began in May, 1966, was the National Academy of Sciences/National Research Council's drug efficacy study to review all new drugs introduced from 1938 to 1962 for which statutory proof of efficacy had not been required when the new drug application was approved. More than 4000 drug products were reviewed in the DESI study. Most were prescription drugs, but 422 OTCs were also included. As the FDA began to implement the DESI findings, the agency learned that more than a few of the OTC products studied were no longer being marketed. Because those that remained represented such a small proportion of over-the-counter drugs on the market, the FDA concluded that a separate review of OTCs was necessary.

Procedure

Primarily because of the sheer numbers of OTCs, the FDA established a review process whereby the ingredients in nonprescription drug products were evaluated on a category-by-category basis. Over 70 product categories arranged by pharmacologic groups have been identified.

The initial review, from 1972 through early 1981, was conducted by 17 advisory panels composed of physicians, pharmacologists, toxicologists, and pharmacists, as well as of nonvoting consumer and industry representatives. Each panel was charged with examining available data relevant to the safety and efficacy of the ingredients and combinations in the product categories assigned to it. Panels were also asked to review existing labeling and to provide FDA with a recommended monograph, which listed the ingredients, combinations, indications and directions for use, warnings, and other conditions relating to safety and effectiveness that the panel believed to be generally recognized as safe and effective (GRAS/GRAE).* Monograph conditions were classified as Category I.

In addition to providing a recommended monograph composed of GRAS/GRAE conditions, panels were also asked to provide a report on other ingredients, combinations, and label claims reviewed but excluded from the monograph because the Panel considered them as unsafe, ineffective, or improperly labeled. These conditions were classified as Category II.

Panel reports often included a third group of ingredients and claims that were reviewed but were not included in the monograph because of insufficient data. These conditions were classified as Category III. According to the agency's procedural regulations, a Category III condition is "one that is excluded from the monograph on the basis of the panel's determination that the available data are insufficient to classify a condition as Category I or Category II and for which further testing is required."[5] In subsequent regulations the FDA stated that "classification of an ingredient or claim in Category III represents a preliminary determination that general recognition of safety and effectiveness can be shown with further testing. Whether such general recognition exists depends on the demonstration of scientific facts by reliable studies."[6]

Following receipt of an advisory panel report covering a product category, the FDA publishes a proposed monograph or order in the *Federal Register*. These are in situations in which no Category 1 (GRAS/GRAE) conditions are identified by the panel. Time is provided for public comment. Later, after reviewing the panel report and additional information submitted during the comment period, the agency issues a tentative final order or monograph. Again, time is provided for filing of written objections or requests for an oral hearing before the commissioner.

After reviewing the objections and data addressed in the oral hearing, if one is held, the agency issues a final order or monograph. Following publication of this document in the *Federal Register*, interested parties have 30 days in which to file citizens' petitions to delay, amend, repeal, or implement the monograph. The

*See Section 201(p)(1), federal Food, Drug and Cosmetic Act; this sets forth criteria for "new" and "old" drug status.

agency's response to such petitions constitutes final FDA action on the matter, from which appeal would be made to the federal courts.

Status

As of 1981, the FDA had published final orders or monographs covering four categories of drug products: antacids, antiflatulents, daytime sedatives, and sweet spirits of niter. No monograph was provided for the latter two categories, and OTC products labeled as daytime sedatives or containing sweet spirits of niter have disappeared from the OTC marketplace.

The FDA maintains that final OTC review orders are substantive, having the force and effect of law. Industry members, however, have contended that the documents should be considered as interpretative.

The FDA has also published 5 tentative final monographs covering antimicrobial agents used in bar soaps and first-aid products, nighttime sleep aids, stimulants, emetics, and antiemetics. Proposed orders or monographs have been published for 32 product categories and final panel reports for 34 other categories are awaiting publication as proposals.

When the last monograph is published, perhaps in 1990 or even later, the FDA's review will have affected every marketed OTC drug product and in many instances monograph statements will be reflected in changed dosages, formulations, and labeling. It is also certain that the review will have an impact on products that entered the market after the review began, as well as those that will enter the market in the future. It was, and remains, the FDA's intention to establish that an OTC product can legally enter the market in only two ways: (1) Through the OTC review; or (2) Through the agency's new drug application process. In both cases, the agency maintains, some sort of formal approval system will be required. The law requires that safety and efficacy of all "new drugs" must be confirmed prior to marketing.* All other OTC drugs must be formulated and labeled in accordance with the provisions of an applicable monograph or face regulatory action.

Even though final monographs exist for only two product categories, and tentative final monographs cover just a few others, manufacturers often have voluntarily chosen to adapt formulations and labeling to conform with advisory panel recommendations or proposed monograph statements. It is expected that this trend will continue as additional OTC review monographs are published.

---

*As defined in Section 201(p) of the federal Food, Drug and Cosmetic Act, as amended, 21 CFR 321(p).

From Prescription to OTC Status Via the Review

Since the Food and Drug Administration began its review of marketed over-the-counter drug products, 22 ingredients and doses previously restricted only to prescription dispensing have been released for use in nonprescription drugs on the basis of recommendations by several of the advisory panels. Many persons, and not only nonprescription drug makers, believe that it is in the public interest to encourage the shift of safe and effective medications from prescription to OTC status in order to improve self-medication and to lower total health care costs. For example, FDA Commissioner Goyan told members of an agency panel on August 9, 1980 that FDA will have to create a committee to consider additional candidates for OTC use once the review process is concluded.

A number of important drugs and doses are included in the list released thus far for use in nonprescription medicines, such as hydrocortisone, oxymetazoline, 4 mg chlorpheniramine, 60 mg pseudoephedrine, three fluoride rinses, dyclonine hydrochloride (as an oral anesthetic), and pyrantel pamoate. These ingredients and new doses are now contained in nonprescription drug products. As the FDA continues to establish monographs for the different product categories in the future, it is possible that other drugs and doses currently restricted to prescription will enter the OTC market.

Pharmacy groups are as yet unclear as to what this will mean to consumers—and to themselves. A recent article speculated that the inclusion of substantial numbers of former prescription drugs in OTCs would lead to expanded opportunities for pharmacists to counsel patrons on the proper use of such products.[7] Pharmacy as a whole, however, may not be ready to perform this function. Although it is true that the average retail pharmacist is in the best and most accessible position to provide counseling when needed, the profession also has an "Achilles' heel": its overall failure thus far to project a strong OTC counseling profile adequately. The profession , though, is "making strides" to change that image, and a number of pharmacy schools have begun devoting a portion of their curriculum to OTC counseling.

Consequences

As a result of the submission of over 18,000 volumes of scientific information in support of OTC ingredients and products to the FDA or to its advisory panels, panel reports and agency monographs published through the OTC review have contributed to greater public acceptance and wider professional recognition of the value of nonprescription drug products in self-medication.

Consumers have already begun reaping the benefits in the form of new and improved products, new and better labeling, and renewed assurances that the nonprescription medicines they buy are safer and more effective than ever before.

It is clear that the twin tides of science and social change are raising self-medication with nonprescription medicines to new levels of sophistication. Companies are committing additional research funds to learn more, to discover new products, and to improve their older, established medications according to the standards of modern science. In addition, farsighted manufacturers are working aggressively to identify additional prescription medicines that can best and safely serve more people through availability over the counter.

Perhaps the most positive result to date of the FDA's OTC review is the development of a strong scientific base for nonprescription drugs. It is clear from this alone that the "patent medicine era" is gone forever, and that OTC monographs will constitute a government seal of approval on entire lines of OTC products. This can only result in more public and professional confidence in nonprescription drugs and drug products.

Role of Self-Medication

Self-medication is the American consumer's first line of defense in health care. Self-treatment with nonprescription OTC products fulfills a series of valuable and sometimes crucial functions for individuals, health care systems, and the national economy. For the individual, self-medication is a familiar, inexpensive, and convenient method of dealing with ordinary health problems that cause discomfort and interfere with the routines of daily living. For health professionals, including pharmacists, self-medication acts as a shield against a deluge of minor complaints by functioning as a selective screening mechanism through which minor and usually self-limiting disorders are sorted out from those requiring professional medical care.

The 1978 edition of the Commerce Department's *U.S. Industrial Outlook* underscored the public health significance of nonprescription medicines:

> Self-medication with proprietary (nonprescription) drugs is a significant factor in the U.S. health care scheme. Escalating costs of health care create a greater need for low cost self-medication than ever before. Seventy-five percent of all illnesses and injuries are initially treated through self-care and OTC medications. If only a small percentage of self-treatment was shifted to medical practitioners, the patient load would disrupt the U.S. health care system.[8]

In 1980, the economist Simon Rottenberg, of the University of Massachusetts, estimated that if only 2% of OTC drug consumers in the United States chose to visit primary care practitioners rather than using self-medication, the annual increase in patients' office visits would be 292 million, a 62% increase. In order to maintain the same quality of consultative care, Dr. Rottenberg calculated that the number of primary care practitioners would have to increase from the present 91,000 to 147,400. The increased cost to produce the additional 56,400 needed doctors would be enormous, perhaps as much as $10 billion.[9]

A study supported by the World Health Organization (WHO) concluded that "medicines are the most common health care resource in contemporary industrial societies," with nonprescription medicines being used an average of 21% more often than prescription drugs in three quarters of the study areas.[10] The WHO international study also confirmed the findings of numerous other investigations that indicated that in the United States and the United Kingdom only one quarter to one third of cases of illness or injury are seen by physicians.[11–13]

It was reported recently that "an astounding seven out of ten consumers self-medicate frequently with OTCs."[14] These data were based on a survey of 2000 family units taken in conjunction with national family opinion. "Self-treatment is especially high among young singles and couples (85%) and among members of large households (76%)," the study found.

Process of Self-Medication

The process of self-medication typically begins with an individual awareness of a symptom or sign of illness or injury, although not all perceived symptoms will be treated. Results of studies of morbidity patterns in the United States and the United Kingdom suggest that between 75 and 90% of the adult population will experience one or more symptoms of illness or injury in a 2- or 4-week period.[12, 15] Less than one third of these symptoms will be brought to the attention of a physician, however.[11]

These studies in the United States and the United Kingdom indicate that 2 basic courses are followed by the population majority not seeking professional medical aid. No therapeutic action will be taken by 7 to 16%, who prefer to tolerate their symptoms. Most people, however, will embark on self-treatment, usually with nonprescription medications. These findings were revealed in the Knapps' 30-week prospective study of 230 households in Columbus, Ohio.[13] In their study medicines were employed in 90.4% of all reported instances of illness or injury. Nonprescription medicines only were taken in 59.1%, prescription drugs only in 19.4%, and prescription and nonprescription together in 11.5%.[13]

In studies conducted in the United States and the United Kingdom, the common cold and other respiratory infections, headache, and gastrointestinal disorders accounted for well over half of all symptoms reported and self-treated (Tables 10-1 and 10-2).[12, 13]

Information Sources

Self-medication usually involves self-diagnosis of signs and symptoms, followed by self-administration of nonprescription medicines without professional supervision. As mentioned previously, a substantial portion of self-care occurs when a well-informed consumer recognizes his own symptoms, chooses a product that will alleviate those symptoms, and administers the medicine at the proper level for the correct duration of dosage. Further, if satisfactory relief is not obtained within an adequate period of time, the informed consumer knows when to discontinue self-medication and seek professional advice.

This scenario occurs in most cases involving self-medication, particularly in the developed countries in which consumers have a wide range of information sources on nonprescription medicines and self-medication, such as advertising, product labeling, advice of health professionals, including pharmacists, books, and the mass media. All these sources can play an important part in the education of consumers for proper self-care and self-medication. It should be stressed, however, that United States law recog-

TABLE 10-1. *Classification of Most Frequently Reported Illnesses or Injuries (Columbus, Ohio, 30 weeks, 1967–1968)*

RANK	CONDITION*	NUMBER	%	CUMULATIVE %
1	Common cold	903	26.7	26.7
2	Headache	534	15.8	42.5
3	Ear and/or throat problems	246	7.3	49.8
4	Gastrointestinal tract problem	241	7.1	56.9
5	Flu	139	4.1	61.0
6	Skin problem	111	3.3	64.3
7	Cuts	110	3.3	67.6
8	Aches and pains	98	2.9	70.5
9	Dental problem	69	2.0	72.5
10	Rectal problem (e.g., hemorrhoids)	67	2.0	74.5
11	Cough	59	1.7	76.2
12	Nerves	52	1.5	77.7

*Because these are self-reported conditions, classifications are not precise.

Source: Knapp, D. A., and Knapp, D. E.: Decision-Making and Self-Medication: Preliminary Findings, *American Journal of Hospital Pharmacy, 29*:1008, 1972, Table 3.

TABLE 10-2. *Symptoms Reported by Adults and Children, United Kingdom, 1969*

SYMPTOM	PERCENTAGE REPORTING SYMPTOMS IN A 2-WEEK PERIOD	
	ADULTS	CHILDREN
Sore throat	12	8
Breathlessness	15	1
Coughs, catarrh, or phlegm	32	17
Cold, flu, or running nose	18	18
Constipation	10	6
Diarrhea	3	3
Vomiting	3	6
Indigestion	18	1
Eye strain or other eye trouble	14	4
Ear trouble	7	3
Faintness or dizziness	8	1
Headaches	38	8
Pain or trouble passing water	2	—
Loss of appetite	6	4
Any problem being under- or overweight	10	—
Nerves, depression or irritability	21	3
Pains in the chest	5	—
Backache or pains in the back	21	1
Aches or pains in the joints, muscles, legs or arms	29	3
Palpitations or thumping heart	6	—
Piles	5	—
Sores or ulcers	4	2
Rashes, itches, or other skin troubles	13	12
Sleeplessness	16	4
Swollen ankles	8	1
Burns, bruises, cuts, or other accidents	9	16
Trouble with teeth or gums	7	12
Undue tiredness	16	2
Corns, bunions, or any trouble with feet	19	2
Women's complaints*	5	1
A temperature	2	3
Any other symptoms	6	3
Number of people (= 100%)	1410	519
Average number of symptoms reported	3.9	1.4

*Asked only of women and girls over 10 years old.

Source: Dunnell, K., and Cartwright, A.: *Medicine Takers, Prescribers and Hoarders*, London: Routledge & Kegan Paul, 1972, Table 4.

nizes that the nonprescription medicine label is the key informational element because its function is to provide all the information—both at the point of purchase and time of use—needed for safe and effective use of the product. OTC labeling must include the following information:

1. The name of the product.

2. The name and address of the manufacturer, packager, or distributor.

3. The net contents of the package.

4. The established name of all active ingredients and the quantity of certain other ingredients, whether active or not.

5. The name of any habit-forming drug contained in the preparation.

6. Cautions and warnings needed for the protection of the user.

7. Adequate directions for safe and effective use.

In 1978 the Opinion Research Corporation sought to determine the extent to which consumers recognize the importance of reading labels of nonprescription medicines, as well as their general understanding of the items of information found on labels.[16] Taking a national sample of 1025 adults, the survey organization found that 98% recognize that label instructions are important and should be read before taking an OTC drug. Eighty percent of the sample identified the categories of information found on labels correctly, and 90% indicated that they would read labels of products having a special tag or sign indicating a change in information.

Groups involved with nonprescription drugs, such as the Proprietary Association, the National Association of Retail Druggists, the American Pharmaceutical Association, and the FDA have all sponsored public education campaigns through mass communication media and other methods to encourage consumers to read labels thoroughly and to use products as directed. That these programs are having some success is suggested by the steady decline in accidental ingestions and hospital admissions involving improper use of OTCs.

The Market

In 1980 American consumers spent about $5.4 billion for nonprescription medicines, up about 11% from the preceding year. About 60% of this total, $3.1 billion, was generated through pharmacy outlets. Despite these totals, consumer expenditures for nonprescription medicines amounted only to 2.3% of the nation's total health expenditures. What does this mean in dollars? It means, for example, that each person spends about $20 annually for nonprescription medicines as compared to $37 for prescription drugs, $46 for dentists, $146 for physicians, over $300 for hospital care, and other sums for other health services, eyeglasses, and medical appliances.[17]

A recent marketing study by Charles H. Kline and Company predicted an 84% increase in United States retail nonprescription drug sales by 1985, and estimated that OTC sales would reach $8.6 billion by that year.[18] The Kline study also found that although 300 or more companies market OTCs, 8 companies, all with sales of $150 million or more in 1979, control about 48% of the market. The companies are McNeil Consumer Products (Johnson & Johnson), Whitehall Laboratories (American Home Products), Glenbrook Laboratories (Sterling Drug, Inc.), Warner-Lambert Company, Bristol-Myers Products, Richardson-Vicks, Inc., and Schering-Plough, Inc.

Marketplace Competition

We have already mentioned one form of competition involving OTCs—that between pharmacies and other retail outlets for a market share of nonprescription medicine sales. Another, more basic competition is among manufacturers of the products themselves. There is much empirical evidence to show that the market for such preparations is, in fact, highly competitive. Many products are close substitutes for one another, often containing identical or similar formulas. Many nationally distributed brands are heavily advertised, although substantial outlays of advertising dollars do not guarantee that a new product will be successful or that an older product will retain a market share. Advertising expenditures do not save inferior products, and neither do discounts and promotional techniques. Products are rejected when substantial numbers of consumers discover their adverse qualities and characteristics and demonstrate dissatisfaction by turning to competing products.

The market failure rate of new nonprescription products is high. It was reported in 1970 that of 308 new OTC drug products introduced 4 years previously, 85% still survived 2 years later but only 55% survived the third year.[19] Nearly everyone familiar with the market has his own list of successes and failures.

Advertising

You should keep in mind that advertising supports self-medication by informing consumers about the nature and benefits of nonprescription medicines and by making marketed products, their ingredients, and their indications for use highly recognizable. Advertising helps consumers to decide which medicine will alleviate their particular symptoms. This is accomplished by (1) making consumers aware of their health and the symptoms of minor illnesses that might affect them; (2) helping identify some causes of those illnesses; and (3) helping consumers to decide whether or not to utilize a nonprescription medicine, seek professional care, or choose some other alternative, such as tolerating the condition while it runs its course.

Because advertising is a principal means of creating awareness of consumers' health needs and bringing to their attention products that can affect their personal well-being, truthful and non-deceptive advertising is essential. Industry codes, sponsored by the National Association of Broadcasters and the Proprietary Association, the nonprescription industry trade group, provide that advertising should not promise more than products can deliver. Advertisers subject their efforts to close in-house legal and medical review. Further review is conducted within the advertising agencies, the media, and various governmental bodies, such as the Federal Trade Commission (for consumer advertising) and the Food and Drug Administration (for advertising to professionals).

In addition to its informational functions in self-medication, advertising has an important economic role. This derives from the widely accepted proposition that the more effectively sellers of products compete with one another, the more and better products consumers will be able to obtain for a given amount of money. The effectiveness of market competition and the effectiveness of advertising are closely linked.

According to a professor of business economics, sellers who fail to advertise their names and locations cannot compete well. An unknown seller is not an effective competitor. If consumers are aware of only half the sellers in the market, the effect is much the same as if there were only half as many firms. Because advertisements are sometimes ignored and often forgotten, and consumers are constantly entering and leaving markets for various products, such advertising must be memorable and repetitive.[20]

Advertising also makes the consumer aware of the existence and attributes of more brands, and it is essential to sellers of new brands to promote competition. New brands are, by definition, unfamiliar to the mass of potential buyers. Advertising is needed to overcome this ignorance.

Throughout the last decade, it has been alleged that the public advertising of nonprescription medicines—especially on television—produces adverse social effects, such as contributing to illicit drug use by young people and to the unsupervised ingestion of medicines by children. These allegations have formed the basis for demands for curtailing or prohibiting advertising of nonprescription medicines on broadcast media or in print.

There has been no substantive evidence to prove these allegations. Since 1970, the Proprietary Association has supported a continuing independent review of the world's scientific literature on the causes of drug abuse and the use of illicit drugs, with special reference to any identifiable role of advertising as a contributing or reinforcing factor. The latest report, dated June 1977, categorically declared that there is no evidence of a causative link between nonprescription medicine advertising and the use of illicit drugs or other forms of drug abuse. The summary also discussed two major studies that investigated this hypothesis. One researcher concluded that "the results suggest that, contrary to often-voiced public concern, television and television advertising of nonprescription [medicines] do not appear to be important influences of drug abuse."[21] The other researcher found a negative relationship between exposure to nonprescription drug advertising on television and the use of marijuana and other illicit drugs.[22]

The issue of drug abuse and the advertising of nonprescription medicines has also been studied by the Federal Trade Commission, the government agency having jurisdiction over consumer advertising. A report of the Commission staff noted that it had reviewed ". . . a number of studies relating to the effect of nonprescription medicine advertising on children. Results show little or no connection between such advertising and drug abuse."[23]

The second hypothesis, that television advertising of nonprescription medicines results in unsupervised ingestion of these products by children, is also without foundation. The frequency of reported fatalities from accidental ingestions of medicines by children in the United States has decreased substantially since 1950, in inverse relation to increasing exposure to television advertising during this period. Accidental ingestions of aspirin, the medicine most frequently involved (and a product heavily advertised on television), have decreased over 75% in the last 9 years. This decline is believed to be a response to a voluntary industry decision to limit packages of children's aspirin to 36 tablets of 1¼ grains each, to the introduction of mandatory safety packaging in 1970, and to government and industry educational programs stressing safe storage of medications in the home.

The Federal Communications Commission, which regulates television and radio broadcasting in the United States, conducted an inquiry into the effects of television advertising of nonprescription medicines on children. Following the inquiry, the Commission denied a petition to prohibit the broadcast of nonprescription medicine advertising until after 9:00 P.M. (by which time it was believed that most impressionable children would be asleep). The Commission stated that ". . . In the absence of empirical evidence to support the claim of a causal connection [between misuse or abuse of drugs and televised advertisements of nonprescription medicines] it would be unreasonable and arbitrary for the Commission to accept the idea that otherwise lawful advertising should be prohibited. . . . [and that it was] unwilling to adopt such regulations on the basis of mere speculation."[24]

Product "Positioning"

The principal purpose of advertising is to communicate. Until about 1970, most advertising for nonprescription medicines was designed to communicate the advantages or features of a product. Advertising is currently designed to create a "position" in the consumer's mind.

The term "positioning" has its roots in the packaged goods field, where the concept was originally called "product positioning." It literally meant the product's form, package size, and price as compared to those of the competition. Positioning is now used in a broader sense to indicate what advertising *does* for the product in the consumer's mind.

Advertising does not work as it once did. One reason may be its pervasiveness. For example, the per capita consumption of advertising in the United States exceeds $100 per year, and many believe that there is a point at which consumers refuse to take more advertising messages into their minds. Advertising industry studies have shown that when consumers are asked to name all the brands they can remember in a given product category, it is rare that anyone will name more than 7—and that's for a high interest category.[25] For low interest product types, the average consumer can usually name no more than 1 or 2 brands. To cope with this kind of complexity, people have learned to simplify. In essence the mind acts as a defense mechanism to protect itself against the barrage of communications, and screens and rejects much that is offered to it. Educational scientists have stated that the mind accepts only new information that matches its prior knowledge or experience, and filters out everything else.[25]

In other words, it is important for a company to create a position for its product in the mind of the consumer, and the position must be the *correct* one. It does no good for National Cash Register to say "NCR means computers"; consumers probably won't accept it. IBM means computers, and NCR means National Cash Register. Examples of proper positioning in the auto rental field are Hertz—No. 1, Avis—No. 2, and National somewhere below. All are successful where it counts—sales growth. Michelob is America's "first premium beer." Seven-Up is the "Uncola" and Nyquil is *the* "nighttime cold remedy."

Recent market research has shown that unless an advertisement is based on a unique idea or position, the message is often put into the mental slot reserved for the leader in that particular product category. Marketers consequently maintain that it is often better to tell the consumer what the product is *not*, rather than what it *is*. Consider again that Seven-Up is the "Uncola," gasoline used by modern engines is "lead-free," and most tires are now "tubeless." All these are examples of how new concepts can best be positioned against older ones.[26]

Marketing/Promotional "Mix"

Advertising is only one element to be considered in the overall strategy of a marketing program. Sometimes the program is called a "marketing mix." Different companies will include different elements in the mix for its products but, as a general rule, most programs include certain basic headings, such as product policy, price policy, channel of distribution(s), logistics, and promotions. These variables become the working tools used by the marketing manager in implementing his program.

Objectives form the strategic basis of promotional planning. Although much of a product's promotion may be directed toward the ultimate purchaser, other promotion is frequently designed to reach the middleman, such as the drug wholesaler or pharmacy buyer, whose efforts are involved with the distribution of the product. Promotion may include such things as co-op advertising, special deals, and quantity discounts and contests, all buttressed by the manufacturer's ongoing advertising for the brand.

An essential base of all strategy involves decisions about time and timing. A firm's marketing management should recognize that it must always be working toward the overall objective of uniting each element of its marketing/promotion mix into an organized and integrated program of action, although an individual strategy is often prepared on behalf of virtually any element of a single brand's marketing mix. Those elements of the mix for which strategies are prepared most frequently include product packaging, pricing, marketing, spending, public relations, copy, media, promotion, testing and research, distribution, and brand varieties. By far the most common of these, if not the most essential, are strategies for marketing, copy, media, promotion, and pricing.[27]

Perhaps the least understood strategy is that of marketing. A primary reason for this is that a marketing strategy often seems to lack the specificity associated with other types of strategy. A copy strategy addresses itself to copy, a media strategy to media. But to what specific element of the marketing mix is a marketing strategy addressed? Marketing strategies normally do not refer to any

TABLE 10-3. *Formats for Strategy Documents*

OUTLINE	DESCRIPTION	EXAMPLES OF POSSIBLE COMMENTS
I. MARKETING STRATEGIES		
A. Objectives	State the unit and/or dollar sales to be achieved, along with any other comments that might further define the brand's overall marketing goals.	Maintain a leadership position in the market. Achieve sales/profits of $ _____ through shipments of _____ . Foster growth by increasing per capita consumption.
B. Strategy		
1. Positioning	Define exactly how the brand is to be positioned in the market relative to its competitive environment.	The only brand that can duplicate the performance of two different products. Offers a major consumer benefit that competition can't match. Highest quality at lowest price.
2. Spending	Describe how the marketing investment is to be spent, in relation to the objectives to be achieved.	Outspend competition two to one. Spend more heavily during peak consumption periods. Spend full available dollars during first year's introduction.
3. Advertising/ Promotion	Refer to any key strategic elements in the advertising and promotion programs that will contribute importantly to achieving the targeted goals.	Capitalize on proven success of basic advertising theme. Use promotion to trade up consumer to more profitable size. Switch from print to TV based on test market success.
4. Other	Comment on any other significant aspects of the brand's basic make-up or approach that will help accomplish its goal.	Expand product into balance of United States. Introduce two line extensions. Offer trade margin parity with competition.

TABLE 10-3. *(Continued)*

OUTLINE	DESCRIPTION	EXAMPLES OF POSSIBLE COMMENTS
II. COPY STRATEGIES		
A. Objectives	State who the target audience is and the basic message to be communicated to this audience.	Convince mothers of young children that they will prefer our product because . . . Convince all teenagers that our product works twice as fast as Brand X.
B. Strategy		
1. Basic Concept	If developed, describe the basic campaign idea that will be used to convey the above message to the target audience.	For people who can't brush after every meal. Leave the driving to us. Put a tiger in your tank.
2. Concept Support	Depending on the campaign approach, state the supporting reasons why the basic message should be believed.	Contains GL 70. Contains a combination of fast acting ingredients. Four out of five doctors recommended. . . .
3. Tone	If appropriate, describe the environmental setting in which the advertising is to be cast.	Contemporary; sincere. Masculine; humorous. Soft; feminine; reassuring. News announcement.
III. MEDIA STRATEGY		
A. Objective	State who the target audience is, the media weight to be applied to this audience, and any other comments that best define the media objectives to be achieved.	Reach young mothers as often as practical. Provide added emphasis in peak consumption periods. Concentrate weight in high growth markets.
2. Strategy	Indicate the media selected for this purpose; the reasons for its selection; and the reach and frequency it will deliver, if appropriate.	TV will continue to be brand's primary medium because . . . Daytime network TV will be used to deliver year-round reach and frequency at maxi-

TABLE 10-3. *(Continued)*

OUTLINE	DESCRIPTION	EXAMPLES OF POSSIBLE COMMENTS
		Nighttime spot will be used in major markets during the high consumption season. Major market newspaper ads will be used to support the summer promotions.
IV. PROMOTION STRATEGIES		
A. Objective	Outline the specific goals of the promotional effort, listing them in the order of their importance.	Stimulate impulse buying in high traffic outlets. Increase distribution. Extend brand trial. Increase frequency of purchase.
B. Strategy	State how these objectives will be achieved, describing the essential make-up of the promotions to be employed.	Offer periodic direct incentives to consumers to purchase in multiple package quantities. Offer two major display allowances to the trade. Drop a 10¢ mail coupon to _____ million homes. Conduct two national consumer-oriented promotions involving self-liquidating premiums.
V. PRICING STRATEGIES		
A. Objective	State the purposes of the recommended retail price structure.	Maintain a gross profit margin of _____ %. Maintain price parity with major competition. Offer consumers a better value on larger sizes.
B. Strategy	If appropriate, explain how these goals are to be achieved.	Increase retail price by 2¢ next June. Reduce the price on the economy size. Immediately follow competition on any price adjustments. Reduce production costs by _____ %.

Source: Ennis, F. B.: *Effective Marketing Management*, New York: Association of National Advertisers, 1973.

one element. Rather, they address themselves to the overall "positioning" of the brand in the market. Table 10-3 contains sample formats for various strategy documents that are commonly employed by marketers of nonprescription medicines.

From the aforementioned it can be seen that nonprescription medications are labeled to be used by consumers in self-treating mild transitory symptoms without professional supervision. Most symptoms and conditions amenable to treatment with nonprescription medicines are called "self-limiting," referring to a condition that runs a definite and limited course, such as a cold, a bruise, or constipation. For the individual, self-medication offers a familiar, inexpensive, convenient, and quick method of dealing with ordinary health problems that cause discomfort and interfere with the business of living. For health professionals, self-medication provides protection against minor complaints. When properly practiced, the process of self-medication functions as a selective screening mechanism through which minor disorders are sorted out from those requiring professional medical and dental care.

The medicines used most frequently by consumers fall into relatively few therapeutic categories. Retail sales of OTC products in all outlets totaled an estimated $5.2 billion in the United States in 1979, approximately 9% higher than in 1978. Sales for prescription or "legend" drugs are approximately twice as much as those for nonprescription medicines.

Nonprescription products are now being reviewed by the Food and Drug Administration and final monographs, when published, will include the ingredients, dosages, combinations, and labeling conditions that are generally recognized as safe and effective for use in nonprescription drug products.

Nonprescription medicines represent a professional opportunity and challenge to the practicing pharmacist to provide professional counseling on proper drug use when requested to do so by consumers. Manufacturers of nonprescription drugs view pharmacists as their partners in providing information to consumers regarding such products. Pharmacists also represent an important market for a manufacturer's distribution, a fact that contributes to his desire to remain on friendly terms.

References

1. Carson, G.: *One for a Man, Two for a Horse,* Garden City, NY: Doubleday & Company, 1961.
2. Kauper, Thomas E.: Letter to Hearing Clerk, FDA, Department of Health, Education and Welfare, February 4, 1974.
3. Schmidt, A. M.: *Federal Register, 39*:19881, 1974.
4. Mercill, A. W.: The Grand Design, PA/FDA Manufacturing Controls Seminar, Cherry Hill, NJ, October 10, 1978.

5. *CFR, 21*:330.10(a)(5)(iii), 1972.
6. *Federal Register, 42*:19139, 1977.
7. Garcha, B.: Is Pharmacy Ready for the Expanding OTC Market, *NARD Journal, 102*:10, 1980.
8. Department of Commerce: *U.S. Industrial Outlook,* Washington, DC: Department of Commerce, 1978, p. 312.
9. Rottenberg, S.: Self-Medication: The Economic Perspective, Presented at a Symposium on Self-Care sponsored by the Proprietary Association, Washington, DC: March 31, 1980.
10. Kohn, R., and White, K. L.: *Health Care—An International Study,* Report of the World Health Organization/International Collaborative Study of Medical Care Utilization, London: Oxford University Press, 1976, p. 223.
11. Fry, J., et al.: *Self-Care: Its Place in the Total Health Care System,* Proceedings of the First General Assembly of the World Federation of Proprietary Medicine Manufacturers, London, 1973.
12. Dunnell, K., and Cartwright, A.: *Medicine Takers, Prescribers and Hoarders,* London: Routledge & Kegan Paul, 1972.
13. Knapp, D. A., and Knapp, D. E.: Decision-Making and Self-Medication: Preliminary Findings, *American Journal of Hospital Pharmacy, 29*: 1010, 1972.
14. Inhorn, M. C.: The Wide World of OTC's, *Drug Topics, 125*:27, 1981.
15. White, K. L., et al.: The Ecology of Medical Care, *New England Journal of Medicine, 265*:885, 1961.
16. Opinion Research Corporation: Public Views on the Labeling of Proprietary Medicines, Princeton: Opinion Research Corporation, 1978.
17. Health Care Financing Administration: in *Product Marketing, 9*:3, 1980.
18. Nonprescription Drugs, Fairfield, NJ: Charles H. Kline and Company, 1980.
19. *Drug Trade News,* February 28, 1970.
20. Pelzman, S.: Statement at the Federal Trade Commission, hearing on proposed antacid trade regulation rule, January 7, 1977.
21. Hulbert, J.: Applying Buyer Behavior Analysis to Social Problems: The Case of Drug Use, Proceedings of the American Marketing Association Annual Meeting, Chicago: 1974.
22. Milavsky, J. R., Pekowsky, B., and Stipp, H.: TV Drug Advertising and Proprietary and Illicit Drug Use Among Teenage Boys, *Public Opinion Quarterly, 40*:457, 1976.
23. Federal Trade Commission staff study, file No. 742-2383, 1975.
24. Federal Communications Commission press release, December 10, 1976.
25. Ries, A., and Trout, J.: Positioning: The Battle for Your Mind, New York: McGraw-Hill, 1981.
26. Trout, J.: Marketing Warfare, Presented at the Proprietary Association's First Annual Marketing Seminar, New York, December 6, 1979.
27. Herpel, G. L., and Collins, R. A.: Specialty Advertising in Marketing, Homewood, IL: Dow Jones-Irwin, 1972.

## PART III

Distribution Channels

## CHAPTER 11

The Manufacturer

MICKEY C. SMITH

Who are the drug manufacturers? In this chapter we will try to answer that question in general terms. But we should point out the following:

1. Companies engaged in the manufacture of pharmaceuticals constitute only a part of what the media likes to refer to as the "drug industry."

2. The manufacture of drugs is only part of the business of many corporations.

3. Many companies whose *main* business is the *manufacture* of drugs have many other businesses as well.

4. Many companies who *market* drugs do not manufacture them.

As with so many aspects of the health-care industry, there is an "official view" of drug manufacturing. In this case it has been stated by the Bureau of the Census, and so we will begin with that view.

Official View

The *United States Census* has defined manufacturers as those engaged in "the mechanical or chemical transformation of inorganic or organic substances into new products."[1] The assembly of component parts or products is considered to be manufacturing. Under this definition, the last *Census of Manufacturers* (1977) found that there were more than 1100 companies manufacturing pharmaceuticals in the United States.

Pharmaceutical manufacturing is divided into three classes: biologic products, medicinals and botanicals, and pharmaceutical preparations.

The biologic products industry includes: "establishments engaged primarily in the production of bacterial and virus vaccines, toxoids and analogous products (such as allergy extracts), serums, plasmas, and other blood derivatives for human or veterinary use."[1]

The medicinals and botanicals industry includes: "establishments engaged primarily in the manufacture of bulk medicinal organic and inorganic chemicals and their derivatives and in processing (grading, grinding, and milling) bulk botanical drugs and herbs."[1]

The pharmaceutical preparations industry includes: "establishments primarily engaged in manufacturing, fabricating or processing drugs into pharmaceutical preparations for human or veterinary use."[1]

Table 11-1 summarizes the size and nature of these industry segments, and indicates the changes that have taken place over recent years. Most notable in this table is the remarkable increase in activity in the Pharmaceutical Preparations segment. During

TABLE 11-1. *Census Statistics: Pharmaceutical Industry*

YEAR	COM-PANIES (NO.)	EMPLOYEES TOTAL NO.	EMPLOYEES PAYROLL ($1,000)	VALUE ADDED BY MANU-FACTURER ($1,000)	VALUE OF SHIPMENTS ($1,000)	SPECIAL-IZATION RATIO	COVER-AGE RATIO
			BIOLOGIC PRODUCTS				
1977	304	15,100	205,400	544,600	896,200	93	74
1967	128	7,400	53,800	109,200	160,000	90	61
1958	110	3,692	16,218	38,947	63,833	89	41
1947	79	2,987	8,474	19,161	37,737	87	57
			MEDICINALS AND BOTANICALS				
1977	179	16,700	249,900	1,235,300	2,025,900	80	73
1967	126	8,400	67,100	243,300	445,200	71	56
1958	114	10,246	62,877	175,817	322,286	72	75
1947	NA*	13,097	42,220	119,525	218,156	73	74
			PHARMACEUTICAL PREPARATIONS				
1977	757	126,000	2,021,200	8,137,000	11,357,100	87	97
1967	875	102,000	821,400	1,881,524	4,096,400	87	94
1958	NA	82,002	466,596	1,881,524	2,591,831	87	94
1947	1,123	65,413	185,497	608,625	941,290	NA	NA

*NA = not available.

Source: U.S. Department of Commerce: *1963, 1967, 1977 Census of Manufacturers,* Washington, DC: Bureau of the Census, 1965, 1969, 1979.

the period 1967 to 1977 the value of shipments for this portion of the industry nearly trebled; inflation may be the cause for part of this increase. During the same period the Biologic Products and the Medicinals and Botanicals sections increased even more.

It may also be seen that companies are currently much larger than in years past. This is primarily due to a combination of both growth factors and the number of mergers within the drug industry. It is noteworthy that in the face of dramatic overall growth of the industry as a whole, the number of companies declined.

The last two columns in Table 11-1 indicate important characteristics of the drug manufacturing industry—its reliance on and involvement with other manufacturing industries. The Specialization Ratio referred to in the first of these two columns indicates the percentage of the total output of the company that can be classified as a product of that industry. Thus, 13% of the output of the Pharmaceutical Preparations segment in 1977 consisted of products that actually fit into other industries.

The last column is primarily an indication of the percentage of all *products* that would be classified within that industry. An important part of what the Census would consider as biologic products or medicinals and botanicals were actually produced by companies classified in other industries. These facts are important in recognizing that the pharmaceutical industry is perhaps even larger than statistics would at first indicate.

Table 11-2 provides data for 1972 and 1977 on the magnitude of various therapeutic categories of the pharmaceutical preparations industry.

Pharmaceutical Manufacturers Association

Perhaps the best, although as yet incomplete, view of the prescription drug manufacturing industry can be obtained from statistics compiled by the Pharmaceutical Manufacturers Association (PMA). In this section we will present data dealing with the members of that association taken from two PMA publications, *The Prescription Drug Industry Factbook* (1980) and the *PMA, 1979–1980 Annual Survey Report.* Both these publications are issued regularly, and you are urged to refer to current editions for updated information. Both contain a wealth of data.

The Pharmaceutical Manufacturers Association is a nonprofit scientific, professional, and trade organization. Its active membership is comprised of 144 firms that are principally engaged in the manufacture of prescription pharmaceutical, medical device, and diagnostic products. The manufacturers promote these products primarily to health practitioners licensed by law to prescribe, administer, and dispense them. Financial support of the PMA is

TABLE 11-2. *Products and Product Classes—Quantity and Value of Shipments by All Producers: 1972 and 1977*

1977 PRODUCT CODE	PRODUCT	NUMBER OF COMPANIES WITH SHIPMENTS OF $100,000 OR MORE (1977)	VALUE OF PRODUCT SHIPMENTS ($ MILLIONS)	
			1977	1972
28340	Pharmaceutical preparations		9670.6	6295.4
28341	Pharmaceutical preparations affecting neoplasms, the endocrine system, and metabolic diseases, for human use	58	903.6	615.4
28342	Pharmaceutical preparations acting on the central nervous system and the sense organs, for human use	108	2258.6	1638.1
28343	Pharmaceutical preparations acting on the cardiovascular system, for human use	61	748.2	385.1
28344	Pharmaceutical preparations acting on the respiratory system, for human use	80	906.3	579.9
28345	Pharmaceutical preparations acting on the digestive or genitourinary systems, for human use	109	1088.3	764.0
28346	Pharmaceutical preparations acting on the skin, for human use	106	616.4	348.5
28347	Vitamins, nutrients, and hematinic preparations, for human use	123	1301.4	690.5
28348	Pharmaceutical preparations affecting parasitic and infective diseases, for human use	70	1291.8	949.0
28349	Pharmaceutical preparations for veterinary use	50	351.0	240.3

Source: U.S. Department of Commerce: *1972, 1977 Census of Manufacturers*, Washington, DC: Bureau of the Census, 1974, 1979.

234

derived mainly from dues based on the annual sales volume of the member firms.

Membership in the association is voluntary and consists predominantly of firms that produce pharmaceuticals under their own labels and are also engaged in significant research and development. Over the past two decades PMA members have been responsible for the research, development, and introduction of more than 90% of the new prescription drugs introduced in the United States and over half the new drugs introduced in the free world. Many of these companies also conduct research of medical devices and diagnostic products.

Table 11-3 presents a 26-year picture of the sales pattern of ethical pharmaceuticals by the industry, both for the United States and worldwide. The picture is one of steady increases in both areas by a multibillion dollar industry. This industry is justly proud of the research and development base that makes such sales figures possible. Research and development figures are shown in Table 11-4, which includes $1.89 billion in total R & D expenditures projected for 1980.

The interesting and vital link between R & D expenditures is illustrated in Table 11-5, which shows sales and R & D expenditures by product class for 1978. The table also provides historical market share data by product class. Nearly 23,000 people were employed in pharmaceutical R & D in 1978 by PMA members.

Research and development expenditures are both important to the vitality of the industry, and are also a cause of concern. Table 11-6 shows the skyrocketing costs of research and development of a new chemical entity from 1967 to 1976. Changes in the regulatory process are cited as a major cause, although not the only one.

Drug Manufacturer Profiles

There is, of course, no "typical" drug manufacturer—they are too diverse, too diffuse, too varied. Some benefit, however, may be gained from a closer look at one or two companies, as contrasted with the macroscopic view of the industry provided in the preceding sections.

We have chosen to focus on 2 of the leaders, Merck and Company, Inc., the first (in July 1979) pharmaceutical-based firm to join the Dow-Jones Industrial 30-company list, and the Upjohn Company. Information for these profiles was obtained from the companies' respective *Annual Reports* for 1980.

Merck and Company posted 1980 sales in excess of $2.7 billion yielding a net income of $415 million, with $234 million being spent for research and development. These figures represent increases over a 10-year period of 228% in sales, 217% in net in-

TABLE 11-3. *United States-Headquartered Firms' Sales and R & D Expenditures, 1954–1980 ($ Millions)*

| YEAR | UNITED STATES SALES*
HUMAN DOSAGE | GLOBAL SALES HUMAN AND VETERINARY[†] | |
		DOSAGE ONLY	DOSAGE AND BULK
1980[‡]	11,069	20,683	21,924
1979	10,444	18,422	19,572
1978	9,156	16,040	17,008
1977	8,233	13,896	15,674
1976	7,669	12,832	13,572
1975	6,895	11,543	12,183
1974	6,083	10,120	10,726
1973	5,507	8,755	9,191
1972	5,018	7,827	8,181
1971	4,667	7,020	7,838
1970	4,322	6,442	6,583
1969	4,008	5,832	6,208
1968	3,655	5,280	5,665
1967	3,226	4,707	5,102
1966	3,011	4,256	4,660
1965	2,779	3,841	4,219
1964	2,479	3,405	3,717
1963	2,313	3,152	3,469
1962	2,199	2,932	3,326
1961	1,954	2,685	2,292
1960	1,905	3,600	NA[§]
1959	1,850	2,500	NA
1958	1,802	2,400	NA
1957	1,742	2,200	NA
1956	1,676	1,900	NA
1955	1,457	1,650	NA
1954	1,252	1,500	NA

*United States' sales of finished prescription and over-the-counter ethical dosage forms.
[†]Global sales are defined to include total ethical pharmaceutical sales within the United States, exports to nonaffiliated firms, and sales abroad by United States affiliates.
[‡]PMA estimates based on member company budgeted figures or estimates.
[§]NA = not available.

Source: Pharmaceutical Manufacturers Association: *PMA, 1979–1980 Annual Survey Report*, Washington, DC: Pharmaceutical Manufacturers Association, 1981, p. 12.

come, and 222% in R & D expense. Nearly $74 million were spent on advertising in 1980.

"Merck is a worldwide organization primarily engaged in the business of discovering, developing, producing, and marketing products and services for the maintenance or restoration of health and the environment." According to the *Annual Report* more than 1000 products are offered in 2 industry segments—Human and Animal Health, and Environmental and Specialty Chemicals.

TABLE 11-4. *Research and Development Expenditures for Ethical Pharmaceuticals: 1978 and 1979 Actual and 1980 Budgeted PMA Member Firms ($ Millions)*

COMPANY-FINANCED R & D EXPENDITURES FOR HUMAN USE PHARMACEUTICALS	1978 ACTUAL	1979 ACTUAL	1980 BUDGETED
Amount spent in United States	$1089.2	$1243.1	$1437.4
Within firm	929.3	1078.2	1232.6
Outside firm	159.9	164.9	204.8
Amount spent in foreign countries	222.0	279.8	337.2
Within firm	198.0	252.8	302.0
Outside firm	24.0	27.0	35.2
Total human use R & D	$1311.2	$1522.0	$1774.6
COMPANY-FINANCED R & D EXPENDITURES FOR VETERINARY USE PHARMACEUTICALS			
Amount spent in United States	$ 69.9	$ 76.7	$ 86.4
Within firm	62.3	69.3	79.0
Outside firm	7.6	7.4	7.4
Amount spent in foreign countries	15.9	19.6	23.8
Within firm	15.2	18.3	22.3
Outside firm	.7	1.3	1.5
Total Veterinary R & D	$ 85.8	$ 96.3	$ 23.8
Total company-financed R & D pharmaceuticals	$1397.0	$1619.2	$1884.8
United States government grants and contracts for company-conducted pharmaceutical R & D	$ 7.0	$ 7.6	$ 6.9
Total expenditures for pharmaceutical R & D	$1404.0	$1626.8	$1891.7

Source: Pharmaceutical Manufacturers Association: *PMA, 1979–1980 Annual Survey Report*, Washington, DC: Pharmaceutical Manufacturers Association, 1981, p. 7.

In 1980 divisions of Merck included:

Kelco Division
Calgon Corporation
Baltimore Aircoil Company
Alginate Industries Ltd.
Merck Chemical Division
Merck Chemical Manufacturing Division

Hubbard Farms, Inc.
MSD AGVET Division
MSD Research Laboratories
MSD International
Merck Sharp & Dohme

(*Text continues on p. 239.*)

TABLE 11-5. *United States Sales and R & D Pharmaceutical Expenditures by Product Class*

PRODUCT CLASS	SALES (%)	GAIN OR LOSS OF MARKET SHARE, 1972–1978 (%)	R & D EXPENDITURES (%)
Central nervous system	23.6	−9.2	16.8
Anti-infectives	15.0	+17.2	18.9
Gastrointestinal and genitourinary	11.8	+10.3	6.2
Neoplasms and endocrine	9.7	−19.2	16.4
Vitamins and nutrients	9.6	+26.3	2.4
Cardiovasculars	9.4	+11.9	16.6
Respiratory system	7.8	+18.2	4.0
Dermatologicals	2.9	−12.1	3.1
Other	10.2	−19.0	12.4

Source: Pharmaceutical Manufacturers Association: *PMA, 1979–1980 Annual Survey Report,* Washington, DC: Pharmaceutical Manufacturers Association, 1981, p. 13.

TABLE 11-6. *Average Discovery Costs and Testing Expenditures Per Marketed New Chemical Entity**

	DISCOUNT RATES							
	MILLIONS OF 1967 DOLLARS				MILLIONS OF 1976 DOLLARS			
	5%	8%	10%	15%	5%	8%	10%	15%
Post-IND test only	10.1	11.5	13.8	15.7	18.5	21.0	25.2	28.7
Post-IND test plus preclinical animal toxicity	11.2	12.9	14.1	17.5	20.5	23.6	25.8	32.0
Allocated discovery cost 3-year allocation period	13.1	16.6	19.6	29.2	24.0	30.4	35.8	53.8
Total	24.3	29.5	33.7	46.7	44.5	54.0	61.6	85.4

*Inasmuch as pharmaceutical R & D requires a capital investment with a return on investment delayed by several years. Professor Hansen has established a "present value" or "capitalized value" to the point of marketing approval for the sums involved. The capitalized value varies with the interest rate considered most appropriate. A selection of alternative discount rates is shown in this table.

Source: Hansen, R. W.: *Regulation and Pharmaceutical Innovation,* Rochester: University of Rochester, 1976.

The last of these is, of course, most closely associated with the drug field. Prescription drug products are promoted by a worldwide staff of approximately 4600 professional service employees. In 1980 products for human health accounted for nearly $2 billion in sales.

The corporate marketing philosophy has been stated as follows: "In all of our marketing efforts, Merck accepts the obligations that we believe are associated with potent medicinals, including not only extreme care in their manufacture but also fair balance and honesty in their promotion." A new program of specialization for the detail staff was established in 1980 to reflect product line characteristics. Under this program representatives will receive extensive training in either musculoskeletal disorders or cardiovascular and infective diseases.

The Upjohn Company had 1980 sales of $1.76 billion and net earnings of $170 million. Nearly $54 million were spent for advertising and nearly $150 million for R & D. Upjohn concentrates on 3 areas—human health, chemical, and agricultural—with the former accounting for about two thirds of the recent sales dollar. The human health segment includes the Upjohn Health Care Services and Laboratory Procedures business as well as drugs. Motrin, introduced in 1974, achieved the other highest first-year sales of any pharmaceutical product. Approximately 40% of the human health care sales in 1979 were made in foreign markets.

The individual seeking a "typical" drug manufacturer is doomed to disappointment because, although drugs constitute the major business of many firms, mergers and acquisitions (Chap. 8) have blurred the once sharp image of the industry.

Mergers and acquisition activities represent 3 key trends within the pharmaceutical industry. First, mergers and acquisitions contribute significantly to market concentration in the pharmaceutical industry in the United States. (The 149 companies that comprise the PMA manufacture about 95% of domestic prescription drugs. Although no single pharmaceutical manufacturer contributes more than 7% of the market, the peculiar structure of the market provides a virtual monopoly owing to the separate, noncompetitive nature of the products.)

Second, there has been a significant trend in the pharmaceutical industry toward diversification. Eli Lilly and Upjohn have reduced their dependence upon pharmaceuticals to around 70% of total sales. In some cases diversification has taken place into areas totally unrelated to pharmaceuticals. Bristol-Myers, for example, has expanded into the movie-making and television businesses. Eli Lilly has entered the commercial livestock market, and Merck has entered the antipollution industry. Typically, however, the largest pharmaceutical firms expand their operations first into the entire range of fields in the health-care market, then into such areas as prepared foodstuffs, animal health care, chemicals, confections, toiletries, household products, and cosmetics.

Third, there has been an attempt on the part of large-scale conglomerates to partake in the profitability of drug manufacturing and sales. Mergers and acquisitions in the pharmaceutical industry have met with unusual success. The typical pharmaceutical firm has rapidly expanded its worldwide sales and decreased its dependence upon strictly pharmaceutical products. It is clear that mergers and acquisitions of existing firms and facilities represent the quickest way for the typical large-scale pharmaceutical firm to gain a commanding position in specific markets within the industry and to expand to growth sectors outside pharmaceuticals.[2]

It is clear that the drug industry is a growth industry however it is characterized. The Wall Street confirmation of this view can be seen in Table 11-7, which shows stock market growth of the big gainers in the 1970s. Further data on industry leaders are given in Table 11-8, which shows products in companies that led in sales in 1980.

Organization for Marketing

In order for a firm to translate its corporate intentions into meaningful action, it must provide an organizational framework that is consistent with, gives meaning to, and provides an operating mechanism for its activities. The organization chart of the firm, if adhered to, can provide a good description of its orientation. Poor organization can hamper efforts founded on the best of intentions. There are various organizational models used in the drug industry.

An example of an internal organizational chart is provided in Figure 11-1. Additional charts and their relationships to operations are included in Chapter 21.

Channels of Distribution

The internal organization that the firm undertakes toward ensuring efficient operations is a precursor to the organization of the total marketing system. Each firm in turn must decide how it will operate within this system. Some decisions that must be made involve the means required to place the manufactured goods in the hands of the ultimate consumer.

For the manufacturer of prescription drugs some of these decisions have already been made. The law requires that at least one

TABLE 11-7. *Top Drug Industry Stock Gainers in the 1970s ($ Millions)**

COMPANY	1969 CLOSE	1979 CLOSE	AMOUNT CHANGE	CHANGE (%)
SmithKline	3812.1	709.5	3102.6	337.3
J & J	4841.3	3169.8	1671.5	52.7
Abbott	2475.7	1031.9	1443.8	139.9
Merck	5445.5	4076.7	1368.8	33.5
Baxter	1612.1	746.1	866.0	116.1
AMHO	4243.1	3385.9	857.2	25.3
Schering	1623.8	917.9	705.9	76.9
Pfizer	2856.6	2175.6	681.0	31.3
Upjohn	1405.2	751.8	653.4	86.9
Revlon	1491.3	870.5	620.8	71.3
Squibb	1718.7	1131.9	586.8	51.8
Searle	1001.3	537.9	463.4	86.1
Bristol-Myers	2420.1	2069.9	350.2	16.9

*Based on the change in total valuation, determined by year-end common stock price times number of outstanding shares.

Source: *F-D-C Reports*, January 7, 1980. Published by F-D-C Reports, Inc., Suite One, 5550 Friendship Blvd., Chevy Chase, MD 20815.

TABLE 11-8. *Top-Selling Products and Manufacturers, 1980*

DRUG	MANUFACTURER	DISEASE OR FUNCTION	YEAR INTRODUCED	SALES ($ MILLIONS)
Tagamet	SmithKline	Peptic ulcer	1977	250
Valium	Hoffman-LaRoche	Muscle relaxant Tranquilizer	1966	230
Inderal	American Home Products	Heart disease Hypertension	1967	200
Motrin	Upjohn	Arthritis	1974	150
Aldomet	Merck	Hypertension	1963	150
Dyazide	Smith Kline	Hypertension	1965	145
Keflex	Eli Lilly	Oral antibiotic	1971	140
Clinoril	Merck	Arthritis	1978	125

Source: Oppenheimer & Company, quoted in *Apharmacy Weekly, 20* (No. 21): 2, 1981. Copyright 1981 by the American Pharmaceutical Association. Reprinted with permission of the American Pharmaceutical Association.

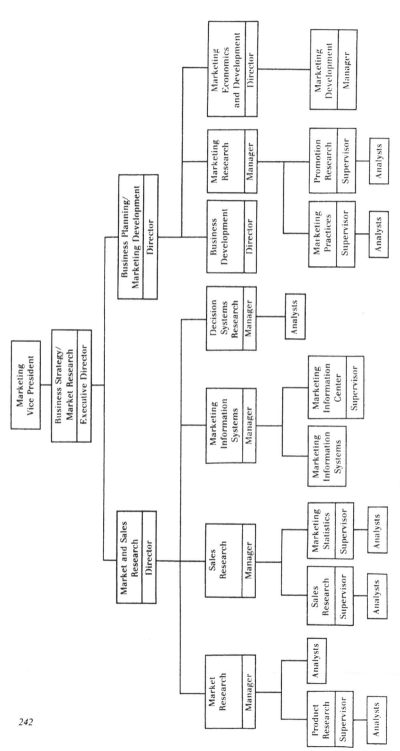

FIG. 11-1. *Marketing organization.*

intermediary stand between the manufacturer and the consumer—i.e., the doctor. It is illegal for the manufacturer to sell legend drugs directly to the patient. The bare minimum, then, as a channel of distribution for prescription drug products would look like this:

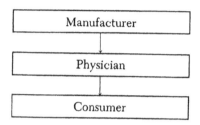

Pharmacists would be quick to point out the need for their services in this distribution process. When the pharmacist is utilized to assist in the *physical* distribution, the role of the physician becomes that of a decision maker. We might then diagram this channel like this:

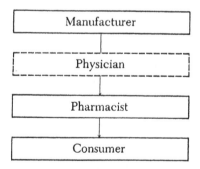

In spite of his pivotal role in drug selection, the physician is not usually drawn into such diagrams.

In the language of drug distribution, the manufacturer who opts to follow this distribution chain is said to "sell direct." The traditional (but by no means only) channel of distribution in the prescription drug field includes the drug wholesaler and looks like the diagram on page 244.

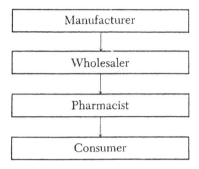

Among the determinants of the channels of distribution are the characteristics of the manufacturer. These include:

1. *Financial capability.* To sell direct is costly, so much so that, even though he may desire to do so, a manufacturer (especially a small one) may find it impossible.

2. *Reputation.* The ability to obtain effective distribution, either direct or indirect, may be heavily influenced by the manufacturer's reputation for integrity and fair dealing.

3. *Manufacturer's policies.* Some pharmaceutical firms have clear-cut policies as they relate to channels of distribution—e.g., Eli Lilly has traditionally distributed only through full service wholesalers. In some cases these policies are so strong that other considerations regarding channel decisions are not important.

Table 11-9 shows trends in use of and sales to various elements of the channel in recent years.

The pharmaceutical industry, like many others, may suffer from superficial analysis of its channels of distribution. Such analysis may result in glossing over the ways in which more than a dozen major industry components impinge upon the activities of each other. A better understanding of the industry can result from viewing the channel as an open system. In this view, input (of many kinds) is received from the environment, operations or a series of operations are performed by the channel on that input, and the transformed input is returned to the environment.[3] These transformations, including addition of time, place, possession, and form utility, are necessary for the product to be complete.

Smooth functioning of the channels of distribution within the pharmaceutical industry relies in large part on general agreement concerning the roles of the respective parties in the channels. Agreement concerning the roles can go a long way toward preventing unpleasant surprises, disappointment, and inefficiency.

TABLE 11-9. *Ethical Pharmaceuticals Manufacturers' Direct Human Use Dosage Form Sales in the United States by Class of Customer, 1969–1979 (Odd Years, Percentage Share of Sales)*

CLASS OF CUSTOMER	1969	1971	1973	1975	1977	1979
Wholesalers	47.6%	46.4%	44.9%	46.9%	49.1%	53.0%
Retailers	29.9	30.0	29.6	27.6	25.5	22.5
Private hospitals	12.2	13.2	14.7	14.7	15.1	14.9
State and local government hospitals	4.0	4.8	4.9	4.6	4.5	4.0
Federal hospitals	2.9	2.8	2.9	2.6	2.7	2.3
Other federal government	1.0	.9	1.2	1.1	1.3	1.4
Practitioners	1.8	1.5	1.4	1.2	1.1	1.2
Manufacturers, repackagers, and other direct sales	0.6	0.4	0.4	1.3	0.7	0.7
Total	100.0%	100.0%	100.0%	100.0%	100.0%	100.0%

Source: Pharmaceutical Manufacturers Association: *PMA, 1979–1980 Annual Survey Report*, Washington, DC: Pharmaceutical Manufacturers Association, 1981, p. 6.

In addition to roles organizational character, defined as being a product of "its method of work, its natural allies, its stake in the course of events, the predispositions of its personnel, and the labels which have become attached to it,"[4] also helps lend stability and predictability to industry relationships. The specific channel member (e.g., wholesaler or retailer) possesses a definite self, distinctive character, and ways of acting and perceiving different from other such organizations. It behaves in accordance with specific roles or sets of prescriptions defining what its behavior should be. The other firms in the distribution channel are able to anticipate its behavior and, similarly, it can foresee the behavior of dependent channel members.[5]

It is patently impossible for each organization in the drug industry to have ready knowledge of the organizational character of all others, although some companies, such as Lilly, McKesson, and Walgreens, have developed such a recognized character. Moreover, in many cases, the character of one organization is known to another one or to a few representatives. Thus, the Syntex detail man *is* the Syntex organization in the experience of the pharmacies in his territory.

The concept of organizational roles also presents problems. This is particularly true because smooth industry functioning is most likely to occur when all parties have a mutual perception of the roles of all organizations in the system. This obviously does not occur quickly, but rather is the result of long-term and increasingly successful performance in a particular role. Other members of the industry, through experience, tend to prescribe

behavior in accordance with their concept of what is correct behavior, and attempt to enforce sanctions if there are deviations.

In spite of the significance of historical developments, evaluation is also an important factor in role perceptions. The super
drugstore, for instance, was originally opposed by almost all segments of the drug industry, whereas its role in the industry is a
pivotal one today.

In considering the importance of role, the United States prescription drug industry is a great industry by almost any standard.
Its products, in spite of their often cited problems, are remarkably
effective. The costs of the drugs to the ultimate customer have
remained remarkably stable. Perhaps most important of all, the
distribution system has been beautifully effective. Of all the components of the health-care system, pharmaceuticals have been the
most accessible. There are pharmacists in almost every small vil-
lage who have made a way of life of having *any* prescription drug
when it is needed. Whereas you might have to travel miles to obtain cobalt therapy, orthodontic services, or even a pediatrician,
the odds are, in any town of more than 1500 people, that any prescription drug will be available. Surely this accomplishment is
something of which all members of the drug industry might be
justifiably proud, and a great deal of mutual pride might be expected as well.

The pharmaceutical industry is obviously a strong and vigorous one. The future is bright. There have been recent concerns
about disturbing trends in prescription patterns, but even these
can be interpreted with optimism. As Steven Chappell (Chap. 6)
has cogently observed:

It is not one or two, but myriad factors that have, over the past half
dozen years, come to operate in the market, and have created some
very confusing patterns in the standard measurements of market activity: prescription data and sales data. These are as follows:

1. More substantial and more frequently applied price increases
since 1973 have created increasing disparities between unit and dollar growth in most pharmaceutical product categories. Due to this
occurrence, the comparison of *dollar* trends with trends in other
measurements of market activity such as prescription data has become a less realistic exercise.

2. Changes have been recorded in the value of the standard unit of
measurement in prescription data—the prescription. Increases in
average prescription size have resulted in fewer refills, and, consequently, fewer total prescriptions. Additionally, and importantly, one
prescription today may, in terms of the number of units of drug it
represents, be the equivalent of two prescriptions in the past.

3. Reductions in prescription activity in certain product categories
appears plausible due to either declines in patient potential, adverse
publicity, questions of efficacy, or concern with abuse potential. Due,
however, to advancing prices *dollar* trends in these product categor-

ies may not reflect declines at all, or to the same extent as do prescription data.

4. The movement away from products that have suffered adverse publicity or questions regarding efficacy to alternate therapy will be wholly reflected in sales data, but not necessarily in prescription data. This is certainly the case when the alternative therapy is available without a prescription; e.g., oral contraceptives to condoms, jellies, foams.

5. The movement from older to newer therapies has generally resulted in a one-for-one trade in *prescription* counts, but a disproportionately upward impact on dollar measures, given the generally considerably higher unit prices of the newer therapy.

6. A growing movement toward the moving of previously legend drugs to over-the-counter status has resulted in a falling off of prescription volume for the products involved. Sales of these products, however, obviously continue and these sales are reflected in sales audit data.

7. Correlations of manufacturer factory sales with prescription or sales *audit* data have become increasingly more difficult because of the purchasing and dispensing of ethical pharmaceuticals by "nontraditional" (and, for the most part, not regularly audited) pharmacy operations—mail order prescription houses, food store prescription departments, HMO or nursing home pharmacies, hospital pharmacies—when serving outpatients.[6]

The manufacturing segment of the pharmaceutical industry is rapidly growing in terms of total sales, although the number of firms in the field is remaining relatively stable. The product classes produced by the industry have varied in importance, depending upon their use and source. A great deal of careful planning should result in a formal, explicit organizational structure, designed to channel all the activities of a firm into the path necessary to ensure efficient delivery of the pharmaceuticals that the firm has prepared.

References

1. U.S. Department of Commerce: *1977 Census of Manufacturers*, Washington, DC: Bureau of the Census, 1979.
2. Murray, M. J.: The Pharmaceutical Industry: A Study in Corporate Power, *International Journal of Health Service, 4*:625, 1974.
3. Hall, A. D., and Fagan, R. E.: Definitions of a System, in *General System*, edited by L. Von Bertalanffy and A. Rapoport, Ann Arbor: University of Michigan Press, 1956, p. 23.
4. Selznick, P.: *The Organizational Weapon*, Glenco, IL: The Free Press, 1960, p. 56.
5. Gill, L. E., and Stern, L. W.: Roles and Role Theory in Distribution Channel Systems, in *Distribution Channels: Behavioral Dimensions*, edited by L. W. Stern, Boston: Houghton Mifflin, 1969, p. 26.
6. Chappell, S. C.: The Prescription Decline: Sense or Nonsense? *Medical Marketing and Media, 15*:21, 1980.

## CHAPTER 12

The Wholesaler

JOHN T. FAY, JR.

Early in 1981, Merrill Lynch was bullish on drug wholesaling. In particular, the firm's financial analysts were attracted to the obvious investment potential of the two largest wholesale distributors in the United States drug industry—Bergen Brunswig Corporation and McKesson Drug Company, a unit of Foremost-McKesson, Inc. "The growing use of sophisticated electronic order entry systems by drug wholesalers," as noted by Merrill Lynch in advice to investors, "has changed drug wholesaling from a labor intensive to a technology intensive business. Whenever this happens the result is the same—innovative companies use technology to increase their market share and improve their profitability."[1]

Marketing experts and industry observers generally agreed with this expression of optimism about the wholesale distribution of pharmaceuticals and health-care products. However, many of these same observers had been pessimistic about wholesaling less than 10 years before. In 1975, for example, the second edition of this textbook stated that "the future is cloudy" for the drug wholesaler, who was characterized further as being "on somewhat shaky ground."[2]

As indicated in Table 12-1, the turnaround in sales and market share began with improved results in 1974, and continues to exhibit steady growth. When the totals compiled by the National Wholesale Druggists' Association (NWDA) for 1980 are compared with those for 1974, an increase of 103% can be seen. After adjusting for inflation, at least half of this growth can be identified as new business.

This success is partially related to major reductions in operating costs from 11.84% of sales in 1974, for example, to 8.60% in 1980. During the same period, inventory turnover improved by 20% and record improvements in productivity were noted in the range of 40 to 50%. Gross margin, in contrast, declined from 13.67% of net sales to 11.22%.

TABLE 12-1. *Prescription Sales and Wholesale Market Shares*

YEAR	UNITED STATES PRESCRIPTION SALES ($ MILLIONS)*	WHOLESALE SHARE (%)[†]	NWDA TOTAL WHOLESALE SALES ($ MILLIONS)[‡]
1964	2,497	48.7	1,615
1965	2,779	48.4	1,836
1966	3,011	47.5	1,944
1967	3,266	47.8	2,101
1968	3,655	47.5	2,118
1969	4,008	47.6	2,297
1970	4,322	46.9	2,397
1971	4,667	46.4	2,503
1972	5,018	45.6	2,671
1973	5,507	44.9	2,889
1974	6,083	45.2	3,230
1975	6,895	46.9	3,760
1976	7,669	48.5	4,115
1977	8,233	49.1	4,482
1978	9,155	51.4	4,910
1979	10,044	53.0	5,470

*Data from Pharmaceutical Manufacturers Association: *Direct Human Use Dosage Form Sales.* Reported as billed (before deducting cash discounts on sales and other marketing expenses), less returns and allowances. Includes sales value of products bought and resold without further processing or repackaging as well as the dollar value of products made from own materials for other manufacturers' resale. Excluded are all royalty payments, interest, and other income.
[†]Data from Pharmaceutical Manufacturers Association: from class of customer analysis.
[‡]Data from National Wholesale Druggists' Association: estimates of active member sales based on operating surveys.

Commenting on the gross margin statistics, NWDA President John M. Morson said that the results reflect "a very substantial reduction in the prices we charge our customers."[3] For the first time in many years, the 1980 *Lilly Digest* reported lower operating costs for community pharmacies. Morson suggested that "wholesalers have contributed to that improved performance through pricing and the systems that offer our customers ways to become more efficient."[3]

Value-added Distribution

New emphasis on a systems approach in marketing by wholesalers supports the traditional argument that wholesaling adds value to products and services. Contemporary applications of computer technology make this possible. With increasing frequency in recent years, pharmacists and drug wholesalers are using computers to improve communication and to reinforce their marketing relationship.

One obvious example is the computerization of order entry and the inventory maintenance process. Among the more obvious benefits are speed, ease of transmission, more efficient service levels, improved turnover rates, reduced cash investment, and balanced delivery schedules. Although the buyer-seller relationship in distribution is generally better than ever before, a basic problem persists. As middlemen, should wholesalers be sales agents for manufacturers or should they be purchasing agents for their customers? To some degree, wholesalers must perform both functions, and the two forms of agency are not mutually exclusive. Current business experience, however, supports the movement toward expansion of the wholesaler's role as purchasing agent for the pharmacist. It is a strategy described by management consultants as "forward integration."

Pharmacists and their wholesalers are working together more closely. This change for the better comes during a period of unusual dynamism in the distribution industry. It is an important and integral part of the structural change now generally recognized by industry observers. McKeon, for example, has made this distinction: "The stability at the macro-wholesale level is misleading. At the micro-level, wholesaling is very dynamic. The channel structure depends upon the time-space-quantity-variety gap between the assortments of sellers and buyers. To the extent that this gap changes, the wholesaling task changes."[4]

In simpler language: the closer you get to the action in wholesaling, the more interesting and innovative it is. The trend line for the wholesalers' market share of prescription sales clearly indicates a turnaround after a period of decline to 1973 and rapid growth since. Computerization and continued application of cost-effective technology are major factors in this growth.

Other factors involved in distribution dynamics include competitive intensity, a changing product-services mix, consolidation of the customer base, new efforts in managerial and marketing continuity, greatly improved productivity, and innovations in pricing strategy. The latter can be illustrated by the current shift to cost-plus pricing that follows by several years the pharmacist's shift from markup to professional fee methods.

Marketing Functions and Transactions

The casual observer of marketing channel practice may wrongly assume that wholesaling is a low growth, unnecessary function that adds an unjustified cost factor to the price paid by retailers and consumers. Easily (but mistakenly) ignored is the value added by wholesale distribution in terms of the utilities of time, place, access, and appropriate quantity.

This lack of understanding derives in part from an initial problem with definitions and descriptive terms. Weiss, for example, has said that there are "wholesalers who manufacture, wholesalers who retail and wholesalers who are uncertain whether they are producers, wholesalers, jobbers, retailers, financiers or whatever."[5] That criticism has limited application to drug wholesaling today.

A clearly stated functional definition has been provided by Lopata, who described a wholesaler as one who:

1. Purchases goods from manufacturers for his own account (as distinguished from the agent, who typically does not purchase for his own account) and resells them to other businesses.
2. Operates one or more warehouses in which he receives and takes title to goods, stores them, and later reships them. (In some cases, he may have goods shipped directly by the manufacturer to the customer, so the goods do not actually pass through his warehouse.[6]

A novel functional approach has been used by Cox and Schutte in a challenge to conventional thinking. They suggested that channel management is best understood with reference to "the physical flow of the goods, the flow of ownership or control, the flow of information, and the flow of money."[7] This distinction, in their view, "makes it possible to determine the precise role of each agency or facility in the channel of distribution."[7]

The customary argument for wholesaling is presented in terms of several basic principles of marketing. Among these are reduced transactions, concentration-dispersion, market proximity, and specialized service. A familiar illustration of an economic justification for the wholesaler's role is the estimate that 600 million transactions annually would be required if 50,000 pharmacies ordered directly each month from 1000 manufacturers.

If this illustration is extended to the extreme of *daily* ordering on a direct basis, some 13 billion transactions would result, an obvious impossibility. This may. be contrasted with the introduction of 250 wholesalers to the model. Assume that 1000 manufacturers deal *weekly* with this group of distributors, who then serve the 50,000 pharmacies *daily*. If 260 working days in a typical year are used as a multiple, the result is 26 million transactions.

$$
\begin{array}{cccc}
1000 & \times & 250 & \times & 52 \\
\text{(mfrs.)} & & \text{(wholesalers)} & & \text{(weeks)}
\end{array}
$$

$$+$$

$$
\begin{array}{cccc}
250 & \times & 200 & \times & 260 & = & 26{,}000{,}000 \\
\text{(wholesalers)} & & \text{(pharmacies} & & \text{(working} & & \text{(transactions} \\
 & & \text{per wholesaler)} & & \text{days)} & & \text{yearly)}
\end{array}
$$

A similar reduction is achieved in order processing, invoicing, and all associated costs, with the genuine advantage of fewer opportunities for error. Computerization of this process overcomes the difficulties of human order takers and depersonalizes inventory control for maximum economic benefit.

Wholesaling, then, *concentrates* merchandise appropriately by assembling an assortment from diverse manufacturers, and *disperses* the right amount to the indicated point of sale in the quantity required (Fig. 12-1). This concentration-dispersion function is often characterized by the terms "sorting" or "breaking bulk." Local availability in response to demand is an important factor in the value added by sorting.

Market proximity in an economic sense refers to local availability and the utilities of place, timeliness, and possession. Next-day delivery from wholesalers is possible virtually everywhere in the United States, and same-day delivery can be achieved in many urban markets. For reasons of cost efficiency, however, there is a trend toward fewer deliveries per week from wholesalers to the pharmacies they serve.

Siecker has provided an interesting example that recognizes this trend and relates it to turnover improvement. He noted that two-thirds of the funds in a typical pharmacy are tied to the purchase and resale of inventory, and he then emphasized the problems of ordering too frequently "because scarce dollars are supporting lazy stock." His example continued with the following:

> If a pharmacy were designed to operate on a two-week order cycle . . . the theoretical inventory turnover would exceed 17 for the year. Obviously, it would be tough to make that figure. But what if 10 turns was a realistic figure for this model? Compare that with the norm of about four turns per year, and suddenly thousands of dollars could be extracted from lazy inventory, easing the cash flow crunch, allowing more flexibility on promotional purchasing and improving return on investment.[8]

Concentration of Purchasing Power

An extension of this reasoning leads to the primary supplier concept. More pharmacists now recognize the benefits that can be obtained by ordering less often from a single wholesaler—a concentration of the purchasing pattern. Similarly, wholesalers are seeking out the best-managed pharmacies in a given market in order to concentrate and improve their customer base.

Some attrition is unavoidable during periods of growth. Improperly managed, underfinanced businesses at both the wholesale and retail levels leave the market to the strongest competi-

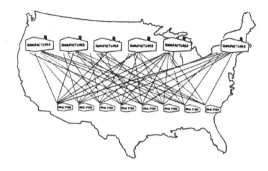

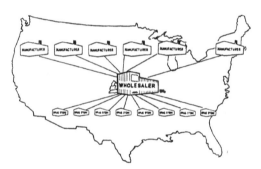

Fig. 12-1. *Schematic illustration of the concentration-dispersion function of the wholesaler.*

tors. One result of this change is a measurable increase in the effectiveness of competition, sharpened and focused by market forces.

The relative numbers of pharmacies and drug wholesalers should be considered here. If we assume approximately 50,000 pharmacies and 500 wholesale houses in the United States, maximum efficiency in the sense of classic economics should be achieved with a ratio of 1 wholesale house serving 100 pharmacies. For many years, however, the operative ratio has been more like 1 to 300, with many pharmacies dividing their purchases among 2 or 3 wholesalers.

Increasing recognition of the primary supplier concept and its decided advantage changes this service ratio. From the former average of 300 pharmacies in a typical wholesaler's customer base, movement toward a smaller base is apparent. Much the same pattern can be observed in the United Kingdom and other countries in which computerization and consolidation have accelerated the survival of the fittest in drug marketing.

Information collected annually by the National Wholesale Druggists' Association has provided statistical details to support these trends. NWDA member firms operate 313 distribution centers that generated $6.55 billion in sales for 1980. This group of businesses accounted for some 85% of the total drug wholesale volume. Accordingly, the entire market approached $7.5 billion from something less than 500 wholesale houses employing about 22,000 people.

This is a relatively small portion of the trillion-dollar market for wholesaling in general—some 300,000 firms employing 5 million people in all classes of trade. However, most analysts agree that drug wholesalers lead the field in terms of sophisticated automation and in consolidation of facilities for cost control and greater efficiency.

A significant part of this success can be traced to fewer than 100 pharmacists who are executives of wholesale drug firms. They are generally chief executives and policy makers. Their influence is exerted throughout the industry in small and large organizations, in privately and publicly owned firms.

Addressing the 1980 year-end sales conference of Bergen Brunswig Corporation, Chairman Emil P. Martini, a pharmacist, described the primary supplier commitment as "causing major changes in the entire economics of the business." Martini argued further that "cost-plus selling and cost-plus-a-fee are quickly eliminating the traditional adversary buyer-seller relationship."[9]

Perceptions of Value Added

An important change in the perception of value added by the wholesale function has been described by Fenstermaker: "Price, so long as it is fair, is no longer the basis of the pharmacist-wholesaler relationship. Business systems and management skill are now appreciated by the customer who is willing to pay for them, not at the lowest price alone, but at a fair price based on the quality of information delivered."[10]

There is much support for this argument in several opinion surveys. The November 1978 issue of *American Druggist* reported on replies from 997 pharmacies to a questionnaire designed to determine "how retailers feel about drug wholesalers." Based on this data, most pharmacists felt good about the relationship and one-third indicated that it was becoming "increasingly close" in the past few years.[10a]

Between 1972 and 1977, wholesale purchases of pharmaceuticals for this sample of pharmacies increased from 61.8 to 67.4%. When asked to compare 1978 and 1977, 52% of the respondents said that they were "buying more merchandise from wholesalers today." Wholesaler salesmen were characterized as "helpful" by 76.9%. Interest in the newer computer-based services was indicated, with nearly 60% of the respondents recognizing a benefit.[10a]

Two years later, *American Druggist* reported the results of a similar survey based on 1144 replies from a randomly selected group of 4000 pharmacies. This response, a relatively high level for a mail study, was seen as a reflection of "the strong interest that exists in the entire subject of wholesaler-retailer relations."[10b]

The October 1980 summary demonstrated increased application of wholesaler-provided services for pharmacists and indicated a general level of satisfaction—64.5% noted that they were "happy with their primary wholesaler." A trend was noted, with the observation that "five years ago, the average respondent did business with 3 wholesalers; today, 2 wholesalers."[10b]

Although 90.7% of the respondents admitted that "they could not get along without the service of a wholesaler," the news was not all good. About one-third reported some degree of discontent. Among the complaints were shorts and omits, return goods policies, delivery schedules, out of stock items, errors in order filling, and poor communications.[10b]

It can be assumed with some confidence that most of these problems are experienced by pharmacists who have not yet made a commitment to a primary supplier. The list of difficulties reads like the opposite of a similar listing of benefits to be derived from conversion to electronic order entry and inventory maintenance.

The January 1981 issue of the *NARD Journal* included comment on 800 replies to a mail survey of its readers. Again, some negative replies and a few apparent misunderstandings were expressed, but 75% of the respondents were using full-service wholesalers and felt that they were "getting their money's worth." Concerning computer-based services from wholesalers, satisfaction was indicated by 67% of the pharmacists in the survey.[10c]

There was clear indication of doubt with reference to pricing and delivery schedules. Some of the respondents questioned the integrity of the wholesaler's pricing structure, and failed to make the connection between increased discounts and reduced delivery frequencies, a "fact of life" in competitive markets. This problem represents an opportunity for the wholesaler, who can argue effectively for the primary supplier concept.

Innovation in pricing by wholesalers is a logical response to competitive intensity in a growing market. It can be estimated reliably that some 25% of wholesalers now offer cost-plus pricing (percentage or fee), and that the practice enjoys increasing application and understanding. Acceptance of this strategy has been facilitated by computerized order entry with invoices in pick sequence, shortened payment terms for customers, and more realistic delivery schedules.

Wholesalers include the following as important influences on their choice of pricing: the method of order entry, frequency of delivery, and the amount of service involved. Daily delivery remains the norm but the trend is toward a reduced schedule. Payment terms for most customers are twice monthly, with a few firms moving to weekly payment.

Policies in Perspective

Pricing decisions are considered by many to be more important in the determination of marketing strategy than any other factor. Price is certainly a major influence on policy at all levels in the distribution channel. An accurate assessment of wholesale pricing in general has been provided by Baumback et al.:

> Price competition is more direct and more intense for wholesalers than at other levels of distribution. A wholesaler has many rivals, including the manufacturer who sells direct, the functional middlemen, and other wholesalers in the same or broader lines. Wholesale prices fluctuate much more than do retail prices or manufacturers' prices because wholesalers operate on narrower margins and are less able to absorb increases in cost, even over a short period of time.[11]

This observation about price fluctuation can be supported by two other considerations. Because wholesale markets are well organized, response to supply and demand factors is particularly sensitive. Competing wholesalers react quickly to changes in the market. Also important is a factor that is often overlooked: a relatively slight change in price to the wholesaler involves large dollar amounts because of the quantities purchased.

The distinction between prices paid by wholesalers (producer prices) and prices *charged* by wholesalers has been a source of confusion in the popular press and governmental surveys. An example is the Bureau of Labor Statistics measure that is now entitled the Producer Price Index; for many years it was incorrectly called the Wholesale Price Index. This index has always reported changes in prices paid to manufacturers by wholesalers, but news stories based on the information would begin routinely with the headline: "Wholesalers Raise Prices Again."

Price is an important determinant of the relationship between manufacturers and wholesalers in the pharmaceutical industry. It has been argued recently that drug wholesalers are now less inclined to be "price-takers" (accepting manufacturers' suggested resale prices and discounting from list) and more inclined to be "price-makers" (adding a charge based upon an increasing variety of services to product cost, largely computer-based).[12]

Because wholesalers distribute the products of hundreds of competing manufacturers, the relative amount of support extended to particular lines is a variable factor. The manufacturer's policy is seen as favorable or not by wholesalers with reference to exclusivity in distribution, gross profit, dollar volume, turnover, and credit terms, among other considerations.

Formerly, a typical reaction of wholesalers to manufacturers who chose to bypass them and sell directly to retailers and hospitals was resentment expressed in lack of sales support. This is understandable when the wholesaler's margin is a function of manufacturers' policy and "suggested" resale prices under the restrictions of list less pricing at wholesale.

As wholesalers apply innovative pricing strategy that frees them from dependence on list prices and shifts them from the position of price-taker to price-maker, the conventional resentment toward direct sellers is tempered by the increased sales that result from pricing their lines competitively. A *policy* favoring wholesale distribution is then more important than pricing or stipulated margins.

It is significant that 10 of the top 20 companies in Table 12-2 are direct sellers by inclination and policy, but the wholesalers' market share for all of these lines is increasing according to the general trend. Order minimums for retailers are a factor of importance. In most cases these minimums have been increasing, but Upjohn maintains direct distribution for nearly 80% of its sales with minimum purchase levels of $50 for the line generally and $100 for a "special purchasing program." Minimum order levels of this size guarantee that the 16 distribution centers operated by Upjohn in the United States will be kept busy.

Conversely, a manufacturer fully committed to wholesaling, such as Burroughs Wellcome, Lilly, Searle, and Smith Kline and French should expect and receive greater support from his wholesaler than that provided to direct sellers. Among the companies that have made this commitment but are not listed with the top 20 in Table 12-2 are Armour, Astra, Boehringer Ingelheim, Dorsey, Endo, Fisons, Hoyt, Knoll, Mead Johnson, Norwich-Eaton, Ortho, Pennwalt, Riker, and others. Although these firms distribute to independent pharmacies exclusively through wholesalers, there are usually differences in policy for chain stores, hospitals, and government agencies. On occasion, these variations have been a source of friction between wholesalers and manufacturers.

TABLE 12-2. *Drugstore Sales Sold Through Wholesalers*
Top 20 United States Pharmaceutical Manufacturers

COMPANY	1982 SALES THROUGH WHOLESALERS (%)	DISCOUNT TO WHOLESALERS (%)
Abbott	57	5
Ayerst	70	16⅔
Burroughs Wellcome	100	16⅔–20
Ciba Geigy	68	16⅔
Hoechst	90	17
Lederle	39	5
Lilly	100	16⅔–20
Merck Sharp & Dohme	45	0
Parke-Davis	28	0
Pfizer	68	5
Robins	69	16⅔
Roche	80	16⅔
Sandoz	86	16⅔–20
Schering	45	2
Searle	100	16⅔–25
Smith Kline and French	100	15–17½
Squibb	30	0
Syntex	93	16⅔
Upjohn	21	0
Wyeth	35	0

Rucker has offered a general summary of differences in manufacturer distribution policies, a challenge for wholesalers:

> Turning to the distribution function, we find three distinct models in use today: (a) some leading firms, such as Eli Lilly, Robins and Smith-Kline utilize wholesalers to distribute more than 90 percent of the pharmaceuticals sold on a non-contract basis; (b) ten large firms follow a diametrical policy and rely heavily on distribution direct to the pharmacy; and (c) all remaining firms fall in a middle category between these two examples. It seems inconceivable that the firms and products found in the respective classifications are so unique that each format represents an optimum social solution for the efficient distribution of drug products. An *a priori* analysis, and supporting empirical evidence, might reveal that maximum system efficiency could be pursued most effectively under model (a).[13]

In suggesting that drug wholesalers distribute all or most products, Rucker warned that limiting factors such as manufacturers' franchise constraints can impede this ideal, as in fact they do.

NWDA Position Statements

The membership of the National Wholesale Druggists' Association, an organization that has served the industry since 1876, includes manufacturers and service agencies with an interest in wholesale distribution. Voting privileges, however, are restricted to wholesalers characterized as active members. NWDA bylaws stipulate these criteria for active membership by a wholesale firm:

1. It must offer credit to customers whose financial condition warrants the extension of credit.

2. It must offer regular sales and customer services through the use of full-time outside representatives.

3. It must provide reasonable and reliable delivery service.

4. It must maintain and own adequate local inventories consisting primarily of drug- and health-related items of a broad variety of suppliers.

5. Its customers must consist for the most part of firms and institutions that are primarily pharmacies not under direct or indirect common ownership with both the wholesaler and each other.

The association has issued periodic statements of position on industry issues, many of which are marketing-related. In 1981, the NWDA published a list of 20 official positions that reflect contemporary thought on topics ranging from national health insurance to the use of polygraphs in employee screening.

Three of these statements express concern about governmental efforts in marketing intervention and cost "control."

MAC/EAC: The NWDA reaffirms its vigorous opposition to Maximum Allowable Cost programs for prescription drugs, Estimated Acquisition Cost plans and federal "Price Guides." These plans are based upon inadequate and untimely price data, questionable scientific reasoning and an illusory promise of cost savings. No public benefit can be derived from this discriminatory intervention in an already over-regulated marketplace.

STATE VOLUME PURCHASE PLANS: The NWDA opposes centralized purchasing schemes tied to ill-conceived competitive bidding, indefensible rebates from suppliers or other approaches that would adversely affect patient care quality and seriously disrupt the drug distribution system. Price cannot be the sole criterion for supplier qualification in any economically sound plan and adequate fees for pharmaceutical service must be provided.

DIRECT PRICE LIMITATIONS: The NWDA vigorously opposes state governmental efforts to limit drug cost reimbursement for pharmacists under Medicaid (Title XIX), to direct prices for certain manufacturers' complete product lines or to limit reimbursement to large size costs for selected, frequently prescribed drugs. Arbitrary plans of this nature and specific reductions from Average Wholesale Price penalize community pharmacies and totally ignore the value-added concept of wholesale distribution.

In addition to concern about governmental encroachment on free market competition, wholesalers have strong opinions about manufacturing practices that have pricing impact. Another three position statements from the NWDA summarize these opinions. The issues involved have been sources of disagreement for many years.

DISCRIMINATORY PRICING: The NWDA rejects as arbitrary and discriminatory the "incremental cost concept" by which some manufacturers rationalize unrealistically low prices to large purchasers other than wholesalers, such as government agencies and institutions, with particular reference to contract bid situations. Each segment of production should carry its fair share of the cost burden. Equally unrealistic and unfair to wholesalers is the practice of selectively favorable pricing to certain classes of purchasers such as rack jobbers, retailers, hospitals, clinics and physicians.

NET PRICING: The NWDA reaffirms its longstanding opposition to the practice known as "net/pricing" by which manufacturers offer products at the same price to all levels of distribution. This practice ignores the obvious need for a service allowance to compensate wholesalers for their function in distribution.

RESALE PRICES: The NWDA believes that manufacturers should publish specific prices at which their products will be sold to wholesalers and refrain from the practice of further suggesting resale prices to be charged by wholesalers to their customers. As responsible businessmen, wholesalers should be free to determine their own pricing schedules individually and independent of manufacturers.

That last sentence emphasizes a trend already in progress that is gaining acceptance throughout the industry, a trend that goes well with the rapid growth of computer-based services offered by drug wholesalers. In this regard, three NWDA positions are related to further automation between wholesaler and manufacturer, a need for standard coding to facilitate computer processing, and recognition by regulatory agencies of the growth in systems applications for pharmacy.

AUTOMATED ORDER ENTRY: The NWDA encourages the growing application of computer systems in order entry, a practice that improves efficiency and service levels to the mutual benefit of manufacturers and wholesalers. Rapidly developing technology demonstrates the obvious value of the clearing house concept with costs shared by both participants in the order process. Confidentiality can be assured and marked improvement achieved with major cost benefit.

CODE AND SYMBOL USAGE: The NWDA recommends that all manufacturers identify each unit of sale with the Universal Product Code, the National Drug Code, or the National Health-Related Item Code in numeric characters as appropriate, and the corresponding use of the UPC Symbol. Further, shipping cases should be marked with the numeric code and the equivalent Distribution Symbol. Similarly, a standardized approach to the identification of solid dose forms is desirable.

COMPUTERIZED STORAGE OF PRESCRIPTION INFORMATION: The NWDA urges all State Boards of Pharmacy to adopt regulations which permit computerized storage and retrieval of prescription information. Numerous patient health protection benefits are available from the use of computers in pharmacy practice. Board regulations allowing the computer to store and retrieve prescription data will facilitate the use of contemporary systems and result in more efficient delivery of pharmaceutical services and improved health care for consumers.

Computers as Agents of Change

Branscomb has described the "spectacular growth and growing pervasiveness of the computer" as "one of the great surprises of modern times."[14] Abelson, reflecting on this phenomenon, concluded that "we are in the early phases of shifts in the economy and in social patterns comparable in magnitude to those of the industrial revolution."[15]

When the first electronic business computer was delivered to General Electric in 1955, Branscomb noted the expert suggestion that, in time, "perhaps 50 companies in the whole country could eventually use 'electronic brains.'"[14] In less than 30 years, the United States has put more than 500,000 general purpose computers into use, and available computing power is growing at the rate of about 40% each year.

Applications of computer services by drug wholesalers on behalf of their customers began in the early 1970s, but the growth since then has been as remarkable as the general trend. In recent years, the NWDA has collected experience data from wholesalers on the utilization of computer-based services provided for pharmacies. The report for August 1981 summarized responses from 94 firms that operated 258 distribution centers (82% of the membership). During the year, another 8000 pharmacies were convinced of the benefits that accompany electronic order entry, according to the report.

Table 12-3 presents some results of the 1981 survey, as compared to similar data for 1979. As indicated, there was growth in all categories of service when expressed in terms of the estimated numbers of pharmacies using the service. For example, the number of pharmacies using electronic order entry almost doubled in the 2-year period, to a total of nearly 32,000.

Customized price stickers are now used by more than 35,000 pharmacies. Also showing a demonstrable increase in usage are shelf labels for inventory control, product movement reports, microfiche systems, and management information reports. Although the latter service has grown in usage, the percentage of wholesalers offering the service has decreased. Other changes worth noting are decreases in the percentage of wholesalers offering

TABLE 12-3. *Computer-Based Services For Pharmacy, 1979–1981*

SERVICE	WHOLESALERS OFFERING (%)		NUMBER OF PHARMACIES USING	
	1979*	1981[†]	1979*	1981[†]
Automated accounts receivable	79	76	5,576	6,041
Customized price stickers	97	96	24,300	35,357
Shelf labels/inventory control	88	97	21,778	31,297
Electronic order entry	91	91	16,685	31,796
Management information report	78	57	8,035	13,705
Product movement report	76	76	9,869	13,865
Third-party processing	50	22	2,862	4,342
Microfiche system	88	75	17,150	25,190
Retail pricing guide	31	47	6,729	9,283
Scientific reorder controls	42	36	6,657	7,956
On-line terminal or in-pharmacy computer	63	39	1,229	1,504
Stock status/special buys:				
Separate report	—	55	10,761	18,327
Microfiche	—	61	9,576	19,218

*Estimates from 95 organizations operating 273 houses (83% of membership).
[†]Estimates from 94 organizations operating 258 houses (82% of membership).

Source: Fraser, W. W.: *NWDA Special Surveys, 1979 and 1981*. Scarsdale, NY: NWDA, 1981, p. 15.

third-party processing and on-line terminals or in-pharmacy computers.

The NWDA estimated that wholesalers spend some $32 million a year to provide these services to customers. Many programs offer a representative package of services to the pharmacist for less than $100 per month. The more obvious measurable benefits include sales increases of the order of $75 to $100 per square foot, an increase in turnover of stock, generally several turns per year, and decreases in inventory costs of 20 to 25%.

Public companies in drug wholesaling regularly report specific results from computer-based services that illustrate these remarkable changes in progress. McKesson Drug Company is the largest of these, with a market share approaching 25%, and is the only national firm. The company operated from 60 distribution centers during fiscal 1981, down from 92 houses in 1974. These larger more efficient centers have posted operating records and have shown extraordinary growth in recent years.

McKesson serves about 14,000 pharmacies and 2000 hospitals. Each distribution center stocks 15,000 products from more than 2500 manufacturers. Overall, about 50,000 different items are found in the McKesson inventory nationwide. The company is a major division of Foremost-McKesson, a diversified corporation that also distributes and manufactures products in the food, chemical, and wine and spirits industries.

The resources available to an organization with annual revenue in excess of $4 billion have been an important factor in McKesson's market share increase and in the development of new services. More than 90% of the company's order lines were received through automated entry procedures in 1981. It was anticipated that the 100% level would be reached in 1983.

Some 12,000 pharmacies were using at least one of the several systems offered by the wholesale firm to its customers for effective shelf management, profit improvement, and reduced investment in inventory. Nearly 7500 of these pharmacies were subscribers in 1981 and 1982 to the complete ECONOMOST program, a comprehensive electronic order entry system that includes pricing protection and control, shelf management procedures and labels, merchandising information, management reports, and other features.

ECONOMOST is organized around retail profit centers in the pharmacy. Sometimes called "fine line classes," these profit centers include more than 100 groups of related products. New participants in the system have their pharmacies rearranged to accommodate the ECONOMOST configuration. All items are assigned a particular location with computer-printed shelf labels.

Reordering is controlled by the item descriptions and by codes on the shelf labels. When the order arrives, it can be shelved quickly because it is shipped to conform to the store layout in the computer's memory. Typically, this saves 4 to 6 hours of labor with each delivery, reduces overstocks and missing items, and makes possible a reduced order schedule—i.e., fewer deliveries per week.

Several types of order entry devices are employed (Fig. 12-2). Portable terminals can enter the necessary information or a touch-tone telephone may be used. A recent system enhancement from McKesson is ECONOSCAN, a wand device that "reads" the product numbers in bar code form (Fig. 12-2*H*). Scanning virtually eliminates errors and reduces order time dramatically.

This systems approach to asset management has found increasing acceptance in hospital pharmacies that formerly acquired inventory directly from manufacturers. Because hospital pharmacies are attracted to the efficiencies of newer wholesaler systems, there has been a readily apparent shift in purchasing practices.

One hospital pharmacist has described a first-year savings of $463,000 from total commitment to a purchasing program using electronic order entry. Based on this experience, Sherrin concluded that "the key to reducing operating or inventory costs is an agreement with a progressive drug wholesaler."[16]

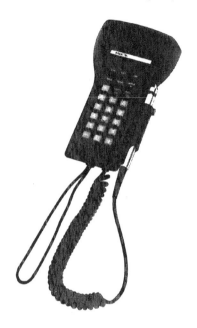

A

B

C

D

(Legend on p. 265.)

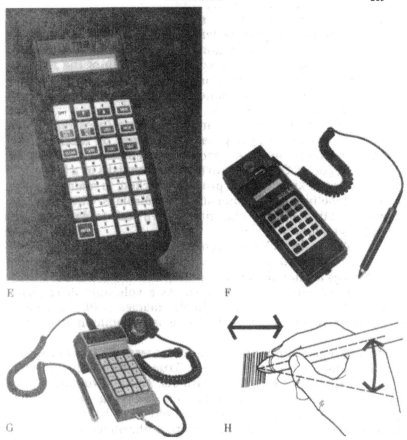

Fig. 12-2. *An assortment of POETs (portable order entry terminals). A, Telxon 716. B, Telxon 101 Manager. C, Telxon 716 (close-up). D, MSI/55. E, MSI/88s. F, MSI/66. G, Azurdata Scorepak. H, ECONOSCAN.*

Retailing Reorganized

Computerization adds the important element of discipline to the order process. There are also wholesaler services available that are not necessarily tied to computers, which impose intelligent controls on marketing practices in the pharmacy. Among these is the relatively new offering from McKesson known as ECONOPLAN. This is a planogram service to assist pharmacists with appropriate item placement and shelf space allocation for each department or major section in the pharmacy. Maximum sales potential is emphasized through merchandising based on reliable product movement information from a variety of sources. ECONOPLAN is intended for the pharmacist who chooses to retain responsibility for merchandising by himself or by his personnel.

The method makes logical shopping easier by positioning large sizes on the right, fast sellers at eye level, and slower-moving items vertically below on gondolas or wall cases. A monthly packet of materials includes a color photograph of the featured department, schematic diagrams for placement, ECONOSCAN shelf labels in planogram sequence, a competitive pricing survey, and merchandising information.

An extension of the service merchandising (occasionally described as rack jobbing) approach is offered by McKesson as COSMcK, a comprehensive space management service for 20 product categories. COSMcK provides regular visits by a McKesson merchandiser to keep shelves properly stocked, to maintain accurate price labeling, and to build attractive displays. Obviously, this allows more time for the pharmacy's own staff to develop sales and serve customers.

VALU-RITE is a McKesson program that provides an opportunity for independent pharmacies to buy products and promote their services as though they were units of a chain, but the advantages of independence are retained. As a voluntary drug chain, VALU-RITE served more than 2000 pharmacies in 1982 as a chain headquarters operation would—there is a common marketing identity.

The concept is similar to one used successfully in other industries, including Associated Grocers, True-Value Hardware, Century 21 Realty, and Best Western Hotels. Another voluntary drug chain was formed in 1981 by Bergen Brunswig and 10 other wholesale firms under the designation of Family Value Drug Centers. Initially there were 20 participating pharmacies.

When McKesson acquired VALU-RITE in 1978, there were 200 members. The voluntary chain became McKesson Drug Company's largest single customer and the largest chain in the United States. A base of 4000 members was anticipated for 1985 to 1986. The major marketing weaknesses of independent pharmacies—limited purchasing and advertising power—are overcome, and the independent's major strengths—local neighborhood convenience, personal service, community involvement, and pride of ownership—are magnified.

Pharmacy design services have been offered for many years by McKesson and other drug wholesalers (Fig. 12-3 and 12-4). A specialized force of pharmacy design consultants operates from McKesson distribution centers to remodel existing pharmacies and to plan and install new facilities. The service includes location analysis to determine and estimate trading areas, drugstore spending patterns, and potential market share available (Fig. 12-5).

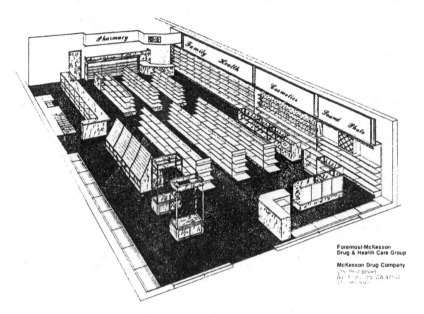

Fig. 12-3. *Pharmacy design. (Source: Foremost-McKesson Drug & Health Care Group, San Francisco.)*

The design of institutional pharmacies and drug distribution systems in hospitals and in extended care facilities is an important aspect of the service available from some wholesalers. McKesson, for example, has a Redi-Med line of equipment that includes applications for the efficient processing of unit-dose medication. A system of medication carts, specialized storage units, and computer-based services has been developed.

Strategic Planning

More than a process or technique, strategic planning is a managerial philosophy. The information ordinarily available to the beginning planner is inadequate. A first step, then, is to improve the information base and to describe accurately what is currently happening. Analytic models are used frequently as aids in plan development.

To build on the information available, and to develop a strategic growth plan for health-care distribution in the 1980s, NWDA retained the services of Booz, Allen & Hamilton.[17] This manage-

Fig. 12-4. *Finished pharmacy. (Source: Foremost-McKesson Drug & Health Care Group, San Francisco.)*

ment consulting firm conducted a major industry inquiry during 1980 and 1981, identifying new opportunities for development in drug wholesaling.*

Booz, Allen's initial report grouped wholesalers into four "levels" or business segments according to sophistication in computer systems, services, and management skills. Level A, about 10% of NWDA firms, includes primarily manual operations with most orders still placed by telephone. Level B firms (33%) have begun the conversion to automation and offer some management services for pharmacists—price stickers and shelf labels, for example. Level C wholesalers (19%) exhibit direct order entry systems for most accounts and have a broader array of services. For the largest segment (38%), in Level D, highly advanced systems are common, and services tailored to individual customer's needs are evolving. Each of the four segments represents a different level of resource investment, with capital requirements increasing steadily from one level to the next.

---

*Several summaries of the Booz, Allen & Hamilton study and a broad assortment of descriptive material about drug wholesaling are available from: National Wholesale Druggists' Association, 105 Oronoco Street, Alexandria, VA.

**Drug Store Location
Analysis Worksheet**

Part 1 Trading Area

Step [1] Determine trading area on map. ☐ Map attached

Step [2] Select source of population figures.

☐ Post Office ☐ Chamber of Commerce ☐ Newspaper Survey ☐ Telephone Company

☐ Personal Survey ☐ Mailing Service ☐ Utility Companies ☐ Developer Site Survey

_____	x _____	= _____
Number of family units	*National average family	Total population of area

Part 2 Total Annual Drug Store Spending in Area

Step [1]

Source of Information	Per Capita Drug Store Spending	Source of Information	Per Capita Drug Store Spending
☐ Sales Mkt Mgmt (Surv Buy Power)	$ _____	☐ Chamber of Commerce	$ _____
☐ Banks	$ _____	☐ U.S. Dept. of Commerce	$ _____
☐ Newspaper	$ _____		
☐ State Pharmaceutical Assn	$ _____		

Step [2]

_____	x _____	= _____
Persons	Per capita spending	Total drug store spending

Part 3 Share Available to Proposed Store

Step [1]	Step [3] Estimated % efficiency of location

Step [1]

	Volume	Amt Trading Area
Store A	$ _____	$ _____
Store B	$ _____	$ _____
Store C	$ _____	$ _____
Store D	$ _____	$ _____
Store E	$ _____	$ _____
Total		$ _____

Step [3] Estimated % efficiency of location

Size	_____ %	Convenient Accessibility	_____ %
Shape	_____ %	Near to Traffic Pulling Merch	_____ %
Front	_____ %	Near to Prescr. Doctor	_____ %
Parking	_____ %	Near to Health Facilities	_____ %
Entrances	_____ %	Near to Public Transportation	_____ %
		Est Average % Efficiency	_____ %

Step [2] Difference total drug store spending and amount of competition in this trading area.

Total spending	$ _____
Amt in this trading area	− $ _____
Total estim. available spending =	$ _____

Step [4] Estimated sales volume of drug store in this location

Total estim. available spending	$ _____
Estimated average % efficiency X	_____
	= $ _____

Part 4 Break Even Sales Volume

Step [1] Min. annual payroll and rent expense

Annual payroll expense	$ _____
Annual rent expense +	$ _____
Total of both =	$ _____

Step [2] Sales volume req. to support this store— (break even point)

Total Expense	$ _____
**Lilly Digest figure −	_____ %
Multiplied by 100 =	$ _____

*Sales & Marketing Management "Survey of Buying Power"
**Current Lilly Digest

S-534 (R3-80)

Fig. 12-5. *Drugstore location analysis worksheet. (Source: Foremost-McKesson Drug & Health Care Group, San Francisco.)*

The analysts cautioned that a wholesaler's position in this classification "is not necessarily a function of size nor is it indicative of the level of success or profitability of the firm."[17] Instead, the segmentation can be used "to help define the nature and extent of the strategic options available." Booz, Allen contended that "size is not a critical factor in achieving competitive economics—efficient, well-managed wholesalers with sales under $20 million are capable of developing a strong market position."[17]

Although consolidation of wholesale facilities and economies of scale resulting from centralization of certain activities were seen as key trends, the study concluded that "a drug wholesaler's profitability is primarily determined by his average account size and his operating efficiency." Voluntaries and franchise arrangements are expected to gain in importance as structures for new value-added services.

In general, Booz, Allen predicted that growth in the 1980s "will be led by drug wholesalers employing an aggressive, service-based, forward integration strategy."[17] A stronger partnership between pharmacists and wholesalers is seen as a necessity based on improvements in management, marketing, and merchandising services, and on appropriate changes in product mix.

A model entitled "Building a Strategy" applies equally well to the pharmacist who recognizes the value of strategic planning. Four elements of a successful strategy were identified in the study: target market, target customer, competitive offering, and required resources.

The last of these elements refers to an investment of funds, people, systems, and facilities to deliver a competitive mix of products and services in the interest of improved health care. This is a marketing investment that pharmacists and wholesalers can and should make together.

References

1. LeConey, M. M.: Financial Analyst Explains Why Investors Like Drug Wholesaling, *Wholesale Drugs, 34* (No. 1):21, 1982.
2. Smith, M. C.: Principles of Pharmaceutical Marketing, 2nd Ed., Philadelphia, Lea & Febiger, 1975, pp. 221, 243.
3. Morson, J. M.: NWDA Regional Meeting Presentation, 1981.
4. McKeon, J. C.: Conflicting Patterns of Structural Change in Wholesaling, in *Marketing Channels,* 2nd Ed., Edited by L. C. Boone and J. C. Johnson, Tulsa: PPC Books, 1977, p. 123.
5. Weiss, E. B., quoted in Lopata, R. S.: Faster Pace in Wholesaling, in *Marketing Channels,* 2nd Ed., Edited by L. C. Boone and J. C. Johnson, Tulsa: PPC Books, 1977, p. 84.
6. Lopata, R. S.: Faster Pace in Wholesaling, in *Marketing Channels,* 2nd Ed., Edited by L. C. Boone and J. C. Johnson, Tulsa: PPC Books, 1977, p. 84.
7. Cox, R., and Schutte, T. F.: A Look at Channel Management, in *Marketing Channels,* 2nd Ed., Edited by L. C. Boone and J. C. Johnson, Tulsa: PPC Books, 1977, p. 14.

8. Siecker, B. R.: The Wholesaler Effect in Pharmacy Management, *American Pharmacy, NS21* (No. 11):34, 1981.

9. Martini, E. P.: Fiscal '80 Best Ever at BBC, *Wholesale Drugs, 32*:8, 1981.

10. Fenstermaker, J. J.: Dynamic Distribution, *Wholesale Drugs, 31*:16, 1980.

10a. Retailers Talk About Wholesalers, *American Druggist, 178* (No. 5):31, 1978.

10b. Independent Drug Store Owners, *American Druggist, 182* (No. 4):24, 1980.

10c. How Independents Perceive Wholesalers, *NARD Journal, 103* (No. 1):21, 1981.

11. Baumback, Lawyer, and Kelley, *How to Organize and Operate A Small Business,* New York: Prentice-Hall, 1973, p. 342.

12. Fay, J. T., Jr.: Wholesale Drug Pricing and Perfect Knowledge, Ph.D. Thesis, Massachusetts College of Pharmacy, 1980.

13. Rucker, T. D.: Reimbursement Policy Under Drug Insurance: Administrative Expediency or Economic Validity, October, 1977. (Unpublished paper.)

14. Branscomb, L. M.: Electronics and Computers: An Overview, *Science, 215* (No. 4534):755, 1982.

15. Abelson, P. H.: The Revolution in Computers and Electronics, *Science, 215* (No. 4534):751, 1982.

16. Sherrin, T. P.: Hospital Pharmacy Cost Containment, *American Critical Care, 1* (No. 1):38, 1981.

17. Booz, Allen & Hamilton Study, available from National Wholesale Druggists' Association, 105 Oronoco Street, Alexandria, VA.

## CHAPTER 13

The Retailer

DEWEY D. GARNER

Educators have found that early in their academic program most pharmacy students do not recognize the importance of studying pharmaceutical marketing. They do not visualize the activities of the community and hospital pharmacy as functions of marketing. It is later, often much later, that they see a career in marketing as their destiny. Table 13-1 lists the career preferences for pharmacy graduates in 1970 and 1980.

Over 80% of all pharmacy graduates will enter the career field of either community or hospital pharmacy. Because someone in each of these fields fits the definition of a drug retailer these graduates will have entered a career of pharmaceutical marketing in a retail establishment. During the decade of the 1970s more graduates wanted to work in hospitals than ever before. Fewer than ever preferred community pharmacy careers and, of those, approximately 50% selected the chains.

The *1977 Census of Retail Trade* defined retailers as "all establishments primarily engaged in selling merchandise for personal or household consumption and rendering services incidental to the sale of goods."[1] In its classification the census included two major types of drug retailers, under miscellaneous retail stores—drugstores and proprietary stores.

Drugstores are establishments engaged in the retail sale of presciption drugs and patent medicines. They may carry a number of related lines, such as cosmetics, toiletries, tobacco, and novelty merchandise, and may operate a soda fountain or lunch counter. These stores are classified on the basis of their usual trade designation rather than on a strict interpretation of commodities handled. Proprietary stores are establishments that generally sell the same merchandise as drugstores, except that prescriptions are not filled and sold.

TABLE 13-1. *Career Choices of Pharmacy Graduating Classes of 1972 and 1980*

CAREER FIELDS	1970	1980
Community pharmacy	67.9%	57.4%
Hospital pharmacy	17.0	23.3
Manufacturing	1.5	2.3
Government	2.0	1.4
Graduate study	8.5	7.2
Other career fields	3.1	2.7
Undecided	—	5.7
	100.0%	100.0%

Sources: The Class of 1972, *American Druggist, 165*:21, 1972; Ratio of Grads Aiming for Hospital Jobs Drops Slightly, *American Druggist, 181*:26, 1980.

For our purposes retailing includes those activities performed by anyone to offer goods and services for sale to the ultimate consumer, and a drug retailer is any outlet providing drugs or health-care services to the patient.

Quantitative Measurement of Importance of Retailing

Data from the *1977 Census of Retail Trade* (the most recent available) showed that the United States' 1.9 million retail stores had sales totaling $723 billion an increase of 58.1% over sales reported in 1972, when the last such census was taken. The 49,510 drug and proprietary stores accounted for $23 billion, an increase of 48.7% since 1972. Drugs account for 1.8% and health and beauty aids for 1.6% of total retail sales.[1]

Table 13-2 provides some indication of the level of sales by type of business. The growth rate in the 1970s of these major types of business was 8 to 10% annually.

Retailing is the third largest employer in the nation, with over 15 million employees. This constituted approximately 18% of all employees in the United States in 1977.[2]

Classification and Extent of Retail Pharmacy Institutions

Classification of retail pharmacies into distinct groups is not as easy as it may seem at first. Historically, retail pharmacies have been divided into three major groups: the apothecary (prescription) shop, the traditional or neighborhood pharmacy, and the super stores. The *Lilly Digest* has classified all pharmacies under

TABLE 13-2. *Total Retail Stores Sales ($ millions) by Type of Retailer*

TYPE OF RETAILING	1977	1978	CHANGE (%)	10-YEAR GROWTH RATE
All retail stores	724,000	798,818	+10.3	+9.4
Durable goods total	247,832	277,916	+12.1	+10.6
Automotive group	148,444	163,668	+10.3	+10.2
Furniture and appliance group	34,761	37,430	+7.7	+9.0
Lumber, building materials, hardware group	38,761	44,125	+14.2	+11.1
Nondurable goods stores total	476,188	520,902	+9.4	+8.9
Apparel group	38,341	37,828	+10.2	+7.7
Men's and boy's wear stores	7,052	7,353	+4.3	+6.9
Women's apparel, accessory stores	13,106	14,660	+11.9	+7.7
Family and other apparel stores	6,693	7,147	+6.8	+7.9
Shoe stores	5,852	6,593	+12.7	+7.2
Eating and drinking places	63,556	70,083	+10.3	+10.4
Food group	158,519	174,458	+10.1	+8.8
Gasoline service stations	58,231	60,884	+4.6	+9.3
General merchandise group	90,133	99,505	+10.4	+8.2
Department stores, excluding mail order	72,333	79,732	+10.2	+7.3
Mail order (department store) merchandise	6,705	7,073	+5.5	+9.0
Variety stores	7,602	7,809	+2.7	+3.1
Drug and proprietary stores	22,918	25,337	+10.6	+8.0
Liquor stores	12,832	13,616	+6.1	+6.6

Source: U.S. Department of Commerce, 1979.

1200 square feet in size with a prescription sales volume exceeding 50% of total sales as an apothecary shop.[2a] A traditional pharmacy is viewed as one usually having 3000 to 5000 square feet, and with a significant out-front sales volume. The super stores are those over 5000 square feet. Actually it would probably be more appropriate to classify many pharmacies with 7500 square feet as traditional pharmacies, because many of the super stores exceed 10 to 30 thousand square feet. Many people view the super stores as being synonymous with chain and discount stores, even though there are also apothecaries and traditional chains.

Under the definition of retailing is also included a number of other institutions to be discussed in this chapter. They include hospitals, health maintenance organizations (HMOs) and other group practice clinics, mail order operations, supermarkets, and drugstores.

Hospitals

In 1978, 6321 hospitals responded to the annual survey of the American Hospital Association. Over 90% of the hospitals with 100 beds offered full-time pharmacy service. Most federal hospitals offered full-time pharmacy service (95.6%) as compared to 71.2% of the nonfederal hospitals.[3]

Differences do exist by region of the country with respect to pharmaceutical service. Table 13-3 indicates that the range of hospitals by region with a full-time pharmacist went from a high of 86% in New England and the Middle Atlantic States to a low of 50% in the West North Central states.

Health Maintenance Organizations and Group Practice Clinics

Health maintenance organizations (HMOs) may be a future market of considerable size for the retail pharmacy. At the first HMO Conference of the National Association of Chain Drug Stores, held in 1981, Dr. Loren Vorlisky, president of the Medcenter Health Plan in Minneapolis, indicated that there were then 240 HMOs serving 9.4 million people. He predicted that by 1990 some 30 million persons and maybe more will be enrolled in HMOs.[4] In 1971 the nationwide enrollment in HMOs was 3.5 million.[5]

TABLE 13-3. *Hospital Pharmacy Service by Region, 1978*

AREA	(NUMBER) HOSPITALS REPORTING	PHARMACY WITH REGISTERED PHARMACIST			
		FULL-TIME		PART-TIME	
		NUMBER	PER-CENT	NUMBER	PER-CENT
United States (Total)	6321	4590	72.6	1221	19.3
By Census division					
1. New England	346	296	85.5	38	11.0
2. Middle Atlantic	754	648	85.9	63	8.4
3. South Atlantic	911	719	78.9	140	15.4
4. East North Central	1011	806	79.7	141	13.9
5. East South Central	485	338	69.7	111	22.9
6. West North Central	809	406	50.2	312	38.6
7. West South Central	821	532	64.8	185	22.5
8. Mountain	410	250	61.0	118	28.8
9. Pacific	774	595	76.9	113	14.6

Source: Adapted, with permission, from: *Hospital Statistics,* published by the American Hospital Association, copyright 1979.

The health maintenance organization was created by federal legislation passed in 1973 (PL93-222) to help alleviate the shortage and inappropriate nature of our health-care services by guaranteeing to provide as well as pay for the enrollee's benefit package. It is based on the following four principles:

1. It is an organized system of health care which accepts the responsibility to provide or otherwise assure the delivery of . . .

2. An agreed-upon set of comprehensive health maintenance and treatment services for . . .

3. A voluntarily enrolled group of persons in a geographic area and . . .

4. Is reimbursed through a prenegotiated and fixed periodic payment made by, or on behalf of, each person or family unit enrolled in the plan.

Because the term health maintenance organization is generic for a prepaid medical plan under which a fixed sum is paid for scheduled benefits over a specified time period, the marketing implications for retail pharmacy are substantial, according to how the pharmaceutical services are provided and how they are reimbursed. Under current programs services are provided through in-house pharmacies or through contractual agreements with outside retail outlets. The mechanism for payment is either fee for service or capitation. Pharmacy managers feel secure with the fee for service approach because it is identical to that of other third-party programs. Many are apprehensive about capitation because it introduces the element of risk associated with the principles of insurance.

Many pharmacies are now contractually involved with HMO programs in the provision of pharmaceutical services. Walgreen Company seems to be taking the lead among drugstore chains in this area. At the company's annual shareholder's meeting in January 1981, President Fred Canning listed HMOs among the major growth areas that Walgreen will be pursuing in the 1980s.[6] Walgreen is now participating in 21 plans in 17 major cities. Canning predicted that HMO growth in the 1980s will increase from a $3.6 billion industry serving 8 million people to a $33.6 billion industry serving 20 million people. Revco, Rite-Aid, and Jack Eckerd Corporation are now also getting into the HMO field.

According to Berkley Bennett, of Washington Counsel/Medicine and Health, a growing number of drug chains may soon be opening stores that do not sell drugs.[7] What they will be selling are sickroom and convalescent supplies. He stated that a freestanding home health-care center can operate with at least 5000 to 6000 square feet of space. People's, Walgreens, Hooks, Stein, Begley, and Medicare-Glaser have already established such stores, or plan to do so.

Walgreen, through its Health Services Division, launched in 1978, is exploring the concept of expanded health centers in 27 of its drug stores. It opened a separate convalescent aids center in the spring of 1978 to probe the potential of this new field of pharmaceutical marketing.[8]

The creation of the freestanding home health-care centers with their emphasis on expanded service may become an important community service to the increasing number of home care patients.

Mail Order Operations

Mail order prescription operations have increased in activity since the Supreme Court voted in 1976 to allow prescription price advertising. This action, coupled with the easing of state restrictions, and aided by an inflation-plagued economy leading more Americans to seek out lower prices, has had a dramatic impact upon the mail order prescription business. More than 25 million prescriptions were filled by mail in 1976, twice the number delivered in 1972.[9]

Historically, much of the mail order operation has been conducted by groups such as the Veterans Administration and various state boards of health and mental health. The largest nongovernmental mail order prescription business in 1976 was conducted by the National Retired Teachers Association-American Association of Retired Persons, handling over 4 million prescriptions. The largest of the profit motive operations was Pharmaceutical Services in Kansas City, with a volume of 200,000 prescriptions annually.[9]

In 1981 the American Nurses' Association offered as a *new benefit* to its members the opportunity to purchase prescription drugs directly from the service agency, Federal Pharmacy Center of Missouri. Their promotional literature to the membership listed "fresh" compounds and exceptional and speedy same-day service as advantages.[9]

Still, the mail order prescription business has had a dubious history of professional respectability. The advent of the mail order firms of the 1950s created a storm of controversy regarding the ethics of mail order practice. The debate centered around the issue of the disruption of the physician-patient-pharmacist relationship. There is also the potential for fraud in the mail order operation, and the need to safeguard the distribution of controlled substances. These feelings have been stated by the National Association of Retail Druggists, the American Pharmaceutical Association (APhA), and other professional pharmacy organizations. In February, 1980, some activities of the APhA in opposition to mail order pharmacy were held to have violated Section 1 of the Sherman Antitrust Act by the United States District Court. Federal Prescription Service, Inc. was awarded $34,000 in damages, automatically trebled under antitrust laws to $102,000. Federal's appeal to the United States Circuit Court claimed that this damage award was insufficient. Oral arguments were heard from later parties in April 1981.[10] The United States Court of Appeals for the District of Columbia overturned the trial court decision and ruled that APhA was not guilty of violating federal antitrust laws on August 12, 1981.[10a] Federal Prescription Service, Inc., appealed the appeal court ruling to the United States Supreme Court. On January 25, 1982, the Supreme Court decided not to review the case and thereby left in place the Appeals Court action.[10b]

It is difficult to speculate on the future for the mail order prescription business. On the one hand it appears that the government may consider a more acceptable view of such operations. On the other hand, federal regulations, such as the maximum allowable cost regulation, state regulations on Medicaid, and local competition could limit the expansion of such activity.

In the nonprescription drug field mail order companies have achieved success. The principal product category offered for many years was vitamins; more recently a myriad of products for weight control and products of natural origin appealing to natural food enthusiasts have been offered.

Discount Stores

The birth of discount outlets, complete with self-service and store departmentalization, can be traced back to the 1880s in this country. However, the growth of high volume, and low price on mass merchandising has been prevalent since the end of World War II. The public has shown a preference for patronizing discount stores because of the convenience of one-stop shopping and low prices. In addition to prescription drugs the discounters offer a variety of product categories that are normally stocked in drug stores (Table 13-4).

To illustrate further the impact that the discounters, supermarkets, and other mass merchandisers have had upon the drugstore, Table 13-5 shows the market share of drugstores for health and beauty aids. Robert Bolger, president of the National Association of Chain Drug Stores, stated that supermarkets are now the number one competitor of drugstore chains.[11]

TABLE 13-4. *Discount Stores Sales by Product Category*

PRODUCT CATEGORY	VOLUME ($ BILLIONS)	SALES PER STORE ($ MILLIONS)	ANNUAL SALES PER SQUARE FOOT ($)	ANNUAL TURNS	INITIAL MARKUP (%)	GROSS MARGIN (%)
Ladies' apparel	6.6	913	91.75	5.3	43	36
Men's and boys' apparel	4.4	608	80.85	3.6	41	35
Automotive	3.5	482	211.27	4.7	35	35
Housewares	3.4	468	91.75	4.2	37	33
Hardware	3.1	427	132.91	3.0	41	36
Health and beauty aids	3.1	429	192.03	4.3	29	23
Consumer electronics	3.0	413	206.44	3.0	26	21
Toys	2.5	344	130.03	3.7	33	26
Sporting goods	2.3	317	124.13	3.5	35	27
Photo and camera	2.2	303	451.91	3.6	23	17
Personal care	1.8	248	257.25	4.2	22	16
Domestics	1.7	238	76.92	3.5	40	35
Stationery	1.2	170	97.32	4.7	44	39
Electric housewares	1.2	165	197.32	4.0	24	16
Records and tapes	1.2	148	157.29	4.4	25	18
Paint	1.1	148	116.50	2.9	43	37
Fabrics and sewing	0.9	119	82.22	2.9	42	36
Jewelry	0.8	106	188.57	3.0	49	42
Glassware	0.4	48	75.98	4.1	42	37

Source: Reprinted by permission of *Discount Store News*, September 24, 1979. Copyright Lebhar-Friedman, Inc., 425 Park Avenue, New York, NY 10022.

TABLE 13-5. *Unit Sales for 25 Health and Beauty Aid Categories for Food, Drug, and Mass Merchandise Outlets in 1980 by Type of Store*

TYPE OF STORE	DOLLAR SALES VOLUME
Drug stores	1,651,154
Food stores	2,813,882
Mass merchandisers	806,913
Total—all stores	5,271,949

Source: Reprinted by permission from *Drug Store News*, January 12, 1981. Copyright Lebhar-Friedman, Inc., 425 Park Avenue, New York, NY 10022.

Drugstores

The most important class of retailers in the drug field is the one known to the public as a pharmacy or drugstore. According to Bureau of Census data there were 44,388 drugstores in the United States in 1977. These establishments employed 92,495 full-time and 20,274 part-time pharmacists.[12]

The total sales volume for drugstores in 1980 was $32,329,228,000, a gain of 11.5% over the sales volume for 1979.[13] Total domestic retail trade sales in 1980 rose less than 7%. These percentages support the hypothesis that drugstores are more immune to recession and depressed economic years as compared to other types of retailers. A breakdown of consumer spending in drugstores by department for 1980 is presented in Table 13-6.

According to the 1980 *Lilly Digest*, 49.8% of the community pharmacy's sales volume was prescription activity,[14] but Barry Downing, board chairman of Associated Druggists, Inc., predicted that nondrug departments will be the big growth users for the future. As people seek the convenience and service of the community drugstore they want to find either a wider variety or sundries-type merchandise—i.e., food, school supplies, toys, housewares, jewelry, and electronic items.[15] Although it may be difficult to predict the future product and service lines of the drugstore, it seems fairly certain that they will continue to prosper. Table 13-7 indicates that the drugstore is one of the strongest survivors among types of retail businesses. Only 2% of them failed in the first 10 months of 1979, one of the lowest failure rates.

STORE SIZE

One means of comparing store size is on the basis of annual sales volume. Table 13-8 contains census data comparing drugstores over 4 decades using this criterion. The trend shows a dramatic increase over time. In 1948 almost half the drugstores had

TABLE 13-6. *1980 Consumer Spending in Drugstores*

DEPARTMENT	SALES VOLUME
Prescriptions	10,880,424
Convenience foods/beverages	3,353,370
Photo products	2,185,239
Tobacco	1,656,892
Magazines/books	1,215,337
Cosmetics	1,192,153
Hair care	1,185,399
Candy/gum	1,087,552
Cough and cold items	657,777
Analgesics	652,606
Vitamins	583,399
Fragrances	511,674
Skin care	502,338
Baby needs	492,442
Dental products	490,475
Stationery	439,680
First aid	411,451
Greeting cards/gifts	395,666
Personal hygiene	346,289
Home health care products	331,139
Optical	326,611
Feminine hygiene	316,727
Shaving products	309,375
Consumer electronics	294,456
Toys/games	272,039
Hardware	247,043
Antacids	242,222
Laxatives	229,627
Hosiery	218,608
Household supplies	172,135
Contraceptives	159,310
Diet aids	156,242
Foot care	118,625

Source: Thurlow, R. M.: 1980 Variety's Hour, *Drug Topics, 125*:5, 1981.

an annual sales volume under $50,000. In 1977 these pharmacies had almost entirely disappeared. The drugstores with over $1,000,000 in sales did not exist in 1948; in 1977 they comprised 12% of the total market. The greatest number of pharmacies in 1977 cluster in the $100,000 to $299,000 sales volume category. Drugstores may also be classified according to the number of employees. Table 13-9 shows census findings for 4 decades of operation. The most striking feature of this table is the disappearance of the one-person store operation, from 12.3% in 1948 to 0.4% in 1977. Currently half the drugstores continue to employ approximately 3 to 9 employees. The proportion of drugstores

TABLE 13-7. *Failures by Type of Retail Business (first 10 months of 1979)*

TYPE OF BUSINESS	NUMBER	%
Food and liquor	320	10.2
General merchandise	46	2.0
Apparel, accessories	301	13.3
Furniture and home furnishings	321	14.2
Lumber, building materials, and hardware	116	5.1
Automotive group	351	15.6
Eating and drinking places	449	19.9
Drugstores	46	2.0
Miscellaneous	395	17.5
Total	2255	99.8*

*Total does not equal 100% because of rounding.

Source: Adapted from Dun & Bradstreet: *Monthly Business Failures*, 54:2, 1980.

with 10 or more employees increased from 23.6% in 1948 to 79% in 1977.

Another way to classify drugstores by size is on the basis of square feet. In Table 13-10 we see stores ranging from 5000 square feet (the independent and convenience stores) to the combination stores, with 40,000 square feet. The expected future growth rate is greatest for the combination and convenience stores.

GEOGRAPHIC DISTRIBUTION

There are differences in retail activity of drugstores in this country according to their geographic region. Among the reasons for these geographic differences are demographic and economic

TABLE 13-8. *Percentage of Stores by Volume of Business (Covers Pharmacies in Business the Entire Year)*

ANNUAL VOLUME	NUMBER OF STORES (%)			
	1948	1958	1967	1977
Under $50,000	44.8	24.5	14.2	2.0
$50,000–99,000	32.4	31.3	19.3	6.1
$100,000–299,000	19.9	37.4	47.9	42.8
$300,000–499,000	2.0	4.4	10.2	19.5
$500,000–999,000	0.8	1.9	6.0	17.3
$1,000,000 or more	0.1	0.5	2.3	12.3
Total	100.0	100.0	100.0	100.0

Source: U.S. Bureau of the Census: *Census of Business, 1963, 1967, and 1977*, Washington, DC: U.S. Government Printing Office.

TABLE 13-9. *Percentage of Drugstores by People Employed*

NUMBER OF EMPLOYEES	PERCENTAGE OF DRUGSTORES			
	1948	1958	1967	1977
0	12.3	9.7	3.5	0.4
1	11.2	8.8	8.4	4.6
2	13.2	11.0	9.4	6.6
3–9	49.4	51.6	50.2	49.5
10–14	9.7	9.6	13.5	18.9
15–19	9.7	4.1	6.2	9.1
20–49	3.7	4.7	8.0	
50–99	0.4	0.4	0.7	10.9
100 or more	0.1	0.1	0.1	0.1
Total	100.0	100.0	100.0	100.0

Source: U.S. Bureau of the Census: *Census of Business, 1963, 1967, and 1977,* Washington, DC: U.S. Government Printing Office.

factors that influence the amount of money spent on products normally stocked in drugstores. Demographic factors such as age, sex, race, and income are most critical because they determine the need for services. The elderly and the extremely young are the greatest users of drugs. Females do most of the purchasing from pharmacies. Income determines the ability to pay, although the Medicaid program has diminished this obstacle to obtaining needed services. The differences become apparent when the country is divided into regions. Table 13-11 presents statistics on total retail sales and retail drugstore sales by geographic division of the United States in 1967 and 1977.

Another important geographic variation in retail drug sales is that between rural and urban regions. In 1979 the top 50 metropolitan areas in the United States accounted for $14,377,919 (50.2%) of total retail drug sales.[16]

TYPES OF OWNERSHIP

The two principal types of ownership in the retail drug field are the independent and the chain. Any company with 4 or more units under the same management is a chain. Table 13-12 indicates the number of establishments by type of ownership. The number of stores has decreased from 51,448 in 1958 to 44,388 in 1977. Independents continue to dominate retail pharmacy in terms of the number of establishments, although the figure has decreased from 92.7% in 1958 to 77.6% in 1977. The predominance of the independents is not as marked when one considers the total sales picture. Furthermore, Table 13-13 indicates that in recent years the chains have been doing considerably better than the indepen-

TABLE 13-10. *Comparison of Drugstore by Size and Square Feet*

	CONVENTIONAL DRUGSTORE		SUPER DRUGSTORE	COMBINATION DRUGSTORE	CONVENIENCE DRUGSTORE
	INDEPENDENT	CHAIN			
Store size (square feet)	5,000	7,500	25,000	40,000	5,000
Sales per store	$500,000	$1 million	$5 million	$12.5 million	$1.5 million
Prescription sales as a percentage of store sales	60	17	10	5	10
Primary market focus	Health care	Health care and general merchandise	Broad general merchandise selection at low prices	One-stop stopping	Convenience items
Expected future growth rate	Negative	Slow	Moderate	Fast	Very fast

Source: Bates, A. D.: Three New Store Formats Will Soon Dominate Drug Retailing, *Marketing News*, 35:9, 1980.

TABLE 13-11. *Geographic Distribution of Total Retail Sales and Retail Drug Activity, 1967 and 1977*

GEOGRAPHIC DIVISIONS*	1967 $	%	1977 $	%	1967 $	%	1977 $	%
New England	18,951,946	6.1	46,101,101	5.2	588,860	5.4	1,356,502	4.7
Middle Atlantic	57,951,153	18.7	134,734,757	15.2	1,675,287	15.3	3,956,171	13.8
East North Central	64,624,911	20.8	170,793,653	19.2	2,316,149	21.9	5,568,217	19.4
West North Central	26,590,953	8.0	70,892,046	8.0	908,125	8.8	2,000,608	7.0
South Atlantic	42,789,060	13.8	140,439,934	15.8	1,675,902	15.3	4,793,783	16.7
East South Central	15,909,404	5.1	50,559,141	5.7	568,611	5.2	1,568,363	5.5
West South Central	27,450,706	8.8	94,556,316	10.7	911,763	8.3	2,687,766	9.4
Mountain	12,209,561	3.9	45,159,718	5.1	532,314	4.9	1,491,723	5.2
Pacific	43,796,625	14.1	134,271,969	15.1	1,753,245	16.0	5,244,601	18.3
Totals	310,274,319	100.0	887,518,635	100.0	10,930,256	100.0	28,667,734	100.0

*States included in divisions are as follows. New England: Maine, New Hampshire, Vermont, Massachusetts, Rhode Island, Connecticut; Middle Atlantic: New York, New Jersey, Pennsylvania; East North Central: Ohio, Illinois, Indiana, Michigan, Wisconsin; West North Central: Minnesota, Iowa, Missouri, North Dakota, South Dakota, Nebraska, Kansas; South Atlantic: Delaware, Maryland, District of Columbia, Virginia, West Virginia, North Carolina, South Carolina, Georgia, Florida; East South Central: Kentucky, Tennessee, Alabama, Mississippi; West South Central: Arkansas, Louisiana, Oklahoma, Texas; Mountain: Montana, Idaho, Wyoming, Colorado, New Mexico, Arizona, Utah, Nevada; Pacific: Washington, Oregon, California, Alaska, Hawaii.

Sources: U.S. Bureau of the Census: *Census of Business, 1967,* Washington, DC: U.S. Government Printing Office; 1979 Regional and State Summaries of Retail Sales, *Sales and Marketing Management, 125:*7, 1980. © 1980 S & MM Survey of Buying Power.

TABLE 13-12. *Number of Establishments by Type of Ownership*

	1958		1967		1977	
	NUMBER	% OF TOTAL	NUMBER	% OF TOTAL	NUMBER	% OF TOTAL
Single units	44,650	86.8	38,000	82.2	31,369	70.7
Stores in 2-unit companies	2,433	4.7	2,199	4.8	2,208	5.0
Stores in 3-unit companies	614	1.2	703	1.5	858	1.9
Stores in 4- or 5-unit chains	485	1.0	531	1.1	750	1.7
Stores in 6- to 10-unit chains	549	1.1	486	1.1	830	1.9
Stores in 11- to 25-unit chains	581	1.1	543	1.2	785	1.8
Stores in 26- to 50-unit chains	466	0.9	662	1.4	507	1.1
Stores in 51- to 100-unit chains	217	0.4	872	1.9	599	1.3
Stores in over 100-unit chains	1,453	2.8	2,248	4.9	6,482	14.6
Totals	51,448	100.0	46,244	100.0	44,388	100.0

Source: U.S. Bureau of the Census: *Census of Business, 1963, 1967, 1977,* Washington, DC: U.S. Government Printing Office.

dents in both prescriptions sales and total sales. In 1980 the chains had an increase in number of prescriptions of 5.4%. The chain stores' total sales were up 15.7% as compared to an increase of 9.5% for the independents.

Drugstores are also classified according to their legal forms of organization. There are three forms of legal organization: the individual proprietorship, the partnership, and the corporation. The individual proprietorship, commonly referred to as a sole proprietorship, has a single owner, the partnership has two or more individuals as owners, and the corporation is an association of three or more individuals chartered under the laws of the state to conduct business as a legal entity. The number of persons involved, their philosophy of conducting business, the availability of capital, and the nature of the business are some factors to consider in choice of legal form of ownership. Table 13-14 gives a breakdown of drugstores by legal forms of organization.

Chains. The data in Tables 13-15 and 13-16 indicate that chain drugstores have strengthened their share of the total drugstore market. In units, and more dramatically in sales volume, they have experienced significant growth; their gain of 15.6% in 1980

TABLE 13-15. *A Comparison of Sales Activity for Independent and Chain Stores for the Years 1978–1981*

	1978	CHANGE (%)	1979	CHANGE (%)	1980	CHANGE (%)	1981
Number of Prescriptions							
Independents	1,080,298,000	+2.0	1,101,720,000	−2.5	1,074,191,000	−6.5	1,004,046,000
Chains	352,104,000	+6.0	373,223,000	+5.4	393,377,000	−0.2	392,404,000
All stores	1,432,402,000	+3.0	1,474,943,000	−0.5	1,467,568,000	−4.8	1,396,450,000
Prescription Dollar Volume							
Independents	$5,939,325,000	+12.1	$6,656,746,000	+7.1	$7,132,628,000	+4.4	$7,450,002,000
Chains	$1,992,907,000	+15.0	$2,292,788,000	+12.4	$2,576,619,000	+11.5	$2,871,719,000
All stores	$7,932,232,000	+12.8	$8,949,534,000	+8.5	$9,709,247,000	+6.3	$10,321,721,000
Total Store Sales							
Independents	$11,775,669,000	+7.3	$12,638,118,000	+9.5	$13,842,135,000	+5.2	$14,565,937,000
Chains	$13,603,198,000	+16.9	$15,907,981,000	+15.7	$18,408,715,000	+15.8	$21,308,140,000
All stores	$25,378,867,000	+12.5	$28,546,099,000	13.0	$32,250,850,000	+11.2	$35,874,077,000

Sources: Number of R$_x$s Filled Drops, but Dollar Volume Rises 8.5%, *American Druggist, 183:17*, 1981; *American Druggist, 184:15*, 1982.

TABLE 13-14. *Number of Drugstores by Legal Form of Organization*

LEGAL FORM OF ORGANIZATION	NUMBER OF ESTABLISHMENTS	%
Individual proprietorship	11,560	26.0
Partnership	2,716	6.1
Corporation	29,944	67.5
Other	168	0.4
Total	44,388	100.0

Source: U.S. Bureau of the Census: Establishment and Firm Size, in *Census of Business*, Washington, DC: U.S. Government Printing Office, 1977, p. 133.

was the highest ever. According to *Drugstore News* their surge of growth was due to inflation, heavy promotion, and aggressive pricing.[17]

There are marketing theory explanations for the success of the chains. Basically their survival depends upon achieving a high sales volume at a low cost. Their size gives them advantages in terms of purchasing power and advertising. Their sales volume allows them to take maximum advantage of quantity discounts. Many perform wholesaler functions through their own warehousing—25 of the chains maintain warehouse facilities in excess of 200,000 square feet.[17]

Chains can have a decided advantage in advertising and promotion because they can realize economies of scale by spreading costs over multiple units. It is possible for them to employ specialized promotion experts to design their advertising campaigns. The messages conveyed to the public center around the two major reasons why people patronize chains—convenience and price. Since the inception of chains in the 1880s they have projected an image of one-stop shopping and lower prices.

The drawing power of chain drugstores has enabled the ownership to acquire the most favorable locations and lease arrange-

TABLE 13-15. *Chains' Strength in Drugstore Market*

YEAR	TOTAL UNITS	CHAIN (%)	INDE-PENDENT (%)	COMBINED VOLUME ($ BILLIONS)	CHAIN (%)	INDE-PENDENT (%)
1970	53,398	30.0	70.0	12.78	55.3	44.2
1975	46,590	39.6	60.4	18.09	66.6	31.4
1980	45,000	43.0	57.0	30.51	77.0	23.0

Source: Reprinted by permission from *Drug Store News*, May 4, 1981. Copyright Lebhar-Friedman, Inc., 425 Park Avenue, New York, NY 10022.

TABLE 13-16. *Ten Years of Chain Drug Growth*

YEAR	CHAIN DRUG SALES (IN $ BILLIONS)	NONCHAIN DRUG SALES (IN $ BILLIONS)	TOTAL DRUG SALES (IN $ BILLIONS)	CHAIN DRUG GAIN	CHAIN DRUG SHARE OF THE MARKET (%)	NUMBER OF CHAIN DRUG UNITS	AVERAGE SALES PER CHAIN UNIT ($)
1980	23.61	6.90	30.51	+15.6%	77.4	19,251	1,226,000
1979	20.43	6.74	27.17	+14.8	75.2	19,764	1,033,000
1978	17.79	7.55	25.34	+13.6	70.2	19,290	922,239
1977	15.66	7.26	22.92	+12.5	68.3	19,221	814,734
1976	13.92	7.19	21.11	+12.2	65.9	18,857	738,187
1975	12.41	7.00	19.41	+13.3	63.9	18,609	666,882
1974	10.95	7.25	18.20	+13.8	60.2	18,192	601,912
1973	9.62	7.20	16.82	+10.2	57.2	18,073	532,285
1972	8.73	6.60	15.33	+11.1	56.9	17,652	494,560
1971	7.86	6.46	14.32	+10.1	54.9	16,839	466,830

Source: Reprinted by permission from *Drug Store News*, May 4, 1981. Copyright Lebhar-Friedman, Inc., 425 Park Avenue, New York, NY 10022.

ments for their stores. Shopping centers are prime targets as business expands into suburban areas.

The breakdown of chain drug sales by department is presented in Table 13-17. No fewer than 10 merchandise categories increased by more than 15% over 1979. Prescriptions, drugs/proprietaries, and toiletries were the top 3 categories by sales volume.

The top 50 drug chains in 1980 according to sales volume are presented in Table 13-18. The top 10 chains took in more than a third of the $30.5 billion spent by consumers in drugstores in 1980. As a group the nation's top 50 accounted for 55% of the market and 71% of the total chain volume.[17]

The top 50 drug chains based upon the number of units in their organization are presented in Table 13-19. Revco, the chain with the greatest number of stores, expanded from only 254 stores in 1970 to 1313 in 1980.[17] In 1978 Revco became the first drug chain in the United States to operate 1000 stores.[18] Although Revco operates the largest number of stores it is the fourth largest in sales volume, behind American, Eckerd, and Walgreen.

Major chains have found that the quickest way to grow is to expand into new markets through the acquisition and merger route. Major acquisition and mergers for 1980 are presented in Table 13-20.

Future growth areas for the chains in the 1980s include the provision of drug services for HMOs, as discussed earlier, and the area of home health care. Because 35% of all health goods and

TABLE 13-17. *Breakout of 1980 Chain Drug Sales*

DEPARTMENT	TOTAL CHAIN DRUG VOLUME ($)	INCREASE (%)	TOTAL SALES (%)	GROSS MARGINS (%)
Prescriptions	4,190,124,000	+15.8	17.7	35–40
Drugs/proprietaries	3,618,410,000	+15.2	15.3	30–35
Toiletries	2,801,890,000	+17.0	11.9	25–30
Cosmetics	1,267,101,000	+17.5	5.8	35–40
Stationery	1,214,816,000	+14.0	5.1	40–45
Tobacco	2,209,390,000	+12.1	9.4	15–20
Candy	909,106,000	+11.0	3.9	25–30
Housewares	1,792,379,000	+16.2	7.6	35–45
Toys	779,648,000	+14.8	3.3	35–40
Photo	1,064,245,000	+16.4	4.5	20–25
General merchandise	1,326,563,000	+15.9	5.6	35–45
D-I-Y	624,959,000	+16.2	2.7	35–45
Grocery/liquor	1,373,931,000	+19.7	5.8	15–20
Misc./promotional	324,451,000	+17.5	1.4	15–20

Source: Reprinted by permission from *Drug Store News,* May 4, 1981. Copyright Lebhar-Friedman, Inc., 425 Park Avenue, New York, NY 10022.

TABLE 13-18. *Top 50 Drug Chains by Sales Volume, 1980*

CHAIN	TOTAL DRUGSTORE SALES (IN $ MILLIONS)	CHAIN	TOTAL DRUGSTORE SALES (IN $ MILLIONS)
1. American	1600*	26. Snyder's	120
2. Eckerd	1521	27. Malone & Hyde	100*
3. Walgreen	1410	28. Medi-Mart	92
4. Revco	1200	29. Duane Reade	80
5. Jewel Cos.	1195	30. Medicare-Glaser	77*
6. Thrifty	970	31. Carl's	75
7. Longs	893	32. Arnold's	74*
8. Pay Less Northwest	751	33. Optel-Mall	60*
9. Rite Aid	745	34. A. D. Clark	56
10. SupeRx	635	35. Big B	50*
11. People's	600	36. White Drugs	48*
12. Pay'n Save	506	37. La Verdiere's	45*
13. Thrift	477	38. Page	45
14. Grary	453	39. Taylor	43
15. CVS	414	40. Pharmacity Drug	40
16. Drug Fair	285	41. Standard	39
17. Dart Drugs	259	42. Begley	37
18. Fay's	243	43. Discount Drug Mart	36
19. Hook	236	44. Kerr	35
20. K & B	225	45. Courtesy	32*
21. Adams	207	46. Ribordy	30
22. Cunningham	203*	47. Rix	29
23. K Mart	200*	48. Carr's Pay Less	28*
24. Perry	153	49. Lewis Self Service	26
25. Genovese	122	50. Muir Drugs	26

*Estimate.

Source: Reprinted by permission from *Drug Store News*, May 4, 1981. Copyright Lebhar-Friedman, Inc., 425 Park Avenue, New York, NY 10022.

services are consumed by the over-65 population, Walgreen recently opened its first store for convalescent aids only.[19] This 6000-square foot unit contains a wide array of hospital supplies and rehabilitation equipment.

Still another area for expansion is the nursing home business. Revco, through its subsidiary Instacare, currently serves more than 100 nursing homes and 10,000 patients.[20] Federal requirements for participation in Medicare have made the nursing home market more attractive to the drugstore industry.

Independents. Although the chain drug outlet continues to grow in importance, it is not time to signal the demise of the independent drugstore. It, too, has certain marketing advantages that allow it to compete effectively. Its strong points are that local own-

TABLE 13-19. *Top 50 Drug Chains: 12,009 Stores*

CHAINS	LOCATION OF HEADQUARTERS	NUMBER OF STORES		NET GAIN
		1980	1979	
1. Revco	Twinsburg, Ohio	1313	1180	+133
2. Jack Eckerd Corporation	Clearwater, Florida	1113	995	+118
3. K Mart	Troy, Michigan	875	700	+175
4. Rite-Aid	Shiremanstown, Pennsylvania	834	752	+175
5. Walgreen Company	Deerfield, Illinois	739	680	+59
6. Thrifty Corporation	Los Angeles, California	529	518	+11
7. SupeRx Drug Stores, Inc.	Cincinnati, Ohio	506	483	+23
8. Peoples Drug Stores, Inc.	Alexandria, Virginia	486	474	+12
9. Jewel Companies	Oak Brooks, Illinois	420	259	+161
10. CVS Stores	Woonsocket, Rhode Island	403	380	+23
11. Adams Drug Company	Pawtucket, Rhode Island	400	425	−25
12. American Stores	Salt Lake City, Utah	395	371	+24
13. Thrift Drug Company	Pittsburg, Pennsylvania	360	357	+3
14. Hook Drugs	Indianapolis, Indiana	252	237	+15
15. Pay Less Northwest	Wilsonville, Oregon	206	146	+60
16. Gray Drug Stores, Inc.	Cleveland, Ohio	183	182	+1
17. Drugfair Stores	Alexandria, Virginia	174	175	−1
18. Cunningham Drug Stores, Inc.	Detroit, Michigan	165	161	+4
19. Mail Drugs	Holbrook, Massachusetts	161	163	−2
20. Malone & Hyde, Inc.	Memphis, Tennessee	160	151	+0
21. Lucky Stores, Inc.	Dublin, California	149	145	+4
22. Sav-On Drugs, Inc.	Anaheim, California	148	135	+13
23. Longs Drug Stores, Inc.	Walnut Creek, California	140	122	+18
24. Union Prescription Centers	Milwaukee, Wisconsin	130	132	−2
25. Pay'n Save Corporation	Seattle, Washington	129	112	+17

26.	HPI Hospital Pharmacies	Los Angeles, California	124	92	+32
27.	Rix Corporation	Auburndale, Massachusetts	115	118	−3
28.	Fay's Drug Company	Liverpool, New York	114	100	+14
29.	Pathmark Drug Stores	Edison, New Jersey	103	99	+4
30.	Medicare-Glaser Corporation	St. Louis, Missouri	96	96	0
31.	Perry Drug Stores	Pontiac, Michigan	96	63	+33
32.	K & B, Inc.	New Orleans, Louisiana	95	84	+11
33.	Dart Drug	Landover, Maryland	74	74	0
34.	Medi-Save Pharmacies	Baton Rouge, Louisiana	65	64	+1
35.	Big "B" Discount Drug, Inc.	Birmingham, Alabama	63	56	+3
36.	Fred Meyer, Inc.	Portland, Oregon	59	56	+3
37.	Snyder's Drug, Inc.	Hopkins, Minnesota	58	57	+1
38.	L. F. Widmann	Lock Haven, Pennsylvania	57	57	+2
39.	King Sooper	Denver, Colorado	53	50	+3
40.	Begley Drug Company	Richmond, Virginia	52	52	0
41.	Genovese Drug Stores	Melville, New York	51	51	0
42.	Taylor Drug Stores, Inc.	Louisville, Kentucky	48	46	+2
43.	Standard Drug Company	Richmond, Virginia	47	45	+2
44.	Medi Mart	Boston, Massachusetts	45	45	0
45.	Hardo Drug Inc.	Northport, Alabama	45	40	+5
46.	LaVerdiere's Super Drugs	Winslow, Maine	44	43	+1
47.	White Drug, Inc.	Jamestown, North Dakota	37	35	+2
48.	Carl's Drug Co., Inc.	Rome, New York	35	34	+1
49.	Arnold's	Detroit, Michigan	34	32	+2
50.	Lomark Discount Drugs	Hamilton, Ohio	29	34	+5

Sources: Business Guides, Inc.; Adapted by permission from *Drug Store News*, May 4, 1980. Copyright Lebhar-Friedman, Inc., 425 Park Avenue, New York, NY 10022.

TABLE 13-20. *Major Mergers and Acquisitions in 1980*

ACQUIRING COMPANY	ACQUISITION	NUMBER OF STORES	LOCATION
Drug King	Disco Drugs	7	California
Eckerd	Post Drugs	7	Texas
	Sav-X	17	Texas
Gray	Drug Fair Stores*	174	Delaware, Maryland, Pennsylvania, Virginia, West Virginia, Washington, DC
Jewel	Sav-On	148	California, Nevada, Texas
Pay Less NW	Pay Less California	61	California, Hawaii, Nevada
Perry	DeKoven	13 stores	Illinois
		13 leased	Illinois, Nebraska, Oklahoma, Texas
Revco	May's	20	Illinois
	Sav-Rite	8	Kentucky
	Skillern's	115	Texas, New Mexico
Walgreen	Rennobohm	17	Wisconsin
	Sage†	5	Texas
	Skaggs stores	5	Missouri

*Pending.
†1981.

Source: Reprinted by permission from *Drug Store News*, May 24, 1981. Copyright Lebhar-Friedman, Inc., 425 Park Avenue, New York, NY 10022.

ership and local management can provide greater flexibility and decisions can be made rapidly. The ownership is in close tune with its patrons, and can better understand their needs and wants.

If the effect of the increase in the number of chain units and the decline in the number of independents on a per store basis is eliminated, the average independent pharmacy did a bigger prescription dollar volume in 1980—$198,642 as compared to $184,154 for the average chain store.[21] The average independent had a 9.6% increase in prescription department dollar volume against a 6.1% increase for the average chain unit.

It is true that the low volume stores, under $150,000 annual sales, are finding it difficult to stay in business. Because they account for 21% of the total drug units but do only 4% of the volume, they may well disappear when the owner retires.[22] However, the future for the large independents seems brighter than ever. Arthur Nielson, Jr., board chairman of A.C. Neilson Company, advised the National Wholesale Druggists' Association to pursue the large independent drugstore. The largest independents "represent the greatest opportunity for drug wholesalers' immediate growth."[23] Neilson called attention to the fact that the large independent has grown in terms of number of stores faster than the chains. From 1972 to 1976 they increased from 16.2% to 23.2%, a 7% gain, while the number of chains has grown only 3.9%.

Franchise. Franchising is an accepted retail institution, which according to the United States Department of Commerce showed its greatest growth between 1974 and 1976, expanding from 339,000 outlets to 458,000 outlets, a 14.7% increase in 2 years.[24]

What is franchising? Basically it is little more than a license to operate a business according to certain stated conditions. It offers the advantage of belonging to a "chain" while maintaining status as an independent business person. Under a franchise agreement the retailer is usually required to pay a franchise fee and to accept certain responsibilities necessary to maintain the chain image. In return, franchise rights include the privilege of buying at reduced rates, selling franchised lines, participating in promotional campaigns, and garnering all the goodwill associated with the trade name of the franchise.

In one respect the franchise operation combines the best of two worlds, the collective management procedures of a large company and the drive and motivation of the independent owner-manager. For the company it allows growth with reduced capital outlay; for the franchise it provides preopening assistance such as site selection and training programs and postopening assistance in promotion, accounting procedures, and management counseling. This is why there are purported to be lower failure rates among franchise operations as compared to nonfranchise independent operations.

There are some potential problems associated with franchises. The franchise may find that all the promised benefits are not forthcoming. The trade name may lack drawing power. The fees and specific starting costs may be greater than expected. Mass purchasing and promotional programs may not reach expectations. Also, there is no guarantee that the franchise name will effectively stimulate people to patronize the pharmacy for their prescriptions and health-related needs.

Probably the best known of the drugstore franchises is Rexall. In recent years there has been an increase in the number of prescription-oriented franchises, such as "Medicine Shoppe." McKesson Drug is currently experimenting with the franchise idea, having opened their ninth and tenth stores in December 1980. According to Roy Milner, president of Foremost-McKesson Drug and Health-Care Group, McKesson went into the franchise program to speed the growth of the independent drug retailer.[25]

Cooperative Chains. Another means whereby independents have attempted to compete with chains is through the formation of a retailer cooperative chain. This voluntary group is formed to realize the economics of group buying or cooperative advertising.

Although the census data are sparse for this type of operation, there seems to be little evidence to indicate that this practice is widespread.

One example of an independent buying cooperative is the Pharmacy Buying Council of Illinois, founded in 1977.[26] This cooperative buys antibiotics for 237 other drug stores.

A Neilson study conducted in 1977 indicated that of the independent drugstores having the largest sales gains, only 34% carried out advertising on their own while the other 66% combined their own with the manufacturers' cooperative ads.[27]

For the independent drugstore of the future to be successful in a marketplace with the larger chain stores, it must be more adept at business matters. Cooperative buying and advertising may enable the independent to compete more effectively.

TYPES OF GOODS OFFERED

Another way to classify retail drugstores is according to the types of goods offered. The most widely used classifications are the prescription-oriented pharmacies and the super stores. Although these distinctions are not precise, they are fairly distinguishable and are frequently analyzed as distinct entities.

Prescription-Oriented Pharmacies. These pharmacies are those whose principal goods are prescriptions and nonprescription health related items. The *Lilly Digest* has classified pharmacies as prescription-oriented if the prescription sales exceed 50% of total sales and the pharmacy is less than 1200 square feet in size.[2a] Table 13-21 presents some significant operating data for the years 1969 and 1978.

Traditional Pharmacies. Although a precise definition of a traditional pharmacy does not exist, there is general agreement that it is independently owned and of moderate size, with prescriptions accounting for 30 to 60% of its total sales volume. A statistical profile of the traditional pharmacy financial operation is presented annually in the *Lilly Digest;* some data are presented in Table 13-22.

Super Stores. Again there really is no precise definition of a super store. Most people equate a super store with the chain discount operations, although there are traditional discount pharmacies and chain prescription shops. Super stores usually carry a vast array of merchandise, and the prescription department represents a significant but much smaller percentage of the total sales volume. Table 13-23 presents a comparison of the operating costs for chain pharmacies (super store operations) in 1970 and 1979. The average sales volume has doubled over the 10-year span.

Tables 13-21, 13-22, and 13-23 reflect significant differences in their comparison of the operating data of prescription-oriented

TABLE 13-21. *Comparison of Operating Costs and Other Data—Prescription-Oriented Pharmacies, 1969 and 1978*

OPERATING DATA	1969	1979
Average sales volume	$123,291	$219,519
Cost of goods sold	57.3%	60.7%
Gross margin	42.7%	39.3%
Rent	4.2%	3.6%
Net profit (before taxes)	8.1%	5.7%
Total income of self-employed proprietor (proprietor's salary and profit)	$24,801	$34,673
Sales per square foot	$171.17	$279.09
Number of prescriptions dispensed	25,181	27,000
Average prescription charge	$4.09	$6.95
Number of hours open weekly	57	53

Source: Prescription Oriented Pharmacies, *Lilly Digest*, 1979, p. 45 (prescription income over 75% of sales), and 1970, p. 27 (prescription income over 75% of sales).

pharmacies, traditional pharmacies and super stores. The super stores average an annual sales volume five times greater than that of the prescription-oriented and traditional pharmacies. Their gross margin is much lower; they fill many more prescriptions despite the lower percentage of prescriptions the total sales, and they are open many more hours weekly.

A comparison of the operating data of prescription-oriented pharmacies to traditional pharmacies indicates that the sole proprietor of the prescription-oriented pharmacies takes home about the same income as does the sole proprietor of the traditional pharmacy. However, this is accomplished by having 40% less in

TABLE 13-22. *Comparison of Operating Costs and Other Data—Traditional Pharmacies, 1969 and 1978*

OPERATING DATA	1969	1979
Average sales volume	$213,710	$345,302
Cost of goods sold	63.8%	65.3%
Gross margin	36.2%	34.7%
Rent	2.5%	2.4%
Net profit (before taxes)	4.5%	3.3%
Total income of self-employed proprietors (proprietor's salary and profit)	$26,582	$35,363
Sales per square foot	$91.71	$140.36
Number of prescriptions dispensed	23,951	26,913
Average prescription charge	$5.90	$6.57
Number of hours open weekly	74	66

Source: Current Trends in Pharmacy Operations, *Lilly Digest*, 1979, p. 7, and 1970, p. 7.

TABLE 13-23. *Comparison of Operating Costs and Other Data—*
Chain Pharmacy Operations, 1970 and 1979

OPERATING DATA	1970	1979
Average sales volume	$845,343	$1,606,756
Cost of goods sold	71.8%	72.0%
Gross margin	28.2%	28.0%
Rent	2.8%	2.7%
Net profit (before taxes)	4.9%	4.2%
Sales per square foot	$111.72	$170.98
Number of prescriptions dispensed	36,471	43,877
Average prescription charge	$3.77	$6.56
Number of hours open weekly	83	84

Source: Current Trends in Chain Pharmacy Operations, *NACDS-Lilly Digest*, 1980, p. 5 and 1971, p. 5.
Note: 1971 was the first edition of *NACDS-Lilly Digest*

annual sales volume and by being open 13 fewer hours weekly. The prescription-oriented pharmacy operates on a much higher gross margin through its concentration on prescription sales.

Marketing Task of the Retail Pharmacist

This chapter has examined the many ways in which the retail pharmacy may operate. As a legal organization the opportunities range from the sole proprietorship to the corporation. By type of goods offered the selection includes the prescription shop, the traditional pharmacy, and the super store. As an owner the primary areas are the chain and independent stores. The hospital market is a mobile alternative for employee pharmacists. The impact of the mass merchandisers (discounter and supermarket) on the retail drugstore has been reviewed.

The retail pharmacy owner's task is basically simple, to go where the customers are, where there are not too many pharmacies. The importance of a good location cannot be overemphasized, because a poor location is a major reason for business failure.

Some of the major reasons for people to patronize pharmacies are convenience, price, variety of merchandise, and types of services offered. The pharmacy owner must identify the segment of the market most appealing to his patrons and compatible with his philosophy of conducting business. An image for the pharmacy compatible with the owner's patronage motivations and philosophy must be created by using proper layout design and promotion. Because of the increased competitiveness within the marketplace, today's pharmacy manager must be a good business person and must employ aggressive marketing techniques to be successful.

The retail sector of our economy is an important and dynamic one. Retail drug distribution is provided in a variety of settings. The future of the industry seems to indicate a growing role for the hospital and chain segments. Although the market share of the small independent has gradually eroded away during the decade of the 1970s, the large independents have recorded their largest share ever. In the final analysis the nature of the retail pharmacy will be molded by the people who compete in the marketplace.

References

1. Bureau of the Census: *1977 Census of Retail Trade—Geographic Retail Trade*, Washington, DC: U.S. Government Printing Office, 1977, Geographic Area Series, pp. V, 28, 52–55, A-8.
2. Current Business Statistics, *Survey of Current Business, 60* (No. 10):11, 1980.
2a. Prescription Oriented Pharmacies, *Lilly Digest, 44,* 1979.
3. American Hospital Association, *Hospital Statistics,* Chicago: American Hospital Association, 1979, p. 192.
4. Glaser, M.: HMO's Should Figure Big in Drugstore's Future, *Drug Topics, 125*:50, 1981.
5. White, R.: HMO's May Offer Profit Potential, *Drug Store News, 3* (No. 3):1, 1981.
6. Epmeier, W.: Walgreen Steps up HMO Thrust, *Drug Store News, 3* (No. 3):1, 1981.
7. Bennett, B.: Free-Standing Home Health Care Center Advocated, *American Druggist, 183*:46, 1981.
8. Walgreen Expands Operations of Its Health Services Unit, *American Druggist, 181*:24, 1980.
9. Mail-Order R_x Field Guide for New Growth, *American Druggist, 174*:59, 1976.
10. Court Hears Arguments in Federal Prescription Case, *Apharmacy Weekly, 20*:72, 1981.
10a. APhA wins Appeal on Mail-order Antitrust Suit, *Apharmacy Weekly, 32*:129, 1981.
10b. Supreme Court Preserves APhA Victory in Mail-Order Antitrust Suit, *Apharmacy Weekly: 21*:17, 1982.
11. Bolger, R. J.: View from the Top, *American Druggist, 183*:20, 1981.
12. Bureau of the Census: *1977 Census of Retail Trade—Retail Subject Series, Drugstores,* Washington, DC: U.S. Government Printing Office, 1977, p. 6.
13. 1980 Variety's Hour, *Drug Topics, 125*:4, 1981.
14. Community Pharmacy Operations—Current Trends in Prescription Department Operations, *Lilly Digest,* 5, 1980.
15. Non-Drug Departments Will Be the Big-Growth Areas, *American Druggist, 182*:54, 1980.
16. Drugstore Sales, *Sales and Marketing Management, 12*:37, 1980.
17. 1980 Sales Jump 15.6% in Chain Drug Stores, *Drug Store News, 3* (No. 9):1, 32, 35, 52, 1981.

18. Revco Becomes the First U.S. Drug Chain with 1000 Stores, *American Druggist, 177*:32, 1978.
19. Walgreen Opens First Store for Convalescent Aids Only, *American Druggist, 182*:24, 1980.
20. Revco Reaps $4 M in Nursing Home R_x Biz, *Drug Store News, 3* (No. 9):3, 191, 1981.
21. Number of R_x's Filled Drops But Dollar Volume Rises 8.5%, *American Druggist, 183*:14, 1981.
22. Glaser, M.: At Last, Unit Sales Takes an Upturn, *Drug Topics, 125*:48, 1981.
23. Pursue Large Independents, Neilson Advises NEDA, *American Druggist, 177*:19, 1978.
24. Marquardt, R., Makers J., and Poe, R.: *Retail Management,* 2nd Ed., Hinsdale, IL: The Dryden Press, 1979, p. 31.
25. Jury Still Out on R_x Franchiser, Says McKesson, *Drug Store News, 3* (No. 9):2, 1981.
26. Independent Buys Antibiotics for More Than 200 Drug Stores, *American Druggist, 178*:13, 1978.
27. Independents Must Sharpen Up, United With Others to Build Buying Power, *American Druggist, 178*:16, 1978.

## CHAPTER 14

Hospitals and Government Agencies

ROGER K. BECKER, RUSSELL F. LEHN,
PHILLIP C. ZARLANGO, and DAVID W. KRUGER

Increasingly, pharmaceutical manufacturers must deal with important groups of customers whose buying power requires special marketing skills and practices. In this chapter we discuss four of these groups: hospitals, the United States government, health maintenance organizations, and Medicare and Medicaid.

Hospitals

As late as the 1960s the marketing of pharmaceuticals to hospitals differed little from the approach taken with the office-based physician. The manufacturer's representative simply promoted drugs directly to the hospital-based physician for use with his hospital patients. The hospital market today and of the future represents a change as well as a major challenge to the pharmaceutical marketer. Factors such as drug selection, purchasing, type of packaging required, the change to more clinically oriented services, and the movement of the practice to the hospital pharmacy in the direction of specialization have all increased the complexity of marketing to hospitals.

We will define the hospital market and examine the complex factors involved in order to determine the impact they have had on the pharmaceutical marketing approach to the hospital market.

Hospital Market

Other than retailers, hospitals are, by far, the largest dispensers of drugs. As they slowly evolve into combinations of inpatient treatment and outpatient centers for ambulatory health care, hospital outpatient pharmacies are becoming a significant source of drug dispensing. In some cases they are competitive with retail pharmacies. Hospital purchases totaled $2.3 billion in 1980, and accounted for 21% of total ethical drug purchases.

The 1980 growth rate of hospitals' ethical drug purchases was 17.5%, as compared to the total United States ethical drug market rate of 12.7%. The compound growth rate of the hospital market over a 4-year period, (1975 to 1978) was 14.2%, as compared to a total ethical drug market compound growth rate of 11.4%. The trend indicates the increasing importance of this market to pharmaceutical manufacturers.

Although a significant change in the size of the hospital market in terms of dollars has been observed, the size of the market in terms of the *number* of hospitals and the number of beds has actually declined (Table 14-1). In the 10-year period from 1968 through 1977, the number of hospitals declined by 1.7%, and during that same period the number of beds declined by 17%. It appears that the increased dollar volume of hospital-dispensed pharmaceuticals can be partially attributed to the large increase in the number of outpatient visits.

TABLE 14-1. *Selected Measures in Registered United States Hospitals*

MEASURE	REGISTERED UNITED STATES HOSPITALS			CHANGE (%)	
	1968	1977	1978	1968–1978	1977–1978
Hospitals	7,137	7,099	7,015	−1.7	−1.2
Beds (1000s)	1,663	1,407	1,381	−17.0	−1.8
Average number of beds per hospital	233	198	197	−15.5	−0.5
Admissions (1000s)	29,766	37,060	37,243	+25.1	+0.5
Average daily census (1000s)	1,378	1,066	1,042	−24.4	−2.3
Occupancy (%)	82.9	75.8	75.5	−8.9	−0.4
Surgical operations	*	18,121,454	17,936,406	—	−1.0
Bassinets	97,319[†]	83,193	80,650	−17.1	−3.1
Births	3,268,431[†]	3,223,699	3,250,373	−0.6	+0.8
Outpatient visits (1000s)	156,139[‡]	263,775	263,606	+68.8	−0.1

*Comparable data not available.
[†]Based only on hospitals reporting newborn data.
[‡]Based only on hospitals reporting outpatient visits.

Source: Adapted with permission from American Hospital Association: *Hospital Statistics*, Chicago: American Hospital Association, 1979. Published by the American Hospital Association, copyright 1979.

Pharmaceutical marketers have traditionally divided the market into two segments: private practice physicians vs. hospital-based physicians (or the private practice market vs. the hospital market). They have ignored what the most recent research indicates is a growing subsegment: the outpatient-ambulatory care market.

Early in 1978, important new data began to emerge. Visits to the outpatient departments of the nation's hospitals were fast approaching half the number of visits of those being made to physicians in private practice. These numbers represent not only the emergency departments but, more importantly, primary and specialty care clinics, onsite group practice clinics, and satellite clinics.

1977 data available from the Department of Health, Education and Welfare, published in April 1979, showed comparisons of office visits with hospital outpatient visits and inpatient admissions (Table 14-2). Significantly, outpatient visits increased 111% as compared to 30% for inpatient admissions. A number of factors appear to be responsible for this trend:

1. Fewer primary care private practice doctors available on off-hours or weekends.

2. An increased trend toward specialization among physicians.

3. A large increase in numbers of residents and hospital staff physicians available to work in clinics.

4. The prevalence of health-care plans that reimburse certain types of medical care only when the services are rendered in the hospital.

5. More hospitals becoming centers in their communities for the latest in medical techniques and equipment.

The trend is expected to continue. It represents an excellent opportunity for pharmaceutical marketers to develop the needed expertise to capitalize on this rapidly growing segment.

The hospital market consists of more than 7000 institutions

TABLE 14-2.

	1965	1977	TREND
Private practice visits	NA*	570,000,000	NA
Hospital outpatient visits	125,790,000	265,437,000	+111%
Hospital inpatient admissions	28,810,000	37,402,000	+30%

*NA = not available.

Source: Department of Health, Education and Welfare, 1977.

with almost 1,400,000 beds. Of these hospitals, over 97% are registered by the American Hospital Association, whose definition of a hospital is the controlling one for the institutions themselves (Table 14-3).

The core of this market is the short-term general hospital, representing over 84% of hospitals and more than 81% of expenditures. The remainder of the hospitals are long-term and federal hospitals.

Federal hospitals are owned and operated by the federal government and include the Veterans Administration Medical Centers, United States Military hospitals of all branches of military service, and Public Health Service hospitals. Nonfederal state and local government hospitals are owned and operated by state, county, and city governments. Nongovernment, not for profit hospitals are owned by various nonprofit organizations such as religious and philanthropic organizations. Investor-owned, for profit hospitals are owned and operated as corporations (and subsidiaries of corporations). Hospital Corporation of America is the largest of this type.

The differences in the types of ownership and control of hospitals have little impact on their operation. All operate general medical and surgical service hospitals. Specialized service hospitals (e.g., psychiatric, pediatric, and orthopedic) are found most frequently in the nonfederal, not for profit area. From a marketing standpoint, this difference in ownership has its greatest impact on drug purchasing and distribution. This is particularly true in fed-

TABLE 14-3. *The United States Hospital Universe: 1979*

HOSPITAL CONTROL	NUMBER OF HOSPITALS		NUMBER OF BEDS	
	TOTAL	REGISTERED, ALL OTHER	TOTAL	REGISTERED, ALL OTHER
United States Total	7,091	6,918	1,393,291	1,372,000
		173		21,291
Federal	353	352	117,015	117,000
				15
Nonfederal	6,665	6,493	1,009,276	988,000
		172		21,276
State and local government	2,141	2,114	214,986	214,000
		27		
Nongovernment (not for profit)	3,528	3,498	692,356	690,000
		30		2,356
Investor-owned (for profit)	921	881	85,428	83,000
		40		2,428

Source: Adapted with permission from American Hospital Association: *Annual Survey of Hospitals,* Chicago: American Hospital Association, 1979. Published by the American Hospital Association, copyright 1979.

eral hospitals, and this impact will be discussed in the following section.

The hospital market may also be described in terms of ownership control by the number of hospitals and size, determined by number of beds (Table 14-4). Most teaching hospitals are in the over-300 bed group, so the major hospital pharmaceutical marketing emphasis is directed to them.

In summary, the size of the market in terms of the number of hospitals and beds has declined, whereas the size of the market in terms of dollars has shown substantial growth. We will now discuss some of the factors that have an impact on the pharmaceutical marketing approach to this growth market.

Hospital Drug Selection

The physician has traditionally been the orderer of drugs. Although he will probably continue to remain important in deciding whether or not a patient should receive medication, the choice of drug, source, and supplier are more frequently being decided by others.

Due to the decline in the number of significant new and patentable drugs and to the increased number of sources of generic and

TABLE 14-4. *Hospitals by Control and Bed Size*

		CONTROL AND BED SIZE				
DESCRIPTION	TOTAL	100 BEDS AND OVER	200 BEDS AND OVER	300 BEDS AND OVER	400 BEDS AND OVER	500 BEDS AND OVER
Hospitals, United States and possessions	6918	3651	2123	1364	886	555
United States hospitals by ownership control						
Government, nonfederal, codes 12–16	2114	844	515	390	310	136
Nongovernment, not for profit, codes 21, 23	3498	2146	1292	789	450	242
Investor-owned for profit, codes 31–33	881	400	129	33	13	4
Government, federal codes 41–48	352	226	168	139	106	70

Source: Adapted with permission from American Hospital Association: *Hospital Statistics*, Chicago: American Hospital Association, 1979. Published by the American Hospital Association, copyright 1979.

nonpatented drugs, hospital pharmacists have expanded their role in the drug selection process. The expanded role and selection authority of the pharmacist has created what is termed "the hospital formulary." This is a list of drugs, classified both generically and therapeutically, which have been approved for use in the institution. In the 1980 American Society of Hospital Pharmacists (ASHP) survey, over 80% of the respondents indicated that they had a formulary system.[1] Except in the case of a new and major single-entity drug, the formulary approval process represents a major challenge for the pharmaceutical marketer.

PHARMACY AND THERAPEUTICS COMMITTEE

The efficient operation of a hospital is dependent on the cooperative efforts of many types of health-care professionals, such as physicians, nurses, pharmacists, and lab technicians, who have independent interests. As a result, many proposed changes are decided by the Pharmacy and Therapeutics (P & T) Committee. This committee has the responsibility of making formulary decisions. It is most commonly comprised of representatives from the various physician specialties, nursing, and pharmacy.

In their hospital promotional efforts pharmaceutical manufacturers will find it increasingly necessary to include or place more emphasis on decision makers other than physicians.

The types of pharmacy input to be considered by committee members when they make formulary decisions are represented in the following question, which appeared in the 1980 ASHP survey:

Check the items that describe your input to the P & T Committee (check as many as applicable):

Provide background information on drugs considered for the formulary.

Provide drug-use experience information for your hospital.

Provide results of formal drug-use review programs.

Provide drug cost data.

Suggest alternate drug entities to replace currently used agents.

Establish or plan drug-use educational programs for hospital staff.

Report medication errors.

Report adverse drug reactions.

Recommend drugs to be stocked in patient care areas.

Consult with physicians (prior to P & T Committee action) who are interested in adding a drug to the formulary.[1]

Another question in the same survey addressed the factors usually considered relevant to individual drug formulary approvals:

> Indicate the importance of the following factors in selecting the source of supply for multi-source drug products at your hospital (circle the appropriate level):
>
> (a) Price
>
> (b) Company reputation
>
> (c) Dosage forms available
>
> (d) Unit-dose packaging
>
> (e) Unit-of-use packaging
>
> (f) Recall and product defect history
>
> (g) Returns policy
>
> (h) Discount and credit policy
>
> (i) Availability of medical information (upon request)
>
> (j) Availability of pharmacokinetic and bioavailability data (upon request)
>
> (k) Availability of stability and compatibility information for injectables
>
> (l) Availability of company quality control information (upon request).[1]

In order to be successful in obtaining drug formulary approval, pharmaceutical representatives must first identify members of the P & T Committee, and then must provide information necessary for a favorable decision. This is not a simple task. It challenges the selling skills of the representative as well as the marketing expertise of the representative's company.

PROMOTIONAL EFFORTS TO PHYSICIANS

Single-source products will continue to be promoted to the physician for brand specification. This, too, presents a challenge to the sales representative, because full-time staff physicians in teaching hospitals are not readily accessible. Residents and interns also play varying roles on influencing and making decisions in teaching hospitals. These roles must be identified in each hospital in order for the pharmaceutical representative to be effective in generating product specification.

In the nonteaching hospital the medical staff is composed primarily of office-based physicians, a situation that provides a different challenge for the pharmaceutical representative. Promotional efforts and materials presented to the physician in the office are generally developed to generate prescriptions for the ambulatory nonhospitalized patient. Because the product benefits presented pertain to this type of patient, physicians generally do not carry their office-prescribing habits over into their hospital practice. To generate hospital prescriptions by office detailing, the pharmaceutical representative must present product benefits as they apply to the physician, to the hospitalized patient, and to the overall clinical situation.

Although formulary approval for a major new drug is not usually a problem, it is a process that must be completed. If the new, single-source product is not considered to be a significant therapeutic advancement, formulary approval may be as difficult to obtain as with multisource drug equivalents. From a marketing standpoint, the appropriate contacts must be made and the necessary information must be communicated.

Purchasing and Distribution

The classic free market forces that normally exist between buyer and seller do not function as distinctly in the purchase of hospital prescription drugs. In the typical model the physician orders the medication, the pharmacist dispenses it, a nurse administers it, a third-party financier pays the cost of it (for a high percentage of patients), and the patient consumes it. To further complicate this process, the pharmaceutical manufacturer is faced with increasingly complex systems of purchasing by hospitals as well as with a shift in the distribution channel for hospital purchases.

BID SOLICITATION AND GROUP PURCHASING

Hospital purchasing in the past 10 years has rapidly shifted to a system of bid solicitation and group purchasing. The crisis in cost containment is again focusing on the costs of drugs and how drugs are purchased. The results of 3 recent studies have revealed similar findings: hospitals are not purchasing drugs effectively or economically. Although figures are not provided, results of another survey by the Government Accounting Office suggested that changes in purchasing with emphasis on group purchasing could save significant amounts in health-care costs. One example described a hospital that saved over $7000 using group purchasing. A 1978 American Society of Hospital Pharmacists drug purchase survey showed that nearly 80% of the respondents were participants in a hospital purchasing group. Nearly 60% of the respondents expected the number of drugs products used in their hospitals to decrease in the next 5 years.[1]

All hospital purchasing groups utilize bid solicitation to obtain competitive and favorable prices. Research has also shown that group purchasing has potential problems in that it requires better planning, more cooperation and information sharing, longer lead times, the determination not to sell out to a drug wholesaler who underbids to prevent the formation of a group, and individual hospital commitments not to purchase later from manufacturers who have lost a bid (a practice commonly known as "back-dooring"). Many hospitals also participate in more than one group. This multiple-group participation presents a major dilemma for the pharmaceutical company, because estimated annual usages are frequently included in more than one bid solicitation. Although pharmaceutical marketers continue to tolerate this practice, it defeats the contractual implication of the bid solicitation and award process.

The hospital pharmacist has largely maintained control of drug purchasing. Because of the technical considerations of drug selection and purchasing, the purchasing agent has not assumed this role. This fact reinforces the importance of having a good business relationship between the purchasing pharmacist and the pharmaceutical sales representative. Without it, the chance of sales success in the hospital market is limited.

PRICING

Due to the increased multisource availability of most frequently used drugs, pricing to hospitals has become increasingly competitive. As late as 1965, many hospitals were paying full retail price for most drugs purchased. Cost containment pressures and the advent of formularies and group purchasing have brought about radical changes in prices paid by hospitals for pharmaceutical products.

Prices offered to bid solicitations (individual hospitals or hospital groups) are usually based on such factors as estimated annual use and individual shipment quantity. Manufacturers have also been willing to price products at a lower level to teaching hospitals. The intent here is to acquaint new physicians with their drugs, with a view to cultivating future prescribing habits. Teaching hospital purchases are also generally greater than those of nonteaching hospitals.

Pharmaceutical marketers have also recognized that, in many cases, when a patient is given an oral drug in the hospital, that same medication will be continued at retail prices when the patient is discharged. Although audits have not been made to measure this retail spill-out, some estimates have placed it as being more than equal to hospital purchases of certain therapeutic classes of oral drugs. In the case of oral antihypertensives, a hospital patient start will frequently generate drug store refills for the rest of the life of the patient.

DRUG WHOLESALERS AS DISTRIBUTORS

Hospitals have traditionally purchased directly from manufacturers because manufacturers were frequently willing to give hospitals a better price in return for contracts and exposure to physicians. In fact, differential pricing to hospitals was often seen as a marketing expense and sometimes treated as such.

With contemporary cost containment pressures, however, hospitals seem more willing to change their source of purchases to wholesalers. Many hospitals feel that, although the purchase price might be slightly higher from a drug wholesaler, the actual cost is less because of reduced inventory levels—especially with the cost of holding inventory at 18 to 30% per year. Additionally, direct purchase administrative costs, including inventory, paperwork, and cost of physical space, are hidden expenses that may also justify purchase at a higher cost from the drug wholesaler, depending upon time and circumstances.

Many drug wholesalers now actively pursue the hospital market by using the same service approach used effectively with retailers—e.g., direct electronic order entry, management and inventory reports, and help in servicing manufacturers' bids and reduction of inventory. For example, the Hospital Corporation of America (HCA) is currently testing a program in which a percentage of the bid price is paid to a local wholesaler to warehouse (depot) the bid products. The program will measure the cost of this approach against the customary ordering and inventory procedures now being used by HCA affiliates. Voluntary Hospitals of America is committed to a pharmacy purchasing program through the wholesaler and is actively seeking traditionally direct-selling manufacturers who are willing to participate in their program. Although many hospitals continue to purchase direct from manufacturers, a rapid change to wholesaler distribution to hospitals (as has been experienced with the retail segment) is anticipated.

A CHANGING PRACTICE

As late as 1970, the role of the hospital pharmacist was not significantly different from that of the retail pharmacist. The hospital pharmacist counted, poured, and dispensed drugs to hospitalized patients; the nursing staff administered the drugs. We have already discussed the expanded role of the hospital pharmacist in regard to drug selection and purchasing. Additionally, the hospital pharmacist has made significant strides in gaining professional status in the hospital environment.

Many hospital pharmacists have upgraded the preparation and distribution of drugs, resulting in better patient care. Two prime examples of upgrading pharmacy services are unit-dose distribution and IV admixture services. Fifteen years ago these systems and services were rare. Today, a high percentage of general hospitals now provide both. Hospital pharmacists have actively pursued many other areas of clinical services (Tables 14-5 and 14-6). Continued advancement into these areas in the 1980s is anticipated.

The expanding role of the hospital pharmacist could be in direct conflict with that of the community pharmacist. Today, the community pharmacist also strives for new roles, and a stronger identity. This conflict will escalate as hospitals extend their role into the community.

The hospital pharmacist's increased importance also presents a selling challenge to the pharmaceutical representative. The clinical pharmacist is exercising greater influence on formulary decisions and on physicians' therapeutic decisions. The representative must be better educated and must possess the necessary clinical knowledge to communicate with the clinical pharmacist. The salesperson must also keep informed of current clinical articles and the latest medical advances. The marketing expertise of the company will be challenged to provide the representative with the technical service and data needed for clinical evaluation. Special packaging will be required to meet the needs of the unit-dose distribution systems, IV admixture services, and outpatient dispensing. Educational services will be increasingly important for in-service and student training. The representative and the company will be successful in this market only if they accept and meet these challenges.

THIRD-PARTY PAY

Third-party reimbursement can be provided either by government programs or by private insurance programs. Medicaid drug benefits cover both in-hospital and out of hospital drug use in nearly all states, although the extent of coverage varies dramatically. Medicare benefits are predominantly for in-hospital care of the elderly, unless they are medically indigent and can qualify for Medicaid. Private insurance generally covers inpatient drugs through basic hospital insurance; outpatient drugs are written into the insurance as an extra.

The high percentage of patients covered for both inpatient and outpatient drugs has minimized the compromising of drug selection and purchasing. Due to competition among pharmaceutical

TABLE 14-5. *Hospital Pharmacy Services Offered on a Daily Basis*

SERVICE	NUMBER OF HOSPITALS OFFERING (%)	
	1978	1979
Monitoring of patient profiles	77.7	85.8
Monitoring drug interactions	69.0	79.7
Drug information service	66.5	77.9
Drug therapy consultation with physician	55.0	60.0
Patient discharge interviews	13.4	13.6
Making rounds with physicians	11.7	10.9
Pharmacokinetic service	6.2	7.7
Administration of drugs to patients	5.4	6.9
Patient admission interviews	4.5	5.6
Working with radiopharmaceuticals	1.5	0.9

Source: *Lilly Hospital Survey,* 1980, p. 23.

companies in efforts to increase their share of this growing market, hospitals have been able to purchase quality products economically through the bid solicitation process and group purchasing. Therapeutic evaluation committees do not compromise necessary therapy for the sake of cost.

However, third-party payers continue to scrutinize patient drug charges, just as hospital administrators continue to look for ways to decrease pharmacy budget expenditures. In order to enjoy a considerable share of this large and growing market, the pharmaceutical marketer will need to be continually conscious of economic factors, remain alert to influences that change these factors, and adopt marketing strategies accordingly.

"GETTING IN THE DOOR"

Most hospitals have established specific procedures that salespeople have to follow in order to gain access to purchasing personnel. These procedures usually involve some type of signing in

TABLE 14-6. *Hospital Pharmacy Services*

SERVICE AVAILABLE	% OF TOTAL	
	GENERAL	SPECIALIZED
In-service education	83.3	90.8
Training program for students	47.1	80.0
Drug utilization review	73.3	75.7
Regular pharmacy bulletin	47.3	72.1
Responding to CPR attempts	26.1	26.9

Source: *Lilly Hospital Survey,* 1980, p. 35.

or registration on the part of the salesperson. In addition, most hospital buyers have specific hours and days when they see commercial representatives. Thus, access to the individuals responsible for drug purchases promises to become even more difficult.

Although procedures become more rigid, it is unlikely that they will be uniformly applied. Salespersons handling products that are highly regarded by the hospital (or those who have earned a certain amount of trust) are often permitted to bypass the rules. These salespeople are permitted to move freely throughout the hospital and to discuss their products with whomever they choose in the hospital. This freedom is a privilege that comes with such status. It is apparent that, even though correct administrative procedures have been established to organize the purchasing process, those procedures are frequently ignored.

Personal contact by sales representatives is still the most widely accepted means of communication. Hospital buyers, however, acknowledge that they also find telephone contact acceptable. This method of selling is one that is presently often ignored by sales representatives. It can be expected, however, to become a necessary and more common method of contact in the multiple decision-maker environment of the hospital.

Hospital Pharmacy Changes

The hospital pharmacy is committed to the clinical movement as reflected in official ASHP policies and in the current literature, and by educational programs for hospital pharmacists. Most hospital pharmacists probably subscribe to the view that, as a matter of survival, the pharmacy must change from a product-oriented technical function to a patient-oriented clinical service. The pharmacy will no longer be thought of as a supply department. The hospital pharmacy in the 1980s will translate its clinical commitment into the widespread implementation of clinical services. The image of the hospital pharmacy will change to that of a department of drug experts.

If current trends continue, the hospital pharmacy will use fewer drugs by strengthening of the formulary system. Dosages will be more specific as drugs become more potent. The hospital pharmacy's services will become more qualitative than quantitative. Expansion of these services will require more diverse packaging, along with more technical information and educational materials.

Purchasing will be carried out by fewer but larger groups, increasing their purchasing power and forcing even greater price competition among suppliers. As indicated earlier, the distribution channel is shifting to the drug wholesaler. Traditional direct-selling suppliers will find it necessary to adapt to this changing preference by hospital pharmacy purchasing.

The pharmaceutical marketer in the 1980s must remain alert to these trends and changes, and must be responsive to them. The hospital market will continue to show substantial growth, with an increasing demand for efficacious drug products of unquestioned quality, and will continue to present an excellent opportunity to the pharmaceutical marketer for increased sales and profits.

United States Government

Selling to government institutions closely parallels selling to the nongovernmental hospital segment of the market. Such activities as creating specifications for products and having them included in the hospital formulary are accomplished only through promotion and detailing to those influential members of the medical hierarchy within each institution.

For the most part, government institutions provide the same services as nongovernmental hospitals. They operate in a broader sense, though, in that they also provide many services in outpatient clinical settings. Before we explore this area, an overview of government medical services is in order. As inevitably happens in discussions about the government, abbreviations and acronyms keep popping up. Because dealing with the government necessitates a familiarity with these terms, they will be included in this discussion on a limited basis.

Department of Defense and Veterans Administration

The two largest segments of the government market interested in buying and dispensing pharmaceuticals are the Department of Defense (DOD) and the Veterans Administration (VA).

The Department of Defense is responsible for providing medical care to active members of the Armed Forces and their dependents stationed both on bases in the United States and throughout the free world, as well as to other authorized requisitioners of the federal government. Requirements for overseas purchases are made by the Medical Directorate's Direct Vendor Delivery Branch for overseas installations through army post offices (APOs) and fleet post offices (FPOs) located in the United States.

The Veterans Administration provides medical care for veterans of the United States Armed Forces via the network of Veterans Administration hospitals located throughout the United States. Some Veterans Administration prescription services are provided via the United States mail. Like the military, the Veterans Administration also provides medical care to both hospitals and outpatient or clinic patients.

In addition to the Department of Defense and the Veterans Administration, the federal government also provides medical care through the United States Public Health Service, the Office of Emergency Planning, the Welfare Administration, and the General Services Administration. As will be discussed in a following section, there is some overlapping in purchasing among the various segments.

Purchasing Volume

In 1978 purchases by the federal government accounted for 3.8% of the purchases of ethical pharmaceuticals from manufacturers. Of these, 2.4% went to federal hospitals, and 1.4% to other federal institutions. This somewhat understates the total government pharmaceutical purchases because it accounts only for purchases made directly from the manufacturer and overlooks purchases made through wholesalers or other sources.

It is estimated that federal government expenditures for 1981 for medical services for this group amounted to $12,388,000,000 divided as shown:

Department of Defense	$5,147,000,000
Veterans Administration	$6,568,000,000
United States Public Health Service	$ 673,000,000

Obviously, these figures include costs of all medical care, not just pharmaceuticals, but it is clear that the government pharmaceutical market is large.

Personnel

Another factor to be considered is the large number of physicians who are exposed to a manufacturer's product and who thus represent potential future purchasers (prescribers) in the domestic marketplace. Although physicians who provide medical care for the Defense Department are actually inducted into military service private physicians, particularly specialists, are also called in and are exposed to the products in use at these facilities.

The number of physicians currently serving in the Armed Forces is almost 9000, 8000 of whom are involved in actual patient care. The other 1000 are found in administrative services or in other nonpatient care positions. Almost all medical specialties are represented by these numbers (Chap. 2).

Patient Characteristics

Products used within the government market generally parallel those used in the domestic market, but there are some differences among the various branches. The Department of Defense serves members of the Armed Forces who, for the most part, are young adults with families. Pharmaceuticals for prevention and treatment of pediatric ailments will therefore be included. Conversely, the Veterans Administration treats patients who, at some time in their lives, served in the Armed Forces. The average patient's age will be much higher in this segment than in the Department of Defense; patients will be predominately males, because only recently has the percentage of females serving in the Armed Forces begun to increase.

This will obviously have an impact on disease incidence, type of treatment, and pharmaceuticals used to treat these ailments. Hypertension, for example, is far more prevalent in patients treated by the Veterans Administration than for those treated by the Department of Defense and, as would be expected, the amount of antihypertensives purchased by the various agencies reflects this difference.

On the other hand, purchases of pediatric pharmaceuticals are almost totally absent in the Veterans Administration. The remaining government agencies, such as the Public Health Service, reflect the more traditional gamut of medical care and treatment as found in the nongovernmental market because these agencies treat the same portion of the population as the domestic market. These differences are important to the pharmaceutical manufacturer in identifying potential markets for particular products, as noted in Table 14-7.

Purchasing Procedures

Government agencies choose from the same array of products generally available to any institution in the domestic market. Their product usage is similarly affected by promotion and detailing, and there exists a transfer of specifications both to and from these two marketplaces, fostered by the movement of health professionals between government and nongovernment facilities. Only after a sufficient demand is created within the government marketplace is there any real change in purchasing procedures.

The Veterans Administration requests and administers annual bids for the Federal Supply Schedule (FSS). This bid is split into 2 parts. Section A includes items not stocked in the Veterans Administration depot that are available from 2 or more known manufacturers (no single-source items are included), and that have a sales volume in excess of $10,000 annually. The Veterans

TABLE 14-7. *Federal Government Awards for Proprietary*
Pharmaceuticals by Class, February 1980 through January 1981

PRODUCT CLASS	% OF TOTAL
Analgesics	3.2
Anesthetics	0.9
Antacids	2.0
Antiarthritics	8.7
Anticonvulsants	0.5
Antihistamines	0.8
Anti-infectives, systemic	14.2
Antiseptics	1.2
Antispasmodics	2.4
Biologicals	1.8
Bronchial therapy	1.2
Cancer therapy	1.5
Cardiovascular therapy	16.8
Contraceptives	0.6
Cough and cold	2.5
Dermatologicals	3.2
Diabetes therapy	1.9
Diuretics	5.0
Hormones	5.3
Hospital solutions	2.7
Laxatives	1.6
Muscle relaxants	1.1
Nutrients/supplements	2.6
Ophthalmic preparations	0.5
Psychotherapeutic drugs	9.2
Sedatives	0.6
Thyroid therapy	1.3
Tuberculosis therapy	0.7
Vitamins	0.8
Miscellaneous ethical	1.8
Crude drugs and chemicals	0.5
All other	2.9
	100%

Source: Federal Government Contracts Award Report, January, 1981, IMS America, Ltd., Ambler, PA 19002.

Administration solicits responses from manufacturers to this bid request, it awards those items it feels is in their best interest, it prints and publishes the catalogs, and it disseminates them to all government agencies.

Section B of the Federal Supply Schedule includes all other products not included in Section A. A manufacturer may respond to Section B of the annual bid by bidding on all products in his catalog, but more generally will bid only on those items that have a more promising potential for government sales. Items accepted under Section A of the Federal Supply Schedule may not be included in Section B. Once the items are accepted under Section B, it is the responsibility of the supplier (bidder) to print and to distribute catalogs or pamphlets with pricing and ordering information. Because of the complexity of the contract numbering nomenclature a detailed discussion will be omitted here, but suffice it to say that contract numbers are assigned for all solicitation requests and contracts.

It is important to note that use of the Federal Supply Schedule, Sections A and B, is mandatory for government agencies. That is, all government agencies must use this as the purchasing source for the products contained within. There also is a $10,000 order limitation per single item. Other terms and conditions of sale vary from supplier to supplier. Quarterly purchase reports, showing purchases by the Veterans Administration, other government agencies, and the total of the two, must be submitted to the Veterans Administration Marketing Center by each manufacturer. It should be understood that "multiple awards" are made under both Federal Supply Schedule sections. In other words, several companies may receive awards for competitive products, at various price levels.

When using the Federal Supply Schedule each Veterans Administration hospital, theoretically, first checks Section A. If the product required is listed the hospital will usually choose the lowest priced product. If the item is not listed in Section A, the institution will refer to Section B, and again will usually purchase the lowest priced item. An important difference between these two sections should be noted. In Section A all products are listed in order of descending price in one catalog. Products in Section B will be listed in separate catalogs containing only products supplied by a given manufacturer. The third choice is direct open market purchases from manufacturers for those products generally not included in Sections A and B. Hospitals may purchase products based on detailing efforts or may issue a "request for quotation."

DEPOT PURCHASES

Both the Department of Defense and the Veterans Administration maintain depots that warehouse products for their user facilities. Products supplied in this manner are items that have achieved a significant sales volume (usually in excess of $10,000 annually) and therefore offer certain economic advantages for central purchasing, billing, and shipping.

For Department of Defense. Once a product achieves a sufficient dollar purchase level, it is reviewed by the Defense Medical Materiel Board (DMMB). This board, located in Frederick, Maryland, is responsible for establishing specifications and standards for new products.

DMMB review includes requests to the manufacturer for the following types of information:

Product formulation.
Stability data.
Expiration dating period.
Shelf life.
Special handling requirements.
Storage requirements, such as refrigeration, protection from light, heat, or freezing, etc.
New drug application information.
Certification requirements (antibiotics).
Patient information.
Commercial pricing information.
Federal Supply Schedule pricing, etc.
Packaging information, which will include a description of the immediate container, closure system, seals, unit quantity, intermediate and exterior shipping containers, together with weight and cube for the shipping container.

The review board may also request data on annual or monthly sales of the product, as well as any other technical or background information from clinical evaluations or medical studies that may be pertinent.

If an item is already available in the depot and a competitive company wishes to bid a product, this process becomes less complicated. The company can request to be put on the bidders' list for that product or group of products; this will ensure receipt of any further bid requests as they are issued.

The Defense Medical Materiel Directorate (DMMD) is responsible for procuring some 16,000 items. The Defense Personnel Support Center (DPSC), located in Philadelphia, is the largest of the Defense Logistics Agency's field activities.

Bid requests for "invitation for bid" (IFB), which are formal advertised requests, must be responded to exactly as requested. Any exception or deviation from specifications, delivery date, etc., will cause the bid response to be rejected. Negotiated "request for proposal" (RFP) or "request for quotation" (RFQ) allows for responses that may take exception to one or more of the bid criteria. Generally the DPSC buys only items that have been previously standardized. Formal bids issued by Defense Personnel Support Center are generally limited to one item per bid request.

For the Veterans Administration. Depot purchasing by the

Veterans Administration is similar to that by the Department of Defense, but the review by the Defense Medical Materiel Board is replaced by a more streamlined version of a specifications group within the Veterans Administration. Bid requests issued by the VA are generally open to negotiation of the bid criteria, and often contain requests for more than one product or group of products.

BID SPECIFICATIONS AND REQUIREMENTS

Both the Defense Personnel Support Center and the Veterans Administration bid requests contain specifications and requirements that must be stringently adhered to if a supplier wishes to be successful in dealing with the government.

Because the number of requirements is quite large, only a few of these will be addressed here to show the procedures involved. There have also been recent developments that indicate a transition from the rigid specifications for government products to a more general acceptance of normal commercial packages, with Military or Veterans Administration exterior case markings. Currently there are also attempts to consolidate purchasing functions by the Military and Veterans Administration into a single shared contract, a procedure that would have obvious advantages for both the government and the supplier. Because larger amounts are being purchased, they permit a lower unit cost to the government and will generally reduce the amount of paperwork and diminish administrative costs for all involved.

These joint requests are titled appropriately JVD bids (joint, Veterans-Defense). Each item ordered by the government, both DOD and VA, is assigned a 13-digit national stock number (NSN). Specification pharmaceuticals are listed under the Federal Supply Class (FSC) class of 6505. The national stock number for a drug, biological, or official reagent would be identified as 6505-XX-XXX-XXXX, in which the Xs would be replaced by any number from 0 through 9. Each bid request specifies the quantity of product desired, including the acceptable plus and minus percentage deviation allowance, and the delivery date (or dates, if the contract is for more than a single shipment), as well as the shipping locations.

Also provided in the bid request is a brief specification data sheet. This includes a description of the product or products requested plus references to other compendium or quality specifications that could be referred to for more detailed product descriptions and requirements. Manufacturing and packaging requirements are provided, ranging from commercial product with exterior government marking, which is the least complicated, to government specification material with government-specified packaging. This latter situation could require manufacturing the products to different specifications and packaging (type of unit package, immediate package, and shipping containers) from those normally supplied by the manufacturer to domestic markets. Obviously, this involves special procedures and may be more costly to the manufacturer.

Additional information included in the bid request pertains to the due date and time that the bid must be received in the contracting office to be considered. A bid response received by the government after the stipulated date and time is considered non-responsive and is eliminated from consideration. The award date, which will generally be stated in number of days following the closing or due date (usually 30 to 60 days), is also provided. Government agency acceptance or rejection of the bid by a formal notice will usually be received during that period. Acceptance criteria—whether or not acceptance and inspection of the material to be delivered will occur at the contractor's plant or at the shipping destination(s)—are also included in the bid specifications.

Information requested to be supplied by the manufacturer or contractor includes bid price and affirmative or negative response(s) as to compliance of the bid requirements (i.e., delivery date, bid specifications, etc.). Included in the bid solicitation will be a section headed Representation, Certification, and Acknowledgments. Most of this information will be in connection with government programs to aid minority and small business ventures.

Also included is a provision entitled "Buy American Act," which requires a manufacturer to list the source of all components or ingredients in the product or products being requested. Preference and price advantage are granted to American-made products over those produced in foreign countries. Certain countries may have "favored" status over other countries, depending on the political dictates of the foreign policy currently in force. Although there is an advantage granted to domestically produced products this price advantage is limited to a fixed percentage over foreign competition, so there is only limited value to this provision.

Pricing to the Government

The overriding premise regarding sales to the government is the "most favored customer" status, which the government expects in all of its dealings. This says that the government is entitled to the *best* price of any customer for the same quantity of goods or materials sold on an equal basis.

There are many other considerations that must be included in developing pricing for government orders. Competition is obviously the leading consideration because only one supplier will be awarded the business for a given bid request, and this award will generally be made according to the lowest price submitted. Exceptions may relate to such considerations as ability to deliver on time and foreign source material versus domestic but, all other considerations being equal, price will be the main determinant.

Government orders are sought by most manufacturers at prices that would be unacceptable and unprofitable if normal accounting practices were followed. The manufacturer generally sells at these reduced prices based on the premise that this is "incremental," or add-on, business.

Generally, no absorption of overhead, such as charges for research costs, product development, sales force expenses, marketing, and administration are covered. With smaller margins than would otherwise be realized from regular sales, the manufacturer may be able to use the government orders to increase manufacturing capacity utilization of otherwise unused production time and facilities. Because of the large size of some government orders, purchasing advantages might accrue to the manufacturer by virtue of increased quantities of raw materials and finishing components involved, which might also favorably affect prices for the domestic product.

An appreciation of the value of the exposure of the manufacturers' products and trademarks to those medical professionals within the government health services system is also important, because these individuals will re-enter the domestic medical market at some future time. Patient exposure, too, is recognized as being of value, particularly with those products having beneficial features, such as taste and appearance, over their competitors.

On the other hand, such factors as increased manufacturing costs incurred because of special handling, increased quality assurance involvement, and more costly administrative procedures must be considered. When applied against the unit cost, these increases will not normally have an appreciable effect on pricing but, where margins are tight, as they generally are in these government bidding situations, they must be taken into account.

Problems in forecasting government requirements must also be considered. Even though the Defense Personnel Support Center issues a quarterly unit forecast, the process of forecasting large production quantities in anticipation of a government bid, which may or may not materialize, must be started well in advance if the manufacturer plans to meet the required delivery dates. This can create large excesses in domestic inventories should the bid be lost to a competitor. In some cases this excess inventory could exceed domestic sales requirements to a point at which the expiration dating might expire before the product is sold. Because of government expiration dating requirements, the product cannot be held for a future government request because too much of the dating period will have elapsed. This requires a constant monitoring and updating of production forecasts for government demands to ensure against these potential problems.

It should be noted that those suppliers who are involved in the basic manufacturing of their products also compete favorably with foreign sources and domestic generic companies.

Government vs. Retail Market

The government market is affected by many factors that do not affect the retail market, such as changes in the size of the military, budget cutbacks, Senate appropriations, war or peace, the military draft, and other political considerations. At any rate, the huge government market is one in which most pharmaceutical manufacturers aggressively seek a larger share.

As might be expected, sales in the government sector occur partially at the expense of the domestic market. This is particularly true of the Veterans Administration, which continues to supply former veterans for the rest of their lives. Other government agencies serving indigent and underprivileged patients authorize medical care that would not otherwise be provided and thus probably do not compete with the domestic market. However, it is only a short step from these agencies to government-funded programs, such as Medicaid and Health Maintenance Organizations, that do have a great impact on the retail pharmaceutical market.

Health Maintenance Organizations

A Health Maintenance Organization (HMO) both insures and dispenses health care. In 1970, a "think tank" named Interstudy coined the term "Health Maintenance Organization" to describe such an institution. Although seemingly recent organizations, HMOs have existed for a considerable time as prepaid health plans. The roots of the prepaid health plan can be traced back to shared cost arrangements for direct health services to Venetian seamen in the thirteenth century.[2] The contemporary HMO began with the formation of the Ross-Loos Medical Group, which served employees of the Los Angeles Department of Water and Power in 1929. By 1933, the Kaiser Foundation Health Plan was started to care for workers on a construction project in the Mojave Desert. As recently as 1970 there were only 25 HMOs in the entire United States. In 1980 there were 240 HMOs dispersed throughout the country, serving over 9 million individuals. From 7 centuries of relative dormancy to a decade of exponential growth—what has happened? Two factors generally recognized as fueling the growth of HMOs are listed on page 324.

1. Intrinsic cost-containment mechanism built into the prepaid health plan.

2. Widespread health-care cost inflation coupled to a large increase in the number of people insured by traditional indemnity fee for service reimbursement organizations.

Financing

The cost-containment mechanisms within prepaid health plans have a direct impact on the marketing of pharmaceuticals to HMOs. HMOs dispense health care to a voluntarily enrolled population; they finance this health care by spreading the cost among all enrolled beneficiaries *and providers* on a prepaid basis. The prepaid aspect of financing health care refers to the practice whereby HMO members prepay their medical fees before their anticipated needs are met, and providers of this anticipated health care are paid in advance of dispensing their professional services.

This is a different means of paying for health care than the traditional fee for service system. The free market method of purchasing health care involves patients (as consumers) who pay a provider an established *fee for each health service* after it has been rendered. Therefore, with most health consumers subscribing to a traditional fee for service insurance plan, the fee is paid on a claim basis, with each claim representing a health service by a provider who is not generally associated with the insurer.

On the other hand, prepaid health plans, such as HMOs, collect money in advance of the demand for payment of provided health services. This money goes into a collective pot and is disbursed to physicians, nurses, hospitals, pharmacies, etc., under a well-controlled system that maintains these providers as salaried or as contractually capitated employees of the HMO. To give additional incentive to restrict provider-controlled demand for prepaid funds, these HMO-associated health professionals often receive some type of bonus for limiting the frequency and expense of their services. Concurrently, these providers generally receive *no* additional payment if their demand for service payment exceeds the prepaid funds available.

Prevention vs. Cure

Woven into the fabric of HMO shared cost is an effort to educate plan members and make services that promote maintenance of good health readily available, such as physicals. This health philosophy is a statement of HMO self-interest in that the general well-being of plan members has a direct relationship to the demand for expensive therapy.

The contrast of cost constraint inherent in prepaid health care versus the generally unrestricted pay incentives of fee for service health care make the following observations noteworthy:

1. As a group, HMO beneficiaries pay 10 to 40% less, including out-of-pocket expenses, for health care than do their fee for service counterparts.[3-5]

2. Researchers drawing from 90 articles encompassing 25 studies from 18 independent research projects concluded that "in 19 of the 25 studies, the general quality of health care, as indicated by the measures applied, was superior to that in fee for service or other settings. Six studies found care to be of similar quality in both settings, and none reported HMO care to be inferior over all."[6]

Another factor of interest to suppliers to the HMO industry is that the government has taken note of these observations and has acted to assist the growth of HMOs. Since the passage of the Health Maintenance Organization Act in 1973 (PL93-222), the growth of HMOs by enrollment and number of plans has been rapid. Several health market studies have projected enrollment growth of HMOs from 9 million persons enrolled in 240 plans in 1980 to more than 19 million enrollees in 450 plans as early as 1988.[7-10]

To market pharmaceuticals successfully to the HMO industry, suppliers must understand not only the cost-containment factors built into the HMO, but also the variety of arrangements that exist between the provider of health care and the insurer reimbursing the provider. Because the term "Health Maintenance Organization" stresses health *maintenance,* and because it has been shown that HMOs accrue the greatest portion of their documented savings by utilizing expensive hospital services approximately 30% less often than patients with fee for service insurance, drug utilization within the HMO accents symptomatic control of incurable chronic illness and high use of drugs capable of curing acute distressing or infectious disease (Table 14-8).[3, 11]

The actual pharmacy benefit of the HMO is provided by a system that attempts to control prescribing practices as well as dispensing costs. Both these factors are important considerations to the drug manufacturer and to the supplier interested in selling to the HMO market.

HMO Classifications

The pharmacy benefit associated with the HMO is usually administered in a format consistent with that of the HMO sponsor. The most widely used general classifications for HMOs are grouped according to three functional distinctions.

TABLE 14-8. *Cumulative Percentage and Number of Prescription Drugs per 1000 Persons per Year Dispensed to Study and Control Groups in Fiscal Year 1972, by Therapeutic Category*

	STUDY GROUP			DC MEDICAID CONTROL GROUP		
RANK	THERAPEUTIC CATEGORY*	CUMULATIVE %	NUMBER PER 1000 PERSONS PER YEAR	THERAPEUTIC CATEGORY†	CUMULATIVE %	NUMBER PER 1000 PERSONS PER YEAR
1	Diuretics	8.3	257	Diuretics	8.3	287
2	Mild analgesics	15.9	236	Mild analgesics	15.6	251
3	Antianxiety agents	23.5	235	Antianxiety agents	22.8	249
4	Antihypertensives	28.7	162	Penicillins	29.5	232
5	Estrogens, progesterones, and oral contraceptives	33.8	159	Antihistamines	35.7	215
6	Expectorants and inhalants	38.8	153	Estrogens, progesterones, and oral contraceptives	41.5	199
7	Penicillins	43.7	152	Antihypertensives	45.8	148
8	Antihistamines	48.0	132	Tetracyclines	49.8	138
9	Tetracyclines	51.8	118	Adrenal corticosteroids	53.6	129
10	Antidiabetics	55.6	117	Bronchodilators	57.2	122

*30 categories account for 90 percent of study group's prescriptions.
†31 categories account for 90 percent of control group's prescriptions.
Note: Eight of ten categories are the same for the study and control groups.

Source: Rabin, D., et al.: Drug Prescription Rates Before and After Enrollment of a Medicaid Population in an IIMO, *Public Health Reports, 93* (No. 1):21, 1978.

GROUP HMO

This type usually owns and operates buildings housing a comprehensive range of health-care services, including the pharmacies they may contain. Group HMOs frequently pay all health professionals, including the pharmacist, on a salaried employee basis, no matter how many actual patients or patient visits these professionals negotiate. Group HMOs do not, as a rule, dispense health care to fee for service patients. Large group HMOs, such as Kaiser Permanente, often own and operate their own hospitals.

STAFF HMO

This type is similar to the group type. However, these HMOs frequently do not own the buildings in which the health professionals work. Staff HMOs generally retain their professional employees on salary, and are comprised of several clinics throughout the service area. These clinics will often provide only a portion of the comprehensive range of health benefits available to enrolled members. These HMOs frequently have capitated contractual arrangements with local hospitals, pharmacies, and other community-based fee for service institutions to provide health care that is not dispensed by their salaried employees. Although many staff-type HMOs serve only plan members, some will also serve non-members on a fee for service basis.

INDIVIDUAL PRACTICE ASSOCIATION HMO

This type costs the least to start up and has recently been appearing in competitive response to the growing enrollment of group-type HMOs. Just as the name implies, Individual Practice Associations (IPAs) generally exist as contractual umbrellas under which individual fee for service physicians provide health care to HMO members on a prepaid or capitated basis. Although the IPA physician devotes varying periods of time for fee for service patients, he will usually care for HMO members under a set monthly fee representing the total number of patients he is likely to see, whether or not he *actually* sees more or less than the number of HMO patients that the fee would cover. IPAs also maintain contractual agreements with community pharmacies, laboratories, and hospitals to build a comprehensive range of benefits for their membership.

It is interesting to note that 65% of all HMO membership is in group HMOs, 20.5% in staff HMOs, and 14.5% in IPAs.[12] Although all HMOs generate prescriptions, not all HMOs will pay for them. As a result, cost control mechanisms such as formularies, maximum allowable cost (MAC), and generic substitution vary considerably and tend to be accented according to the HMO providing pharmacy benefits.

As might be anticipated, IPA and staff HMOs are not as cost-coordinated as group HMOs, and are more likely to use substitution and MAC to contain pharmacy costs. Group HMOs have the greatest control over their employed physicians and pharmacists, and usually own the pharmacy and its inventory. As a result, formularies are more easily administered in the group HMO. Group HMOs, with the greatest enrollment, are also frequently capable of buying drugs at the best price because of their volume purchasing power. These factors, as well as the type of pharmacy operation actually used by the HMO, are important variables to consider when suppliers to the industry plan market strategy to sell to HMOs.

Pharmacy Classifications

Just as there are three functional distinctions for HMO types, there are also three types of operative pharmacy groupings. Although these groupings closely parallel the HMO types and are usually associated in kind with their HMO sponsor, there are many variations and hybrid affiliations.

IN-HOUSE PHARMACIES

These are usually owned and controlled by the HMO corporation, which employs pharmacists for the purpose of dispensing drugs to plan members. These pharmacies are generally part of group HMOs and serve plan members almost exclusively while strongly discouraging fee for service retail trade.

LIMITED PHARMACY NETWORK

This dispenses drugs to HMO members through pharmacies that are usually independently owned, with the pharmacists receiving their pay from the owner of the pharmacy. Therefore, limited pharmacy networks are comprised of a limited number of community pharmacies within the HMO service area, some of which may also conduct fee for service retail trade or may serve only HMO plan members on a claim-processing or capitated basis. It is possible, for instance, for staff HMOs to have independently owned and operated pharmacies at each clinic location.

OPEN PHARMACY NETWORK

This is similar to the pharmacy plan used by most traditional indemnity or fee for service insurance programs. Within the open pharmacy network, HMO plan members are free to go to any pharmacy located in the HMO service area and obtain drug benefits. This type of network is often used by IPA-type HMOs. All pharmacies in the network serve fee for service customers, and payment for serving HMO members is usually obtained through a claim-processing mechanism.

Regardless of the type of pharmacy network used by an HMO, most HMO plans require a copayment from the beneficiary receiving the drug service each time a prescription is filled. Generally speaking, the lowest copayments are observed in plans having in-house pharmacies, because that type of pharmacy is usually best cost-controlled within the operational requirements of the HMO. As may be imagined, limited and open pharmacy networks are more difficult to control in terms of inventory costs and dispensing fees, and most are likely to have guidelines from the HMO that encourage generic substitutions and MAC.

Drug Utilization

At the present time, 3 new prescriptions per year per enrollee are generated by HMOs in the United States, representing over $220 million for new prescriptions alone.[10, 13–18] This prescription volume is approximately 11% less than the national fee for service new prescription rate of 3.36 prescriptions per person per year. HMO cost controls have some impact on the generation of new prescriptions; these are market forces that must be recognized by suppliers to the industry.

Concomitant with various direct types of drug cost containment are various means employed by HMOs for controlling prescribing practices. Not only do HMOs attempt to limit use of hospitals, but group HMOs and the reimbursement incentives built into staff and IPA HMOs also attempt to match the expense and facility of the health-care practice to the needs of a patient. For example, physician extenders, such as nurse practitioners and physician assistants, will often be the first, and frequently the only, members of the health-care team to see HMO patients. If a patient requires further medical attention, then he may be referred to a physician and then, if necessary, to a specialist, and possibly on to a hospital or specialized treatment center. As a result, physician extenders are sometimes granted limited prescribing responsibilities, and are targeted as recipients of promotional drug information offered by suppliers marketing to HMOs.

In one study HMO physicians were asked to identify the number of detail men typically seen each month. "Responses indicated that detail man contact occurred only infrequently, if at all. Nearly 38% of physicians indicated that they were contacted an average of less than once per week."[19] It was noted in this study that low detail man contact was in part due to organizational policy. It was also noted that HMO physicians tended to use literature-based sources for general drug information, with HMO colleagues proving to be the most influential factor in encouraging initial prescribing of a new drug.

As already noted, the sale of drugs to and through HMOs is primarily influenced by the prepaid incentive for cost containment. The actual cost-containment mechanisms used by an HMO vary according to the type and functional characteristics of the HMO as well as according to the type of pharmacy network used to administer the drug benefit.

Future Considerations

The cost-containment success of the HMO industry should attract more attention as health-care consumers, including the government (as funders of Medicare and Medicaid), become more aware of the inflationary effects of increasing health-care costs. Presently, the government is strongly encouraging enrollment of Medicare and Medicaid populations in HMOs. The demonstration phase of HMO feasibility testing and governmental investigation ended with the signing into law of Bill PF 95-559 on October 14, 1978.

These 1978 HMO amendments essentially proclaimed governmental endorsement for the HMO concept. "Many believe that reliance on fee for service medicine, coupled with virtually no attempt to modify the supply or organization of health services, has led to many of the programs' (Medicaid/Medicare) problems."[20]

It is apparent that HMOs have an established place among health-care institutions. "Therefore, we suggest that in addition to HMO growth on a national level, suppliers to the industry need to consider the likelihood of a transformation of certain market areas into competitive health systems. . . ."[10]

Medicare and Medicaid

Social health legislation received its impetus during the depths of the Depression. In the years that followed, several pieces of social legislation had a significant impact upon the health-care system. It was not until the passage of the Kerr-Mills Act in 1960, however, that the push for increased drug services began. The American public's empathy towards the poor and the elderly peaked in the mid-1960s, which led to the passage of two key amendments to the Social Security Act: the Medi*care* Amendment (Title XVIII) and the Medi*caid* Amendment (Title XIX). The implementation of these two amendments has been the focal point for increased government involvement and interest in drugs and drug costs. In fact, the social legislation of the 1960s sensitized the government to a much stronger involvement with the entire drug distribution system.

Objectives

The object of Medicaid is to provide access to health care for needful families with dependent children and for the aged, blind, and disabled, whereas Medicare is a federally run health insurance program for those 65 and older, and for some under 65 who are disabled. Because most states offer outpatient pharmaceutical benefits under state medical assistance programs (Medicaid), and Medicare does not, this section will limit itself to an analysis of state medical assistance programs and their impact on pharmaceutical manufacturers.

Basic Services vs. Optional Services

Title XIX of the Social Security Act *requires that certain basic services be offered* in any state Medicaid program:

1. Inpatient hospital services.

2. Outpatient hospital services.

3. Laboratory and x-ray services.

4. Skilled nursing facility services for individuals 21 and older.

5. Home health-care services for individuals eligible for skilled nursing services.

6. Physician services.

7. Family planning services.

8. Rural health clinic services.

9. Early and periodic screening, diagnosis, and treatment for physical and mental defects for eligibles under 21.

In addition to basic services, states may provide a number of other services, if they elect to do so, including drugs, eyeglasses, private duty nursing, intermediate care facility services, inpatient psychiatric care for the aged and those under 21, physical therapy, and dental care.

Each state must determine the scope of services offered. They also generally determine the reimbursement rate for services, except for hospital care. In the latter case, states are required to follow the Medicare reasonable cost payment system, unless they have approval from the Secretary of Health and Human Services to use an alternate payment system for hospital care.

The federal government pays a percentage of the expenditures incurred by each state in providing Medicaid care and services to eligible recipients. The federal government's share is referred to as FMAP (Federal Medical Assistance Percentage). The federal share of state medical vendor payments is determined by a statutory formula designed to provide a higher percentage of federal matching funds to states with low per capita incomes, and a lower percentage of matching funds to states with higher per capita incomes.

Under the formula, if a state's per capita income is equal to the national average per capita income, the federal share would be 55%. If a state's per capita income exceeds the national average the federal share is lower, with a statutory minimum of 50%. If a state's per capita income is lower than the national average the federal share is increased, up to a maximum of 83%; however, no state currently receives more than 77.55%.

The actual formula used in determining the state and federal share is as follows:

$$\text{state share} = \frac{\text{state per capita income}}{\text{national per capita income}} \times 45$$

The federal share is equal to 100% minus the state's share, with a minimum of 50% and a maximum of 83%. The formula provides for squaring both the state and national average per capita incomes. This procedure magnifies any differences between the state's income and the national average. Consequently, the federal matching to lower income states is increased and federal matching to higher income states is decreased; however, the statutory minimum of 50% eliminates much of the skewing effect on higher income states.

Vendor Payments for Drugs: Maximum Allowable Cost

On July 1, 1974, South Dakota added prescription drug services to its Medicaid program. This brought to 50 the number of jurisdictions offering the drug benefit. Total Medicaid vendor payments have increased almost 800% since 1965 and 130% since 1970. Table 14-9 shows vendor payments by state for prescribed drugs for fiscal years 1974 to 1979.

Due largely to tremendous increases in medical care expenditures under public assistance programs, Caspar Weinberger, then Secretary of Health, Education and Welfare, in 1975 introduced

TABLE 14-9. *Vendor Payments for Prescribed Drugs Under Title XIX of the Social Security Act, Medical Assistance Programs for Fiscal Years 1974–1979 ($ thousands)*

STATE	1974	1975	1976	1977	1978	1979*
Total	$706,746	$816,453	$959,951	$1,018,221	$1,088,238	$1,232,582
Alabama	12,123	15,643	15,730	16,694	18,349	22,277
Arkansas	6,321	11,960	14,221	14,133	15,813	18,832
California	87,957	96,156	119,881	135,324	148,496	171,214
Colorado	6,856	7,458	8,343	8,790	9,684	9,622
Connecticut	7,124	9,079	10,864	12,092	13,420	14,750
Delaware	1,248	1,342	1,614	1,518	1,603	1,845
District of Columbia	4,843	5,779	6,524	5,170	4,428	4,935
Florida	11,764	18,878	19,604	23,148	22,684	33,238
Georgia	16,753	25,929	26,771	29,449	34,074	36,886
Guam	†	†	†	†	†	†
Hawaii	2,372	2,747	3,999	4,725	4,469	5,121
Idaho	1,331	1,503	1,762	1,669	1,894	2,316
Illinois	56,945	64,907	66,629	66,353	70,579	86,057
Indiana	11,416	12,505	16,512	19,539	21,189	21,845
Iowa	5,260	6,607	8,547	9,027	11,089	13,240
Kansas	7,415	8,364	10,072	11,307	10,715	12,312
Kentucky	10,698	12,009	12,896	12,041	11,590	13,334
Louisiana	10,931	25,755	34,316	29,417	33,847	39,395
Maine	3,745	3,825	5,762	6,170	7,094	8,284
Maryland	15,869	17,282	17,634	14,102	12,581	15,872
Massachusetts	24,157	28,776	29,750	26,784	27,909	37,065
Michigan	36,933	43,713	50,566	46,611	53,470	59,436
Minnesota	13,160	12,831	16,423	17,031	18,583	20,647
Mississippi	16,256	19,677	23,949	19,611	24,312	27,710
Missouri	11,685	12,923	15,991	17,663	20,282	21,582
Montana	1,135	1,706	1,723	2,220	2,360	2,498
Nebraska	4,528	4,709	5,496	5,634	6,306	6,942
Nevada	916	1,165	1,502	1,008	1,092	1,468
New Hampshire	2,071	2,738	2,489	2,730	2,791	3,058
New Jersey	19,725	24,509	24,865	29,627	33,913	39,089
New Mexico	2,828	3,130	3,805	4,174	4,163	4,442
New York	86,851	86,183	100,242	103,200	89,882	99,720
North Carolina	16,599	18,281	22,604	26,310	26,695	29,131
North Dakota	1,766	2,146	1,955	2,218	2,397	2,571
Ohio	38,351	34,339	38,597	38,445	38,786	46,104
Oklahoma	90‡	14	3,601	5,730	6,086	7,433
Oregon	3,180	4,174	5,282	6,042	7,360	6,766
Pennsylvania	29,664	24,853	44,716	60,711	70,439	70,950
Puerto Rico	16,884	21,862	21,270	23,270	20,833	16,332
Rhode Island	4,876	5,304	5,878	6,356	6,475	6,847
South Carolina	4,569	7,371	10,419	11,857	11,513	14,371
South Dakota	—	1,560	1,247	1,206	1,453	1,683
Tennessee	12,439	17,853	23,789	26,504	30,852	34,234
Texas	32,224	37,468	44,383	48,731	52,267	58,536

(Continued on p. 334.)

Table 14-9. *(Continued)*

STATE	1974	1975	1976	1977	1978	1979*
Utah	2,286	2,424	2,826	2,985	3,494	3,782
Vermont	2,103	2,414	2,794	2,911	2,909	3,027
Virgin Islands	326	301	466	248	441	342
Virginia	14,224	13,911	12,709	15,032	17,479	20,519
Washington	10,448	11,891	13,021	13,337	13,456	14,695
West Virginia	3,256	3,710	6,482	7,061	7,754	8,523
Wisconsin	12,245	16,788	19,430	22,308	28,889	31,704

*State data submitted directly to NPC. *Exceptions:* Delaware, Hawaii, Pennsylvania, South Carolina—data reported on HHS-NCSS 2082 B(3), Section B(3).
†No data reported.
‡Oklahoma money payments include $17 per month for drugs for all adult public assistance programs. (Title XIX Vendor Drug Program not implemented until FY-76, July 1, 1975.)
Note: No Title XIX vendor drug program as of FY-79: Alaska, Arizona, Wyoming (Arizona—no Title XIX Medicaid Program).

*Source (except for 1979 column): Research Report B-5 (prepublished Table Q-3), FY-78 (preliminary), Office of Research, Demonstrations and Statistics, Office of Research, Medicaid Program Data Branch, Health Care Financing Administration, Department of Health, Education, and Welfare. (Data obtained July 1979; now the Department of Health and Human Services, HHS.)

the concept of determining the maximum reimbursement for drug costs to health-care programs that receive full or partial funding from the federal government. Secretary Weinberger assured the American public that the new system of placing ceilings on the amount of money which the federal government would pay for drugs (maximum allowable cost) would in no way influence the quality of pharmaceuticals being utilized by the public and private sectors of the health-care system. The final set of maximum allowable cost (MAC) regulations, as approved on July 28, 1975, applies only to those drugs that are widely available from more than one source—manufactured by more than one firm. The regulations limit reimbursement for multisource drugs to the lowest of:

1. The maximum allowable cost price of the drug, if any.

2. The acquisition cost of the drug plus a reasonable dispensing fee.

3. Or the provider's usual and customary charge to the general public for the drug.

There have been many objections to this program. The most frequently expressed is that the direct and indirect administrative costs of such a program exceed any possible savings. This conclusion was supported by results of a study by PRACON, Inc., a Washington, DC-based consulting firm.[22] This study concluded that the use of regulatory authority to establish arbitrary price guidelines (MAC) may result in complex administrative systems that drive up program costs rather than result in appreciable savings.

The administrative cost of the California Medi-Cal Program, which imposed cumbersome administrative controls over price and availability, was 8% of the total payments for drugs, while the Texas program that adopted effective utilization controls was only 3%. Also, through utilization management, Medicaid patients in Texas used 10% fewer drugs per capita than in California.

The MAC regulations have prompted several pharmaceutical firms to manufacture and distribute multisource drugs at competitive prices. This does not necessarily lead to increased demand for these products by the purchasing pharmacist. Unless prescribers (physicians) increase the number of prescriptions written, the most likely outcome for the specific pharmaceutical manufacturer will be lower margins on total sales. The multisource drug market has a basically inelastic demand. This is illustrated by the inability to expand demand for a generic pharmaceutical in relation to the unit price of the product. Manufacturers, therefore, are forced to concentrate their efforts on patent-protected items that produce sufficient profits for supporting ongoing research and development. The federal government has simply succeeded in shifting a portion of the financing for prescription drugs to a segment of the private sector that requires new patent-protected pharmaceuticals.

Research and quality-oriented manufacturers cannot operate innovatively and efficiently under a lowest price reimbursement system. Emphasis on "price only" criteria for drug selection would be at the expense of quality health care, and would have a severe impact on research and, in turn, on future drug development.

The administrative burden imposed by Medicaid, along with payment ceilings, has led to a deteriorating financial condition for many retail pharmacies. As gross margins have gradually decreased and operating expenses have increased, net profit has fallen. In spite of the extra time and expense required for filling Medicaid prescriptions, reimbursement has been less than that normally paid for private-pay prescriptions. The dispensing fees have fallen behind real world costs. Because regulated fees will always lag if data must be extensively collected and analyzed, a "usual and customary" system has been recommended to permit prices to respond to the marketplace. The National Association of Retail Druggists prefers the term "marketplace pricing" instead of the "usual and customary" for dispensing a prescription, because the former term reflects all current operating costs, a reasonable profit, and a return on the investment.

The future of drug benefits under Medicaid would seem to depend, in part, on the government's recognition that the retail pharmacy must be compensated for the task of filling prescriptions. Continued cost-cutting strategies, coupled with insufficient adjustment of fees, puts the administrative burden on the retailer. This, in turn, may force the choice of the lowest priced generic (regardless of quality) and decrease the likelihood of providing any other pharmacy services. The possibility of driving the smaller retailer out of business is greatly increased, along with the probability that fewer pharmacies will choose to participate in the program. In the end, the pharmacist's support of these programs must encompass the reimbursement for the drugs being dispensed and the impact of price ceilings upon the pharmacy's business and professional services.

Formularies: Open vs. Closed

Faced with the challenge of stretching budgets to meet the constantly increasing needs of Medicaid recipients, government administrators and legislators often devise fiscal strategies directed to specific benefit categories such as pharmaceuticals. It is not surprising that some states adopt restrictive drug formularies with little thought of the impact associated with increased utilization of other, more costly health services.

A drug formulary can be described as a predetermined list of products available for selection by the dispensing pharmacist. An open formulary generally contains all major therapeutic classes of drugs and most brand names and branded generics within each class. A closed formulary is restrictive. Generally only one or two products are allowed within any therapeutic class and, occasionally, entire categories are eliminated, such as vitamins, hematinics, and minor tranquilizers.

In May 1980, the National Pharmaceutical Council published a report supporting their hypothesis that increased health-care expenditures are caused by restrictions placed on Medicaid drug programs.[21] Two states were chosen for the study, Louisiana and Texas. During the study periods, Texas retained an open drug formulary while Louisiana implemented a restrictive formulary.

The principal findings of the study revealed that while prescription expenditures decreased in Louisiana by $4.1 million, other program expenditures rose by $15.1 million. These results reinforced the study's hypothesis that restricting access to certain drugs increases the demand for nonprescription services such as outpatient hospital visits, physician visits, and nursing home days.

The Texas Medicaid Program, which maintained an open formulary, did not exhibit the large utilization increases found in

Louisiana. Between 1976 and 1977, the overall "constant dollar" increase in total health-care expenditures was $4.08 per Texas recipient versus $23.69 per Louisiana recipient.

Pharmaceutical manufacturers have undertaken a concerted effort to communicate the benefits of maintaining and promoting open drug formularies. Access to appropriate drug therapy has proven to be the most cost-effective method of treating disease states that are so prevalent in the poor, aged, and disabled.

Some companies hire and train special government affairs representatives whose sole function is to monitor Medicaid activity at the state level and to ensure that each Medicaid administrator is familiar with the company's products. Because many states maintain special Medicaid drug formularies, every effort must be made to ensure adequate product representation. Government affairs representatives spend considerable time preparing proposals for inclusion of their products on these formularies. Each proposal stresses therapeutic advantage, price advantage, and possible replacement of an existing product with their product.

Most pharmaceutical manufacturers do not maintain special field personnel for the purpose of monitoring Medicaid activity. They usually rely on local representatives to follow developments in this area and to report changes or opportunities for new business. Home office personnel then prepare the necessary reports and arrange presentations at state formulary committee meetings.

Capitation

Concern over the rapidly escalating costs of health care has spawned a variety of cost-containment schemes over recent years. One reimbursement formula that has emerged relatively recently is the concept of capitation. Broadly defined, capitation of pharmaceutical services is a reimbursement method whereby a provider of pharmaceuticals (retail pharmacy) is paid a uniform per capita fee per program eligible (welfare patient) based on the average utilization of pharmaceuticals for a specified period of time. The rate of capitation (payment to pharmacist) is generally inclusive of both product acquisition cost and professional dispensing fee.

It seems likely that interest in single service capitation as a cost-containment mechanism will be a major issue of debate among government, industry, and health-care providers in the 1980s. Because a manufacturer's major interest is the potential effect of capitation on pharmaceutical services, we will focus our comments on this aspect of the issue.

Proponents of a capitation system as a reimbursement mechanism for pharmaceutical services suggest that there are three parties who benefit under such a system: the program administrator, the pharmacy practitioner, and the patient. The opponents of the capitation system question the concept from the points of view of quality of care, administration, financing, and overall value to the parties involved. Capitation, they have argued, creates a two-tier system of delivery for pharmaceutical services—the private versus the public or third-party patient. Cost containment becomes the primary goal for the third-party-supported tier, and can result in the discriminatory practice of dispensing a lower level of product quality and service in order to stay within capitation reimbursement allowances.

Capitation has an impact on the quality of care by setting up an "adverse selection principle"; that is , it is a system that provides pharmacies with an economic incentive to avoid high utilizers, and rewards them for retaining low utilizers of pharmaceutical services. Patients with high levels of need, such as the debilitated and elderly, become undesirable as enrollees and may be bounced back and forth from pharmacy to pharmacy. This creates a situation whereby there is a lack of continuity of care that may prove both physiologically and therapeutically detrimental to the patient. Most service-oriented pharmacies are less likely to participate in such a system, because capitation does not reward the delivery of increased levels of service but rather encourages the delivery of minimal services.

Although currently in its infancy, the capitation "movement" as an alternative mechanism for reimbursement of pharmaceutical services appears to be developing as a major new attempt to contain costs in the drug sector of the nation's health-care delivery system. It represents another artificial constraint on the free market system, along with restrictive formularies, substitution, and MAC, to achieve administrative expediency at the expense of the quality of patient care. Many feel that the goals of quality care and cost economy can best be accomplished by promoting a free market incentive system that rewards innovation and productivity. Although short-term cost savings may result from capitation experiments, it is likely that administrative and other hidden costs may soon overtake any savings resulting from implementation of such programs.

Future Considerations

The short- and long-term prospects for adequate health care for the indigent, the disabled, and the aged are now more uncertain than at any time in the past quarter-century. Inflation and an uncertain economy will lead to more poverty and, inevitably, to more illness. At the same time, the great public hospitals and the social programs that lessen the effects of poverty—food stamps, school lunches, neighborhood health centers, Medicaid—are being cut back by the government. Like Great Britain and other countries, the United States has discovered that free health care can be expensive.

Perhaps the major weakness of the Medicaid concept and other social programs is a lack of sufficient incentives to encourage preventive health care and realistic utilization of services. Many possible solutions have been proposed for reducing expenditures while maintaining current levels of care:

1. Drug utilization review programs.

2. PSROs (Professional Service Review Organizations).

3. Copayment plans for prescriptions (patient pays part of fee).

4. Greater utilization of HMOs by welfare recipients.

5. Capitation.

If the future for the poor is dim, do the pharmacist and the manufacturer have reason for optimism? Has the trend been established for additional market intrusion by the government at the costly expense of the free enterprise system? What happens when a pharmacist is forced to select products from a list of only the cheapest drugs? There results a significant negative effect, not only on the professionalism of community pharmacy, but also on the ability of manufacturers to generate revenues for the development of new pharmaceutical products. Today's research and development cannot be funded from selling tomorrow's innovations. Pharmacy's free selection from existing products will help preserve and encourage an atmosphere that permits the development of safe, effective, and reasonably priced medicines. Arbitrary pressure from the government to select the cheapest product possible does not appear consistent with the future economic viability of pharmacy or research-oriented manufacturers.

References

1. American Society of Hospital Pharmacists: *1980 ASHP Hospital Survey,* Washington, DC: 1980.
2. Seward, E. W., and Fleming, S.: Health Maintenance Organizations, *Scientific American, 243* (No. 4): 647, 1980.
3. Luft, H.: How Do Health Maintenance Organizations Achieve Their Savings?, *New England Journal of Medicine, 298* (No. 24):1336, 1978.
4. Colfin, K., Neisuler, R., et al.: Utilization of Preventive Services by Poor, Near-Poor, and Non-Poor Members of an HMO, presented at the American Pharmaceutical Association Annual Meeting, Los Angeles, October, 1978.

5. Sparer, B., and Anderson, A.: Utilization and Cost Experience of Low Income Families in Four Group Practice Plans, *New England Journal of Medicine, 89*:67, 1973.
6. Williamson, J., et al.: Quality of Health Care in HMOs Compared to Other Settings, Johns Hopkins University, 1979. (Unpublished.)
7. Department of Health, Education and Welfare: National HMO Development Strategy Through 1988, Washington, DC: U.S. Government Printing Office, Publication No. (PHS) 79-50111, September, 1979.
8. Viable Force, *The White Sheet,* No. 8, 1980.
9. Market Researcher Sees Big Growth for HMO Suppliers, *HMO Focus* (HHS OHMO), *3* (No. 5):7, 1980.
10. The Likely Impact of a Competitive Health Care System, Interstudy HIMA Report 80-3, Minneapolis: 1980.
11. Rabin, D., et al.: Drug Prescription Rates Before and After Enrollment of a Medicaid Population in an HMO, *Public Health Reports, 93* (No. 1):16, 1978.
12. OHMO 4th Annual Report to the Congress, Public Health Service, DHEW Publication No. (PHS) 79-13058, September, 1978.
13. Johnson, R., et al.: Examining the Annual Drug Utilization of A Cohort of Low Income Health Plan Members, *Medical Care, 17* (No. 6):581, 1979.
14. West, S., et al.: Drug Utilization Review in an HMO, *Medical Care, 15* (No. 6):507, 1977.
15. Hardigan, H. R., et al.: Distribution and Cost of Drugs in Pharmaceutically Decentralized Health Maintenance Organization, *Contemporary Pharmacy Practice, 3* (No. 1):29, 1980.
16. Johnson, R.: Drug Services and Costs in HMO Prototypes, *American Journal of Hospital Pharmacy, 30*:415, 1973.
17. Sparer, G., et al.: Utilization and Cost of Low-Income Families in Four Prepaid Group Practice Plans, *New England Journal of Medicine, 89*: 191, 1973.
18. Middleton, J., and Dee, D.: HMOs—Days of Future Passed, *American Pharmacy, NS20* (No. 10):43, 1980.
19. Christensen, D., and Wertheimer, A.: Sources of Information and Influence on New Drug Prescribing among Physicians in an HMO, *Social Science and Medicine, 13A*:313, 1979.
20. Vignola, M. L., et al.: Medicaid Beneficiaries in Health Maintenance Organizations: Utilization, Cost, Quality, Legal Requirements; An Annotated Bibliography, Washington, DC: the American Public Welfare Association and Department of HHS, 1980.
21. Hefner, D. L.: Cost-Effectiveness of a Restrictive Drug Formulary, Louisiana vs. Texas, Washington, DC: National Pharmaceutical Council, 1980.
22. Sudovar, S. G., Jr., and Rein, S. D.: Managing Medicaid Drug Expenditures, Nutley, NJ: PRACON Inc., for Roche Laboratories, 1978.

Competitive Practices

Economic and Competitive Aspects of the Pharmaceutical Industry

DOUGLAS L. COCKS

The pharmaceutical industry, especially at the manufacturing level, has been the focus of much academic interest involving several disciplines. The industry has been of special interest to economists because it has one of the most extensive data bases, which allows the empiric testing of various hypotheses concerning competition, the effects of regulation, and other economic phenomena. In turn, a fairly extensive literature on the industry has developed. The Kefauver hearings of the late 1950s and early 1960s were the initial forums in which economists could use the data on the industry to generate economic analyses.[1] These analyses continued with the Nelson hearings of the mid- to late 1960s.[2] From these studies, economists were able to establish a body of academic literature that focused primarily on the competitive aspects of the pharmaceutical industry. This pre-1970 literature provided a generally consistent viewpoint of the economics of the industry.

As with many intellectual and academic pursuits, the analysis of the economics of the pharmaceutical industry has gone through what can be described as a dialectical process, through which theses are first formulated and certain antitheses are then generated. From the conceptual conflict formed by these competing theses and antitheses, a set of syntheses, or even a synthesis, can be formulated. This may be the intellectual process that is occurring relative to the study of the economics of the industry.

Beginning about 1970, economists began to investigate alternative explanations and hypotheses (antitheses) concerning the economics of the pharmaceutical industry. It is the purpose of this chapter to provide a fairly comprehensive review and interpretation of both the pre- and post-1970 sets of literature on this subject. In addition to the summary of the literature, it is hoped that

. . .

the discussion contained in this chapter will provide a basic bibliography for those who want to investigate and interpret the economic literature for themselves.

In addition to consideration of competitive characteristics, economists have also studied the impact of regulation on the industry. For the most part, this literature appearing after about 1970, was concerned with the effects of the 1962 Drug Amendments.[3-7] A summary of studies that have assessed the economic impacts of drug regulation will also be provided. It is hoped that this chapter will give a better understanding of the operation of and environment surrounding the modern pharmaceutical industry.

Elements of Standard Economic Theory

Pure Competition

Economists have traditionally emphasized the market model of pure competition as the hallmark for assessing and judging the degree of economic efficiency in the production and consumption of goods and services in a particular marketplace. This model is a theoretical construct that not only provides a means of determining economic efficiency but also depicts how consumers and producers collectively interact to establish the prices and quantities of goods and services available.

According to theory, pure competition can exist when certain necessary conditions are evident. One of these is the homogeneity of product. This means that the products offered by different producers are essentially the same, and consumers cannot differentiate among these products; therefore, they are indifferent, in terms of product characteristics, to the goods being offered by individual firms or suppliers.

Another necessary condition for pure competition is that there are many buyers and sellers of a product in a given market. There are so many buyers and sellers that no one buyer or seller can influence the price of the goods or the quantity provided to the market.

The lack of external or contrived constraints on market activities is another necessary condition for pure competition. This means that market participants, buyers or sellers, cannot, in a collective manner, form associations to restrict the flow of resources, establish prices, or otherwise control various aspects of economic activity. This condition precludes the existence of such entities as cartels and labor unions.

The final necessary condition for theoretical pure competition is that there is complete mobility of resources. Economic resources are components of labor and capital (machines, equipment, buildings, etc.) that go into the production of goods and services. Under this condition, these resources are free to move across all the markets that comprise an economy, and they move according to the priorities established by these markets.

Perfect Competition ·

Economic theory also considers what is known as "perfect competition." Perfect competition requires the same necessary conditions as pure competition, but adds the necessary condition of complete information. All market participants must have complete information about market conditions. Therefore, both buyers and sellers have exact knowledge about the prices, quantities, qualities, and characteristics of all goods, services, and resources associated with particular markets.

When the conditions of pure or perfect competition are met, economic theory predicts that maximum economic efficiency will be achieved. This is an efficiency represented by the characteristic that the consumers of all goods and services in the economy receive the exact quantities they desire at the prices they are willing to pay. The prices that are paid reflect the relative costs of the resources used in the production of the goods and services. In turn, these costs reflect the characteristic that the resources used are employed in their most profitable manner and, thus, reflect the most desired use for consumers relative to all the alternative uses of these resources.

For producers, the conditions of pure or perfect competition imply that all goods and services will be produced at the lowest cost possible. Producers will maximize profits but, because of the competitive process associated with market interactions, all profits will be normal. Profit rates may differ, but these differences will reflect only the differences in the supply and demand risks associated with a particular market activity. Under these conditions, firms will simply accept the prices that are given to them by the marketplace and will determine the quantity of output that will maximize their profits—the quantity at which the difference between their total revenue and total costs is the greatest.

Within the theoretical context of the model of pure competition, price is the major concern. Price is the economic parameter on which consumers make economic choices, and on which firms or producers concentrate in order to determine what quantity they are willing to supply to the market. Within this framework, firms are merely price takers.

In studying the economic characteristics of individual industries, the application of the concepts contained in the theoretical construct of pure competition falls under the economics subdiscipline known as "industrial organization."[8] Industrial organization attempts to assess the competitive characteristics of particular industries. The conventional methodology that has been established is known as the "industrial organization paradigm." This focuses on the structural, conduct or behavioral, and performance elements of the industry being studied.

Applications of Economic Theory

Early Analyses

Much of the early literature on the economics of the pharmaceutical industry utilized the industrial organization framework. It is possible to summarize the structure-conduct-performance approach by reviewing the literature on the industry, much of which came out of the Kefauver and Nelson hearings.[9-19] Generally, these studies concluded that there is a misallocation of resources in the production of ethical pharmaceuticals—that is, the prices of drugs are too high relative to the costs of producing them and too high relative to consumers' desires. According to the underlying theory, this results in a less than optimum quantity of the goods provided.

STRUCTURAL CHARACTERISTICS

There are several structural characteristics that are considered important within the industrial organization framework, and these were emphasized in pre-1970 pharmaceutical industry studies. The concept of concentration is a primary element of structure. Concentration is the share of economic activity attributed to a certain number of firms in an industry or market. This economic activity could be the share of such things as total assets, employees, or sales.

The most widely used measure of concentration is the share of sales for the leading firms in a given industry or market. In studying the pharmaceutical industry, the focus of analysis was the therapeutic category. The individual therapeutic categories were considered to be the relevant "economic markets." It was felt that these therapeutic categories are highly concentrated—a large percentage of the total sales of a given therapeutic category is controlled by a few firms, usually four to eight. This high concentration was considered at least a preliminary indication of economic control and "market power."

The second structural characteristic emphasized in the earlier literature was the relatively high degree of price insensitivity of the demand for drug products—inelastic demand. Feldstein made an overall estimate of the price elasticity of demand for pharmaceutical products, an estimate that was relatively low.[20] Five main reasons were given for this relatively low price sensitivity: (1) the one who pays for the product (the patient) is not the one who makes the purchase decision (the physician); (2) drug patents establish a high degree of exclusivity for a product that denies competition from substitutes; (3) the promotion and advertising of ethical drugs impede the ability of physicians to consider all possible substitutes of drug therapy completely; (4) associated with promotion is the notion that drug firms' research and development programs produce products that are not necessarily different from existing products—research and development generates artificial product differentiation; (5) at the time of the earlier studies most states had antisubstitution laws, and it was assumed that these laws decreased the substitutability of "equivalent" drug products.

A third structural characteristic attributed to the pharmaceutical industry is the existence of "entry barriers." Entry barriers legally prevent rival firms from entering an industry or particular market or, if entry is not legally precluded, the effort and cost of entering prevents competitors from increasing the total quantity of drug products available to consumers. The entry barrier emphasized most was the drug patent. This is the legally constituted preemption of the duplication of unique chemical substances.

The early literature also emphasized product differentiation as an entry barrier. Two aspects of this product differentiation were thought to exist. First, the research and development activity of the industry was considered to be directed primarily toward the achievement of relatively slight scientific and chemical differences. Small firms were said to be precluded from these activities due to the great expense necessary to achieve this type of product differentiation. Second, pharmaceutical promotion, for the most part through the pharmaceutical sales representative, was felt to be a substantial entry barrier. Only the largest firms could have the necessary amount of promotional clout to make a significant impact on a given drug market.

BEHAVIORAL CHARACTERISTICS

The second dimension of the industrial organization framework studied was the conduct or behavior of firms in the industry. Price rigidity for products in various therapeutic categories has been presented as evidence of oligopolistic pricing behavior, in which firms either explicitly or tacitly coordinate their prices.

Price rigidities involving broad-spectrum antibiotics and cortico-steroid hormones are examples of pricing rigidity in the industry.[13]

It was argued that another aspect of the behavioral characteristics of the industry was that product competition, as opposed to price competition, prevails such that large firms engage in extensive promotion of their brand name products. It was felt that large firms stress the greater quality of these brand names over the generic products of smaller firms. This activity enhances the ability of firms to tacitly agree on prices. Steele has stated two reasons why he felt that the large firms' claims were not totally founded: (1) drugs listed in the *U.S. Pharmacopoeia* and the *National Formulary* are subject to the same standards of efficacy, content, and excellence; (2) smaller firms have been subject to greater regulatory scrutiny by the Food and Drug Administration than have larger firms.[17]

The final behavioral characteristic of the industry emphasized in the earlier literature was the product differentiation promulgated through the industry's research and development efforts. Products similar to existing products were developed and patented (this has become known as "molecule manipulation"), offered as new products, and then promoted widely in order to maintain what has been described as "monopoly power." Comanor has attributed the large amount of product obsolescence that exists in the industry as indicative of this type of behavior.[10]

PERFORMANCE CHARACTERISTICS

The last element of the industrial organization paradigm is performance. Performance is what "society" wants or expects from an industry or market that acts competitively.

The performance characteristic of an industry that is the major focus of attention is the rate of return of the individual firms, as well as the collective return to the leading firms. There are several measures of the rate of return. The one that appears most often in a popular context is the return on sales, the ratio of income to sales. This measure does not have real significance in economic terms. Surrogate measures of the economic rate of return that have been utilized are the return to stockholders' equity (the ratio of income to the dollar value of stockholders' equity) or the return to investment (the ratio of income to the dollar value of a firm's investment).

Relatively and persistently high rates of return (either to stockholders' equity or to total investment) were observed for the pharmaceutical industry. The concern over this follows from the theoretical notion that returns cannot remain above "normal" if there are no constraints (entry barriers) within an industry. When returns are high resources will be attracted to that production activity without these constraints. This in turn increases available supplies and applies downward pressure to prices. This is apparent from the theory of pure competition. If there are constraints returns can remain high, supplies will be restricted, and prices will be higher than they would be without the constraints. An implicit concern over relatively high rates of return is that they represent an inequitable distribution of income going from the consumers of pharmaceuticals to the producers of these products.

Pricing performance has also been considered to be important. Through evidence gathered at the Kefauver hearings, it was concluded that the prices of brand name products are substantially greater than the marginal cost of producing the product. Under the theory of pure competition, prices will equal marginal costs unless artificial constraints exist.

It was also observed that there are differences between the prices of brand name drugs and the prices of generic products. It was assumed that the prices of generic drugs are equal to their marginal manufacturing costs, including a normal return. These price differentials suggest the existence of "monopoly power."

The next performance characteristic to be considered from the earlier literature was the progressiveness of the industry. Progressiveness concerns the ability of the industry's research and development facilities to develop "socially" desirable new products—products that represent significant breakthroughs in medical therapy. Associated with this is the question of whether or not the patent system in its present form provides the necessary incentive to ensure a flow of these products from the industry.

The early economic analysts acknowledged that there had been a few innovative products coming from the industry, but the emphasis in the literature reiterated some testimony from the Kefauver hearings. It was felt that the value of the industry's research and development programs has little social significance; most medically significant new drugs were said to have come from outside the industry. The claim was that the firms engaged in "molecule manipulation," which produces differentiation—that is, merely changing the molecular structure of a compound so that it does essentially the same thing as existing products but may be called something else.

Productivity is another aspect of progressiveness that was considered important. This is productivity in the technical-economic sense, which observes the rate of change in the ratio of physical output to productive inputs (usually labor or physical capital, or both). The early literature did not look at individual firm or industry productivity directly. Comanor did study the issue of research and development "productivity," and concluded that the industry did not display positive efficiencies in research and development.[11]

Essentially the early literature on the economics of the industry was an application of the industrial organization paradigm— structure, conduct, and performance, concluding that the pharmaceutical industry exhibits the characteristics of a "classic coordinated oligopoly." The result, according to the theory and its early applications, is a transfer of income from the consumer to the producer that is not justified by the producer's contribution to the economic welfare of society. Thus, there is an alleged misallocation of resources in the production of ethical pharmaceuticals; the prices of drugs are too high relative to the costs of providing them and too high relative to consumers' desires. This results in a less than optimum quantity of goods being produced.

Refinements in Economic Theory

The basic theories of the firm and the competitive process underlying the pre-1970 assessment of the economics of the pharmaceutical industry are the standard approaches in the discipline of economics. It is recognized by many economists that these theories may be inappropriate for studying specific industries, as is the use of the industrial organization paradigm. This does not mean, however, that these theories are not useful, for at the least they perform the didactic function of describing a form of the market system.

In looking at certain industries, it may be more appropriate to use theories that incorporate elements of dynamics.[21] Theories of dynamics generally observe the factors that generate changes in firms, among firms, and in markets. Dynamic theories may focus on the factors that cause "disequilibrium" in markets, as contrasted to the "static" standard theory that focuses on the state of "equilibrium," in which the prices of goods are equal to the marginal costs of producing those goods. According to a dynamic theory, if this equating of cost and price does not exist it may be just temporary and the market will naturally cause the "efficient" state to occur. A dynamic theory may also emphasize that disequilibrium and, thus, a difference in marginal cost and price, is an aspect of the incentives that result in innovation and progress. In economic terms, the price-marginal cost difference is the opportunity cost for innovation, and when this cost is recognized then, by definition, cost does equal marginal cost, and the dynamic approach has the same result as the pure competition static approach in terms of economic efficiency. This requires a "subjective" evaluation of the "social" nature of that cost that is a source of controversy among economists.

The concept of opportunity cost is a core element of analysis for both the static and dynamic theories of competition. The basic notion of opportunity cost is that the true cost of an economic resource (a unit of capital or labor) is what is foregone when that resource is used to produce something else. The value of the next best alternative use of a particular resource is the cost of that resource—in economic terms, its opportunity cost.

This apparent agreement between the static and dynamic approaches to a basic theoretical concept may be somewhat misleading. There is really a lack of agreement on how to measure real economic costs. The static approach implicitly assumes that a precise calculus is available to determine the cost of economic resources. The dynamic approach explicitly recognizes that "costs are ultimately subjective evaluations of the utility of foregone alternatives, the value of what could have been produced with the resources now being used to produce one's product."[22]

An analogy illustrates the difference between the static and dynamic approaches to the study of competition in a given industry. The static theory is similar to a photograph that shows the conditions of competition at a point in time. The dynamic theory is similar to a motion picture that shows events over a period of time. The photograph cannot pick up the changes that occur when the competitive process of the market is operating. Dynamic theories are developed to obtain a clearer understanding of the competitive aspects of change in the marketplace.

Dynamic theories of the competitive process attempt to identify those characteristics that cause change. This is change that affects the number and identity of the firms in a market, change that may generate new products and production processes, and change that can influence the prices that are charged by competing firms.

A dynamic theory that has been applied to the pharmaceutical industry is relatively simple in that it focuses on a primary characteristic of the industry, the relatively large amount of research and development (R & D) that is carried out by many pharmaceutical firms. This research and development effort attempts to produce new products that are medical advances and may thus be economically attractive.

Within the context of this dynamic theory research and development and resulting innovation, or striving for innovation, serve as catalysts for two competitive effects. The first is that pharmaceutical innovation provides a relatively inexpensive means of reducing the cost of alternative therapies. The replacement of tuberculosis hospitals with antitubercular agents and the replacement of the iron lung with polio vaccines are classic examples of low cost drug therapies effectively competing with high cost alternative therapies. Antibiotic therapy, cardiovascular drugs, antiulcer agents, and antiarthritic agents are examples that may not be so dramatic, but their economic implications are equally important.

The second competitive effect recognized by the dynamic theory is that all new products cannot be dramatic innovations, even though the incentive is great for pharmaceutical firms to introduce "significant breakthroughs." Many product introductions may provide only marginal advances in therapy, but what may be as important is that they provide price competition for existing drug therapies.

Thus, with research and development serving as the means of promoting innovative competition, as well as the standard static price competition, "consumer welfare" approaches a maximum in the static, short run sense as well as in the dynamic, long run sense.* This dynamic theory hypothesizes that the natural economic state is that which is depicted by the static "monopoly" model, and that competition through innovation provides a systematic eroding of "preferred" market positions. This, in turn, generates systematic price competition as product innovations enter the marketplace. Therefore, the dynamic theory sees market activity as a process. Standard static economic theory has a tendency to ignore this process and concentrates on market conditions at certain points in time.

This subtle distinction between the two theories is important when studying an industry such as the pharmaceutical industry. The "products" of the industry, particularly the products of firms heavily committed to research and development, are not merely the physical substances represented by a given chemical or set of chemicals. These products represent a whole set of utility-enhancing characteristics that require "subjective evaluations of the utility of foregone alternatives,"[22] and the dynamic theory hypothesizes that the marketplace, through the relative prices of individual products, is capable of determining comparative values—therapeutically and, thus, economically.

There is another aspect of the concept of economic cost to be considered that relates to what is known in economics as the "theory of the firm." Consideration of this theory of the firm is important because it incorporates a more comprehensive aspect of the true economic opportunity costs of the development and manufacture of pharmaceutical products.[23] This application of the theory of the firm has its roots in the earlier work of Coase,[24] but the refinements that can be applied to the pharmaceutical industry come from the more recent work of Williamson.[25]

The essence of the theory is that in many instances in the com-

---

* "Consumer welfare" is a technical economic term that is not related to welfare in the sense of providing to the needy. The term relates to the economic efficiency of markets providing the maximum amount of goods at the lowest price.

plex United States economic system there are situations in which the use of markets is relatively resource-costly. Contrary to the assumptions of the pure competitive model, it is recognized that the acquisition of pertinent market information requires the use of economic resources. These resources are needed to ascertain information about prices, quality, and other factors necessary for making rational economic decisions.

In response to this, the economic system seems to develop institutional arrangements that economize on the inefficiencies that would be generated if "external" markets were used. These external markets are the market conditions recognized by the model of pure competition, which assumes that there are many buyers and sellers. The application of Williamson's theory rationalizes this response and stresses the importance of internal organization in what is referred to as "hierarchies."[25]

Williamson's theory of internal organization is mainly an explanation of the efficiencies that can be gained from vertical integration. As applied to the pharmaceutical firm, a special form of vertical integration is considered. This is the integration in which pharmaceutical firms undertake to produce currently existing products and to engage in research and development programs for the production of future products. It is felt that this is of great importance because of the types of public policy applied to the industry and the types of analytical elements relevant in forming this public policy.

There are two basic considerations as to why it is efficient to have both characteristics—current product production and new product production—existing in one firm. The first one relates to corporate finance and sources and the use of cash flows in the firm. The second characteristic relates to the efficiencies that can be gained by resorting to internal markets within the firms as opposed to external markets that are considered in conventional microeconomic theory, in which there is a market response to two possible sources of "market failure" such that the opportunity costs of using internal markets are less than those of using external markets. The first of these sources of market failure is the inherent capital market failure that can be associated with complex activities, such as research and development. This is exemplified by the notion of a pharmaceutical firm going to a banker with a loan proposal for a major research and development project. The cost of assembling and organizing the information so that it may be communicated to the layman would be relatively high. Added to this would be the greater uncertainty of obtaining funding for the project. Having the funds come from internal sources, the cash flows generated by the existing product line, economizes on productive resources. The second of these possible market failures considers the specific activities involved in carrying out research and development and the actual production and marketing of pharmaceuticals. It appears there are many opportunities for lowering transactions costs when the internal market of the firm is utilized.

More Recent Analyses

Since about 1970 several empirical studies of the economics of the pharmaceutical industry have been conducted. To a certain extent these studies address the issues that are considered in the dynamic theories of competition and the firm.

Before summarizing the more recent literature on the economics of the pharmaceutical industry, we should put into perspective what is felt to be the basic point of departure from the earlier studies. To do so it is essential to depict the nature of a pharmaceutical firm conceptually.

In considering a pharmaceutical firm there may be two polar cases. At one end of the spectrum there is the generic producer who, for the most part, produces only a "physical" product. At the other end of the spectrum there is the research and development-intensive producer, who not only produces the physical product but also produces a "bundle" of services and activities that may be important economically. These include the research and development capabilities to produce new products and to improve existing products, both from the standpoint of improving their therapeutic characteristics and reducing the costs of production and costs of getting the product to the patient.

A concomitant element of these research and development capabilities is the production and dissemination of the knowledge of the therapeutic aspects of a particular product. This knowledge includes, but is not limited to, determining what the product is and what it will do. The knowledge production and dissemination process begins with the development of a new product and continues over its period of use.

The research and development-intensive firm may also provide services through the maintenance and support of the distribution system that gets pharmaceutical products to patients.

The two characteristics of the research and development-intensive firm—i.e., the physical product and bundle of research and development services—are really inseparable. The current physical product generates the cash flows that produce the research and development capability, which, in turn, generates new products. New cash flows are generated from these new products that are important for increasing the body of knowledge about the production aspects of previously existing products and about the therapeutic characteristics of the firm's total product line, which may be important to physicians and their patients.

Given this conceptual view, it is possible that the competitive driving force in the pharmaceutical industry comes from a substantial number of firms that are closer to the research and development-intensive producer end of the spectrum. Empirical analysis has identified at least 22 firms that could be characterized as research and development-intensive, and it is likely that there are more.[26] This conceptual view also suggests that there is actually more economic "value" in the research and development-intensive product and, thus, there may be a higher product price when this value is perceived by the marketplace.

As previously mentioned, one of the most important aspects of the pre-1970s literature is that these studies were essentially static in nature. What needs to be considered is change and the factors that induce change—the dynamic view. This change orientation is important from the point of view of analyzing the research and development-intensive firm.

An aspect of the pharmaceutical industry's inherent dynamism is the amount of turnover in the market position that occurred among the top 22 drug firms for the period 1965 through 1975. On the average, a pharmaceutical firm changed 4.7 positions in market rank during this period. According to the theory of oligopoly, as suggested by the industrial organization paradigm, it is necessary that there be stability among the firms in order for the tacit and implied coordinating activities of these firms to be maintained. The kind of instability evident in the pharmaceutical industry would indicate that this oligopoly relationship has not been established.

In the original study in which this kind of turnover analysis was made, the average pharmaceutical firm changed 4.1 positions in market rank in the period 1962 through 1972. This study observed the turnover among the top 21 firms. Thus, comparing the 2 periods—1962 through 1972 compared with 1965 through 1975—there actually was an increase in instability in the industry, suggesting that the possibility of oligopolistic coordination is precluded even further.

In studying the question of whether or not a coordinated oligopoly exists among pharmaceutical firms, the kind of turnover that occurs suggests that it would be difficult to establish common objectives among the number of firms comprising the research and development-intensive portion of the industry. This is especially true when these firms are engaged in highly technical activities.*

---

* For a more formal exposition of this concept as it applies to the pharmaceutical industry, see D. L. Cocks: Commentary, in *Issues in Pharmaceutical Economics*, edited by R. I. Chien, Lexington, MA: Lexington Books, 1979, pp. 53–61.

There is a fair amount of disagreement among economists as to the relevance of concentration. The concept of concentration is basically static. Even on this static basis, however, the pharmaceutical industry does not have the classic characteristic of an oligopoly. Compared with many industries, the industry is not concentrated because it took 22 firms to obtain 76% of the industry's sales in 1975. In 1972 it took 21 firms to garner the same 76%. Thus, the industry became slightly less concentrated. In addition, the top four firms accounted for only 27% of the industry's sales.

These data suggest that there is a high degree of market instability among the leading firms in the pharmaceutical industry. A basic question then arises as to the forces that cause this kind of instability. Results of a previous study indicate that an important source of this instability is the innovative activity of drug firms, as represented by the introduction of new chemical entities (NCEs).[26] It was noted that firms gaining or maintaining market position did so by introducing more new products than the firms that lost market position. No statistical significance could be attributed to market instability and innovation, but insight was provided in regard to the dynamic characteristics of the industry; this may be the result of a significant amount of research and development activity among a relatively large number of firms.

Another static structural characteristic is the existence of entry barriers. The dynamic element exhibited by the high degree of firm turnover suggests that entry barriers do not really exist in the industry. The entry barrier issue was extensively investigated by Telser and colleagues.[27] This study determined that market entry was substantial in the industry and, as economic theory would predict, drug prices tended to fall as a response to entry. Drug promotion and research and development expenditures were felt to be the primary entry barriers in the pharmaceutical industry. It was also determined that there is a direct relationship between the rate of market entry and the level of promotional intensity.[27] Therefore, entry into drug markets is facilitated by drug promotion—detailing, advertising, etc.

Related to both the static and dynamic characteristics of an industry is the issue of prices. Table 15-1 presents several alternative price indexes for pharmaceuticals. All these indexes show essentially the same pattern of price movement for prescription drugs. Overall, drug prices have been increasing only slowly over the indicated time period. Much of the increase occurred in the later years because of the high rate of increase in general inflation. When these drug prices are compared to the price index in the last column, a relative decline in prescription drug prices may be noted.

In regard to the conduct issue of price rigidity, a study by Cocks

TABLE 15-1. Selected Pharmaceutical Price Indexes (1967 = 100)

YEAR	LARGE R&D INTENSIVE	BLS* PHARMACEUTICAL PREPARATIONS— WHOLESALE	BLS CONSUMER PRICE INDEX— PRESCRIPTIONS	PMA-FIRESTONE† WHOLESALE PRICE INDEX	BLS-CONSUMER PRICE INDEX— ALL ITEMS
1967	100.0	100.0	100.0	100.0	100.0
1968	100.3	99.0	98.3	99.1	104.2
1969	101.8	99.5	99.6	100.1	109.8
1970	103.1	99.2	101.2	101.0	116.3
1971	105.4	99.0	101.3	102.9	121.3
1972	104.0	99.1	100.9	102.4	125.3
1973	101.1	99.9	100.5	102.7	133.1
1974	100.9	104.2	102.9	109.3	147.7
1975	108.2	113.2	109.3	116.2	161.2
1976	114.2	120.3	115.2	123.8	170.2
1977	120.6	125.4	122.1	131.7	181.5
1978	125.4	131.9	131.6	138.8	195.4
1979	127.4	141.2	141.8	146.1	217.4
1980	138.1	153.7	154.8	158.9	246.8

Sources:
* BLS—Bureau of Labor Statistics.
† PMA—Pharmaceutical Manufacturers Association; index prepared and developed by John M. Firestone, Professor of Economics (ret.), University of the City of New York.

and Virts found that data used in earlier drug-pricing studies were obtained from published price lists, which do not necessarily reflect actual prices paid.[28] A similar conclusion was reached by Stigler and Kindahl in a study of several industrial markets.[29] They found that published price lists tend to be rigid and do not reflect the behavior of actual transaction prices accurately. For nationally sold products, actual transaction prices tend to be lower and display a much more flexible behavior pattern than do catalogue prices.

Unfortunately, transaction prices are not readily observable. Therefore, Cocks and Virts used actual retail transaction prices of selected prescription drugs to compute retail price indices.[28] These findings were then translated into conclusions about manufacturers' prices by assuming that pharmacists' fees and wholesalers' margins remained essentially constant. This study calculated price changes between 1962 and 1971 for several leading drugs in each of ten product markets and calculated an aggregate price index for each market. Prices of more than one half of the product groups were found to decline during this period. The average price decline for the two leading pharmaceutical products in each of the ten product markets exceeded 8%.

Price rigidity, as an aspect of conduct, is a key part of what economists call the theory of oligopoly. This theory states that oligopolists, comprising a small number of firms, establish tacit arrangements so that prices will not fluctuate widely. According to the theory, if prices do not remain rigid, the implicit coordination among the firms will break down. Several mechanisms have been discussed to explain how this price coordination can occur. One of these is known as the kinked demand hypothesis. Primeaux and Smith tested this hypothesis as applied to the pharmaceutical industry.[30] Their study concluded that the theory is not applicable to the industry and therefore price rigidity conduct does not seem to exist.

Reekie studied the issue of whether or not physicians are responsive to price.[31] His study presented empirical evidence that physicians are indeed aware of relative prices, especially in the context of comparative therapeutic advantages of different drugs. A study by Pauly outlined the theoretical aspects of how physicians exhibit this price sensitivity.[32] Another study by Reekie on the Dutch pharmaceutical industry confirmed the price competitive characteristics of the industry, and this price competition reflects the relative price sensitivity of physicians.[33]

The available data suggest that there is much greater price flexibility, and thus price competition, in the pharmaceutical industry than has generally been assumed. Competition in prices within several sets of competing drugs has produced a downward trend in prices in relation to the prices of other consumer products. Moreover it has been shown that, in general, list price stability is not evidence of lack of competition. A comprehensive review of economic literature by Demsetz did not reveal any relationship between price changes and market structure over a broad range of industries.[34]

Another conduct or behavioral issue that has been addressed is the role of drug promotion. The early view was that promotion was not really designed to inform physicians but, rather, its purpose was merely to persuade physicians to choose a particular product among products that were roughly equivalent in the therapeutic sense. As stated previously, Telser and co-workers found that drug promotion was important for inducing price competition in drug markets.[27] A comprehensive study by Leffler suggested that large social benefits are evident from drug product promotion, especially because this promotion is associated with important new drugs.[35]

Focusing on the rate of return of the industry as the primary static performance characteristic, the rates of return observed in early economic literature on the industry were accounting rates, and not economic rates. Economic rates must be used to judge economic efficiency. Accounting rates of return do not consider research and development expenditures as an asset or as an investment paving the way for future products. Rather, accounting practice treats research and development as an expense, just as supplies would be treated. Therefore, when economic efficiency is being assessed, adjustments must be made to show research and development funds for what they really are—an investment, rather than an expense. This concept has been endorsed by the staff of the Federal Trade Commission.[36] When research and development expenditures are treated as an investment, several studies showed that the economic rate of return for the pharmaceutical industry is similar to the rate for all industry.[37–43]

The static framework has never explicitly considered the productivity of the industry as an aspect of performance. In the dynamic sense, this is an important consideration, for productivity measurements are time-related. Several studies have indicated that the pharmaceutical industry, especially the research and development-intensive portion of the industry, exhibits a significantly greater rate of productivity change when compared with industry in general.[44–47]

Another important aspect of the progressiveness of the industry is the issue of the therapeutic and medical contributions of pharmaceutical firms. The early literature suggested that private industry did not really contribute to major therapeutic advances. To the contrary, however, there are examples in which private firms did make important contributions to medical therapy. The development of antituberculosis agents, which eliminated the need for tuberculosis hospitals, represents a significant reduction in the cost of treatment of the disease.

Polio vaccine represents another major contribution to medical therapy. Although the vaccine was not originally discovered by private firms, its mass scale production was a significant aspect of industry's involvement.

The development of the major tranquilizers represents another area in which relatively low cost drug therapy replaced the comparatively costly hospital treatment of many forms of mental illness. These tranquilizers significantly reduce the number of hospital beds for persons with mental disease.[48]

A more recent example of a fairly substantial medical contribution in which a drug replaced a significantly higher cost mode of therapy is ulcer treatment. The product cimetidine has been shown to reduce the cost of alternative treatment significantly—hospitalization and surgery.[49]

Finally, the medical contribution of the private pharmaceutical industry does not necessarily have to be as demonstrable as suggested by the preceding examples. The whole history of advancements in antibiotic therapy provides evidence of how the industry's competitive process contributes to the advancement of medical treatment. It began with the discovery of the sulfonamides and progressed through the development of the penicillins, the broad- and medium-spectrum antibiotics, and the cephalosporins, and can even include the aminoglycosides for the treatment of very serious infections.

In the early 1970s Deutsch evaluated the research performance of the industry. He concluded that "The evidence presented here suggests that the contribution of firm-sponsored drug research to improve social welfare has been large."[50]

The progressiveness characteristic of "social" contribution can also be related back to the static conduct concept. The early literature concluded that, from a conduct standpoint, the industry's research was primarily directed toward "molecule manipulation" to differentiate between similarly acting products. This notion probably arose because of a lack of appreciation of the research and development process in the industry.

To summarize the recent economic literature on the economics of the industry, the question of the pharmaceutical industry's economic efficiency is essentially a theoretical consideration. Earlier conclusions were shown to have been based on either questionable economic methodology or possibly on irrelevant data. Although profits remain high, the relevance of these measures is strongly questioned. Studies of economic profit—economic return on investment—demonstrate levels consistent with "workable competition" and, thus, fulfill the economic criterion for efficiency.

Concentration as an indicator of oligopoly is being questioned by economists. In addition, it has now been shown that, although many prescription drug markets do have products and firms in leadership positions at any particular moment, this is to be expected when innovation is occurring. Over time, these positions of leadership change, indicating competitive forces at work. Prescription drug marketing has not been shown to be a barrier to entry but, rather, has been shown to be both a means to entry and a response to entry.

A reasonable hypothesis is that research and development have become virtually the key to the industry's competitive structure. These produce new competitive products that initially may represent preferred market positions but that will invariably lead to price competition in one form or another (in the static sense) as, for example, new antibiotics compete with older antibiotics. In addition, research and development and manufacturing technology have been shown to be effective generators of efficiency that lead to cost containment, price competition, or both.

It appears that much of the industry's apparent profitability—accounting profits related to accounting measures of assets employed—is, in reality, part of the "cost" of research and development. Much of the price of products of research and development-oriented firms reflects the values or costs of research and development. There is no question that a society could have the benefit of today's drugs with today's quality standards at prices lower than those presently being charged by manufacturers. Any number of mechanisms are available to "wring out" the costs of research and development from today's drug prices. But these same research and development costs of today will contribute to lower prices in the future in four ways:

1. Some research and development leads to future treatments that are less costly than those of today, even though the prices of such drugs may seem high in isolation (in some cases, new drugs can make treatment possible where none was available before).

2. Some patented new drugs quickly result in direct price competition with previously introduced drugs, patented or not patented.

3. Effective, successful patented new drugs stimulate competitive research that often yields better and lower-priced products to challenge the original drugs.

4. The industrial environment and activities in research and

development-oriented firms may lead to a high level and growth of productivity, which contribute substantially to slowing the growth of relative drug prices, even in periods of high inflation.

Economic Effects of Pharmaceutical Industry Regulation

As previously discussed, the availability of a consistent and relatively comprehensive data base has given economists the opportunity to study various aspects of the industry. One of the areas studied most extensively is the effects of regulation.

Supply Side Regulation

There are two main economic effects of regulation. One category can be described as the economic effects of supply side regulation. The studies that have considered this aspect attempted to determine the economic impact of the regulation associated with the Food and Drug Administration (FDA). These began with several doctoral dissertations; the pioneering study was that of Jadlow.[8] There have been several other studies, generally doctoral dissertations, that attempted to assess the effects of the 1962 Drug Amendments to the 1938 federal Food, Drug, and Cosmetic Act, which was the focus of Jadlow's original study.[4, 51] The general conclusion to be drawn from these studies is that the 1962 Drug Amendments had a significant negative impact on the research and development productivity of pharmaceutical firms.

The studies just discussed concentrated on pharmaceutical firms and the industry. Peltzman attempted to assess the effects of FDA regulation—again primarily the 1962 Drug Amendments—on consumers.[52] It has been estimated that the value of reduced innovation for consumers costs $300 million to $400 million annually.

Duke University Professors of Economics Henry G. Grabowski and John M. Vernon have provided further analyses of the impact of regulation on the economics of the industry. A principal finding of their research is that the generation of innovative new products is becoming more highly concentrated in large multinational pharmaceutical firms.[53] Grabowski has also found evidence that new drugs are generally introduced in foreign markets much sooner than they are in the United States.[54] This is known as the "drug lag," which was first identified and measured by Lasagna and Wardell.[55, 56]

An important reason for these phenomena is the sheer cost of introducing new drug innovations—new single chemical entities. Hansen has estimated that the cost of innovating and developing a new single chemical entity is in excess of $50 million in 1976 dollars.[57] This cost determination incorporates an assessment of direct dollar outlays, a normal return on investment, and inflation. In 1980 dollars this cost was around $70 million.

In addition to the supply side regulation associated with the FDA, there are other regulatory agencies that affect the operation of pharmaceutical firms. An important economic aspect of this type of regulation is its social opportunity cost—that is, what society gives up for the kinds of regulation that are in effect. Something that may be given up is productivity improvement, as concluded by a large United States pharmaceutical firm. It was determined that, if the excessive regulation from just seven federal agencies could have been eliminated in 1 year, that firm's rate of productivity improvement in that year would have been twice what it was. Of course, the FDA was by far the major contributor to this negative productivity effect.[47]

It is important to note that this assessment of regulatory impact was not based on the elimination of the goals of regulation, but rather was based on the assumption that the goals could be achieved differently from the way mandated by the federal agencies. It was assumed that firms could achieve these goals if left to their own devices.

Another manifestation of supply side drug regulation is the impact on effective patent lives. United States patent law grants a 17-year period of exclusivity to unduplicated pharmaceutical agents. With pharmaceuticals, a patent is generally applied for when the compound is discovered. Subsequent to this, the compound must be tested and must adhere to all the FDA regulatory requirements contained in the IND (investigational new drug) and NDA (new drug application) processes. Because the FDA regulatory process must be completed before a new drug can be marketed, the effective patent life is shortened. The longer the regulatory process, the shorter the patent life. Wardell and Eisman have shown that FDA regulation reduces the effective life of pharmaceutical patents to approximately 9 to 10 years.[58] The importance of this is that it is much more difficult to recoup the high costs alluded to previously.

Demand Side Regulation

The study of the effects of demand side regulation has not been as comprehensive as that of the supply side, both because the effects of such regulation are much more subtle and because the data to study demand side consequences are not as readily available. In order to address the effects of demand side regulation, it is necessary to put into context the way in which this type of regulation may affect pharmaceutical firms, especially research and development-intensive firms. The overall context in which to view this type of regulation is how it affects the cash flows and the expectations of cash flows of firms. Because the major source of funds for research and development-intensive pharmaceutical firms is from internally generated cash flows, this type of regulation is very important.[59]

Demand side regulation is not as monolithic as supply side regulation in that it is not as focused on one agency or activity, such as the FDA. Examples of demand side regulations include the efforts to repeal states' antisubstitution laws, policies to limit reimbursement under public assistance programs (the Maximum Allowable Cost program for Medicaid is an example), formularies, and the various efforts to enhance generic drugs.

These types of regulation are demand side regulation because they are public policies designed to constrain the use of certain manufacturers' products and the prices that can be charged for these products. There is a direct logic chain from increased regulation to increased costs for firms to a reduction in new innovations. To understand the impact of demand side regulation it is necessary to understand the implications of the internal markets that were discussed previously, as well as the importance of cash flows as the primary source of pharmaceutical research and development funding.[23, 59]

Virts has identified one of the most significant aspects of demand side regulation in the pharmaceutical industry, the fact that many of the effects of this type of regulation are long run in nature.[60] It may be possible to show short-term benefits from these policies but, when the long-term effects are taken into account, the policies may not be beneficial. The primary long-term effect would be the reduction in innovation. The logic flow here is that a reduction in cash flows reduces the amount of funds available for research and development, and reduced research and development lead to fewer new single chemical entities, thus reducing the potential for price competition.

An additional characteristic of demand side regulation is one that illustrates a basic economic principle, and it also relates to the difficulty of measuring the impact of this type of regulation. Economists generally consider various factors as being "at the margin." What is the effect of the next incremental unit of regulation? The incremental unit of regulation, especially this demand side regulation, may be extremely important.

In economic analysis the optimal level of an activity is that level at which the difference between the cost of that activity and the benefit of that activity is the greatest. An equivalent statement is that the optimal level is the point at which an additional unit of the activity is associated with additional costs that are identical to the additional benefits that are generated—that is, marginal cost equals marginal benefit. The policy dilemma is that this basic principle is never really considered, which is especially apparent in the proliferation of demand side regulation that has occurred recently.

It is obvious that it is impossible to identify the individual effects of either supply side regulation or demand side regulation precisely in the pharmaceutical industry. A recent study implicitly, and in combination, has assessed the economic impact of both types of regulation. Virts and Weston estimated the expected rate of return (in 1976 terms) to pharmaceutical research and development.[61] This estimate incorporates the Hansen assessment of the cost of developing a new single chemical entity.[57] In addition, the study estimated the cash flows that could be generated from the "typical" new single chemical entity. This estimate is primarily based on the actual market success of many recently introduced new drug innovations.

In addition to estimating the cost and expected cash flows associated with new drug innovations, the Virts-Weston study measured the number of firms that were able to introduce new drug innovations in three time periods—1954 to 1958, 1963 to 1967, and 1972 to 1976. The data from the study show that there was a significant reduction in the number of firms able to introduce new innovations in the 1963 to 1967 and 1972 to 1976 periods as compared with the 1954 to 1958 period.

These data strongly suggest that the return to pharmaceutical research and development is below that which could be earned in alternative investments in the economy. This is not to suggest that individual drug firms will not fare well, but rather that the return to the industry's research and development is not economically attractive. Given the extensive nature of both supply and demand side regulation, it is obvious that this is a major contributing factor to the decline in the industry's expected rate of return.

References

1. Senate Committee on the Judiciary, Subcommittee on Antitrust and Monopoly: Hearings on Administered Prices in the Drug Industry, 86th Cong., 2nd Sess., 1967 and 1968.
2. Senate Select Committee on Small Business, Subcommittee on Monopoly: Hearings on Competitive Problems in the Drug Industry, 90th Cong., 1st and 2nd Sess., 1967 and 1968.
3. Bailey, M. N.: Research and Development Costs and Returns: The U.S. Pharmaceutical Industry, *Journal of Political Economy, 80*:70, 1972.
4. Cocks, D. L.: The Impact of the 1962 Drug Amendments on R and D Productivity in the Ethical Pharmaceutical Industry, PhD thesis, Oklahoma State University, 1973.

5. Grabowski, H. G., Vernon, J. M., and Thomas, L. G.: The Effects of Regulatory Policy on the Incentives to Innovate: An International Comparative Analysis, in *Impact of Public Policy on Drug Innovation and Pricing*, edited by S. A. Mitchell and E. A. Link, Washington DC: the American University, 1976.

6. Grabowski, H. G.: *Drug Regulation and Innovation*, Washington DC: American Enterprise Institute, 1976.

7. Jadlow, J. M., Jr.: The Economic Effects of the 1962 Drug Amendments, PhD thesis, University of Virginia, 1970.

8. The leading textbook in this area is by Scherer, F. M.: *Industrial Market Structure and Economic Performance*, 2nd Ed., Chicago: Rand McNally, 1980.

9. Comanor, W. S.: The Drug Industry and Medical Research: The Economics of the Kefauver Committee Investigations, *Journal of Business*, *39*:12, 1966.

10. Comanor, W. S.: Research and Competitive Product Differentiation in the Pharmaceutical Industry in the United States, *Economica*, *31*:372, 1964.

11. Comanor, W. S.: Research and Technical Change in the Pharmaceutical Industry, *Review of Economics and Statistics*, *47*:181, 1965.

12. Costello, P. M.: Economics of the Ethical Drug Industry: A Reply to Whitney, *Antitrust Bulletin*, *14*:397, 1969.

13. Costello, P. M.: The Tetracycline Conspiracy: Structure, Conduct and Performance in the Drug Industry, *Antitrust Law and Economics Review*, *1*:13, 1968.

14. Kefauver, E.: *In A Few Hands: Monopoly Power in America*, New York: Pantheon, 1965.

15. Markham, J. W.: Economic Incentives in the Drug Industry, in *Drugs in Our Society*, edited by P. Talalay, Baltimore: Johns Hopkins University Press, 1964, pp. 163–173.

16. Schiffin, L.: The Ethical Drug Industry: The Case for Compulsory Patent Licensing, *Antitrust Bulletin*, *12*:893, 1967.

17. Steele, H.: Monopoly and Competition in the Ethical Drugs Market, *Journal of Law and Economics*, *5*:131, 1962.

18. Steele, H.: Patent Restrictions and Price Competition in the Ethical Drugs Industry, *Journal of Law and Economics*, *17*:198, 1964.

19. Walker, H. D.: *Market Power and Price Levels in the Ethical Drug Industry*, Bloomington: Indiana University Press, 1971.

20. Feldstein, M. S.: Advertising, Research and Profits in the Drug Industry, *Southern Economic Journal*, *35*:239, 1969.

21. Fisher, F. M.: Diagnosing Monopoly, *Quarterly Review of Economics and Business*, *19*:7, 1979.

22. Vaughn, K. I.: Economic Calculation Under Socialism: The Austrian Contribution, *Economic Inquiry*, *28*:535, 1980.

23. Cocks, D. L.: Applied Microeconomics and the Business Economist, *Business Economics*, *14*:55, 1979.

24. Coase, R. H.: The Nature of the Firm, *Economica*, *NS 4*:386, 1937.

25. Williamson, O. E.: *Markets and Hierarchies: Analysis and Antitrust Implications*, New York: the Free Press, 1975.

26. Cocks, D. L.: Product Innovation and the Dynamic Elements of Competition in the Ethical Pharmaceutical Industry, in *Drug Development and Marketing*, cited by R. B. Helms, Washington, DC: American Enterprise Institute, 1975, pp. 225–254.

27. Telser, L. G., Best, W., Egan, J. W., and Higinbotham, H. N.: The Theory of Supply with Applications to the Ethical Pharmaceutical Industry, *Journal of Law and Economics, 18*:449, 1975.
28. Cocks, D. L., and Virts, J. R.: Pricing Behavior of the Ethical Pharmaceutical Industry, *Journal of Business, 47*:349, 1974.
29. Stigler, G. J., and Kindahl, J. K.: *The Behavior of Industrial Prices,* New York: National Bureau of Economic Research, 1970.
30. Primeaux, W. J., Jr., and Smith, M. C.: Pricing Patterns and the Kinky Demand Curve, *Journal of Law and Economics, 19*:189, 1976.
31. Reekie, W. D.: Price and Quality Competition in the United States Drug Industry, *Journal of Industrial Economics, 26*:223, 1978.
32. Pauly, M. V.: *Doctors and Their Workshops,* Chicago: University of Chicago Press, 1980.
33. Reekie, W. D.: Price and Quality Competition in Drug Markets: Evidence from the United States and the Netherlands, in *Drugs and Health,* edited by R. B. Helms, Washington, DC: American Enterprise Institute, 1981, pp. 123–139.
34. Demsetz, H.: Two Systems of Belief About Monopoly, in *Industrial Concentration: The New Learning,* edited by H. J. Goldschmid, H. M. Mann, and J. F. Weston, Boston: Little, Brown, 1974, pp. 164–184.
35. Leffler, K. B.: Persuasion or Information? The Economics of Prescription Drug Advertising, *Journal of Law and Economics, 24*:45, 1981.
36. Bureau of National Affairs, Inc.: FTC Annual Line of Business Report Program, *Securities Regulation and Law Report,* D-1, 1973.
37. Ayanian, R.: The Profit Rates and Economic Performance of Drug Firms, in *Drug Development and Marketing,* edited by R. B. Helms, Washington, DC: American Enterprise Institute, 1975, pp. 81–96.
38. Bloch, H.: True Profitability Measures, in *Regulation, Economics, and Pharmaceutical Innovation,* edited by J. D. Cooper, Washington, DC: American University, 1976, pp. 147–157.
39. Clarkson, K. W.: *Intangible Capital and Rates of Return,* Washington, DC: American Enterprise Institute, 1977.
40. Cocks, D. L.: Comment on the Welfare Cost of Monopoly: An Inter-Industry Analysis, *Economic Inquiry, 13*:601, 1975.
41. This reference has been deleted.
42. Schwartzman, D.: *The Expected Return from Pharmaceutical Research,* Washington, DC: American Enterprise Institute, 1975.
43. Stauffer, T. R.: Profitability Measures in the Pharmaceutical Industry, in *Drug Development and Marketing,* edited by R. B. Helms, Washington, DC: American Enterprise Institute, 1975, pp. 97–119.
44. Brand, H.: Productivity in the Pharmaceutical Industry, *Monthly Labor Review, 80*:9, 1974.
45. Cocks, D. L.: The Measurement of Total Factor Productivity for a Large U.S. Manufacturing Corporation, *Business Economics, 9*:7, 1974.
46. Cocks, D. L.: Drug-Firm Productivity, R & D, and Public Policy, *Pharmaceutical Technology, 1*:21, 46, 1977.
47. Cocks, D. L.: Company Total Factor Productivity: Refinements, Production Functions, and Certain Effects of Regulation, *Business Economics, 26*:5, 1981.
48. Peltzman, S.: The Diffusion of Pharmaceutical Innovation, in *Drug Development and Marketing,* edited by R. B. Helms, Washington, DC: American Enterprise Institute, 1975, pp. 15–25.
49. Geweke, J. F., and Weisbrod, B. A.: Some Economic Consequences of

Technological Advance in Medical Care: The Case of a New Drug, in *Drugs and Health,* edited by R. B. Helms, Washington, DC: American Enterprise Institute, 1981, pp. 235–271.

50. Deutsch, L. L.: Research Performance in the Ethical Drug Industry, *Marquette Business Review, 17*:129, 1973.

51. Caglarcan, E.: Economics of Innovation in the Pharmaceutical Industry, PhD thesis, George Washington University, 1977.

52. Peltzman, S.: An Evaluation of Consumer Protection Legislation: The 1962 Drug Amendments, *Journal of Political Economy, 81*:1049, 1973.

53. Grabowski, H. G., and Vernon, J. M.: Structural Effects of Regulation in the Drug Industry, in *Essays on Industrial Organization in Honor of Joe Bain,* edited by R. Masson and P. D. Qualls, Cambridge: Ballinger, 1976, pp. 181–205.

54. Grabowski, H. G.: *Drug Regulation and Innovation,* Washington, DC: American Enterprise Institute, 1976.

55. Lasagna, L., and Wardell, W. M.: The Rate of New Drug Discovery, in *Drug Development and Marketing,* edited by R. B. Helms, Washington, DC: American Enterprise Institute, 1975, pp. 155–163.

56. Wardell, W. M.: Developments in the Introduction of New Drugs in the United States and Britain, 1971–1974, in *Drug Development and Marketing,* edited by R. B. Helms, Washington, DC: American Enterprise Institute, 1975, pp. 165–181.

57. Hansen, R. W.: The Pharmaceutical Development Process: Estimates of Development Costs and Times and the Effects of Proposed Regulatory Changes, in *Issues in Pharmaceutical Economics,* edited by R. I. Chien, Lexington, MA: Lexington Books, 1979, pp. 151–181.

58. Eisman, M. M., and Wardell, W. M.: The Decline in Effective Patent Life of New Drugs, *Research Management, 21*:18, 1981.

59. Grabowski, H. G., and Vernon, J.: The Determinants of Research and Development Expenditures in the Pharmaceutical Industry, in *Drugs and Health,* edited by R. B. Helms, Washington, DC: American Enterprise Institute, 1981, pp. 3–20.

60. Virts, J. R.: Economic Regulation of Prescription Drugs, in *Issues in Pharmaceutical Economics,* edited by R. I. Chien, Lexington, MA: Lexington Books, 1979, pp. 195–209.

61. Virts, J. R., and Weston, J. F.: Expectations and the Allocation of Research and Development Resources, in *Drugs and Health,* edited by R. B. Helms, Washington, DC: American Enterprise Institute, 1981, pp. 21–45.

## CHAPTER 16

Advertising

MAX A. FERM
and
MICKEY C. SMITH

The purpose of advertising ethical pharmaceutical products is no different from that of advertising any other product—namely, to produce an awareness that will favorably motivate the subject to utilize (or prescribe) your product. The major differences lie in the restrictions placed upon ethical pharmaceutical advertising by the availability of suitable advertising media and government regulation on both the federal and state levels.

Compared to other consumer use products, advertising in the ethical pharmaceutical market is extremely restricted. By definition the ethical pharmaceutical market "prohibits" communication directly with the consumer. Mass advertising media, such as television, radio and national magazines, as well as local mass advertising media such as newspapers and billboards, are not utilized. Exceptions to this do exist, and these will be presented in the discussion of space media analysis.

Media

The traditional pharmaceutical advertising media for exposing a product message are professional journals, magazines, or newspapers, direct mail, convention, or hospital displays, and service items such as educational films, medical illustrations and photography, office supplies, textbooks, and the like. In recent years an attempt has been made to utilize other advertising media, such as video tape cassettes, closed circuit TV, and radio.

For the most part, companies in this industry with sizable promotional expenditures have limited the advertising department to space media and direct mail media, while the balance of promotional expenditures is usually administered by the sales promotion department. The distinction between the responsibilities of the advertising department and those of the sales promotion department can best be described by their different methods of communicating the selling message—the advertising department primarily employs written or visual messages, while the sales promotion department primarily relies upon the use of sales personnel in personal, primarily oral, presentations.

Space Media

Space expenditure represents the amount of money spent for advertising in journals, magazines, and newspapers. The growth in this area of promotion through the 1960s was significant. In 1957 the total expenditure for ethical pharmaceutical space advertising in the United States was $26,785,000 as compared to $101,000,000 in 1969, almost a fourfold gain.

Over the past few years, due in great part to increasingly stringent Food and Drug Administration regulations, relatively few new pharmaceuticals have reached the marketplace. Space expenditures from 1969 through 1972 remained constant at about $101,000,000. By 1980 the figure was more than $170,000,000. However, the actual number of advertising pages purchased dropped from 110,000 in 1969 to 93,000 in 1972, and was roughly the same in 1980. The constant cost for fewer pages is directly related to an inflationary increase in publication space rates resulting from higher costs of labor, paper, and postage.

Earlier a distinction was made between journals, magazines, and newspapers, with the difference between them being in the editorial content. Journals, for the most part, offer technical information relating to an individual's professional practice. The *Journal of the American Medical Association, Archives of Internal Medicine, GP,* and the *Journal of the American Pharmaceutical Association* are examples of professional journals. *Medical Economics, American Druggist,* and *Dental Management* are in the magazine category because their editorial content is not specifically devoted to the scientific aspects of the reader's training, but is nonetheless important to the business side of professional practice. Newspapers require no definition and include publications such as *Medical Tribune, Family Practice News,* and *Drug Topics.*

Before a decision can be reached in the selection of specific publications, they should be analyzed according to available data. This information is almost always supplied by the publisher and appears in the form of a rate card for the publications in question.

If this is not available from the publisher then alternate sources, the *Standard Rate and Data Service* or the *Health Media Buyer's Guide* (Fig. 16-1) can be used. These publications provide pertinent information describing all publications in the field.

Space media are often described and analyzed in terms taken from portions of the publisher's rate card. For example, it will be noted that the publication can be distributed in two ways—paid or controlled. A paid journal is sent to physicians on the basis of a subscription or as a result of a portion of their organizational dues being applied to pay for the journal. "Controlled" indicates that the publication is sent at no cost to the recipient. If the publisher selects the names of those who will receive his publication rather than using a subscription list, it is classified as controlled media. Each publication will list the number of recipients. If this number is large and includes an audience of most medical specialties located throughout the United States, it is considered to be a mass circulated publication. A specialty journal, on the other hand, limits its circulation to one specialty, and even though its distribution may be national, it cannot be classified as mass media.

Publications are issued at regular intervals and, as a result, they can be described in terms of frequency—weekly, monthly, semimonthly, or whatever the publisher deems to be a necessary number of issues to cover the purpose of the journal adequately. Obviously, to be current and of interest, newspapers have to be issued more frequently than the average clinical publication.

It is always of interest to examine the cost of a single advertising page in relation to the total number of recipients. This analysis is obtained by using the following formula:

$$\frac{\text{cost per ad page}}{\text{circulation} \div 1000} = \text{cost per thousand circulation (CPM)}$$

For example, a journal shows 100,000 circulation and lists the cost of a black and white page at $1,000.00:

$$\frac{\$1,000}{100,000 \div 1,000} = \$10 \text{ per thousand circulation}$$

The importance of this figure (CPM) is easily understood when one considers that two publications may charge the same price for a single advertising page yet offer a wide difference in circulation.

Another factor to be considered before buying space in a publication would be the size of the advertising page, which is stated in relative terms such as large, medium, or small. This information is particularly important if the proposed advertisement is too large to be displayed properly on a small page and therefore requires an

FREQ.	S2x PG. RATE	CURR. RATE CARD	CIRC.	Journal of the American Medical Association		ESTAB.	AFFIL.	ANN. SUB. RATE	VERIF.
Weekly	3,100.	1/80	Pd./C.			1883	Yes	36.00	▽BPA

AFFILIATION: American Medical Association.

EDITORIAL DIRECTION: The mission of this journal is education: to inform its readers of progress in clinical medicine, pertinent research, and landmark evolutions in other areas as they interface with medicine. It is a forum for open and responsible discussion, and publishes various directories, medical news items, letters, original papers, abstracts, questions & answers, obituaries, and practice opportunities.

SERVICES TO ADVERTISERS AND READERS:
Quarterly Advertising Reaction Studies: Conducted by Hagen Communications. Feb. 9, May 11, Aug. 17, Nov. 30, 1979.

Sundry Marketing Services: Profile of Medical Practice, Socioeconomic Issues of Health, Annual U.S. Distribution of Physicians, competitive media analyses, Group Practice Studies, Syndicate Readership Studies.

Special Issues in 1979: Contempo (3/30); Annual Meeting, AMA House of Delegates (Official Call) (6/1); Index Issue (6/29); Continuing Education for Physicians (9/7); Interim Meeting, AMA House of Delegates (Official Call) (10/5); Winter Scientific Meeting Issue (10/26); Medical Education in the U.S. and Index Issue (12/28).

Advertising placement: Interspersed.
Split-runs available.
Adv./Edit. ratio: 45%:55%.

PUBLISHED weekly by the American Medical Association, 535 N. Dearborn St., Chicago, Ill. 60610. Tel. (312) 751-6742.

Vice-President, Publishing: John T. Baker
General Sales Manager: Joe Dennehy
Editor: William R. Barclay, M.D.
Executive Managing Editor: Robert Mayo
Director, Dept. of Advertising Communications: Thomas J. Carroll
Director, Dept. of Advertising Sales: Raymond J. Christian

ADVERTISING SALES OFFICES:
American Medical Association
East: 600 - 3rd Ave., Ste. 700, New York, N.Y. 10016. Tel (212) 867-6640. Eastern Sales Manager: Robert C. Corcoran. Salesmen: Mark Attler, Wilbur Tice, Clifford Vanderhoof.
Midwest/West: 535 N. Dearborn St., Chicago, Ill. 60610. Tel. (312) 751-6752. Midwest/Far West Salesman: James Anton; Midwest: William J. Healy, Alice Harvey; Northern Salesman: Thomas J. Carroll.

Rate & Mechanical Information:

BLACK & WHITE RATES: EFFECTIVE JAN. 1980

	1 ti	6 ti	13 ti	26 ti	39 ti	52 ti	65 ti	78 ti
1 page	3405	3355	3305	3235	3170	3100	3035	2965
2/3 pg	2970	2920	2880	2820	2755	2705	2645	2585
1/2 pg*	2340	2300	2270	2215	2175	2125	2085	2035
1/3 pg	1710	1675	1655	1620	1585	1550	1515	1485
1/6 pg	870	860	845	820	805	790		

	91 ti	104 ti	156 ti	208 ti	260 ti	312 ti	416 ti
1 page	2895	2825	2755	2690	2645	2585	2535
2/3 pg	2525	2465					
1/2 pg*	1985	1940					
1/3 pg	1450	1415					

*Horizontal only

EARNED RATES: ROB - Earned rates are based on freq. Space purchased by a parent company & its subsidiaries may be comb. for computation of earned rate. Ea. pg. of a unit or ea. frac. pg. will be counted as 1 insertion toward earned rate. Inserts - Full-run & demo/geographic preprinted insert pgs. count toward earned freq. disc. based on the pgs. chgd. per ad unit. Exception - Single leaf inserts backed up with AMA or Public Service Ad at adv. expense, earns 1 "pg." toward freq. computation.

COMBINATION RATES: Adv. running at least 13 full pgs. in JAMA along with 13 1/2-pg. or larger units in American Medical News (full-run or demo) during a 12-mo. period may comb. freq. in ea. for computation of add'l. freq. discs. Once the min. have been satisfied, fracs. may be added for computation of even lower earned rates.

INSERT RATES: Inserts will be billed at pg. for pg. based on the B&W freq. Demo/Geographic inserts, consult pub.

COLOR RATES: Std. $320. Mtd. $425. 4/c 1x $1,120, 6x $1,090, 13x $1,040, 26x $1,010, 39x $985, 52x $960. (May be comb. with AM News national & demo units toward 4/c freq. disc.)

BLEED: No chg.

COVERS: 2nd 35%. 4th 50%. 4th when used in conj. with 3rd 30%.

INSERTS: Chgs. based on B&W rate for ea. pg.

SPECIAL POSITIONS: All positions other than covers on a guar. basis, 10%.

COMMISSION/CASH DISCOUNT: 15%/2% 10 days.

PUBLICATION TRIM SIZE: 8-1/8 x 10-13/16.
PAGE is 3 cols.
PRINTING PROCESS: Web offset.
TYPE OF BINDING: Perfect.

UNIT SIZES:	Non-Bleed Sizes:		Bleed Sizes:	
	Width	Height	Width	Height
Full page	7	10	8-3/8	11-1/16
2/3 pg	4-5/8	10	5-1/4	11-1/16
1/2 pg (horiz)	7	4-7/8	8-3/8	5-7/16
1/3 pg (vert)	2-1/4	10	3	11-1/16
1/3 pg (horiz)	4-5/8	4-7/8		
1/6 pg (vert)	2-1/4	4-7/8		

INSERTS: Size 2-pg. 8-3/8 x 11-1/16; size 4-pg. same (folded). Wgt. consult pub. Keep all live matter 3/8" away from trim edges.

REPRODUCTION REQUIREMENTS: Offset film pos. Halftone screen 133-line. Rotation of colors: Blue, red, yellow, black. Material held 1 yr.

CLOSING DATE: 34 days prior to issue date.
ISSUANCE DATE: Fri.
MAILING POINT: Brookfield, Wis. 53005.
MAILING ORGANIZATION: W. A. Krueger Co.

SHIPPING INSTRUCTIONS: Contracts & Insertion Orders to American Medical Association, Adv. Dept., 535 N. Dearborn St., Chicago, Ill. 60610. Reproduction Material to AMA Publication, c/o W. A. Krueger Co., 12821 W. Blue Mound Rd., Brookfield, Wis. 53005.

JAMA-3	Third Run 10/10/79
Revisions: Rates	

(continued on next page)

Fig. 16-1. *Sample page,* Health Media Buyer's Guide.

added expenditure for more space. Also, some publishers refuse to disturb the editorial matter by allowing advertisements to appear within the text of the journal, but restrict advertisements to positions preceding or following the editorial content. This front or back placement is usually referred to as "stacked" ad placement as compared to run-of-book (ROB), in which advertising is interspersed throughout the publication. Because it is the editorial con-

JOURNAL OF THE AMERICAN MEDICAL ASSOCIATION (cont'd.)

Circulation by Medical Specialty:

Physicians Primary Specialty	Total Qual. Copies	Office Based Prac.	Interns/ 1st yr. Residents	Residents	Full Time Hosp. Staff	Total Hosp. Based	Total Patient Care
Aerospace Medicine	185	71	———	7	33	40	111
Allergy	867	810	———	———	11	11	821
Anesthesiology	7,786	5,721	———	390	810	1,200	6,921
Broncho-Esophagology	4	3	———	———	———	———	3
Cardiovascular Diseases	4,396	3,373	———	8	325	333	3,706
Dermatology	3,177	2,533	———	260	123	383	2,916
Diabetes	133	108	———	———	3	3	111
Emergency Medicine	1,839	1,163	———	41	510	551	1,714
Endocrinology	534	308	———	3	27	30	338
Family Practice	16,303	13,445	581	1,087	340	2,008	15,453
Gastroenterology	1,593	1,219	———	1	87	88	1,307
General Practice	26,943	25,357	5	81	502	588	25,945
Gen. Preventive Med.	225	66	———	14	13	27	93
Geriatrics	188	112	———	———	27	27	139
Gynecology	774	697	———	———	18	18	715
Hematology	670	340	———	1	64	65	405
Hypnosis	18	17	———	———	———	———	17
Immunology	27	9	———	———	2	2	11
Infectious Diseases	301	101	———	1	28	29	130
Internal Medicine	33,070	25,420	1,478	2,618	1,049	5,145	30,565
Laryngology	4	4	———	———	———	———	4
Legal Medicine	39	13	———	———	2	2	15
Neoplastic Diseases	290	219	———	———	25	25	244
Nephrology	680	434	———	———	60	60	494
Neurology	2,008	1,329	———	246	143	389	1,718
Neurology, Child	83	50	———	———	17	17	67
Neuropathology	34	13	———	———	5	5	18
Nuclear Medicine	483	267	———	30	111	141	408
Nutrition	41	50	———	———	———	———	22
Obstetrics	64	50	———	———	9	9	59
Ob. & Gyn.	17,239	15,132	248	662	364	1,274	16,406
Occupational Med.	1,428	909	———	6	28	34	943
Oncology	462	304	———	3	24	27	331
Ophthalmology	7,378	6,148	23	500	166	689	6,837
Otology	66	59	———	———	3	3	62
Otorhinolaryngology	3,634	2,841	———	329	171	500	3,341
Pathology	5,370	2,652	101	443	1,221	1,765	4,417
Pathology, Clinical	445	235	———	———	104	104	339
Pathology, Forensic	115	55	———	4	4	8	63
Pediatrics	15,914	13,677	352	599	390	1,341	15,018
Pediatrics, Allergy	212	174	———	2	7	9	183
Pediatrics, Cardiology	154	75	———	4	31	35	110
Pharmacology, Clinical	150	23	———	———	9	9	32
Phys. Med. & Rehab.	881	425	———	69	238	307	732
Psychiatry	8,272	5,110	178	719	1,054	1,951	7,061
Psychiatry, Child	837	504	———	57	86	143	647
Psychoanalysis	301	286	———	———	5	5	291
Psychosomatic Med.	37	22	———	———	1	1	23
Public Health	633	123	———	3	30	33	156
Pulmonary Diseases	1,243	700	———	1	158	159	859
Radiology	6,650	4,776	———	321	903	1,224	6,000
Radiology, Diagnostic	3,067	2,137	———	223	434	657	2,794
Radiology, Pediatric	83	49	———	———	20	20	69
Radiology, Therapeutic	838	584	———	48	123	171	755
Rheumatology	553	423	———	———	16	16	439
Rhinology	6	6	———	———	———	———	6
Surgery, Abdominal	318	283	———	———	11	11	294
Surgery, Cardiovascular	841	702	———	———	51	51	753
Surgery, C & R	445	393	———	6	10	16	409
Surgery, General	20,825	16,837	602	1,324	792	2,718	19,555
Surgery, Hand	240	202	———	2	12	14	216
Surgery, Head & Neck	116	88	———	———	15	15	103
Surgery, Neurological	2,104	1,666	———	142	126	268	1,934
Surgery, Orthopedic	7,968	6,528	———	467	365	832	7,360
Surgery, Pediatric	195	156	———	———	19	19	175
Surgery, Plastic	1,623	1,357	———	91	58	149	1,506
Surgery, Thoracic	1,307	1,011	———	57	95	152	1,163
Surgery, Traumatic	52	40	———	———	6	6	46
Urology	4,445	3,748	———	228	200	428	4,176
Other Specialty	1,493	644	———	24	97	121	765
Other Unspecified	4,429	2,096	733	303	292	1,328	3,424
Total Copies to Physicians	225,148	176,454	4,301	11,425	12,083	27,809	204,263
Hospitals	2,021						
Nursing Homes	172						
Med. Libs., Schools, Assns.	967						
Med. Students	18,248						
Others Allied to Field	16,729						
GRAND TOTAL	263,285						

JAMA-3 cont'd.   Third Run 10/10/79

Revisions: Circulation

(continued on next page)

Fig. 16-1. *(Continued.)*

tent that is of interest to the reader, run-of-book is preferred by most advertising managers because such placement increases the probability that their ad will be seen.

Probably the most important description that can be applied to a publication relates to its ability to document the number of actual readers for an average issue, as well as the potential number of viewers for an average advertisement. This is called readership, and it is of greater significance than circulation. Not all medical or allied publications can supply this information, because it requires expensive, well-controlled studies to develop meaningful results.

A number of media research companies have developed techniques for determining readership of medical publications. This work has been supported by the pharmaceutical industry with individual drug companies subscribing to various media audits. One of the early media studies conducted for the industry by an outside media service attempted to establish the Average Issue Audience of ten mass audience publications in which advertising was heavy. Personal interviews were held among physicians who were led through a copy of each publication included in the survey, article by article, ostensibly to determine their interest in editorial content. The particular issues tested had already been published and distributed a month or so before, so a respondent who had looked into the copy prior to the interview period could recognize material he had seen just recently. Such positive identification would establish him as a "reader."

It was soon discovered that these studies had limited application. Personal interviewing was expensive and time-consuming, and only a handful of publications could be tested in one interview session before respondent and interviewer fatigue set in. This technique was soon supplanted by the mail questionnaire, a far less expensive way of gathering readership data and one that could cover many more publications, specialty as well as mass audience.

The mail questionnaire is sent to a sample of physicians selected so as to be representative of the total physician population. A photograph of the cover of each publication included in the study is reproduced for identification purposes (Fig. 16-2). Respondents are asked to estimate a range or degree of reading activity, regarding number of issues and number of pages, for each publication they receive. Results are presented to subscribers as a series of tables, ranking the publications in terms of stated reader involvement.

Issue audience studies apply to editorial audience—they measure the number of physicians who claim to look into or read a publication—but they do not provide information relating to reading patterns or traffic through a publication. In other words, they do not measure advertising audiences. Readers handle different publications in different ways. Some will read a technical journal cover to cover while others may check the table of contents first and then turn to a selected article or articles. With newspapers, the tendency is to scan or thumb through the pages. The problem for the media planner is further compounded, because advertising may be stacked in some publications and interspersed in others. Given these variables, it is quite possible for a publication to be widely read in terms of editorial content and yet be a poor medium in which to place advertising.

From the mid-1960s on, more and more publications have engaged in research which documents their ability to deliver readers to a page of advertising. Called Ad Page Exposure (APX), these studies measure the number of physicians who are exposed to a unique message placed on a page where advertising would normally appear, the unique message being the physician's own name handwritten across a blank white page. The placement of the test page within the issue is rotated to cover eight different ad page positions, so that findings may be presented for an "average" ad page. Each test copy is mailed to each physician in the sample in normal fashion, and he has no advance knowledge that his copy has been altered in any way. Approximately 10 weeks after the issue is mailed, the physician is called (via telephone) and asked if he had read that particular issue and, if so, did he recall seeing his name. A "yes" answer qualifies him as part of the advertising audience of the publication.

More recently, a modification of the APX technique, the "check" or "perfect coupon" study, has achieved wide acceptance among advertisers. Instead of the physician's name on the test page, a personalized bank check, usually for $5.00, constitutes a unique offer. The bank statement listing the checks cashed also establishes a minimum number of physicians who were exposed to the page.

Issue Audience and Ad Exposure studies represent basic criteria among many that are useful in comparing and evaluating media. Depending on marketing objectives and strategies, which vary from product to product and for a given product over time, other factors, to greater or lesser degree, must also be evaluated. Weeklies may be particularly valuable for a new product, because their frequent publication allows for a rapid buildup of advertising impressions. If market potentials vary significantly by physician specialty, geographic region, or city size, journal circulation patterns should conform to market characteristics. Some journals are selected because of prestige value, others because of preferred ad position options, such as the back cover.

Other criteria, of a more qualitative nature, such as differences in sensory effects (relating to "climate" or "mood" created by various editorial content), may also be considered. Judgment and belief in the reliability of our yardsticks will determine the weight we assign each variable. If we were to define *ideal* media research, it would be the measurement of the sales effect of the same ad or ad campaign placed in different journals. Realistically, however, ideal research requires an ideal environment and involves far more sophisticated research techniques than are currently available. Lacking the ideal, efforts should be directed to-

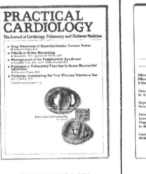
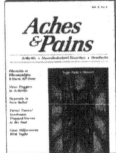

PRACTICAL CARDIOLOGY

1. Do you ☐ receive in your name
☐ see someone else's or library copy
☐ not see

2. Number of ISSUES looked into per YEAR
☐ None ☐ 1-33% ☐ 34-66% ☐ 67-100%

3. Number of PAGES looked at per ISSUE
☐ None ☐ 1-33% ☐ 34-66% ☐ 67-100%

ACHES & PAINS

1. Do you ☐ receive in your name
☐ see someone else's or library copy
☐ not see

2. Number of ISSUES looked into per YEAR
☐ None ☐ 1-33% ☐ 34-66% ☐ 67-100%

3. Number of PAGES looked at per ISSUE
☐ None ☐ 1-33% ☐ 34-66% ☐ 67-100%

YOUR PATIENT & CANCER

1. Do you ☐ receive in your name
☐ see someone else's or library copy
☐ not see

2. Number of ISSUES looked into per YEAR
☐ None ☐ 1-33% ☐ 34-66% ☐ 67-100%

3. Number of PAGES looked at per ISSUE
☐ None ☐ 1-33% ☐ 34-66% ☐ 67-100%

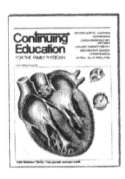

EMERGENCY MEDICINE

1. Do you ☐ receive in your name
☐ see someone else's or library copy
☐ not see

2. Number of ISSUES looked into per YEAR
☐ None ☐ 1-33% ☐ 34-66% ☐ 67-100%

3. Number of PAGES looked at per ISSUE
☐ None ☐ 1-33% ☐ 34-66% ☐ 67-100%

CONTINUING EDUCATION FOR THE
FAMILY PHYSICIAN

1. Do you ☐ receive in your name
☐ see someone else's or library copy
☐ not see

2. Number of ISSUES looked into per YEAR
☐ None ☐ 1-33% ☐ 34-66% ☐ 67-100%

3. Number of PAGES looked at per ISSUE
☐ None ☐ 1-33% ☐ 34-66% ☐ 67-100%

ANNALS OF INTERNAL MEDICINE

1. Do you ☐ receive in your name
☐ see someone else's or library copy
☐ not see

2. Number of ISSUES looked into per YEAR
☐ None ☐ 1-33% ☐ 34-66% ☐ 67-100%

3. Number of PAGES looked at per ISSUE
☐ None ☐ 1-33% ☐ 34-66% ☐ 67-100%

Fig. 16-2. *Sample portion of mail questionnaire.* (From Annual Study of Medical Journal Readership. Fort Washington, PA, Healthcare Communications, 1980.)

ward the practical—building on techniques already at hand.

All the previous descriptions, and many more, are significant to an advertising manager who is charged with the responsibility of selecting the most efficient publications for selling his product.

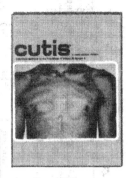

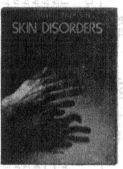

ECONOMIC DISCLOSURE

1. Do you   ☐ receive in your name
     ☐ see someone else's or library copy
     ☐ not see

2. Number of ISSUES looked into per YEAR
   ☐ None ☐ 1-33% ☐ 34-66% ☐ 67-100%

3. Number of PAGES looked at per ISSUE
   ☐ None ☐ 1-33% ☐ 34-66% ☐ 67-100%

SKIN & ALLERGY NEWS

1. Do you   ☐ receive in your name
     ☐ see someone else's or library copy
     ☐ not see

2. Number of ISSUES looked into per YEAR
   ☐ None ☐ 1-33% ☐ 34-66% ☐ 67-100%

3. Number of PAGES looked at per ISSUE
   ☐ None ☐ 1-33% ☐ 34-66% ☐ 67-100%

CUTIS

1. Do you   ☐ receive in your name
     ☐ see someone else's or library copy
     ☐ not see

2. Number of ISSUES looked into per YEAR
   ☐ None ☐ 1-33% ☐ 34-66% ☐ 67-100%

3. Number of PAGES looked at per ISSUE
   ☐ None ☐ 1-33% ☐ 34-66% ☐ 67-100%

FAMILY PRACTICE RECERTIFICATION

1. Do you   ☐ receive in your name
     ☐ see someone else's or library copy
     ☐ not see

2. Number of ISSUES looked into per YEAR
   ☐ None ☐ 1-33% ☐ 34-66% ☐ 67-100%

3. Number of PAGES looked at per ISSUE
   ☐ None ☐ 1-33% ☐ 34-66% ☐ 67-100%

CURRENT CONCEPTS
IN SKIN DISORDERS

1. Do you   ☐ receive in your name
     ☐ see someone else's or library copy
     ☐ not see

2. Number of ISSUES looked into per YEAR
   ☐ None ☐ 1-33% ☐ 34-66% ☐ 67-100%

3. Number of PAGES looked at per ISSUE
   ☐ None ☐ 1-33% ☐ 34-66% ☐ 67-100%

JOURNAL OF FAMILY PRACTICE

1. Do you   ☐ receive in your name
     ☐ see someone else's or library copy
     ☐ not see

2. Number of ISSUES looked into per YEAR
   ☐ None ☐ 1-33% ☐ 34-66% ☐ 67-100%

3. Number of PAGES looked at per ISSUE
   ☐ None ☐ 1-33% ☐ 34-66% ☐ 67-100%

Fig. 16-2. *(Continued.)*

To gain a better understanding of the terminology and its use-fulness, this part of Chapter 16 is devoted to a typical exercise of space media analysis. Let us assume, for example, that we have the assignment to prepare a space schedule for an oral narcotic analgesic consisting of APC with codeine. To begin we must look beyond the previously mentioned publisher information to first determine our market. By referring to IMS, the *National Disease and Therapeutic Index* (NDTI), previously described in Chapter 6,

TABLE 16-1.

APC W CODEINE — 40002 — GEN — TAB/CAP — Jan 65–Dec 65 Class 40 3 Page 1411

EST. U.S. APPEAR. (,000)

Sample Data:	12 MOS	QTR
Drug Appearances	1318	252
Drug Uses	241	44
	265	48

MD

MD	12 MOS NO.	%	QTR %
GP/PT	900	68	75
Into C. Ga	154	12	3
Surg.	133	10	15
Obg.	73	6	7
Ped.	5	—	—
E.N.T.	5	1	—
Oph.	8	—	—
Derm.	—	—	—
Allerg.	—	—	—
Urol.	6	—	—
Proct.	2	—	—
P. & N.	—	—	—
Osteo.	35	3	—
TOT.	1318	100	100

SEX

SEX	12 MOS NO.	%	QTR %
Male	526	40	46
Female	787	60	54
TOT.	1313	100	100
Unspec.	5		

AGE

AGE	12 MOS NO.	%	QTR %
Under 1	5	—	—
1–2	11	1	—
3–9	91	7	—
10–19	541	41	14
20–39	421	32	42
40–59	250	19	32
60 +	—	—	13
TOT.	1318	100	100
Unspec.	—		

ISSUANCE

ISSUANCE	12 MOS NO.	%	QTR %
Hosp. Ord. Admin.	500	42	52
Disp.	236	20	13
Rx Rec'm'nd	451	38	32
Sample	11	1	2
TOT.	1197	100	100
Unspec.	121		

VISIT

VISIT	12 MOS NO.	%	QTR %
First	580	45	57
Subseq.	699	55	43
TOT.	1279	100	100
Unspec.	39		

THERAPY

THERAPY	12 MOS NO.	%	QTR %
New	629	52	61
Continued	570	48	39
TOT.	1199	100	100
Unspec.	120		

CONCOMIT.

CONCOMIT.	12 MOS NO.	%
Use Alone	402	31
W/TC 21	142	11
W/TC 46	126	10
W/TC 22	125	10
W/TC 41	118	9
W/TC 07	76	6
W/TC 40	53	4
W/TC 97	52	4

REGION

REGION	12 MOS NO.	%
East	237	18
Midwest	541	41
South	269	20
West	272	21
TOT.	1318	100

FORM

FORM	12 MOS NO.	%	QTR %
Tab Cap	1318	100	100
Liquid	—	—	—
Oph	—	—	—
Otic	—	—	—
Nasal	—	—	—
Inj.	—	—	—
Top.	—	—	—
Supp.	—	—	—
A.O.	—	—	—
TOT.	1318	100	100
Unspec.	—		

LOCATION

LOCATION	12 MOS NO.	%	QTR %
Office	704	54	49
Home	52	4	4
Hosp.	505	39	47
Teleph.	36	3	—
Other	—	—	—
TOT.	1298	100	100
Unspec.	20		

DIAGNOSIS

Code	DIAGNOSIS	12 MOS. NO.	%	QTR. %
17	Accidents and Poisoning	363	25	36
800	Fractures	98	7	9
840	Sprains and Strains	71	5	15
920	Contusion Crushing	66	5	6
870	Laceration Open Wound	41	3	2
980	Oth Accidents Poisoning	39	3	—
850	Head Injuries	16	1	6
950	Inj Nerves Spinal Cord	12	1	—
830	Dislocations	11	1	—
940	Burns	5	—	—
18	Spec Cond W O Sickness	297	21	25
Y07	Postpartum Observation	157	11	17
Y10	Medical Surg Aftercare	134	9	8
Y100	Surgical Aftercare	134	9	8
Y06	Prenatal Care	6	—	—
08	Dis of Resp System	263	18	20
470	Common Cold	45	3	4
475	Acute URI Multiple Sites	33	2	2
481	Influenza W Oth Resp Sym	33	2	5
473	Acute Tonsillitis	26	2	—
491	Bronchopneumonia	23	2	2
472	Acute Pharyngitis	23	2	—
519	Pleurisy	15	1	2
500	Acute Bronchitis	12	1	2
471	Acute Sinusitis	12	1	—
513	Chronic Sinusitis	9	1	3
492	Prim Atypical Pneumonia	8	1	—
501	Bronchitis Unqualified	8	1	—
490	Lobar Pneumonia	6	—	—
493	Pneumonia Other Unspec	6	—	—

DESIRED ACTION

DESIRED ACTION	12 MOS. NO.	%	QTR. %
Pain Relief	652	49	49
Analgesic	497	38	34
Symptomatic	42	3	4
Relieve Headache	30	2	2
Pain Relief & Antipyretic	28	2	3
Antipyretic	12	1	—
Antipyretic & Antitussive	11	1	—
Analgesic & Antitussive	8	1	3
Pain Relief & Sedative Unspec	6	—	—
Analgesic & Antipyretic	6	—	—
Antitussive	6	—	2
Sedative Day & Sedative Night	5	—	—
Pain Relief & Narcotic	5	—	—
Antipyretic & GI Antispasmodic	5	—	—
Relieve Cramps	4	—	2
Sedative Night	3	—	2
Total	1318	100	100

Source: IMS America, National Disease and Therapeutic Index.

we can obtain the specific use characteristics for APC with codeine. Table 16-1 (taken from *NDTI*) indicates that there are six physician groups currently using generic APC with codeine to any significant degree. This can be seen in the category marked MD, which indicates the percentage of use by specialty for this particular product.

More sophisticated findings can be obtained by determining the percentage of the physician population (physician universe) that each of these specialties represents, and then comparing this with the percentage of use by specialty, as can be seen in Table 16-2. This will provide a weighted factor and may, for example, indicate that although the GP/PT specialists category uses 68% of the drug, they only represent 35% of the physician population, indicating a much greater than average use per physician. For the purpose of media analysis within the scope of this chapter, it would be sufficient to say that emphasis will be applied to sell the general practitioner (GP), internist, surgeon, obstetrician, ophthalmologist and osteopath. By promoting to these selected physicians we are affecting nearly 100% of the current prescribers.

The first consideration is to reach through advertising the greatest possible audience at the lowest possible cost. This goal can be attained by purchasing mass media aimed at all specialties or by selecting individual specialty journals. Further refinements, if indicated, can be made by selecting regional mass or specialty media. To demonstrate in a cursory manner the method employed in media analysis, we have limited this portion of the chapter to a comparison of two mass space media and two specialty space media.

A typical analysis chart should at least include the method of receipt (paid or controlled), readership information, quantities of practitioners receiving the journal and particularly those indicated by *NDTI* as users, cost per advertising page, and cost per thousand. A more definitive analysis can be obtained by using

TABLE 16-2. *Comparison by Specialty of Physician Use of APC/Codeine and the Physician Population*

PHYSICIAN SPECIALTY	% OF USE FOR APC/CODEINE	% OF UNIVERSE (UNITED STATES)
GP/PT Spec.	68	35
Int. C. Ge.	12	14
Surgery	10	15
Ob/Gyn	6	7
Ophthalmology	1	4
Osteopathy	3	6

Source: Lea Associates: % of Use for APC and Codeine, *NDTI*, Drug Volume: 1411, 1965; Lea Associates: % of the Universe, *NDTI*, Drug Volume: 1422, 1966.

readership and cost per ad pages figures to arrive at a cost per thousand users, given the cost per ad page and quantity of the desired specialties contained within the total circulation figures.

Let us assume that we have a one-page black and white advertisement and we must develop criteria for choosing either *Journal "A"* or *Journal "B."* By referring to Table 16-3 we can analyze the various characteristics of importance for promoting APC with codeine. Columns 2 through 6 are the circulation figures for the desired physician specialties. It can be quickly seen that the major variation in circulation among the desired audience exists in Column 7 (osteopaths). In this case *Journal "A"* is an official publication of physicians and is not freely circulated among osteopaths. The 106 osteopathic circulation indicated for *Journal "A"* would represent osteopath subscribers.

The second variation in circulation can be found in Column 1. *Journal "B"* reaches approximately 26,500 more physicians than does *Journal "A."* Among the desired audience, however, *Journal "B"* can only account for approximately 11,800 additional osteopaths. A deeper analysis of the remaining surplus circulation (approximately 15,000) would have to reveal use by our selected specialties in hospitals in order to be considered as a valuable bonus.

If we turn our attention to Columns 8 through 10 we can view the cost analysis. Although *Journal "B"* costs $480 per page more than *Journal "A,"* the total circulation cost per thousand varies by only 90 cents. On this basis, *Journal "B"* is comparable in cost to *Journal "A"* in spite of the $480 page difference. However, we had shown earlier that our prime interest is to reach those medical specialties indicated in Columns 2 through 7. Column 10 reveals the cost per thousand for these specialties. The difference begins to widen in this area of analysis, but again, not to any significant degree. When one considers that the total prime specialty circulation of *Journal "B"* is approximately 125,500 (plus a possible prime hospital audience in the surplus circulation), then the $2 per thousand difference will not be the deciding factor. To prove this point, multiply the $2 per thousand difference by 125.5 thousand (circulation), which yields $251, and compare this with the difference in page cost ($480). You would not be paying a premium for reaching the audience.

If a choice between these two publications must be made, then further investigation is required. One area that might be further analyzed is the GP circulation alone. A market research service indicated that the GP was by far the most important group among these specialties.[1] By dividing the number of GPs into the ad cost and multiplying the result by 1000, the cost per thousand GPs can be determined. In this case *Journal "A"* shows that the cost per thousand general practitioners is $35.11, while *Journal "B"* is $44.43. The difference widens and becomes significant.

TABLE 16-3. *A Media Analysis Comparison of Two Mass Circulated Medical Publications*

| PUBLICATION | CIRCULATION | | | | | | | AD COST (8) | CPM AD UNIT (9) | CPM AD UNIT COL. (10) |
	TOTAL (1)	GP (2)	INTERNIST (3)	SURGEON (4)	OBSTETRICIAN/ GYNECOLOGIST (5)	OPHTHIAL- MOLOGIST (6)	OSTEOPATH (7)			
*Journal "A," paid weekly**	210,448	60,495	21,814	16,199	12,501	5,818	109	$2,120.	$10.07	$34.98
Journal "B," controlled weekly	236,925	58,514	21,601	15,876	11,688	5,868	11,961	$2,600.	$10.97	$36.98

* Paid from membership dues.

Under certain circumstances this information may be sufficient to arrive at a decision, but of greater importance would be any available data signifying the degree of readership for each publication. If, for example, *Journal "B"* had demonstrated greater readership, a completely new set of figures would be developed. The formula in this case is

$$\frac{\text{cost per ad page} \times 1000}{\text{circulation} \times \text{\% of readership}} = \text{cost per thousand readers}$$

Let us assume that *Journal "B"* has proved that 80% of the general practitioners regularly read this publication. The analysis would then show a cost per thousand GP readers of $55.54:

$$\frac{\$2,600 \times 1,000}{58,514 \times 80\%} = \$55.54$$

On the other hand, if *Journal "A"* demonstrated a 60% GP readership, their cost per thousand GP readers would be $58.41.

$$\frac{\$2,120 \times 1,000}{60,495 \times 60M} = \$58.41$$

Many factors influence the decision of which publication to select. Not all variations have been included in the previous discussion, but it should provide some understanding of the considerations that must be employed to justify an expenditure of money for space advertising in mass publications.

In specialty space media the analysis becomes quite specific, because only one type of physician is being sought, in this instance the surgeon. Because some general practitioners have a secondary specialty (surgery), they may subscribe to a surgical journal. The *National Disease and Therapeutic Index* has indicated that general practitioners are good drug users for APC with codeine.[1] Therefore this additional general practitioner circulation becomes a bonus in the selection of a surgical journal.

For the purposes of comparison we have selected two surgical journals, *Surgery "X"* and *Surgery "Y."* Both these publications are paid circulated and issued monthly. Table 16-4 indicates the characteristics previously described for mass circulated publications. One important difference exists, and that is a further definition of circulation in terms of domestic and foreign subscribers.

In this case we are particularly interested in the domestic circulation and we have analyzed our costs on this basis. A detailed discussion appears to be unnecessary because the variations, par-

TABLE 16-4. *A Media Analysis Comparison of Two Specialty Surgical Publications*

	CIRCULATION				AD COST	CPM AD UNIT	CPM SURGEONS
PUBLICATION	TOTAL	DOMESTIC	GP	SURGEONS (GENERAL)			
Surgery "X," paid monthly	11,400	9,461	321	5,251	$340.	$36.17	$65.38
Surgery "Y," paid monthly	15,109	11,745	389	9,002	$300.	$25.69	$33.33

ticularly the cost per thousand general surgeons, are significant. This analysis has been brought to your attention because many paid specialty journals, unlike mass circulated publications, have acquired meaningful foreign circulation which must not be overlooked.

Direct Mail

The use of direct mail has a distinct advantage over space advertising in that it can be directed to specific individuals rather than groups of individuals. A premium is paid for this advantage because on a per contact basis direct mail is more costly. It is, however, a separate medium and requires understanding of the facilities available to be employed properly.

The American Medical Association (AMA), for the most part, provides basic lists used in medical promotion to franchised mailing houses, from whom they are available. An AMA royalty fee is included in the mailing house charge each and every time the list is used. Lists are supplied on computer tape and are frequently revised because inaccurate lists give rise to undelivered mail, which adds a heavy burden to the cost of this medium.

Lists are available in almost any manner desired. One can purchase the use of physicians' names by specialty, age, type of practice, state or county of practice, and other statistics.

A description of these lists and the meaningfulness of various categories have been amply described in Chapter 2.

Direct mail, in addition to its selectivity, permits the use of promotional techniques not readily available in space media. For example, past experience has shown that physicians are not easily motivated by coupon insertions in journals, while product requests from the physicians can be obtained in the form of self-addressed business reply cards included with direct mail promotional material. This is an important consideration because it establishes a relationship between manufacturer and physician that can be measured and utilized.

The mailing of samples, either by request or unsolicited, is another advantage offered when mail is used. The use of samples, when permitted, is a valuable promotional tool that provides the physician with an opportunity to gain experience and ease in the use of a drug prior to a formal prescription.

When a campaign is developed, various types of mailing pieces are employed by manufacturers. Some of these are in the form of self-mailers, envelope mailers, letters, or box mailings. The least expensive is the self-mailer, which requires no envelope and is usually prepared as a jumbo card (two sides) or a four-page mailer. A mixture might include all or several of these types, each one printed in sufficient quantity to be used more than once. For example, one might select three individual pieces, each mailed three times for a total of nine mailings. Testing has repeatedly proved that when business reply cards are employed for measuring responses and a proper mixture of styles is available, one can anticipate an almost equal response the first time a particular mailing piece is used and the third time it is repeated.[2]

Other studies with business reply cards as the measurement have focused upon the difference in response that can be obtained by altering such factors as the introduction of a letter, the use of postage stamps instead of printed indicia, personalization, and other variations.[2]

Although direct mail is a desirable medium, it has a major disadvantage. Unlike journals, which offer an editorial environment designed to appeal to the physician's need to improve clinically, economically, or culturally, the average mailing piece is obviously promotional in design. The challenge is to create interest while delivering a selling message.

One device employed to overcome this drawback is the preparation of a manufacturer-sponsored journal, or "house organ." This provides the advantages of both types of media by offering an interesting editorial format with direct mail specificity. It is an expensive means of promotion that has recently found favor among advertisers. The preparation of editorial matter incurs the majority of cost because it requires additional staff not required for advertising needs. For this reason companies have been formed to gather the editorial material. By specializing in one area—such as news or clinical abstracts—a single staff of writers can be employed for the preparation of several "house organ" magazines appealing to different physician specialties.

In the last 5 years a noticeable trend has evolved relative to the content of advertising. The rapidity of technologic change coupled with the licensure requirement to obtain continuing education credits (CEU) has stimulated advertisers to promote education usually related to their product specialties. As a result the advertising content is less oriented to product promotion than it is to program promotion. This allows the program itself to be the medium for the product. In essence it is no different from a newspaper or magazine advertising itself on television.

Media Mix

Having reviewed past and recent published studies, it can only be concluded that there is no known formula for spending promotional budgets correctly. This is not to say that previous information is worthless, but rather it would be preferable to say that it is limited. Physicians who are asked their preference of media are not nearly as reliable as measuring sales results following the use of specified media. The value of media for all new products cannot be as valid as the experience gained from evaluating a single product's performance. For this reason, a simple yet meaningful method for measuring accurately the relative value of various media for a given product has been developed. The sole criterion for reading results is the difference in sales resulting from a fixed expenditure. It should be remembered that the pharmaceutical industry, like all other industries in our capitalistic system, rates success in terms of sales and resultant profits, and no research findings can substitute for this.

To demonstrate the Media Mix Test, we will work with a product currently in the marketplace. By examining Figure 16-3, it may be noted that the United States has been divided into three equal sales regions to enable the differences in the regions to be measured accurately. If this had been a new product, the country would have to be divided into equal corporate sales regions rather than equal sales regions. If it is assumed that a budget of $300,000 has been allocated for journals and direct mail advertising, $100,000 total expenditure to each area may then be allotted. By applying the various percentages for areas A, B, and C, we have weighted journals in Area A, weighted direct mail in Area B, and have set control of equal media weight in Area C. For example, in Area A $80,000 for journals and $20,000 for direct mail would be allocated. This would be reversed in Area B, while in Area C each medium would receive $50,000. It is understood that all other influences, particularly detailing, would be exerted uniformly throughout the country.

Although it is possible to use Area A for journals only, and Area B for direct mail only, an artificial situation would be established because no influence should be overlooked. In our experience, this test need not run for an entire year. Six months is usually sufficient to read the results. The balance for the promotional year can then be used to incorporate the findings of the test.

Direct mail in the Media Mix Test is easily controlled by in-

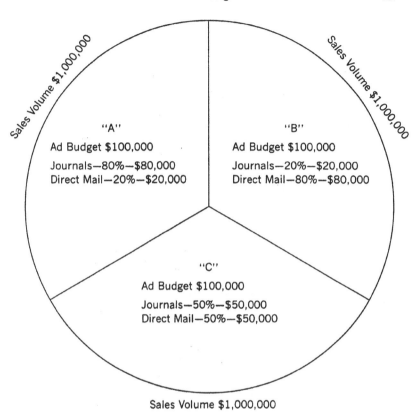

Fig. 16-3. *Media Mix Test Model.*

creasing or decreasing the frequency of the mail. Journal advertising, however, does present a problem of control. If national media
exposure is desired, it must be used under test conditions. Most
journals allow for this under one of two conditions: (1) inserts
rather than run-of-book ads are used; or (2) in those areas of reduced journal spending the advertiser must substitute another
product ad so that the journal may have that page occupied by a
product of the same company. Assuming that the creative concept
provides the proper "position" for the product and is properly executed for the appropriate medium, the results of this test will determine the proper balance of expenditure for direct mail and
journal advertising. It is understood, of course, that more than
these two media make up a complete promotional mixture. Other
influences will be reviewed in Chapter 17.

As with journal advertising, techniques have been developed to
assess exposure to direct mail ads. One of several available tech-

niques is Clark-O'Neill's Mail Ad Exposure (MAX). That firm's description of the technique and some of its results follows:

> The MAX technique is thoroughly objective, statistically reliable and identical to APEX or Ad Page Exposure (which measures the percentage of doctors who see your ads in medical journals). To take advantage of this service, clients tell their Clark-O'Neill Account Executive of mailings they wish to test. A projectable number of physician names (400) is randomly selected from the mailing list.
>
> For each selected test name, a personalized handwritten check, usually $5.00, is prepared and tipped inside the direct mail piece. Since the check can be found only if the mail has been opened and seen, the returned checks reflect actual mail ad exposure. The test group and the balance of the mailing, identical in outward appearance, are then merged geographically and are mailed together.
>
> Cashed checks are returned to the First Jersey National Bank in Jersey City, New Jersey. They are processed through a special research account and results are accumulated for a 10-week test period. At the conclusion of the test, two types of exposure scores are reported to the participant; adjusted and unadjusted. Unadjusted scores reflect the *total* number of checks returned. Adjusted scores reflect checks which have been *self*-exposed. In other words, adjusted scores represent checks actually found by the physician himself. This is determined by the answers to two questions on the back of the check:
>
> 1. Did someone else bring this check to your attention?
> 2. If someone else brought this check to your attention, would you ordinarily have seen this mail?[3]

In 1978 some MAX scores were:

Average Exposure—Self-Mailers: 29.4%
Average Exposure—Polybags: 33.0%
Average Exposure—Envelope Mailers: 35.8%
Average Exposure—Series Mailers: 43.2%
Average Exposure—Newsletters: 44.6%
Average Exposure—Dimensional Mail: 57.5%
Average Exposure—*All* Types of Mail: 40.6%[3]

Advertising Audits and Research

Among the audits described in Chapter 6 were those of journal and direct mail advertising. Examples of each of these are presented in Figures 16-4 and 16-5.

In addition to using audits to monitor the advertising activity of a firm's competitors, it is also important to know the effectiveness of one's own advertising. St. Pierre has asked how one goes about selecting the appropriate advertising testing methodology with the large number of research methods currently available for studying pharmaceutical advertising.[4] Regardless of the testing medium employed, the first step in the selection of an appropriate test methodology is to identify exactly what the advertising is designed to accomplish—its objective(s).

The advertising objectives could be any one or all of the following:

1. To generate product awareness ——→ *RECALL*

2. To communicate *new* information ——→ *COMMUNICATION*

3. Increase interest or product usage

4. To generate positive convictions ——→ *PERSUASION*
about the product

Once the objective(s) of the advertising have been identified, the objectives of the research can be determined and the appropriate test methodology(ies) can thus be selected:

1. If the execution is designed to generate awareness of the product's name, naturally a test that includes a measure of recall would be recommended.

2. If an execution is designed primarily to convey a message or explain a therapeutic or medical rationale, a test that includes the examination of the communication abilities of the execution would be in order.

3. If the objective of the execution is to increase prescribing or usage interest or change or reinforce current beliefs about the product, a test that is capable of measuring the execution's persuasiveness would be in order.

When selecting the appropriate test vehicle, all the objectives of the advertising must be taken into consideration. Thus, if there are multiple advertising objectives (and there usually are), the research technique employed must be able to measure the execution's performance in all the relevant areas.

In his review of advertising research alternatives, St. Pierre listed 23 market research organizations and 7 journals that conduct pretests on ads. He also found and described 26 organizations and 48 journals that offered some kind of post-testing service.[4]

Social Criticism of Drug Advertising*

Advertising prescription drugs in print, especially in medical journals, has been the subject of critical comment for at least 25 years. This criticism has ranged from expressions of concern for the aesthetics of such promotion to calls for its total elimination.

* This section has been adapted from a presentation by Smith, M. C., at the conference, Proper Prescribing: Conflicting Signals, Mount Sinai School of Medicine, New York, May 19, 1981.

(Text continues on p. 394.)

Fig. 16-4. Sample journal audit. (IMS America, Inc.)

NATIONAL MAIL AUDIT
DECEMBER 1978
TABLE D
CLASS RECAP
PAGE 0 3

DOLLARS (000), # ADS, CIRC (000)

USC		1977 DEC	1977 YR-TO DATE	JAN	FEB	MAR	APP	MAY	JUN	JUL	AUG	SEP	OCT	NOV	DEC	CURR. 12 MOS	YR-TO DATE	YR-TO DATE % CHG 77/78
09200 ANTIARTHRTCS, TOPCL	$	5	22	3		3	1	3	1	5	3		10	31	2	16	16	-27
	# AD S	2	6	1		2	1	2	1	3	2		1	4	1	10	10	+67
	CIRC	3	86	19		33	16	31	14	31	18		25	111	11	143	143	+67
09300 GOUT-SPECIFIC PRPS	$		194	52				5	17	32	3					174	174	-10
	# AD S		18	4				1	1	8	2					25	25	+39
	CIRC		718	217				10	50	155	18					736	736	+3
SAMPLE	$		7															
	# AD S		1															
	CIRC		11															
10100 PTY ANTIARTHRT TOP	$		12		14		18	6	7			13			2	15	15	+29
	# AD S		3		1		1	1	2			1			1	4	4	+33
	CIRC		82		42		57	30	61			45			11	102	102	+25
11000 ANTICOAGULANTS	$		52			31	6	4	1	9						42	42	-20
	# AD S		5			4	1	1	1	1						3	3	+4
	CIRC		181			33	22	12	2	31						129	129	-28
12000 ANTICONVULSANTS	$		79			31	13	3	9	23	8	13			18	38	38	-52
	# AD S		15			4	2	1	1	2	2	3			2	8	8	-47
	CIRC		715			97	42	10	29	75	21	45			36	93	93	-87
13100 ANTIDIARRH W/O ANTNF	$	55	424	33	6	22		3				13	31	2	12	97	97	-77
	# AD S	3	31	3	2	2		1				2	3	1	1	13	13	-58
	CIRC	191	968	125	35	19		10				45	31	20	20	352	352	-64
SAMPLE	$		28															
	# AD S		2															
	CIRC		28															
14000 ANTIHIST. SYSTEMIC	$	55	581	59		31	13	81	155	96	109	133	102	17	50	851	851	+47
	# AD S	8	66	7		4	1	9	13	11	9	12	10	5	8	91	91	+38
	CIRC	133	1555	193		97	40	154	302	261	170	232	235	26	133	1880	1880	+21
SAMPLE	$	20	247	17		22		30	37	33	33	36		11	9	231	231	-6
	# AD S	8	8	1		2		3	1	1	3	3		2	2	17	17	+113
	CIRC	17	348	15		19		36	58	52	51	58		14	12	315	315	-1C
15111 TETRACYCLINES	$	7	7			6		8					7	5	11	41	41	+478
	# AD S	1	1			1		1					1	1	2	6	6	+500
	CIRC	12	12			14		15					5	13	24	75	75	+525

NC INDICATES NO CHANGE   HI,% INDICATES OVER 999%

O INDICATES LESS THAN I

NATIONAL MAIL AUDIT
DECEMBER 1978

TABLE D

DOLLARS (000), # ADS, CIRC (000)

CLASS RECAP
PAGE D 4

USC / measure	1977 DEC	1977 YR-TO DATE	JAN	FEB	MAR	APR	MAY	JUN	JUL	AUG	SEP	OCT	NOV	DEC	CURR. 12 MOS	YR-TO DATE	YR-TO DATE % CHG 77/78
15112 TETRACYC.CONGENERS																	
# ADS	2	85						16							21	21	-76
$ ADS	1	10						1							5	5	-50
CIRC	4	268						12							76	76	-72
15120 CHLORAMPHENICOL																	
# ADS					2					1	1		1	2	2	2	
$ ADS					1					1	1		1	2	2	2	
CIRC					9					4	4		3	57	11	11	
15130 CEPHALOSPORIN																	
# ADS		111	22		17	5			34			2		26	106	106	-4
$ ADS		10	1		1	1			2			1		2	8	8	-20
CIRC		387	166		58	16			116			5		90	391	391	+1
15140 ERYTHROMYCIN																	
# ADS	17	83								12			26	10	48	48	-42
$ ADS	2	13								2			2	1	5	5	-62
CIRC	32	407								61			66	28	155	155	-62
15151 AMPICILLIN																	
# ADS		1									2				2	2	+223
$ ADS		2									1				1	1	-50
CIRC		12									24				24	24	+96
15152 AMOXICILLIN																	
# ADS	110	506	35	28	73	31	80	72	2	56	61	34	10		486	486	-4
$ ADS	7	82	3	1	8	3	6	6	2	3	3	2	1		37	37	-55
CIRC	296	2143	115	76	182	127	260	115	6	140	159	52	26		1339	1339	-38
SAMPLE																	
# ADS	7	88			18										18	18	-79
$ ADS	1	12			2										2	2	-83
CIRC	9	104			22										22	22	-79
15153 PENICILL.BRD.SPFCT																	
# ADS		97	2		2					16		11	22	34	87	87	-10
$ ADS		10	1		2					1		2	2	5	12	12	+20
CIRC		204	3		2					43		11	35	75	173	173	-15
15170 AMINOGLYCOSIDES																	
# ADS	28	36			4								23		27	27	-25
$ ADS	4	6			1								2		3	3	-50
CIRC	60	70			5								38		43	43	-40
15180 BRD/MED SPEC.OTHER																	
# ADS		20															
$ ADS		2															
CIRC		64															
SAMPLE																	
# ADS		7															
$ ADS		1															
CIRC		7															

O INDICATES LESS THAN 1   NC INDICATES NO CHANGE   HI% INDICATES OVER 999%

Fig. 16-5. *Sample direct mail audit.* (IMS America, Inc.)

NATIONAL MAIL AUDIT

DECEMBER 1978

DOLLARS (000), # ADS , CIRC (000)

EXPENDITURES BY CLASS

PAGE G 15

PRODUCT		1977 YR-TO DATE	JAN	FEB	MAR	APR	MAY	JUN	JUL	AUG	SEP	OCT	NOV	DEC	CURR. 12 MOS	YR-TO DATE	YR-TO DATE % CHG 77/78
10100 PTY ANTIARTHRT TOP BANALG ONEAL J F	$ ADS CIRC	4 1 21					6 1 30							2 1 11	8 2 41	8 2 41	+100 +95
IODEX LAMBDA P+	$ ADS CIRC	4 1 30						3 1 31							3 1 31	3 1 31	NC +1
IODEX METHYL SAL LAMBDA P+	$ ADS CIRC	4 1 30						3 1 31							3 1 31	3 1 31	NC +8
CLASS TOTAL 10100 PTY ANTIARTHRT TOP	$ ADS CIRC	12 3 82					6 1 30	7 2 61						2 1 11	15 4 102	15 4 102	+29 +33 +25
11000 ANTICOAGULANTS COUMACIN ENDO	$ ADS CIRC	51 4 176		14 1 42		18 1 57			9 1 31						42 3 129	42 3 129	-18 -25 -27
HEPARIN SOC RIKER LABS	$ ADS CIRC	1 1 5															
CLASS TOTAL 11000 ANTICOAGULANTS	$ ADS CIRC	52 5 181		14 1 42		18 1 57			9 1 31						42 3 129	42 3 129	-20 -40 -28
12000 ANTICONVULSANTS CELONTIN PARKE-DAVI	$ ADS CIRC	15 3 160				2 1 8									2 1 8	2 1 8	
DEPAKENE ABBOTT LAB	$ ADS CIRC																

O INDICATES LESS THAN 1   NC INDICATES NO CHANGE   HI% INDICATES OVER 999%

NATIONAL MAIL AUDIT
DECEMBER 1978 — DOLLARS (C00), # ADS, CIRC (000)

EXPENDITURES BY CLASS
PAGE G 16

PRODUCT		1977 DEC	1977 YR-TO DATE	JAN	FEB	MAR	APR	MAY	JUN	JUL	AUG	SEP	OCT	NOV	DEC	CURR 12 MOS	YR-TO DATE	YR-TO DATE % CHG 77/78
12000 ANTICONVUL SANTS																		
DILANTIN PARKE-DAVI	$ ADS		15															
	# ADS		3															
	CIRC		160															
MILONTIN PARKE-DAVI	$ ADS		16															
	# ADS		3															
	CIRC		160															
MYSOLINE AYERST	$ ADS		19				4				4				7	16	16	-19
	# ADS		2				1				1				1	3	3	+50
	CIRC		59				14				15				7	36	36	-39
TEGRETOL GEICY	$ ADS		2				2									2	2	
	# ADS		1				1									1	1	
	CIRC		16				8									8	8	
ZARONTIN PARKE-DAVI	$ ADS		5					4	1		4				11	20	20	+300
	# ADS		1					1	1		1				1	4	4	
	CIRC		15					12	2		6				29	49	49	+218
CLASS TOTAL 12000 ANTICONVUL SANTS	$ ADS		79				6	4	1		8				18	38	38	-52
	# ADS		15				2	1	1		2				2	8	8	-47
	CIRC		715				22	12	2		21				36	93	93	-87
13100 ANTIDIARRH W/O ANTNF																		
COLONIL MALLNCKRDT	$ ADS	52	213	31												15	15	-64
	# ADS	2	2	2												2	2	-11
	CIRC	174	651	111												30	30	-58
IMODIUM ORTHO	$ ADS		2					3	9	23		13	2	1	12	77	77	
	# ADS		1					1	1	2		1	1	1	1	8	8	
	CIRC		1					10	29	75		45	5	6	20	273	273	
INFANTOL W PARG PINK FIRST TEXA	$ ADS		1															
	# ADS		1															
	CIRC		5															
LOMOTIL SEARLE	$ ADS	3	181	3									1	1		5	5	-97
	# ADS	1	19	1									1	1		3	3	-84
	CIRC	17	284	14									22	14		50	50	-83
PAREPECTOL IN ROKER	$ ADS		28															
	# ADS		2															
	CIRC		28															
SAMPLE	$ ADS		28															
	# ADS		2															
	CIRC		28															

O INDICATES LESS THAN 1   NC INDICATES NO CHANGE   HI% INDICATES OVER 999%

In an extensive policy-related analysis of the pharmaceutical industry Hornbrook has analyzed the interrelationship between promotional intensity and dynamic changes in market structure.[5] Hornbrook's analysis included *total* promotional expenditures and did not specifically address print advertising. He found, in any case, that promotion has a "pro-competitive effect"—that is, it acts as a means of market entry; ". . . promotion is not strictly a tool of the large dominant pharmaceutical firms: small firms can and do use advertising and detailing to make inroads on the market shares of the leaders."[5]

Perhaps the most damning criticism of advertising, if substantiated, would be that it results in inappropriate prescribing—either too much, too little (hardly likely), or the wrong drug. A comprehensive review of the literature on this subject has been published.[6] The weight of *published* evidence lends little credence to the idea that journal advertising, alone, has a major effect on prescribing—for good or for ill.

It is likely that considerable evidence of the effects of advertising on prescribing volume exists in the files of drug manufacturers who have certainly conducted marketing research in this area. For obvious competitive reasons manufacturers do not publish such research. Consequently, our review was limited to published work.

A further limitation imposed on this review was the inclusion only of studies showing outcomes; either prescribing must be shown to have changed, or physicians must have stipulated that the advertisements had such an effect. Not included were studies showing that the physician read the advertisement or remembered the advertisement. Although logic supports the view that ads read or recalled affect prescribing behavior, evidence of such an effect was required for the study to be included.

There has been some additional research done since the review cited above. In one of the few published studies linking advertising and prescribing, Walton presented the following summary:

> A sample of 1,000 physicians in private practice, stratified by specialty, made a total of 35,400 observations of 354 ads, which appeared in medical journals, between Autumn 1976 and Winter 1977. The evidence adduced provides reliable support for the postulated linkage between physicians' awareness of medical-journal advertisements and subsequent enhanced prescribing, a linkage that is more than a series of coincidences.
>
> In real terms 95 percent of the ads were associated with positive prescribing behavior patterns. Specifically, within 60 days following a quarterly period of advertising exposure, physicians who recalled ads went on to be prescribers of the products advertised in consistently

larger proportions than those who did not recall ads. Moreover, the risk that this behavior was due to chance is minute:
· For the complete set of observation $p < 0.0001$;
· for every subset studies, $p < 0.001$. except in one subset, where $p < 0.004$.
Beyond a reasonable doubt in all instances!

Recognition of ads by physicians appears to be central to intensified prescribing in the postexposure period.[7]

Kalb has reviewed the literature on the effects of various influences on prescribing. He noted previous studies that indicate that print advertising serves "principally as a channel of information rather than one of persuasion."[8] In his own research involving 210 physicians responses to a questionnaire, 70% said that they were *not* influenced to prescribe a product based on reading a medical journal advertisement.

Two additional points are salient:

1. It should not be surprising to find that advertising *does* influence prescribing, because that is its primary mission.

2. An increase in prescribing of a given drug as a function of advertising is not necessarily bad. Such a judgment requires data on the alternative that the physician would have chosen had he not prescribed the drug in question.

Statements such as "Drug companies encourage the use of pills as cure-all"[9] are troublesome. First, there is no support for such a statement; indeed, it is indefensible. Second, even if it were true, who is encouraged by the drug companies—the physician, who is either already leaning toward this view or too easily swayed in this direction? Usdin, in a response to criticism of advertising, has posed this question: "Are physicians really dullards who await instructions from detailmen and Madison Avenue? If so, blame our medical education system as well as the manufacturers."[10]

What is largely missing from all discussions of drug advertising is a statement by the patient. At which point does patient input, either individual or collective, become part of the equation? Because the patient, or a surrogate, ultimately pays the bill, it does not seem illogical to suggest that he have some input into the information gathering decision. For instance, would the patient prefer to pay a higher price for the drug, including an information component for advertising and other forms of promotion, or (perhaps) a somewhat higher price for the services of a physician who (possibly) must spend more of his time gathering, assessing, and acting upon information gathered?

Two recent studies may have important implications for advertising review. In the first of these an experimental study was undertaken to assess the impact of governmental regulation on the believability of prescription drug advertising.[11] The specific variables investigated were symbolic impact and fair balance. Mock advertisements (Fig. 16-6) were developed for four tricyclic antidepressant drugs. Symbolic impact was operationalized by portraying the advertisements as originating from United States medical journals (regulated), or Mexican medical journals (unregulated). Fair balance was operationally defined as the inclusion of a brief summary in the advertisement. A nonrandom sample of 24 physicians saw 4 advertisements representing the 4 treatment combinations. On a self-administered questionnaire, they indicated their confidence in the information contained in the advertisement. A 2-factor, repeated measures randomized block factorial design was employed in the analysis. The results indicated that the presence of fair balance was significantly associated with higher levels of believability; the symbolic impact factor was nonsignificantly associated with believability. There consequently appears to be a perception that FDA regulation of drug ads results in ads that are more believable.

The second study results argued, to a degree, against the purported effect of journal advertising on prescribing.[12] Again, however, it is not possible to isolate the effect of advertising from other informational media. In this study, briefly, we selected as a sample the most frequently prescribed brand-name drug in each of 20 major therapeutic classes used by the National Therapeutic Audit. We determined the advertised uses of the drugs from ads for each appearing in medical journals in 1976, and determined the actual uses of the drugs from physician reports in the *National Disease and Therapeutic Index*. We found that only 3 of the 20 drugs were used totally as indicated by the advertisements. The largest discrepancies were found among "related, but unmentioned" uses for tranquilizers, antiarrythmics, antidiabetics, and antidiarrheals. These findings, too, are interesting, but only 20 drugs were involved, and the effect of the advertising must certainly be viewed as equivocal.

Rheinstein, whose job it is to see to the proper advertising of prescription drugs, has noted that actions by the FDA include:

• About 5 requirements of remedial ads per year.

• About 300 required cancellation of ads per year.

• Seizure of a drug product about every 1 or 2 years.[13]

He does not report, and we do not know, what the denominator of this regulatory activity is. He does note that 31 of the 35 medical

Depression in elderly patients needs unique therapy, Thyamel provides it.

Depression in elderly persons differs in significant respects from depression in younger ages. The elderly depressed patient is more severly depressed – and depressed for longer periods of time. Older patients also experience recurrences of depression sooner. So, special therapy is needed to meet the challenge of depression in the elderly.

Thyamel is that therapy...the drug of choice for the elderly patient suffering from depression.

Thyamel remains safe even after prolonged use – which is important for the longer-lasting depressive episodes in the elderly.

Thyamel is compatible with most other medications which diseases among the elderly may necessitate.

Brief Summary

Indications: Endogenous depressive illness

Contraindications: Known hypersentivity

Warnings: Use with caution in patients with a history of glaucoma, ureteral or urethral spasm. Should not be used in children under 12. Safe use during pregnancy has not been established

Precautions: Reduce dosage, or alter treatment, if serious adverse effects occur. Close supervision required when given concomitantly with anticholinergic drugs

Adverse Reactions: Dry mouth, blurred vision, constipation, paralytic ileus, urinary retention, dizziness, skin rash, nausea and vomiting.

How Supplied: Tablets of 10 mg and 25 mg

For safety, for effectiveness...Thyamel is the drug of choice for depression among the aged.

Fig. 16-6. *Mock advertisement (Larson, L. N., et al.: Government Regulation and the Believability of Prescription Drug Advertising, Drug Intelligence and Clinical Pharmacy, 11:338, 1977.)*

journals with 70,000+ circulation are "controlled circulation"—that is, supported by advertising.

The complexity of the issue may be illustrated by a somewhat farfetched example. Journals that solicit advertising do not promise to influence prescribing: they promise readership. The journal that needs advertising, then, must produce contents that draw readers, and in this sense advertising may act indirectly to improve editorial quality (if readership is a measure of that quality). By the same token, however, the journal that does not accept advertising but relies on subscriptions must also produce readership, or logic demands that the number of subscriptions will decrease. (It is recognized that some journals are part of a membership "package" and thus may or may not be read, but do not depend upon readership for survival.)

Journal advertisements may, and probably do, affect prescribing in the presence of other prior, subsequent, and coterminous stimuli. Separation of the effects of the advertisements from these other stimuli, and separation of the good effects from the bad effects, is possible but unlikely outside the artificial, experimental situation.

The journal advertising of prescription drugs is a topic for which "controversial" is not an adequate descriptor. Scientific study of the issues has been sparse, and rhetoric has been abundant. Attempting to cut through the latter, what do we really know? Not necessarily in order of importance, nor necessarily complete, is this list:

1. A great deal of money is spent on journal advertising.

2. Some indeterminate amount of this money results in:
   a. More needed information for prescribers from the journals that are supported by the ads.
   b. Some needed information for prescribers from the ads themselves.

3. Someone, the patient or some third party, pays for the cost of the advertising.

4. An objective cost-benefit analysis of the above has not been conducted and is probably impossible.

5. The effect of such advertising is more reminder than direct persuasion, but it must play some additive role in the milieu of drug promotion and information.

References

1. Lea Associates: National Disease and Therapeutic Index, January, 1965–December, 1965, Ambler, PA: Lea Associates, 1966.
2. Shaller-Rubin Company: *The Value of Direct Mail,* unpublished study, New York: Shaller-Rubin Company.
3. *The Clark-O'Neill Indicia,* May 1978.
4. St. Pierre, P.: *A Comprehensive Review of Advertising Testing,* New York: Medicus Communications, 1979.
5. Hornbrook, M. C.: Market Structure and Advertising in the U.S. Pharmaceutical Industry, *Medical Care, 16*:90, 1978.
6. Smith, M. C.: Drug Product Advertising and Prescribing: A Review of the Evidence, *American Journal of Hospital Pharmacy, 34*:1208, 1977.
7. Walton, H.: Ad Recognition and Prescribing by Physicians, *Journal of Advertising Research, 20*:39, 1980.
8. Kalb, C. D.: Psychological Motivation in Physician Prescribing Habits, *Medical Marketing and Media, 13*:43, 1978.
9. Butler, R. N.: Public Interest Report No. 19—The Overuse of Tranquilizers in Older Patients, *International Journal of Aging and Human Development, 7*:185, 1976.
10. Usdin, G.: The Coin Needn't Smell: A Response to the Seidenbert Thesis, *Mental Hygiene, 55*:32, 1971.
11. Larson, L. N., et al.: Government Regulation and the Believability of Prescription Drug Advertising, *Drug Intelligence and Clinical Pharmacy, 11*:338, 1977.
12. Usman, S., Marshall, C., and Smith, M. C.: Differences Between Actual and Advertised Uses of Drugs: A Replicated Study, *Journal of Advertising Research, 19*:65, 1979.
13. Rheinstein, P. H.: Considerations in the Regulation of Prescription Drug Promotion, in *Perspectives in Pharmacy,* edited by A. I. Wertheimer and N. L. Suntrup, Minneapolis: University of Minnesota, 1980.

## CHAPTER 17

Detailing and Other Forms of Promotion

TED KLEIN

Pharmaceutical Selling

First let us define our terms, and agree on what we will be calling the people who see physicians, dentists, pharmacists, and nurses with the purpose of influencing these health-care professionals to buy, recommend, or prescribe a product. In mid-1981 (when this chapter was written) I asked 75 sales managers of the top United States-based pharmaceutical companies to tell me what name they used to describe the people they ask to call on health-care professionals.

Throughout my 30-year career in the business, I and most others have called them detailmen or detailers. We are obviously using an archaic terminology, because my survey results showed that the preferred term is pharmaceutical sales representative (PSR). The second most often used term is salesman. No one who answered the questionnaire used detailmen or detailers to describe their field force. One respondent, who employs over 500 territory managers, told me that the title "detailmen" was "offensive."

At the beginning of this century, William Osler, one of the best known and respected physicians in the United States, warned his colleagues that "'the drug-house drummer' was a dangerous enemy to the virility of the general practitioner."[1]

Eighty years later there may be many physicians who neither like, trust, nor feel that they need pharmaceutical companies to send them "drummers," but they are a minority. Most professionals who are actively involved in providing health care see and apparently enjoy meeting representatives of pharmaceutical companies, with the tacit understanding that these people are sent to influence them to use or to prescribe a product.

In 1976, Harcourt Brace and Jovanovich completed a well-executed and carefully planned study of what over 500 physicians think about pharmaceutical sales representatives.[2]* (They called these people detailmen in their questionnaire.) Of those physicians who completed the questionnaire, it was found that 80% see 6 or fewer PSRs a week, and of these, 7.4% see 6 a week, 9.1% see 5 a week, 12.7% see 4 a week, 18.4% see 3 a week, 20.3% see 2 a week, and 9.5% do not see PSRs at all. Only 2.1% see 10 or more a week. General practitioners see more PSRs than do any other physician surveyed, including general practitioners, obstetricians and gynecologists, pediatricians, and surgeons.

When asked specifically why they see these people, most practicing physicians said that they see them to obtain samples and information about new products.

The physicians were asked to rank the companies in order of excellence in the overall quality of their field force. The top ten firms, in order of ranking by the physicians, were:

1. Eli Lilly and Company

2. Merck Sharp & Dohme

3. The Upjohn Company

4. Parke-Davis (division of Warner-Lambert Company)

5. Abbott Laboratories

6. Smith Kline & French Laboratories

7. Lederle Laboratories

8. Wyeth Laboratories

9. Roche Laboratories

10. Ciba Pharmaceutical Company

When asked to assess the value of the average PSRs, 14% of the 500 respondents said that they were generally excellent, 60% good, 19% fair, and 3.6% poor. Almost 58% reacted well to the concept of female representatives, 8% were not enthusiastic, and 27% had no opinion either way.

One of the reasons why physicians see pharmaceutical sales representatives is to obtain technical information about prescription drugs. Seventy-one percent of those surveyed were satisfied that they were getting accurate technical information from the manufacturer's PSRs, but 16.5% were not. Seventy percent felt that they were provided "fair balance" in the information presented, and 21% were not convinced that they were hearing the complete story.

*For more information about the survey, contact Mr. Bern Rogers, 757 Third Avenue, New York, NY 10017.

Sixty-one percent favored the elimination of unsolicited mailed samples, asking that only written requests for samples be considered, while 24% felt that unsolicited samples by mail were fine. Only 1 in 10 of the physicians surveyed wanted detailmen to be "certified by the government." (See the section "Certified Medical Representatives" for a description of the Certified Medical Representative Institute, Inc.)

Hospital Pharmacists' Opinions of Pharmaceutical Representatives

Each fifth year since 1955 the editors of *Pharmacy Times* have asked 400 chief hospital pharmacists the same 15 questions in eight categories. Here is my summary of the 1980 results as compared to answers from the 1960 survey.

	1960	1980
Think that PSRs take too much of their time	28%	35%
Believe they tie up staff time	23%	43%
Think that hospital medical representatives are using pressure tactics	26%	39%
Were in favor of hospital exhibits	67%	77%

Evaluation of Detailing by Retail Pharmacists

Robbins has reported on an "image" survey conducted among retail pharmacists.[3] Of the 280 respondents, 92 (32.9%) rated the pharmaceutical industry as excellent, or very good, 47.5% as good, and 19.7% as fair or poor. Ten characteristics were considered:

1. Quality of products.

2. Frequency of detail calls.

3. Level of knowledge of detailers.

4. Helpfulness with inventory control.

5. Helpfulness with return goods.

6. Promptness of merchandise delivery.

7. Manufacturers desire to do business.

8. Extent of research orientation of manufacturer.

9. Frequency of new product introduction.

10. Extent of support for pharmacy.[3]

Table 17-1 summarizes how five pharmaceutical companies were rated by practicing pharmacists.

TABLE 17-1. *Summary of Company Ratings*

COMPANY	MEAN RATING*	NUMBER OF DETAILMEN	
Lilly	1.55	1060	
Roche	1.91	728	
Schering	2.36	579	$r = 0.945$
Robins	2.41	542	
Winthrop	2.88	458	

*1 = excellent; 5 = poor.

Source: Pharmaceutical Marketing Research Group.

Measurement of Effect of Pharmaceutical Representatives

Obviously the best measure of whether or not a salesperson is paying his way is to determine if the actual sales in the area served is affected by his presence. In pharmaceutical marketing this is difficult to assess, for many reasons. First, a substantial number of patients usually do not have a prescription filled in the area covered by a given salesperson. For example, I used to see a physician in New York City, but lived in a New Jersey suburb (25 miles from my doctor's office). I generally had my prescriptions filled at a pharmacy close to my home. Thus, the actual sales of my prescriptions were probably credited to a PSR other than the one who called on my physician.

Moreover, increasing numbers of people are using mail order to save money on many prescription drugs. The National Retired Teachers Association reported that in 1980 over 4.5 million prescriptions were filled in their 9 mail order pharmacies.[4]

Researcher Katherine Caraccioli noted that the American Hospital Association reported a 111% increase in out-patient department visits to hospitals over the 12 years from 1965 to 1977.[5] Over 265 million visits were recorded. A fair estimate is that at least every patient received one or more prescriptions not covered by any auditing of sales calls to hospital physicians.

IMS America's *National Detailing Audit (NDA)* issues monthly reports on their panel.* The physician is asked to keep a diary on the company PSRs he sees, the products discussed, and the amount of time spent discussing each product. These diaries are then mailed to IMS for tabulation. About 1000 to 1200 individual office-based physicians of all ages in 19 major specialties partici-

*The organizations that study detailing activity and the effectiveness of detailing consulted for this chapter were IMS America, Ltd., Ambler, PA 19002, and Drug Distribution Data, Inc. (DDD), A Subsidiary of IMS America, Ltd., Wayne Interchange Plaza 1, Wayne, NJ. See also Chapter 6.

pate in the survey on a monthly basis. Data gathered from this sample panel are projected to national estimates.

In a typical month IMS reports approximately 1.5 million calls by PSRs on physicians in office-based practice, and some 4 million product details covering 4500 different products. Sixty percent of these details involved the leaving of a sample by the PSR with the physician. They also report to the marketer who buys their services on how many calls were made on physicians by their PSRs, and the specific products that were discussed.

DRUG DISTRIBUTION DATA

According to their sales pamphlet, Drug Distribution Data (DDD) is "a sales management and marketing tool which provides pharmaceutical sales data on a geographic basis." Marketers can track sales down to zip code levels so that they can compare their sales with those of competitors product by product. Thus, by using DDD, a marketer should be able to know how his PSRs are doing.

As of mid-1981, about 36 pharmaceutical companies used this service, which measures over 90% of all indirect sales for over 400 wholesalers and warehousing chains in the United States. Over 12,000 pharmaceutical products are audited.

The system works in this manner. The wholesaler and chain warehouses send DDD on computer tape order, which are copies of warehouse withdrawal data for all audited items. Participating manufacturers also supply DDD with data on their direct unit sales. DDD then converts the unit sales into dollars, using the current prices given to them by the manufacturer. A uniform price is then assigned to every item. Each transaction is then stored in one of 21,000 zip codes. Included in this data base are over 50,000 pharmacies, 17,000 physicians, who give or sell patients prescription drugs (dispensing physicians), and 7400 hospitals—a total of 150,000 outlets.

Manufacturers use these data to tell them the actual sales and sales potential by zip code for each product. Using the data they set sales goals, evaluate performance of each salesperson, and then determine the kind of help needed (where, and by whom). Many DDD customers use the data for such purposes as testing advertising and devising special promotional techniques. The reports show dollar sales, percentages of contribution by product, performance, comparing markets with each other, and market shares of a product.

COST OF PHARMACEUTICAL SALES

No one knows how much the industry spends on pharmaceutical sales. The most recent estimate I have seen is $600 million in 1980, as compared to approximately $184 million in 1965.[6]

In mid-1981 I made a survey of sales managers of the largest 75 pharmaceutical marketers (about half completed the questionnaire). I asked how many physicians each representative was asked to call on each year, each month, and what the average, including bonus, was for these people after they had been working for 2 years.

The cost estimated by the sales manager or vice president of sales to call on general practitioners varied from a high of $80 (from a full-line company with over 300 representatives) to a low of $11 per call for a small specialty firm with 160 on its sales staff. There seems to be a difference in opinion on what these costs are when you consider how other industries compute the cost of a sales call. In 1981 it was reported that it cost an "industrial" marketer $137.02 for a sales call.[7] IMS America used a cost per call figure of $28 in 1980 based upon surveys of participating companies to determine the direct costs of keeping a PSR in the field.

Other highlights of my 1981 survey include the following:

- Seventy-eight percent of the pharmaceutical representatives are men.

- Most companies have a training requirement of 35 days for the first year (initially, 14 days).

- Most have a hospital sales force.

- The average PSR receives $22,500 annual salary (after 2 years on the job).

- The PSR is expected to complete 150 calls on non-specialist physicians per month.

- Turnover averages 12% per year.

- It costs about $2500 to recruit a PSR.

- Most companies plan to keep the same number of PSRs on their staff in 1982, as compared to 1980. Few will add people, and no one reported plans to reduce the field force in 1982.

Training: Certified Medical Representatives

As far as I know there is no college that offers a formal training program for pharmaceutical sales representatives. A good number of people who are representatives come from a variety of backgrounds. Not long ago pharmacists were heavily recruited; some companies accepted only graduates of pharmacy schools, but this is not so today.

Training usually begins at the home office. Initially, from 2 to 4 weeks will be spent providing the recruit with basic information that will become the bedrock of facts on which to build more detailed information.

Patricia McKeen, Executive Vice President of our company, Medical Marketing Distaff (MMD) since 1969, has participated in well over 300 industry sales training programs. MMD provides sales people for many national and local health-care marketers. She believes that the best training for a PSR comes from actual experience in the field. "We found that the average detail call lasts about 5 minutes. In that time you have less than 600 words to use to give the professional your message. This includes time for his comments and questions."

In 1966 several individuals, including some physicians, founded the nonprofit educational organization now known as the Certified Medical Representative (CMR) Institute, Inc.* It is the only independent organization that provides advanced education to people in pharmaceutical sales. According to the organization, "the CMR program was established as a resource available to the health-care field, providing a professionally recognized basic educational standard to all medical representatives."

To receive CMR certification an individual must pass examinations in courses for a total of 34 credits. There are 6 required courses: anatomy, pharmacology (in 2 parts), physiology, medical terminology, and *governmental* relations. Ten or more electives are also offered, including courses in biochemistry, microbiology, psychology, pharmaceutical industry, clinical drug interactions, and an introduction to disease states. They are college level courses, and may be considered as postgraduate work. Examinations are given twice a year across the nation in "examination centers" located in major colleges and universities, and all are administered by a proctor.

It usually takes a student, devoting about 1 hour per course per week, about 2½ years to complete the home study course. It costs $1170 for the entire course if the student's company pays an annual fee of $5000 to belong to the organization. If not, the same program costs the individual about $1780.

As of this writing over 1500 people have passed the CMR examinations. The average graduate is about 33 years old, with 6½ years work experience. Of these, 45% are college graduates with degrees in science and 29% with degrees in business, but virtually all held BA degrees when they entered the program.

---

*The Certified Medical Representative Institute, Inc., is located at 4316 Brambleton Avenue SW, Roanoke, VA 24018, telephone (703) 989-4596.

Hospital Selling

There are about 8200 hospitals in this country, almost all of which allow sales calls by pharmaceutical sales representatives. Generally these calls begin with a visit to the Chief Pharmacist.

Getting the product accepted by the Hospital Formulary Committee, usually composed of various department heads (who serve on a rotating basis), is the key to selling prescription drugs in the hospital. Often the only two permanent members of the committee are the Hospital Administrator and the Chief Pharmacist. This committee is responsible for deciding which medicines are allowed into the hospital. If the committee does not accept a new pharmaceutical product it is not impossible to obtain the drug, but it can be difficult for a physician who wants to prescribe it. (He can obtain enough of a nonformulary approved product to treat one patient, but has to go through a good deal of paperwork each time he wants to use it.)

One of the best ways to get hospital sales is for the PSR to prove to the hospital pharmacist that he is able to provide services to the hospital staff. The most effective service is giving technical information about the hospital use of prescription drugs, and one of the easiest ways to provide this information to many of the staff physicians, nurses, and pharmacists is to set up an exhibit. This is usually comprised of explanatory panels that can be set up on a table, which describe a product as it should be used in the hospital.

According to Ben Teplitsky, Pharmacy Editor of *Pharmacy Times,* who was Chief Pharmacist for 2 1000-bed hospitals, there are 4 key planning steps for a successful hospital exhibit:[8]

Planning Exhibits. This is most often done without the direct action of the pharmaceutical sales representative. The sales management of the company is usually responsible for planning. However, the individual representative, according to Mr. Teplitsky, should make certain that the home office knows what he can tell them about seasonal interest, hospital requirements as to size, and number of people needed to work the exhibit (larger hospitals need at least two representatives for each exhibit).

It is also a good idea to issue invitations to the hospital staff to make sure that the people the PSR wants to see know that he is going to be there, but the PSR should not do this unless he has permission from the hospital pharmacist, administrator, or whoever is acting as his contact. Bulletin board posters are also worthwhile.

Setting up Exhibits. The PSR must be sure to comply with hospital rules. Furniture should not be moved unless permission is given. Teaching aids that have been tested should be used.

During Exhibits. An adequate supply of literature should be available, and the exhibit should never be left unattended. The physicians, pharmacists, and nurses should be allowed to ask questions. If they stay around a commercial exhibit, chances are that they are interested in the product. The PSR should allow them to ask before starting to say something they don't want to know.

After Exhibits. The PSR should clean up, and should be sure to send thank-you notes to all who have been of help. It is a good idea to keep a record of the questions asked, and to tell the Chief Pharmacist what the staff wanted to know about the products. This can be of real value to the pharmacist who needs information on what the physician is interested in.

Conventions

Many pharmaceutical companies pay convention expenses—displays, travel, etc.—to help improve their company's relations with the sponsoring medical organization. Exhibiting at conventions is often a political decision, and not a marketing one. One executive recently admitted to me:

> In the two or three minutes they spend at our booth, we don't expect physicians to get a great deal of information about our products. However, we believe that they will miss us if we aren't there. Often the yearly medical meeting is expected to generate enough income from pharmaceutical companies' exhibits to keep the entire organization alive for another year. Since the officers of the organization are also usually the leaders in the medical specialty, being an exhibitor at their meeting shows them that you are keenly aware of your responsibility to help keep the society solvent. These physicians remember things like this when asked to conduct clinical studies on a new product.

TABLE 17-2. *1965–1979 Attendance at National General Meetings**

YEAR	AMA	AAFP	AOA	ACS[†]
1965	24,270	1,850	1,640	2,170
1970	16,040	3,200	2,100	10,190
1972	11,060	4,800	2,090	12,010
1974	8,000	4,000	2,400	10,070
1976	3,800	4,150	2,300	12,580
1977	3,000	3,620	2,300	11,600
1978	2,100	4,900	2,290	12,840
1979	—	3,500	2,300	9,750

*Was considered a general meeting rather than a specialty meeting, due to the diverse nature of the practices of its membership.
[†]Abbreviations for the above: AMA (American Medical Association); AAFP (American Association of Family Physicians); AOA (American Osteopathic Association); ACS (American College of Surgeons).
Source: Klein, T. Courtesy of Health Care Exhibitors Association, 1980.

The Health Care Exhibitors Association celebrated its fiftieth year in 1980. On the occasion of this anniversary the organization sponsored a study of medical meetings, some results of which are shown in Tables 17-2, 17-3, and 17-4. Along with members of the Professional Convention Managers Association, a series of focus group sessions were conducted that led to additional research.

A review of some facts and opinions obtained shows that medical meetings can be an excellent communications medium. Here are some highlights of this survey:

- Ninety percent of all physicians attend at least one meeting a year. The average physician goes to 4, and 16% attend 10 or more.
- Fifty percent of general practitioners attend their societies' meetings, but 70% of all specialists attend specialty meetings.
- Sixty-five percent of family physicians surveyed felt that they received some value from the meetings, compared to 90% of the specialists.

When asked why they attended medical conventions, most pharmaceutical companies listed these answers (in order of importance):

1. To promote our products.
2. To gain exposure within the medical organization.
3. To reach hard to see physicians (who do not see our people, but do come to meetings—especially those doctors in small towns).
4. To be seen along with our competition.
5. To support our sales force.
6. To introduce a new product. (This can be the most important reason if there is a new product to introduce.)

Medical equipment manufacturers do not have the same priorities; they attend meetings to obtain direct sales and leads for sales. In 1970, the average pharmaceutical company exhibited at 21 general meetings and 13 specialty meetings, and in 1980 at 26 general meetings and 22 specialty meetings. They attend roughly the same number of national meetings as pharmaceutical companies, as well as many more regional meetings.

Continuing Medical Education

A few years ago not many marketers provided substantial funding in their budgets to help support post-graduate professional education programs. Several companies did pay all expenses for

TABLE 17-3. *Number of Professional Attendees at National Specialty Meetings*

YEAR	OBSTETRICS/ GYNECOLOGY	AMERICAN COLLEGE OF CARDIOLOGY	ORTHOPEDIC SURGERY	HOSPITAL PHARMACY
1965	2880	1670	1800	850
1970	2650	4170	4000	850
1972	2800	4750	4440	1250
1974	3200	5440	5100	1500
1976	3100	6590	5500	2200
1977	3210	7000	6130	2430
1978	3500	7200	7000	3400
1979	3830	7540	7400	4100

Source: Klein, T. Courtesy of Health Care Exhibitors Association, 1980.

physicians and pharmacists (and sometimes their spouses) to tour their manufacturing and research facilities. On occasion, a manufacturer would pay the cost of a scientific exhibit for medical meetings.

Increasing Physician Participation

Continuing Medical Education (CME) has now become a subject of greater interest to a large number of health-care marketing experts. A survey completed in mid-1980 showed that 26 states

TABLE 17-4. *Membership Meeting Attendance*

	MEMBERSHIP FIGURES			MEETING ATTENDANCE FIGURES		
	1970	1979	% Change	1970	1979	% Change
American Medical Association	210,000	170,000	−19	16,040	2,100	−37
American Academy of Family Practitioners	32,000	45,600	+43	3,200	3,500	+9
American Orthopedic Association	10,900	14,000	+28	2,100	2,300	+10
American College of Surgeons	34,100	42,000	+23	10,190	9,750	−4
American College of Obstetricians and Gynecologists	14,000	21,500	+54	2,650	3,830	+45
American College of Cardiology	5,500	9,500	+73	4,170	7,540	+81
American Orthopedic Surgeons Association	6,200	7,800	+26	4,000	7,400	+35
American Hospital Pharmacists Association	7,000	18,000	+157	350	4,100	+382

Source: Klein, T. Courtesy of Health Care Exhibitors Association, 1980.

required physicians to take some post-graduate education courses.[9] The American Medical Association issued 34,617 Physician Recognition Awards for the years 1970 to 1980, as compared to 14,795 in 1969 to 1970. Seventeen state medical societies now require evidence of postgraduate education for membership.

The American Academy of Family Physicians is the pioneer medical society that requires a physician to have CME credits in order to retain membership. Its closely regulated program began in 1947. Some other organizations that require CME include the American Association of Neurological Surgeons, the American College of Emergency Physicians, the American Psychiatric Association, and the American Society of Abdominal Surgeons.

Many pharmaceutical marketers recognize the importance of helping specialists keep up with CME credits. (Table 17-5). According to the American Medical Association, in the nation's 90 medical schools in 1978 to 1979, over 8000 courses for physicians were presented, with over 220,000 hours of instruction. Some 665,000 physicians registered for these sessions.[9]

Sophisticated marketers can provide product-related information to those who take these courses by ensuring that the organizing faculty has access to experts who know their products. Moreover, many sponsors of the teaching programs welcome industry films, videotapes, slides, and other educational materials that can be used as part of the programs.

Today many manufacturers support lengthy and extensive postgraduate teaching programs lasting from 1 to 2 days. The invited physicians hear well-planned lectures by outstanding experts. Travel, hotel, and meals, and entertainment of spouses will often be paid or subsidized by a pharmaceutical marketer.

Reaching Physicians Via CME

In 1979, the American Medical Association spent $37,700 (exclusive of AMA staff time) to study how physicians keep up to date on advances in medicine.[10] The words "continuing medical education (CME)" were used to describe various programs whereby physicians were asked to designate how often they participated in each of 19 different activities. Of the 8600 or so physicians in the AMA sample, 3563 completed the questionnaires, including both AMA and non-AMA members. Taking note of the results of this research is worthwhile for anyone interested in knowing just how physicians rate themselves when it comes to how they keep up on medical progress.

Reading medical journals is still the primary activity for physicians interested in knowing what's new in medicine. The average physician who answered the questionnaire spent 5.5 hours a week on medical reading (internists spent an average of 6.5 hours).

TABLE 17-5. Report of Activity in Continuing Medical Education for the Years 1978–1979

	NUMBER OF INSTITUTIONS	NUMBER OF COURSES PRESENTED	TOTAL HOURS OF INSTRUCTION OFFERED	NUMBER OF PHYSICIANS REGISTERED FOR ALL COURSES	NUMBER OF INDIVIDUAL PHYSICIANS REPRESENTED IN TOTAL REGISTRATION	COURSES CANCELLED
Medical schools	90	8,044	222,649	665,882	175,724	98
Hospitals	273	9,229	191,372	383,167	97,885	78
City, county, and state medical societies	27	1,603	5,090	108,971	23,505	1
Specialty medical societies and academies of general practice	168	1,543	24,000	222,892	116,859	94
Voluntary health agencies	16	31	374	14,524	4,507	5
Other schools of public health, post-graduate medical schools, and government agencies	92	1,699	74,262	75,532	41,411	120
Total	666	22,149	517,747	1,470,968	459,891	394

Source: Journal of the American Medical Association, 224:1118, 1980.

Thus, according to this survey, print still seems to be one of the best ways to reach prescribing physicians with a message.

The next most cited medium was "consultation" or "discussion" with other physicians. An average of 4.09 hours per week was reported for this activity. Less than 1 hour a week was spent on listening to physician radio news, tapes, or watching films or TV programs.*

According to the 1979 AMA study, physicians spent an average of 12.73 days in 1979 attending CME courses. Of these, 19% said that they committed over $5000 annually to attend these sessions. All physicians spent an average of $969 for CME-related travel, $400 for professional society dues, and about $300 for materials, books, journals, self-assessment courses, etc. The $5000 per physician per year may not seem like much, but it is a tremendous amount of money considering that there are now about 170,000 office-based practicing physicians under the age of 65.

The pharmaceutical marketer who takes time to study how his company can help physicians help themselves learn is bound to do well in raising the physician's conscious appreciation of the contribution.

Public and Professional Relations

The Pharmaceutical Manufacturers Association (PMA) lists about 108 members in its public relations section. In 1981 I surveyed the 20 largest, because few more than that have a formal public relations program or department.

It is interesting to note that in an industry besieged with public relations problems there are not that many highly-trained public relations professionals. In 1981, of the members of the PMA (who sell about 90% of all prescription drugs in this country), there were still few on staff trained in public relations. Most do report, fortunately, to the Chief Executive Officer (80%). Annual budgets range from $250,000 to $2,000,000.

Most public relations professionals in the pharmaceutical industry, according to my survey, spend their time as follows:

Financial	20.0%	Conventions	1.8%
Product	11.0%	Legislative	12.8%
Advertising	1.6%	Employee	12.2%
Public relations	6.6%	Other	10.0%

---

*The Physician Radio Network now has over 80,000 special FM receivers in physicians' offices and homes. Each day, every day, a new 1-hour program with medical news, interviews, discussions, and pharmaceutical commercials is broadcast 24 times.

Financial Relations

A primary task of those who provide financial public relations help to publicly-owned companies is to work with the Chief Financial Officer to comply with all Securities and Exchange Commission (SEC) regulations for release of information. Many of these firms employ outside financial relations experts who will provide help with stockholder programs, meet with the drug analysts employed by stockbrokers, and keep open communications links with writers for the drug trade and business press.*

Product Publicity

The significant activity in product publicity for prescription drugs is usually associated with the launching of the product. At that time a good deal of money can be spent on the announcement and on press information about the new drug.

New product publicity usually includes distribution of a press kit that provides the following:

1. News releases.

2. A background report on the indications for which the drug has been approved, and a listing of the drug.

3. Photographs of the product (for the trade media).

4. Interviews, pictures, and biographies of those responsible for the development of the product are often provided.

There are very few professional publications that provide information to physicians and dentists about new drugs.† Pharmacists, nurses, and other health professionals usually rely on paid journal or direct mail advertising and visits by professional representatives for prescribing information on a new drug. A great deal of effort is spent by sophisticated public relations people, however, in getting lay media to cover the launching of a new drug, or even to report new indications for an already established product.

---

*I believe that some of the most knowledgeable people in the drug business are drug analysts assigned to cover the industry by the top brokerage firms. Many now have teams of experts, including physicians as well as those knowledgeable in business. These people will cover obscure research conferences looking for information on drugs in early trials. The newletters published in Britain's *Scrip* provide information about drugs available or being used in research throughout the world, usually years ahead of what will be reported in this country. Their address is Scrip, 200 Norm Glebe Road, Suite 902A, Arlington, VA 22203.

†Public Relations Aids, a firm in New York that specializes in lists and mailing services, maintains a computer service that lists all publications received by physicians that routinely print new drug publicity announcements; many also include a photo of the trade package.

Major new products are often discussed on network television within a few days after they are available for prescription. This is the result of a carefully planned public and professional relations program created and implemented by the manufacturer. At the same time the company must exercise care so as not to violate FDA regulations, or to raise the hopes of patients unduly—nor does it want to "run up" the stock price beyond what is fair and reasonable. There is no doubt that many people, including physicians and patients, first hear about the availability of a new drug from television, a national news magazine, or daily newspapers, and not from a medical journal.

When it takes 5 to 10 years and $40 to 80 million to launch a new prescription product, drug marketers will usually pull out all publicity stops when a new drug is ready for marketing. There are even many large companies who begin publicity in professional and lay media 1 or 2 years *before* the product is ready for market to help build a legitimate interest in their new drug. Here, for ethical and regulatory reasons, the approach tends to be conservative, or the company may be charged with undue "touting."

Not to be dismissed lightly is the important part that public relations experts can play in defending controversial products, such as birth control pills, certain tranquilizers, antibiotics, and others that occasionally are scrutinized by the FDA, congressional critics, consumer advocates, and others at both national and state levels.

Once a product is on the market, a manufacturer usually relies on public relations help to obtain TV time and newspaper interviews for a physician who has been involved in research on the drug, or even for one who is well known and is willing to take the time to talk directly to the public about what he or she considers to be a real advance in medicine or medical care. Much time and money are also spent to have products discussed at professional meetings, where the scientific and sometimes the lay press can be invited to cover the proceedings. News of a product discussed at these scientific sessions, often held during the annual meetings of many medical organizations, finds its way into the professional and lay media as news coverage by science writers. Some of these meetings or symposiums are paid for by manufacturers prior to the launching of an important new product, specifically to inform key opinion leaders about the drug.

Community Relations

Publicity about a company, its contributions as a good citizen in the community, promotion of news regarding its pharmaceutical representatives, and even sponsorship of health fairs is part of the public relations effort of many pharmaceutical companies. A hallmark in community relations, related to product promotion, was the "Sabin on Sunday" program financed largely by Pfizer Laboratories when its polio vaccine was marketed. There is no question that the public relations effort for these programs was largely responsible for the success of the product.

Of the many companies that have an aggressive community relations involvement, few have as effective a program as that supported by Syntex. This Palo Alto manufacturer spends over $500,000 a year for its community public relations capital contribution, and its art gallery and auditorium provide free space to local organizations.

Employee Relations

Most pharmaceutical manufacturers assign public relations staff either to help with employee relations, or to take over the entire responsibility for all written material. They will send out news releases on such matters as new employees and promotions. Public relations professionals write and produce company newsletters or newspapers, which are sent to all employees, and at least one company produces daily TV programs for its employees. Some employee publications are administered by the personnel departments, but writing professionals and publications are usually more effective when under the aegis of public relations or public affairs departments.

The Pharmaceutical Manufacturers Association recognizes the importance of company publications by sponsoring an annual contest for the best work done in both continuing and special publications, as well as for the best overall communications program for employees.

Media Contact

The number of marketers who have full-time professionals working with the lay press on a regular basis is increasing. The tasks assigned to media experts often include not only product publicity, but also promotion of health-related information in which the marketer's product may never be mentioned at all.

Future Considerations

Health-care professionals now have many ways to learn about prescription drugs, medical devices, and diagnostic products. For most, finding time to see the professional representative seems to be increasingly difficult, yet few marketers planned to have fewer PSRs on their staffs in 1982 as compared to 1981. There is a belief that the more sales people you have, the greater the sales. It also seems that in the years to come, however, nontraditional media will play an increasingly important role. I believe that soon creative cable television, plus the individual use of satellite receivers (using your own "dish" to tune directly in on a satellite) will be a preferred way for physicians to get information about the evergrowing array of medical products. Just as there is now a special radio for physicians (Physicians Radio Network), I predict that within a few years physicians will have their own TV channels. It will be a reactive system so that the viewer will be able to participate in programs by simply pushing buttons on a device attached to each set.

PSRs will still be working, but in newer, more efficient ways. Traditional face-to-face selling will never be abandoned. Human contact will always have values beyond those that technology can provide. At the same time, a more diverse promotional mix will help companies to serve the health professionals more proficiently.

References

1. Somers, H. H., and Somers, A. R.: *Doctors, Patients and Health Insurance*, Washington: the Brookings Institute, 1966, pp. 103–104.
2. *Doctors on Detailing*, survey conducted for Harcourt Brace and Jovanovich, New York, 1978.
3. Robbins, J.: *Pharmacy: A Profession in Search of a Role*, Stanford, CT: Navillus Publishing, 1979.
4. Personal communication.
5. Caroccioli, K.: The Untapped Segment of the Pharmaceutical Marketplace, *Medical Marketing and Media, 15*:23, 1980.
6. Medical Exhibitors Association: *The Evolving Environment for Medical Meetings*, New York: Medical Exhibitors Association, 1980.
7. What's Doing, *American Business* (press report), *10*:6, 1981.
8. Teplitsky, B.: 28 Tips for Detailmen Regarding Hospital Exhibits, *Pharmacy Times*, 44:82, 1978.
9. Anon.: Continuing Education Activities, *Journal of the American Medical Association, 244*:1118, 1980.
10. *Continuing Medical Education Newsletter, 10* (No. 1), 1981.

## CHAPTER 18

Retail Competition—
The Community Level

ARTHUR KOORHAN

Drugstores have evolved from places in which medications were extemporaneously compounded, and proprietary (patent) medicines and health-related sundries could be purchased, to diverse retail pharmacies. The diversity runs from the physically small (under 2000 square feet) "professionally" oriented shops to the 50,000 square feet-super drugstores. The original "corner drugstore," which because of its long hours and accessibility began to stock and sell many nondrug convenience items, has become a major force in the general retail marketplace while still maintaining a connection to its health-related role.

There is little doubt that the community pharmacy is a special case among retailers. The pharmacy is presently undergoing what sociologists refer to as the "professionalization" process. In its efforts to attain full status among the other health professions, there has been a tendency to act as though the more "crass" commercial aspects of the distribution of drugs did not exist. Simultaneously with the professionalization of pharmacy practice, the demand for marketing skills has risen. These apparently divergent demands often focus on the same individual.

Efforts have been made to trade the term "retail druggist" for "community pharmacist." In fact, the very term "retail" is anathema to many members of the profession. Nevertheless, from a marketing point of view, the community pharmacy retains many characteristics of a retail institution, and as such warrants attention in any study of pharmaceutical marketing. In any case there is still every evidence of pharmacies engaging in active competition with one another, and this competition is the primary focus of this chapter. Although this discussion will be primarily concerned with prescription drugs, by far the majority of retail drug outlets continue to derive a substantial portion of their income from nonprescription sources. Therefore, I have found it necessary also to consider the significance of these nonprescription items.

Retail Competition Components

The principal means by which the retail establishment gains a differential advantage over competitors are location, price, promotion, buying, personnel, and service; and combinations of these.

Location

The location of a community pharmacy may be a critical factor to its survival. A number of studies of consumer preference have shown convenience (location) to be an important factor in the selection of a pharmacy.

The pharmacist is at the mercy of the same type of directed demand as the drug manufacturer. Pharmacies have therefore traditionally been located in close proximity to physicians and to medical centers. There is a particular value in receiving a patient's first prescription because of the potential for refills, as well as the possibility of filling prescriptions for other members of the family.

The pharmacist who is contemplating the establishment of a new pharmacy should engage in market research of the same nature as that in which the manufacturer takes part. Socioeconomic qualities of the population in the immediate area of the proposed location must be determined, as well as those of the whole community. The pharmacist should determine if the economy of the community is viable and if the supply of health professionals is adequate. Socioeconomic variables will determine the economic future of the pharmacy, and will also help the pharmacist to decide on the type of pharmacy image to project. As noted in Chapter 3, the ability to match the image of the pharmacy with the self-images of most of the customers will be a big determinant of success.

A good community market research survey would take a close look at the nature and location of the competition. As we shall see in "Nature of Competition" in this chapter, the competition may include more than just other drugstores. It would be of little benefit, for example, to learn that the community was largely employed by a single manufacturing plant if it was not also determined that part of the benefit program of the employees included obtaining prescriptions at a reduced rate through the company infirmary. The existence and type of prepayment programs in the community may also be of critical concern, primarily because many of these programs tend to limit profitability and encourage discounting of the patient's copayment, thus eroding the profit potential.

The pharmacist entrepreneur must avoid venturing capital into a situation that cannot be thoroughly examined in advance. Traffic flow, parking facilities, access to public transportation, the draw and stability of neighbor tenants, and demographics of the surrounding population are among factors to be considered before entering the arena as a retail competitor. Contact and consultation with local city planners, zoning boards, and real estate developers will also assist in the decision-making process. A physically small room in which prescriptions will be the source of a significant portion of the volume will need a proximate population having a favorable mix of older persons; if the room size will be larger the proximate population would favor young marrieds, who have 1 or 2 children and own their own homes, with the houses less than 10 years old, 6000 to 10,000 square foot-pharmacies with broad merchandise lines do well and grow with a newer, neighborhood.

Wertheimer, in a paper presented in 1970, described a study of the distance traveled by patients to various types of pharmacies in one community. His findings and conclusions are illuminating:

Neighborhood independent pharmacies drew 63.2% of their prescription trade from within one-half mile. Many variables produce this situation and must be mentioned. Population density varies greatly within communities and the location of professional pharmacies is usually quite different from that of neighborhood pharmacies.

Professional pharmacies tend to exist near medical centers, clinics and hospitals and many of these institutions are located in non-residential areas and in areas of a different character than purely residential locations. It is observed that most, or approximately 90%, of prescription trade came from within a three-mile distance for three categories of stores: chain pharmacies, shopping center pharmacies, and neighborhood independent pharmacies. The difference between these types of pharmacies generated nearly all of their prescription trade (98.4%, 97.2%, 99.2%), while discount operations generated 90.1% of their prescription volume with a similar distribution (89.2%) for professional pharmacies.

What the pharmacy manager must weigh is the cost of operating and advertising versus the expected gains to be derived. One full page weekly for 52 consecutive weeks in a local newspaper costs annually $75,969.00. The effect and cost of just this type of advertising should be examined by pharmacy managers. Clearly, the neighborhood independent pharmacy has lower costs especially in rent and advertising expense than do chain and discount type pharmacies. Pharmacists must keep in mind that prescription consumers reside within some set distance from their pharmacy in planning services and facilities as well as in designing promotional campaigns.[1]

Table 18-1 shows the relationship of business mix to location. Note the square footage and volume mix for each category.

Chain stores select locations using sophisticated techniques to make the same determinations as independents. The force of their advertising and promotions, however, makes them less dependent on such factors as physician location and the appeal of neighbor tenants. Chain stores profile the population in the catchment area and place special emphasis on the nature of and proximity of competition. Table 18-2 shows the relationship of business mix for chains to location. Note the square footage and volume mix for each category.

There is much that may be learned from studying Tables 18-1 and 18-2. Note, for example, that a comparably located chain store is two to three times the size of the independent. Note also that the average gross sales range from two to four times higher for the chain but that prescription department sales are generally less. (The trend, however, for sales growth in the prescription area is more favorable to chains.) Total expenses as a percentage of sales are less in chain stores) but net profit before taxes are generally higher (except for those in medical office buildings). Note the number of stores located in medical office buildings by both chains and independent operations, and then note the expense, volume, and profit figures for the reasons for comparative purposes.

Price

After the location has been chosen the price policy must be determined. For an independently owned operation some of the same factors considered as when selecting the location must be brought in once again to help determine the price policy. A neighborhood with a heavier density of senior citizens may be more prescription price-conscious than a younger mix, but the latter may be more responsive to lower prices for household needs, such as disposable diapers, for example. Convenience remains a dominant reason for selecting a retail pharmacy, but the appeal of lower prices is hard to overcome. What is important for the independent owner is to achieve a proper balance between the two, thus establishing a reputation for "fair" pricing.

Chain stores have generally built their reputations on a low price image, and need only to continue advertising and promo-

(Text continues on p. 426.)

TABLE 18-1. Summary of Independent Pharmacy Operations According to Location

AVERAGES PER PHARMACY	DOWNTOWN (596 PHARMACIES)		NEIGHBORHOOD (478 PHARMACIES)		SHOPPING CENTER (248 PHARMACIES)		MEDICAL, OFFICE BUILDING (187 PHARMACIES)	
Sales								
Prescription	$166,331–	48.6%	$175,824–	51.4%	$185,140–	44.0%	$198,784–	77.7%
Other	175,930–	51.4%	166,118–	48.6%	235,449–	56.0%	56,936–	22.3%
Total	$342,261–	100.0%	$341,942–	100.0%	$420,589–	100.0%	$255,720–	100.0%
Cost of goods sold	224,317–	65.5%	226,190–	66.1%	277,824–	66.1%	152,999–	59.8%
Gross Margin	$117,944–	34.5%	$115,752–	33.9%	$142,765–	33.9%	$102,721–	40.2%
Expenses								
Proprietor's or manager's salary	$ 22,902–	6.7%	$ 23,683–	6.9%	$ 26,641–	6.3%	$ 23,180–	9.1%
Employees' wages	40,287–	11.8%	39,583–	11.6%	48,502–	11.5%	27,376–	10.7%
Rent	6,555–	1.9%	7,601–	2.2%	12,235–	2.9%	11,107–	4.3%
Heat, light, and power	3,150–	0.9%	3,192–	0.9%	3,961–	0.9%	814–	0.3%
Accounting, legal, and other professional fees	1,337–	0.4%	1,504–	0.5%	1,977–	0.5%	1,500–	0.6%
Taxes (except on buildings, income, and profit) and licenses	4,871–	1.4%	5,244–	1.5%	6,238–	1.5%	3,944–	1.5%
Insurance (except on buildings)	3,525–	1.0%	4,096–	1.2%	4,289–	1.0%	2,657–	1.1%
Interest paid	2,325–	0.7%	2,042–	0.6%	2,698–	0.6%	1,263–	0.5%
Repairs	1,100–	0.3%	1,146–	0.4%	1,362–	0.3%	512–	0.2%
Delivery	1,305–	0.4%	1,654–	0.5%	1,467–	0.3%	1,608–	0.6%
Advertising	4,886–	1.4%	3,472–	1.0%	4,800–	1.2%	1,677–	0.7%
Depreciation (except on buildings)	3,170–	0.9%	2,936–	0.9%	3,556–	0.9%	1,937–	0.8%
Bad debts charged off	467–	0.1%	479–	0.1%	502–	0.1%	522–	0.2%
Telephone	1,140–	0.4%	1,271–	0.4%	1,500–	0.4%	1,280–	0.5%
Miscellaneous	8,671–	2.6%	8,222–	2.4%	10,479–	2.5%	9,539–	3.7%
Total expenses	$105,691–	30.9%	$106,125–	31.1%	$130,207–	30.9%	$ 88,916–	34.8%
Net profit (before taxes)	$ 12,253–	3.6%	$ 9,627–	2.8%	$ 12,558–	3.0%	$ 13,805–	5.4%
Add proprietor's withdrawals	22,902–	6.7%	23,683–	6.9%	26,641–	6.3%	23,180–	9.1%

(Bracketed subtotals spanning the expense items: Downtown 10.5%, Neighborhood 10.4%, Shopping Center 10.2%, Medical, Office Building 10.7%)

Total income of self-employed proprietor (before taxes on income and profits)	$35,155– 10.3%	$33,310– 9.7%	$39,199– 9.3%	$36,985– 14.5%
Value of inventory at cost and as a percent of sales				
Prescription	$20,023– 12.0%	$20,984– 11.9%	$21,740– 11.7%	$24,416– 12.1%
Other	39,975– 22.7%	34,820– 21.0%	48,694– 20.7%	7,075– 12.4%
Total	$59,998– 17.5%	$55,804– 16.3%	$70,434– 16.7%	$31,221– 12.2%
Annual rate of turnover of inventory	3.9 times	4.2 times	4.1 times	5.0 times
Size of area and sales per square foot*	sq. ft.	sq. ft.	sq. ft.	sq. ft.
Prescription	362 $455.32	360 $491.28	396 $470.94	462 $439.27
Other	2,158 81.57	2,108 79.03	2,855 83.48	676 88.73
Total	2,520 142.27	2,468 147.81	3,251 133.12	1,138 257.86
Sales per dollar invested in inventory				
Prescription	$8.31	$8.38	$8.52	$8.23
Other	4.40	4.77	4.84	8.05
Net profit per dollar invested in inventory	$0.204	$0.173	$0.178	$0.442
Number of prescriptions dispensed				
New	11,833– 45.9%	13,077– 48.3%	13,968– 49.5%	15,054– 54.8%
Renewed	13,921– 54.1%	13,977– 51.7%	14,272– 50.5%	12,423– 45.2%
Total	25,754–100.0%	27,054–100.0%	28,240–100.0%	27,477–100.0%
Prescription charge	$6.46	$6.50	$6.56	$7.23
Number of hours per week				
Pharmacy was open	64 hours	68 hours	70 hours	53 hours
Worked by proprietor	44 hours	42 hours	44 hours	38 hours
Worked by employed pharmacist(s)	32 hours	34 hours	39 hours	27 hours

*Based on averages of pharmacies that reported all data.

Source: *Lilly Digest*, 1979.

TABLE 18-2. *Chain Drugstore Operations According to Location*

AVERAGES PER PHARMACY	DOWNTOWN BUSINESS DISTRICT (149 PHARMACIES)		NEIGHBORHOOD (151 PHARMACIES)		NEIGHBORHOOD SHOPPING CENTER (796 PHARMACIES)		REGIONAL SHOPPING CENTER (169 PHARMACIES)		MEDICAL OFFICE BUILDING (15 PHARMACIES)	
Sales										
Prescription	$228,550	18.3%	$276,285	19.3%	$301,428	17.9%	$294,159	16.3%	$172,153	33.5%
Other	1,022,120	81.7%	1,152,525	80.7%	1,384,864	82.1%	1,511,683	83.7%	341,316	66.5%
Total	$1,250,670	100.0%	$1,428,808	100.0%	$1,686,292	100.0%	$1,805,842	100.0%	$513,469	100.0%
Cost of goods sold	877,348	70.2%	1,027,490	71.9%	1,220,165	72.4%	1,297,462	71.8%	315,247	61.4%
Gross margin	$373,322	29.8%	$401,318	28.1%	$466,127	27.6%	$508,380	28.2%	$198,222	38.6%
Expenses										
Manager's salary	$23,869	1.9%	$27,436	1.9%	$26,592	1.6%	$28,422	1.6%	$21,883	4.3%
Employees' wages	131,594	10.5%	137,179	9.6%	156,536	9.3%	165,908	9.2%	66,642	13.0%
Rent	31,975	2.6%	36,323	2.5%	45,994	2.7%	47,691	2.6%	34,036	6.6%
Utilities (including telephone)	11,430	0.9%	13,351	0.9%	17,406	1.0%	15,807	0.9%	5,563	1.1%
Insurance, licenses, and taxes (except on profit) [10.6%]			[10.1%]		[11.9%]		[9.8%]		[9.3%]	
Repairs	23,063	1.8%	22,805	1.6%	23,227	1.4%	29,362	1.6%	18,853	3.7%
Advertising	3,994	0.3%	3,863	0.3%	5,130	0.3%	5,406	0.3%	1,626	0.3%
Depreciation (except on buildings)	21,890	1.7%	16,787	1.2%	27,514	1.6%	28,362	1.6%	2,653	0.5%
Supplies	7,636	0.6%	8,405	0.6%	10,244	0.6%	10,357	0.6%	5,563	1.1%
Headquarters fee	6,302	0.5%	7,122	0.5%	8,449	0.5%	7,861	0.4%	5,645	1.1%
All other direct store expenses	37,588	3.0%	37,318	2.6%	51,024	3.0%	43,125	2.4%	14,080	2.7%
	21,957	1.8%	30,039	2.1%	27,769	1.7%	26,024	1.5%	7,053	1.4%
Total expenses	$321,298	25.6%	$340,608	23.8%	$399,885	23.7%	$408,325	22.7%	$185,597	35.8%
Net profit (before taxes)	$52,024	4.2%	$60,710	4.3%	$66,242	3.9%	$100,055	5.5%	$14,625	2.8%

Value of inventory at cost and as a percent of sales

	Col 1	Col 2	Col 3	Col 4	Col 5
Value of inventory at cost and as a percent of sales					
Prescriptions	$ 23,492– 10.3%	$ 28,125– 10.2%	$ 27,820– 9.2%	$ 29,112– 9.9%	$ 23,087– 13.4%
Other	152,532– 14.9%	162,154– 14.1%	213,711– 15.4%	222,511– 14.7%	71,998– 21.1%
Total	$ 176,024– 14.1%	$ 190,279– 13.5%	$ 241,531– 14.3%	$ 251,623– 13.9%	$ 95,085– 18.5%
Annual rate of turnover of inventory	5.0 times	5.5 times	5.2 times	5.3 times	3.4 times
Size of area and sales per square foot*	sq. ft.	sq. ft.	sq. ft.	sq. ft.	sq. ft.
Prescription	351 $587.22	374 $701.98	406 $681.87	445 $644.60	357 $501.33
Other	5,661 168.90	5,894 171.60	9,384 137.92	8,636 162.73	2,646 138.16
Total	6,012 267.23	6,268 271.03	9,790 241.38	9,081 273.23	3,003 183.21
Sales per dollar invested in inventory					
Prescription	$9.73	$9.82	$10.83	$10.10	$7.46
Other	6.70	7.11	6.48	6.79	4.74
Net profit per dollar invested in inventory	$0.296	$0.319	$0.274	$0.398	$0.154
Number of prescriptions dispensed					
New	17,478– 51.6%	21,965– 52.8%	25,214– 54.4%	24,023– 53.8%	13,265– 54.8%
Renewed	16,423– 48.4%	19,616– 47.2%	21,138– 45.6%	20,664– 46.2%	10,958– 45.2%
Total	33,901–100.0%	41,581–100.0%	46,352–100.0%	44,687–100.0%	24,223–100.0%
Prescription charge	$6.74	$6.64	$6.50	$6.58	$7.11
Number of hours per week					
Pharmacy was open	75 hours	81 hours	86 hours	82 hours	62 hours
Worked by manager	47 hours	45 hours	46 hours	46 hours	46 hours
Worked by employed pharmacist(s)	69 hours	74 hours	83 hours	88 hours	41 hours

Source: *Lilly Digest* (Chain Stores), 1980.

tional activities to maintain this image. Independents with lower prices must advertise this in order to gain advantage for themselves because of their pricing policy. Low prices without advertising will take too long to create the desired impression in the shopper's mind.

The ability of retail drug outlets to utilize price as a device to increase patronage levels depends in part on the importance of price in the mind of the consumer. Thus, when times are prosperous, low prices can be expected to lose some of their appeal. Low prices may also bring profit margins to a low level, with little margin for error. Usually the cost of lowering prices also means that some cutbacks in other competitive activities will be necessary. Finally, any government or private prescription program that combines a free prescription service with free choice of vendor will serve to minimize the ability of prescription price to serve as a competitive weapon.

Today's patients are more product-conscious. Also, they are more aware of the legal requirements that the product name appear on the prescription label and that the prescription prices be posted. Consequently, much of the secrecy about prices charged for and the actual names of prescription drugs has been removed. The operator who advertises the savings available through the use of generic drugs also makes an impression on the marketplace. A shift of prescription volume from independent operations to chain and other advertising operations has occurred because of the impact of advertising.

The subject of price must also include a discussion of pricing philosophies and methods. Pricing philosophy should recognize the appeal of certain products to important population segments, as well as recognize the needs of the pharmacy owner. Many pharmacies, for example, choose to dispense oral contraceptive drugs at prices just above and even below actual product cost. Others price hypoglycemic products in the same manner. Their philosophy is that increasing sales to women of childbearing age or to the elderly will lead to success.

Methods for pricing prescriptions vary with owners. In general, the most common methods for pricing prescriptions are a professional fee (dispensing fee) plus cost, markup on cost, and a combination of a professional fee plus a markup.

The professional (dispensing fee) technique that has gained much popularity in the past decade arrives at the final retail price by adding a preset fee to the cost of the product used in each prescription. This fee is determined by totalling all the overhead (expense) factors associated with prescription preparation, and then adding an increment for profit, resulting in the fee per prescription. The same fee is applied to each prescription regardless of the ingredient cost. The advantage of this system is that it recognizes the professional service provided by the pharmacist instead of relating the final price to the product cost. The disadvantage of this system is that it is not competitive to "mark up" pricing for low cost products, and it does not recognize the price imaging derived from the low pricing of high velocity drugs, such as oral contraceptives. A more subtle disadvantage of this system is that third-party payers may first adopt the concept and then become intransigent about adjusting the fee upward. A third unforeseeable disadvantage is the inflexibility of the fee; it does not respond promptly to inflation extremes.

The markup on cost method of pricing takes the cost of the product and moves it up by a predetermined percentage that has been tested to ensure the pharmacist of a proper return on investment. The markup percentage can be varied by product, therapeutic category, and turnover. This system provides the pharmacist with a competitive tool that allows sufficient pricing flexibility to establish the "low price image" yet provides a price that reacts to the cost of the commodity. The disadvantage of this system is that it is only commodity cost-oriented, and applies the cost of the professional service unequally.

The most promising system is a combination of these two. All cost factors other than the professional service are boiled down to a percentage markup, and then a fee based only on the service provided is added. The fee can be made product-specific, if necessary, thus providing some competitive flexibility. Recently the profession has identified the need for an additional fee (called an administrative fee) to offset the costs of preparing and submitting claims to third-party payers.

The matter of pricing for certain population segments, such as senior citizens, and pricing for a prepaid subscribers copayment plan for prescriptions covered by insurance cannot be overlooked. Independent pharmacists and chain pharmacy owners have identified the competitive advantage of the higher utilization of prescription drugs by certain population segments, and then offering that group a discount on the regular price. In certain areas this form of inducement is so commonly applied that it provides no advantage to any retail pharmacy and is expected. A similar technique is used in discounting the patient's copayment portion of prepaid prescription coverage. In a community with a high number of third-party paid prescription insurance enrollees, discounting the copayment has become the most significant marketing strategy that can be adopted by a pharmacy. It should be noted that no matter how low prices are, someone else can have lower prices.

Promotion

Promotion of pharmaceutical services at the community level cannot be entirely divorced from price considerations, because many larger retailers use price as the central theme in their promotions. Most promotion at the retail level is conducted through radio, TV, and local newspapers. Other media utilized include direct mail, door-to-door circulars, "package stuffers," and the Yellow Pages. Many wholesalers will assist the pharmacist to select merchandise and to obtain promotional allowances for local advertising of nationally known brands of over-the-counter products.

From a professional point of view, it would seem that promotion of the community pharmacy should deal more with public relations than with advertising if it is to be in keeping with the current process of professionalism. Within these limits it is still possible for the pharmacist to engage in considerable promotional activity. The promotional budget for the average American pharmacy has been about 1.5% of sales. A pharmacy with sales of $200,000 a year might thus expend $3000 on promotion. It has been stated that newspapers or circulars is probably the most frequently used medium for retail pharmacy advertising. For the small- to medium-sized pharmacy in anything but a large city, it is probably also the most effective. Newspaper ads offer the pharmacist an opportunity to express himself creatively. Most local newspapers are able to provide layout and retail store advertising specialists.

There are firms that specialize in preparing independent pharmacy circular advertising. Their services include supplying the merchandise (at an attractive price), guaranteeing the sales, mailing or distributing the circular, and advising on in-store merchandising. These programs are equivalent to chain store promotions.

This does not mean that a pharmacist cannot draft effective advertising on his own. Trade publications frequently feature success stories of this type. There are enough cliché-ridden newspaper messages about "our competent personnel" and "fresh drugs" to recognize that some danger does exist for the customer to assume that amateurish efforts in advertising carry over into the prescription department. It must be noted, however, that the local pharmacist is in a position to convey appropriate community themes in the pharmacy's advertising if he is talented in this direction.

The use of radio spots can be an effective means of promotion for the community pharmacist if they are properly conceived and presented. The pitfalls and opportunities are much the same as for the newspaper, but with the added difficulty of writing copy that sounds good on oral presentation.

Opportunities may arise for the community pharmacist to work with a local program that is connected to nationwide promotional efforts. Most of these occasions are connected with advertising campaigns for drug products. There are also opportunities to promote the prescription department in connection with such events as National Pharmacy Week, National Poison Control Week, and Community Health Week.

Other promotional techniques frequently used by chain versus chain or chain versus independent advertisers include the following:

1. Coupons good for a reduction from the regular price of a new (or transferred refill) prescription.

2. A "free with a prescription" offer for a desirable item.

3. Drawing type of give-aways (e.g., cars, TVs, trips).

4. Less tangible give-aways, such as poison antidote charts, health-related literature, poison-proofing the home.

There is no limit to innovative promotional ideas but as soon as a successful promotion is developed, it will be copied (and often improved upon) by the competition. The function of successful promotions is to increase the traffic coming into the pharmacy and to familiarize the service area with the pharmacy's name and location.

Buying

Buying really means selling—buyers purchase merchandise for sales, and a prudent buyer purchases only enough merchandise to ensure maximum turnover. Sound inventory management creates success in a pharmacy whether it is a large or small operation. Buying acumen is another differential advantage that is related to price. Low prices are not possible for long unless the pharmacist has bought the drugs at a price that is to the pharmacy's advantage. For the small pharmacist, acting independently, there is little opportunity to engage in really sophisticated purchasing practices. Most opportunities lie in the pharmacist's ability to forecast sale trends accurately, take advantage of special buying opportunities, act on cash discounts, and control inventory.

The importance of astute buying is reflected in developments discussed in previous chapters. The franchise operation has as one of its prime advantages the ability to make purchases at lower prices. The chain store, which has grown to be such a force in the retail drug field, also has group buying as a reason for its existence. Finally, drug co-ops have been formed specifically to allow products to be sold at lower prices to participating pharmacies.

The pharmacist with a keen marketing and professional mind seldom has to delay filling a prescription because the drug is not in stock. This assumes that he has a thorough knowledge of the professional community in the area, and also is familiar enough with current pharmaceutical literature to know the characteristics of new products as they are introduced.

The problems associated with stocking an independent pharmacy represent only a fraction of the problems associated with stocking a small, medium, or large chain. Buying beyond a 30-day turnover time, no matter how low the price, can be more destructive than paying a higher price and turning the item more frequently. An item yielding 25% profit turning 12 times a year is more profitable than one yielding 40% profit turning 7 times a year.

This must all be carefully considered when making buying decisions. Using the wholesaler as a resource to obtain dating terms, and off-invoice discounts must not be overlooked.

Personnel

Selection, training, and retention of satisfactory personnel is vital to the success of the community pharmacy. The process can be divided into categories, including recruitment, training, placement, and motivation. Regardless of the size of the pharmacy, the employer must seek out sources for employees, establish a training program, match the talent and aptitude of the employee to the job assignment, and establish programs to motivate and retain those employees who can contribute to a successful operation.

Obviously the larger the units or number of units operated demands more specialization by the owner's organization. Large chains employ individuals who recruit pharmacist-managers by visiting colleges of pharmacy and business colleges. Training programs vary from a one-time review of store policy and procedures to an elaborate ongoing multimedia program. Job assignments should be based on the appraisal by the interviewer or supervisor, and should follow the principle of not placing a square peg in a round hole. The investment in recruiting and training personnel needs the protection afforded by short-range motivational and long-range retention programs. No matter what the size of the pharmacy, some rewards can be accrued for productivity and longevity. No community pharmacy can truly be successful when staffed with less than competent personnel.

No owner, regardless of outstanding ability, can succeed without properly trained assistants. One surly employee can alienate the most loyal customer.

The selection of personnel to provide service is potentially the greatest competitive weapon. Pharmacy has a long tradition of service among retail institutions. W. C. Fields satirized this to the point of ridicule in a short film entitled "The Pharmacist." In the film the pharmacist (Fields) grovels, whines, and makes obeisance to a grumpy customer who eventually purchases a postage stamp. The pharmacist, undaunted, presents the customer with a large oriental vase, the give-away of the week. In another segment he agrees to deliver a half-box of cough drops (he agreed to break up the package) some 15 miles out of town.

Consumer surveys have shown the services of the pharmacy to be important to them, but not uniformly so. The success of the discount stores attest to that. The services traditionally expected of the community pharmacy are interest-free credit and free delivery, neither of which are available through most discount stores.

The marketing rationale behind any service depends on its ability to ensure repeated patronage by the customer and members of his family. Although it is recognized that both credit and delivery services do serve this purpose to a degree, it is also true that these services are vulnerable to abuse. Because the discount or chain store operates on a cash-and-carry basis, there is a temptation to use the family pharmacy only when it is needed, and to use other outlets when funds and time permit.

Pharmacists are currently reviewing new types of services that are actually preferable from both the professional and marketing viewpoints. The service with the most potential at this time seems to be the maintenance of records of a family's health. This is attractive from the standpoints of both business and public health. (It is required by at least one state board of pharmacy.) The complete family health record would chronicle not only the prescriptions actually received by members of the family, but also their use of nonprescription medications, drug allergies, special health problems, and expenditures. If a family receives this kind of service there is less incentive to shop around. At year's end the family knows it can depend on a complete statement for income tax purposes, and it also knows that health information needed by themselves or their physician is readily accessible. This is a strong competitive weapon, one on which the physician has relied for a long time, and one that is difficult to attack by price competition.

Chains and many independent pharmacies have installed on-line or "stand-alone" data retention and processing systems. On-line systems are connected via phone lines to a remote computer on which patient records are stored along with other data, such as drug movement, third-party billing, and reconciliation. Stand-alone systems are essentially the same but the computer (usually a mini- or microcomputer) is located in the pharmacy. Computerization shortens prescription preparation time, provides tax records, displays medication records, detects possible drug interactions or possible allergic reactions, over- (or under-) utilization, polypharmacy, and polyprescribers, and prepares third-party billing. This tool improves service, can thus be used as the keystone of a marketing program. Ultimately consumers will demand computerized pharmacies.

Another service that offers a tremendous competitive advantage is the 24-hour pharmacy. Maintaining a 24-hour pharmacy cannot always be cost-justified but, in an urban area, a limited number of such stores will attract much support. Many chains and large independents have used the 24-hour store successfully.

Recently a newer idea has become established. We shall call it the "one-stop health goods and services shop." In such a store the consumer can find the following under one roof: a pharmacy, health and beauty aid shop, optical shop, and a durable medical equipment (DME) shop. Add to this an audiology department and some dental chairs, and we have the basis for this concept. The attraction this holds for consumers is self-evident and, as prepaid insurance coverage for DME, optical, audiology, and dental care proliferate, utilization of these services will increase, thus expanding the demand and need for providers of these services.

Scrambled Merchandising and the "Wheel of Retailing"

Various marketing students have called attention to a phenomenon in the retail field known as the "wheel of retailing." This term describes rather well the pattern of retailing that has evolved in this country, and that has particular relevance to the drug field. The hypothesis suggests that new types of retailers will emerge as low status, low margin, low price operators, who will offer more services and acquire more elaborate establishments as they become successful. These changes require increased investment and result in higher operating costs that, in turn, necessitate higher prices. With the higher prices again comes vulnerability to competition by newer low status, low margin, and low price outlets.

It is difficult at present to evaluate just how far the wheel of retailing has turned in the drug field. There are obvious examples of drugstore chains that have passed the low budget stage, but there are also many stores that logically fit the description of those with operators in the first stage of this evolutionary process.

The retail drug field is a tempting and logical one for the entry of the operator who aims at short-term profits. The popular press provides free advertising through continued emphasis on high drug prices. The drugstore owner who is willing to cut back on service can find a lucrative return in retail drugs, particularly in the short run. This technique is not quite as effective in the prescription area, which requires considerably more attention, but it can also be utilized there. If the customer knows which drug he is taking, is familiar with the price, and is willing to pay cash and pick up the prescription, he is least likely to be swayed by other arguments for continuing to patronize his regular pharmacy.

As retailers continually investigate various areas of opportunity to determine the ideal mixture of goods and services, it is natural that there will occasionally be areas of overlap among retailers in the type of goods offered. One text has referred to this competition among different types of dealers and distributors who sell the same commodity as "conglomerate market competition."[2] Insofar as this term refers to the reverse of the situation—competition for sales of many different types of commodities by the same basic type of retailer—there is probably no better example of the concept than the drugstore.

The pharmacy at one time limited itself to dealing only in health-related products. Literally every type of good imaginable has been offered for sale in the pharmacy, particularly since World War II. Television comedians refer, with good reason, to going to the drugstore for a set of tires. The tendency toward "scrambled merchandising" has become so prevalent, particularly among certain chain stores, that we often find the "tail wagging the dog"— that is, the store has long since ceased to be a drugstore in anything but name.

Many in pharmacy have complained vigorously about the sales of drug products by such outlets as food stores, department stores, and discount stores. In fairness it must be noted that concern has also been expressed over the tendency of the traditional drug outlet to offer nonhealth-related items for sale. There is ample marketing explanation for both of these tendencies and, if the situation were not complicated by two factors—the use of professional staff and the special consideration due merchandise that affects health—they might be largely ignored and allowed to solve themselves through the dynamics of the marketplace.

Factors Influencing Scrambled Merchandising

In the case of the larger chain operations, which are generally owned by nonpharmacists who are thoroughly committed to pharmacy as a retail operation, it is somewhat easier to understand the reasons for the proliferation of goods in the retail drugstore. But scrambled merchandising is not limited to the big operators—it occasionally finds its way into even the smallest pharmacy. The reasons for this vary according to the type of pharmacy, but certain basic causes may be cited:

1. The character of the pharmacist's market.
2. Changes in consumer shopping habits.
3. Interconnectedness of demand.
4. Efforts to increase store traffic.
5. Pressure from the manufacturer.
6. Common costs in the retail outlet.

CHARACTER OF PHARMACIST'S MARKET

The importance of the character of the market in which the pharmacy operates is particularly apparent in the rural setting. In the small community with limited retail opportunities the pharmacist often finds it necessary to provide some of the missing retail services. Thus, we may find the pharmacist serving as the only local source of such items as jewelry, crystal, photographic supplies, and light snacks, in addition to prescriptions and other health-related services. Often these items are added in direct response to a customer request. It should also be noted that in many instances these product lines are subsidizing the prescription department. Putting it another way, if the pharmacist did not engage in these other merchandising activities, the prescription volume might be insufficient to support the pharmacist, and the community would be deprived of prescription services. Although it is true that this constitutes a considerable waste of the training that the pharmacist has received, pharmacy's leaders have as yet produced no economically sound alternative.

CHANGES IN CONSUMER SHOPPING HABITS

The change in shopping habits that has done the most to encourage the expansion of product lines in the pharmacy and other retail outlets is self-service, another development that has come about since World War II. The willingness of customers to serve themselves without the assistance of clerks has allowed the addition of more open display space and additional new products without the necessity of significant labor cost increases. The fact that customers are willing to purchase health-care items without advice must be attributed, at least in part, to a generally more knowledgeable public in regard to health matters. Television has certainly contributed to this development. Humorous and vastly simplified explanations of the way in which patent medicines treat common minor ailments have given people confidence in their ability to choose self-medications. Network television also has made the products easily recognizable on the self-service shelf.

Health and its care have also become a favorite topic for the mass publications. People are now more interested in and willing to talk about health matters. This newfound knowledge inspires confidence in self-service shopping and, in spite of the uproar within pharmacy, to the average consumer, plucking a bottle of aspirin from a supermarket shelf is no different from doing the same thing in a self-service drugstore. It seems possible that the cavalier treatment accorded medicines for self-medication in discount stores, TV advertisements, food stores, and many pharmacies has contributed to a certain lack of respect that seems to exist for prescription drugs. From a marketing viewpoint it makes little sense to expect a customer to approach the prescription as the product of a professional service when it is obtained in an atmosphere of "help yourself" and "caveat emptor." A basic conflict of image occurs, which in the average community source of drugs, is more "drugstore" than "pharmacy." Furthermore, there is considerable evidence that the customer likes it this way.

The situation described above has not gone unrecognized. A new concept in the offering of prescription and nonprescription drugs has now appeared, which will be presented here because its success requires some change in consumer shopping habits. In 1965 the American Pharmaceutical Association introduced the Pharmaceutical Center, a physical and conceptual renovation for pharmaceutical distribution at the retail level (Fig. 18-1).

A pharmaceutical center's most dramatic innovation is the complete absence of displayed merchandise. Nonprescription products are available, but only upon request and through the pharmacist. There is no scrambled merchandising, and no self-service. Such centers have been enthusiastically received by the profession, and the numbers in operation are increasing. The fact that they can be successful is attested to by their survival. Still to be answered, however, is the question of how much influence they will have on the total prescription marketing picture. It is theoretically possible for the concept to become so widespread as to become a real deterrent to the practice of discount prescription pricing. The total effect of a pharmaceutical center as a marketing phenomenon will depend upon the following:

1. The number of pharmacists who are willing to initiate this type of operation.

2. The viability of a center in various markets (e.g., the rural town described previously).

3. The extent to which the public can be made to accept this new concept. (It is possible that at least some classes of people will be alienated by this atmosphere.)

Fig. 18-1. *A reception desk and a health information center make up an important part of Emerson's Pharmaceutical Center. Source: McKesson and Robbins.*

4. The importance of congruity in the image presented by the retail establishment (depending on Factor 3). If the center is widely accepted by pharmacy and by the public, the public may no longer be willing to accept its prescription services in any but this merchandise-free setting.

5. The demand for consultative services.

From the point of view of many in pharmacy, this certainly represents an opportunity for the community pharmacy to get off the wheel of retailing and mitigate its vulnerability to yet another cycle. There is no assurance that this is an immediate prospect, however, although 100 such centers were opened in the 2 years after the concept was introduced.

INTERCONNECTEDNESS OF DEMAND

A principal reason that early ventures toward expanding offerings in the retail store seemed logical was that the newly offered item was in some way related to those traditionally carried. Thus, in the pharmacy, cosmetics were health-related, at least indirectly. It has been said that a person who comes into a drugstore wants either to "feel better, look better, or smell better." If cosmetics are sold, why not costume jewelry? Costume jewelry? How about watches? And so it goes. What began as a direct relationship has deteriorated to third- and fourth-generation relationships—or to no relationship at all. There is at least a marketing rationale for selling products that show certain demand characteristics.

In respect to violation of the principle of interconnectedness of demand, the pharmacy is often more guilty than the institution it so frequently criticizes, the supermarket. Food and drugs have a natural association. Both are necessities, both are health-related, and both are usually taken by mouth. It is thus a little disconcerting to recall the vigorous protests raised by pharmacists when it was first proposed to sell saccharin and infant formulas in grocery stores. This is made particularly striking when the wide variety of completely unrelated merchandise displayed in many pharmacies, including perishable and nonperishable food items, is considered.

EFFORTS TO INCREASE STORE TRAFFIC

The use of scrambled merchandising to increase store traffic finds a marketing justification for traditionally low traffic establishments, such as furniture and jewelry stores. Although the pharmacy is traditionally a high traffic type of retail outlet, nothing compares with the traffic generated by offering low-priced milk or bread.

PRESSURE FROM MANUFACTURERS

Many pharmaceutical manufacturers are now subsidiaries of larger conglomerate corporations. Other drug manufacturers are so large as to have nondrug subsidiaries of their own. This creates some situations in which the manufacturer finds it desirable to offer new nondrug products through the traditional retail outlet, the community pharmacy. The reverse situation can also exist, in which the drug manufacturer finds that relationships with other types of retail establishments encourage the sale of drug products through them.

The effects of manufacturers "cents off label" packaging and redeemable coupons appearing either in print advertising or direct mail should be also mentioned. Manufacturers, not unlike retailers, are aware of mass market potentials. In addition to traditional marketing techniques, they have introduced coupons and "cents off" packaging as a sales stimulus, and their proliferation can be overwhelming. The retailer who redeems coupons may find it necessary to employ extra personnel or to pay a service for obtaining the reimbursement. The popularity of coupons in depressed times has led to promotional techniques such as double value for coupons when redeemed with the purchase.

Similarly, a predictable movement of routine packaging becomes meaningless when the same product is packaged in a "cents off" label. The normal inventory often lies dormant because of competition with itself. These pressures often place the retailing pharmacist (or any other retailer) in between the allegorical rock and hard place, particularly when promotion-minded aggressive competition uses both programs to gain advantage.

COMMON COSTS IN RETAIL OUTLETS

The most tempting reason for adding yet another product category to the merchandise line is that every sale will yield pure profit. With the exception of the prescription department it is difficult to trace costs of operation to any particular type of product. Heat, ventilation, utilities, and management costs are all spread over the entire store inventory, regardless of its nature. Given a common pool of costs, it is then tempting indeed to add another item free of charge. Of course, it is technically proper to allocate costs proportionately to goods carried, and theoretically no product should get a free ride in the determination of the cost of carrying it. These points are usually overlooked, however, and the proliferation continues.

Research is needed on the effect of the cluttered appearance of many drugstores in regard to point-of-purchase displays and eventually to sales. The impact on store image would also be interesting to determine, as would the number of the tempting little additions that eventually become merchandise burdens. One thing is certain, and that is that scrambled merchandising seems to be self-perpetuating. It has its element of revenge, as when one retailer counters a competition's infringement on his product area with a similar retaliatory move.

Effects of Scrambled Merchandising

There can be little doubt that the effects of the scrambled merchandising tendency upon pharmacy have been profound, with implications beyond the field of marketing. Pharmacy finds its image blurred. Neither the public nor the pharmacist may be quite clear on just which role is proper. Most pharmacists are prevented from an all-out effort of entrepreneurship by a quite natural urge to assume professional status. The marginality of their position tends to dilute both professional and business efforts. The pharmacist may, in fact, be forced into a position that results in his performing an inadequate job in both areas. Certainly the pharmacist was not properly trained to sell the potpourri of unrelated merchandise that may clutter the shelves, and futile efforts to do so may hinder the proper practice of pharmacy. One wonders whether a few visionary leaders, knowledgeable in the field of pharmaceutical marketing (a field still viewed with considerable distaste by many pharmacy educators), might have foreseen, and perhaps even prevented, some of these developments in their seminal stages 25 years ago.

From the marketing viewpoint the effects of scrambled merchandising may be more apparent. One obvious effect is that on price. Different types of establishments have different cost structures, permitting considerable price variation. Also, many retailers use price pressures alone as a means of market entry. Marginal operators soon find price competition to be an impossible means of survival. The natural tendency, then, will be toward various methods of nonprice competition. In pharmacy this has taken the direction of greater service. The pharmacy press has pointed out to the independent operators (and quite rightly) that service is one form of competition that their competitors in chain and discount operations find hardest to duplicate. Such services as delivery, credit, and maintenance of family health records are important forms of nonprice competition. More chains, though, are providing the latter two services, especially with the acceptance of credit cards.

McCarthy has discussed the classification of prescriptions in this context.[2] He noted that, upon first examination, the prescription would logically be classed as a specialty item because a specific product is sought and the price paid will be that which is asked. He pointed out that price comparisons on prescriptions are often embarrassing or at least impractical, although the practice has been encouraged by consumer organizations and the American Medical Association. For this reason prescriptions are likely to be taken where it is most convenient—e.g., near the physician's office or near the patient's home. The pharmacist who places competitive emphasis on service is, then, attempting to place that *service* into the realm of a specialty good. Insofar as this endeavor is successful, the individual pharmacist may be able to thwart the efforts of other drugstores that view prescriptions as homogeneous shopping goods and place all of their competitive eggs in the price basket.

Other developments expected following in the wake of widespread scrambled merchandising include increasing competition by brand name, greater responsibility for promotion placed on the manufacturer, and increased pressure for restrictive legislation. Improved communications media such as television have served to heighten the public's awareness of brand names. In the "scrambled" situation this is important to distinguish a good product from the many others clamoring for the attention of the customer. The tendency for many types of outlets to handle a product encourages the development of private label merchandise lines for the concomitant monopoly power. Thus we see Walgreen products sold exclusively in their pharmacies. Independent pharmacies have attempted to duplicate this process by purchasing prepackaged products to which they (or the manufacturer) attach their store label. Often overlooked by independents, however, is the need to promote these private brands through either personal selling or advertising. Many pharmacists have found private brand merchandise, available "exclusively" at their establishment, gathering dust years later because of failure to recognize this fact.

The manufacturer can be expected to engage in what is known as pull-type promotion. The product can be promoted so effectively that the retailer will be forced to stock and sell it by sheer weight of consumer request. The manufacturer may be forced into this position due to the desire on the part of the retailers to engage in competition using their private brand. Pull-type promotion is old hat to pharmacists, because it has constituted 99% of all promotion for prescription drugs in the past. All promotion was directed to the physician, with the manufacturer assured of the pharmacist's cooperation in stocking the product once the first prescription appeared.

Pharmacy has been accused of adopting a "there oughta be a law" policy throughout much of its history. Probably the longest battle of this type was the fight for passage of a national fair trade law (later referred to as quality stabilization). In other actions pharmacy has attempted to induce passage of legislation restricting sales of certain (or all) health-related items to pharmacies. These efforts have ranged from eliminating sales of contraceptive devices in filling stations to the establishment of third—and even fourth—classes of drugs whose sale would be limited to pharmacies and pharmacists.

Pharmacists have not been too successful in their pursuit of these restrictive goals, even though it was possible to combine the elements of protection of the public health and the health of small business (traditionally a soft spot in legislative hearts) in their arguments. In one case, however, pharmacists were more successful. In a 1973 ruling the United States Supreme Court reversed the

Liggett decision of 1928 and upheld a North Dakota statute requiring that the majority ownership of pharmacies be in the hands of North Dakota-registered pharmacists in good standing. The nationwide effects were expected to depend upon actions taken by the individual states, but for those interested in the supremacy of "independent" pharmacy it stood as a landmark decision. The decision of the North Dakota and Supreme courts was upheld as reflecting the interest of the citizens of that state. The North Dakota law not only requires 51% ownership but in-person supervision by the owner. Most other states have been reluctant to introduce similar legislation because of the difficulty in proving that such restrictive legislation is truly in the public interest.

Even though the picture is considerably complicated by the health and professional elements of community pharmacy, the potential for success in any battle for restrictive legislation is probably summed up best in the following two quotes: "It is hard to legislate against the dynamics of the marketplace in a free enterprise society."[3] ". . . entrepreneurs must work with what the market can and will accept rather than with what they would like to impose upon it."[2]

Nature of Retail Competition

Heterogeneity in the marketplace is most in evidence at the retail level. Each store is truly unique in at least one respect—location. Retailing is also characterized by an extremely dynamic competitive situation with whole classifications of retail stores appearing or disappearing, and with shifts in geographic pattern and in the nature of retail assortments.

Newer types of outlets are now merchandising all types of drugs, health, and beauty aids, including the following:

1. Chains operating leased departments in discount outlets and opening their own discount stores.

2. Food chains buying up drug chains.

3. Discount chains putting in their own or leased drug departments.

4. Labor unions opening their own pharmacies.

5. Mail order prescription houses.

6. Hospital clinic pharmacies.

7. Prescription services supplied by employers as a fringe benefit.

8. Group practice medicine, including pharmacy services.

9. Door-to-door drug retailing.

10. Drug retailing by department and variety stores.

11. In-house HMO pharmacies.

12. Vitamin products sold in health food shops.

Traditionally retail pharmacies were segmented into three major types: the traditional or neighborhood pharmacy, the prescription shop, and the super store. Until recently, discussions of retail competition in the drug field confined themselves to these three types of outlets, usually from the point of view of the neighborhood pharmacy. Recently, however, there is evidence that competition is approaching from other directions, and more importantly it has made itself felt in the prescription department.

A more unexpected source of competition has been the hospital outpatient dispensing area. In the sense that it deals with the ultimate consumer the hospital has always fit, at least loosely, the definition of a retailer. It has not been until recently, however, that the community pharmacist has shown concern over the hospital as a potential source of competition. Outpatient or ambulatory care services provided by the hospital are justified by hospital pharmacists because of the perceived vacuum that exists between needed follow-up care and care as currently provided by community pharmacies. This vacuum could result in the avoidable expense of readmission to the hospital.

This competitive force may have a significant impact on the kind of care provided by community practitioners. For example, there is a growing need for in-home provision of hyperalimentation and related nutritional services, but community pharmacies have not yet dealt with this need, whereas hospital pharmacies are equipped to provide this service. It is expected that some community pharmacy owners will recognize the advantage of providing this service.

Certainly the retail pharmacy will find itself at a severe disadvantage if it attempts to compete routinely with the hospital pharmacy. The most obvious inequity is the tax-exempt status of most hospitals, as is frequently pointed out by the pharmacists concerned. Almost equally important, however, is the pricing structure followed by many drug manufacturers when dealing with hospitals. Many community pharmacists contend that hospitals receive discounts not available to community pharmacists, and that the discounts are offered simply because they are hospitals rather than as a result of any advantage to the producer in terms of quantity sales or decreased costs.

A pharmacy group received a favorable decision after filing a lawsuit against manufacturers for what was termed discriminatory pricing practices to hospitals that provided outpatient prescription services in direct competition with community practitioners. As a result of the ruling, direct-selling distributors of prescription merchandise must make certain that competitive pricing is confined only to drugs intended for inpatient use. Nevertheless legal loopholes still exist, which allow direct sellers to meet a local competitive price.

Another newer source of competition comes from the Health Maintenance Organization (HMO). Theoretically HMOs thrive by preventing critical illness, as opposed to existing health-care delivery systems that provide "catastrophic" care. Larger "bricks and mortar" HMOs maintain on-site pharmacies or contract with certain community pharmacies to provide services at a controlled cost. Other HMOs, known as Independent Provider Associations (IPAs), contract with some existing health-care providers for services, thus limiting the marketplace.

The effects of the physician-owned pharmacy or the drug dispenser as a competitor are diminishing, but they still affect the marketplace. What is more anticompetitive is the independently owned pharmacy located within the clinical setting. Legislation has been enacted that restricts physician ownership and imposes pharmacy-like requirements on the dispensing physician, but some areas of the country are still seriously affected by this type of competition.

Effects of Prepaid Drug Programs on Retail Competition

The nature of retail competition changes dramatically with a significant increase in the numbers of people covered by prepaid insurance (or government) prescription benefit programs. The nature of retail competition is also affected by the amount of the beneficiary's liability for the prescription. In general, the number of prescriptions issued and filled increases as more people are covered by prepaid prescription programs. At the same time a significant change in the quantity of drug per prescription also takes place. The profitability per prescription decreases, however, because of reimbursement techniques.

Government Programs

The government program that has had the greatest impact on retail competition is Medicaid (Title XIX). The Medicaid program was designed to provide indigent persons with first-class health care based on the premise that access to good health care is a right, and not a privilege. Indigent patients usually pay nothing for this service but can be required to pay a small amount of the cost. Despite this idealistic commitment, there were many obstacles to its achievement, not the least of which is an unsound reimbursement policy for the provision of pharmacy services.

This policy states that a pharmacy will be reimbursed at the lesser of a cost (subject to definition) plus a fee as compared to a pharmacy's usual price. Cost is sometimes defined as the average wholesale price (AWP) but more often as the estimated actual cost (EAC), which is usually less than the AWP, or the actual acquisition cost (AAC), which may be less than either the AWP or the EAC, but not more. For certain multisource products a maximum allowable cost (MAC) is also established. The amount of the fee and the choice of EAC, AWP, or AAC is determined by each state. States are required to conduct fee surveys periodically, and are allowed to adjust fees accordingly. A recent ruling permits states to allow pharmacies to add an administrative fee to offset the cost of the paperwork associated with the billing for these services.

As a practical matter, most states have failed to respond promptly or adequately to the need for fee adjustments and, in many instances, have lowered the fee or failed to pay promptly (or both) because of lack of funds. Because the provision of pharmacy services is an optional benefit under Title XIX some state programs do not include drug coverage, and other states have contemplated eliminating the drug benefit. Many states have restricted the benefit through use of a formulary or by simply eliminating a drug or class of drugs from coverage.

With all of this as background, it is clear that in certain geographic areas having large Medicaid populations usual prices will be established at or above the maximum paid by Medicaid, and competition will be based primarily on location and service. Self-paying clientele shopping in this environment may be faced with a higher average retail price because of the dominance of the government program. Chain stores tend to abandon this market because of the lack of profitability at usual prices. A competitive force is thus eliminated that, by its nature, tended to keep prices for all drugstore articles at a fairly low level.

Private Programs

Because the automobile industry, as a result of collective bargaining, has agreed to provide coverage for a significant portion of the cost of prescription drugs to their employees and their families, privately insured prescription programs have grown to a great extent. In some states 40% of the population is covered and, in some cities in those states, 75% of the population is covered.

Private insurance programs usually follow the pattern of paying the cost (as they define it) plus a fee, less a flat portion paid by the beneficiary, for each prescription drug covered by the program when dispensed in a quantity consistent with the program's parameters. The flat portion paid by the beneficiary is known as the "copay" (shorthand for copayment liability), less commonly known as the "deductible" or "shared cost." This copay generally varies from $0 to $3 (although $4 and $5 programs exist), with $2 being the most common figure. (My own figures show that in Michigan there is equal distribution between $2 and $3 programs.)

Surprisingly, when viewed in retrospect, competition concentrates almost exclusively on discounting the copay. It is strange that patients who pay only a small portion of their prescription costs usually try only to reduce this cost rather than find pharmacies that provide more meaningful patient services. My personal experience is that, in a third-party paid prescription environment, the most effective marketing tool available is discounting the copay. Because private insurers are generally slow to improve the fee structure, sometimes indicating the copay discounting as a reason, and because the cost of ingredients increases more rapidly than fees as a result of inflation, choice of product, and prescription modality, the profitability of third-party paid prescriptions is being reduced. Some of this burden is then passed, disproportionately, to the pricing of cash-paid prescriptions.

Is the Independently Owned Drugstore Doomed?

An FDA Commissioner once predicted the demise of the corner drugstore, but this prediction failed to materialize. It was accurate only in that the drugstore moved from the corner to a position adjacent to a supermarket (or other merchants) and expanded its size and inventory. Implicit in the words "corner drugstore" was the connotation of independent ownership. It is true that chain drugstores have obtained more significant portions of both the prescription and out-front marketplace. It is equally true that some chains have broken both the 1000-store and billion-dollar volume barriers, but many independents have fared equally well and, in fact, have begun to expand into multiunit operators.

In 1980 43% of all community pharmacies were chain (undefined) stores.[4] These stores had 77% of total drugstore sales. In 1970 only 30% of all community pharmacies were chain stores, with 55.8% of drugstore sales. Extrapolation of these figures shows that the average chain store's volume in 1980 exceeded $1,200,000, and the annual prescription volume exceeded $200,000.

Defining chain stores as four or more commonly owned and operated but separately located drug stores reduces these figures somewhat, but they are still impressive. What these numbers really say is that (1) successful drugstore operations are expanding their share of market and (2) as independents establish successful operation patterns they tend to become multiunit operators, thus altering their statistical characterization from independent to chain.

In order to consider whether there is a future for the independent drugstore, it is necessary to break down prescription business into two functions: the distributive function and the professional function.

Distributive Function

The distributive function is often described as the "count, pour, lick and stick" process of prescription preparation. This is the basis of retail drugstore prescription competition. The charge for the prescription should be the sum of the costs of the ingredients, the investment, the overhead, and the prescription preparation, and an increment for profit. This total is defined as the drug distribution cost. To this may be added the additional cost resulting from the professional function.

Ingredient cost can be reduced by more efficient buying and through the exercise of product selection. The prescription preparation cost can be reduced through the use of ancillary personnel, counting machines, and computer technology. The overhead cost can be reduced by increasing productivity and volume. The profit increment is usually linked primarily to the ingredient cost and to the other costs, so therefore it is reduced accordingly. Chain stores and independently owned pharmacies that can control and reduce their drug distribution costs will remain and thrive in the marketplace.

Professional Function

The professional function are generally defined as one that is knowledge-based and independent of commodity costs. Medication profile review, monitoring of under- or overutilization of drugs, detection of problems associated with polydrug or polyprescribers, proper dosing, and storage are examples of professional functions.

Until payment for professional functions becomes separated from payment for distributive functions, providers of these functions will either not be a viable competitive force in the marketplace or, if they are, will have to subsidize the additional costs from other income.

If independently owned or chain drugstores equate their policies with recovering the cost of both functions from their prescription prices, their position in the marketplace will diminish. Thus, prescriptions will be provided by pharmacists who practice either in their own establishment or who are employees. Price competition will continue to draw the majority of patients until the need for the pharmacist's professional talent is sufficiently recognized, and is paid for as a separate item. Until that time, retail competition will continue to deal primarily with the cost of the distributive function.

References

1. Wertheimer, A. I.: Geographic Pharmacy Trading Patterns, Paper presented to the American Pharmaceutical Association Academy of General Practice, 1970. Washington, D.C.
2. McCarthy, E. J.: *Basic Marketing, A Managerial Approach,* Homewood, IL: Richard D. Irwin, 1964, pp. 508, 510.
3. Staudt, T. A., and Taylor, D. A.: *A Managerial Introduction to Marketing,* Englewood Cliffs, NJ: Prentice-Hall, 1965, p. 302.
4. *Drug Store News,* 1981.

## CHAPTER 19

International Marketing

BARRIE G. JAMES

Marketing drugs internationally is neither an unique or a new phenomenon. Many pharmaceutical companies, both United States-based and foreign-owned, have marketed ethical drugs outside their country of origin over an extended period of time.

The impetus for the international development of the pharmaceutical industry, the way in which companies organize for overseas marketing, and the international operating environment for multinational pharmaceutical companies, although similar in many respects to other industries, have many unique business characteristics. Similarly, although close comparisons between the domestic and international approaches to marketing pharmaceuticals can be made, there are a number of distinct differences in both degree and in kind between the two types of marketing.

Developmental Impetus

Various interrelated factors have accelerated the move from the domestic to the international marketing of pharmaceuticals, particularly since the end of World War II:

- The continuous advances in pharmaceutical technology leading to the development of more efficacious drugs with lower side-effects profiles and the ability to produce large quantities of drugs.

- Worldwide public demand for higher quality and greater quantities of ethical drugs, aided by the formation of public and private health-care systems that were themselves a product of government interest and involvement in the well-being of the population at large.

- The continuous conversion by physicians to the prescribing of more sophisticated and effective drugs.

- Relative economic and political stability combined with a large growth in real incomes in the industrialized countries.

Environment for International Marketing

The demand for ethical drugs is reflected by the environment of the marketplace. In international marketing there are a number of environmental factors influencing demand.

Demographic Characteristics

Total population size, growth and birth rates, age and sex distribution, degree and trends of urbanization, occupational profiles, education, affluence, and real reductions in inequalities of access to health care are major demand determinants.

Disease Incidence and Trends

Mortality and morbidity are important demand factors. Birth and infant mortality, diseases of the elderly and middle-aged, and intractable ill health in all age groups exert considerable pressures on both the total and specific demands for ethical drugs.

In industrialized countries the main disease problems, which are expected to continue, are those linked to degenerative diseases, a feature of the aging population such as respiratory diseases, and mental illness. In developing countries disease patterns tend to be a function of a combination of poor education, low public and personal health-care standards, poverty, malnutrition, and high birth rates. In less developed countries drugs tend to be relied on more heavily than in industrialized countries due to the lower per capita number of available physicians and hospital facilities. Drugs tend to constitute a higher proportion of total health-care costs in the less developed countries because they reduce physician time and the use of high-cost hospital facilities. Generally, the lower the socioeconomic and technological profile of a country, the higher is the physician reliance on drugs as a compensatory factor.

Social Environment

Affluence has increased population mobility and in turn transportation accidents, industrialization and technological innovation have increased industrial hazards, the pace and pressures of modern living have potentiated mental illness and violence, changes in morality have increased the incidence of abortions, venereal disease, and drug addiction, and excesses of eating, drinking, and smoking have all served both to change and increase the demand patterns of ethical drugs. In general, the more complex the environment, the more complex are health problems and their treatment.

Health-Care Systems

The increasing availability of public and private health-care systems to large sections of the world's population, particularly in the industrialized nations, has greatly affected the demand for ethical drugs. Although the concept of government responsibility for public health care is fairly old, the practical application is entirely a twentieth century phenomenon. Governments initially became involved in the regulation of health-care standards, providing partial financial support, and have moved gradually into the area of direct provision of health-care systems.

The current provision of health-care systems throughout the world falls largely between the extremes of the almost completely free enterprise system of the United States, which has low levels of public funding and control, to the Soviet Union, which operates a completely public-financed and controlled health-care system with no private services. Even the United States is now moving into the area of public services, because both the Medicaid and Medicare programs are beginning to gather momentum, and complete public health-care services have even been proposed.

Many health-care systems have introduced measures to reduce overprescribing by the physician and overconsumption by the patient. In the former case the number of prescriptions is monitored, and in the latter case the level of reimbursement for drugs is partially covered by the health-care system.

Almost all governments today require registration of ethical drug products. That is, the government accepts the manufacturers' claims that the product is efficacious and that the drugs' effects are acceptable within certain defined conditions and dosage levels. This acceptance is based either on the government's own trials of the product or on those carried out by the manufacturer, which have been conducted under defined conditions. Registration of an ethical drug product is an indispensable requirement if a drug product is to be marketed successfully.

Climatic Conditions

Climatic conditions lead to varying demand levels for certain types of products, whether they are seasonal, such as anti-allergy products, or one time, such as the severity and duration of winter on the incidence of respiratory diseases. Differing climates produce different demand levels. For example a high British incidence of respiratory ailments can be contrasted with endemic tropical disease in West Africa. Public and personal health-care standards also affect demand patterns significantly. Short-lived epidemics, such as the influenza epidemic of the Hong Kong variety in 1967 to 1968, and the Hungarian strain of 1974 to 1975, influence demand patterns in the short-term period for certain types of drugs.

Medical Practice

Both the quality and quantity of medical assistance available, and diagnostic and treatment techniques, which vary widely, influence consumption patterns in both the type and form of administration of ethical drugs.

In developing countries combination drugs are frequently used as a "shotgun" therapy, in which mixed infections are presumed to be present in an environment whether neither the patient nor the government can afford the time or cost of lengthy diagnoses. In certain countries, mainly the more developed ones, the antibiotic chloramphenicol is restricted to the treatment of typhoid fever, owing to its side-effects, whereas in other countries, often less developed, it is the most favored broad-spectrum antibiotic. In North America and Britain, suppositories are little used, while in many Latin countries the use of suppositories is one of the main forms of drug administration.

The overall number of physicians in both general and specialist practice, the number of physicians under contract to public and private health-care systems, the educational level and local standards of medical practitioners, the number of patient visits per physician, the number of drugs prescribed per visit, the average price per drug prescription, and the unit volume of drugs supplied per prescription are also critical factors that affect the demand for drugs.

Organizational Approaches

The first approach by many drug companies to overseas markets was the export of finished goods in response to orders obtained from company-appointed agents. For example, Schering AG of Germany established an agent, Schering and Glatt, in New York in 1894 to handle its business in the United States. An extension of this export policy was company-operated sales forces overseas that fed export orders to the parent company. An early example of formation of a company export sales force was in 1919 when

Eli Lilly sent salesmen to China, Mexico, and the Philippines.

To manage this low-risk and low-cost operation the early organization structures were simple, designed to handle the basically administrative nature of credit and shipping to overseas customers. In most respects the Export Departments, as they were usually called, lacked the scale and depth of operations of their domestic counterparts, and were heavily dependent on their domestic associates for both the supply of finished goods and various support services.

Although some companies had established overseas operations between the 1880s and 1920s, until the late 1940s the industry was split between fine chemical companies, who developed and produced active ingredients, and dosage formulators, who packaged pharmaceuticals for sale to retail outlets. The availability of many new synthetic compounds during the 1940s and 1950s revolutionized the pharmaceutical industry and led to both forward and backward integration, which produced the modern fully integrated pharmaceutical company. The availability of a wide range of synthetic compounds and the advent of public health-care systems, coupled with a surge in economic prosperity and political stability, created a tremendous growth in the international pharmaceutical market. At this point many governments began to exert pressure, through regulatory and tariff barriers, for the indigenous production of drugs.

These circumstances required a local presence, either through a surrogate, such as a licensee or a joint venture partner, or by the company itself. The former routes tended to be adopted by the smaller companies, who lacked the resources for global expansion or in areas that were subject to either political or economic uncertainty or in which the market because of size was uneconomic or too complex.

For those companies that selected a direct investment strategy, various new demands were placed on the Export Department, which required a new and integrated approach to servicing these demands. For example, the need for direct investment created a demand for expertise in financing, building, equipping, maintaining, staffing, and operating overseas facilities. As the number of these facilities increased a larger, more formalized and sophisticated infrastructure was required to administer, service, and monitor activities in as many as 50 countries on 5 continents. The demands were such that most large scale American-based pharmaceutical companies had, by the mid-1960s, renamed their overseas operations center as the International Division, which more adequately reflected both the role and size of the foreign business interests of these companies.

This change in operating philosophy came somewhat later for

the Americans than for the Europeans. The domestic markets in Europe are much smaller than that of the United States; for example, the typical Swiss pharmaceutical company obtains 95 to 97% of its sales volume outside Switzerland and German companies 60 to 70% outside their home market, in contrast to domestic companies, few of whom obtain more than 50% of their pharmaceutical sales revenue outside the United States. The European companies were in fact more international far sooner than their American counterparts because of both business and geographic necessity. By the early 1980s a further change in organization was beginning to occur in the United States.

The growing similarity between regulatory demands in various countries, new communications technology, and the increasing costs of research and development began to require that a coordinated approach be taken to managing the entire pharmaceutical operation as a single business rather than as disparate domestic and international divisions. Although some companies maintain separate operating divisions under a central pharmaceutical management other companies, such as Syntex, are in the process of consolidating their entire pharmaceutical operations under one management as a strategy to meet the new challenges posed by a market which now has to be viewed as a global market rather than as a number of individual markets separated by political boundries.

International and Domestic Pharmaceutical Marketing

Differences of Degree

Although the United States vies with Japan as the largest single drug market in terms of sales volume, the United States only represents less than 25% of the free world pharmaceutical market. A major position in the United States market is strategically important to any drug company, but if this policy is conducted to the exclusion of securing similar positions in the major markets, which are collectively larger than that of the United States, the strategic value of a global business operation is weakened.

The marketing of ethical drugs in a market as competitive and as large in both population and geographic area such as the United States is a formidable task. The American marketer is faced with 50 integral markets in which it is possible and normal to launch a new product or to revise marketing tactics simultaneously. The international marketer, however, is faced with a much larger scale of operations in over 100 countries, which range in size from approximately that of the United States market, such as Japan, to as small as that of the Republic of Nauru in the Pacific, with a population of 8000.

Differences in Kind

The international marketer is faced with a number of major differences between the United States and overseas markets in the kind of business that international pharmaceutical marketing entails. Differences in culture, language, religious convictions, political affinities, climatic conditions, and economic circumstances are immediately apparent. These factors influence government attitudes toward health care, the medical infrastructure, the quality and quantity of health-care delivery, and diagnostic and treatment practices, which in turn affect consumption patterns in both types and forms of ethical drugs used.

In many respects the American drug market is both highly sophisticated and relatively mature. Although this position is shared by a number of markets in northern Europe, Canada, and Australasia many markets in Latin America, Africa, and Asia are largely embryonic and are in rapid phases of growth. These differences in kind require an individualized approach according to country in order for a company to maximize its opportunities among a large number of dissimilar circumstances.

Le Défi Américain and European Revenge

After World War II many American-based drug companies followed the trend of United States businesses in establishing overseas operating companies, complementing companies such as Parke, Davis that began operations in London as early as 1891. These companies were in an excellent position both to attain and maintain market leadership in many countries immediately following 1945. German companies, which had dominated both research and world trade in pharmaceuticals up to 1939, were no longer an effective force with their research teams disbanded, their factories gutted, and their patents void. In addition, various countries with substantial pharmaceutical companies, such as France, the Netherlands and Britain, were undergoing reconstruction as a result of the war. Only the Swiss companies were in a position to react competitively to the United States challenge in a significant manner.

The key factor behind the early success of the American drug companies was technological leadership. A number of important pharmacologic innovations in United States, particularly in the antibiotic and corticosteroid fields, produced a virtual revolution in the pharmaceutical marketplace.

Technological leadership coupled with adequate resources and a lack of organized competition enabled many of the larger American drug companies to secure important market positions individually and these companies, in several large markets, became collectively the largest national group of companies. A wave of American companies established overseas operations in the late 1940s and 1950s that complemented the companies established earlier, and were in turn complemented by a number of medium-sized American companies, such as Schering-Plough, which began a major expansion during the mid- to late 1960s. In the late 1970s these companies were, in turn, augmented by newer companies such as Dow, Revlon, and Syntex that, primarily through acquisition, sought to broaden the international aspect of their pharmaceutical operations.

Although this competition would normally have increased the level of United States participation in foreign markets, various factors inhibited further American market penetration. No company or country has a long-term exclusive position in pharmaceutical technology, because the patent system alerts competitors to new technology. In addition to developing existing pharmaceutical technology significant new technological advances were made in Europe; for example, Denmark (purified insulin), Germany (diuretics), France (antihistamines), Sweden (anethestics), Switzerland (vitamins and tranquilizers) and Britain (beta blockers and semisynthetic penicillins). Japan also (antibiotics and cytostatic agents) became a new source of innovation. Along with the increase in technological competition was the dampening effect in the United States of the Kefauver-Harris Amendment in 1961 to the Food, Drug and Cosmetic Act of 1938, which imposed serious regulatory controls over the American-based companies that made pharmaceutical research and development a more time-consuming and costly endeavor.

Aiding this challenge to United States supremacy were a number of additional factors. Many of the large European and Japanese companies were themselves part of larger organizations that, attracted by the high margin of specialty chemicals, provided considerable funding for their pharmaceutical subsidiaries. In some countries both the nationalism and protectionism of indigenous companies inhibited the expansion of foreign-owned companies, including those from the United States.

The growth of these foreign competitors, who had the technological capability, financial resources, and a pressing need to amortize the increasing costs of pharmaceutical research and development over a worldwide rather than a national market has led to a strategy of attempting to penetrate the American domestic market. Although a number of the larger foreign-based companies have operated in the United States for many years (Hoffmann LaRoche—1905, Burroughs-Wellcome—1906, Ciba-Geigy—1921) the big influx of foreign companies into the American market only occurred during the 1970s. A further factor that encouraged foreign interest in the American market was the steady decline in the parity of the United States dollar against the major foreign currencies from the mid-1970s, which lowered the cost and therefore the risk of building up business operations in the United States.

The preferred entry route into the American market during the 1970s was almost exclusively through the acquisition of a local company. This entry strategy followed the low risk attitude of the new competitors who sought to augment their policy of minimizing entry costs in a large volume and large geographic market by purchasing the expertise and experience necessary to negotiate the critical interface with government and the multifaceted marketing system.

The circular effect of the American challenge overseas and the foreign counterchallenge in the United States market illustrates the fluidity of competition within the pharmaceutical industry on a global scale, and discounts any theory of long-term exclusivity of company or country dominance in the marketplace.

Future Considerations

The universality of need and usage of pharmaceutical products, the increasing economic interdependence of the world, and the growth in communications technology suggest that the pharmaceutical business must be viewed as a global market rather than as a collection of disparate national markets. Although this is reality in the macro sense for the corporate allocation of resources for research and development, finance, manpower, and production capacity, marketing in a micro sense must be fully geared to individual market characteristics and nuances, to specific local regulations, and to promotion techniques appropriate for gaining a market share in a highly competitive environment. The greatest challenge to future success for the multinational pharmaceutical company will be the effectiveness of the balance struck between resource allocation on a corporate level and the flexibility for marketing the end product efficiently in a collection of heterogeneous markets that have widely differing operating characteristics.

## PART V

Controls

CHAPTER **20**

Internal Controls

ALFRED A. MANNINO

An athlete who consistently excels in a particular sport may be described as having "good control" in that he exhibits the ability to coordinate his resources—speed, power, agility, and skill—with the rules of the sport in a manner that results in victory most of the time. The word "control," therefore, can be closely associated with the word "success," at least in this limited context: the athlete who controls the environment of his sport frequently wins, while the one who does not control the environment rarely wins.

This special relationship of control and success extends into other areas, as well; it may be readily observed in many different activities, from operating an automobile to obtaining an education to pursuing a career in a business or profession. Furthermore, the key element of control—the coordination of resources with rules—remains constant from one activity to another. Expanding on the automobile analogy, for example, we find that the driver who is able to coordinate his automotive resources (steering, acceleration, braking, and mechanical potential) with the traffic rules (regulations and accepted procedures) is "in control"—and he will probably experience little trouble in reaching his destination. But the driver who is not able to coordinate these resources and rules stands a good chance of being "out of control"—and the probability of a safe arrival becomes a matter of conjecture.

Similarly, a marketing company that places a great deal of emphasis on controlling its business environment is more likely to achieve its goals and objectives than is a company that just lets nature take its course. The marketplace is extremely complex and perpetually demanding; companies that cannot control their own activities have very little hope of surviving the competitive pressures for long. For this reason, most successful marketing companies can point to effective internal controls that they regularly use as guides for their planning, production, distribution, and marketing.

Internal controls, of course, cannot guarantee success for a marketing company—there are no guarantees in a truly competitive, free enterprise system. Internal controls, though, can be instrumental in helping a company prevent the antithesis of success—failure. The halls of the bankruptcy courts are strewn with the empty husks of marketing companies that missed too many opportunities and risked too much, and postmortem examinations of those companies would probably reveal that they did not have effective internal controls to provide them with advance warning of the problems that eventually proved fatal.

Role of Internal Controls

A pharmaceutical marketing company* is a highly complex organization that requires the application of many different business disciplines and the allocation of many different resources. Even a small company will become involved in the full range of marketing activities sooner or later: laboratory research, product development, production, packaging, financial planning, personnel administration, advertising, professional communications and, of course, sales. In this respect, the potential for organizational complexity, all pharmaceutical marketing companies are similar.

There is another point of similarity, one that is grounded in the utmost simplicity—a pharmaceutical marketing company will exist only as long as it continues to fulfill patient needs and investor desires. Fulfilling patient needs means contributing in some way to better health care; fulfilling investor desires means providing a reasonable return on investment.

This fundamentally simple fact of business life is often overlooked by the industry observer or company manager who becomes involved in the complexities of day-to-day operations; unfortunately, it is an oversight that can prove to be painfully expensive. If a company successfully meets both these standards, fulfilling patient needs and investor desires, it will assure its own continuity in the marketplace. If a company fails to meet either of these two standards, however, it will eventually cease to exist as a company; physicians just will not prescribe, and patients will not buy, products that do not contribute to better health care. By much the same token, investors will not be inclined to support a company that does not provide a reasonable return on investment.

---

*In the context of this chapter, the term "pharmaceutical marketing company" is used to denote a profit-oriented organization that develops, manufactures, and distributes pharmaceutical products. Most of the internal control principles suggested here, however, are applicable in some degree to wholesalers and retailers as well.

Between the organizational complexity and the fundamental simplicity lies a serious problem: how does a manager coordinate the various business disciplines and resources so that patient needs and investor desires are consistently fulfilled? The problem can be illustrated by two pieces of data: industry sources estimate that it requires an average of 8 years of effort and more than $50 million of investment to bring a new pharmaceutical product to the marketplace from the time of discovery to first sale (this average includes time and money expended on compounds that never become actual products for one reason or another). A pharmaceutical marketing company can ill afford errors in judgment, timing, or positioning when such numbers are involved, and errors are quite possible, given the complexity of the organizational structure and the company's interrelated activities.

The solution to the problem, or at least the part of the solution that will be dealt with in this chapter, is to control as much as possible the various disciplines and resources involved in bringing a product to the marketplace and keeping it there successfully for its anticipated lifetime. The word "control" in this sense simply means *effective management.* Individual internal controls, therefore, are simply management tools used in the normal course of business.

Internal controls can take many different forms, from routine interoffice communications to sales representatives' daily call reports to more sophisticated computerized budget and expense statements (specific examples will be outlined later in this chapter). Some internal controls are occasionally criticized by line personnel as being nothing more than "unnecessary paperwork" and "administrative red tape," and this may be the case if the controls are not properly conceived and carefully structured. Internal controls can be extremely valuable, however, if they reflect certain positive qualities. Effective internal controls, for example, should be pragmatic (workable), comprehensive (broadly inclusive), intelligible (easily understood), and measurable (capable of being evaluated). In addition, internal controls should be useful, and this is perhaps the most important quality they can have. A manager uses controls to make his job easier and his work better, so a control mechanism should not present obstacles to efficiency nor become a burden to accomplishment. Inherent within this quality of usefulness is the stipulation that internal controls should be self-motivating; they should offer clearcut rewards ("If I use this control, my project will be completed on time") and impose specific penalties ("If I don't use it, my project will not be completed on time"). This aspect of reward and penalty helps to ensure the actual application of internal controls once they are established within the company.

The need for effective internal controls has grown more acute in recent years, and the controls subsequently initiated by pharmaceutical marketing companies in response to this need have become considerably more complex. The heightened level of health-care sophistication has played its part, of course; rapid molecular development, advanced diagnostic procedures, and greater awareness by both physicians and patients—all of these have presented new challenges to marketing managers.

Operating costs in all areas have continued to climb, creating serious problems for companies that want to remain competitive. Tougher governmental regulations and more involved testing and licensing procedures have dramatically increased the amount of time, labor, and paperwork required to bring a new product to the marketplace. Research and development expenses alone have more than tripled in the last 10 years, with an estimated 80% of the industry's research and development (R & D) budgets earmarked for new products. These financial pressures are made even more significant by the fact that companies can no longer count on having the full 17 years of patent protection after introducing a new product. The patent clock starts ticking when the product is discovered and—if it takes an average of 8 years to move from discovery to first sale—a company only has about 9 years in which to recover the developmental costs.

The role of internal controls in a pharmaceutical marketing company is an important one, important because controls are essential if a manager is to properly execute his responsibilities to his own personal goals, to his department's function, and to his company. By extension, it can also be inferred that internal controls are instrumental in helping a company meet the standards required for continued existence—that is, the fulfillment of patients' needs and the fulfillment of investors' desires.

Controllable Aspects of Marketing

Under ideal conditions a company would be able to control all aspects of marketing, thereby developing a new pharmaceutical product effortlessly, bringing it to the marketplace smoothly, and capturing universal awareness, total acceptance, and maximum sales volume immediately. Unfortunately, ideal conditions do not now exist and are unlikely to come into existence. There will always be the possibility of snags in the development process, there will always be competition, and there will always be problems with communications, awareness, and acceptance. The manager in a pharmaceutical marketing company, therefore, must simply adapt to whatever conditions are encountered and try to control what can be controlled.

Not all factors, of course, can be controlled. There are quantitative and qualitative aspects of marketing that offer varying degrees of opportunity and challenge. To a large measure, the quantitative aspects of marketing are directly controllable and the qualitative aspects are not, although it is sometimes possible to influence the qualitative aspects and thereby control them indirectly. To clarify this point, consider the art of poetry. Essentially, the poet has four resources with which to work: words, rhyme, meter, and imagery. Of these four aspects of poetry, the first three are quantitative—they can be measured accurately and the poet can, consequently, control them with reasonable certainty. But the fourth aspect, imagery, is qualitative; it cannot be premeasured because its value (or weight or impact) depends on how the reader subsequently perceives it and reacts to it. The poet, therefore, cannot control the effect of imagery directly, but he can influence how it will be perceived by carefully selecting imagery that is universal and profound—and in this manner he exercises indirect control.

The same principle applies in marketing. A manager in a pharmaceutical marketing company can almost always establish direct control over the quantitative aspects of marketing, such as product characteristics (e.g., molecular structure, efficacy, and packaging) and corporate risks or resources (production costs, pricing levels, size and activity of the sales force). The qualitative aspects of marketing, however, such as public awareness and individual motivation of sales representatives, can be controlled only insofar as the manager can influence them. This can usually be done by properly utilizing certain controllable quantitative aspects of marketing; increased advertising can raise public awareness, for example, and periodic evaluation of individual effort can improve the performance of sales representatives.

It should be apparent from what has been discussed so far that some factors are more controllable than others. The corollary—an important one—is that some factors are less controllable than others. Interestingly, these less controllable aspects of marketing are those that tend to cry out the loudest for the initiation of effective internal controls, primarily because they can subsequently determine the company's degree of success. It is a relatively simple matter, for example, to manage the size of the sales force because size is quantitative and, therefore, is directly controllable; all that needs to be done is to add or subtract qualified people. It is generally difficult, on the other hand, to manage the effectiveness of the sales force because effectiveness is qualitative in nature and is subject only to indirect control. Given these aspects of the sales force, size and effectiveness, most managers would agree that internal controls are potentially more valuable when they are applied to the less controllable of the two.

Appropriate Control Points

There are literally hundreds of different control mechanisms that can be developed within the flow of product evolution and the framework of a pharmaceutical marketing company. Although most may be tried almost anywhere, this does not mean that they will be automatically successful; a manager may discover that a control mechanism is nonproductive, or even counterproductive, if it is applied at the wrong point. An internal control designed to monitor the level of expense accounts, for example, would undoubtedly be ineffective if the control point were centered at the regional sales management level, with no control authority extending to national management. It is important, therefore, to specify what is to be controlled and to know where the appropriate control points are.

With respect to the first half of this equation—specifying what is to be controlled—there are three basic categories of controllable resources: time, money, and events. The time category may be specified by the manager as either an active span (days, weeks, or months) or as a static point on the calendar (a deadline). Money is a category that consists of dollars budgeted, spent, or received; as such, everything that can be translated into dollars is considered money, including the time and labor of managers, staff, and employees. The events category includes all actions, activities, and projects; filling out a call report and drawing up a budget are events, as are the completion of a product brochure, the convening of a staff conference, and the filing of documentation required by federal regulations.

The second half of the equation, knowing where the appropriate control points are, is equally straightforward; time controls are appropriate and useful wherever timing is decided or applied, money controls are properly initiated wherever finances are allocated, spent, or collected, and events controls are applicable wherever actions, activities, or projects are planned or completed. Notice that the control points are described as being most appropriate at those personnel levels at which authority actually exists—that is, where timing is decided or applied, where finances are allocated, spent, or collected, and where projects are planned or completed. A control mechanism would be inappropriately applied at a level at which the individual did not have both the responsibility and the authority to exercise it.

Up to this point, the basic control categories and control points have been presented so that they appear to be quite simple, but there is a caveat: nothing is ever as simple as it seems. The flow of product evolution from concept to discontinuance involves thousands of complex interactions between time, money, and events, not to mention the many levels of authority that exist within the company's organizational structure and the innumerable spheres of influence in the marketplace that exist outside the structure. These complex interactions and spheres of influence call for internal controls of a highly sophisticated nature if the company is to coordinate and manage the resources at its command effectively.

The actual number and scope of internal controls suitable for a particular pharmaceutical marketing company will, of course, vary according to certain factors. The size and economic involvement of a company, for example, both have direct bearings on the number of controls it will need to initiate and their complexity. A small company with a relatively low dollar volume may be easier to control than a large company with a high dollar volume. On the other hand, a small company with a high dollar volume may find it necessary to employ rather sophisticated control mechanisms to protect its investment.

The activity spectrum of a company is also important in determining how many controls are appropriate and how extensive they should be. Some manufacturers deal only with wholesalers, and their control programs would not necessarily be complex. Manufacturers dealing directly with wholesalers, retailers, physicians, and the buying public, however, as well as with corporate shareholders, potential investors, and the financial community, usually find that a greater number of more sophisticated controls are needed in order to ensure that time, events, and money are handled efficiently and effectively.

The success of any single control mechanism largely depends on a series of value judgments that are applied at the control point by the individual with the responsibility and the authority. These value judgments are (1) initial evaluation, in which the need for a control is weighed and the control mechanism is planned, (2) implementation, in which the planned control is introduced and applied to the system, (3) reevaluation, in which the results of the control are periodically measured to see if it is working, and (4) adaptation, in which the control is changed or modified—or even abandoned—if it is not working properly.

In addition, a control mechanism must have one other characteristic if it is to be effective—it must be easy to use, requiring little or no thought or effort on the part of those who apply it. As mentioned previously, one positive quality of a control mechanism is that it makes a manager's job easier and his work better. A control that is difficult to use will only get in the way of efficiency, and will eventually fall of its own weight.

Another point should be stressed in this discussion of appropriate control points. Of the three categories of controllable resources—time, events, and money—time is probably the most critical because it is the major limiting factor on what may be accomplished by an individual. There are only so many hours in a working day and, once those hours have been expended, there is no way to make more. For this reason, a company is wise to initiate comprehensive time controls so that managers are encouraged to set priorities on their time, and subsequently on money and events as well.

Flow of Product Evolution

Brief mention has been made of the flow of product evolution; this is a term that requires clarification if the significance of the role played by internal controls in a pharmaceutical marketing company is to be fully comprehended. The flow of product evolution is connected directly to a pharmaceutical marketing company's primary raison d'être: the fulfillment of patient needs. A company is formed for the simple purpose of developing a product or products that will be effective for certain recognized diseases, ailments, or symptoms. These diseases, ailments, or symptoms describe the patient needs that are to be fulfilled. At some point in time these needs may be unfulfilled in the sense that there is no effective compound available or that existing compounds have certain undesirable side-effects. The physician may recognize the need but until a pharmaceutical company recognizes it and begins to work on fulfilling it, the flow of product evolution does not begin. Consequently, many future products have not yet even entered the flow of product evolution.

Once the patient need is recognized, however, the flow begins. The product proceeds through various stages: concept, discovery, creation, distribution, communication, exchange, return, and discontinuance. At each stage of a product's evolution there are numerous opportunities to apply effective controls that can help the marketing company achieve fulfillment of the patient need. There are also numerous opportunities *not* to apply controls, thereby risking failure.

At the concept stage, for example, it is possible to recognize the need and still misjudge its extent, a situation that can lead to overestimating the potential demand for the product. Similarly, the other stages in the flow of product evolution present significant opportunities and risks:

1. Discovery involves research and development, testing, and licensing, all expensive and time-consuming procedures.

2. Creation calls for production, packaging, and pricing.

3. Distribution entails the complex functions that make the product available at both the wholesale and retail levels.

4. Communication is required to advertise, promote, and explain the product's features, benefits, and applications to the health-care professionals who ultimately influence the product's usage.

5. Exchange occurs when the product is actually purchased at the retail level.

6. Return is necessary whenever a product is overstocked at the retail level, when there is product damage during shipping, or when there is diminished demand.

7. Discontinuance occurs at the end of a product's life cycle when it becomes obsolete, is replaced, or begins to show little or no profit for the marketing company.

It is simplistic, therefore, to think of internal controls only in terms of "product out, money in." The flow of product evolution is enormous in scope and challenge. The manager of a pharmaceutical marketing company who understands this will apply himself to learning the potential value of various control mechanisms and initiating them wherever practical to ensure the success of his company's products in the marketplace.

Organizing for Optimal Control

A pharmaceutical marketing company is a highly complex organization, a fact that need not cause anyone a great deal of concern because, although the word "complex" sometimes has undesirable connotations, there is really nothing undesirable or troublesome about complexity, as long as a certain degree of organization is applied. Biologic life, itself, is a highly complex matter, but the inhabitants of this planet have been able to manage well, thanks primarily to the structured organization that regulates the interactions of various life forms.

The basic organizational tool in a marketing company is a table of organization. Its purpose is to categorize the various business disciplines and resources clearly, establish levels of responsibility and authority, and delineate the paths of direction, instruction, and reporting. Properly applied, the table of organization can simplify the planning process, speed the flow and volume of work, and aid in the achievement of long range objectives and short-range goals. In this sense, the table of organization serves as a sort of overall control mechanism and as such warrants some discussion here.

It is probably safe to say that no two companies are organized exactly alike. A company's size, scope of activities, and marketing objectives—along with numerous other factors, including the personalities of top management—all influence the form of the table of organization. It is therefore impossible to present a single organizational model and to suggest that it should apply to all companies. Instead it is better merely to outline a hypothetic model stipulating that, however logical it may appear, such an organizational structure may not actually exist anywhere in the world of marketing.

Figure 20-1 shows such a hypothetical table of organization for daily business operations. Notice that the company's business disciplines have been segmented into five different categories or divisions—finance, administration, operations, research and development, and marketing—and that the vice president of each of these divisions reports directly to the president, who in turn reports directly to the board of directors. In this table of organization the functions of the finance, administration, operations, and research and development divisions have not been thoroughly detailed, while the marketing division has been detailed to a greater extent. The marketing division is organized into three distinct departments: marketing planning, market research, and sales. The first two are essentially involved in planning and development, while the latter has the responsibility of actually implementing the plans in the marketplace. The casual observer might conclude that a pharmaceutical marketing company's efforts are centered on its sales staff, but this table of organization clearly shows otherwise. The planning and development activities are at least as critical as the sales activities, especially if proper internal controls are utilized.

One other point should be emphasized in this discussion of the daily organization of a company. Any division within a company may be operating in a vacuum, so to speak, thereby losing contact with what is happening elsewhere within the company. The marketing division, for example, could easily pursue its own promotional efforts for a new product and might introduce the product to the market months before the manufacturing division is ready to fill orders. Or, the research and development division could encounter obstacles in its work, thereby creating unexpected delays that would have an adverse effect on the marketing division. In order to ensure continuing communications and avoid potentially serious problems, the table of organization provides for top level coordination between divisions; there are established liaisons, and therefore vital control points, between the vice presidents of marketing and finance, of marketing and operations, and of marketing and research and development.

The organizational structure detailed in Figure 20-1 may be suitable for most daily business operations, but it falls short of providing the type of control necessary for company-wide, special

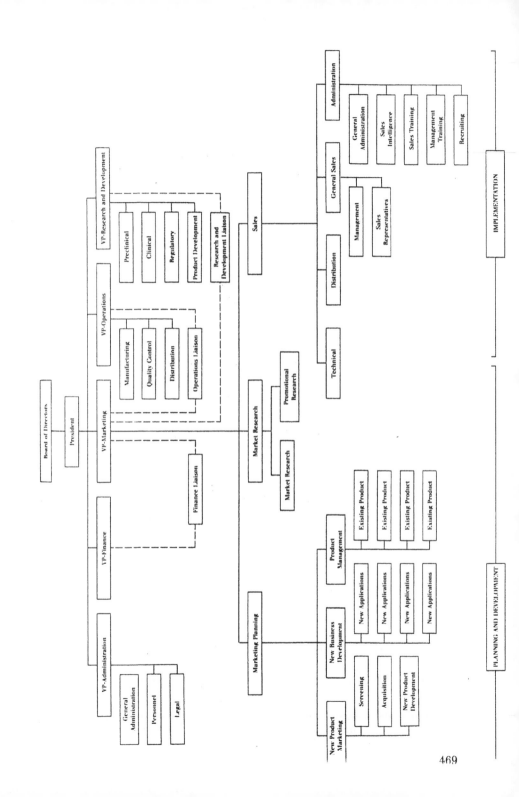

Board of Directors

President

VP-Administration
- General Administration
- Personnel
- Legal

VP-Finance

VP-Marketing

VP-Operations
- Manufacturing
- Quality Control
- Distribution
- Operations Liaison

VP-Research and Development
- Preclinical
- Clinical
- Regulatory
- Product Development
- Research and Development Liaison

Finance Liaison

Marketing Planning

Market Research
- Market Research
- Promotional Research

Sales
- Technical
- Distribution
- General Sales
  - Management
  - Sales Representatives
- Administration
  - General Administration
  - Sales Intelligence
  - Sales Training
  - Management Training
  - Recruiting

New Product Marketing
- Screening
- Acquisition
- New Product Development

New Business Development
- New Applications
- New Applications
- New Applications
- New Applications

Product Management
- Existing Product
- Existing Product
- Existing Product
- Existing Product

PLANNING AND DEVELOPMENT

IMPLEMENTATION

469

effort projects, such as the development of a new product from discovery to first sale. The reason for this is that the day-to-day table of organization shown is vertical in nature (the lines of responsibility and authority run vertically through each division), and does not allow for adequate coordination of activities horizontally between divisions. (The exception, of course, would be an interdivisional liaison such as the one just discussed, but this contact is generally considered to be more of a checkpoint than a structure for bringing a multitude of diverse disciplines and resources into play.)

One approach to controlling company-wide, special effort projects is outlined in Figure 20-2; which depicts an organizational structure for developing a new product. Notice that this hypothetical table of organization is comprised of three separate groups, one consisting of the company president and the divisional vice presidents (New Product Steering Committee), one consisting of selected staff members from the various divisions (New Product Development Team), and the other consisting of a group known as Program Management.

The members of the New Product Steering Committee serve permanently and are responsible for providing direction, approving plans, and coordinating the activities of the New Product Development Team with the activities of the rest of the company. The members of the New Product Development Team, on the other hand, are assigned on a temporary basis—for the duration of a particular project—and have the responsibility of actually developing the new product as well as the authority to use other company resources from any division as the need arises. Once the new product has been introduced into the marketplace, the New Product Development Team is disbanded, the product becomes the responsibility of a product manager in the marketing division, and the day-to-day organizational structure becomes applicable. The Program Management group is another permanent organization charged with monitoring the activities of all programs and projects—developmental and in place—and, in this capacity, serves to provide the necessary ongoing horizontal control mentioned previously.

Internal Control Mechanisms

Time and Computerized Call Report System

Probably every pharmaceutical marketing company in the country uses some form of call report system to evaluate how their sales representatives spend their time in the field. If there are

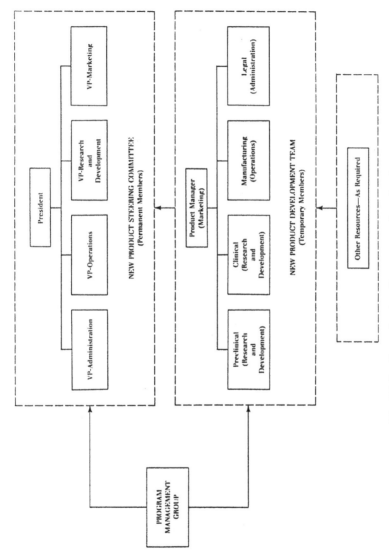

Fig. 20-2. *Organization for new product development*

some companies that do not use such a system, they are not paying enough attention to their most valuable and least renewable resource—time. A sales representative has only so many hours in a day and only so many days in a year to call on physicians, pharmacists, and hospitals. Even a half-day lost for some reason means that he is a half-day behind in the job his company expects him to do, and he will never be able to make up that half-day. In order for a company to be absolutely certain that its products are being presented properly according to the product manager's plan, the company needs to know how its representatives are utilizing their time.

The Computerized Call Report System shown in Figure 20-3 (in an abbreviated form) is not a babysitting procedure designed to force representatives to account for their time; professional sales representatives do not require, and would be offended by, such a procedure. Instead, the call report system outlined here is designed to provide management with some vital information: which products were presented during the reporting period, the physician specialties to which they were presented, the number of samples left behind, the number of physicians seen and their percentage of the total physician population in the representative's territory, and the average number of physicians seen in the course of a week during the reporting period, as compared with the average for the last four reporting periods. In addition the work summary indicates where the available time was spent if the sales representative was not making calls in his territory, a convenient way to see if sales meetings, vacations, or illness influenced the number of calls made.

The type of call report system shown in Figure 20-3 is initiated by the sales representative in the field. After each physician call, the representative fills out a card, providing the raw data for the computer. At the end of the day these cards are mailed to the company's headquarters. The data is processed there and the final computer printout is prepared. The printout shown here is for the end of a quarterly reporting period but the information could be made available at any time, thereby providing management with an up to date accounting of each sales representative's time—and a valuable control tool.

Events, Quarterly Tactics Composite, and Time and Events Schedule

Controlling the flow of events, ensuring that specific things are done by specific dates, becomes more difficult as the number and complexity of events increase. If one's only responsibility, for example, is to see to it that a letter is mailed before quitting time

TERRITORY/REPRESENTATIVE: 3101/DOE, JOHN W.   PERIOD: FOURTH QUARTER   ENDING: DEC. 31

PRODUCT DETAILED	CURRENT PERIOD DETAILS			CURRENT PERIOD PHYSICIANS DETAILED BY SPECIALTY									NUMBER OF SAMPLES LEFT	
	PRIMARY	SECONDARY	REMINDER	GP/FP	IM	CD	UROL	PD	GE/GI	N/NS	EM	OTHER	CURRENT PERIOD	FY TO DATE
Product A	22	12	78	68	16	3	1	12	1	1	2	8	915	3576
Product B	12	8	87	61	15	1	—	14	1	—	3	12	590	1948
Product C	10	4	25	6	1	—	13	12	—	2	—	4	152	260
Product D	165	47	35	156	46	8	1	1	6	—	4	25	2044	4720
Totals	209	71	225	291	78	12	15	39	8	3	9	49	3701	10504

CLASS	PHYSICIANS SEEN: CURRENT PERIOD				LAST FOUR PERIODS	
	POPU- LATION	NUMBER SEEN	PERCENT COVERAGE	WEEKLY AVERAGE	NUMBER SEEN	WEEKLY AVERAGE
1	2613	420	16.1	32.3	1291	24.8
2	834	37	4.4	2.8	147	2.8
3	852	24	2.8	1.8	120	2.3
4	3063	6	.2	.5	23	.4
Totals	7362	487	6.6	37.4	1581	30.3

WORK SUMMARY		
NUMBER OF DAYS	CURRENT PERIOD	FY TO DATE
Available	91.0	365.0
Worked	65.0	260.0
Off territory:	26.0	105.0
Sick	1.0	5.5
Vacation	.0	14.0
Holiday	3.0	7.0
Sales meeting	5.0	28.0
Sales training	1.5	5.0
Medical meeting	2.5	2.5
Vacant	13.0	43.0
Unreported	.0	.0

Fig. 20-3. *Computerized call report system*

today, there is no real cause for concern; it is a relatively simple chore. But if one's responsibility includes writing 24 letters, typing them, addressing and stamping the envelopes, and dropping the letters in the mailbox, then things start to get busy—especially if one must first call the printer and have the letterhead stationery printed.

Figure 20-4 represents a small part of a larger control mechanism used by one pharmaceutical company to outline promotional tactics and to ensure that the tactics are carried out on schedule. In this case the chart covers a period of 3 months (the second quarter of the year) and applies only to direct mail promotions for a single product. (In actual practice, the chart would include four or more tactical media in addition to direct mail—e.g., journal advertising, promotional material, etc.). The Tactics Composite at the top of the form provides a description of each mailing, a brief outline of each component of the mailing, the theme, target and audience, quantity needed, and mailing date. The Time and Events (T & E) Schedule shown lists each individual stage of production through which the promotional material must go before being mailed—for example, the promotional specifications must go to the advertising agency by a certain date, the copy and layout must be back from the agency by another date, and the compliance forms must be submitted by a certain time. All these job functions must be checked off on time in order for the mailing to go out as scheduled.

If one or more production job functions are not completed on schedule then the product manager is alerted by his T & E schedule; he immediately adjusts the subsequent job functions deadlines, reschedules the mailing, and notifies the other departments within the company as well as any wholesalers or retailers who might be involved. After all, these other marketing centers plan many of their events around the promotional efforts of the company and could experience serious problems if all promotional events were not properly coordinated. A tactics composite and T & E schedule such as the one shown in Figure 20-4 can be valuable in ensuring that coordination of effort.

Money and Departmental Expense Budget

Over the years businesses have developed many methods for controlling the flow of money, both in and out. Some of these control mechanisms are simple and some are complex; some are quite successful, some not quite so successful, and some do not work at all. This chapter does not purport to present a selection of these money control mechanisms, nor to argue their relative merits. It is sufficient to make one point: in the context of marketing, it

PRODUCT: ABC OINTMENT   QUARTER: SECOND   PROMOTIONAL MEDIUM: DIRECT MAIL

TACTICS COMPOSITE

DESCRIPTION	COMPONENTS	THEME	AUDIENCE	QUANTITY	MAIL DATE
Initial mailing	Brochure, samples, letter	Concepts in cardiology	Cardiologists, gastroenterologists	40 M	7/06
User mailing	Brochure, letter	Dosage availability	ABC ointment users	31 M	8/10
Monograph reprint	Editorial, ad reprint, letter	Concepts in cardiology	Cardiologists, gastroenterologists	40 M	9/14
Sample fulfillment	6 × 20 g-ointment, letter	Sample fulfillment	Responders	2 M	9/15
Wholesaler mailing	Fact sheets, selling sheets, letter	Profit potential	Wholesalers	5 M	8/15

TIME AND EVENTS (T&E) SCHEDULE

JOB FUNCTION	COMPLETION DATE		
	JUL.	AUG.	SEP.
Promotional specifications to agency	Done	Done	4/16
Copy and layout due from agency	Done	4/25	5/21
Compliance submission date	4/01	5/05	6/01
Approved copy and layout to agency	4/20	5/25	6/21
Mechanical due from agency	5/09	6/15	7/11
Mechanical to printer	5/19	6/25	7/21
Printed material from printer	6/06	7/10	8/06
Ship to mailing house	6/16	7/20	8/16

Fig. 20-4. *Quarterly tactics composite and T & E schedule*

is the responsibility of each individual manager to control the cash flow so that the company can prevent out-of-cash situations and meet its expense and timing obligations.

Figure 20-5 shows a basic departmental expense budget for one product assigned to one product manager. Each general budget item (e.g., journal advertising, direct mail, product literature) is allocated a certain amount of money for the year, which is then allocated by the product manager to cover certain monthly events. This is all done using the guidelines laid down by an overall, management-approved marketing plan; the product manager is subsequently evaluated by his adherence to this plan, both in terms of what is happening and how much it is costing.

A computer tracks each budget item or account and provides a monthly and quarterly printout of expenses charged to each account. By comparing the departmental expense budget (the plan) with the computer printout (the actual expenditures), the product manager can easily and conveniently see how closely he is following the marketing plan with regard to allocated money. If he has spent too much one month, he will probably want to cut back on expenses the next month. If he has spent too little, however, he may want to spend more the next month in order to get back in sync with the budget and with the marketing plan. Companies utilizing this type of money control mechanism generally believe that it is just as much a mistake to spend under budget as to spend over budget, because underbudget spending means that the marketing plan is not being implemented properly and that the product is not receiving the promotional thrust management originally intended.

Sales and Distribution/Inventory Monitoring System

Not too many years ago most marketing companies tended to measure their daily operations simply in terms of unit sales—the more product they could move through the door, the better off they thought they would be. Unfortunately for many companies, this approach to marketing ignored the fact that it is very easy for the distribution pipeline to become clogged with excess product. Consumer sales can suddenly decline for any number of reasons, causing overstocked shelves at the retail level, overstocked warehouses at the wholesaler level, and overstocked inventories at the manufacturing level. The result of such a situation is economic chaos all along the marketing chain.

Marketing companies have gone to great lengths to develop data collection and evaluation systems that can provide current information regarding the status of their products in the distribution pipeline. A simplified example of one such system is shown in

DEPARTMENT: __MARKETING PLANNING__   ACTIVITY: __PRODUCT MANAGEMENT__   PRODUCT: __ABC OINTMENT__

BUDGET ITEM: ACCOUNT TITLE	ACCOUNT NUMBER	JAN	FEB	MAR	APR	MAY	JUN	JUL	AUG	SEP	OCT	NOV	DEC	ACCOUNT TOTALS
Medical meetings	9322	—	500	500	500	1,000	1,000	500	1,000	1,000	1,000	500	500	8,000
Journal advertising	9350	4,000	4,000	—	10,000	10,000	10,000	26,000	20,000	25,000	20,000	20,000	15,000	164,000
Direct mail	9351	—	3,000	—	14,500	13,500	7,000	13,500	—	16,500	—	13,500	—	81,500
Product literature	9352	13,000	—	—	13,000	—	—	1,000	—	—	1,500	—	—	28,500
Direct mail samples	9365	3,000	3,000	4,000	3,000	3,000	4,000	3,000	3,000	4,000	3,000	3,000	4,000	40,000
Detail samples	9366	41,000	—	—	21,000	—	—	10,500	—	—	10,500	—	—	83,000
Monthly totals		61,000	10,500	4,500	62,000	27,500	22,000	54,500	24,000	46,500	36,000	37,000	19,500	
Quarterly totals				76,000			111,500			125,000			92,500	
Yearly total														405,000

Fig. 20-5. *Departmental expense budget*

Figure 20-6. Systems such as this were designed to provide reliable information regarding three key factors: (1) the number of
units of specific products that were shipped to retailers by wholesalers during a month (withdrawals); (2) the number of units of
specific products wholesalers had on hand at the end of a month
(inventory); and (3) the number of months' supply that inventory
constitutes for wholesalers (based on the previous month's withdrawal activity and expressed as a fraction—e.g., 1.5-months' supply equals 45 days and 0.1-month's supply equals 3 days).

Using a distribution/inventory monitoring system similar to
this, a company can learn a great deal about how its products are
performing in the distribution chain. The company's product
managers can then make appropriate plans to correct any apparent problems. In Figure 20-6, for example, XYZ tablets were reported in January as having only 8.592 million withdrawals from
wholesaler inventories, leaving the wholesalers with 133.2 million
units of the product—a 16 months' supply. Knowing that this inventory level was much too high, the product manager initiated a
sustained promotional program at the retail store and consumer
levels. By August, withdrawals had increased by about 5 million
units per month. Equally important, wholesaler inventories were
gradually reduced to a 4.5 months' supply—an improvement, certainly, but still not an acceptable level from a wholesaler's point of
view.

A distribution/inventory monitoring system can indicate when
a product is selling steadily, when its sales are oscillating up and
down, when it is experiencing the growth side of its life cycle, and
when it is on the decline near the end of its life cycle. All these
factors, and more, are of considerable importance to a pharmaceutical marketing company if it expects to control its many activities. One of the more important functions of a control mechanism
such as the one shown in Figure 20-6, however, is to provide a
valuable service to the marketing company's wholesalers and retailers by avoiding, wherever possible, those circumstances that
could lead to either overstock or out-of-stock situations.

Sales Performance and Evaluation by Territory

Individual performance by a company's field sales representatives is a qualitative factor that can be controlled only insofar as it
is possible to influence certain quantitative factors. As such, it is
an enormously complicated problem. Nevertheless, most companies realize the value of improving individual performance and
have made major progress by initiating evaluation techniques that
allow them to measure performance and to take corrective action
when appropriate. In the past, the term "corrective action" fre-

WHOLESALE AND CHAIN WITHDRAWALS AT MONTH'S END
(In thousands of units—number of months' supply shown in parentheses)

PRODUCT NAME	JAN	FEB	MAR	APR	MAY	JUN	JUL	AUG
ABC ointment—60 g	72,944 (1.5)	81,552 (1.3)	69,004 (1.2)	72,706 (1.0)	73,504 (1.1)	66,115 (1.2)	75,813 (1.9)	85,373 (1.4)
LMN caps—250s	20,598 (1.2)	22,662 (1.1)	21,314 (1.2)	24,000 (0.9)	21,182 (1.2)	20,147 (1.3)	20,763 (1.3)	21,740 (1.2)
XYZ tablets—100s	8,592 (16)	9,852 (12)	9,792 (11)	9,816 (9.8)	10,692 (7.7)	10,776 (7.1)	13,920 (4.9)	13,692 (4.5)

WHOLESALE AND CHAIN INVENTORY AT MONTH'S END
(In thousands of units—number of months' supply shown in parentheses)

PRODUCT NAME	JAN	FEB	MAR	APR	MAY	JUN	JUL	AUG
ABC ointment—60 g	112,629 (1.5)	109,315 (1.3)	80,816 (1.2)	74,271 (1.1)	77,271 (1.1)	76,198 (1.2)	145,082 (1.9)	115,918 (1.4)
LMN caps—250s	24,392 (1.2)	24,100 (1.1)	25,630 (1.2)	21,499 (0.9)	24,287 (1.2)	25,092 (1.3)	27,022 (1.3)	25,535 (1.2)
XYZ tablets—100s	133,200 (16)	119,376 (12)	107,364 (11)	95,832 (9.8)	82,164 (7.7)	82,500 (7.1)	67,656 (4.9)	61,800 (4.5)

Fig. 20-6. *Distribution/inventory monitoring system*

quently meant dismissal, but this is no longer the case. Marketing companies would much prefer to retain their experienced sales personnel and to help them improve their performance by providing additional training and counseling. In some cases, a problem with performance might be solved by reassigning a sales representative to another territory or by modifying the size of the existing territory.

Whatever the case, a company must first have a system with which to measure actual performance. An example of such a system is shown in Figure 20-7. The key to this system is that actual gross sales dollars (Total Retail Dollars on the computer printout) are considered only secondarily; instead, the primary emphasis is placed on how well each representative has done in relation to the calculated potential of his territory.

This potential is shown on the printout in Figure 20-7 as the Year-to-Date Market Value Index, a figure representing the percentage of sales the company might expect from that particular territory. The percentage itself is based on actual past sales performance as reported by the major pharmaceutical marketing companies participating in the system. Territory 3101, for instance, J. Doe's, territory, has a market value index of 1.47, which indicates how much J. Doe *could* sell in his territory if he were getting his fair share. According to the printout, J. Doe's sales are substantially above the market value index for his territory, with a sales index of 1.77 for the year and 1.86 for the last reported month. J. Doe's performance index, therefore, is 121 for the year and 122 for the month, which simply means that J. Doe is performing about 20% better than to be expected in this particular territory.

A sales performance evaluation by territory, such as this one, can be most useful in pinpointing sales problems of one sort or another. The printout in Figure 20-7 makes it clear, for instance, that W. Allen is performing close to the potential for his territory for the year (with a year-to-date performance index of 107), although he obviously experienced some trouble, probably temporary, last month (when his monthly performance index fell to 54). Other problems may also be seen in Figure 20-7. Both R. Brown and his company may benefit by assigning him to another territory other than 3104, preferably a territory that has a better market value index; as it is, he is doing as well or better than the potential for his territory, but the territory, with a market value index of only 0.85, is obviously too small. On the other hand, P. Johnson in territory 3105 is in trouble for a different reason. His performance index for the year is only 85, no doubt a result of the fact that his territory is too large for one person to handle (the market value index is 3.11). What the company should do is reduce the geo-

MANUFACTURER: ABC COMPANY

PERIOD ENDING: MARCH 31

TERRITORY OR AREA	REPRESENTATIVE	YEAR-TO-DATE MARKET VALUE INDEX	TOTAL RETAIL DOLLARS		SALES INDEX		PERFORMANCE INDEX	
			CURRENT MONTH	YEAR-TO-DATE	MONTH (%)	YEAR-TO-DATE (%)	MONTH (%)	YEAR-TO-DATE (%)
3101	Doe, J.	1.47	37,747	145,462	1.86	1.77	122	121
3102	Smith, A.	1.87	71,831	217,076	3.54	2.65	191	142
3103	Jones, K.	1.15	39,324	147,478	1.94	1.80	174	157
3104	Brown, R.	0.85	17,377	83,278	0.86	1.02	96	120
3105	Johnson, P.	3.11	34,873	146,894	1.72	1.79	83	85
3106	Allen, W.	1.16	39,324	147,478	0.64	1.24	54	107

Fig. 20-7. Sales performance evaluation by territory

graphic size of P. Johnson's territory, possibly giving the excess to
R. Brown's territory in order to eliminate the inequities.

Overall Control and Management by Objectives

In the course of day-to-day business it becomes easy to lose
sight of long-term objectives. The importance of the year-end profit figures, for example, may tend to fade into the background as a
manager focuses intently on the quarterly report that must be submitted today, on the pressing personnel problem that just will not
go away, or on the sales literature that is delayed at the printer
because the color separations are not right. No matter how honor-
able the intentions, it is possible to forget the intensity with which
we pledged ourselves to particular areas of self-improvement
12 months ago; generalized job objectives and New Year's resolu-
tions are similar in this respect.

Figure 20-8 shows an example of a control mechanism that can
be used to keep good intentions on the right track. This form, or
one similar to it, is used by managers in many companies to establish general objectives for themselves, to detail specific goals that
will ensure achievement of those objectives, to stipulate certain
methods by which performance toward those objectives and goals
may be measured, and to set dates for evaluation. Each manager
writes his own evaluation form, which is then reviewed by his
supervisor and amended if necessary. Eventually both parties
agree to the substance of the objectives, goals, and measurements.
The evaluation form is referred to frequently on a regular basis so
that the manager may continually evaluate his own performance
and make greater efforts if he finds himself falling short of reaching his goals.

In addition to the general objectives and specific goals shown
in Figure 20-8 (planning and sales/profit), a typical individual
evaluation might include the following performance categories:
expense management, forecasting, personal development, reporting, marketing materials, and profit improvement. If such a control mechanism is to be used successfully, however, it must have
three basic qualities. First, the manager must be able to set his
own goals, guided only by the company's overall plans and his
supervisor's counsel. Second, the general objectives must be
translated into specific and achievable goals, so that language
such as "prepare a strategic business plan for each product assigned" becomes action-oriented: "plans to be submitted . . . ,"
"plan to include . . . ," "submission of plans to be completed . . . ."
Finally, the manager's performance toward the specific goals
must be measurable in some substantive way—by an audit, by
indisputable data, or by confirmation by his supervisor.

NAME: __JOHN W. DOE__

GENERAL OBJECTIVES	VALUE (%)	SPECIFIC GOALS	METHOD OF MEASURING PERFORMANCE	EVALUATION PERIOD
I. *Planning objectives:* Prepare a strategic business plan for each product assigned (to include 1- and 3-year plans per division requirements)	20	A. Plans to be submitted covering all assigned products. B. Plan to include flex contingency section, fully allocated profit-and-loss statement for next FY, and pro-forma statement for 3 years C. Submission of plans to be completed prior to beginning of third quarter	Submission and acceptance of plans on schedule	Third quarter
II. *Sales/profit objectives:* Effectively manage and coordinate the marketing of all assigned products to achieve sales, profit contribution, and market penetration goals of the product line	15	A. *XYZ antacid:* 1. Maintain market share above 18% 2. New prescriptions for fiscal year to exceed 875,000 3. Gross product profit contribution to equal or exceed profit plan	A. IMS audit data B. Market research reports C. End-of-year gross profit figures	Fiscal year
		B. *ABC ointment:* 1. Attain an 8% market share of the anti-anginal market 2. New prescriptions for the product line to exceed 750,000 3. Gross product profit contribution to equal or exceed profit plan	A. IMS audit data B. Market research reports C. End-of-year gross profit figures	Fiscal year

Fig. 20-8. *Partial format for individual evaluation of performance*

Other Control Mechanisms

In this chapter we have discussed only a few of the hundreds of control mechanisms currently in use by pharmaceutical marketing companies. Even within the limitations of a single controllable category there are dozens or different ways to approach the same problem, so that the control mechanism used by Company A to monitor the production of promotional literature, for example, may be totally different from that used by Company B for the same purpose. It is possible therefore for a manager to move from one company to another and be confronted with new and challenging control mechanisms every step of the way. This should not be a cause for concern; if the control works for a company, it should be retained. The significant point to remember for a manager who reads this chapter is the importance of being able to specify what is to be controlled and to know where the appropriate control points are.

## CHAPTER 21

External Controls

GARY C. WILKERSON
and
MICHAEL A. PIETRANGELO

Pharmaceutical marketing is influenced by a variety of external controls. These controls may be imposed by numerous factions, including congressional enactment at both the federal and state levels, judicial decisions, public opinion stimulated by journalists and public interest groups, and industry or peer pressure resulting in self-regulation. They may be applied directly, such as limitation of production quotas of controlled substances, and indirectly, such as restrictions on drug advertising and pricing.

The most obvious encroachment on free and unrestrained marketing of pharmaceuticals is congressional enactment of federal and state statutes, regulations, and ordinances. In the United States, promulgation of major federal laws directly affecting prescription and over-the-counter (OTC) drugs frequently resulted from public pressure stimulated by exposure and adverse reaction to pharmaceuticals and their methods of manufacture and distribution. For example, serving as impetus for passage of the 1938 Federal Food, Drug and Cosmetic Act, was the tragedy in which numerous deaths occurred following ingestion of Elixir of Sulfanilamide. This disaster expedited approval of the act and represented the first congressional activity in this area in over 30 years. Additionally, the European experience in the early 1960s with thalidomide, a drug available in the United States at that time only on an experimental basis, precipitated passage of the Harris-Kefauver Amendments to the 1938 Act requiring, among other things, that drugs be proven effective as well as safe.

State legislatures have also been active. Their passage of anti-substitution laws, preventing pharmacists from substituting a generically equivalent drug for a brand-name medication pre-scribed by a physician, directly affect pharmaceutical marketing. These state enactments have been subjected to severe criticism in recent years.

The judiciary has had a profound effect upon the marketing of pharmaceuticals. Courts have considered cases involving a broad spectrum of issues that affect pharmaceuticals. For example, deci-sions involving the culpability of corporate officers exercising apparent supervisory authority, or the lack of it, in the manufac-ture and distribution of foods and drugs have had a substantial impact on both industries by imposing strict criminal liability in certain instances. Furthermore, recent holdings by federal judges and appellate courts regarding premarket clearance of new drugs and the procedures and requirements will therefore not affect marketing strategies of pharmaceutical companies lightly.

Public opinion, influenced by muckrakers such as Upton Sin-clair and Samuel Hopkins Adams and public interest organiza-tions such as the Health Research Group and the American Asso-ciation of Retired Persons, has proved a decisive weapon. These authors and organizations have significantly affected public policy and opinion about such issues as the need for food and drug legis-lation, repeal of antisubstitution laws, development of patient package inserts, and safety and efficacy requirements for drugs. The decade of the 1970s has revealed an ever increasing power wielded by these organizations, particularly in the legislative arena.

Lastly, but its effect should not be minimized, the pharmaceuti-cal industry and its member firms, individually and collectively through trade organizations, have been active in developing regu-lations and guidelines directly affecting the marketing of its prod-ucts. For example, in an effort to protect and ensure the strength, quality, and purity of medications, companies have assisted in the development and implementation of good manufacturing prac-tices (GMPs). By permitting Food and Drug Administration (FDA) investigators to view and inspect manufacturing processes and records, even beyond that required by law, companies have helped the FDA to become aware of the industry's capabilities and current practices. Then, responsive to the FDAs proposed GMP regulations, as published in the *Federal Register,* drug firms have participated actively by suggesting amendments and corrections to these through filing of formal comments.

Another example of self-regulation is the industry's use of safety packaging for aspirin products. Responsive to a relatively small but nonetheless significant number of accidental ingestions of aspirin-containing products by children, manufacturers have instituted a voluntary practice of distributing these products only in safety containers. This activity preceded and resulted in the legal requirement for safety closures and containers by the Consumer Product Safety Commission, and is an example of self-imposed industry restraints affecting the marketing of pharmaceuticals.

The philosophy of self-regulation is not only limited to drug companies. As pharmaceutical firms grew and diversified, many acquired cosmetic businesses. The practice of imposing voluntary manufacturing standards for drug products naturally affected corporate management of the cosmetic subsidiaries. Cosmetic manufacturers have developed many voluntary programs, including (1) voluntary registration of cosmetic product establishments, (2) voluntary filing of cosmetic product ingredient and cosmetic raw material composition statements, and (3) voluntary filing of cosmetic product experiences. These reports are submitted to the FDA in conformity with standard procedures described in the *Code of Federal Regulations.*

The extent and complexity of external controls, including government statutes and regulations, court decisions, public interest groups, and voluntary standards affecting the marketing of pharmaceuticals have necessarily transformed a "trade" previously concerned with tonics, bitters, and swamp root into a most highly sophisticated, mechanized, and regulated industry. As a result of these controls, pharmaceutical marketing must be recognized as a "pervasively regulated" industry.[1]

Government Controls

Federal Laws and Regulations

Table 21-1 lists various federal laws that have influenced the marketing of pharmaceuticals both generally and specifically.

Legislation specifically governing pharmaceuticals traces its origins to muckraking articles and books, two national tragedies, and the efforts of Dr. Harvey Washington Wiley. In this age of sterile parenteral products and the realization that it requires $70 million to develop a new drug entity and approximately 8 years to secure FDA approval to market the product,[2] it is interesting to reflect on the historical facts that resulted in the passage of the first federal legislation for food and drugs. The quality of drug products now taken for granted was the primary issue when Dr. Wiley created his "Poison Squad."

In the 1800s leading remedies included Kick-A-Poo Indian Sagwa and Mrs. Moffat's Shoo-Fly Powders for drunkenness. Notwithstanding inadequate government controls over label claims to cure such remedies, the most serious problems concerned adul-

TABLE 21-1. *Federal Legislation*

LEGISLATION	YEAR PASSED
General Applicability	
Sherman Antitrust Act	1890
Federal Trade Commission Act	1914
Clayton Act	1914
Robinson-Patman Act	1936
Miller-Tydings Act	1937
Wheeler-Lea Act	1938
Lanham Trademark Act	1946
McGuire-Keogh Act	1952
Fair Packaging and Labeling Act	1966
Consumer Product Safety Act	1972
Environmental Legislation	
Solid Waste Disposal Act	1965
Clean Air Amendments	1970
Federal Water Pollution Control Act Amendments	1972
Resource Conservation and Recovery Act	1976
Specific to the Drug Industry	
Food and Drug Act	1906
Harrison Narcotic Act	1914
Federal Food Drug and Cosmetic Act	1938
Durham-Humphrey Amendments	1951
"Harris-Kefauver" Amendments	1962
Drug Abuse and Control Amendments	1965
Drug Abuse Prevention and Control Act	1970

teration of foods and drugs. Because of minimal government regulation, diseased meat was prevalent. Consequently, as early as 1879, European countries acted to restrict meat importation from the United States, and by 1888, 11 countries prohibited importation of American pork products.[3]

The first domestic attempts to resolve these problems were measures promulgated by the states. Agricultural chemists such as Samuel Johnson paved the way by exposing adulteration in the fertilizer industry. For this reason, state departments of agriculture were given jurisdiction over these statutes. Acting separately, however, states could not protect themselves adequately against adulterated goods in interstate commerce. Additionally, it was difficult for a manufacturer to comply with the highly individualized state requirements. The time was ripe for a strong-willed individual to seize the initiative, capture the public imagination, and call for the passage of federal legislation.

Harvey Washington Wiley, MD, born and educated in rural Indiana, became the first Professor of Chemistry at Purdue University. In 1883, after 9 years at Purdue, he was appointed Chief

Chemist of the United States Department of Agriculture. Because of the controversy surrounding the use of food preservatives and their alleged tendency to interfere with the process of digestion, Dr. Wiley selected 12 volunteers who pledged to consume no food or drink other than that provided at a specially prepared "hygienic table." The experiment began on December 16, 1902, and continued until December 17, 1904. The food was spiced with preservatives such as boric acid, borax, salicylates, sulfurous acid, and other chemicals. Publication of this experiment caused widespread notoriety, with the press referring to the volunteers as Dr. Wiley's "Poison Squad".[3]

Concurrent with Dr. Wiley's activities, the issues of drug and food adulteration were vigorously attacked in many periodicals, including the *Ladies' Home Journal* and *Collier's Weekly*. Perhaps the most significant campaign waged by muckrakers was the novel by Upton Sinclair, *The Jungle*. Sinclair described the distribution of diseased meat rejected by government inspectors that was salvaged from dumps, loaded on carts, intermingled with clean meat, and sold. Although more than 100 food and drug bills were introduced into Congress from 1879 to 1906, an unwilling Congress acted only after public outrage was spurred by these articles and by a health tragedy. In 1902, 12 children died from tetanus contamination of diphtheria antitoxin.[4]

As a result of 25 years of work by Dr. Wiley and the direct involvement of President Theodore Roosevelt, the Pure Food and Drug Act was passed by Congress and signed by the President on June 30, 1906, effective January 1, 1907. This statute represented the first federal enactment that specifically affected the marketing of pharmaceuticals. It prohibited shipment of adulterated drugs in interstate commerce. Additionally, it formally recognized the *United States Pharmacopoeia* and the *National Formulary* as official compendia that established legal standards for drugs. Unfortunately, however, the act did not prohibit false therapeutic claims but only false and misleading claims as to the identity of a drug. Furthermore, the mildness of the penalties did not provide sufficient deterrent effect.[3]

The first case considered by the Supreme Court involving the new act demonstrated its inadequacies. In this instance, the defendant was charged with delivering for shipment in interstate commerce certain misbranded packages of drugs labeled "Mild Combination Treatment for Cancer." A divided court held that, under existing law, delivering for interstate shipment drugs that the defendant knew represented false therapeutic claims did not constitute misbranding. As drafted, the act prohibited only false statements regarding the identity, strength, quality, and purity of the ingredients.[5] As a direct consequence of this ruling, Congress enacted the Sherley Amendment that prohibited false and misleading therapeutic claims for drug products.

Administration of the Pure Food and Drug Act and its attendant jurisdiction of pharmaceuticals remained in the Bureau of Chemistry of the Department of Agriculture until 1927. The Food and Drug Administration was then created within this department. In 1940, the FDA was transferred to the Federal Security Agency, the predecessor of the Department of Health, Education and Welfare, which subsequently became the Department of Health and Human Services.

Although the act served to correct many perceived deficiencies in the production and distribution of pharmaceuticals, it still did not require evidence of safety prior to marketing, nor did it regulate the advertising of drugs. These deficiencies were dramatically illustrated by another tragedy.

Responding to the increasing demand for a liquid dosage form of currently available sulfanilamide capsules, the Chief Chemist for S. E. Massengill Company developed an "elixir." The product previously was used to treat infections caused by hemolytic streptococci. The chemist, who joined the firm in 1935 subsequent to employment with other pharmaceutical companies, developed a solvent that served as a suitable vehicle for the drug. Because the 1906 act did not require premarket safety testing, no animal or human toxicity studies were performed prior to marketing.[6]

Distribution of the Sulfanilamide Elixir commenced on September 4, 1937. The FDA received initial mortality reports on October 14. Seizure was ordered October 16, and the FDA discovered that 240 gallons had been manufactured. Eleven gallons and 6 pints were dispensed on prescription or sold over the counter. Approximately one half of this amount was consumed, resulting in over 100 deaths.[3] It was subsequently learned that the chemist used diethylene glycol as the solvent, a relatively unknown compound at that time. Today, however, it is used in automotive antifreeze.

It is interesting to note that the court order for seizure of the substance was not founded on allegations that the drug was adulterated or unsafe. Rather, the product was labeled as an "elixir," which necessarily implies an alcoholic solution. The product contained no alcohol and was therefore misbranded. Accordingly, if it had been properly labeled as a solution rather than as an elixir, no violation would have occurred.

This tragedy, coupled with books authored by F. J. Schlink and Arthur Kallet, *100,000,000 Guinea Pigs,* and Ruth Lamb, *American Chamber of Horrors,* detailing hazards caused by current manufacturing practices of foods, drugs, and cosmetics, aroused public pressure and overcame government inertia. As a result the Federal Food, Drug and Cosmetic Act was passed.[7] The act identified certain prohibited acts, including introduction into interstate commerce of any food, drug, or cosmetic that is adulterated or misbranded.[8] Furthermore, any person who violated the prohibited acts was to be imprisoned not more than 1 year nor fined more than $1000, or both.[9] A second conviction would result in imprisonment up to 3 years and a $10,000 fine.[10] Additionally, the new act sanctioned multiple seizures in cases of adulteration but permitted only a single seizure if an article were misbranded.[11]

Provisions regarding the advertising of drugs were of critical significance to the marketing of pharmaceuticals. At issue was enforcement jurisdiction for false advertising. Should the Federal Trade Commission (FTC) or the FDA assume responsibility for these provisions in the new bill? The FTC actively lobbied against sharing jurisdiction with the FDA. The Proprietary Association (the trade organization of OTC drug manufacturers), the United Medicine Manufacturers of America, and the Institute of Medicine Manufacturers supported FTC. Its principal congressional advocates included Senator Clark (Missouri) and Representative Lea (California).

The central objection against assigning drug advertising responsibilities to the FTC was the restriction imposed by the Supreme Court in the *Raladam* case. This decision limited FTC authority only to false advertising in which an injury to competition could be shown.[12] Pharmacist-legislators Wheeler and Lea sought to overrule the *Raladam* decision and give the FTC responsibility for advertising by congressional enactment. They drafted the Wheeler-Lea Amendments to the Federal Trade Commission Act. This measure was introduced by Senator Wheeler, passed by the Senate, and referred to the House Committee on Interstate and Foreign Commerce, chaired by Representative Lea. Under the guidance of the chairman, the bill quickly passed the House.

The Wheeler-Lea Amendments prohibited dissemination of any false advertising for the purpose of inducing, directly or indirectly, the purchase of food, drugs, devices, or cosmetics. Such actions constitute unfair or deceptive practices under the Federal Trade Commission Act. An advertisement is false when misleading in any material respect. Furthermore, omission of any material fact may result in a misleading advertisement.[13] As the commission noted in *FTC vs. Sterling Drug, Inc.*, the Wheeler-Lea Act abolished the rule of caveat emptor. The consumer has a right to rely upon statements contained in advertising and, if the advertisement has the capacity or tendency to deceive, its language contravenes the law.[14]

Passage of the Wheeler-Lea Amendments resolved the issue of regulation of drug advertising. It must be remembered, however, that the FDA still retained jurisdiction over labels and labeling.*

The 1938 act required drug packages to be labeled with adequate warnings and directions for use. Drugs not so labeled were deemed misbranded. However, an exemption from the "directions" requirement existed for medications not necessary for protection of public health.[15] After World War II many pharmaceutical companies that had previously restricted marketing of their products through professional channels began labeling all packages for prescription sale. This created a problem because the statute required adequate directions for use unless otherwise exempted.

Then, in 1948, the Supreme Court handed down its landmark decision in *U.S. vs. Sullivan.* In this case a pharmacist, who purchased properly labeled sulfathiazole from a wholesaler, removed 12 tablets from the bulk container, placed them in a pill box, labeled it "sulfathiazole," and sold it to a patient. The court held that the pharmacist violated the misbranding provision of the act by not providing adequate directions and warnings for use to the customer.[16]

Following this decision, Congress passed the Miller Amendment, which clearly extended to wholesale and retail establishments liability for violation of the act. Pharmacists consequently became concerned over possible prosecution for selling legend drugs over the counter, even though such actions were not expressly prohibited by the 1938 act. There obviously existed a need for the statutory definition of prescription drugs. Two pharmacist-legislators, Representative Carl Durham (North Carolina) and Senator Hubert Humphrey (Minnesota), sponsored such legislation. Supported by the National Association of Retail Druggists and by the FDA, the Durham-Humphrey Amendment to the Food, Drug and Cosmetic Act became law on October 26, 1951.[17] In effect, this measure provided for the existence of two classes of drugs, those dispensed pursuant to a prescription and those sold over the counter.

Three general categories of prescription drugs were defined in the amendment:

1. Hypnotic or habit-forming drugs that are specifically named in the law, and their derivatives, unless specifically exempted by a regulation.

---

*Label is defined by the act as a display of written, printed, or graphic matter upon the immediate containers of any article. (21 U.S.C. §321(k).) Labeling means all labels and other written, printed, or graphic matter (1) upon any article or any of its containers or wrappers, or (2) accompanying such article. (21 U.S.C. §321(m).)

2. A drug that is not safe for self-medication "because of its toxicity or other potentiality for harmful effect, or the method of its use, or the collateral measures necessary to its use."

3. A "new drug" that has not been shown to be safe for use in self-medication, and that, under the terms of an effective new drug application, is limited to prescription dispensing.[17]

Additionally, it amended the act by (1) restricting the dispensing of legend drugs pursuant only to prescription, oral or written (with certain exemptions) and (2) prohibiting the refilling of such prescriptions without the expressed authorization of the prescriber (oral and written in appropriate circumstances).[18]

It further required that all prescription medications, prior to dispensing to the patient, bear the following statement: "Caution: Federal law prohibits dispensing without a prescription" (hence the name "legend" drugs).[19] This measure directly affected the marketing of prescription pharmaceuticals. Drug firms discovered the need and benefit of physician advertising by the use of detail men (salesmen), medical journals, and direct mail. However, the companies tended to describe the therapeutic *advantages* of their drugs, neglecting to identify side-effects and contraindications. Consequently, the drug manufacturers were replacing medical schools as principal sources of drug information.[20]

The FDA recognized the need for the physician to have all necessary information for each medication he prescribed at his disposal. Accordingly, the "full disclosure" regulations were promulgated. These regulations required that the label specify, among other things, the format for full disclosure, including the kind and amount of active ingredient and the dosage. Although these changes corrected numerous deficiencies, important modifications are still to be made.

The most significant amendments to the 1938 act were the Harris-Kefauver Amendments of 1962. Senator Estes Kefauver (Tennessee) held a series of hearings in the late 1950s and 1960s that questioned the marketing and pricing methods of the pharmaceutical industry. Then, in late 1961, the thalidomide tragedy unfolded.

Thalidomide was a tranquilizer-sedative marketed by Chemie Grunenthal in West Germany as an OTC. The product was distributed for approximately 3 years before Dr. Leng, a pediatrician at the University of Hamburg, discovered and reported to the company that it caused phocomelia, a birth defect in infants. By this time several thousand infants had been affected.[6]

Although the product was not distributed on a nationwide basis in the United States, the William S. Merrell Company conducted clinical trials with it. Approximately 30,000 patients were tested and other firms performed animal tests. Dr. Frances Kelsey, the FDA medical officer assigned to review new drug applications (NDAs) for thalidomide, questioned existing safety data and, primarily for this reason, the drug was never approved for use in the United States. In the absence of appropriate data, applicants were advised of the necessity of generating such data or, alternatively, including in labeling a statement that safety of the product during use in pregnancy had not been established.[6]

The European experience was reported in early 1962, at which time all domestic clinical trials were terminated. All new drug applications were either rejected or withdrawn—public condemnation and legislative reaction was swift. Another tragedy, therefore, provided impetus for congressional activity, and in 1962 the Harris-Kefauver Amendments were passed unanimously.

These amendments have significantly affected the marketing of pharmaceuticals in the United States by requiring substantial evidence of efficacy for drugs approved between 1938, the enactment date of the act, and 1962. Of course, "new" drugs introduced after 1962 must also comply with this standard. Consequently, introduction of new drugs was necessarily delayed for several years because of the extensive testing required. Target dates for the production, ordering, and receipt of labels and packaging, and shipment of the finished product, required new time schedules, and there were considerable increases in premarket expenditures. Also, the patent life of new chemical entities consequently decreased.

Because of these and other restrictions imposed on the marketing of new drug products, the amendments have been subject to extensive litigation. Section 505(d) requires the FDA to reject any application that lacks substantial evidence that the drug will have the effect it purports. It goes on to define substantial evidence as that which consists of adequate and well-controlled investigations, including clinical trials.[21]

The increased burdens on industry have been substantial. For example, in one instance the FDA rejected submitted studies conducted by Cooper Laboratories in support of an NDA on grounds that each study had at least one deficiency. A federal court sustained the agency's decision, holding that the submissions did not meet the substantial evidence test.[22] Additionally, the Supreme Court in *Weinberger vs. Hynson, Westcott & Dunning*[23] rejected the use of testimonial evidence, stating that "[T]he substantial evidence requirement reflects the conclusion of Congress, based upon hearings, that clinical impressions of practicing physicians do not constitute an adequate basis for establishing efficacy.'"*

As noted previously, drugs approved between 1938 and 1962 also required efficacy review. Because of the massive number of medications approved during this era, and because of the manpower limitations at the agency, the FDA contracted with the National Academy of Sciences and its National Research Council to conduct the required efficacy review for approximately 3000 drug products. This program was termed the Drug Efficacy Study Implementation (DESI). Each product reviewed is classified as either effective, probably effective, possibly effective, or ineffective. If the FDA finds a drug to be less than effective, the manufacturer may submit additional data to the New Drug Evaluation Office. If its decision is to upgrade the product to "effective" status, a notice is published in the *Federal Register.* If the drug is classified other than effective, the company is provided with a notice of opportunity for hearing before an administrative law judge. Only one hearing has been held, however, and two are currently in progress. The DESI study commenced in 1968 and, by 1980, had examined more than 2000 products and removed almost 900 products from the market because of a lack of effectiveness. As is evident, the DESI program has substantially affected marketing strategy.

One of the most important concepts resulting from the Harris-Kefauver Amendments was the abbreviated new drug application (ANDA). This policy arose from the need to review thousands of generic drug products so affected. Rather than require duplication of the basic safety and efficacy data submitted by manufacturers of pioneer drugs, the agency permitted "me-too" generic manufacturers of pre-1962 drugs to submit only manufacturing and bioequivalency data. The mechanism for submission of these data was the ANDA.[24]

Because of lengthy delays incurred for completing the DESI review, a suit was filed in October 1972 by the American Public Health Association and the National Council of Senior Citizens. The court thereafter set certain dates by which segments of the DESI Review were to be finished, and stipulated that by October 11, 1976, final reports had to be issued.[25] The FDA was unable to meet these deadlines. The Public Citizens Litigation Group then filed a petition seeking to reopen the case.[26] The court in this instance required completion of the review by June 1984.[27]

It must be remembered that the ANDA program applies only to generic counterparts of pioneer drugs approved from 1938

---

*Companion cases decided the same day affirming the agency's summary judgment to avoid holding a full hearing on each NDA withdrawal necessitated by DESI are: *Ciba Corp. vs. Weinberger,* 412 U.S. 640; *Weinberger vs. Bentex Pharmaceuticals,* 412 U.S. 645; *U.S. vs. Pharmaceutical Corp. vs. Weinberger,* 412 U.S. 655. See also *Upjohn Company vs. Finch,* 422 F. 2d 944 (6th Cir. 1970).

through 1962. What policy should the FDA employ for reviewing and approving generic drugs first available for marketing after 1962? FDA again chose not to require duplicative safety and efficacy for "me-too" drugs of their pioneer counterparts. Firms only needed to submit an application detailing safety and efficacy data as listed in published literature, so-called "paper" NDAs.

Unfortunately, unlike ANDA policy and procedures, the FDA did not publish this policy decision in the *Federal Register*. Pioneer drug firms discovered something amiss when the agency approved an NDA filed by IMS, Inc. in January 1979 for furosemide injectable. Responding to a request for copies of documents submitted under the Freedom of Information Act, a memorandum was secured that identified the genesis of the "paper NDA" program.[28]

Because pioneer drug manufacturers did not have the opportunity of notice and comment regarding implementation of this policy, as they did for ANDAs, a suit was filed in an attempt to provide such opportunity to comment and to assist the development and molding of the paper NDA policy.[29] The matter is now within the federal jurisdiction of and will be decided by the federal judiciary. Consequently, the courts will enjoy a major role in shaping, developing, and implementing new drug approval policy in the United States.

This was not the first time that courts have so participated. The judiciary has frequently served as an external control on pharmaceutical marketing, as noted in the *Sullivan, Raladam, Johnson, Massengill,* and *Sterling* cases cited previously. Additionally, in *U.S. vs. Dotterweich,* the court found that an employer can be held strictly liable for acts committed by his employees.[30] In this case, a drug repackaging firm purchased an OTC drug from a manufacturer, repackaged it, and shipped it to customers. Later, the firm and its chief executive officer were charged with introducing a misbranded and adulterated drug into interstate commerce. At trial the corporation was acquitted but Dotterweich was convicted, even though he had no personal knowledge of the violations. The court found that public health and welfare demands a high standard of care be imposed on the pharmaceutical industry. Therefore, an employer will be held accountable for the acts or omissions of his employees if performed within the scope of their employment.

This principle of strict liability was subsequently reaffirmed by the Supreme Court in *U.S. vs. Park,* a 1975 case.[31] In this instance, FDA investigators repeatedly inspected and issued citations to Acme Supermarkets for holding food products in unsanitary conditions. The president, Park, acknowledged that he was responsible for warehouse sanitation and was personally aware of violations at his Baltimore and Philadelphia facilities, but the conditions remained uncorrected. The jury found, and the Supreme Court affirmed, strict criminal liability.

These cases have firmly established in our jurisprudence the principle that corporate officers will ultimately be held responsible for criminal acts or omissions by their employees.

Throughout the years attention has also been focused on controlled substances. In 1970 Congress passed the comprehensive Drug Abuse Prevention and Control Act.[32] This repealed prior statutes, including the Harrison Narcotic Act of 1914[33] and the Drug Abuse and Control Amendments of 1965,[34] and consolidated under one title jurisdiction for barbiturates, amphetamines, and other controlled substances. This act regulated the marketing of narcotics and dangerous drugs by federal registration, contrasting with the Harrison Narcotic Act that controlled such activity through imposition of a tax. Enforcement jurisdiction for the act was entrusted to the Drug Enforcement Agency within the Justice Department. Direct marketing restrictions imposed on drugs subject to this act include production quotas, limitations on prescription orders and refills, storage requirements, and informational data about the prescriber, dispenser, and patient to be recorded on the prescription.

One additional statute concerning major federal enactments specifically regulating pharmaceuticals deserves mention. Although not affecting pharmaceuticals directly, the Medical Device Act of 1976 concerns products related to health care that are frequently produced by pharmaceutical companies.[35] This measure established a premarket clearance scheme not unlike that for new drugs. It requires submission by manufacturers of a premarket notification form at least 90 days prior to marketing. The FDA, through its Bureau of Medical Devices, then classifies the proposed device into one of the following categories: (1) Class I—General Controls; (2) Class II—Performance Standards; and (3) Class III—Premarket Approval.[36] These categories provide increasingly stringent conditions for a proposed device according to its complexity and the need to ensure its safety and efficacy.

Up to this point attention has been devoted principally to federal statutes and to their impact on pharmaceutical marketing. The effect of federal regulations (as distinct from statutes) however, promulgated under statutory authority, has in many instances been as dramatic. Examples include current good manufacturing practices and man-in-the-plant and patient package insert regulations.

The 1962 Kefauver-Harris Amendments to the 1938 Federal Food, Drug and Cosmetic Act, specifically Section 501(a)(2)(B), state that a drug is deemed adulterated if the methods, facilities, or controls employed in manufacture, processing, packaging, and storing do not conform to "current good manufacturing processes."[37] Accordingly, current good manufacturing practices (GMPs) regulations were initially promulgated in 1963 and updated in 1971 and 1979.[38] Their intent was to establish certain minimum standards to be met by pharmaceutical manufacturers thereby ensuring quality, purity, strength, and potency of finished drug products. Indeed, the legislative history of the 1962 amendments demonstrate that Section 502(a)(2)(B) was included to raise the standards of all manufacturers to the level of current industry "good manufacturing practices."

Requirements established include minimum standards for plant facilities and equipment, control of drug components, containers and closures, training and experience of personnel, written procedures, and expiration dating. The financial obligations necessitated by compliance were significant. Firms spent millions of dollars modifying existing facilities and hiring additional personnel.

The so-called "man-in-the-plant" regulations were intended by the FDA to eliminate the practice of listing a company as manufacturer of a product on drug labels when its contact with the manufacturing process was minimal, at best. For example, one firm might hire a subcontractor to perform the actual manufacturing process and merely place a quality control person at the subcontractors plant. The finished product label, however, would then contain no reference to the actual manufacturing company, the subcontractor.

Several aspects of this practice were the subject of hearings before the Subcommittee on Monopoly and Anticompetitive Activities of the Senate Select Committee on Small Business in November 1977 and, in 1980, before the House Subcommittee on Oversight and Investigations of the Committee on Interstate and Foreign Commerce. The consensus of these committees and the FDA was that continued use of the man-in-the-plant policy misleads consumers and health-care personnel in regard to the actual manufacturer of a specific drug product.[39]

To correct this practice, the FDA promulgated regulations that defined the term "manufacturer" for purposes of drug labeling as any firm that "performs all of the following operations that are required to produce the product: 1) mixing; 2) granulating; 3) milling; 4) molding; 5) tableting; 6) encapsulating; 7) coating; 8) sterilizing; and, 9) filling . . . containers."[40] As a result of comments filed by pharmaceutical firms, the FDA included an "escape" clause that permitted use of the designations "distributed by" or "marketed by." As a consequence, the name of the actual manufacturer still need not appear on the label. Although it appears that this provision contravenes the spirit and intent of the regulation, it is consistent with requirements of the statute that provide that a drug product is misbranded under §502(a) if its labeling does not identify the manufacturer, packer, *or distributor* (emphasis added).[41] Even with this escape clause, it became necessary for many drug companies to alter their marketing practices by modifying their product labeling.

Another FDA regulation has significantly affected pharmaceutical marketing practices by requiring distribution of package inserts to patients with each new prescription for ten drugs or drug classes. Although not a new concept, expansion of the program to include other than estrogenic substances has been the subject of considerable debate.* The FDA intends to evaluate the success of this program prior to expansion of patient package inserts (PPIs) for other pharmaceutical products.

This age of consumerism dictates that patients receive more information about drugs prescribed for and taken by them, but there is still considerable controversy regarding the amount and manner of information to be disseminated. Physicians and other health-care personnel cite decreasing compliance with dosage requirements when patients are made aware of potential side-effects of drugs. Pharmacists claim inability to stock and distribute PPIs for all prescription products. Industry argues that marketing costs must necessarily increase and be passed on to patients. These arguments are countered by those of consumer groups, who contend that patients have an inherent right of access to all available information about their medications.

If the program is expanded to include all prescription drugs, one result may be a redirection of advertising toward consumers in an attempt to create a consumer demand for a particular drug product or brand of drug product. This would represent a departure from current prescription marketing practices.

The PPI program was "temporarily" stayed as a result of President Reagan's Executive Order that delayed implementation of all regulations pending review of their need by his administration.[43]

Additional regulations that may represent the most significant impact on the OTC drug industry were those creating the OTC Review. These regulations, published by the FDA in May 1972, initiated a most ambitious review of drug ingredients, and their concentrations, dosage schedules, formulations, and labeling.[44] The purpose of the review was to establish uniform standards for the safety, efficacy, and labeling of nonprescription medicines. Because of the vast number of marketed drug products, the FDA

---

*In 1970 the FDA required distribution of a patient package insert with oral contraceptives.[42]

decided to examine ingredients rather than commercial products. Even with this modified approach, it was discovered that up to 1000 ingredients were involved. The FDA thus created seventeen panels organized according to pharmacologic categories to examine the ingredients. Each panel reviews available literature and considers submissions from industry, consumer groups, and interested parties. It then issues a report to the FDA containing recommendations. The FDA reviews the report and publishes a Proposed Monograph for public comment in the *Federal Register.* The Monograph classifies ingredients and labeling claims as follows:

1. Category I—generally recognized as safe and effective.

2. Category II—generally recognized as unsafe or ineffective.

3. Category III—more study needed to determine general recognition of safety and efficacy.

Upon review of comments filed by interested parties in response to the Proposed Monograph, the FDA then issues a Tentative Final Monograph. Comments may again be made, which are then reviewed, and a Final Monograph issued. All OTC products must conform to ingredient and labeling requirements by the effective date of an applicable Final Monograph or be subject to seizure.[44]

Perhaps the most important marketing effect of the OTC Review is the prohibition by the FDA against the use of synonyms of Category I-approved labeling claims. The agency announced its intention to permit manufacturers to use only the exact wording as identified in the Monographs. Although industry has strenuously argued that certain terms approved by the FDA for Category I status are meaningless to the lay public, and that companies should be permitted to substitute more easily understood terms, the agency has steadfastly rejected these arguments. For example, "antitussive" is an approved Category I term, but "helps relieve coughing" or "stops coughing" is not. "Antiflatulent" is a Category I label claim for products that alleviate gas symptoms, but "antigas" is not. The list is very extensive.

Two lawsuits affecting the OTC Review deserve mention. There was the so-called Category III suit, in which public interest organizations (Health Research Group (HRG) and Public Citizen, Inc.) objected to the FDA's continued permission to market products containing Category III ingredients during the Proposed Monograph to Final Monograph stages.[45] Manufacturers whose OTC products contained such ingredients were permitted to obtain additional data to support moving an ingredient from Category III to Category I during this interval. It was the position of HRG that, once ingredients were classified as being in Category III, the products containing these ingredients were illegally marketed because they were not generally recognized as safe and effective and therefore had to be removed from the marketplace.[46] Judge Sirica agreed, holding that the Category III regulations were unlawful. The court's principal objection to the FDA's practices was that the agency permitted continued marketing of products containing Category III ingredients for a specified period of time (until the effective date of Final Monograph) when it had no authority to do so. The court, however, failed to require removal of these products from the market. Although this decision might have drastically affected pharmaceutical marketing, the practical effect has been minimal because the FDA has continued its practice of permitting the marketing of Category III ingredients up to date of the Final Monograph.[45]

An additional suit that went to the heart of the entire OTC Review was that of the *National Association of Pharmaceutical Manufacturers and the National Pharmaceutical Alliance vs. FDA.*[47] In this case, the trade association of generic manufacturers challenged the force and effect of the monographs promulgated by the FDA. At issue was whether or not the regulations were merely interpretive, declaring the FDA's opinion of the Federal Food, Drug and Cosmetic Act, or binding, substantive regulations with which manufacturers must legally comply. The court held that the OTC Review regulations enjoyed the full force and effect of law, violation of which could subject OTC medicines to seizure.

Antitrust and Trade Regulations

The external controls so far discussed are specific to the pharmaceutical industry. There are numerous antitrust statutes and trade regulations, however, that are applicable to all business entities engaged in or affecting interstate commerce.

The cornerstone of the federal regulation of business activity was the 1890 Sherman Antitrust Act.[48] Congress perceived a need to prohibit the proliferation of activity similar to that engaged in by the Standard Oil Company of Ohio. In the late 1800s, John D. Rockefeller and his associates united several small refineries to obtain favorable treatment from the railroad industry. Under the Standard Oil banner, the company prospered and exerted considerable influence on the Erie, New York Central, and Pennsylvania railroads, thereby receiving rebates on shipments and information regarding competitors' products and their shipments. The stockholders then created a trust and turned over their stock certificates to certain trustees for tax purposes. By 1872 all but three or four of the approximately 40 refineries in Ohio had been acquired by the Standard Oil Trust. The power wielded by the group was significant.

In response to these anticompetitive practices, Senator John

Sherman (Ohio) introduced the Sherman Antitrust Act. The act stated that "every contract, combination in the form of trust or otherwise or conspiracy, in restraint of trade or commerce among the several States, or with foreign nations, is hereby declared to be illegal" (Section 1). Additionally, it provided that "every person who shall monopolize, or attempt to monopolize, or conspire with any other person or persons, to monopolize any part of the trade or commerce among the several states, or with foreign nations, shall be deemed guilty of a misdemeanor . . ." (Section 2).[13]

Although the act provided the intended benefits of reducing monopolies and increasing competition, its broad language did not anticipate increasingly complex business arrangements. To meet this need, Congress passed the Clayton Act in 1914.[49] The Clayton Act differed from the Sherman Act in two basic ways. First, the Clayton Act prohibited actions that *may* result in future anti-competitive practices. Additionally, it addressed certain business arrangements specifically, such as exclusive dealing arrangements, acquisitions, and mergers, among others, rather than identifying general prohibitions.

Section 2 of the Clayton Act, as amended, generally made it unlawful for any person to discriminate in price, services, or facilities where its effect may be to lessen substantially competition or to create a monopoly.[50] (This section will be explored in greater detail later.)

Section 3 prohibited a seller from conditioning a sale of goods on the provision that the purchaser will not deal in goods of a competitor of the seller when the effect of such an arrangement may decrease competition substantially or tend to create any monopoly.[51] Essentially, this section proscribed three types of business practices: (1) tying agreements (forcing a customer to buy a second item when he purchases the first item); (2) exclusive dealing arrangements (precluding a buyer from purchasing the subject commodity from anyone other than the seller); (3) requirements contract (requiring a buyer to purchase all of his needs from the seller).

Section 7 of the act prohibited any company from acquiring the assets or stock of another where its effect may substantially lessen competition.[52] This provision was intended to combat the development of large conglomerates whose intention is to acquire a dominant share of a market. Section 7A imposed notification requirements and a waiting period on companies that intended to make significant acquisitions.[53]

Section 8 prohibited interlocking directorates and corporate officers in certain instances.[54]

Although the Clayton Act sought to eliminate discriminatory pricing practices, it expressly exempted price differences based on quantity, thus giving large firms a purchasing advantage. A 1934 congressional inquiry confirmed the fact of chain store growth and the corresponding decline of independently owned stores.[55] Consequently, Congress acted to amend Section 2 of the Clayton Act by passing the Robinson-Patman Act in 1936.[56] As amended, Section 2 consisted of six subsections:

1. Section 2(a) made it unlawful for a seller to discriminate in prices for goods of "like grade and quality" when the requisite probable competitive injury results, unless the discrimination is "justified" by one of the several defenses found in that subsection and in subsection (b) of Section 2.[57]

2. Section 2(b) provided, first, that when a prima facie case of discrimination in price, services, or facilities is proven, the person charged with the violation bears the burden of rebutting those charges by justifying his actions; and second, that when a seller's discrimination is "made in good faith to meet an equally low price of a competitor, or the services or facilities furnished by a competitor," the prohibitions of subsections (a), (d), and (e) shall not apply.[58]

3. Section 2(c) forbade the payment of "brokerage" fee and similar allowances to buyers or their representatives, "except for services rendered in connection with the sale or purchase of goods."[59]

4. Section 2(d) prohibited the payment, by the seller, for any services or facilities furnished by the buyer in connection with the processing, handling, or sale of products, unless such payment is available to all other competing customers "on proportionally equal terms."[60]

5. Section 2(e) forbade a seller to furnish services or facilities to any purchaser in connection with the sale of a commodity for resale, unless the seller also furnishes such services of facilities to all purchasers "on proportionally equal terms."[61]

6. Section 2(f) made it unlawful for buyers "knowingly to induce or receive a discrimination in price" prohibited by Section 2.[62]

It is important to note that the Robinson-Patman Act did not prohibit differential pricing per se. Rather, it required that each purchaser have the opportunity to buy on equally favorable terms. Quantity discounts are permissible if all purchasers can so participate.

Exceptions to the basic premise of antitrust philosophy are the fair trade laws enacted by the states. These laws are somewhat misnamed because they identify and sanction methods employed by manufacturers to set prices for trademarked goods at the retail level. To guard against destructive price wars and to meet the ever-increasing demand for the protection of goodwill that was attached to trademarked commodities during the Depression era, Congress enacted the Miller-Tydings Act in 1937, thereby exempting fair trade practices from the antitrust laws.[63] This federal amendment enabled states to pass fair trade statutes that permitted a manufacturer to set the retail price for his trademarked goods.

The Supreme Court, in *Schwegmann vs. Calvert Distillers Corporation,* however, held that the Miller-Tydings Act did not encompass retail outlets that had not signed agreements with a manufacturer to refrain from selling below a certain price, so-called nonsigners.[64] Therefore, nonsigners to such contracts could sell below the fair trade price. In 1952 Congress responded by passing the McGuire-Keogh Act, which amended the Federal Trade Commission Act and permitted enforcement of vertical (manufacturer to wholesaler to retailer) price-fixing agreements, even against retailers who had not signed such contracts.[65]

The validity of fair trade laws has been upheld by the Supreme Court,[66] but many state constitutions have banned them. Additionally, because of the great expense involved, manufacturers were reluctant to pursue violators. Furthermore, a period of severe inflation and an increasing demand for active antitrust enforcement led to the passage by Congress in 1975 of the Consumer Goods Pricing Act, which repealed both the Miller-Tydings and McGuire-Keogh Acts, thereby abolishing state fair trade laws and practices by preemption.[67]

Still another antitrust statute affecting and serving as an external control on the marketing of pharmaceuticals was the 1914 Federal Trade Commission Act. The impetus for passage of this law was identical to that of the political and business influences that led to the passage of the Clayton Act, as discussed previously. This act established the Federal Trade Commission (FTC), which is composed of a chairman, a political appointment of the President, and four commissioners, also appointed by the President for staggered 7-year terms. The commission exercises jurisdiction principally by enforcement of the Federal Trade Commission Act and the Clayton Act, as amended by the Robinson-Patman Act. The FTC enjoys significant power to investigate commercial activities by exercising functions such as conducting hearings, issuing subpeonas requiring production of documents and testimony, and issuing cease and desist orders and trade regulation rules.[55]

It must be remembered, however, that although the FTC has exclusive jurisdiction of the Federal Trade Commission Act, it has only concurrent jurisdiction with the Department of Justice for enforcement of the Clayton Act. The Justice Department has exclusive control over the Sherman Antitrust Act.

As originally enacted, the Clayton Act prohibited only unfair methods of competition in commerce. The FTC could therefore act only if competitors were injured as a result of the business actions of a particular company. Responding to the Supreme Court decision in *FTC vs. Raladam*,[12] Congress enacted the Wheeler-Lea Amendments in 1938, thereby expanding jurisdiction of the act to encompass "unfair or deceptive acts or practices."[68] This extended the FTC's power to act and protect the public without regard to competition.

The FTC may act through formal or informal proceedings. Formal procedures resulting in issuance of a cease and desist order may be enforced by civil penalty. Each day of violation constitutes a separate offense. The financial penalty may be collected by a civil suit filed by the Justice Department. The commission's informal enforcement program includes FTC guides, advisory opinions, and trade regulation rules (TRRs).

With enactment of the Magnuson-Moss-Warranty-Federal Trade Commission Improvement Act of 1975, Congress greatly enhanced the FTC's power to seek consumer redress for unfair and deceptive practices. Although the FTC had authority to promulgate TRRs prior to passage of this amendment, its ability to enforce them was significantly enhanced with its passage. The FTC's only mechanism for enforcement had previously been a cease and desist order. The FTC may now apply directly for judicial relief, including recision and reformation of contracts, refund of money, return of property, payment of damages, and civil penalties.[69]

Passage of these amendments to the FTC Act also initiated a more active TRR program. Of particular interest to and having a direct impact on the marketing of pharmaceuticals were the Claims and Antacid Warnings TRRs. These separate proceedings, if enacted, would profoundly affect the advertising of nonprescription drugs. The OTC Drug Claims TRR, published in November 1975, permitted the advertising of only the exact claims approved as Category I in the Final Monographs promulgated by the FDA.[70] No synonyms or words of similar import were acceptable, even if the public understood other language more clearly. Accordingly, the test imposed by the proposed Drug Claims TRR was not whether the unapproved term was untruthful, misleading or unfair but, rather, was it on an approved list? If not, it was illegal per se and, therefore, unavailable for use. A violation of the exact language runs afoul of the TRR and therefore violates the law because all TRRs, once enacted, have the full force and effect of law.

As required, the FTC provided public notice and opportunity for comment on the proposed Drug Claims TRR. OTC manufacturers were unanimous in their opposition to the TRR as written because it restricted meaningful information available to consumers unduly, thus precluding the use of language necessary to provide adequate information for lay use of medicines. The purpose of advertising is to convey general product awareness to the public. Advertisers must communicate in easily understood terms, but use of the term "antitussive" instead of "cough suppressant" does not accomplish this.

The FTC must have been persuaded by these arguments because, on February 11, 1981, the commission decided to terminate this rule making proceeding, rejecting its staff's position completely.[71]

The Antacid Warnings TRR, unlike the Drug Claims TRR, did not take the form of a predrafted proposed rule but was a series of questions for determining the need to recite "cautions" in OTC drug advertising and, specifically, to determine whether antacid label caution's required by the Antacid Final Monograph should appear in advertisements.[72] Again, industry participated actively in the rule making procedure. At issue was the fundamental principle of whether the FTC acted beyond its statutory grant in proposing that advertising to consumers contain all precautionary statements required on antacid labels by the FDA. The Wheeler-Lea Amendments had granted authority to the FTC to ban unfair and deceptive practices. It further conferred jurisdiction on the FTC for OTC drug advertising. Could the FTC, though, take action against an antacid advertisement that contained only truthful claims merely because it did not also list all precautionary statements? Moreover, did the consumer really expect a television advertisement to state all instances in which a product should *not* be used, or used with caution?

These issues will continue to receive attention as the FDA completes the rule making process. Its final decision, certain to be litigated extensively, will have a decided affect on pharmaceutical marketing.

The FTC, on June 4, 1975, published a proposed trade regulation rule, the Prescription TRR, that would have preempted state laws that prohibited the advertising or dissemination of prescription price information. The commission felt that such restrictions contributed to artificially and unduly inflated prescription prices. Without these restrictions, consumers could secure more favorable prices and thereby save a substantial amount of money.

Its need was obviated, however, by the Supreme Court decision in *Virginia State Board of Pharmacy et al.* vs. *Virginia Citizens Consumer Council, Inc. et al.*[73] In this case the court ruled that commercial speech—the freedom to advertise prescription prices—is protected by First Amendment freedoms, applicable to the states through the Fourteenth Amendment's due process clause. Both the consumer and society have strong interests in the free flow of commercial information. State restrictions on such rights are preempted by the Constitution. This decision accomplished by judicial fiat that which the Commission intended by its proposed rule. Therefore, further efforts were discontinued.

Other statutes and regulations serve as additional external controls, and merit some discussion. The Federal Hazardous Substances and Consumer Products Safety Acts, and the Poison Prevention Packaging Act of 1970 (PPPA), enforced by the Consumer Products Safety Commission (CPSC), have affected the marketing of pharmaceuticals by requiring the use of special labels and packaging.[74] For example, under the authority of the PPPA, regulations were promulgated requiring safety packaging for aspirin-containing products.[75] Considerable planning by pharmaceutical marketing personnel was required. By the effective date of these regulations, aspirin manufacturers had to order and receive new safety caps and containers, test them according to required protocols, and be prepared to market the new packages without interruption of shipment or sales of the product to their customers.[76]

Other Federal Laws

Additional federal laws affecting pharmaceutical marketing include environmental statutes and regulations. Implementation of the Clean Air Amendments of 1970 and the Federal Water Pollution Control Act of 1972 require careful planning and consideration by corporate management prior to construction of new facilities or expansion of existing plants.[77, 78] Certain geographic areas that do not meet federal air quality standards have been designated as "nonattainment areas." If a pharmaceutical plant is located within such a region, the management may discover that plans for plant expansion resulting in increased pollutant discharge may run afoul of federal regulations. In this instance, expansion may occur only if other companies within the region, or other discharge sources within the subject plant, decrease emissions so that expansion does not significantly increase overall pollutant discharge.[79]

A third environmental statute, the Resource Conservation and Recovery Act Amendments to the Solid Waste Disposal Act, passed by Congress in 1976, created "cradle to grave" responsibility for hazardous wastes.[80] Although manufacturers and distributors of pharmaceuticals are normally not thought to deal in hazardous substances, many chemicals used in manufacturing processes are subject to the act and its regulations. The increased costs necessitated by compliance are incorporated into the profit and loss structure for each drug product, and are reflected in the sales price of each item. As pharmacists and consumers are well aware, monthly price increases are commonplace, due partially to these environmental measures.

State Laws and Regulations

When Congress exercises a granted power, the federal legislation enacted may displace or preempt state law under the Supremacy Clause of the Constitution. In the absence of congressional activity, states may enact measures that affect commerce within their boundaries. State antisubstitution laws represent an example of local governmental activity in the absence of federal preemption, and serve as yet another form of external control on the marketing of pharmaceuticals. These statutes, generally enforced by State Boards of Pharmacy, the licensing and disciplinary agencies for pharmacists, prohibit a pharmacist from dispensing any product other than the specific brand of medicine prescribed by licensed practitioners. Physicians and dentists are thus assured of the specific identity and quality of medicines ingested or applied by their patients. In response to the limitations imposed by these laws, pharmaceutical firms have directed most of their marketing and advertising efforts to prescribers, rather than to pharmacists.

The consumer movement of the 1970s, spearheaded in the health-care field by the American Association of Retired Persons (AARP) and by the Retired Teachers Association (RTA), has resulted in the repeal of antisubstitution laws in all but two states (Texas and Indiana). Pharmacists, in most instances, may now substitute a less expensive generic equivalent for brand-name medications when filling prescriptions. If the prescriber wishes to ensure, however, that the drug item dispensed is exactly what he prescribes, he may so require by checking a box on the prescription form that says "Dispense as Written," or by signing a signature line containing this designation. Consequently, pharmacists have assumed the principle role of selecting the specific manufacturer's brand to be dispensed to the patient. Accordingly, pharmaceutical companies have now redirected their marketing and promotional efforts to include pharmacists.

Recent activity by State Boards of Pharmacy (Minnesota and New York) and by some state legislatures (Connecticut; Section 20-166) has created certain marketing problems for the industry. The FDA now permits over-the-counter sale of up to 0.05% topical hydrocortisone, previously available only with a prescription. The Connecticut legislature enacted a statute prohibiting sale of this compound except by a registered pharmacist. This effectively restricted the marketing of hydrocortisone in Connecticut to retail and hospital pharmacies, thereby preventing distribution by mass merchandisers and supermarkets. Because of these restrictions and the resultant general availability of the medication to consumers, this statute has since been repealed.

Additional state controls include enactment of "Green River" ordinances, prohibiting door-to-door selling, and "Blue Laws," requiring Sunday closing of retail establishments. Fair trade laws were noted earlier.

Industry Controls

Pharmaceutical manufacturers have initiated numerous voluntary programs affecting the marketing of their products. In an effort to protect public health and welfare, individual companies and their trade associations have developed guidelines concerning numerous industry practices.

The Pharmaceutical Manufacturers Association (PMA) has adopted several voluntary policies to which its member companies subscribe. For example, the PMA voluntarily agrees with and would support federal legislation concerning the following:

1. Prohibit the giving of prizes, premiums or items of value to members of the health professions as incentives or rewards for the prescribing or dispensing of medical products.
2. Prohibit the inspection of prescription files in retail or hospital pharmacies by pharmaceutical company representatives.
3. Require that samples of prescription products be distributed on written request only, with detailed record-keeping and accountability.
4. Require appropriate documentation in matters of bioavailability, bioequivalence and therapeutic equivalence.
5. Require that the name of the manufacturer appear on every prescription product label when it differs from that of the distributor.
6. Require FDA to conduct regular, effective drug plant inspection programs in a uniform manner, at least annually, in companies both large and small, and to uniformly enforce current good manufacturing and laboratory practice regulations.
7. Require that companies maintain adequate records and have the skilled manpower and facilities necessary to handle investigation of adverse drug effect reports.
8. Require expiration dating on all prescription drug products, with a maximum expiration period of five years.
9. Require, where feasible, that each individual tablet, capsule, or

other solid dosage form of a prescription drug carry the identifying mark of the manufacturer.
10. Require that the name of the prescription product appear on the patient's prescription container, except when the doctor directs otherwise. (PMA Board Resolution)

A most visible program is the Code of Advertising Practices of the Proprietary Association, the trade association of OTC drug manufacturers. Promulgated in 1934, the 22-point code addressed issues such as the substantiation of claims, efficacy of active ingredients, unnecessary use of medicines, and sanctions against prizes and gimmicks.

Additional voluntary measures employed by manufacturers for OTC drugs include the quantitative disclosure of active ingredients on drug labels, expiration dating identifying a product's shelf life, refraining from bulk mail sampling, "flagging" labels to advise consumers of significant changes in products, and using safety packaging for aspirin-containing medicines. Many of these programs are now mandated by law, but their origins may be traced to industry standards that were voluntarily established.

The philosophy of discretionary codes has been extended from medicines to cosmetics. As corporations diversified, pharmaceutical firms acquired cosmetic companies.* Influenced perhaps by the actions of its pharmaceutical company counterparts, the Cosmetic, Toiletries and Fragrances Association (CTFA), the trade association of cosmetic houses, embarked on numerous voluntary programs. For example, in 1979 the CTFA filed a Citizen's Petition with the FDA requesting promulgation by the agency of good manufacturing practice (GMP) regulations for cosmetics. Cosmetic GMPs require major capital spending for plant expansion and improvement, and cosmetic firms intend to ensure protection of public health and the quality and purity of cosmetics, particularly "eye area" products. Promulgation of these regulations will achieve that goal throughout the industry.

Furthermore, several major cosmetics companies have provided extensive funding for the establishment of the Cosmetic Ingredient Review (CIR). The purpose of the CIR is to identify ingredients for which there is a reasonable certainty of safety for use in cosmetics. Cosmetic firms would then refrain from using any ingredients identified by the CIR as lacking appropriate safety information.

Additional voluntary standards adhered to by the pharmaceutical and cosmetic industries include guidelines established by the

---

*For example, Schering-Plough acquired Maybelline Company; Eli Lilly & Company acquired Elizabeth Arden; E. R. Squibb & Sons acquired Charles of the Ritz Cf. Revlon, Inc. and Norcliff Thayer and U.S. Vitamin, or its assets.

National Association of Broadcasters and by the National Advertising Division of the Better Business Bureau. Also, the major television networks have established specific substantiation requirements. Manufacturers and their advertising agencies have participated in these programs for years.

Social Controls

It has been said that "In the final analysis it is society itself which controls all marketing activities."[81] Society is often mirrored in the comments of its journalists. As noted earlier, the muckrakers have played an important role in the development of laws (external controls) affecting pharmaceutical marketing. Upton Sinclair (*The Jungle*), Samuel Hopkins (*The Great American Fraud*) and, more recently, Martin Gross (*The Doctors*) and Morton Mintz (*The Therapeutic Nightmare*, reissued as *By Prescription Only*) have contributed to the increased awareness and education of the American consumer. In certain instances their writings spurred congressional activity where only inertia had existed.

Consumer activists groups such as the Health Research Group, Public Citizen, Inc., the AARP, and the RTA, whose policies reflect the social consciousness of the consumer, have proved formidable adversaries in litigation and in formal rule making hearings and procedures. Also, industry itself has demonstrated a social consciousness by developing voluntary standards and codes individually and through its trade associations—in essence, self-regulation.

Congressional enactment at federal and state levels, judicial decrees, participation of consumer organizations, and discretionary programs instituted by pharmaceutical companies have served as external controls influencing and shaping the marketing of pharmaceuticals in the United States. As a direct result, the manufacture, distribution, and marketing of pharmaceuticals must surely be a "pervasively regulated" industry.

References

1. *Marshall vs. Barlow's, Inc.,* 436 U.S. 307 (1978).
2. Rogart, M.: Paper NDA's and ANDA's for Post-1962 Drugs—The Pioneer Manufacturer's View, presented at the fall FDLI Conference, Washington, DC, December, 1981.
3. Wilson, S.: *Food and Drug Regulations,* Washington, DC: American Council on Public Affairs, 1942, pp. 14, 22, 57, 130–131.
4. History of Drug Regulation, *GMP Reports, 1* (No. 1), 1979.
5. *U.S. vs. Johnson,* 211 U.S. 488 (1911).
6. Kaluzny, E.: *Pharmacy Law Digest,* Milwaukee: Douglas-McKay, 1974, pp. 166.14–166.16.

7. Federal Food Drug and Cosmetic Act, 21 U.S.C. §301 *et seq.* (1938).
8. 21 U.S.C. §331(a).
9. 21 U.S.C. §331(a).
10. 21 U.S.C. §331(b).
11. 21 U.S.C. §334(a)(1).
12. *Federal Trade Commission vs. Raladam Co.*, 283 U.S. 643 (1931).
13. Stickells, A. T.: *Federal Control of Business*, San Francisco: Bankroft-Whitney, 1972, pp. 57, 105.
14. *Federal Trade Commission vs. Sterling Drug, Inc.*, 317 F2d 669 (2nd Cir.)(1963).
15. 21 U.S.C. 351(f).
16. *U.S. vs. Sullivan*, 332 U.S. 633(1948).
17. 21 U.S.C. 353(b)(1).
18. 21 U.S.C. 353(b)(1) and (2).
19. 21 U.S.C. 353(b)(4).
20. Jansen, W. F.: Pharmacy and the Food and Drug Law, *American Pharmacy, NS21* (No. 4):33, 1981.
21. 21 U.S.C. §355(d)(5) and (6).
22. *Cooper Laboratories vs. Commissioner, Fed. FDA*, 501 F2d 772 (D.C. Cir. 1974).
23. 412 U.S. at 630.
24. *Federal Register, 35*:11273, 1970.
25. *American Public Health Association vs. Veneman*, 349 F. Supp.
26. *American Public Health Association et al. vs. Patricia Harris, et al.*, Civil Action No. 70-1847 (Sept. 24, 1980).
27. Winding Down the DESI Review, *American Pharmacy, NS21* (No. 2):28, 1981.
28. Memorandum of Dr. Marion J. Finkel, Associate Director for New Drug Evaluation, FDA Bureau of Drugs, to Division Directors, July 31, 1978.
29. *Hoffman-LaRoche, Inc. vs. Califano*, Cir. No. 79-1150 (D.D.C. 1979).
30. *U.S. vs. Dotterweich*, 320 U.S. 277 (1943).
31. *U.S. vs. Park*, 421 U.S. 658 (1975).
32. 21 U.S.C. 801 *et seq.*
33. Former 21 U.S.C. 4701 *et seq.*
34. Former 21 U.S.C. 360 *et seq.*
35. *Public Law* 94-295 (May 28, 1976).
36. §513(a)(1).
37. 21 U.S.C. 351(a)(2)(B).
38. *Federal Register, 43*:45014, 1978.
39. *Federal Register, 43*:45615, 1978.
40. *Federal Register, 45*:25776, 1980.
41. 21 U.S.C. §352(b)(1).
42. *Federal Register, 35*:9001, 1970.
43. Executive Order No. *12229* (1981).
44. *Federal Register, 37*:9464, 1972.
45. *Cutler vs. Kennedy*, 475 F. Supp. 838 (D.D.C. 1979).
46. 21 U.S.C. 352(a) and (f).
47. 487 F. Supp. 412 (S.D.N.Y. 1980).
48. 15 U.S.C. §1–7.
49. 15 U.S.C. §12 *et seq.*
50. 15 U.S.C. §13.

51. 15 U.S.C. §14.
52. 15 U.S.C. §18.
53. 15 U.S.C. §15A. This section was added as part of the Hart-Scott-Radino Antitrust Improvements Act of 1976.
54. 15 U.S.C. §19.
55. Hills, C. A.: *Antitrust Advisor,* New York: McGraw-Hill, 1971, pp. 234–235, 322–323.
56. 15 U.S.C. §13 *et seq.*
57. 15 U.S.C. §13(a).
58. 15 U.S.C. §13(b).
59. 15 U.S.C. §13(c).
60. 15 U.S.C. §13(d).
61. 15 U.S.C. §13(e).
62. 15 U.S.C. §13(f).
63. 15 U.S.C. §1.
64. 341 U.S. 384 (1951).
65. 15 U.S.C. §45.
66. *Old Dearborn Distributing Co. vs. Seagram Distillers Corp.,* 299 U.S. 183 (1936).
67. *Public Law* 94-145, 89 Stat. 801 (1975).
68. Chap. 49, Sec. 3, 52 Stat. 111, March 21, 1938, 15 U.S.C. §45 as amended.
69. 15 U.S.C. §57b(b).
70. *Federal Register, 40*:52631, 1975.
71. *Federal Register, 46*:24585, 1981.
72. *Federal Register, 41*:14534, 1976.
73. 44 U.S.L.W. 4686 (U.S. May 24, 1976).
74. 15 U.S.C. §1471-75.
75. 16 C.F.R. 1700.15(a) and (b).
76. 16 C.F.R. 1700.20.
77. 42 U.S.C. §1857 as amended.
78. 33 U.S.C. §1251 *et seq.*
79. Rodger, W. H.: *Environmental Law,* St. Paul: West Publishing, 1977, p. 273.
80. 42 U.S.C. §6912 *et seq.*
81. Smith, M. C.: External Controls, *Principles of Pharmaceutical Marketing,* 2nd Ed., Philadelphia: Lea & Febiger, 1975, p. 401.

Suggested Readings

The list that follows contains additional sources of information, opinion, and background on the pharmaceutical industry. The list is not intended to be exhaustive, nor is every item on the list recommended. Those included *do* provide a reasonably representative list of "places to start" for the serious student of pharmaceutical marketing. Some, although out of date, are presented for their historical value. The reader is also referred to the references at the end of each chapter. No attempt has been made to list articles in the periodical literature.

Index

In addition to standard business, pharmacy, medical, and social science indices, the reader is also referred to the *Pharmaceutical News Index* (PNI). This source indexes a variety of publications of drug industry newsletters, most notably *F-D-C Reports* (the "Pink Sheet"), an invaluable weekly news publication.

Periodicals

The standard business, pharmacy, and medical press contain regular articles of interest and relevance to pharmaceutical marketing. Some specific periodicals of note are listed below.

Medical Marketing and Media
Drug and Cosmetic Industry
The Pharmaceutical Executive

Books

The reader is cautioned that this is only a partial list of books, some of which may be out of print. It should also be noted that an exceptional amount of information is contained in the proceedings of various congressional investigations (Kefauver, Nelson, Kennedy, etc.). It would be helpful to begin with the *Catalogue of Government Publications* or a good documents librarian.

American Enterprise Institute: *New Drugs: Pending Legislation,* Washington, DC: American Enterprise Institute, 1976.

Arnow, E. L.: *Health in a Bottle: Searching for the Drugs that Help,* Philadelphia: J. B. Lippincott, 1970.

Bond, R. S., and Lean, D. F.: *Sales, Promotion, and Product Differentiation in Two Prescription Drug Markets,* Staff Report, Bureau of Economics, Federal Trade Commission, Washington, DC: U.S. Government Printing Office, 1977.

Chien, R. I. (Ed.): *Issues in Pharmaceutical Economics,* Lexington, MA: Lexington Books, 1979.

Cooper, M. H.: *Prices and Profits in the Pharmaceutical Industry,* Oxford: Pergamon Press, 1966.

Davies, W.: *The Pharmaceutical Industry—A Personal Study,* Oxford: England, Pergamon Press, 1967.

Dowling, H. F.: *Medicines for Man,* New York: Alfred A. Knopf, 1970.

Fletcher, F. M.: *Market Restraints in the Retail Drug Industry,* Philadelphia: University of Pennsylvania Press, 1967.

Harris, G. D.: Pharmaceutical Marketing, in *The Pharmaceutical Industry,* edited by C. M. Lindsay, New York: John Wiley & Sons, 1978.

Helms, R. B. (Ed.): *Drug Development and Marketing,* Washington, DC: American Enterprise Institute, 1975.

Hornbrook, M. C.: *Market Determination and Promotional Intensity in the Wholesale-Retail Sector of the U.S. Pharmaceutical Industry,* Rockville, MD: National Center for Health Services Research, Department of Health, Education, and Welfare, 1976.

James, B. G.: *The Future of the Multinational Pharmaceutical Industry to 1990,* New York: John Wiley & Sons, 1977.

Keller, B. G., and Smith, M. C.: *Pharmaceutical Marketing: Anthology and Bibliography,* Baltimore: Williams & Wilkins, 1969.

Lindsay, C. M. (Ed.): *The Pharmaceutical Industry,* New York: John Wiley & Sons, 1978.

MacCullum, D. H.: *Drug Industry Price and Cost Trends,* New York: Faulkner, Dawkins, and Sullivan, 1975.

Measday, W. S.: The Pharmaceutical Industry, in *The Structure of American Industry,* 5th Ed., edited by W. Adams, New York: MacMillan, 1977 (extremely useful introduction despite some questionable judgments).

Mintz, M.: *By Prescription Only,* Boston: Beacon Press, 1967.

Olson, P. C.: *Marketing Drug Products,* New York: Topics Publishing, 1964.

Peltzman, S: *Regulation of Pharmaceutical Innovation: The 1962 Amendments,* Washington, DC: American Enterprise Institute, 1974.

Pharmaceutical Manufacturers Association: *Prescription Drug Industry Fact Book,* Washington, DC: Pharmaceutical Manufacturers Association, various years.

Reekie, W. D.: *The Economics of the Pharmaceutical Industry,* London: MacMillan, 1975.

Seidman, D: *Protection and Overprotection: The Politics and Economics of Pharmaceutical Regulation,* Washington, DC: Social Science Research Council Center for Coordination of Research and Social Indicators, 1976.

Silverman, M., and Lee, P. R.: *Pills, Profits and Politics,* Berkeley: University of California Press, 1974.

Smith, M. C.: *Principles of Pharmaceutical Marketing,* 1st and 2nd Eds., Philadelphia: Lea & Febiger Publishers, 1969, 1975.

Talalay, P. (Ed.): *Drugs in Our Society,* Baltimore: Johns Hopkins Press, 1964.

Index

Numerals in *italics* indicate figures; "t" following a page number indicates tabular material.

Abbreviated New Drug Application
(ANDA), 198, 495
Academic market, physician, 38–40
Acquisition, business, 173–176, 239–
240, 290, 294t
Ad page exposure studies, 375
Adulterated drugs, 497–498
Advertising, 369–399
audits and research in, 388–389,
390–393
believability of, government regulations and, 396, *397*
direct mail, 384–386
drug, social criticism of, 389, 394–
398, *397*
federal control of, 491
inappropriate prescribing and,
394–395
journal, prescribing and, 398
media in, 369–388
media mix, 386–388, *387*
nonprescription drug, 218–221
objectives of, 389
patient and, 395
product positioning by, 221–222
professional practice, 7
space media, 370–384
Aesthetic needs, 89
Age, of consumer, 27
drug mentions of, 32t–33t
of patient visiting physician, 28–
29, 28t
of physician, 38
Alcon, 178
Allergan, 178
American Academy of Family Physicians, 411
American Marketing Association, 25
American Pharmaceutical Associa-
tion, advertising and, 7
Ampicillin, 193
Antacid Warnings TRR, 506
Antibiotic therapy, 360
Antisubstitution laws, 192–193
Antituberculosis agents, 360
APhA seal, 105
Apothecary shop classification, 274
Armed Forces physicians, 315
Armour, 178
Aspirin, 220

Audits and surveys of pharmaceutical marketplace, 120–131,
122t, 125t, 127t–130t
Aureomycin, 192
Automated order entry, 260

Back-dooring, 309
Barriers to pharmaceutical market-
ing, 6–9
Bid solicitation, hospital, 308–309
Bid specifications, government, 320–
321
Bioavability profile, 197–198
Biologic products industry, 232
Boots Co., 199
Brand loyalty, 188
Brand name, 190
Business combinations, 173, 174t–
175t
Business opportunity connotation of
market, 10, 11t
Business planning and research,
145–149
Business reply cards, 385
Buyer, 69
Buying, 429–430

Call Report System, Computerized,
470–472, *473*
Capitation, 337–338
Cash flow control, 474–475
Census data, 116
Cents off packaging, 437–438
Certified Medical Representative
Institute, Inc., 406
Chain stores, 286–291, 288t–293t
breakdown by department of, 290,
290t
generic drugs and, 204
location of, 421, 424t–425t
mergers and acquisitions by, 290,
294t
number of units in organization
of, 290, 292t–293t
sales activity for, 287t
sales statistics of, 445–446
sales volume of, 290, 291t

Chain stores (*Continued*)
  strength in drug market of, 288t
  ten years' growth of, 289t
Change from normal in sickness,
  90–92
Charge establishment, 7
Chiropodists, 41
Chiropractors, 44
Chlorpromazine, 150
Cimetidine, 360
Clayton Act, 502–503
Clean Air Amendments, 507
Clinical serendipity, 150
Clinical trials planning, 136–137
Code and symbol usage, 260
Code of Advertising Practices of
  Proprietary Assoc., 510
Commercialism, 7
Commodity approach to marketing,
  18–19, *20*
Community relations, 415–416
Competition, economics and, 343–
  368
  nonprescription drugs and, 218
  perfect, 345–346
  pure, 344–345
  retail, 418–447
  static vs dynamic approach to,
    351–352
Compliance, cost factors in, 107–108
  encouraging, 108–109
  factors affecting, 105–108, *107*
  patient, 105–109, *107*
  patient income and, 106
  patient response and, 108
Compliance behavior model, 106–
  107, *107*
Computer, pharmacy use of, 431–
  432
  prescription information storage
    by, 261
  project management and, 164–165
  wholesalers and, 249–250
Computerized Call Report System,
  470–472, *473*
Concentration of market, 346–347
Concentration-dispersion function of
  wholesaler, 252, *253*
Conglomerate(s), 176
Conglomerate diversification, 177
Conglomerate market competition,
  433
Consumer, 12, 27–29, 28t, 30t–35t
  advertising and, 395
  age of, 27
  compliance of, 105–109, *107*
  decision making in health matters
    by, 89–109
  drug therapy expectations of, 109

income level of, 27–28, 106
motivation of, 88–114
orientation of, 17
sex of, 27
shopping habits of, 434–436, *436*
spending in drugstores by, 281t
Consumer Goods Pricing Act, 504
Continuing medical education, 410–
  413, 412t
Contributions of pharmaceutical
  marketing, 6
Controlled media, 371
Convalescent aids business, 291
Conventions, selling at, 408–410,
  408t, 410t
Cooperative chain stores, 295–296
Copy strategies, 224t
Corporate development, 143
Corporate planning perspectives,
  143–145
Corporate technoscientific success,
  142, *143*
COSMcK, 266
Cosmetic(s), 184–185, 185t
Cosmetic, Toiletries and Fragrances
  Association, 510
Cosmetic Ingredient Review, 510
Cosmetic manufacturers and self-
  regulation, 487
Costs, drug, 107–108
Custom research service, 120

Death rate, age-adjusted, selected
  causes of death and, 45t
Decision makers' market, 38–40
Decision making, 68–69
Decline in product life cycle, 65
Defensive projects, 157
Demand, aggregate, 26
  artificial, 7
  derived, 53–54
  directed, 54
  elasticity of, 50–52, *51*
  expansibility of, 49
  inelasticity of, 50–51, 347
  interconnectedness of, 437
  primary and selective, 54–55
  seasonal, 52–53, *53*
  third-party payment and, 52
Demand side regulation, 363–365
Dentists, 40–41
Department of Defense (DOD),
  314–315
  characteristics of population, 316
  depot purchasing by, 318–319
  physicians in, 315
Depot purchasing, 318–320
Derived demand, 53–54

Dermatological Research Laboratories, 179
Detail audit, 130t
Detailing, 400–417
Detailmen, 400
Development personnel, 145, 146t
Direct mail advertising, 384–386
Direct mail audit, sample, *392–393*
Directed demand, 54
Discount stores, 278, 279t–280t
Discriminatory pricing, 260
Disease incidence, 44–46, 45t
Distribution, channels of, 240–247, 245t
  generic drug, 200–203
  hospital, 308–313
  manufacturer, 258
  value-added, 249–256
Distribution/inventory monitoring system, 476–478, *479*
Diversification, 172–189, 178t
Divestiture, 184
Domestic marketing, 453–454
Dosage form, 136
Dow Chemical Co., 176
Drugs, adulterated, 497–498
  attributes of, new drug adoption and, 74–75
  development of, 152–156, 153t–156t
    NDA wait in, 155t
    phases of, 152, 153t–156t
    pre-industrial phase of, 153t
    research phase of, 153t
  HMO utilization of, 329–330
  hospital selection of, 305–308
  Medicare and Medicaid payment for, 332–336, 333t–334t
  newly marketed in 1957–1958, 56, 57t–58t
  patent life of, 363
  patient expectations and, 109
  perceived vs intrinsic value of, 8
  proprietary, government-awarded, 316, 317t
  quality of, 8
  recent development of, 5
  social criticism of advertising for, 389, 394–398, *397*
  therapeutic category of, percentage distribution by, 32t–33t
  top 100 most prescribed, 59t–61t
Drug abuse, 220
Drug Abuse Prevention and Control Amendment, 497
Drug adoption process, 72–73, *82*
Drug Distribution Data, 404
Drug Efficacy Study Implementation (DESI), 495

Drug lag, 362
Drug manufacturer profiles, 235–240
Drug pushing, pharmaceutical industry, 7
Drug use, path analysis of, 93, 100, *101*
Druggist, 104, 418
Drugstore, 104, 280–298. See also *Pharmacy*
  chain, 286–291, 288t–293t
  consumer spending in, 281t
  cooperative chain, 295–296
  definition of, 272
  distributive function of, 446
  franchise, 295
  geographic distribution of, 282–283, 285t
  independent, 291–295
  independently owned, 445–447
  legal form of organization of, 288t
  percentage of by people employed, 283t
  percentage of by volume of business, 282t
  professional function of, 446–447
  size and square feet comparison of, 284t
  store size of, 280–282, 282t–284t
  total sales volume of, 280
  types of goods offered by, 296–298, 297t–298t
  types of ownership of, 283–296, 286t
Drugstore location analysis worksheet, *269*
Drugstore purchase audit, 122t
Durham-Humphrey Amendment, 492–493

Economic approach to marketing, 18–19, *20*
Economic connotation of market, 10
Economic status of person visiting physician, 28–29, 28t, 106
Economic theory, applications of, 346–362
  competition and, 343–368
  concentration of market in, 346–347
  early, 346–350
  entry barriers in, 347
  inelastic demand in, 347
  molecular manipulation and, 348
  perfect competition in, 345–346
  price rigidity in, 347–348
  product competition in, 348
  product obsolescence and, 348
  productivity in, 349–350

Economic theory (*Continued*)
  progressiveness and, 349
  pure competition in, 344–345
  rate of return and, 348–349
  recent, 354–362
  refinements in, 350–354
  standard, 344–346
  static vs dynamic, 350–352
  theory of firm and, 352–353
ECONOMOST, 263
Econoplan, 265–266
ECONOSCAN, 263
Education, continuing medical,
  410–413, 412t
Effectiveness, efficiency vs, 8–9, 9t
Emotional buyer, 69
Employees, drugstore, 283t
Employee relations, 416
Entry barriers, 347, 356
Equivalency tests for generic drugs,
  197–198
Estimated Acquisition Cost plans,
  259
Estrogen, conjugated, 193
Ethical OTCs, 208
Ethical pharmaceuticals, 235, 236t,
  237t
Exchange, complex, 12
  interactive, 12–14
  pharmaceutical market, 15, *15*
  requirements of, 12
Exchange flows, functional approach
  and, 18, 19t
  institutional, 18
  major, 12, *13*
Expansion, external, 173–177, 174t–
  175t
  growth and, 172–173
  problems with, 189
  reasons for, 188–189
Expenditure, annual, for prescription
  drugs, 30t–31t
  health services and supplies under
  public programs, 42t–43t
Expense budget, departmental,
  474–476, *477*
Exploratory research, 151
External controls, 485–513
  governmental, 487–508
  industry, 509–511
  social, 511
  state, 508–509
External expansion, 173–177,
  174t–175t

Facilitating functions, 18
Fair trade laws, 503–504

Family health record, 431
Family Value Drug Centers, 266
Federal Food, Drug, and Cosmetic
  Act, 485
Federal legislation, 487–501, 488t
Federal price guides, 259
Federal Supply Schedule (FSS),
  316–318
Federal Trade Commission Act,
  504–507
Financial relations, 414
Firm, theory of, 352–353
Fisher-Stevens physicians' practice
  profile, 38, 39t
Flow of product evolution, 466–467
Focus group technique, 132
Food and Drug Administration, 490
Food chain store operation, 186
Foreign expansion, 187
Foreign investment, 187, 188t
Foremost-McKesson, 262–263
Formulary, hospital, 306
  decisions on, 306
  drug approval for, 307
  open and closed, Medicare and
    Medicaid and, 336–337
Four Ps, 17
Franchise drugstores, 295
Functional approach to marketing,
  18, 19t

Generic drugs, 190–205
  branded, 194–195
  chain stores and, 204
  current market for, 198–203
  drug product selection and, 193–
    194
  equivalency tests of, 197–198
  growth of, 196–197
  history of, 191–192
  laws concerning, 192–194
  liability insurance and, 204
  manufacturer's name on, 193
  manufacturing of, 202–203
  marketing and distribution of,
    200–203
  pharmacist's selection of, 195–196,
    192t
  promotion of, 203–205
  reliability of, 204
  return goods policy for, 204–205
  size, shape, and color of, 199–200
Geographic market area determination, 9–10
Goods, marketing of, 6
  offered by drugstores, 296–298,
    297t–298t

Good Manufacturing Practices (GMP), 486, 498
Government, U.S., 314–323
  as market, 42t–43t, 44
  bid specifications and requirements of, 320–321
  controls of, 487–508
  depot purchases by, 318–320
  pricing for, 321–323
  proprietary pharmaceutical awards by class, 316, 317t
  purchasing procedures of, 316–321
  purchasing volume of, 315
  retail market vs, 323
Grays, 176
Gross margin statistics, 248–249
Group practice clinics, 275–277
Growth and expansion, 172–173
Growth stage of new product, 64

Handbook of Prescription Drugs, 54
Harris-Kefauver Amendment, 485, 493
Hazardous Substances and Consumer Products Safety Acts, 507
Health and beauty aid sales, 280t
Health Care Exhibitors Assoc., 408–410, 408t, 410t
Health care industry, drug firm expansion into, 186–187
Health Maintenance Organizations, 275–277, 323–330
  classifications of, 325–328
  competition and, 443
  drug utilization by, 329–330
  financing of, 324
  future of, 330
  group type, 327
  individual practice association type, 327–328
  pharmaceutical marketing and, 325, 326t
  pharmacy classification in, 328–329
  prevention vs cure in, 324–325
  staff type, 327
Health Media Buyers' Guide, 371, *372–373*
Historical data, 116
Hoffman-La Roche, 165–168
Home health-care center, 276–277
Horizontal business combinations, 184
Horizontal integration, 176
Hospital(s), 301–314
  administrative control of, 304, 304t

as market, 301–305, 302t–303t
bid solicitation and group purchasing by, 308–309
control and bed size of, 305, 305t
drug selection in, 305–308
drug wholesalers and, 310
gaining access to, 312–313
outpatient visits to, 303, 303t
pharmacists in, 310–311, 402
pharmacy and therapeutics committee of, 306–307
pharmacy changes in, 313–314
pharmacy in, 442–443
pharmacy services offered by, 275, 275t, 312t
physicians in, promotion to, 307–308
prices paid by, 309–310
purchasing and distribution in, 308–313
selling in, 407–408
statistical measures of, 302, 302t
third-party pay for drugs in, 311–312
Hospital formulary, 306
Hospital purchase audit, 121–123, 122t
House organ, 385
Hydrocortisone, 508–509

Ibuprofen, 199
Illness or injury, classification of frequently reported, 215t
Income level, consumer, 27–28, 106
Independent drug store, 287t, 291–295
Individual evaluation of performance, 482, *483*
Industrial controls, 509–511
Industrial organization approach to marketing, 18–19, *20*
Industrial organization paradigm, 346
  behavioral characteristics of, 347–348
  performance characteristics of, 348–350
  structural characteristics of, 346–347
Ineffectiveness, 8–9
Inefficiency, 8–9
Inelastic demand, 347
Information flow, 12
Innovation in Marketing, 46–47
Institutional approach to marketing, 18
Insurance programs, private, 444–445

Intermediate consumer market, 46–47
Internal controls, 459–484
  appropriate, 464–466
  ease in use of, 465
  events as, 464–465
  marketing and, 462–463
  mechanisms of, 470–484
  money and departmental expense budget as, 474–476, *477*
  money as, 464–465
  number of, 465
  organization and, 467–470, *469, 471*
  overall control and management by objective as, 482, *483*
  quarterly tactics composite and time and events schedule as, 472–474, *475*
  role of, 460–462
  sales and distribution/inventory monitoring system as, 476–478, *479*
  sales performance and evaluation by territory as, 478–482, *481*
  time and computerized call report system as, 470–472, *473*
  time as, 464–465
  value judgments about, 465
Internal organization, Williamson's theory of, 353
International marketing, 448–456
  climatic conditions and, 450–451
  demographic characteristics and, 449
  developmental impetus of, 448–449
  disease incidence and trends and, 449
  domestic vs, 453–454
  environment for, 449–451
  foreign investment in US, 454–456
  health-care systems and, 450
  medical practice and, 451
  organizational approaches to, 451–453
  social environment and, 449–450
Introduction stage of new product, 63
Issue audience studies, 374–375

Jewel Co., 186
Joint venture, 176
Journals, 370
Journal advertising, prescribing and, 398
Journal audit, sample, *390–391*
"Junkies," American, 7

Kaiser Permanente, 327
Kinked demand hypothesis, 358
Kroger Co., 186

Labeling, OTC, 217
Lannett issue, 198–199
Lay referral system, 91
Legislation, effects on expansion and diversification of, 187
Levitt, Theodore, 46
Liability, employer, 496–497
Liability insurance, 204
Life cycle, product, 56–65, *62*
Location of pharmacy, 419–421, 422t–425t
Logistics functions, 18

McGuire-Keogh Act, 504
McKesson Drug Co., 262–263, 295
McKesson & Robbins, 180
Magnuson-Moss-Warranty-Federal Trade Commission Improvement Act of 1975, 505
Mail, generic promotion by, 203
Mail Ad Exposure technique, 388
Mail order operations, 277–278
Mail questionnaire for advertising research, 374, *376–377*
Man-in-the-plant regulations, 498–499
Managerial approach to marketing, 17
Manufacturer, 231–247
  distribution characteristics of, 244
  generic drugs, 202–203
  legal definition of, 498–499
  official definition of, 231–233, 232t
Market, actualization of, 12, *13*
  analysis of, 115–138
  behavior of, 48–67
  business opportunity connotation of, 10, 11t
  character of, scrambled merchandising and, 434
  concentration of, 346–347
  connotations of, 9–10, 11t
  definition of, 25
  hospital as, 301–305, 302t–305t
  identification of, 25–47
  marketing and, 11–14, *13*
  measurement of, 115–116
  mechanism of, 10
  nonprescription drug, 217–226
  pharmaceutical, actualization of, 16
  place connotation of, 9–10
  potential of new products and, 157, 158t

proximity of, 252
sample of, 115–116
separations in, 11t
size connotation of, 10
statistics and census data for, 116
valuation dimension of, 10
Market shares of top drugs, 61t
Marketers, 12
Marketing, activities of, 12
controllable aspects of, 462–463
definition of, 12
data on, 133–137
  analysis and interpretation of, 133–135
  applications and uses of, 135–137
  clinical trials and, 136–137
  dosage form and, 136
  measurement and, 134
  methodology and, 133–134
  premarketing planning and, 137
  question formulation and, 133
  questioning of, 134–135
functions of, 18
generic drugs and, 190–205
international, 448–456
management in, major steps in, 17
normative theory of, 14
organization in, 240, *242*
pharmaceutical, approaches to study of, 16–21
  definition of, 14–16
  functional approach to, 18, 19t
  industrial organization approach to, 18–19, *20*
  institutional approach to, 18
  managerial approach to, 17
  systems analysis approach to, 20–21, *21–22*
positive theory of, 14
retail pharmacist and, 298–299
system of, 20–21, *21*
Marketing research, company, 132–133
complications in, 119
group homogeneity and, 119
pharmaceutical market and, 117–119
product choice decisions in, 118
research subjects in, 118
services of, 120–131, 122t, 125t, 127t–130t
Marketing strategy documents, 223t–225t
Marketing-promotional mix, 17, 222–226, 223t–225t
Marketing-research interface, 141–171

Markup on cost method, 427
Maslow's list of needs, 89
Maturity stage of new product, 64
Maximum Allowable Cost programs, 259, 334–335
"Me-too" drugs, 17
Measurement data, 116
Media advertising, 369–388
Media contact, 416
Media mix advertising, 386–388, *387*
Media strategies, 224t–225t
Medical care sought, 93, 94t–96t
Medical contribution of pharmaceutical firms, 359–360
Medical Device Act of 1976, 497
Medical education, continuing, 410–413, 412t
Medicare and Medicaid, 330–339
basic vs optional services of, 331–332
capitation and, 337–338
future of, 338–339
open and closed formularies and, 336–337
retail competition and, 443–444
vendor payments for drugs by, 332–336, 333t–334t
Medicinals and botanicals industry, 232
Meprobamate, 150
Merchandising, scrambled, 432–441
Merck & Co., 176
profile of, 235–239
R & D at, 144
Merger, 184, 239–240, 290, 294t
Middlemen, 46
Miller Amendment, 492
Miller-Tydings Act, 504
Milliken, John T, & Co., 179–180
Misconceptions about pharmaceutical marketing, 6–9
Model Drug Product Selection Law, 194
Molecular manipulation, 65–66, 348, 349, 360
Morbidity, 45
Mortality, 45
Motrin, 199

National Center for Health Statistics, 29
National Detailing Audit, 403–404
National Formulary, 489
Needs, Maslow's hierarchy of, 89
Net pricing, 260
New chemical entity (NCE), cost of development of, 144, 363

New chemical entity (NCE) *(Continued)*
  research and development costs
    of, 235, 238t
New drugs, marketed in 1957–1958,
    56, 57t–58t
  publicity for, 414–415
New horizon research, 147
New product, development of, orga-
    nizational structure for, 470,
    471
  introduction of, 62–65
  market potential of, 157, 158t
Newspaper advertising, 428
Nonprescription drugs, 206–226. See
    also *Over-the-counter (OTC)*
    drugs
  advertising of, 218–221
  definition of, 207–208
  market for, 217–226
  marketing/promotional mix and,
    222–226, 223t–225t
  marketplace competition and, 218
  product positioning of, 221–222
Normative theory of marketing, 14
Nurses, 41, 44
Nursing home business, 291
NWDA, membership in, 259
  position statements of, 258–261

Obsolescence, product, 348
Office visit audit, diagnosis, 129t
  drug class, 127t
  individual drug, 128t
Oligopoly, 355, 358
One-stop health goods and services
    shop, 432
Opportunity cost, 351
Optical centers, 186
Order entry, automated, 260
Organization, as internal control,
    467–470, *469*, *471*
  marketing, 240, *242*
  marketing channel and, 245–246
"Orphan" drugs, 17
Osteopathic physicians, 40
OTC Drug Claims Rule, 505–506
Outpatient visits, 303, 303t
Over-the-counter (OTC) drugs. See
    also *Nonprescription drugs*
  counseling and, 212
  federal control of, 499–501
  labeling of, 217
  review by FDA of, 208–213
    background of, 208–209
    consequences of, 212–213
    prescription drugs and, 212
    procedure in, 209–211
    status of, 211

Paper NDAs, 496
Parke-Davis and Co., 173
Patent medicines, 191, 206
Patents, 191, 347, 363
Path analysis of medicine use, 95,
    100, *101*
Patient. See *Consumer*
Patient package inserts (PPI), 499
Payment flow, 12
Payment sources for prescription
    drugs, 30t–31t
Performance, individual evaluation
    of, 482, *483*
Personnel, community pharmacy,
    430–432
Pfizer, 176
Pharmaceutical care, 16
Pharmaceutical Center, 435, *436*
Pharmaceutical industry, census
    statistics on, 232–233, 232t,
    234t
  concentration of, 356
  demand side regulation of, 363–
    365
  entry barriers in, 356
  generic drugs and, 193
  instability of, 356
  magnitude of therapeutic categor-
    ies in, 234t
  medical contribution of, 359–360
  price rigidity and, 356–358
  pricing and, 356–359, 357t
  productivity of, 359
  promotion by, 359
  ranking based on sales of, 180,
    181t
  rate of return of, 359
  research and development in,
    354–355
  research performance of, 360
  supply side regulation of, 362–363
Pharmaceutical Manufacturers
    Assoc., 233–235, 236t–238t,
    509–511
Pharmaceutical marketing, market-
    ing research and, 117–119
  restrictions on, 117
  target of, 117
  unique aspects of, 118
Pharmaceutical preparations indus-
    try, 232
Pharmaceutical sales representative,
    400–406
  cost of, 404–405
  Drug Distribution Data and, 404
  hospital pharmacists and, 402
  measurement of effect of, 403–405
  physician and, 401–402
  retail pharmacists and, 402–403

training of, 405–406
Pharmacist, generic drug selection
    by, 195–196, 192t
    hospital, 310–311, 402
    professional standing of, 104
    retail, 298–299, 402–403
Pharmacy. See also *Drugstore*
    choice of, 103
    computer-based services for, 262t,
        431–432
    design services for, 266, *267–268*
    graduates in, career choices of,
        272, 273t
    HMO, 328–329
    hospital, 313–314, 312t
    patient attitudes towards, 103–105
    patronage motives and, 102–105
    prescription-oriented, 296, 297t
    sales personnel of, 430–432
    services of, 431–432
    subjective utility of, 103
    traditional, 274, 296, 297t
    24-hour, 432
Pharmacy and Therapeutics Com-
        mittee, 306–307
Pharmacy Buying Council of Illinois,
        296
Physician, 29, 38–40, 36t–37t, 39t
    academic market and, 38–40
    age of, 38, 76
    age, color, economic status of
        patients of, 28–29, 28t
    drug adoption process of, 72–73,
        82
    government-employed, 315
    hospital, promotion to, 307–308
    innovator/traditionalist counts of,
        38, 39t
    nonhabitual choice process of, 70,
        72
    osteopathic, 40
    patient visits by source or place of
        care to, 34t–35t
    pharmaceutical sales representa-
        tives and, 401–402
    prescribing habits of, 68–87
        Applied Management Sciences
            study of, 76
        decision making process in, 81,
            82t
        drug attributes and, 74–75
        drug information and, 81–86,
            83–85
        information sources and, 77–79,
            77t–78t
        job satisfaction and, 76–77
        negative factors in, 75
        peer influence in, 74
        phases of, 75

professional source vs commer-
        cial sources and, 75–76
    studies of, 73–79
    variables in, 74
    primary specialty of, 36t–37t, 38
    veto power of, 26
Physician assistants, 44
Physician panel, 126, 127t–129t
Physician Radio Network, 413
Physiologic needs, 89
Place connotation of market, 9–10
Planned obsolescence, 66–67
*PMA, 1979–1980 Annual Survey
        Report,* 233
Podiatrists, 41
Poison Prevention Packaging Act of
        1970, 507
Polio vaccine, 360
Positive theory of marketing, 14
Pre-industrial phase of drug devel-
        opment, 153t
Premarketing planning, 137
Prepaid drug programs, 443–445
Prescribing process, decision-
        making, 70, *71*
    habits in, other professionals and,
        79
    physician, 68–87
    psychotherapeutic, 80
    psychotropic drugs and, 79–81
    inappropriate, advertising and,
        394–395
    information in, 7, 81–86, *83–85*
    journal advertising and, 398
    nonhabitual choice in, 70, *72*
    rational, 17
    variables in, 70
Prescription, data on, sales data vs,
        246–247
    definitions of, 110
    functions of, 109–113, 111t–112t
    information on, computerized stor-
        age of, 261
    latent functions of, 111–113, 112t
    manifest functions of, 110, 111t
    repeat, 112–113
    sick role status and, 111–112
    unfilled, 105–106
Prescription audits, 124, 125t
Prescription drugs, annual expendi-
        tures and sources of payment
        for, 30t–31t
    channel of distribution for, 243–
        244
    definition of, 207–208
    legal definition of, 492–493
    OTC status and, 212
Prescription Drug Industry Factbook,
        233

Prescription trade regulation rules (TRR), 506
Prescription-oriented pharmacies, 296, 297t
Price, determination of, value in use in, 8
  direct limitations of, 259
  growth stage and, 64
  posting of, 105
  quantity and, 49–50
  resale, 260
  rigidity in, 347–348, 356–358
  service vs, 439
Price guides, federal, 259
Price indexes, pharmaceutical, 356, 356t
Pricing, 7
  discriminatory, 260
  economic theory and, 356–359, 357t
  federal government and, 321–323
  hospitals and, 309–310
  marketplace, 335
  net, 260
  performance and, 349
  retail competition and, 421, 426–427
  strategies in, 225t
  wholesale, 256–257
Primary demand, 54–55
Private insurance programs, 444–445
Procaine, 150
Producer, 12
Producer Price Index, 256
Product competition, 348
Product development, 141–143
Product differentiation as entry barrier, 347
Product evolution, 466–467
Product flow, 12
Product life cycle, 56–65, 62
  decline in, 65
  growth stage in, 64
  introduction stage in, 63
  length of, 65
  maturity stage in, 64
  saturation stage in, 64–65
Product manager, 165–168
Product movement, 116
Product obsolescence, 348
Product positioning, 221–222
Product production, 353–354
Product publicity, 414–415
Product research manager, 162–164
Productivity, industry, 349–350, 359
Professional (dispensing fee) technique, 426–427
Progressiveness of industry, 349

Project management, 161–165, 161, 163t
  computerized, 164–165
  interdisciplinary teams in, 161–162, 161
  one-page status summary of, 165, 166
Project selection, 157–161, 159t
Project team organization, 162, 163t
Promotion, drug, 359
  generic drug, 203–205
  pull-type, 440
  retail competition and, 428–429
  strategies in, 225t
  to hospital physicians, 307–308
Promotional elasticity, 49
Promotional media audit, 126, 130t
Propranolol, 150
Proprietary medicines, 190, 208
Proprietary stores, 272
Prospect, 26
Psychiatric decision-making, 80
Psychotherapists, 80
Psychotropic drugs, 79–81
Public and professional relations, 413–416
  community relations and, 415–416
  employee relations and, 416
  financial relations and, 414
  media contact and, 416
  product publicity and, 414–415
Public programs and expenditures for health services and supplies, 42t–43t
Publications for industry news, 132
Publicity, product, 414–415
Pull-type promotion, 440
Purchasing, depot, government, 318–320
  hospital, 308–313
  hospital group, 308–309
  US government, 316–321
  Veterans Administration, 316–318
Purchasing power concentration, 252–254
Purchasing volume of federal government, 315
Pure Food and Drug Act, 489
Puritan attitudes, 7

Quackery in 1880s, 206
Quality, drug, 8
Quantity, price and, 49–50
Quasimarketing functions, 18

Race of person visiting physician, 28–29, 28t

Radio spots, 428
Rate of return, 359
Rational buyer, 69
Readership, medical publication, 373–374
Recombinant DNA, 150
Redi-Med line, 267
Regulation, demand side, 363–365
  supply side, 362–363
Resale prices, 260
Research, 149–156, 153t–156t
  approaches to, 150
  assessment areas in, 169–170
  business planning and, 145–149
  drug development in, 152–156, 153t–156t
  environment for, 141–143
  exploratory, 151
  functions of, 170
  incentives for, 170–171
  marketing inputs in, 156–157
  new drug development and, 153
  personnel in, development personnel vs, 145, 146t
  perspectives of, 145
  planning in, 145–148
  productivity in, 169–171
  project management in, 161–165, 161, 163t
  project selection and, 157–161, 159t
Research and development, costs of, 235, 236t–238t, 361
  economic theory and, 354–355
  lower prices through, 361–362
  marketing data in, 135–136
  static vs dynamic approach to, 351–352
Resource(s), unproductive use of, 7–8
Resource Conservation and Recovery Act, 507
Retail business failures, 282t
Retail competition, 418–447
  buying and, 429–430
  location of pharmacy and, 419–421, 422t–425t
  Medicaid and, 443–444
  nature of, 441–443
  personnel and, 430–432
  prepaid drug programs and, 443–445
  pricing and, 421, 426–427
  private insurance programs and, 444–445
  promotion and, 428–429
Retail druggist, 418
Retail market, government vs, 323
Retail pharmacy, new locations of,

186. See also *Drugstore; Pharmacy*
  prescription audits in, 124, 125t
  purchase audit in, 121, 122t
Retail sales audit, 131
Retailer, 272–300
Retailing, classification and extent of, 273–298
  quantitative measurement of, 273, 274t
  reorganization of, 265–267, 267–269
  wheel of, 432
Return, rate of, 348–349
Return goods policy, 204–205
Revco, 176, 290
Revlon Co., 185
Rexall, 295
Richardson-Merrell, Inc., 176
Robinson-Patman Act, 503
Roerig Co., J. B. 176

Safety needs, 89
Sales, conventions and, 408–410, 408t, 410t
  data on, prescription data vs, 246–247
  discount store, 279t
  distribution channel and, 244, 245t
  distribution/inventory monitoring system and, 476–478, 479
  health and beauty aid, 280t
  hospital, 407–408
  independent vs chain stores and, 287t
  pharmaceutical, 400–406
  pharmaceutical manufacturers rank based on, 180, 181t
  prescription, wholesale market shares and, 249t
  research and development expenditures and, 235, 238t
  total retail, type of retailer in, 274t
Sales patterns of ethical pharmaceuticals, 235, 236t
Sales performance evaluation by territory, 478–482, 481
Samples, mailing of, 385
Sandoz diversification, 184
Saturation stage of new product, 64–65
Schering-Plough, 182t–183t
Scrambled merchandising, 432–441
  common costs and, 438
  consumer shopping habits and, 434–436, 436
  effects of, 438–441
  factors influencing, 433–438

Scrambled merchandising (*Continued*)
  interconnectedness of demand in,
      437
  manufacturer pressures and,
      437–438
  market character and, 434
  price vs service and, 439
  store traffic increase and, 437
Searle, G. D., & Co., 182t–183t
Seasonal demand, 52–53, *53*
Selective demand, 54–55
Self-actualization needs, 89
Self-medication, decision process in,
      100
  information sources for, 215–217
  process of, 214–215, 215t–216t
  role of, 213–214
Separations in pharmaceutical
      marketing, 10, 11t
Services, marketing of, 6
  pharmacy, 431–432
  price vs, 439
Sex of consumer, 27, 32t–33t
Sharp & Dohme, 176, 179
Sherley Amendment, 490
Sherman Antitrust Act, 501–502
Shopping habits, consumer, 434–436,
      436
Sickness career, change from nor-
      mal in, 90–92
  decision steps in, 89–90, *90*
  need for help and, 93–100, 94t–99t
  particular treatment or setting
      type in, 102–105
  patient compliance and, 105–109,
      107
  rights of, 111–112
  significance of change in, 92–93
  type of help needed in, 100
Sickroom and convalescent sales,
      276–277
Size connotation of market, 10
SmithKline, business activity
      changes of, 182t–183t
  diversification of, 184
  R & D at, 144
Social controls, 511
Source or place of care and patient
      characteristics, 34t–35t
Space media advertising, 370–384
  ad page exposure studies for, 375
  analysis of, 377–384, 378t–380t,
      382t, 384t
  cost per thousand circulation in,
      371
  growth in, 370
  issue audience studies for, 374–375
  mail questionnaire and, 374, *376–
      377*

readership and, 373–374
  stacked vs run-of-book ad place-
      ment in, 372–373
Specialization, 172–189
  definition of, 177–179
  physician, 36t–37t, 38
Standard Industrial Classification, 10
State laws and regulations, 508–509
State volume purchase plans, 259
Substantial evidence requirement,
      494–495
Sulfa drugs, 66
Sulfanilamide elixir, 490
Super stores, 274, 296, 298t
Supply and demand, 48–55
Supply curve, 49, *49*
Supply side regulation, 362–363
Swan-Meyers Co., 180
Symptoms, frequency of, medical
      care sought and, 93, 94t–96t
  ranking of, frequency and medical
      care sought in, 93, 97t–99t
  reported by adults and children,
      216t
  seriousness of, 91–92
  significance of, 92–93
Syndicated research service, 120
Systems analysis approach to mar-
      keting, 20–21, *21–22*

Tactics composite, quarterly, 472–
      474, *475*
Tagamet, 144
Target market, 17
Task Force on Prescription Drugs,
      17
Telephone in generic promotion, 203
Television advertising, 220–221
Thalidomide, 493–494
Theory of firm, 352–353
Therapeutic categories, 234t
Therapeutic drugs as markets, 10
Third-party payment, 52, 311–312
Time and events schedule, 472–474,
      475
Tolerance threshold, 91
Top drug industry stock gainers,
      241t
Top-selling products and manufac-
      turers, 241t
Trade regulation rules, 505–506
Trademarks, 191
Tranquilizers, 360
Transaction functions, 18

United States Adopted Name
      (USAN), 190

United States Pharmacopoeia, 489
Upjohn, direct distribution by, 257
  profile of, 239–240
  project team organization of,
    162–163, 163t
Use right flow, 12
Utilities, intangible, 8

VALU-RITE, 266
Valuation, objective exchange, 10
Value of drug, 8
Value-added distribution, 249–256
Vertical business combinations, 184
Vertical integration, 176
Veterans Administration (VA), 514–
  515
  depot purchasing by, 319–320
  population characteristics in, 316
  purchasing by, 316–318
Veterinarians, 41

Walgreens, 176, 277
Warehouse withdrawal audit, 123
Warner Lambert Co., 173
Water Pollution Control Act, 507

Wheel of retailing, 432
Wheeler-Lea amendments, 491–492
Wholesale market shares, 249t
Wholesale Price Index, 256
Wholesaler, 248–271
  computers and, 261–263, 262t,
    264–265
  concentration-dispersion function
    of, 252, *253*
  drug, 186
  drugstore sales sold through, 257,
    258t
  economic justification of, 251
  functional definition of, 251
  hospitals and, 310
  marketing functions of, 250–252,
    253
  pricing by, 256–257
  purchasing power concentration
    and, 252–254
  strategic planning of, 267–270
  value-added distribution by, 249–
    256
Wiley, Harvey Washington, MD,
  488–489
Women in health care market, 27
Worldwide expansion, 184